GENDER

AND ANTHROPOLOGY

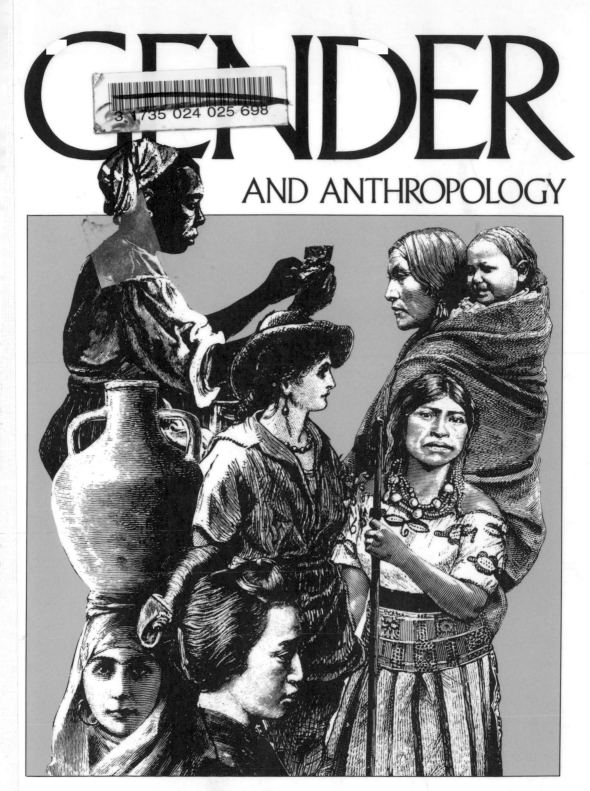

Critical Reviews for Research and Teaching

Gender and Anthropology

Critical Reviews for Research and Teaching

Edited by
Sandra Morgen

American Anthropological Association, Washington, D.C.

Published by the
American Anthropological Association
1703 New Hampshire Avenue, N.W.
Washington, D.C. 20009

Additional copies of *Gender and Anthropology:*
Critical Reviews for Research and Teaching
are available for purchase:

$15 AAA members
$20 Nonmembers

Please make checks payable to the
American Anthropological Association,
and send to the above address.

Library of Congress Cataloging-in-Publication Data
Gender and anthropology :   critical reviews for research and teaching   /   Sandra Morgen, editor.
       p.   cm.
    ISBN 0-913167-33-9
    1. Women—Cross-cultural studies. 2. Anthropology—Study and teaching (Higher). 3. Sex role—
Cross-cultural studies. I. Morgen, Sandra.
    GN479.7.C75   1989
    305.42—dc20   89-27355
                                                                                                          CIP

ISBN 0-913167-33-9

Funding for this project was made possible by the U.S. Department of Education, Fund for the Improvement of Postsecondary Education.

TABLE OF CONTENTS

Continued on next page

Acknowledgments and Dedication

This book represents the culmination of a three-year project which is built on the strong foundation of feminist scholarship and activity in the field of anthropology. As such there are many people to thank—those who made a specific contribution to this project, and the many others whose vision and work has made feminist anthropology such a vibrant and strong scholarship. These acknowledgments are restricted to those who made a direct contribution to this project, though I hope all of those who have helped to build feminist anthropology know we appreciate their groundwork.

The Advisory Board for the Gender and the Anthropology Project deserves all of our gratitude for the commitment they made to this project. Lynn Bolles, Ruth Borker, Johnnetta Cole, Jennie Joe, Louise Lamphere, Jane Lancaster, Janet Spector, and Kay Warren each helped to inaugurate this project and ensure its success. From the planning at Board meetings to the reading of proposals, chapters, Director's reports and queries; to the words of advice and encouragement that came throughout the years, each Board member gave her unique perspective and special skills to the project.

The Faculty Evaluators for this project carefully read drafts of each of the book chapters and provided feedback to authors for their final revisions. Each chapter owes some of its accessibility and success to George Ashley (Holyoke Community College), Catherine Coles (Dartmouth College), Diana Crader (University of Southern Maine), Ralph Faulkingham (University of Massachusetts), David Kideckel (Central Connecticut State), Lynn Stephen (Northeastern), Alan Swedlund (University of Massachusetts), Judy Tizon (University of Southern Maine), and Deborah Winslow (University of New Hampshire).

We owe a tremendous debt of gratitude to the Fund for the Improvement of Post-secondary Education, which funded this project, and to our project officers Tom Carroll and Jamie Lewis. I wish particularly to thank Tom Carroll, who believed in this project and made working with FIPSE very rewarding.

There are many people in the AAA to thank. Eugene Sterud was always accessible and supportive, and he went the extra mile to support the project intellectually and financially. Rick Custer was masterful with a manuscript that needed a lot of final readying for production. Noni Batu and then Jean Stewart worked with FIPSE and the project to balance books, budgets, and file all the necessary financial reports.

I owe my deepest day-to-day gratitude to Karen Gaul, the project assistant from 1987 to 1989. Karen, a graduate student in anthropology at University of Massachusetts, helped in all phases of the project; she applied her wide-ranging intellectual, organizational, artistic, and social skills independently, cheerfully, and thoughtfully. She was a joy to work with, and I expect her to continue to contribute to the development of feminist anthropology through her own work. I also want to thank Paulla Ebron, Jeanine Maland, Joyce Conlon, and other graduate students at University of Massachusetts who helped out at different points in the project.

There are a host of other friends and colleagues to thank, each of whom gave me benefit of counsel or specific help over the past three or four years. Holly Mathews and Pat Beaver helped to write the proposal to the AAA for seed money for this project; Sylvia Forman was always there to help with both day-to-day needs and as an "insider" when the project was discussed at AAA Executive Committee meetings. Carol Stack, Karen Sacks, Anna Tsing, and Laurie Price were good counsel and support.

I want to thank the Women's Studies program at the University of Massachusetts for letting this project spread out in its space when we have so little, and Ann Williams, the Women's Studies secretary for helping us understand and negotiate the University of Massachusetts bureaucracy. Five Colleges Incorporated hosted our 1988 meetings with faculty evaluators, lending its support to the work of the project.

One other aspect of the Project on Gender and the Curriculum, not included in this book but essential to its overall success, was the "textbook project." Five teams of textbook authors and consultants examined some of the leading textbooks used in introductory anthropology to consider ways to broaden and deepen their coverage of women and gender. Thank you for the fine work you did—Lila Abu-Lughod, Louise Lamphere, Yolanda Moses, Nancy Scheper-Hughes, and Ida Susser. Textbook authors Dan Bates, Carol Ember, Melvin Ember, Marvin Harris, William Haviland, and Conrad Kottak deserve our thanks for their willingness to allow their texts to be scrutinized, and for their careful consideration of the feedback by the project consultants. Mary Moran, codirector of the textbook project, was an invaluable colleague throughout the work of this endeavor.

During the course of this project, Board member and chapter author Ruth Borker lost a battle with cancer, and we all lost a wonderful colleague. We dedicate this publication to the memory of Ruth and to Michelle Rosaldo, Nancy Tanner, and Eleanor Leacock. Along with many others, they have helped make feminist anthropology a vital, living enterprise.

Gender and Anthropology: Introductory Essay

Sandra Morgen
University of Massachusetts, Amherst

The dramatic development of anthropological research on women and on gender over the past two decades has profound implications for research and teaching in anthropology. This research has produced critiques of the ways women have been represented in anthropology and has generated a host of new questions and approaches for exploring women's experiences in their historical and cultural variety. *Gender and Anthropology: Critical Reviews for Research and Teaching* is the culmination of a three-year project designed to help bring the insights of this new research to the teaching of anthropology. Drawing on the work of feminist anthropologists in all the subfields, this book demonstrates the value of examining gender and women's lives in all areas of anthropological inquiry.

Feminist critiques of anthropology have exposed the pervasiveness of both androcentric (male bias) and Eurocentric assumptions and representations of women in anthropology. As early as 1971 Sally (Linton) Slocum argued that most anthropological research and theory focused primarily on male activities or on male perceptions of female activities, including the ''man-the-hunter'' theory, which effaced women's place in human evolution. Since then, others have built on her insights, documenting the failure of the field of anthropology to fully explore human experience because of its neglect of women and of gender as a dimension of social life. During the past twenty years cultural anthropologists, anthropological linguists, archaeologists, primatologists and physical anthropologists, equipped with new questions, frameworks, and a recognition of gender bias in traditional anthropology, have produced a wealth of new data and theory which encourages us to appreciate and understand gender as a fundamental aspect of social relations of power, individual and collective identity, and the fabric of meaning and value in society.

This book is about both *women* and *gender,* and about the particular historical relationship between scholarship on women (i.e., the anthropology of women) and theories about gender. While there has been some important work on gender which begins from the analysis of male experience (for example, Herdt 1982; Whitehead 1981; Williams 1986), I would argue that the search by feminist anthropologists for theoretical frameworks and analytical categories to understand women's experiences has been the most significant factor in the elaboration of research and theory on gender. Indeed, Henrietta Moore has recently argued that ''feminist anthropology has made its most distinctive contribution through demonstrating why an understanding of gender relations must remain central to the analysis of key questions in anthropology and in the social sciences as a whole'' (1988:195).

Feminism and Anthropology

In the mid-1970s several publications, *Women, Culture and Society* (Rosaldo and Lamphere 1974), *Toward An Anthropology of Women* (Reiter 1975) and *Women and Men: An Anthropologist's View* (Freidl 1975) signaled the beginnings of feminist anthropology. While any number of important works (especially Brown 1970; Freidl 1967; Goodale 1971; Leacock 1972; Slocum 1971) predated the publication of these books (enough in fact to warrant the publication of Sue Ellen Jacob's 1971 bibliography *Women in Perspective: A Guide for Cross Cultural Studies*), a new era had begun as women became *central* to the research and theoretical agendas of both younger and more established scholars.

Feminist anthropologists of the early to middle 1970s explicitly denied that women's roles, status or relationships with men are biologically determined. Each of these books makes a case for understanding cultural variability in women's lives and for examining social and cultural explanations for that variability, particularly as culture mediated the meanings and constraints of biology on human behavior and social organization. Interestingly enough, the systematic study of the intersection of biology and culture in the production of gender has not been a focus of much feminist anthropological research. The fundamental question—What difference does sex difference make?—is a highly politicized question, one that will not be well answered until the feminist critique of science (Fausto-Sterling 1985; Hubbard and Lowe 1979; Keller 1985; Sayers 1982) begins to affect the process of scientific research.

These three works (Rosaldo and Lamphere, Reiter, and Freidl) each acknowledge the pervasiveness of women's subordination, although in quite different ways. Rosaldo and Lamphere presume the "universality" of women's subordination or sexual asymmetry. Reiter finds that "sexual inequality appears widespread and the institutions in which it is embedded have a long and complex history" (1975:11). And Freidl argues that a degree of male dominance exists in all known societies, but that cultures that rely on different subsistence technologies display different degrees of male dominance. The question of the pervasiveness of women's subordination, particularly the issue of universality, became a major focus of debate among feminist scholars for much of the decade.

Even more important than these different positions on the question of the universality of women's subordination are the divergent approaches to the study of women heralded in these three texts. The three lead articles in *Women, Culture and Society* together provided a framework for examining sexual asymmetry, which defined women's culturally articulated role as "mother" as the ultimate source of women's subordination. Rosaldo argued that despite the variety of cultural interpretations of "woman" and "mother" found in the ethnographic record, women's childbearing and childrearing roles provide the basis for an opposition between a "domestic" and a "public" sphere (or orientation) in all human societies, an opposition that constitutes the basis of hierarchical gender relations (1974). At the level of cultural analysis, Sherry Ortner examined the interrelationship between three binary oppositions (male:female, culture:nature, public:domestic) elaborating Rosaldo's model (1974). Nancy Chodorow examined how all of this is played out and reinforced generationally through the socialization of children (1974). While acknowledging variation in women's roles and status, this framework made central the task of explaining what was presumed to be similar in women's condition cross-culturally (i.e., a universal subordination to men). This framework also assumed the centrality of motherhood in women's lives, in cultural constructions of gender, and in the organization of families and social structure.

The major alternative approaches in the feminist anthropology of the period were heralded in Reiter's collection, in Freidl's book, and, as Lamphere recently pointed out (1987), in many of the other articles in *Woman, Culture and Society*. All of these took more seriously differences in women's roles and statuses across time and space, and emphasized the analysis of women's productive activities and relations. Almost all of the articles in the Reiter anthology examine women's roles in production, from Sally Slocum's extremely influential article on the importance of gathering in the evolution of *Homo sapiens;* to ethnohistorical studies such as Judith Brown's examination of Iroquois women; to the rich case studies from Latin America, Africa, Oceania, Europe, and China. Many of these articles were clearly influenced by Marxist perspectives, and even those not explicitly indebted to Marxist theory tended to acknowledge the importance of a historical understanding of the development of male dominance.

An important theme in the Reiter collection is the proposition that egalitarian gender relations existed among some foraging peoples before contact with Europeans and colonization. The egalitarian hypothesis, as it has come to be known, was proposed by Eleanor Leacock (1972, 1978) building on the work of Friedrich Engels. Taken together the articles present a compelling critique of traditional anthropological theory for ignoring women's roles in production and/or presuming a natural (and biological) basis for the sexual division of labor. These twin failings of anthropology—neglect and presumption—have obscured both the conditions under which women have achieved considerable power and autonomy in certain cultures at particular historical moments (Draper, Sacks, and Brown, for example) and the historical dynamics of women's subordination, most particularly the consequences of the rise and spread of capitalism.

If Freidl's book shares with the Reiter collection a focus on women's labor and women's roles in production, it differs substantially both theoretically and methodologically. Freidl examined differences in male and female roles, status, and power in societies characterized by foraging and horticultural subsistence technologies. While she was concerned with exploring the consequences of different subsistence technologies for the sexual division of labor and of differential allocations of power for relations between men and women, she also noted variations among foragers and horticulturalists. Freidl concludes that male control over women is related to men's extradomestic activities and their prerogatives to exchange valued goods and services beyond the domestic unit. The development of an evolutionary model to explain differences in degrees and kinds of women's subordination is also found in another influential book from this period, *Female of the Species,* by Martin and Voorhies (1975).

Throughout most of the 1970s much of the discourse of feminist anthropology focused on "women's subordination," "women's status" and "sex (or gender) roles." This period was marked by two related concerns: the search for an explanation for either the universal or the historically developed subordination of women, and the development of frameworks to examine women's status cross-culturally. Even as many scholars presumed women to be subordinate to men across time and place, there was a keen awareness that women's roles, and their relative power and autonomy, varied considerably in different cultures.

As Lamphere has argued, anthropologists who turned their attention to the study of women may have had their consciousness raised by the larger women's movement, but their methodological and theoretical "toolkits" came from their traditional training in anthropology (1987:17). Thus, she argues, different theorists chose to examine women from the vantage points of social structure, cultural analysis and symbolism, cross-cultural analysis, or historical materialism, because of their particular training and theoretical allegiances. However, beyond this, tradition molded early feminist scholarship in even more basic ways. As groundbreaking as it was to problematize the issue of gender asymmetry, much feminist theory continued a grand old tradition in anthropology, albeit with a progressive twist. The study of women's lives and gender was often separated from the analysis of men's lives, the complexity of relationships between men and women, and from a larger discussion of social relations of power in culture(s).

At the risk of oversimplification, let me suggest three main "streams" of feminist scholarship that followed from this work, and that had matured into significant bodies of scholarship by the early 1980s:

1. Following primarily from the theoretical framework in Rosaldo and Lamphere, a body of scholarship has developed that focuses on the *social or cultural construction of gender* as primarily shaped by and expressed in the roles and meanings of motherhood, kinship, and marriage. Two of the main collections of this work are *Nature, Culture and Gender* by Carol MacCormack and Marilyn Strathern (1980) and *Sexual Meanings* by Sherry Ortner and Harriet Whitehead (1981). Henrietta Moore argues that this work tended to examine gender as a symbolic construction, and she identifies its creative force as emerging from the dilemma of how to account for both the variability in cultural understandings of gender and the universality of women's subordination (1988:13). As this research developed in the mid- to late 1980s, some theorists focused primarily on the social construction of gender, emphasizing the analysis of social structure (for example, Collier 1987), while others, examining the cultural construction of gender, relied more heavily on the analysis of culture and symbol, following from the frameworks developed by Ortner and Whitehead.

2. Following from the theoretical perspective in Reiter, and the work of historical materialists such as Eleanor Leacock, scholarship developed that focuses on gender as it is historically constructed and as it relates to class (and in the work of some scholars, to race and ethnicity) in the constitution of social relations of power and changes in the mode of production. As Moore has noted, this research tends either to reject or problematize the thesis of universal gender asymmetry (1988:30). Two of the most influential works in this tradition are Karen Sacks' *Sisters and Wives* (1979) and the collection *Women and Colonization* by Mona Etienne and Eleanor Leacock (1980). The emphasis on unraveling the historical processes that have shaped gendered experience and meaning has centered on the impact of colonialism and global capitalism on indigenous societies, particularly as these forces changed relations of production and precolonial, precapitalist social and political formations.

3. Like Freidl, some feminist scholars used the comparative method to analyze different variables that explain differences in women's status, role, authority and/or power cross-culturally. In this work there is less theoretical concern with the concept of gender and more with the refinement of concepts such as women's status and the development of models that correlate gender-related activities, characteristics, or roles with measures of economic, social, and political power. Within this literature there are some, like Freidl (1975) and Martin and Voorhies (1975) who work with a relatively small number of cases, moving from the intensive comparison of these cases to their cross-cultural hypotheses. Others draw on large numbers of cases, sometimes using data from the Human Relations Area Files (HRAF), applying sophisticated statistical methodology in their search for cross-cultural generalization. Two representative books in this tradition are Alice Schlegel's *Sexual Stratification* (1977) and Peggy Sanday's *Female Power and Male Dominance* (1981).

By the early 1980s each of these streams of feminist anthropology had produced at least two major theoretical volumes that articulated the developing perspectives in the field. In addition, there were a number of important collections about women in different culture areas (Beck and Keddie 1978; Hafkin and Bay 1976; Nash and Safa 1976; Oppong 1983; Wolf and Witke 1975) and a proliferation of important ethnographies focusing on women and gender, among the most widely read being Carol Stack's *All Our Kin* (1974); Margery Wolf's study of Taiwanese women (1972); Marilyn Strathern's study of Mt. Hagen women (1972); Annette

Weiner's restudy of the Trobriand Islanders (1976); and Marjorie Shostak's study of the !Kung (1981).

During the last two decades feminist perspectives have also been developing in primatology (Altmann 1980; Fedigan 1982; Hrdy 1981; Lancaster 1975, 1976, 1978; Rowell 1974, 1984; Small 1984); the study of human evolution (Dahlberg 1981; Slocum 1971; Tanner 1981; Tanner and Zihlman 1976; Zihlman 1978); the study and critique of social biology and sociobiology (Hrdy 1981; Leacock 1981; Leibowitz 1978); and anthropological linguistics (Borker 1980; Gal 1978; Harding 1975; Philips 1980; Philips et al. 1987). Although there has been a sharing of feminist research and theoretical development across the subfields, the debates and historical development of scholarship are quite different from archaeology, physical anthropology, and linguistics than what I have briefly discussed above for cultural anthropology.

The anthropological study of gender and language owes much of its theoretical center to the work of sociolinguists on sex differences in language (see especially Lakoff 1975). In both Susan Philips's article in the 1980 *Annual Review of Anthropology* and the chapter by Borker and Maltz in this collection it becomes clear that much of this work tries to develop a cross-cultural perspective (e.g., Abrahams 1975; Gal 1978; Harding 1975; Lederman 1980; Schieffelin 1987) and a theoretically more sophisticated understanding of paradigms of power and dominance (Borker 1980; O'Barr and Atkins 1980; Warren and Bourque 1985) than is often found in the literature on gender and language. The work in this field examines both the ways in which gender is encoded and given particular meaning in language and how gender differentiates speech behavior. Borker and Maltz (this volume) argue that this research is important not only for what it can contribute to the anthropological study of language and culture, but because it focuses attention on "cultural repertoires, choices, strategies and constraints, and the power of the cultural code itself," topics of more general interest to cultural anthropologists.

A major focus of much of the scholarship on women and gender by feminist archaeologists and physical anthropologists has been the articulation and development of the challenge to the "man-the-hunter" version of human evolution. As Zihlman details in her chapter, the earliest critiques of man-the-hunter centered on the ways that women had been denied an active role in human evolution by the focus on hunting and the neglect of gathering; and by androcentric assumptions about pair bonding, sexual behavior, and nonhuman primate and hominid social organization. Over the past fifteen years feminist primatologists, human biologists, and students of human evolution have moved from this initial critique to new research that radically revises our understandings of dominance and bonding among primates; the importance of female activities (especially foraging and parenting) and female choice (sexual selection) in human evolution; and our reconstructions of human prehistory.

In recent years feminist critiques of archaeology and the study of human prehistory have escalated (Conkey and Spector 1984; Gero 1985; Gibbs 1987), but as Spector and Whelan argue (this volume), a feminist archaeology is a vision for the future. According to Spector and Whelan, two important areas of research structuring an archaeology of gender are the analysis of the evolutionary development of gender differentiation and the formation of gender-based hierarchies. Even the raising of these questions poses a challenge to the ways prehistory is generally constructed by anthropologists, who tend rather uncritically to read directly from biological sex differences to a presumed gendered division of labor and power throughout human existence. Meanwhile, exciting new ethnohistorical work on the rise of the State (Gailey 1987; Silverblatt 1987, 1988) makes important empirical and theoretical contributions to this larger effort of gendering reconstructions of prehistory and historicizing the development of gender hierarchy and social stratification.

Development of the Anthropology of Women and Gender

The developments in feminist anthropology discussed above were influenced by a number of factors, among the most important being (1) reflection and debate among its practitioners; (2) debates in anthropology as a whole; and (3) critique and theoretical elaboration in the interdisciplinary field of Women's Studies. I will briefly discuss each of these factors. I have chosen to discuss reflection and debate among feminist anthropologists by examining review articles that both mark and have stimulated major developments in anthropological scholarship on women and gender. The explosion of anthropological work on women and gender since 1975 has warranted major review articles in *Signs,* a major feminist interdisciplinary journal (Atkinson 1982; Lamphere 1977; Rapp 1979; Stack et al. 1975), in the *Annual Reviews in Anthropology* (Mukhopadhyay and Higgins 1988; Quinn 1977); and elsewhere (Rogers 1978). These reviews have served the field by reviewing the wealth of new literature and by posing important questions and critiques of major directions in the literature.

In 1977 Naomi Quinn was questioning the advisability of searching for one "key variable" to explain women's status in society, recommending that future studies "treat women's status as a composite of many different variables, often causally independent from one another" (1977:183). Challenges to the Rosaldo/Ortner/Chodorow framework had multiplied so that Quinn (1977), Lamphere (1977) and Rogers (1978) could reflect on the meaning of ethnographic counterexamples and on the epistemological concern that the framework itself was shaped by the gender ideology of modern Western Europe and the United States. It is clear from all the reviews through 1980 that the most contested issues were the debate over the egalitarian hypothesis (Leacock) and over the applicability and limitations of Rosaldo's "domestic/public" framework.

But by the 1980s the center of the debates had begun to shift; Rapp's 1979 review forecasts these important changes. Rapp argues that feminist anthropology was moving away from "a unitary discussion of gender as either egalitarian or hierarchical . . . realizing the need for more subtle understandings of the variety of female experiences both within and between cultures" (1979:500). She identified a number of other exciting tendencies in the field, including studies of "changing political and economic relations in traditional societies" (1979:504), Marxist-feminist attempts to understand relations of reproduction as well as relations of production, and studies of "female traditions and activities inside the sexually segregated domains" (1979:511).

In 1980 Rosaldo published an article that included a self-critical reflection on the ethnocentrism of her formulation of the "domestic-political" opposition, and by the following year she and Jane Collier had published an influential article that proposed a new framework for analyzing gender in small-scale societies (1981). Collier and Rosaldo's model focuses on brideservice societies and examines how social relations, including male dominance, are structured by marriage. This article, like most of the others in the collection *Sexual Meanings* (Ortner and Whitehead 1981) argues that cultural constructions of gender are not simply or primarily shaped by the dynamics of political economy, the argument so eloquently argued in Sack's influential book *Sisters and Wives* (1979).

By this point the theoretical models of both feminist political economists and those employing cultural analysis had benefited from the debates within feminist anthropology. More feminist cultural anthropologists now took seriously both relations of production and (what Marxist-feminists called) "relations of reproduction," or (what the cultural analysts examined as) the politics of kinship and marriage. Differences among women within particular cultures were more carefully addressed, and in some cases were central to the analysis of the dynamics of gender (e.g., Sacks's 1979 distinction between sisters' and wives' relations to the means of production and Collier's 1987 distinction between brideservice and equal and unequal bridewealth societies). But the distance between the explanations and assumptions of those doing cultural analysis and those doing political economy only seemed to widen with the elaboration of each body of theory.

Jane Atkinson's 1982 review of feminist anthropology noted that these two camps had each contributed different but important legacies: Marxist-feminists leading the way in historical analysis, with the "non-Marxist camp" displaying a "strong commitment to comparative study" (1982:246). The historical analysis of Marxist feminists tended to focus on a rigorous analysis of the impact of capitalism and the rise of the State on gender relations. This literature emphasized change in gender roles, relations, and ideology within a society as a result of changes in production and contradictions between the forces and relations of production. Cultural analysts, on the other hand, while attending to the detailed investigation of the cultural construction of gender in particular societies, developed comparative frameworks to understand gender in its symbolic and ideological manifestations cross-culturally, one of the most important of these being Ortner and Whitehead's model of "prestige structures" (1981).

The debate between political economists and cultural analysts was not restricted to feminist anthropology, but was mirrored in the field of sociocultural anthropology as well. Far from being a field unto itself, feminist anthropology was influenced by and contributed to the emerging trends and the theoretical debates within the field (Tsing 1987). For example, while neo-Marxists were calling into question economic reductionism and the applicability of traditional class analysis, feminist political economists were demonstrating the gender specificity of class experience (e.g., in the process of proletarianization) and the intersection of gender- and class-based stratification and inequality. On another front, feminists, inspired by both developments in the study of kinship and the study of gender, mounted a challenge to traditional kinship studies (Collier, Rosaldo and Yanagisako 1982; Rapp 1982; Tsing and Yanagisako 1983). In a recent book, *Gender and Kinship,* based on a 1982 international conference in Bellagio, Collier and Yanagiasko argue that "gender and kinship are mutually constructed. Neither can be treated as analytically prior to the other" (1987:7).

If feminist anthropology has been both influenced by and a major "player" in some of the most significant theoretical rethinking and debate in the field, this is rarely recognized. Nowhere in cultural anthropology has the tendency to marginalize this scholarship, denying its central contribution to the "cutting edge" of anthropological thought been more apparent than in the current reflexive movement in anthropology. In 1986 Marcus and Fischer published *Anthropology as Cultural Critique,* a book that was pivotal in calling attention to what they call a "crisis of representation" in anthropology and the other human sciences. Marcus and Fischer argue that the central issue for contemporary anthropology is the self-conscious reflection on the writing of ethnography toward the end of developing a "historically and politically sensitive interpretive anthropology [that] . . . reconstructs fieldwork, the cultural other, and the concept of culture itself as the framing points for the field of ethnographic representation" (1986:166). While there are a number of references to gender in the book, and the index claims two references to "feminism," at no time do the authors credit feminist anthropology for its pioneering work on the issue of *representation* (primarily the representation of women); its well-documented concern with both male bias and other forms of gender bias (Scheper-Hughes 1983) as these have constructed notions of otherness; its tradition of self-reflexivity (e.g., Rosaldo 1980); or the efforts of some of its practitioners in writing ethnographies that give voice to subjects and that reveal multiple versions of realities within a cultural context.

Each of these contributions were also overlooked by Clifford and Marcus in their explanation of their failure to include any feminist anthropologists in either the conference or volume based on the conference at the School of American Research held in 1984. Clifford and Marcus asserted that "[f]eminism had not contributed much to the theoretical analysis of ethnographies as texts" (1986:20). The "partial truth" of this statement speaks more to the narrowness of their vision of what is important in assessing the "politics of ethnography"—they explicitly defend a focus on "the rhetorical and contextual theory we wanted to bring to bear on ethnography" (1986:20)—than on the actual or potential value of feminist insights on this issue.

This is not the only example of how the dominant tradition within the field has obscured, or sometimes co-opted, the work of feminists. Adrienne Zihlman's chapter on human evolution in this volume speaks passionately about the continued failure of major figures in the field to credit the research of feminists for changes in models of human evolution that dominate the field today, particularly the work on the importance of foraging and mother-child units in human evolution.

If it has been difficult to summarize the scholarship of feminist anthropologists during the 1970s, the task of assessing the burgeoning feminist anthropology of the 1980s is even more so. I leave much of this to the excellent chapters that follow in this book, which, because they take on more discrete portions of the literature, can examine trends and arguments in greater detail. One can also turn to Henrietta Moore's new book *Feminism and Anthropology* (1988). There are, however, several important themes that characterize this scholarship that I will address here, which will also demonstrate some of the ways that contemporary feminist anthropology has been influenced by theoretical developments in the interdisciplinary scholarship in Women's Studies.

Moore argues that the "anthropology of women" was the precursor to today's *feminist anthropology*, which she defines as "the study of gender, of the interrelation between women and men, and of the role of gender in structuring human societies, their histories, ideologies, economic systems, and political structures" (1988:6). It is noteworthy that Louise Lamphere's recent review of feminism and anthropology is subtitled "The Struggle to Reshape Our Thinking about Gender" (1987). Moore and Lamphere are not arguing that women are no longer the center of most feminist research; rather, they believe that the central theoretical agenda concerns gender as both cultural construction and social relation. If the anthropology of women demonstrated that ethnographic description and theory was woefully incomplete without understanding women and women's lives, contemporary feminist anthropology goes further, revealing the centrality of gender as an analytic concept in understanding human culture and society.

But here is the catch. One of the most significant and yet elusive aspects of current research on women and on gender is this: even as we are calling for and demonstrating the value of examining gender as an analytic category—which, like race, ethnicity, class or caste, tends to be crucial in the construction of both group identity and structures of power in society—we simultaneously recognize the need to deconstruct the category "gender." In other words, we need to understand how history, culture, politics, and economic factors coalesce in the construction of gender in specific historical/cultural contexts. Contemporary feminist anthropology has forcefully shown that *gender is a profoundly important analytical concept* and that what *gender is or means* in any particular culture at a specific historical moment must be explored and not presumed.

Thus, one of the most significant characteristics of current feminist research is its rigorous attention to the cultural and historical specificity of gender, a trend that has led away from global theorizing about "women" and toward more attention to individual cases and comparisons that are more attuned to particular historical, regional, and cultural contexts. Some of the most important new thinking on gender has come from the various efforts of scholars to deconstruct the meaning of "woman"/"womanhood" (for example, Collier and Yanagisako 1987) and to examine women's multiple roles, statuses, and positions within the power structures of societies, particularly as those are shaped by age, kinship, marital status, race, ethnicity, and class (for example, Bookman and Morgen 1988; Cole 1986; Nash and Fernandez Kelly 1983; Ong 1987; Robertson and Berger 1986; Sacks 1988; Sudarkasa 1986; Zavella 1987). This is increasingly accomplished by giving greater voice to women as subjects who speak through oral history, life history, texts such as their poetry and other creative expression, and through some of the experimental "new" ethnography (for example, Abu-Lughod 1987).

One of the most important influences on the redirection of feminist theory in general, and feminist anthropology in particular, to explore differences *among* women (rather than privileging male-female difference as the most important matrix for understanding gender) has come from the theoretical work of women of color. (This is an extensive literature, but see for example Carby 1982; hooks 1984,1989; Hull et al. 1982). While Marxist-feminist anthropology has examined the interrelationships between gender and class, and feminist anthropologists in general have painted a portrait of rich diversity in women's lives cross-culturally, much feminist theory, *including much feminist anthropological theory,* has hung on to assumptions about commonalities among women that feminists of color have revealed to be ethnocentric, racist, and neo-imperialistic. In the face of this criticism, which is even more true of mainstream anthropological theory, feminist anthropology is engaged in the exciting process of critical reexamination of its assumptions, its methodologies, and its theories. And as each of the chapters in this book makes clear, this scholarship is a rich source for material on a wide variety of important anthropological subjects.

Women and Gender in Anthropology: Past, Present, and Future

Before the 1970s, discussion of women and women's lives in ethnography was most commonly found in chapters on personality or sex roles, and on marriage, family, and kinship. There were not many studies that focused primarily on women, although those that were continue to be regarded as important (especially the work of Phyllis Kaberry 1939, 1952; Margaret Mead 1935, 1950; and Ruth Landes 1938). Anthropological theory tended to neglect gender as an analytical category, and women appeared mainly as the pawns of men's exchanges in kinship theory (where at least they were mentioned!). Moreover, despite the high status of a few women in the field (notably Margaret Mead and Ruth Benedict) and the relative openness (for a social science) of anthropology to women, the story of the history of anthropology and anthropological theory is most often told with only limited reference to women practitioners; Gacs, Khan, McIntyre, and Weinberg 1988 make this point and offer resources to correct this in *Women Anthropologists: A Biographical Dictionary* (1988).

Anthropology textbooks well into the 1970s restricted their attention to women and/or gender to two main areas—in discussions of "sex roles and personality" or in discussions of kinship and family. Why did the field restrict its examination of women or gender to those two areas? Two related explanations must be considered, one having to do with intellectual history and the other with Western patriarchal notions about gender.

One of the first anthropologists to focus her research on women, and in particular on the cultural construction of gender and cultural variability in sex roles, was Margaret Mead

(1935, 1950). Mead was very clear about her focus in *Sex and Temperament in Three Primitive Societies:*

> This study is not concerned with whether there are or not actual and universal differences between the sexes, either quantitative or qualitative. It is not concerned with whether women are more variable than men, which was claimed before the doctrine of variability exalted variability, or less variable, which was claimed afterwards. It is not a treatise on the rights of women, nor an inquiry into the basis of feminism. It is, very simply, an account of how three primitive societies have grouped their social attitudes towards temperament about the very obvious facts of sex difference. [1935:viii–ix]

Mead's work established the role of culture in conditioning male and female roles and personalities, and she interpreted the importance of that work as the insight it offered "into what elements are social constructs, originally irrelevant to the biological facts of sex-gender" (1935:ix). As the above statement indicates, Mead understood long before contemporary feminism that women tend to "lose out" in their portrayals in social and biological theory.

Even today Mead's work is very likely to be used to discuss women and the cultural construction of gender in textbooks and courses in introductory anthropology. Because Mead's theoretical work was largely in the field of culture and personality, when her work is used to discuss women it tends to be framed in the conceptual language she used—which has to do with *sex roles,* gender and personality, and psychology. So we see, in contemporary anthropology, the survival of a "sex roles" and personality approach to the study of women, particularly in general anthropology, long after "culture and personality" ceased to be a dominant theoretical framework in the field.

In mid-20th-century North American anthropology, research or theoretical concerns about women were encompassed by the ascendant theoretical frameworks of structural functionalism and structuralism. During this period, women entered anthropological theory mainly through studies of family and kinship. While women remained visible in anthropological theory, they did so largely as pawns rather than as social actors, and it was rare that women's voices informed or were central to ethnographic description or theory.

However, intellectual history is only part of the story. The most compelling reasons why anthropologists think and teach about women primarily in relation to personality, kinship, and family is because they share unexamined Western assumptions about gender. A central theme of Western cultures is the importance of distinguishing differences (usually oppositions) between men and women and presuming that those differences manifest themselves in psychological differences that shape sex roles and relationships between men and women. Moreover, that women and gender must be considered when (and often only when) thinking about the family and about kinship also reflects patriarchal ideas about the place of women in culture and society. I will not dwell any further on how powerful our own cultural constructions of gender have been in shaping our "scientific" study of human nature and evolution and of culture, except to suggest that despite two decades of the feminist unraveling of Western epistemology, many gender-biased notions remain to be dethroned (see recent discussions by Collier and Yanigasako 1987; Errington and Gewertz 1987; Strathern 1988).

Dominant anthropological understandings of gender are revealed not only by where anthropology textbooks and theory do discuss women and/or gender, but also by where those discussions are conspicuously absent. Two of the most striking examples of this absence are in our teaching of human evolution and of stratification, power, and political economy. As Adrienne Zihlman argues so eloquently in her essay (this volume), the challenge to the "man-the-hunter" version of human evolution was one of the first feminist arguments about androcentrism in anthropological theory. Despite the extensive development of the gathering hypothesis and revisionist work on hominid diet, dentition, and tool use, according to Fedigan (1986) and Zihlman (1985) theories of human evolution have failed to fully grasp the importance of the feminist challenges and reconstructions. Zihlman argues that for the most part feminist work has been dismissed, ignored, or co-opted. Even when textbooks present a reconstruction of our human past that acknowledges that women gathered and sometimes hunted, hunting (and male activity and adaptation) remains at the center of the story of human evolution, whether it is focused on hominidization or the rest of the pre-agricultural past.

In light of the wealth of feminist work that examines gender asymmetry as a fundamental component of social structure and/or political economy, it is also striking that most textbooks discuss stratification and political economy without discussing gender. Even textbook authors who have made an effort to incorporate the new research on women and gender in their books tend to separate, or "ghettoize," these discussions from their general analysis of power and politics in society. For example, in each of the last three editions of *Culture, People, Nature* Marvin Harris has justified his exclusion of the study of "sex hierarchies" from the chapter on stratification (which is to examine the "principal varieties of stratified groups found in state level societies") with the following explanation:

> Sex hierarchies are conventionally distinguished from class hierarchies. We will do the same and postpone the discussion of sex hierarchies to Chapter 20 (Gender Roles and Human Sexuality). This distinction rests on the fact that class hierarchies include both sexes, whereas sex hierarchies refer to the domination of one sex by another within and across classes. Moreover, unlike class hierarchies, sex hierarchies occur in bands, villages, and chiefdoms as well as in states. [1988:397]

This "convention," to use Harris's word, is highly problematic, and the exclusion of gender from discussions of stratification and social relations of power is commonplace in most anthropology textbooks, and in most anthropological theory. Harris presumes that stratification by sex is significantly different from class-, race-, caste-, or ethnic-based forms of stratification, in part because "class hierarchies include both sexes," whereas sex hierarchies are found within and across classes. While this is indisputably true, race, ethnic, and probably caste hierarchies are also found within and across classes.

Even more important, by separating the exploration of gender, race, ethnicity, caste, and class—this approach makes impossible the realization of what I would argue is one of the most important insights of feminist anthropology—that to understand stratification, domination, or political economy we have to investigate the constitution of social relations of power within a culture without presuming the primacy or unimportance of different principles that structure inequality or define group identity or categorical membership (Morgen 1987). In other words, gender, race, ethnicity, caste, and class are best analyzed as they intersect in creating social relations of power, and as different historical, cultural, and political-economic processes shape the configuration of power within a society.

This brief discussion of evolution and stratification exemplifies my main point—that the new research on women and on gender has the potential to transform the ways we think and teach about a wide range of topics beyond sex roles and personality, kinship, and the family. The authors in this volume cover many of the topics we teach about in introductory anthropology—human evolution, principles of archaeology, language and culture, the intersection of biology and culture in shaping human life, ritual, politics, the economy, colonialization, "development," contemporary social issues and other topics that are illuminated by examining women's lives and theorizing about gender. Not only does this breadth of coverage provide the teacher of introductory anthropology with a great deal of material to incorporate throughout his/her course, but it demonstrates how fundamentally feminist scholarship questions prevailing "truths" in the field and points in new directions for teaching and research.

Using *Gender and Anthropology: Critical Reviews for Research and Teaching* as a Curriculum Guide

This guide has been developed to help teachers of undergraduate anthropology incorporate the new scholarship on women and gender into their courses, particularly introductory courses. There exists within many sectors of the academy a deep chasm between research and teaching. Both of these endeavors are as likely to be indicted by college faculty for stealing time away from the other as they are to be seen as guiding or reinforcing the other. In the same vein, it is rare to find the newest and the most exciting research findings immediately translated into introductory courses. These courses tend to be regarded as forums for inculcating the "basics" of a discipline.

This guide is intended to help bridge the gap between new research scholarship and undergraduate teaching in anthropology by bringing the insights and findings of recent anthropological research on women and gender to bear on curricular questions. Under the auspices of the American Anthropological Association, the Project on Gender and the Curriculum commissioned anthropologists with expertise in one of ten culture regions or eight subfields or special topics to write the chapters that make up the core of this guide. Each chapter contains (1) a conceptual essay that analyzes the important themes, debates, literature, and background information that contextualize (2) two specific curricular suggestions and (3) resources offered by the author for inclusion in introductory courses. This guide, taken as a whole, makes a powerful case for permitting the insights of this scholarship on women and gender to inform teaching (and research agendas) that are not strictly "about women" but that to recognize women as full, visible actors in society and culture. Each of the chapters of this guide demonstrates how the new scholarship on women can lead to changes in the stories we tell our undergraduates about human evolution, human nature, culture, and cultural diversity. The extraordinary developments in feminist scholarship over the past two decades provide us with insightful critiques of some prevailing anthropological paradigms, offer new ways of thinking and teaching about old questions, and raise some exciting new questions for our field as a whole.

We have organized this curriculum guide to provide resources for faculty to mainstream the new research on women and gender into introductory anthropology. By "mainstreaming" we mean incorporating material on women's lives and considering gender as a fundamental category of identity and social structure *throughout* courses. This differs substantially from an approach that reserves discussion of these topics to one particular book chapter, ethnographic example, or course topic/section. By encouraging "mainstreaming" we do not mean to suggest that course sections or entire courses on women and gender are not important. Quite the reverse—because issues about the changing roles of women are of great interest to many of our students, organizing courses so they include the topic *is* important. Our point is that if this is the only strategy taken by an instructor or a textbook author, then students may learn that information about women is marginal and that women themselves can be regarded as peripheral or secondary.

The specific organizations of this guide—by culture region and selected subfields—emerged from a recognition that the issues, the debates, and the pace of research on women and gender varied across the subfields of anthropology, and, within sociocultural anthropology, by culture regions. Because feminist anthropologists today emphasize the historical and cultural specificity of women's experience, and because many anthropologists tend to use ethnographic material from cultures and culture regions they know the most about, we decided to use a culture area rather than an institutional or topical approach to organizing much of the sociocultural material. Financial limitations precluded our ability to cover all culture regions in the guide. Although we do not have chapters on Europe, the Soviet Union, Canada, the Arctic or most of Oceania (there is a chapter on Aboriginal Australia), there are some excellent overview and bibliographic references available on these areas available elsewhere (e.g., Maltz 1988; Sinclair 1986).

This project was funded by the U.S. Department of Education, with the primary mandate being to foster change in introductory anthropology courses in U.S. colleges and universities. A major concern in selecting authors of individual chapters was to ensure their familiarity with the introductory anthropology course as taught in these institutions. The major drawback of this approach is the tendency for the chapters to reflect American anthropological scholarship on women and gender. We are the inheritors of a strong Eurocentric bias, and this book only just begins to crack this. While some of the chapters draw on the work of indigenous anthropologists, on the whole the guide reflects the fact that U.S. feminist anthropology still remains rather firmly rooted in a Eurocentric grounding.

Taken as a whole, this guide does cover most of the important topics and issues taught in introductory anthropology. The chapters by Zihlman, Fedigan and Fedigan, Spector and Whelan, and Lancaster examine important issues in human evolution and the reconstruction of early hominid life and prehistory. Major paradigms in physical anthropology are challenged and alternative frameworks are presented in the chapters on human evolution, for example in Zihlman's discussion of debates about the importance of women and foraging in models of evolution. Fedigan and Fedigan explain how new pictures of primate life have followed from recognition of the importance of lifelong female bonds among primates and from the different views of primate female sexuality and intra-group patterns of dominance. Lancaster examines the intersection of biology and culture in her discussions of fertility and infertility; she poses disturbing questions about trends in human female fertility and in cultural and psychological response to reproductive risks in the context of the global differentials in resources within and between cultures. A number of these chapters reveal how androcentric assumptions undergird major assumptions and theories about our human past and anthropology's strategies for describing that past. Spector and Whelan propose heightening the awareness of students about androcentrism through a critical reading of textbooks and creative exercises that engage students in the process of decoding gender as it might be expressed in material culture.

The issues of ethnocentrism, and the intertwining of Western racial and gender biases in descriptions and analysis of non-European cultures comes up in a number of the chapters. Hale's discussion of the literature on the Middle East makes a powerful case for the centrality of gender bias in the ethnography of that region. She exemplifies her point in discussion of dominant anthropological frameworks for understanding Islam, sexuality, and intepretations of veiling. In a similar vein, Bolles and D'Amico-Samuels credit gender and Eurocentric bias in the literature on the Caribbean for its failure to understand the reasons for or the meaning of the prevalence of matrifocality in that region.

Each of the major domains of social life or institutions of culture are examined in several of the chapters focused on specific culture areas. The most extensive discussions of family and kinship can be found in the chapters on the Caribbean, China, Southeast Asia, Africa, India and the United States. Religion, ritual, and ceremony are most fully explored in the chapters on China, Aboriginal Australia, and India. Women's involvement in politics is a major focus of chapters on the Middle East, Latin America, India and the United States.

Women's roles in production and the changing nature of women's work are highlighted in the chapters on Africa, Latin America, Southeast Asia, Aboriginal Australia, Native North America and the United States, and in the chapter on development. The chapter on China considers the politics of fertility control, and issues concerning women and health care in the United States are central in Mulling's chapter on gender and social policy. While the article by Jacobs and Roberts provides the most detailed examination of women's sexuality and the relationship between the cultural construction of gender and of sexuality, there are additional discussions in the chapters on American Indians, Sub-Saharan Africa, and the Middle East. Finally, Borker and Maltz examine the ways that gender identity, gender roles and the experience of gender are reflected in and reinforced by language. *mereeen*

      Two topics are so frequently addressed throughout the guide that they deserve particular discussion here—the cultural construction of gender and socioeconomic transformation, particularly the impact of colonialism and capitalism on women's lives. While these two lines of inquiry are sometimes examined together, they also represent the two most significant, and often divergent, theoretical approaches in contemporary feminist anthropology. The discussion of the cultural construction of gender in anthropology is as old as Margaret Mead's New Guinea–based work on sex roles, personality formation, and the construction of the self. What any individual chapter in this guide shows and what the guide as a whole makes indisputable is the tremendous variability and complexity of the cultural construction of gender.

Some of the chapters focus on ritual as an arena in which gender comes to have meanings that are created and sometimes contested (for example, chapters by Anagnost, Burbank and Fruzzetti). Ong shows how the competing discourses of multinational corporations, Islamic religious ideology, and local culture shape cultural constructions of "woman" in the fast-changing societies of Southeast Asia. A number of the chapters reveal the ways race, ethnicity, and class specify the experience and the meaning of gender in particular historical contexts (Bolles and D'Amico-Samuels, Nash, Susser, Mullings).

The importance of analyzing gender as an integral aspect of structures of power and domination in societies is a theme that echoes in most of the discussions of socioeconomic change throughout this volume. For example, the chapters on the Caribbean and on Latin America show both the gender-differentiated impact of colonialism and slavery on indigenous peoples and the ways gender intersected with race and class in the ruling ideologies that buttressed post-conquest social and political formations. Anagnost's discussion of the politics of gender in revolutionary Chinese society underscores the complexity of analyzing social change by pointing to both the disjunctures between revolutionary ideology and practice and the material and ideological constraints that shape the political construction of gender. Finally, a number of the chapters explicitly address women's active involvement in revolutionary and grassroots political movements (especially the chapters on the Middle East and the United States).

Just as we have tried to provide the widest possible coverage of culture areas and subdisciplinary specialization in this guide, we have also made an effort to represent the diversity of theoretical perspectives most current in feminist anthropology. While many of the authors of chapters include either some reference to or a discussion of research on women in the culture area, subfield, or topic from theoretical perspectives other than hers/his, that diversity is probably best represented by our choices of authors themselves. Thus, some of the authors focus more on political economy; others privilege cultural, symbolic, sociobiological, or other explanatory frameworks.

We consider this theoretical diversity a strength of the project, and hope that it helps underscore the important recognition that feminist anthropology is really feminist anthropologies. Nevertheless, though authors of different chapters in this guide would be likely to disagree with each other over approach, explanation, and/or the political implications of their scholarship, they do share a fundamental desire to see women and gender more central in anthropological research and teaching. To the extent that this book helps to achieve this incorporation it will have succeeded in its primary goals—strengthening the ability of anthropology to be a science of humankind and to address important issues affecting the diverse peoples of the world.

References Cited

Abrahams, Roger
  1975   Negotiating Respect: Patterns of Presentation among Black Women. Journal of American Folklore 88(347):58–80.
Abu-Lughod, Lila
  1987   Veiled Sentiments: Honor and Poetry in a Bedouin Society. Berkeley: University of California Press.
Altmann, Jeanne
  1980   Baboon Mothers and Infants. Cambridge: Harvard University Press.
Atkinson, Jane M.
  1982   Review Essay: Anthropology. Signs 8(2):236–258.
Beck, Lois, and Nikki Keddie, eds.
  1978   Women in the Muslim World. Cambridge: Harvard University Press.
Bookman, Ann, and Sandra Morgen
  1988   Women and the Politics of Empowerment. Philadelphia: Temple University Press.
Borker, Ruth
  1980   Anthropology: Social and Cultural Perspectives. *In* Women and Language in Literature and Society. Sally McConnell-Ginet, Ruth Borker, and Nelly Furman, eds. Pp. 26–44. New York: Praeger.
Brown, Judith
  1970   A Note on the Division of Labor by Sex. American Anthropologist 72:1073–1078.
  1975   Iroquois Women: An Ethnohistorical Note. *In* Toward an Anthropology of Women. Rayna Reiter, ed. Pp. 235–251. New York: Monthly Review Press.
Carby, Hazel
  1982   White women listen! Black Feminism and the Boundaries of Sisterhood. *In* The Empire Strikes Back: Race and Racism in 70's Britain. Birmingham University Centre for Contemporary Cultural Studies, eds. Pp. 212–235. London: Hutchinson.
Chodorow, Nancy
  1984   Family Structure and Feminine Personality. *In* Woman, Culture and Society. Michelle Rosaldo and Louise Lamphere, eds. Pp. 43–66. Stanford: Stanford University Press.
Clifford, James, and George Marcus
  1986   Writing Culture: The Poetics and Politics of Ethnography. Berkeley: University of California Press.
Cole, Johnnetta
  1986   All American Women: Lines That Divide, Ties That Bind. New York: Free Press.
Collier, Jane
  1987   Marriage and Inequality in Classless Societies. Stanford: Stanford University Press.
Collier, Jane, and Michelle Rosaldo
  1981   Politics and Gender in Simple Societies. *In* Sexual Meanings: The Cultural Construction of Gender and Sexuality. Sherry Ortner and Harriet Whitehead, eds. Pp. 275–329. Cambridge: Cambridge University Press.
Collier, Jane, Michelle Rosaldo, and Sylvia Yanagisako
  1982   Is There a Family: New Anthropological Views. *In* Rethinking the Family: Some Feminist Questions. Barrie Thorne and Marilyn Yalom, eds. Pp. 25–39. New York: Longman.

Collier, Jane, and Sylvia Yanagisako
  1987   Gender and Kinship: Essays toward a Unified Analysis. Stanford: Stanford University Press.
Conkey, Margaret, and Janet Spector
  1984   Archeology and the Study of Gender. *In* Advances in Archaeological Method and Theory,
        Volume 7:1–38. New York: Academic Press.
Dahlberg, Frances
  1981   Woman the Gatherer. New Haven: Yale University Press.
Duley, Margot, and Mary Edwards
  1986   The Cross-Cultural Study of Women: A Comprehensive Guide. New York: Feminist Press.
Errington, Fred, and Deborah Gewertz
  1987   Cultural Alternatives and Feminist Anthropology: An Analysis of Culturally Constructed Gen-
        der Interests in Papua New Guinea. Cambridge: Cambridge University Press.
Etienne, Mona, and Eleanor Leacock
  1980   Women and Colonialization. New York: Praeger.
Fausto-Sterling, Anne
  1985   Myths of Gender: Biological Theories about Men and Women. New York: Basic Books.
Fedigan, Linda
  1982   Primate Paradigms: Sex Roles and Social Bonds. Montreal: Eden Press.
  1986   The Changing Role of Women in Models of Human Evolution. Annual Review of Anthro-
        pology 15:25–66.
Freidl, Ernestine
  1967   The Position of Women: Appearance and Reality. Anthropological Quarterly 40(3):97–108.
  1975   Women and Men: An Anthropologist's View. New York: Holt, Rinehart and Winston.
Gacs, Ute, Aisha Khan, Jerrie McIntyre, and Ruth Weinberg
  1988   Women Anthropologists: A Biographical Dictionary. New York: Greenwood Press.
Gailey, Christine
  1987   From Kinship to Kingship: Gender Hierarchy and State Formation in the Tongan Islands. Aus-
        tin: University of Texas Press.
Gal, Susan
  1978   Peasant Men Can't Get Wives: Language Change and Sex Roles in a Bilingual Community.
        Language in Society 7(1):1–16.
Gero, Joan
  1985   Socio-politics and the Woman-at-home Ideology. American Antiquity 50(2):342–350.
Gibbs, Liv
  1987   Identifying Gender Representation in the Archeological Record: Contextual Study. *In* The
        Archeology of Contextual Meanings. Ian Hodder, ed. Pp. 79–89. Cambridge: Cambridge Univer-
        sity Press.
Goodale, Jane
  1971   Tiwi Wives. Seattle: University of Washington Press.
Hafkin, Nancy, and Edna Bay
  1976   Women in Africa. Stanford: Stanford University Press.
Harding, Susan
  1975   Women and Words in a Spanish Village. *In* Toward an Anthropology of Women. Rayna Rei-
        ter, ed. Pp. 283–308. New York: Monthly Review Press.
Harris, Marvin
  1988   Culture, People, Nature: An Introduction to General Anthropology. New York: Harper and
        Row.
Herdt, Gilbert
  1982   Rituals of Manhood: Male Initiation in Papua New Guinea. Berkeley: University of California
        Press.
hooks, bell
  1984   Feminist Theory: From Margin to Center. Boston: South End Press.
  1989   Talking Back: Thinking Feminist, Thinking Black. Boston: South End Press.

Hrdy, Sarah
  1981   The Woman That Never Evolved. Cambridge: Harvard University Press.
Hubbard, Ruth, and Marian Lowe
  1979   Genes and Gender II: Pitfalls in Research on Sex and Gender. New York: Gordian Press.
Hull, Gloria, Patricia Bell Scott, and Barbara Smith
  1982   All the Women Are White, All the Blacks Are Men, But Some of Us Are Brave. Old West-
          bury, NY: Feminist Press.
Jacobs, Sue Ellen
  1971   Women in Perspective: A Guide for Cross Cultural Studies. Urbana: Illinois University Press.
Kaberry, Phyllis
  1939   Aboriginal Women, Sacred and Profane. London: G. Routledge.
  1952   Women of the Grassfields. London: H. M. Stationery Office.
Keller, Evelyn Fox
  1985   Reflections on Gender and Science. New Haven: Yale University Press.
Lakoff, Robin
  1975   Language and Women's Place. New York: Harper Colophon Books.
Lamphere, Louise
  1977   Review Essay: Anthropology. Signs 2(3):612–627.
  1987   Feminism and Anthropology: The Struggle to Reshape Our Thinking about Gender. *In* The
          Impact of Feminist Research in the Academy. Christie Farnham, ed. Pp. 11–33. Bloomington:
          Indiana University Press.
Lancaster, Jane
  1975   Primate Behavior and the Emergence of Human Culture. New York: Holt, Rinehart and Win-
          ston.
  1976   Sex Roles in Primate Societies. *In* Sex Differences: Social and Biological Perspectives. M. S.
          Teitlebaum, ed. Pp. 22–61. Garden City: Anchor Press.
  1978   Sex and Gender in Evolutionary Perspective. *In* Human Sexuality: A Comparative and De-
          velopmental Perspective. H. Katchadourian, ed. Pp. 51–80. Berkeley: University of California
          Press.
Landes, Ruth
  1938   The Ojibwa Woman. New York: Columbia University Contributions to Anthropology, Vol-
          ume 31.
Leacock, Eleanor
  1972   Introduction to F. Engels, The Origin of the Family, Private Property, and the State. New
          York: International Publishers.
  1978   Women's Status in Egalitarian Society: Implications for Social Evolution. Current Anthro-
          pology 19(2):247–254.
  1981   Myths of Male Dominance. New York: Monthly Review Press.
Lederman, Rena
  1980   Who Speaks Here? Formality and the Politics of Gender in Mendi. Journal of the Polynesian
          Society 89(4):479–498.
Leibowitz, Lila
  1975   Perspectives on the Evolution of Sex Differences. *In* Toward an Anthropology of Women.
          Rayna Reiter, ed. New York: Monthly Review Press.
  1978   Females, Males, Families: A Biosocial Approach. North Scituate, MA: Duxbury Press.
MacCormack, Carol, and Marilyn Strathern
  1980   Nature, Culture and Gender. Cambridge: Cambridge University Press.
Maltz, Daniel
  1988   Anthropological Bibliography of Women in Europe. Washington, D.C.: American Anthro-
          pological Association, Society for the Anthropology of Europe.
Marcus, George, and Michael Fischer
  1986   Anthropology and Cultural Critique. Chicago: University of Chicago Press.
Martin, Kay, and Barbara Voorhies
  1975   Female of the Species. New York: Columbia University Press.

Mead, Margaret
    1935   Sex and Temperment in Three Primitive Societies. New York: William Morrow.
    1950   Male and Female: A Study of the Sexes in a Changing World. New York: William Morrow.
Moore, Henrietta
    1988   Feminism and Anthropology. Minneapolis: University of Minnesota Press.
Morgen, Sandra
    1987   Gender, Cultural Specificity and Anthropological Theory. A paper presented at the annual
           meeting of the American Anthropological Association.
Mukhopadhyay, Carol, and Patricia Higgins
    1988   Anthropological Studies of Women's Status Revisited: 1977–1987. Annual Review of An-
           thropology 17:461–495.
Nash, June, and Maria Patricia Fernandez-Kelly
    1983   Women, Men and the International Division of Labor. Albany: State University of New York
           Press.
Nash, June, and Helen Safa
    1976   Sex and Class in Latin America. New York: Praeger.
    1986   Women and Change in Latin America. South Hadley, MA: Bergin and Garvey.
O'Barr, William, and Bowman Atkins
    1980   "Women's Language" or "Powerless Language"? *In* Women and Language in Literature
           and Society. Sally McConnell-Ginet, Ruth Borker, and Nelly Furman, eds. Pp. 93–110. New
           York: Praeger.
Ong, Aihwa
    1987   Spirits of Resistance and Capitalist Discipline: Factory Women in Malaysia. Albany: State
           University of New York Press.
Oppong, Christine
    1983   Female and Male in West Africa. London: George Allen and Unwin.
Ortner, Sherry
    1974   Is Female to Male As Nature Is to Culture? *In* Woman, Culture and Society. Michelle Rosaldo
           and Louise Lamphere, eds. Pp. 67–88. Stanford: Stanford University Press.
Ortner, Sherry, and Harriet Whitehead
    1981   Sexual Meanings. Cambridge: Cambridge University Press.
Philips, Susan
    1980   Sex Differences and Language. Annual Review of Anthropology 9:523–544.
Philips, Susan, Susan Steele, and Christine Tanz
    1987   Language, Gender and Sex in Comparative Perspective. Cambridge: Cambridge University
           Press.
Quinn, Naomi
    1977   Anthropological Studies of Women's Status. Annual Review of Anthropology 6:181–225.
Rapp, Rayna
    1979   Anthropology: A Review Essay. Signs 4(3):497–513.
    1982   Family and Class in Contemporary America: Notes toward an Understanding of Ideology. *In*
           Rethinking the Family. Barrie Thorne and Marilyn Yalmon, eds. Pp. 168–187. New York: Long-
           man.
Reiter, Rayna (Rapp)
    1975   Toward an Anthropology of Women. New York: Monthly Review Press.
Robertson, Claire, and Iris Berger
    1986   Women and Class in Africa. New York: Africana Press.
Rogers, Susan
    1978   Woman's Place: A Critical Review of Anthropological Theory. Comparative Studies and So-
           cial History 20:123–162.
Rosaldo, Michelle
    1974   Women, Culture and Society. A Theoretical Overview. *In* Women, Culture and Society.
           Michelle Rosaldo and Louise Lamphere, eds. Pp. 14–42. Stanford: Stanford University Press.
    1980   The Uses and Abuses of Anthropology. Signs 5(3):389–417.

Rosaldo, Michelle, and Louise Lamphere
1974   Women, Culture, and Society. Stanford: Stanford University Press.
Rowell, Thelma
1974   The Concept of Dominance. Behavioral Biology 11:131–154.
1984   Introduction to Section I: Mothers, Infants and Adolescents. *In* Female Primates: Studies by Women Primatologists. Meredith Small, ed. Pp. 13–16. New York: Alan Liss.
Sacks, Karen
1979   Sisters and Wives: The Past and Future of Sexual Equality. Westport, CT: Greenwood Press.
1988   Caring by the Hour: Women, Work, and Organizing at Duke Medical Center. Urbana: University of Illinois Press.
Sanday, Peggy
1981   Female Power and Male Dominance. Cambridge: Cambridge University Press.
Sayers, Janet
1982   Biological Politics: Feminist and Anti-feminist Perspectives. New York: Methuen.
Schieffelin, Bambi
1987   Do Different Worlds Mean Different Words? An Example from Papua New Guinea. *In* Language, Gender and Sex in Comparative Perspective. Susan Philips, Susan Steele, and Christine Tanz, eds. Pp. 249–260. Cambridge: Cambridge University Press.
Scheper-Hughes, Nancy
1983   The Problem of Bias in Androcentric and Feminist Anthropology. Women's Studies 10(2):109–116.
Schlegel, Alice
1977   Sexual Stratification: A Cross-Cultural View. New York: Columbia University Press.
Shostak, Marjorie
1981   Nisa: The Life and Words of a !Kung Woman. Cambridge: Harvard University Press.
Silverblatt, Irene
1987   Moon, Sun and Witches: Gender Ideologies and Class in Inca and Colonial Peru. Princeton: Princeton University Press.
1988   Women in States. Annual Review of Anthropology 17:427–460.
Sinclair, Karen
1986   Women in Oceania. *In* The Cross-cultural Study of Women. Margot Duley and Mary Edwards, eds. Pp. 271–289. New York: Feminist Press.
Slocum, Sally (Linton)
1971   Woman the Gatherer: Male Bias in Anthropology. *In* Women in Cross-Cultural Perspective. Sue Ellen Jacobs, eds. Urbana: University of Illinois Press. Reprinted in Toward An Anthropology of Women. Rayna Reiter, ed. New York: Monthly Review Press.
Small, Meredith
1984   Female Primates: Studies by Women Primatologists. New York: Alan Liss.
Stack, Carol
1974   All Our Kin. New York: Harper and Row.
Stack, Carol, Mina Davis Caulfield, Valerie Estes, Susan Landes, Karen Larson, Pamela Johnson, Juliet Rake, and Judith Shirek
1975   Review Essay: Anthropology. Signs 1(1):147–160.
Strathern, Marilyn
1972   Women in Between: Female Roles in a Male World, Mt. Hagen, New Guinea. London: Seminar Press.
1988   The Gender of the Gift: Problems with Women and Problems with Society in Melanesia. Berkeley: University of California Press.
Sudarkasa, Niara
1986   "The Status of Women" in Indigenous African Societies. Feminist Studies 12(1):91–103.
Tanner, Nancy
1981   On Becoming Human. Cambridge: Cambridge University Press.

Tanner, Nancy, and Adrienne Zihlman
   1976   Women in Evolution. Part I: Innovation and Selection in Human Origins. Signs 2(3):585–
      608.
Tsing, Anna
   1987   Changing Frameworks in Feminist Anthropology. Paper presented at the annual meeting of
      the Northeastern Anthropological Association, Amherst, Massachusetts.
Tsing, Anna, and Sylvia Yanagisako
   1983   Feminism and Kinship Theory. Current Anthropology 24(4):511–516.
Warren, Kay, and Susan Bourque
   1985   Gender, Power and Communication: Women's Responses to Political Muting in the Andes.
      In Women Living Change. Susan Bourque and Donna Devine, eds. Pp. 255–286. Philadelphia:
      Temple University Press.
Weiner, Annette
   1976   Women of Value, Men of Renown: New Perspectives in Trobriand Exchange. Austin: Texas
      University Press.
Whitehead, Harriet
   1981   The Bow and the Burden Strap: A New Look at Institutionalized Homosexuality in Native
      North America. *In* Sexual Meanings. Sherry Ortner and Harriet Whitehead, eds. Pp. 80–115. Cam-
      bridge: Cambridge University Press.
Williams, Walter
   1986   The Spirit and the Flesh: Sexual Diversity in American Indian Culture. Boston: Beacon Press.
Wolf, Margery
   1972   Women and the Family in Rural Taiwan. Stanford: Stanford University Press.
Wolf, Margery, and Roxanne Witke
   1975   Women in China. Stanford: Stanford University Press.
Zavella, Patricia
   1987   Women's Work and Chicano Families: Cannery Workers of the Santa Clara Valley. Ithaca:
      Cornell University Press.
Zihlman, Adrienne
   1978   Women in Evolution, Part II: Subsistence and Social Organization among Early Hominids.
      Signs 4(1):4–20.
   1985   Gathering Stories for Hunting Human Nature. A Review Essay. Feminist Studies 11(2):365–
      377.

1

Woman the Gatherer: The Role of Women in Early Hominid Evolution

Adrienne L. Zihlman
University of California, Santa Cruz

Orientation

The purpose of this module is to provide guidance for incorporating women and their activities into discussions of hominid evolution and early hominid life. "Woman the gatherer" developed as a countertheme to "man the hunter" in order to generate an image of women as active and autonomous participants in the evolutionary process and in early hominid society. It is a view consistent with evolutionary principles and takes into account a wide range of information. Complementary information can be found in chapters by Fedigan and Fedigan, Lancaster, and Spector and Whelan.

An Approach to Studying the Past

This module focuses on the early stage of human evolution some 2 to 4 million years ago. For this period of time there is minimal direct information to assist us. Consequently, reconstructions of the human past often rely on assumptions based upon cultural values and stereotypes or individual experience. However, there is available "indirect" information about the evolutionary process, about our close relatives, and about contemporary people who live a nomadic way of life.

Because this module presents an evolutionary perspective, several kinds of information are relevant: time, fossil record, living species and the evolutionary process.

1. *Time* establishes when events happened in the past and makes it possible to determine their sequence and duration (for example, when human physical characters appear during pre-

history). But other events also are of interest: Did food sharing come before or after gathering? Did a sexual division of labor appear in the earlier stages of human evolution or perhaps much later, when more permanent settlements emerged? The time chart (Table 1) provides a general sequence of events for orientation and discussion.

2. *Fossil Record*. The direct evidence for events some 2–4 million years ago consists of fossil bones and teeth, and later, stone artifacts, uncovered in eastern and southern Africa. From teeth and bones we identify the fossils as hominid (in the human family) and can measure brain and tooth size, limb length, and proportions. Within general parameters, this evidence offers possibilities for inferring diet and development from the teeth, locomotion from the pelvic and foot bones, brain size from the skull, and body size from joints and limb bones. The early fossils record that a human form of bipedal locomotion emerged much earlier in time than did a large brain.

3. *Living Species*. Fossils cannot speak with a distinct voice. Therefore the past (direct) evidence must be integrated with present (indirect) evidence of living species in order to explain human prehistory. For example, genetically chimpanzees are the closest living relatives to humans. Thus, it is not surprising that early hominids resemble chimpanzees in many features of brain size, dental development, and joint and bone structure. Chimpanzee behavior cannot be identical to that of early hominids; nonetheless, it provides a basis for speculating about some aspects of early hominid behavior, such as object manipulation, communication, and social bonds.

Modern gathering-hunting societies illustrate the interrelationships of several aspects of behavior—for example, how food is obtained and processed, by whom and with what kinds of tools; and how subsistence intersects with other activities such as food sharing, care of children and women's work. An approach to the past that combines the fossil and archeological record with the behavior of living chimpanzees and foraging peoples offers ways to look at women's activities and to place hunting and male activities into perspective.

4. *Evolutionary Process*. Evolution by natural selection means three things: individuals in a population survive to adulthood, they mate and produce offspring, and they rear their offspring to reproductive age. Given mammalian, and specifically primate, reproduction, females are central in producing and rearing offspring and are a limiting resource in population expansion. Therefore an evolutionary perspective of past human societies must consider the female life cycle and reproductive effort.

To ensure that women are included in the human species, I avoid the use of the generic *man* and adopt the term *humans*. Language shapes our perspective and can structure our thinking. Phrases like "the evolution of man," "the social life of early man," or "mysteries of mankind" are cases in point.

The Evolution of Social Life: Contrasting Hypotheses

Behavior does not fossilize, yet it is behavior rather than bones and teeth alone that interests us about human evolution. Reconstructions of human behavior that developed during the 1960s (and are still very much in evidence) can be summarized as "man the hunter." This view of human evolution is known for its emphasis on meat eating and hunting and on the activities of males. According to this view, distinguishing features of the human way of life encompass a diet in which meat is a main item, in contrast to the presumed vegetarian apes; hunting by males as a means to obtain it, and consequently an early division of labor by sex; pair bonding so males would share meat with their mates and offspring and ensure social

Table 1.
Time Chart: Major Events in Human Evolution

Time Scale (Years before present)	Events	Possible Interpretation of Way of Life
10,000	Domestication of plants and animals in the Old World	Major changes in family and gender relationships? Food sources concentrated; Permanent settlements
100,000	Spread of *Homo sapiens* throughout Old World	Gathering-hunting well developed
500,000	Origin of *Homo sapiens* in Africa Humans in Europe and northern Asia	Expanding resource base Beginning of single hunting in temperate regions?
1,000,000	Human populations expand to Southeast Asia	Gathering successful in habitats outside Africa
2,000,000	Bone tools, evidence of digging Stone tools; some in association with animal bones; some bones with cutmarks	Effective procurement of plant foods (digging) Occasional butchering of large animals for meat Predation continues Expanding home range size
3,000,000	Hominid fossils in East and South Africa—2 species?	Collecting and sharing wide range of plant foods; predation on small animals
3,500,000	Fossil hominid footprints at Laetoli; hominid jaws and teeth *Australopithecus*	Early hominids adapting to savanna collecting dispersed foods bipedally with organic tools
5,000,000	Divergence of humans and chimpanzees (molecular evidence)	
6-8,000,000	Savanna mosaic habitat becomes widespread in Africa	

stability within the group; and the loss of estrus and acquisition of continual sexual receptivity of females to attract males.

The gathering hypothesis or "woman the gatherer" was developed as a corrective to the omission of women and women's activities in traditional reconstructions; this perspective is useful for keeping gender in human evolution. When first proposed, this view emphasized both the importance of plant foods in the diet and gathering as a method for obtaining plants and small animals for food and as an impetus in the development of the human way of life (Linton 1971; Tanner and Zihlman 1976; Zihlman and Tanner 1978).

In the hunting hypothesis, early hominid behavior is interpreted as a result of men's hunting activities: bipedal locomotion, tool using and making, food sharing, formation of pair bonds, and the sexual division of labor. In contrast, the gathering hypothesis stresses that obtaining plant foods with tools, especially by women, was the basis for the human way of life, and that plants were major food items, a focus for technological innovation and for changes in social behavior. Behaviors once thought to be exclusive to a hunting way of life are equally if not more important to a gathering one: upright posture, bipedal locomotion, and the ability to walk long distances and carry; sharing food, making and using tools; having knowledge and communicating about the environment. Women as well as men were developing these skills.

The gathering hypothesis has been seen in opposition to hunting and as exclusively about women. But a more central issue is timing: when did hunting emerge in human evolution and what preceded it? It is likely that innovations around plant foods developed in the earliest stages of human evolution and that hunting came later in time. There is a great deal of information from the fossil record, studies of the behavior of chimpanzees, and the role of women in contemporary gathering-hunting societies to support the gathering hypothesis. Evidence for utilizing meat from large animals by early hominids appears in the archeological record almost 2 million years after the first appearance of hominids. Unequivocal evidence for hunting is much later in time.

The Fossil Record and Its Interpretation

Direct evidence from the australopithecine fossils dated from between 2 and 3 million years ago provide information on diet and development from dentition, locomotion from pelvic and foot bones, hand function from hand bones and body proportions from skeletal remains.

Dentition

All early hominids have large, well worn, thickly enameled molar and premolar teeth. Relative to estimated body size, these teeth are larger than they are in any contemporary ape or human. The corresponding muscles of mastication—the temporalis and masseter—have left well-developed markings on the skull and jaws. These features are associated with a dental mechanism effective for grinding foods that are tough or foods from the ground that are gritty and wear down the teeth (Wallace 1975). The dental mechanism of early hominids is convergent with that of bears and pigs. Thickly enameled posterior teeth are also found among primates, such as orangutans and cebid monkeys, which dentally process fruits with tough outer coverings.

The dental evidence is consistent with an omnivorous diet that probably included various kinds of fruits, seeds and nuts, fibrous vegetation, as well as roots and tubers from underground. Early hominids were very likely eating some animal protein, and their dentition does not rule this out. But features of the chewing apparatus point to a diet that contained many items that required dental preparation. At this early stage in evolution, tool use for extensive preparation of food, such as pounding or cooking, was probably not well developed.

Recent studies on rate of tooth formation and eruption have changed our ideas about the developmental pattern and chronological age of individual fossil hominids (Beynon and Dean 1988). Previously it was supposed that australopithecine maturation was prolonged, as in modern humans, and was a departure from the faster developmental rate in apes (Mann 1975). These new studies now indicate that dental formation is similar to that of chimpanzees, and that growth and development were on a faster rather than a slower track.

Canine teeth in early hominids are small, about the size of the incisors, and show little variation. In contrast, canine teeth of male monkeys and apes are usually notably larger than those of females and are associated with male-male competition or defense against predators. The small canine teeth in hominids indicate little difference in function between females and males but suggest changes in social interaction, especially between males, and in antipredator strategies.

Locomotor Anatomy

Bipedal locomotion is a defining characteristic of the human family, the *Hominidae*, and its hallmark is endurance rather than speed (Zihlman and Brunker 1979). There is evidence for this form of locomotion by 3.5 mya based on hominid footprints from Laetoli, Tanzania, although the fossil hominid pelvis, lower limbs and foot bones retain a number of chimpanzee-like features (Leakey & Hay 1979; Stern and Susman 1983). A new first metatarsal almost 2 million years old resembles that of humans more than apes, but its joint surface suggests that the characteristic toe-off mechanism of human gait was absent (Susman and Brain 1988).

Brain and Body Proportions

More recently discovered fossils indicate that the cranial capacity of hominids between 2 and 3 million years ago is well within the range of chimpanzees (Falk 1987). Brain reorganization as deduced from preserved surfaces of fossil brains may have been minimal and more similar to an ape than to a human pattern. A partial skeleton almost 3 million years old (AL 288, called "Lucy") preserves arm and thigh bones and suggests the body proportions were intermediate between chimpanzee and humans. Compared to chimpanzees, early hominids probably had a lower center of gravity, which would have increased stability in an upright position. Because the fossils are rarely complete or even nearly so (the famous Lucy has 40% of the entire skeleton), it is difficult to establish body size and its range in the population. Some of the fossils, like Lucy, are very small; other individual bones, such as the thigh or foot bones, are quite large. At this time it is not clear how many species of hominids these bones represent and what size range might have existed within each species. This information is important for establishing how much bigger in body size males might have been than females.

Hand Bones

Modern human hands have short straight finger bones, well-developed thumb bones and associated muscles, and a mobile palm. In contrast, ape hands have long, curved robust fingers, relatively small thumb bones and associated muscles, and limited mobility in the palm. Fossil hand bones of 3 million years ago are still quite curved and bear resemblance to those of African apes (Susman et al. 1984). However, the palm region indicates greater mobility than that of apes and the potential to grip objects and strongly manipulate them (Marzke 1983). At these hominid sites (Hadar, Ethiopia) no objects are preserved that can be interpreted as hominid tools.

But at a fossil site about 2 million years of age (Swartkrans) newly discovered hominid hand bones and tools are preserved together. The thumb bone suggests well-developed muscles and an ability to firmly grasp tools (Susman 1988). The associated stone and bone artifacts show signs of having been used for digging.

Animal Bones and Stone Tools

For many years the animal bones that had accumulated in South African caves along with the hominids were thought to be the result of hominid activities. Subsequent research on these and other sites demonstrates that bones may accumulate and be modified by natural processes, such as weathering, sorting and transporting by water, trampling by animals, and collecting, breaking, and destruction by carnivore predators and scavengers.

Some of this early research involved comparing the bone collecting behavior and consumption patterns of several species of carnivore, including hyena, cheetah, leopard, porcupine, and owl, with human food remains from Middle and Late Stone Age archeological sites (Brain 1981). This analysis provides a compelling argument that the bone accumulations in the caves were the result of hunting behavior of carnivores (primarily leopards) and that the early hominid bones at the same sites were remains of the hunted and not the hunters.

Stones (and a few bones) with unmistakable signs of wear or workmanship show up in the archeological record between 2 and 2.5 million years ago. These implements consist of flakes, choppers, and unmodified pieces that show wear or are of foreign materials transported from another area. The function of stone tools is not always obvious. But now microscopic study of wear patterns on some stone implements suggest that they were used for cutting soft plant materials, for scraping and sawing wood and for cutting animal tissue (Keeley 1977; Keeley and Toth 1981). Flake tools and choppers could have been used to clean, cut up, and pound plant foods, for preparing effective wooden implements or for bashing open marrow cavities of long bones for marrow. New bone tools from Swartkrans found with hand bones and mentioned above show a polish similar to that produced experimentally on bones used for digging in hard ground.

The association of animal bones, stone tools, and hominid remains from East African sites led to the conclusion that the bones were the debris accumulated by hominids at home bases (Isaac 1978). More recent studies indicate that bone breakage and concentration may be due primarily to carnivore activities and make it unlikely that these areas are campsites or home bases as once thought (Potts 1984, 1988).

At a few sites between 1 and 2 million years ago, cutmarks on animal bones may have been made by stone tools and suggest that the hominids were butchering large animals (Bunn 1981; Potts and Shipman 1981). But there is no evidence that the animals butchered were killed by human actions, and it is difficult to establish with any certainty how early people obtained meat prior to 130,000 years ago (Klein 1987). Animal bone and stone tool associations may reflect a mixture of hominid and carnivore activities (Potts 1988).

Supporting Information from Chimpanzees and Foraging Peoples

The fossil and archeological record of 2–3 million years ago give insight about diet, development, locomotion, and manipulative skills of early hominids. Animal bone accumulations, stone and bone implements and associations with bones help sort out hominid from carnivore activity. Information about chimpanzee behavior offers suggestions about the kinds of behavior that might have been present in the ancestral ape population, and contemporary gathering-hunting societies illuminate the nature of women's roles in a nomadic way of life.

Molecular Data

During the 1960s new techniques to study the genetic material of living species revealed that chimpanzees and gorillas were the closest living relatives to humans and the two groups may have separated some 5 million years ago, rather than 20 or 30 mya, as previously thought (Sarich and Wilson 1967). Recent techniques comparing DNA indicate that chimpanzees and humans are more closely related to each other than either is to the gorilla (Sibley and Ahlquist 1984; Williams and Goodman 1989). This close genetic relationship between chimpanzees and humans suggests that the common ancestor to both groups may have resembled chimpanzees more than any other primates. Behaviors observed in chimpanzees may have been present in the common ancestor and early hominids.

Chimpanzee Behavior

Chimpanzees in their natural habitat are more similar to humans in a number of behaviors than previously recognized or appreciated. For example, chimpanzees, like humans and most other primates, are best described as omnivorous because they eat a variety of both plant and animal foods; they are not strictly vegetarian (Harding and Teleki 1981). Their diverse diet includes a preponderance of fruits, supplemented by insects and small animals. It is likely that the early hominids, even if relying primarily on plant foods, also preyed upon small animals for food.

Chimpanzees also prepare and use tools, occasionally walk bipedally and communicate social and environmental information (Goodall 1986). Both females and males modify and use materials in a variety of ways—leaves as sponges, twigs as probes to obtain termites, rocks and sticks as hammers to crack open nuts and as missiles. Female chimps spend more time than males fishing for termites and in cracking open nuts more efficiently (Boesch and Boesch 1984; Goodall 1986). The most significant variable related to the sex difference in frequency and efficiency in nut cracking may be social. Adult males prefer to maintain visual contact with other group members and often stop the activity in order to engage in social interactions. Adult females in contrast, continue cracking nuts even if there is a conflict or if the group moves on.

Sharing food among chimpanzees was first reported in the context of predation and eating meat, with adult males sharing more frequently (Goodall 1968; Teleki 1973). As more data were collected, it became apparent that plants are widely shared, and over half the instances occur between mother and offspring pairs. Most of the food shared is plant material and most sharing (in 86% of instances) is between related individuals (McGrew 1975; Silk 1978).

Among pygmy chimpanzees *(Pan paniscus)* food sharing seems to occur more frequently than is the case for *Pan troglodytes* (Kano 1982; Kuroda 1984). Juvenile animals are the most frequent recipients, and adult females are donors four times more often than are adult males.

Long-term studies on several species of free-ranging primates demonstrate that chimpanzees, like other primates, form relationships between mothers and offspring and among siblings that endure throughout life. These small family groups form the social core in most primate species. Primatologists discovered that rank and status in the group passes from mothers to their offspring, a contrast to previous assumptions that dominance rank is something earned simply by the fighting abilities of big and strong males (Sade 1972; see Fedigan and Fedigan module).

Chimpanzee social organization is flexible (fission-fusion type) and suited to ranging over many square miles in search of food. Groups change in size and composition and are not headed by a leader male. Friendships and kin ties influence the day to day associations of animals. An extensive communicative repertoire of postures, gestures, vocalizations and facial expressions permits varied and complex responses to different social situations.

Like group composition, sexual activity is variable with several patterns: opportunistic or noncompetitive mating where a female in estrus may mate with several different males during a single cycle; or a short-term exclusive relationship where a male prevents other males from mating with his temporary mate; or a consortship where a male and female leave the group for a week or more and remain away from other chimpanzees (Tutin 1979). No single mating pattern accurately describes this highly social species.

Female chimpanzees spend most of their adult life pregnant and lactating and invest more time and energy in rearing offspring than do males. Adult males in chimpanzee groups are generally protective of all infants and young; and through patrolling territorial boundaries maintain the home range of the chimpanzee community from neighboring males.

In their omnivorous diet, object manipulation, social development, flexibility in sexual activity, and fission-fusion social organization, chimpanzees may resemble the early hominids and illustrate the active role females play in this range of activities. There is a tendency to emphasize the differences between chimpanzees and ourselves. But for this early period of human evolution it is instructive to emphasize our similarities with chimpanzees and the continuity between the ape ancestor and the earliest hominids.

Gathering-Hunting Peoples

A nomadic, gathering-hunting way of life persisted in some form from the time of human origins 5 million years or so ago. Only after about 10,000 years ago did human populations begin to settle down in some parts of the world, to cultivate plants and domesticate animals. Therefore, modern-day nomadic peoples provide a more realistic model for helping to conceptualize early hominid societies than do Western industrialized ones.

The significance of gathering first became apparent at the same conference on "hunting-gathering" peoples, where Washburn and Lancaster and Laughlin presented their ideas on hunting (Lee and DeVore 1968). Several studies reported that the majority of tropical hunter-gatherer groups in Africa, Asia, Australia, and North America subsists mainly on plant foods gathered by women, or on fish, and much less by hunting per se. In actuality most such groups are "gatherer-hunters," which led Lee and DeVore (1968) to conclude that vegetable foods were probably always available and that early hominid women likely played an active role in subsistence—collecting food, making and using tools, as well as caring for infants.

The savanna mosaic environment illustrated by the bushveldt and woodlands of the Kalahari in southern Africa contains many species of plants that are used for food, medicine, and materials for making many kinds of tools. One population, for example, utilizes 80 plant species as food, 11 of which are staple items in the diet. These include various types of melon, beans, roots, tubers, leaves and gum; they are tasty, nutritious, abundant, predictable and accessible. These people also hunt or gather some 50 kinds of animals, though their role in overall diet varies seasonally (Tanaka 1980). The heavy reliance on plant foods of tropical savanna gatherer-hunters contrasts with earlier assumptions that the main food items in a savanna environment would necessarily be meat.

The task of gathering food falls primarily to women. They go out collecting, often with other women, carrying their nursing infants, their digging implements and sharpening stone; the kaross, a garment made of animal skin, serves as a baby sling, as well as a container for gathered food (Lee 1968, 1969). The work effort of women is considerable, and they frequently walk long distances and carry heavy loads. It is not unusual for a woman to return home after a journey of several miles, carrying the equivalent of 75% of her body weight in food, firewood and baby (Lee 1979; Peacock 1985). Among the Kalahari San, women carry their babies continually for the first two years, an estimated 2400 km, which decreases to 1800 km in the third year and 1200 by age four (Lee 1979). Children of this age weigh from about 6 to 15 kg, which is added to the food and goods a woman might carry. After children are weaned they remain in camp with other adults and children while the mother again goes out gathering. Women are responsible for about 90% of child care (Lee 1979).

Women also contribute protein to the diet. Killing birds and small mammals with a club or collecting tortoises and insects can be considered a form of gathering. Women may report back to camp on the animals and tracks observed while gathering, and this information may be used later by men during hunting. Men also gather food, but this may consist of picking and eating plants while hunting, though occasionally men return from hunting with plants, birds' eggs, or firewood. Women among the Kalahari San do not hunt by bow and arrow, but in some cultures they do (Estioko-Griffin and Griffin 1981).

Overall, the picture of women we now have from gathering-hunting societies is one of active, mobile individuals, who walk long distances, carry heavy loads, and contribute a major source of food to their families. They prepare food, use tools, and at the same time become pregnant, lactate, and care for children.

Early Hominid Behavior from a Woman's Perspective

Locomotion and Travel

Bipedal locomotion is a terrestrial, savanna adaptation for covering long distances while carrying food and water, digging sticks, objects for defense, and offspring. A large home range is necessary for obtaining the widely dispersed resources on the savanna, especially of plant foods. The evidence suggests that both women and men engaged in these activities.

For women there are social aspects of bipedal locomotion. A hominid mother probably carried and nursed her baby almost continually for three years, as do chimpanzees and women in foraging societies. Without a grasping foot like that of chimpanzees to cling to their mother's hair, hominid babies could not hold on to their mothers as well. Consequently the mother had to take a more active role in carrying the infant. A sling for support might have been an early hominid "tool" that would have freed the mother's arms and hands for other activities.

Tool Making and Using

Stone tools persist better through time than food plants or implements made from organic materials, but both were probably important in early hominid subsistence (Lee 1968). Given the importance of organic tools among gatherer-hunters and the facility of chimpanzees with grass stems and twigs and wooden hammers, many implements used by early hominids were probably made of organic material and used for digging. This type of implement may represent a straightforward transition from chimpanzee termiting sticks to the simple, multi-purpose digging tools of modern gatherer-hunters (see Spector and Whelan, this volume). Similarly, the stones used by chimpanzees for cracking open nutshells would not be readily recognized as tools in the archeological record.

Development and Learning

If the hominid way of life depended upon bipedal locomotion and making and using tools, then from a child's point of view, the gathering way of life required extended time to acquire motor and cognitive skills. In turn, it required a long dependence on adults (Zihlman 1983). An early hominid child could not be physically independent until it was weaned and could walk long distances. For chimpanzees this occurs about age 5, but a contemporary child does not develop the stamina to walk long distances until about age 8.

A young chimpanzee does not master the art of termiting with tools until about age 5, and skills for cracking open nuts with stone and wooden hammers are not developed until adolescence. Presumably it would have taken an early hominid child at least 5 years to learn motor and cognitive skills for using tools effectively. Learning these, as well as social skills, would have taken place within the protective social environment of the mother and group, and so equipped the young to survive, reproduce and rear offspring.

Mating Patterns and Sexuality

Although early hominid mating patterns are usually presented as monogamous or pair bonded, these suggestions can only be speculative. Nonetheless, I would conjecture that mating patterns were variable, as they are among chimpanzees, and stress flexibility and female choice. The dependency of young after weaning would have been facilitated if males, as well as females, shared food and cared for the young. The males need not have been the biological fathers. They might have developed friendships that have been described for female and male baboons and chimpanzees. Females might view males with these traits as more sexually attractive and so choose them as mates. The small canine teeth in early hominids suggest that social changes occurred among early hominids, perhaps a reduction in aggression among males, and between females and males, compared to chimpanzees.

Sexual Division of Labor

The nature of a sexual division of labor and when it developed during human evolution have been major issues for theories of human evolution. In human societies it is reciprocal and expected. Among chimpanzees there are differences in frequency of tasks by sex and by age, but there is no formalized sharing or exchange. Early hominids were probably more similar to this pattern than to that of gatherer-hunters. My own view is that the sexual division of labor as we know it today probably developed quite recently in human evolution, perhaps in the Later Pleistocene when hunting begins to be effective, or even later when people began to live in settlements and give up a nomadic way of life.

Summary

Information derived from the fossil record, primate behavior, and gatherer-hunters gives a firm basis for delineating women's reproductive, economic, and social activities and contributions to human evolution. We can conclude that women made and used tools to obtain food for themselves, as well as to sustain their young after weaning; walked long distances; and carried food and infants bipedally on the African savannas (Tanner 1981; Tanner and Zihlman 1976). It is also reasonable to conclude that hunting did not emerge at the earliest stage in human evolution. Rather, hunting probably developed much later in human history and derived from the technological and social base in gathering (Zihlman 1978, 1981).

There are limitations to what the record of human prehistory can reveal about the behavior of women and men. Details of social behavior can never be known with any certainty and will always be a focus for conjecture and debate. But a balanced understanding of human evolution should incorporate women as well as men, children as well as adults into the picture and include the range of activities throughout the life cycle on which natural selection acts, rather than a narrower focus on one or two of them. It is as much through the willingness to incorporate the available information as it is through the information itself that we can gain a more complete view of our ancient human ancestors.

References Cited

Beynon, A. D., and M. C. Dean
  1988   Distinct Dental Development Patterns in Early Fossil Hominids. Nature 335:509–514.
Boesch, C., and Helwig Boesch
  1984   Possible Causes of Sex Differences in the Use of Natural Hammers by Wild Chimpanzees. Journal of Human Evolution 10:585–593.
Brain, C. K.
  1981   The Hunters or the Hunted? An Introduction to African Cave Taphonomy. Chicago: University of Chicago Press.
Bunn, H. T.
  1981   Archaeological Evidence for Meat-Eating by Plio-Pleistocene Hominids from Koobi Fora and Olduvai Gorge. Nature 291:574–577.
Estioko-Griffin, Agnes, and P. Bion Griffin
  1981   Woman the Hunter: The Agta. *In* Woman the Gatherer. F. Dahlberg, ed. Pp. 121–151. New Haven: Yale University Press.
Falk, Dean
  1987   Hominid Paleoneurology. Annual Review of Anthropology 16:13–30.
Goodall, Jane
  1968   The Behaviour of Free-living Chimpanzees in the Gombe Stream Reserve. Animal Behavior Monographs 1:165–311.

      1986   The Chimpanzees of Gombe. Cambridge: Harvard University Press.
Harding, R. S. O., and G. Teleki, eds.
      1981   Omnivorous Primates: Gathering and Hunting in Human Evolution. New York: Columbia
              University Press.
Isaac, G. L.
      1978   The Foodsharing Behavior of Protohuman Hominids. Scientific American 238(4):90–108.
Kano, T.
      1982   The Social Group of Pygmy Chimpanzees *(Pan paniscus)* of Wamba. Primates 23:171–188.
Keeley, L. H.
      1977   The Functions of Paleolithic Flint Tools. Scientific American 237(5):108–126.
Keeley, L. H., and N. Toth
      1981   Microwear Polishes on Early Stone Tools from Koobi Fora, Kenya. Nature 293:464–465.
Klein, R. G.
      1987   Reconstructing How Early People Exploited Animal: Problems and Prospects. *In* The Evo-
              lution of Human Hunting. M. Nitecki and D. Nitecki, eds. Pp. 11–45. New York: Plenum.
Kuroda, S.
      1984   Interaction over Food among Pygmy Chimpanzees. *In* The Pygmy Chimpanzee: Evolutionary
              Biology and Behavior. R. L. Susman, ed. Pp. 301–324. New York: Plenum.
Leakey, Mary D., and R. L. Hay
      1979   Pliocene Footprints in the Laetolil Beds at Laetoli, Northern Tanzania. Nature 278:317–323.
Lee, R. B.
      1968   What Hunters Do for a Living or How to Make Out on Scarce Resources. *In* Man the Hunter.
              R. B. Lee and I. DeVore, eds. Pp. 30–48. Chicago: Aldine.
      1969   !Kung Bushman Subsistence: An Input-Output Analysis. *In* Ecological Studies in Cultural
              Anthropology. P. Vayda, ed., Pp. 47–79. Garden City, N.Y.: Natural History Press.
Lee, R. B., and I. DeVore
      1968   Man the Hunter. Chicago: Aldine.
Linton, Sally
      1971   Woman the Gatherer: Male Bias in Anthropology. *In* Women in Cross-Cultural Perspective.
              Sue-Ellen Jacob, ed. Champaign: University of Illinois Press. Reprinted under Sally Slocum in
              Toward an Anthropology of Women, 1975 R. Rapp Reiter, ed. Pp. 36–50. New York: Monthly
              Review Press.
Mann, Alan
      1975   Paleodemographic Aspects of the South African *Australopithecines.* Anthropology Publica-
              tions No. 1. Philadelphia: University of Pennsylvania Press.
Marzke, M.
      1983   Joint Functions and Grips of the *Australopithecus afarensis* hand, with Special Reference to
              the Region of the Capitate. Journal of Human Evolution 12:197–211.
McGrew, W. C.
      1975   Patterns of Plant Food Sharing by Wild Chimpanzees. Proceedings of the 5th Congress, in-
              ternational Primatology Society (Nagoya, Japan). Pp. 304–309.
Peacock, Nadine
      1985   Time Allocation, Work and Fertility among Efe Pygmy Women of Northeast Zaire. PhD dis-
              sertation, Harvard University.
Potts, R.
      1984   Home Bases and Early Hominids. American Scientist 72:338–347.
      1988   Early Hominid Activities at Olduvai. Hawthorne, N.Y.: Aldine de Gruyter.
Potts, R., and Pat Shipman
      1981   Cutmarks Made by Stone Tools on Bones from Olduvai Gorge, Tanzania. Nature 291:577–
              580.
Sade, D. S.
      1972   A Longitudinal Study of Social Behavior of Rhesus Monkeys. *In* Functional and Evolutionary
              Biology of Primates. R. H. Tuttle, ed. Pp. 378–398. Chicago: Aldine.

Sarich, V. M., and A. C. Wilson
  1967   Immunological Time Scale for Hominid Evolution. Science 158:1200–1203.
Sibley, C. B., and J. Ahlquist
  1984   The Phylogeny of the Hominoid Primates as Indicated by DNA-DNA hybridization. Journal of Molecular Evolution 20:2–15.
Silk, J. B.
  1978   Patterns of Food Sharing among Mother and Infant Chimpanzees at Gombe National Park, Tanzania. Folia Primatologica 29:129–141.
Stern, J., and R. L. Susman
  1983   The Locomotor Anatomy of *Australopithecus afarensis*. American Journal of Physical Anthropology 60:279–318.
Susman, R. L.
  1988   Hand of *Paranthropus robustus* from Member I, Swartkrans: Fossil Evidence for Tool Behavior. Science 240:781–783.
Susman, R. L., and T. M. Brain
  1988   New First Metatarsal (SKX 5017) from Swartkrans and the Gait of *Paranthropus robustus*. American Journal of Physical Anthropology 77:7–15.
Susman, R. L., J. T. Stern, and W. L. Jungers
  1984   Arboreality and Bipedality in the Hadar Hominids. Folia primatologica 43:113–156.
Tanaka, J.
  1980   The San Hunter-Gatherers of the Kalahari. Tokyo: Tokyo University Press.
Tanner, Nancy
  1981   On Becoming Human. New York: Cambridge University Press.
Tanner, Nancy, and Adrienne Zihlman
  1976   Women in Evolution: Innovation and Selection in Human Origins. Signs 1(3 pt. 1):585–608.
Teleki, G.
  1973   The Omnivorous Chimpanzee. Scientific American 228 (I):33–42.
Tutin, Caroline E. G.
  1979   Mating Patterns and Reproductive Strategies in a Community of Wild Chimpanzees *(Pan troglodytes schweinfurthii)*. Behavioral Ecology and Sociobiology 6:29–38.
Wallace, J. A.
  1975   Dietary Adaptations of *Australopithecus* and Early *Homo*. In Paleoanthropology, Morphology and Paleoecology. R. H. Tuttle, ed. Pp. 203–223. The Hague: Mouton.
Williams, S. A., and M. Goodman
  1989   A Statistical Test That Supports a Human/Chimpanzee Clade Based on Noncoding DNA Sequence Data. Molecular Biology and Evolution 6:325–330.
Zihlman, A. L.
  1978   Women in Evolution, Part II. Subsistence and Social Organization Among Early Hominids. Signs 4(1):4–20.
  1981   Women as Shapers of the Human Adaptation. *In* Woman the Gatherer. Frances Dahlberg, ed. Pp. 75–120. New Haven: Yale University Press.
  1983   A Behavioral Reconstruction of *Australopithecus*. *In* Hominid Origins: Inquiries Past and Present. K. J. Reichs, ed. Pp. 207–238. Washington, D.C.: University Press of America.
Zihlman, A. L., and Lynda Brunker
  1979   Hominid Bipedalism: Then and Now. Yearbook of Physical Anthropology 22:132–162.
Zihlman, A. L., and N. Tanner
  1978   Gathering and the Hominid Adaptation. In Female Hierarchies. L. Tiger and H. Fowler, eds. Pp. 163–194. Chicago: Beresford Book Service.

Annotated Bibliography

The following sources may be assigned to students or used by the instructor to focus discussions or prepare lectures on some aspect of the role of women in evolution.

Bleier, Ruth
  1984   Science and Gender: A Critique of Biology and its Theories on Women. New York: Pergamon Press.

  Covers a range of topics with useful discussions on the brain and human "nature," hormones and sex differences, and man the hunter. Of particular interest is Chapter 5, "Theories of Human Origins and Cultural Evolution: Man the Hunter," which critiques the theory, but also makes the important point that no single factor or event can provide *the* key to human evolution.

Boesch, C., and H. Boesch
  1984   Possible Causes of Sex Differences in the Use of Natural Hammers by Wild Chimpanzees. Journal of Human Evolution 13:415–440.

  Adult female chimpanzees more frequently than males perform the most difficult techniques of using hammers (stone and wood) to crack open several kinds of nuts for food. The differences appear during adolescence and seem to be affected (among other variables) by differences in female vs. male social behavior and perhaps the need of adult females for higher caloric and protein content.

Brain, C. K.
  1981   The Hunters or the Hunted? Chicago: University of Chicago Press.

  This superb book represents pioneering work that attempts through experiments and detailed observations to account for the bone accumulations in the South African hominid-bearing caves. A thorough investigation, including experiments (what bones remain after carnivore meals, how are they broken, etc.); the conclusion is that carnivores are mainly responsible and that hominids were dietary items.

Dahlberg, Frances
  1981   Woman the Gatherer. New Haven: Yale University Press.

  Collection of articles on female primates and women cross-culturally. In particular, see the articles by W. McGrew on female chimpanzees, Estioko-Griffin and Griffin on hunting among Agta women, and Zihlman on evolutionary perspective of women, including discussion of gathering activities and sexual dimorphism.

Estioko-Griffin, Agnes
  1986   Daughters of the Forest. Natural History 5:37–42.

  A popular account of Agta women of the Philippines who hunt game animals and still raise their children. Demonstrates flexibility in women's activities, in contrast to the stereotype that women do not hunt.

Fedigan, Linda
  1986   The Changing Role of Women in Models of Human Evolution. Annual Review of Anthropology 15:22–66.

  The review begins with the historical context of human evolution models as far back as the 19th century and discusses their fate. It then moves into the 20th century and covers the contribution of primate, ethnographic, and material evidence to scenarios of early human social life. The controversies and issues are presented and evaluated clearly.

Harding, R. S. O., and Teleki, G., eds.
  1981   Omnivorous Primates: Gathering and Hunting in Human Evolution. New York: Columbia University Press.

  Excellent selection of 14 articles on primates, fossil hominids and modern people, which illustrates diets as variations on the theme of omnivory and the role of hunting and eating meat. R. Harding reviews primate diets in the wild; G. Teleki focuses on chimpanzees; R. Gould on Australians; R. Harako on pygmies in Zaire; G. Silberbauer on Kalahari peoples, and more.

Hrdy, Sarah Blaffer, and W. Bennett
1981 Lucy's Husband: What Did He Stand For? Harvard Magazine 46:7–9.

Discussion of Lovejoy's theory on the origin of bipedal locomotion and female sexuality, with a light touch.

Klein, Richard
1987 Reconstructing How Early People Exploited Animals: Problems and Prospects. *In* The Evolution of Human Hunting. M. H. Nitecki and D. V. Nitecki, eds. Pp. 11–45. New York: Plenum Press.

Evaluates the associations of animal bones and stone tools at early hominid sites in order to discover how humans were exploiting animals. His analysis concentrates on Middle Pleistocene sites (about 500,000 yr) in Spain, which, during the 1960s, were widely cited as proof of big game hunting. For some early and middle Pleistocene sites the artifacts suggest that people killed some of the animals and the bones damaged by stone tools indicate some butchering. Not until the Middle Stone Age about 100,000 years ago does hunting appear effective, and by the Later Stone Age in Africa (40,000 yr) there was a major advance in the "human ability to extract protein from nature" (p. 39).

Lee, Richard B., and I. DeVore, eds.
1968 Man the Hunter. Chicago: University of Chicago Press.

Classic collection of articles based on conference of same name, with articles on hunting in human evolution, (e.g., Washburn and Lancaster; Laughlin), but also information on women's gathering efforts, such as Richard Lee's article on Kalahari !Kung.

Lee, R. B.
1979 The !Kung San: Men, Women and Work in a Foraging Society. Cambridge: Cambridge University Press.

Summary of his extensive field work; of particular interest, Chapters 9 "Men, Women and Work" and 11 "Production and Reproduction"—discussion of work effort, hunting, women's work, mobility and birth spacing.

Linton, Sally
1971 Woman the Gatherer: Male Bias in Anthropology. *In* Women in Perspective. S. E. Jacobs, ed. Pp. 9–21. Urbana: University of Illinois Press. Reprinted under Sally Slocum in Toward an Anthropology of Women. Rayna R. Reiter, ed. Pp. 36–50. 1975. New York: Monthly Review Press.

Important historical article that first put forth the idea of woman the gatherer in early human evolution and pointed out the bias in interpretations and the unbalanced emphasis on men and their activities.

Marshall, Lorna
1976 The !Kung of Nyae Nyae. Cambridge: Harvard University Press.

Very useful for providing information on activities of women and men. In particular, Chapter 3, "Plant Foods and Gathering" and Chapter 4, "Animal Foods and Hunting" document in detail these foods and the activities associated with them.

Perper, T., and Carmel Shrire
1977 The Nimrod Connection: Myth and Science in the hunting model. *In* The Chemical Senses and Nutrition. Pp. 447–459. New York: Academic Press.

This gem provides some interesting insights into the historical threads connecting hunting with the Old Testament.

Potts, Richard
1988 Early Hominid Activities at Olduvai. Hawthorne, N.Y.: Aldine de Gruyter.

Thorough review of the formation process of sites and how bones and stones get together. Brings together information on trying to figure out the behavior of early hominids, including the new work on cut marks and the ways they can occur on bones. Reviews previous ideas and research, including Glynn Isaac's. Also useful is Home Bases and Early Hominids (American Scientist 72:338–347), which concludes that the stone accumulations once thought to be home bases are not supported by recent analyses.

Tanaka, Hiro
   1980   The San: Hunter-Gatherers of the Kalahari. A study in Ecological Anthropology. Tokyo: University of Tokyo Press.

Chapter 1 is an excellent documentation of everyday life and the range of activities and material culture with good illustrations. Chapter 2 deals with the foods eaten and how they are obtained.

Tanner, Nancy M.
   1981   On Becoming Human. New York: Cambridge University Press.

Tanner proposes chimpanzees as a model to represent protohominids and develops the gathering hypothesis. Discusses the record of early humans and its interpretation. Particularly useful are its images of women and portrayal of women's activities.

Tanner, N., and A. Zihlman
   1976   Women in Evolution. Part I: Innovation and Selection in Human Origins. Signs 1 (3, part 1):585–608.

Discusses the role of women as initiating the direction of human evolution through their activities related to gathering and sharing food. Emphasizes the interrelationship of subsistence with social behavior and care of offspring.

Zihlman, A. L.
   1978   Women in Evolution. Part II: Subsistence and Social Organization among Early Hominids. Signs 4(1):4–20.

Discusses the possible role of women during the first 2–3 million years of human evolution drawing on the fossil and archeological evidence.

   1982   The Human Evolution Coloring Book. New York: Harper and Row.

A source book for basic information on primates and human evolution. Provides representations of female primates and women and depicts behaviors involving women.

   1987   American Association of Physical Anthropologists Luncheon Address, 1985: Sex, Sexes and Sexism in Human Origins. Yearbook of Physical Anthropology, no. 30.

Personal history of the gathering hypothesis and how it has been received in physical anthropology.

Zihlman, A. L., and J. M. Lowenstein
   1983   A Few Words with Ruby. New Scientist, 14 April.

Through an interview with a 3-million-year-old woman we get an idea of life on the savanna from Ruby's point of view.

Bibliographic items useful here and annotated in other modules:

Conkey, Margaret, and Janet Spector
   1984   Archaeology and the Study of Gender. Advances in Archaeological Method and Theory 7:1–38. New York: Academic Press. (Spector/Whelan module).
Fedigan, Linda
   1981   Primate Paradigms. Montreal: Eden Press. (Fedigan module).

Goodall, Jane
    1986   The Chimpanzees of Gombe. Cambridge: Harvard University Press. (Fedigan module).
Hrdy, Sarah, and G. C. Williams
    1983   Behavioral Biology and the Double Standard. *In* Social Behavior of Female Vertebrates. S.
        K. Wasser, ed. Pp. 3–17. New York: Academic Press. (Fedigan module).
Lancaster, Jane
    1985   Evolutionary Perspectives on Sex Differences in the Higher Primates. *In* Gender and the Life
        Course. A. Rossi, ed. Pp. 3–27. Chicago: Aldine. (Lancaster module).
Shostak, Marjorie
    1983   Nisa: The Life and Words of a !Kung Woman. New York: Vintage. (Lancaster module).

Course Component 1: Gender and Tools

Objectives

To examine female and male differences in tool using and associated activities among chimpanzees and gathering-hunting peoples in order to help students think about possible early hominid technology and activities associated with women.

Resources

Films.   *Jane Goodall Studies of the Chimpanzee. Tool Using.* 1978 National Geographic Society. 17th and M Streets; Washington D.C. 20036.
    Bitter Melons. An overview of daily life of the Kalahari San gatherer-hunters.
    The Wasp Nest. A group of women and children while gathering and socially interacting. Both from the San Film Series, Documentary Educational Resources, 24 Dane Street, Somerville, Massachusetts 02143; 617/666-1750.

Readings.   For instructor or to assign to students (see bibliographies for complete reference).
    Chimpanzees: Boesch and Boesch (1984); McGrew in Dahlberg (1981); Goodall (1986) Chapter 18.
    Gathering-hunting people: Lee (1968, 1979); Marshall (1976) Chapters 2, 3, 4; Tanakaq (1980) Chapters 2, 3; Estioko-Griffin & Griffin in Dahlberg (1981).
    Evolutionary perspective: J. B. Lancaster (1968) On the Evolution of Tool-using Behavior. American Anthropologist 70:56–66; Tanner (1981) Chapter 9; Potts (1988); Klein (1987); A. Zihlman (1982) Part V.

This exercise has three components that may be used separately or in combination.

1. *Chimpanzees*

Not until long-term studies were carried out in several habitats did it become known that there are differences between female and male chimpanzees in skill level and time spent in using tools.
    Both sexes use tools made from organic and stone materials. Tools are used in connection with insects, nuts, and water. Two factors are important: caloric needs and social behavior. From tool-using activities, females may obtain more calories, which are necessary for

reproduction. Females seem to be more willing to spend time and effort in tool-using activities that are less social, whereas males seem to focus more on other animals.

Questions for discussion:

What materials are used in tool-using contexts?
What foods are obtained through tool-using?
What sex differences exist in frequency of activities? Why?
What differences exist in skill level?
When do the sex differences appear during the life cycle and what might this mean?
How would the kinds of tools used by chimpanzees be recognizable in the archeological record?
What does the behavior of chimpanzees suggest about the behavior of past populations (especially about female hominids) as read in the fossil record?

2. *Contemporary Gathering-Hunting Peoples*

When field research focuses on subsistence activities, we learn that time and skill are involved in finding, obtaining, and processing many species of plant foods. Women most frequently engage in these activities, but men also do on occasion. The digging stick, though simple in appearance, requires skill to make and use and is an important multipurpose tool. Remember to include slings and containers as tools.

Questions for discussion:

What kinds of tools are used to obtain plant foods?
What kind for animal foods?
What kind of materials are used and how long have they been available? (e.g., iron or metal tipped arrows)
What plant resources require tool processing?
In what ways are plants processed? (e.g., cutting, pounding, chopping)
How many kinds of plants are utilized and what kind of knowledge is needed to find and process them? (e.g., seasonal plants, underground roots and tubers)
What is the role of women in these activities? of men?
Given this information what kinds of considerations must be made for the archeological record?

3. *Early Hominids of 2 to 4 Million Years Ago*

There are no stones or bones recognizable by archeologists showing modification much before 2 million years ago. About that time stones and bones appear in association at several hominid sites: Olduvai Gorge in East Africa and Sterkfontein and Swartkrans in South Africa. The sites are very different, and archeological research is devoted to discovering the conditions under which bones and stones become associated in these different sites (cave vs. open air). Furthermore, experiments that duplicate markings on ancient stones and bones can help interpret early human activities. For example, C. K. Brain suggests that bone fragments were used in digging in hard earth because the polish and striations on them can be duplicated.

Questions for discussion:

What kinds of objects have been found in early sites?
How do we know the objects might have been made or used by early hominids?

What other kinds of tools might have been used and why are they not present?
How might these tools be used in connection with plants? with animals? for procurement? for processing? with other activities?
Who might be doing these activities?
How much difference between females and males might there have been in these activities and why?
What reasons can you think to give to support the idea that there was not yet a division of labor by sex?
What are the limitations of our knowledge from the archeological record?

Course Component 2: Images of Women and Men in Prehistory

Objectives

To raise awareness about how women have been depicted in evolutionary reconstructions; to question the assumptions underlying these depictions; to focus on or create more positive images of women in prehistory.

This exercise can utilize whatever materials are easily available. Because positive images are less readily available, this exercise may focus closely on less positive or directly negative images, define why they are negative and raise awareness about underlying assumptions. The project can focus on materials from the library or on films. The following are a few examples.

The Popular Press. Magazines such as *Time, Newsweek,* and most recently *U.S. News and World Report* (27 February 1989) occasionally have stories, even cover stories on human evolution, and issues of *National Geographic* (especially April 1979 and November 1985) are useful.

Time-Life books are a good source; for example, *Early Man* by Clark Howell (1965) and *The Emergence of Man* series (1972), in particular the first and second volumes, "The Missing Link" and "The First Men" (this cover is quite interesting).

There are historical changes. The most positive depiction of women's activities are found in the November 1985 cover story "The Search for Early Man." These reconstructions of early hominid social life can be used for comparison with some earlier and more negative ones.

Questions for discussion:

Are women or female figures present? If not, this might be a point for discussion.
Assuming female figures are present, are the figures identified as women? If so, how?
Location: Where are the women placed? Foreground? Background? What does this suggest about their position in the group? Contrast this to where the men placed are in the illustration.
Body posture: Are women pictured standing, sitting, moving? How about the men?
Activities: In what kinds of activities are the women engaged? Are they holding or using tools? What activities are men doing? Is the range of activities for men greater than for women?
Demeanor: Where are the women looking (out, down)? Do they appear to be afraid? timid? in charge? Are women depicted burdened with children? as leaders? dependent? marginal? How are men depicted?

Overall, what kind of impression is conveyed about early hominid society? Is it women or men who are doing the work, sharing food, caretaking, making or using implements?
Is a sexual division of labor implied? How do these characterizations fit with what you have learned in this course?
How might reconstructions of the past reflect our own cultural stereotypes of what are proper roles for women and men?
With knowledge of nonhuman primates and gatherer-hunters, what kind of picture might you construct of early hominid life?

Book Chapters.   Using similar questions as above, this variation compares chapters in two books about early human evolution.

Nancy Tanner's *On Becoming Human* has a number of positive images of women which may be useful in addressing the above questions. Use Chapter 9, "Gathering and the Australopithecine Way of Life," which discusses a way of life that centers on women as active participants in society and engaged in many activities. They are depicted as mobile, socially central, and autonomous.

Contrast Tanner's chapter with one that deals with the same time period in human evolution but presents a very different image of women.

In Donald Johanson and Maitland Edey's *Lucy: The Beginnings of Humankind* (1981, Simon & Schuster), Chapter 16, "Why Did Lucy Walk Erect? Is It a Matter of Sex?" argues that early hominid women had to stick close to home (be less mobile) in order to decrease infant mortality. They were cared for by males and a female served as a male's "own private gene receptacle" (p. 334).

Films.   The following films can be used in two ways: to ask questions about the depiction of women in prehistory (using the questions presented above) *but also* how women and women scientists are depicted.

Lucy in Disguise (Smeltzer Films, P.O. Box 315, Franklin Lakes, NJ 07417) is overtly about "the discovery and interpretation of early man."

Watch closely how women are depicted. How is Lucy (presented as an animated figure), who lived some three million years ago, depicted? (alone, vulnerable, unaware and not paying attention and so she is eaten by a crocodile).

How are women (scientists) depicted? They are not identified, but are presented as teachers of children or assistants, in the background.

The Making of Mankind a six-part series by the BBC, hosted by Richard Leakey. Several of the parts are useful for this exercise. How are the women presented? Are they identified? Are any presented as scientists or authorities?

Contrast this with the National Geographic film *Mysteries of Mankind,* which was aired early 1988. Here women as scientists are prominent, which is appropriate given the significant number of women scientists in the discipline.

In the context of these discussions, the article by Linda Fedigan, "The Changing Role of Women in Models of Human Evolution," provides an informative historical perspective for students.

2

Gender and the Study of Primates

Linda Marie Fedigan
University of Alberta

Laurence Fedigan
University of Alberta

General Trends in Primatology in Relation to Feminist Scholarship and Our Perception of Female Primates

There is at least one striking parallel between the well-known field of ethnography and that of the lesser known primate ecology: both have had a history of producing descriptions of social life in which females played shadowy, secondary roles while the males performed on center stage. Or, to paraphrase Burbank's comment (1989) on ethnographic studies of Australian aborigines, females were portrayed as barely animate objects in a landscape peopled by males. In both cases, little anthropological attention was paid to reporting the details of female lives, whereas the lives and social interactions of males were disproportionately described. Rather than being a conspiracy to suppress one-half of the story, this bias seems to have resulted from the well-known human disposition to see and hear preferentially that which fits our preconceptions. In primatology, this bias was also to some extent a natural outcome of the fact that males in many of the earliest-studied species were larger and exhibited more dramatic behavior, such that the observer's eye was drawn to these individuals first. Since anthropologists are trained in institutions (and come from societies) in which men are accorded at least public control of social organization, it is not surprising that early descriptions of primate society mirrored these human patterns (see comments by Haraway 1983, 1986; Hrdy 1984, 1986; Hrdy and Williams 1983).

From the 1950s, when extensive primate field studies were first initiated, into the 1960s and 1970s, primate social organization commonly was believed to be founded upon a stable male dominance hierarchy. Indeed, in some descriptions a rigid male hierarchy was portrayed as equivalent to the entire "social organization." That is, males were thought to be socially central as well as powerful and competitive, and the network of male relationships was described as dyadic, linear, and constant. Female primates were described as dedicated mothers to small infants and sexually available to males in order of the latter's dominance rank, but otherwise of little social significance.

The first type of evidence to weaken this model came from longitudinal studies of well-known individuals and groups. These studies provided the evidence that members of most primate societies are biologically related to each other through the females of the group, whereas the males are only temporary residents. Until recently, the common practice in Western primatology was for each individual graduate student to find a group to study for a year or so and then return to complete a degree and find a job, often never to see the study subjects again. However, a few exceptional projects, such as studies of rhesus macaques on Cayo Santiago Island, of baboons in Kenya, and of chimpanzees in Tanzania, were begun in the late 1950s and early 1960s, and were then maintained over the years by perseverant individuals or teams of researchers.

In addition, Japanese primatologists, trained in a discipline independently created in the East (Asquith 1986), characteristically cooperated in teams to produce life history studies of well-known individuals and groups of monkeys. Their papers, first translated into English in 1965 (Imanishi and Altmann 1965), reported that Japanese monkeys live in societies made up of related and closely bonded females, who remain in their natal groups throughout their lives, whereas mature males transfer frequently between groups. It was not until nearly a decade later, as similar descriptions began to accumulate from other longitudinal studies of cercopithecine monkeys, that the implications became clear to primatologists. The growing recognition that in the majority of primate species, mother-offspring (especially mother-daughter) bonds do not end at weaning, but continue over lifetimes, led to the description of primate "matrilineal" systems and a gradual shift in perception to social organization as based on lifelong female bonds. In part because nonhuman primates cannot be interviewed, it took years of patient observation to recognize that in most primate societies males come and go, playing only cameo roles, whereas females remain to carry the plot.

Around the same time that longitudinal data started to become available in the mid-1970s, a critique of the male-hierarchy model of social life was spearheaded by Thelma Rowell (1974; see also 1972). A few years earlier, Bernstein (1970) had demonstrated that monkey "dictators" did not exist, in that no one individual in the group was necessarily the winner of different types of conflicts in all types of social settings. Or to put it more technically, he showed that different measures of dominance between the same individuals in a given group of primates did not necessarily correlate, and further, the top-ranking ("alpha") individual in a hierarchy could be reduced to the lowest ranking by manipulation of the social/environmental context.

Rowell used such evidence, as well as her many years of experience in studying captive and free-ranging baboons, to argue that dominance as traditionally conceived was a very limited and learned aspect of social relationships, which was far more characteristic of stressed experimental animals than of primates in nature. Her controversial, landmark paper initiated a widespread debate and reassessment of the meaning of dominance in primate social life. In it, she asked the polemical question: "Is our own species more than usually bound by hierarchical relationships, at least among the males, who have written most about this subject?" (1974:132). To put her paper into context, evidence was becoming abundant at that point in the history of primatology that for animals as intelligent and as dependent upon social learning as primates, asymmetrical power relationships could not be determined by simple biological variables such as age, weight, and sex, nor by the straightforward expedient of who can physically defeat whom in a dyadic interaction. Indeed, the literature was becoming replete with examples of individuals who were old, ill, toothless, or otherwise physically weak, exercising important forms of control over other members of their groups. As the outdated, mechanistic model of dominance began to crumble under the weight of conflicting evidence and theoretical questionings, researchers acknowledged that nonhuman primates exhibited considerable sophistication in their attempts to exert control over each other, and in their power relationships. Some workers even argued that we may describe these relationships and interactions in terms of "primate politics" and "social strategies" (Bernstein 1981; Strum 1982; deWaal 1982). Although disputes continue over the exact degree and significance of competition, most researchers today would agree that primates live and function in intricate (nonlinear, nondyadic) social networks in which skillful and sentient individuals attempt to both predict and manipulate the interactions and reactions of others.

The two changes in our understanding of primate societies just outlined—the recognition of lifetime female bonds and the reconceptualization of dominance—produced a curious reversal in our portrayal of males and females, evident when we compare descriptions in the literature from the 1960s (e.g., Chance 1968) to the 1980s (e.g., Fedigan 1982). As noted by Jane Lancaster (1973), in a most prescient and popular article (see also Lancaster 1975, 1976, 1978), the early model of primate society saw males as competitive cornerstones of the group, whose enduring bonds cemented a stable social order, whereas females were uninterested in hierarchies, unable to organize themselves stably, and tended to engage in dominance interactions that were inconsistent squabbles. Lancaster referred to this point of view as a scientific statement of folk beliefs about the differences between men and women. Today primatologists would agree that the situation in most primate groups is, at least in some respects, the opposite of this description.

By the late 1970s, primatologists had begun to focus upon how and why individuals of both sexes cooperate in some situations and compete in others. New theoretical models in evolutionary theory, such as kin selection and reciprocal altruism, had suggested mechanisms which might cause, or at least facilitate, cooperation in males and both competition and cooperation in females. Some earlier theorists such as Tiger (1969) and Tiger and Fox (1971) had argued that female primates were not capable of cooperation or strong bonding, but a wealth of field data soon showed that the opposite was true, and kin selection theory provided an evolutionary explanation for the easily demonstrable strength of female bonding. Inclusive fitness, the key concept of kin selection theory, concerns the individual's ability to produce and rear offspring *and* her ability to help her relatives produce and rear offspring, both of which contribute to that individual's reproductive success. Since closely related animals share common genes, there are both direct and indirect mechanisms for contributing genetic material to the next generation. Most primate societies are made up of biologically related clusters of females, and thus cooperation between these group members helps to ensure the inclusive fitness of each.

Somewhat paradoxically, early views of primate females also held that they were noncompetitive and sexually passive. This was largely the result of sexual selection theory, developed by Darwin a century ago to explain secondary sex differences between males and females. He argued that males generally must compete for access to females, so the males are both ardent and assertive. Females, on the other hand, especially female mammals, produce relatively few offspring, and in order to ensure the best possible fathers for their few young, remain reluctant to mate, and choosy in regard to mating partners. Stereotypes of the noncompetitive, sexually reluctant female primate were forced to undergo revision, again due to a combination of antithetical field data and new theories of behavior. Research reports from a variety of species began to accumulate, many of them studies of female primates by women primatologists, which documented repeatedly that female monkeys and apes are sexually assertive, and in some situations, highly competitive. Although female primates do sometimes compete with each other for access to preferred male mates, most female-female competition is over access to the resources necessary to sustain them and their offspring. In those few primate societies *not* made up of related females, such as howler monkeys, females are noted for high levels of competition and low levels of cooperation. Even in societies made up of related females, competition does occur between biologically more distant relatives and between groups. From an evolutionary or adaptive point of view, it is clear that better access to resources should enhance a female's ability to produce and rear offspring (that is, should enhance her reproductive success). Theorists also began to suggest ways in which females would benefit from sexual assertion, and in some situations, from mating with a variety of males.

Sarah Hrdy (1984) has identified this recognition that evolutionary forces act directly upon females, as well as upon males, as one of the three major reasons for the shift in perception of female primates that occurred in the 1970's. Her other two proferred reasons are methodological improvements within the subdiscipline and an impetus from outside the field arising from the women's movement. To these three we would add the continuing and swelling flow of young women scholars into the field, who may have been drawn in, at least partly, under the influence of a few strong early role models. To conclude this section on general trends in primatology over the last three decades, we will consider these suggested reasons for the trends in turn.

As we indicated, the 1970s were a very active decade in the field of evolutionary theory, especially theories of behavior. Although controversial within the discipline of anthropology and for the larger community of Western social scientists and feminists, there is little doubt that the ferment of activity that has taken place under the rubric of "sociobiological" scholarship has contributed to major breakthroughs in our perceptions of the behavior of female animals. Often criticized as sexist, especially because of the early formulations, both sociobiologists and their opponents have participated in debates over scientific depictions of sex roles that could not help but chip away at old, simplified stereotypes, as both sides honed and revised their arguments. Sociobiological theories have been developed in the past decade that have attempted to explain why females are selected to form strong cooperative bonds in some situations (mainly kin selection theory) and to compete fiercely in others (mainly refinements of natural and sexual selection theories), in contrast to previous evolutionary models that had assumed that differential selection operated directly only on males.

The second reason for increasing recognition of female primate importance suggested by Hrdy was commonsense improvement in methodology. One of these improvements has already been outlined above—the desirability, and in many cases, necessity, of long-term data. Many subdisciplines of anthropology have now recognized the better understanding that results from longitudinal studies, but this is especially true in primatology, where our subjects are long-lived, responsive to social tradition, and yet silent on the history of their relationships. The other major improvement in methodology was simple, yet far-reaching in impact. In a highly influential paper on sampling methods in animal behavior, Jeanne Altmann (1974) pointed out that each individual must be observed for equivalent amounts of time before comparative statements of any kind can be made. The relevance of this consideration to studies of females is that prior to this point, most observational research had been done through opportunistic sampling. Whatever caught the researcher's eye or came first to their attention was recorded. Since, in many primate species, the males are larger and more noticeable, much more male than female behavior was recorded, and in some studies, individual females were not even discriminated. Jeanne Altmann called for an end to generalizations resulting from a biased focus on certain attention-attracting individuals, and the methodological improvements that resulted from her important paper facilitated better, more complete descriptions of the behavior of female primates.

Hrdy's third reason was the strong suggestion from the women's movement to examine our subjects with a female perspective; in other words, a deliberate and ideological shift in the way we conduct our research. A number of disciplines have felt the impact of the simple directive from feminist theory to begin asking questions about the subject matter from the female point of view. Hrdy points to Lancaster's 1973 paper, "In Praise of the Achieving Female Monkey," as a prime example of this approach. Lancaster and other women primatologists (e.g., Thelma Rowell, 1984) also have suggested that women, because of their common experience as *females*, may possess an enhanced ability to empathize with, and to comprehend, the behavior of their subjects.

We would like to suggest here another implication of the thinking on science that resulted from the women's movement and feminist scholarship, and that may play a role in the shifting perception of female primatologists that began in the 1970s. This is the question of whether women scientists might see the world somewhat differently from men and thus practice their science, and approach their subject matter, in a distinctive, although not necessarily unitary, manner (cf. Keller 1983, 1985). Several scholars in the social studies of science (e.g., Bleier 1984; Fee 1983, 1986; Gilligan 1982; Messing 1983) have suggested that Western women scientists tend to be holistic and integrative thinkers, who, as a result of differential socialization practices, may be more attuned than men to the complexities and subtleties of social interactions, and less satisfied with reductionist principles of analysis (Keller 1983, 1985, 1987). They argue further that the values traditionally defined as feminine may lead women to be generally more persistent and patient, willing to wait for the material to speak for itself rather than forcing answers out of it, and envisioning themselves as more connected to the subject matter than in control of it. This is not to argue that individual men may not share some of these proclivities, nor that all men may not be capable of developing these capacities, but "whether consciously articulated or not, women carry the seeds of an alternative ontology, epistemology and ethics" (Fee 1986:47). Although such generalizations clearly must be approached with caution, we will argue later that a comparison of the work of several women primatologists to that of the men who preceded them in one specific research area of primatology could be seen to offer some support to this argument.

Because of the dearth of information on the lives of female animals that resulted from the early focus on males, an initial part of the feminist challenge to existing ideas in animal behavior and primatology had to involve simply the collection of data on what female prosimians, monkeys, and apes actually do. A spate of books began to appear in the 1980s documenting the lives of female animals, especially primates, and in the process providing evidence to help demolish the old sex role stereotypes (e.g., *Female Primates*, edited by Small [1983]; *Social Behavior of Female Vertebrates*, edited by Wasser [1981]; *Primate Paradigms*, by Fedigan [1982]; *Females of the Species*, by Kevles [1986]; *The Female Animal*, by Elia [1985]; *The Woman Who Never Evolved*, by Hrdy [1981]; *Strategies of Being Female*, by Shaw and Darling [1984]).

Many of these studies on females were conducted by women primatologists, either out of empathy for other members of their sex and/or for ideological reasons and/or because research on female primates was one of the exciting and uncharted areas of the subdiscipline. Several reviews of the resulting books (e.g., Bielert 1986; Fedigan 1984; Haraway 1986; Small 1985) have noted that women form a large and increasing proportion of primatologists, although quantitative documentation of this point is as yet sparse. Many of these younger women were trained under male primatologists, so it will take a social historian to document how and to what extent their work was facilitated by the early presence of the few, very prominent women in the discipline, such as Thelma Rowell, Alison Jolly, Phyllis Jay, Jane Goodall, Dian Fossey and Jane Lancaster (see Haraway 1989). The importance of female role models has been documented previously for other disciplines, and will likely prove to be the case here, although we cannot ignore the fact that many male primatologists have been receptive to and/or influential in attempts to redress previous imbalances in sex role research. The objective of this essay is to highlight the contribution of women to our changing perspective on primate social life, rather than to provide a representative history of the roles that both men and women have played in our discipline. Perhaps more so than in the related fields of social anthropology and animal behavior, male practitioners of the science of primatology have been active in changing our ideas about female behavior and biology (see, for example, the theoretical papers by Richard Wrangham 1979, 1980). However, without denying the role of those men, what is emphasized here is that women have been major forces in the research and thinking of the past 15 years that has led to a shift in our general perception of primate societies.

Specific Examples of the Contribution of Women to Primatology

Following the discussion of very general trends in the perception of sex differences and social life in primates given in the previous section, we will continue with an example of one species that has been continually and intensively studied from the 1950s to the present, and that specifically illustrates the major revisions in our perception of primate behavior, and the reasons for that revision having taken place. Although research on the chimpanzee will be discussed at the end of this section to exemplify one remaining point, the majority of this section will trace a selected history of field studies on the common or savannah baboon (*Papio cynocephalus,* for simplicity here to include olive, yellow, and chacma).

The baboon is chosen for three reasons. First, a survey of introductory textbooks in anthropology published over the last 15 years shows unequivocally that if any *one* primate species is selected for a detailed description, it will be the baboon, with the chimpanzee being the second most popular choice. Unfortunately, there is an inevitable time lag between the initial dissemination of new research findings to specialists and the ultimate appearance of such revisions in general introductory textbooks. Therefore, most texts published right up to the mid-1980s continued to describe baboons as had the researchers of one or two decades ago, and fail to refer to much of the new work, which will be briefly described here and in the annotated bibliography.

The second reason for the focus on baboons in this section is that it was the original research in the 1950s on this particular species, generalized to *all* primates, which produced the model of social organization based on male competition and cooperation. For reasons that are not entirely clear, except that baboons are abundant and relatively amenable to field study, research on this type of primate has been both the source of the original male-biased model and also has given rise to many of the criticisms and countervailing views that brought about a minor paradigm revolution in primate sex role studies. Finally, baboons are chosen as an extended, specific example because they have been, until recently, the favorite species from which to draw analogies to humans. In many introductory anthropology textbooks, scenarios of early human social life are presented that are built directly or implictly on what we thought we knew about baboon society.

Our first glimpse of baboon society in the wild came from short field studies by Washburn, DeVore and Hall (DeVore 1964; Hall and DeVore 1965; Washburn and DeVore 1961). Although their studies lasted only a few weeks to a few months, their tightly constructed descriptions had a powerful influence on the general impression most anthropologists came to hold of primate behavior, perhaps because these were the first primate field studies to achieve wide publicity, and also because the type of society portrayed may have appealed to Western folk beliefs about human and primate nature. Their original scientific findings were parlayed into many secondary sources, popular articles, and films, achieving wide dissemination in various media and even forming a substantial component of an extensively used elementary school social science curriculum ("Man: A Course of Study").

As portrayed by Washburn and DeVore in particular, baboon society consisted of multi-male groups in which a few powerful, central males lived with a number of physically weaker adult females and their immature young, in a stable, tightly organized and cohesive group. It was suggested that when baboons had, as a species, left the safety of the trees for the rigors and benefits of life in the open savannah, it was necessary to abandon the relaxed social system characteristic of forest-dwelling primates. Instead, they adopted a rigidly controlled, hierarchical social structure in which males cooperated to protect the group, but competed for access to females, and thus ruled over females and young as a necessary part of their dominant and aggressive role. Several militaristic metaphors and analogies were present in these original descriptions of baboons. Groups were referred to as "troops," and much attention was paid to mechanisms for group defense against outside attacks, a defense carried out by pugnacious males, whose bodies were described as fighting machines.

One concept from these early studies that was to give rise to much controversy and many publications was the manner in which a group of baboons travel or forage across an open area. Washburn and DeVore (1961) described baboons as always traveling in a fixed pattern consisting of a few high-ranking adult males and females with young at the center, and an outer circle of the adolescent males on the periphery. Envisioned as concentric circles, and sometimes described as DeVore's "army-model" of baboon society, this formation was thought to be a social defense mechanism, in that a rapidly approaching predator would first encounter and attack the most expendable group members, the adolescent males. Should the baboons have more time to detect predators, it was believed that all males would come forward, or remain stationary, in order to place themselves between the danger and the more vulnerable group members, forming a protective phalanx while the females and young ran for the safety of the trees.

In the late 1960s and early 1970s, Thelma Rowell began to publish the results of her five-year study of baboons (Rowell 1966, 1972) and many of her descriptions of their social life differed significantly from the Washburn/DeVore model. In particular, she noted that baboons do not rest or travel in concentric circles (she attributed the pattern to artificial feeding during the DeVore study), and she reported that when attacked by predators or frightened by any other major threat, the entire group would flee with the unencumbered, long-legged males at the front, and the females carrying the heaviest infants coming last. Since Rowell's description, several baboon researchers have devoted themselves to the question of pattern during group movement, and although opinion varies as to the type of pattern or indeed the presence of any pattern other than random (e.g., S. A. Altmann 1979; Harding 1977; Rhine and Westland 1981), it is clear that nothing so simple or male-determined as DeVore's original army-formation occurs in baboon groups.

Thelma Rowell did not confine her reports of her own research findings and her criticisms of the Washburn/DeVore model to group travel patterns. She also described baboon society as loosely structured, with no specialized male roles or male orientation, but rather mobility of males between groups and fidelity of mothers and offspring to natal groups and ranges. She saw few aggressive encounters and was unable to detect any consistent pattern of individuals as winners or losers, that is, no detectable dominance hierarchy. This, in part, led her to write the influential 1974 paper calling for a reassessment of our understanding of dominance and social control, a paper that was discussed in the previous section of this review. Rowell compared baboon behavior in a variety of environmental settings, including captive and diverse field conditions, and found her results to be quite variable in the different settings. The recognition that even within one species, individuals and groups may behave quite variably led to an increasing wariness among primatologists about premature generalizations, and an awareness that the behavior of our subjects is more flexible and complex than we had first thought.

Some ten years later, Jeanne Altmann began to publish some of the results of her longitudinal study of baboon mothers and infants. Although the Altmann husband and wife team has played a pivotal role in much of our understanding of baboon ecology and demography, here we will focus upon one aspect of the work that speaks directly to our perception of female baboons. In the original Washburn/DeVore study (and in many others that were to follow), females were not discriminated individually and were portrayed primarily as passive recipients of male baboon actions (e.g., females were protected and defended by males, and they were sexually available to males roughly in order of the latter's dominance ranks). Females also were described as wholly dedicated mothers, to the extent that the reader assumed they did little else than care for their young. Jeanne Altmann's book (1980) helped to flesh out the picture of what adult female baboons *do* with their lives, in their daily activities.

Although nonhuman primate mothers do expend enormous amounts of time and energy in direct reproductive activities, they also must acquire enough food to sustain themselves and their unweaned young, and they must socialize in order to survive successfully in a social group. Their knowledge of the range in which they have grown up, of the history of the group and the relationships of its members, and their responsibility to their dependent young, all ensure that in comparison to males, female baboons hold essential information and key positions leading to social power. Altmann's analysis of the activity patterns of female baboons demonstrated, as other researchers have shown for other primate species, that females lead full social and productive (in terms of food-getting) lives, *as well as* performing the reproductive roles to which researchers have tried to consign them. The evidence from her book, along with her pivotal paper on unbiased sampling techniques, has been a major contribution to the task of bringing female baboons out of the shadows and into the light of scientific depictions of social life.

In the late 1970s, Robert Harding, Timothy Ransom, and Robert Seyfarth published papers arguing that baboons establish complex social affiliations, and criticizing oversimplified views of how aggression and dominance operate, and determine reproductive success in baboon society (e.g., Harding 1977, 1980; Ransom & Ransom 1971; Ransom 1979; Seyfarth 1976, 1977, 1978). But it was two women, Barbara Smuts and Shirley Strum, who fully developed their arguments and provided extensive supportive documentation in their books and articles published in the 1980s (e.g., Smuts 1983a,b,1985; Strum 1982, 1983a,b, 1987).

An important hypothesis in primatology, which one could say has taken on dimensions of a "received truth," is the idea that dominant males have first access to receptive females and therefore produce more offspring, and experience greater reproductive success, than do subordinate males. Despite numerous criticisms of the theory and methods surrounding this assumed correlation between dominance and reproductive success, and the sweeping generalizations that preceded testing of the model, the idea is still considered sacrosanct by many primatologists, and baboons are often cited as the prime example of its veracity (see Fedigan 1983 for a review of this topic). Both Smuts and Strum supplied data and arguments to directly contradict the dominance = reproductive success model. Smuts found no correlation between male dominance and reproductive success (indeed, she had great difficulty even determining a male dominance hierarchy). In her book (1985) she focused in particular on another social phenomenon that seemed to her to be more closely related to reproductive success than dominance, and that is reciprocal friendships between adult males and females. Although others had described these special relationships (e.g., Altmann 1980; Strum 1983a; Seyfarth 1978), Barbara Smuts was the first to document that rather than mating in order of male dominance rank, females mated preferentially with males with whom they had a previous "special relationship." Furthermore, these same males were the likely fathers and protectors of the infants of their female friends. Smuts argued that there were several types of "competitive success" exhibited by older resident males that reflected maturity and learned social skills not yet acquired by younger males. A major contribution of her book is the convincing documentation and portrayal of the social and evolutionary significance of cross-sex friendships in baboons.

Shirley Strum has spent nearly two decades studying several adjacent groups of baboons residing in Kenya, with a particular focus on one group known as the "Pumphouse Gang." In her book (1987), she describes how, having trained under Washburn at Berkeley, she began her fieldwork in 1972 with a tidy, well-constructed picture in her mind of baboon society, a picture based on a set of powerful, simplifying assumptions about males as the driving force behind social cohesion, and mothers and young revolving around these hubs of society. She quickly began to observe patterns in the baboons that complicated and contradicted these initial assumptions. Males did not seem to resort to physical aggression very often, but they did seem to spend an inordinate amount of time working out their own relationships and trying to achieve some degree of social stability among themselves. On the other hand, females were able to depend on assistance from family and relatives that came almost automatically, and they were less preoccupied with constant jockeying for position. As noted by Schaller in the Foreword to Strum's book, it is entirely to her credit that when her observations collided with preconceived ideas, she willingly accepted a new vision. For although Washburn has shown a willingness to modify his ideas over time (and indeed Washburn trained several of the women who later criticized his work and provided the evidence and new approaches to replace his own ideas), the majority of primatologists, especially baboon specialists, did not provide a sympathetic audience for Shirley Strum's interpretation of baboon behavior.

Her problems began when she discovered that in her study group, males seldom engaged in physical confrontations, and when they did interact agonistically, it was difficult, if not impossible, to determine consistent winners and losers of such confrontations. Male baboon dominance hierarchies, if they existed at all in her groups, were certainly not linear or consistent. She found that younger, incoming males tended to initiate the confrontations that occurred, perhaps as much to determine the network of social alliances and to find their position within it, as for any desire to actually gain some resource. In any case, older resident males often ceded such confrontations to the younger males who initiated them, so that the latter would be scored by a researcher as dominant over the former. However, Strum found that when highly desired "resources" were at issue, such as meat from vertebrate prey, or proximity to an estrous female, the older, long-term males always walked away with the prizes. Thus, she concluded (1982) that for her study groups, male dominance was inversely correlated to competitive (especially mating) "success," a conclusion that was either ignored or hotly rejected by many primatologists. Like Thelma Rowell before her, Shirley Strum discovered there are vested interests in the traditional views of male dominance and great resistance to a different version. To this day, one can read journal articles in primatology stating as an accepted fact that dominance determines reproductive success, and that no one has ever found anything but a positive correlation between these two variables.

If not dominance, what, in the view of these researchers, does account for the "success" of older resident males? Both Barbara Smuts and Shirley Strum have explored the role of male "social strategies" in general, as providing a variety of alternatives to aggression. Their books document how male baboons must "finesse" their way to success, by relying on systems of social reciprocity which they must actively construct. As Strum says, experience, skill, and the ability to manipulate others are essential. "Real power resided with those who were 'wise,' rather than those who were 'strong,' those who could mobilize allies rather than those who try to push through with brute force'' (1987:151). Following in the tradition of Washburn, Strum does feel that there are lessons for humans in the findings from baboons. However, her writings imply that these lessons reside not in the biological underpinnings of human behavior as so many have asserted previously, but rather in the alternatives to aggression that are available to any intelligent species such as those in the Order Primates.

We have provided this extended example of how four women—Thelma Rowell, Jeanne Altmann, Barbara Smuts, and Shirley Strum— have changed the course of thinking on baboon social life, not to deny the role that men have played in baboon studies and the development of primatology as a discipline (or to set them up as "straw men"), but rather to begin to elucidate how women, both deliberately and because of their distinctive life experiences, may contribute in important ways to our discipline. In reading the works of these four women, one common theme is how the baboons themselves provide the ideas and the answers, often in direct contradiction to theoretical or popular preconceptions. All four of these women provide revisionist views on their subject matter, views that have helped to replace original reductionist analyses with more sophisticated understandings of sex roles and social bonds. By a willingness to let their material "speak to them" through the process of extended field observations, and by crediting to their animals mental and social abilities that often are reserved just for humans, these researchers demonstrate the sense of connectedness to their subject, which has been described as frequently characteristic of women scientists. Along with integrative thinking and a respect for complexity, it has been suggested that women researchers tend to be patient and perseverant, more interested in detailed understanding than in sweeping generalizations. Indeed, these four baboon researchers (and many male primatologists as well) could only have drawn their conclusions from longitudinal study. However, there is little doubt that for professionals and public alike, the paragon of patience in animal behavior studies is Jane Goodall. We would like to turn briefly to her work in order to complete this section.

As McGrew (1986:323) has noted, Jane Goodall is simply the most famous primatologist ever; she defines our "science for the world at large much as Margaret Mead did for cultural anthropology." Like Margaret Mead she has both benefited and suffered from that notoriety. In part because Goodall did not enter primatology by "coming up through the ranks" as it were (she worked as a secretary before Louis Leakey recommended her for National Geographic support to study chimpanzees) it was not uncommon for many years to hear her work disparaged by colleagues, even after she completed her doctorate at Cambridge University. Throughout the historical stage in primatology covered in this essay (approximately 1960–87), Jane Goodall has been painting and repainting, casting and recasting, our increasingly multifaceted perception of chimpanzees as highly individualistic and intelligent social beings. She has demonstrated a continuing concern to document the life stories of known individuals, even when studies of the individual were out of vogue in primatology:

> When I began observing chimpanzees in 1960, the concept of individuality in nonhuman animals was unpopular in scientific circles. In fact, the first technical paper I submitted for publication was returned by a major periodical with the suggestion that a few alterations be made: where nad written "he" and "she" or "who," these had been crossed out and "it" or "which" had been substituted. [1986:90]

Her ability to maintain her own vision of how research should continue to be done at the Gombe Stream Reserve Center in the midst of political controversy and the glare of publicity is matched only by her one-woman campaign over the years to maintain and enhance living conditions for chimpanzees at Gombe and around the world. It often seemed that with each passing year, a new and startling revelation about chimpanzee behavior at Gombe would be made, and whereas many of the secondary players and sources would quickly issue proclamations about the true nature of chimpanzees (and thus of humans by analogy), Goodall would continue to work and watch, collecting bits of information and mulling them over with the patience necessary to put together a very complex puzzle. This is not to say that Goodall did not publish over the years of her study. Apart from many journal articles and a monograph, she published two popular books, and most recently a massive (600 pages), lavishly illustrated and documented summary of her 25 years of research at Gombe. The book has received accolades in both the popular and scientific press (e.g., McGrew 1986; Trevethan 1987; Wrangham 1987). Goodall has said repeatedly that had she stayed with her study of chimpanzees "only" for ten years (a long study by most standards), our view of these animals would be incomplete and misleading. Wrangham (1987) describes how a renowned male scientist declared Goodall to be absurd to continue with her work after 1971, because it had all been done already. However, it is only since 1971, in the second and third decades of her study, that we have begun to appreciate the extremes of both altruism and violence of which the chimpanzees are capable. Many questions about their behavior remain unanswered, but Goodall works on at Gombe.

Concluding Points

We began this essay with a suggested similarity between ethnography and primate ethology. We would like to conclude with a second similarity: in both fields a few outstanding women have established reputations for their ability to work well under very difficult field conditions, and thus have made it acceptable for women to do so. Like Margaret Mead, Peggy Golde, and Laura Bohannan in cultural anthropology, women such as Dian Fossey, Birute Galdikas, and Jane Goodall have been a source of inspiration to many young women preparing for primatological field work. Unlike the disciplines of animal behavior and arctic biology, for example (where academic folklore still promotes the view that women cannot withstand the hardships of fieldwork), within the fields of ethnography and primatology, women have worked successfully in some of the most arduous situations. A few popular books written by and about primatologists document the difficulties these women encountered working in remote parts of tropical countries, in terms of political, personal, and health problems (e.g., Fossey 1983; Mowat 1987). It has been suggested to us more than once that many women enter and practice primatology in order to work with cute, little, furry animals. However, research with primates in the wild is far removed from the "cute response" invoked in most people by infant monkeys and apes in the circus and the petting zoo. Adult primates in nature seldom strike the researcher as sweet or simply entertaining. These animals spend most of their time engaged in the quotidian, if life-sustaining, search for adequate food; violence is a fact of life in some species, and a few species and situations actually involve danger to the researcher. This is not to exaggerate the "adventure" aspect of primate fieldwork, but to make it clear that many aspects of fieldwork are not in the least romantic, that nonhuman primates are only cute in very limited situations, and that women, like men, are probably drawn into the field for a number of reasons, including the presence of successful role models.

What we regard as misinterpretation of why many women practice primatology (as an extension of their maternal feelings to sweet little animals) does lead us to an important, if controversial issue in feminist approaches to science. This is the feminist critique of the dichotomy traditionally invoked in science between reason and feeling. Within primatology, anthropomorphism (the attribution of human characteristics, especially feelings, to animals) has taken on the status of a taboo. And yet, renowned researchers such as George Schaller and Thelma Rowell have said that much of what we understand about the behavior of our closest relatives we do through intelligent empathy. In other words, we project our feelings onto our subjects in order to better understand them, and we assume they have feelings at least somewhat like our own. As one critic of the traditional goal of objectivity in science has said:

> In such feminist imaginings, the scientist is not seen as an impersonal authority standing outside and above nature and human concerns, but simply a person whose thoughts and feelings, logical capacities and intuition, are all relevant and involved in the process of discovery. [Fee 1986:47]

In a discipline quite distant from primate behavior, it also has been suggested that significant insights into scientific questions may be achieved through a suspension of the traditional dichotomy of feeling and reason, or subject and object. In her discussions of the life and work of Barbara McClintock, Evelyn Fox Keller (1983, 1985) notes that this genius in the area of corn genetics (McClintock was belatedly acknowledged with a Nobel Prize) developed an extraordinary rapport with individual corn plants and their constituent chromosomes. McClintock herself believes that she developed her scientific powers and made her discoveries, because the longer she studied the maize chromosomes and sought to distinguish and understand them, the more she felt that they became a part of her, they became her friends, and she forgot herself as separate from them. At least two women primatologists have spoken candidly about emotional involvement with their subjects as the very secret of their scientific success:

> I readily admit to a high level of emotional involvement with individual chimpanzees without which, I suspect, the research would have come to an end many years ago. [Goodall 1986:cover]

> Peggy taught me that you can have strong emotions, such as the special attachment I felt for her, and still do good science. The two were not, as I had once thought, mutually exclusive. . . . Techniques could still be systematic and rigorous, data could still be safeguarded from bias, interpretations could still be put on a firm quantitative footing. Best of all, feeling strongly about baboons made the science more rewarding. [Strum 1987:203]

As well as this sense of connectedness or integration with subject matter, there are several other distinctive characteristics described for Barbara McClintock as a scientist, and sometimes listed as ideologically desirable by feminist scientists, or simply differentially present in women due to socialization and life experiences. Many of these also are exhibited by the women primatologists whose work has been covered here. A short list of these traits would be: (1) a special respect for individual differences and proper attention paid to gaining insight from the exceptional case; (2) a belief that the complexity of nature exceeds our own imaginative possibilities and that reductionist solutions demonstrate insufficient humility in the face of such complexity; (3) a reluctance to impose an a priori or premature theoretical design on the material, but rather a desire to listen to the material, to let the research matter guide one as to what to do next, to develop a "feeling for the organism"; and (4) the ability to persist under difficult circumstances, particularly lack of recognition and respect from colleagues.

At the risk of repetition we would like to reiterate that none of these are biological capacities exclusive to women. Rather they are traits that some have argued to be more characteristic of women due to socialization practices and ideological directives. An alternate view suggests that women have been so scarce in the development of the sciences, that the successful ones have had to transcend traditional scientific as well as gender socialization processes, so that their qualities are those of the "outsider" and thus have rather different implications (Keller 1983, 1985, 1987). The ability to critique and reform traditional science

with a new and different vision is available to both sexes. Indeed, within the feminist literature, the past decade of primatology is often singled out as a model of nonsexist research and
theory, because both men and women readily have acknowledged former biases and worked
to rectify them. In particular relation to this essay, men have been involved in the developing
critique of the concept of dominance and in the revision of the early baboon models of primate
social organization.

Many of the significant women primatologists would be reluctant to call themselves (or
to be labeled!) feminists, so that there may not as yet be a well-developed and self-conscious
feminist school of thought within primatology. However, it is clear that there is a strong fe-
male-informed point of view prevalent in the subdiscipline today. We have begun to move
beyond the stage of simply critiquing past androcentrism and cataloging the details of female
lives. That is, we have begun to ask meaningful questions and to develop adequate understandings about differences between the sexes that reflect not Western folk beliefs, but rather
what our observations of the organisms themselves tell us. As Keller (1985) points out, traditional science has had as its main goal, prediction, the power to control and manipulate
objects in such a way that certain predicted events will happen. Many primatologists today
would agree that our science should have a different goal: "not prediction per se, but understanding; not the power to manipulate, but empowerment—the kind of power that results from
an understanding of the world around us, that simultaneously reflects and affirms our connection to that world" (Keller 1985:166).

Acknowledgments

We wish to thank Jeanne Altmann, Evelyn Fox Keller, Barbara Smuts, Shirley Strum, and Thelma
Rowell for their very helpful comments on this module. We also thank the eight anonymous reviewers
and Sandra Morgen, the project director, for their constructive criticisms. The final responsibility for
the content of this essay is, of course, our own.

References Cited

Altmann, J.
   1974   Observational Study of Behavior: Sampling Methods. Behaviour 49:227–267.
   1980   Baboon Mothers and Infants. Cambridge: Harvard University Press.
Altmann, S. A.
   1979   Baboon Progressions, Order or Chaos? A Study of One-Dimensional Group Geometry. Ani-
      mal Behavior 27:46–80.
Asquith, P. J.
   1986   Anthropomorphism and the Japanese and Western Traditions in Primatology. *In* Primate On-
      togeny, Cognition and Behavior Developments in Field and Laboratory Research. J. Else and P.
      Lee, eds. Pp. 61–71. New York: Academic Press.
Bernstein, I. S.
   1970   Primate Status Hierarchies. *In* Primate Behavior: Developments in Field and Laboratory Re-
      search. L. A. Rosenblum, ed. Pp. 71–109. New York: Academic Press.
Bernstein, I. S.
   1981   Dominance, the Baby and the Bathwater. Behavioral and Brain Sciences 4:419–457.
Bielert, C.
   1986   Review of *Female Primates: Studies by Women Primatologists*. International Journal of Pri-
      matology 7:221–223.

Bleier, R.
    1984   Science and Gender: A Critique of Biology and its Theories on Women. New York: Pergamon
        Press.
Burbank, V. K.
    1989   Gender and the Anthropology Curriculum: Australian Aborigines. *In* Gender and Anthropol-
        ogy: Critical Reviews for Teaching and Research. S. Morgen, ed. Washington, D.C.: American
        Anthropological Association.
Chance, M. R. A.
    1968   The Social Bond of Primates. Primates 4:1–22.
DeVore, I.
    1964   Primate Behavior. *In* Horizons of Anthropology. S. Tax, ed. Pp. 25–36. Chicago: Aldine.
Fedigan, L. M.
    1982   Primate Paradigms: Sex Roles and Social Bonds. Montreal: Eden Press.
    1983   Dominance and Reproductive Success in Primates. Yearbook of Physical Anthropology
        26:91–129.
    1984   Sex Ratios and Sex Differences in Primatology (A review of *Female Primates: Studies by
        Women Primatologists*). American Journal of Primatology 7:305–308.
Fee, E.
    1983   Women's Nature and Scientific Objectivity. *In* Women's Nature: Rationalizations of Inequal-
        ity. M. Lowe and R. Hubbard, eds. Pp. 9–27. New York: Pergamon Press.
    1986   Critiques of Modern Science: The Relationship of Feminism to Other Radical Epistemologies.
        In Feminist Approaches to Science. R. Bleier, ed. Pp. 42–56. New York: Pergamon Press.
Fossey, D.
    1983   Gorillas in the Mist. Boston: Houghton Mifflin.
Gilligan, C.
    1982   In a Different Voice: Psychological Theory and Women's Development. Cambridge: Harvard
        University Press.
Goodall, J.
    1986   The Chimpanzees of Gombe: Patterns of Behavior. Cambridge: Belknap Press.
Hall, K. R. L., and I. DeVore
    1965   Baboon Social Behavior. *In* Primate Behavior: Field Studies of Monkeys and Apes. I. De-
        Vore, ed. Pp. 53–110. New York: Holt, Rinehart and Winston.
Haraway, D.
    1983   Signs of dominance: From a Physiology to a Cybernetics of Primate Society. Studies in the
        History of Biology 6:129–219.
    1986   Primatology is Politics by Other Means. *In* Feminist Approaches to Science. R. Bleier, ed.
        Pp. 77–118. New York: Pergamon Press.
    1989   Primate Visions: Gender, Race, and Nature in the World of Modern Science. New York: Rout-
        ledge.
Harding, R. S. O.
    1977   Patterns of Movement in Open Country Baboons. American Journal of Primatology 47:349–
        354.
    1980   Agonism, Ranking and the Social Behavior of Adult Male Baboons. American Journal of
        Physical Anthropology 53:203–216.
Hrdy, S. B.
    1984   Introduction to Section II. Female Reproductive Strategies. *In* Female Primates: Studies by
        Women Primatologists. M. F. Small, ed. Pp. 103–109. New York: Alan R. Liss.
Hrdy, S. B., and G. C. Williams
    1983   Behavioral Biology and the Double Standard. *In* Social Behavior of Female Vertebrates. S.
        K. Wasser, ed. Pp. 3–17. New York: Academic Press.
Imanishi, K., and S. A. Altmann, eds.
    1965   Japanese Monkeys. Edmonton: University of Alberta Press.

Keller, E. F.
1983 A Feeling for the Organism: The Life and Work of Barbara McClintock. New York: W. H. Freeman.
1985 Reflections on Gender and Science. New Haven: Yale University Press.
1987 The Gender/Science System: Or, is Sex to Gender as Nature is to Science. Hypatia 2:37–59.
Lancaster, J. B.
1973 In Praise of the Achieving Female Monkey. Psychology Today. September.
1975 Primate Behavior and the Emergence of Human Culture. New York: Holt, Rinehart and Winston.
1976 Sex Roles in Primate Societies. *In* Sex Differences: Social and Biological Perspectives. M. S. Teitelbaum, ed. Pp. 22–61. Garden City: Anchor Press.
1978 Sex and Gender in Evolutionary Perspective. *In* Human Sexuality: A Comparative and Developmental Perspective. H. Katchadourian, ed. Pp. 51–80. Berkeley: University of California Press.
McGrew, W. C.
1986 Goodall and Gombe, Review of *The Chimpanzees of Gombe: Patterns of Behavior*. Nature 323:30.
Messing, K.
1983 The Scientific Mystique: Can a White Lab Coat Guarantee Purity in the Search for Knowledge about the Nature of Women? *In* Women's Nature: Rationalizations of Inequality. M. Lowe and R. Hubbard, eds. Pp. 75–88. New York: Pergamon Press.
Mowat, F.
1987 Women in the Mists: The Story of Dian Fossey and the Mountain Gorillas of Africa. New York: Warner Books.
Ransom, T. W.
1979 The Beach Troop of Gombe. Lewisburg: Bucknell University Press.
Ransom, T. W., and B. S. Ransom
1971 Adult Male-Infant Relations among Baboons *(Papio anubis)*. Folia Primatologica 16:179–195.
Rhine, R. J., and B. J. Wertland
1981 Adult Male Positioning in Baboon Progressions: Order and Chaos Revisited. Folia Primatologica 35:77–115.
Rowell, T. E.
1966 Forest-living Baboons in Uganda. Journal of Zoology (London) 149:344–364.
1972 The Social Behaviour of Monkeys. Baltimore: Penguin Press.
1974 The Concept of Dominance. Behavioral Biology 11:131–154.
1984 Introduction to Section 1: Mothers, Infants, and Adolescents. *In* Female Primates: Studies by Women Primatologists. M. F. Small, ed. Pp. 13–16. New York: Alan R. Liss.
Seyfarth, R. M.
1976 Social Relationships among Adult Female Baboons. Animal Behaviour 24:917–938.
1977 A Model of Social Grooming among Adult Female Monkeys. Journal of Theoretical Biology 65:671–698.
1978 Social Relationships among Adult Male and Adult Female Baboons, II: Behavior throughout the Female Reproductive Cycle. Behaviour 64:3–4.
Small, M. F.
1985 Review of *Social Behavior of Female Vertebrates*. American Journal of Physical Anthropology 66:98–100.
Smuts, B. B.
1983a Dynamics of Social Relationships between Adult Male and Female Olive Baboons: Selective Advantages. *In* Primate Social Relationships: An Integrated Approach. R. A. Hinde, ed. Pp. 112–116. Oxford: Blackwell.
1983b Special Relationships between Adult Male and Female Baboons: Selective Advantages. *In* Primate Social Relationships: An Integrated Approach. R. A. Hinde, ed. Pp. 262–266. Oxford: Blackwell.

    1985   Sex and Friendship in Baboons. New York: Aldine.
Strum, S.
    1982   Agonistic Dominance in Male Baboons: An Alternative View. International Journal of Primatology 3:175–202.
    1983a   Use of Females by Male Olive Baboons. American Journal of Primatology 5:93–109.
    1983b   Why Males Use Infants. *In* Primate Paternalism. D. Taub, ed. Pp. 146–185. New York: Van Nostrand Rinehold.
    1987   Almost Human: A Journey into the World of Baboons. New York: Random House.
Tiger, L.
    1969   Men in Groups. New York: Random House.
Tiger, L., and R. Fox
    1971   The Imperial Animal. New York: Dell.
Trevathan, W.
    1987   Review of *Chimpanzees of Gombe*. American Journal of Primatology 73:409–410.
deWaal, F. B. M.
    1982   Chimpanzee Politics: Power and Sex among the Apes. New York: Harper and Row.
Washburn, S., and I. DeVore
    1961   Social Behavior of Baboons and Early Man. *In* Social Life of Early Man. S. L. Washburn, ed. Pp. 91–103. Chicago: Aldine.
Wrangham, R. W.
    1979   On the Evolution of Ape Social Systems. Social Science Information 18:335–368.
    1980   An Ecological Model of Female-bonded Primate groups. Behaviour 75:262–300.
    1987   Ordinary Chimpanzees. Review of *The Chimpanzees of Gombe*. American Journal of Primatology 13:77–79.

Annotated Bibliography

Altmann, Jeanne
    1980   Baboon Mothers and Infants. Cambridge: Harvard University Press.

Using data from a well-known group of baboons (''Alto's Group'') that has been studied by a team of researchers since 1971, this book focuses on the reproductive lives of female baboons, especially the relationships of mothers to their dependent infants. Jeanne Altmann's emphasis on the time and energy constraints placed on females, because they must forage and socialize as well as mother their young, demonstrates that even nonhuman primate females manage to arrange their reproductive activities (nursing, mating) around their fundamentally necessary subsistence activities. This is contrary to the traditional picture of an adult female monkey or ape as little more than a ''baby-making machine.'' Altmann's work also pioneers the study of monkey mothers living in complex, free-ranging groups, as opposed to living in solitary or dyadic laboratory conditions, and thus documents the many variables (and stresses) that come into play in the mother-infant relationship under natural conditions.

Fedigan, Linda Marie
    1982   Primate Paradigms: Sex Roles and Social Bonds. Montreal: Eden Press.

An overview of research on sex differences in primate behavior. Fedigan's book attempts to rectify the male-dominated view of primate societies prevalent in the 1960s and 1970s, by emphasizing the significant and often central role of females in primate societies. The book is divided into five sections. The first introduces the primates and the basic information and issues in the study of primate behavior which may be useful as background to the general anthropology reader, and the second covers the major concepts in primatology (aggression, dominance, kinship, etc.) which are necessary for understanding theories of sex differences in behavior. The third section focuses on the ontogeny and development of behavior in young primates, the fourth provides field descriptions of the social lives of nine primate species, and the fifth section examines the perspectives on sex differences offered by various derivatives of evolutionary theory. Although primatology is a fast-changing discipline, and many of the androcentric biases described in this 1982 book are in the process of being alleviated, this work remains the only attempt to provide a synthesis and overview of the revisionist primatology now underway, often at the field sites and work tables of female primatologists. As such, it should be of value to the anthropologists who would like to incorporate the "female point of view" into their understanding and teaching of this subdiscipline.

Goodall, Jane
  1986   Chimpanzees of Gombe: Patterns of Behavior. Cambridge: Belknap University Press.

Although this is a very large and long book, if you can read only one major work in primatology, it should be this one. Jane Goodall is, without doubt, the founding mother of primate field studies, and this volume is a testament to her skills, her stamina and her "feeling for the organism." Designed for both the specialist and general reader, and written in Goodall's usual clear and accessible style, no one can come away from this book unimpressed by what one persistent, hard-working, patient woman can accomplish in the discipline of primatology. Summarizing 25 years of study on 85 individually known chimpanzees, the book is lavish with photographs, data, and word pictures that convey her understanding of chimpanzee behavior. Somewhat like Richard Leakey in hominid paleontology, Jane Goodall had to earn acceptance in the academic community because she did not enter the discipline in the traditional way, and because the public has always loved her best. This book has enough data analyses to satisfy most of the quantitatively minded specialists, but more important, it synthesizes an incredible volume of information into 19 highly readable chapters on traditional topics in primatology, such as territoriality, dominance, sexual behavior, grooming, and feeding. Especially her "Who's Who" chapter should bring the animals alive for the general reader. Goodall's latest book is a splendid natural history of our closest living relative spoken in the evocative voice of a remarkable woman scientist.

Hrdy, Sarah B.
  1981   The Woman That Never Evolved. Cambridge: Harvard University Press.

A unique attempt to combine a sociobiological and a feminist approach is found in the works of Sarah Blaffer Hrdy. The core of her argument (which has been taken up in various forms of different works) is that the noncompetitive, sexually passive, consistently nurturant female primate, human or otherwise, is a mythological creature that never evolved, but was created instead from the androcentric perceptions of male scientists. Hrdy's own research and reviews of the research of others, especially that of other women primatologists, leads her to conclude that in many circumstances female primates are selected to be sexually active to the point of promiscuity, competitive to the extent of harming the lives of other females, and devious to a Machiavellian degree in their relations with adult males. This is not a pretty picture of primate female nature, but Hrdy believes that women have to come to terms with what she sees as the biological reality of competition and the resulting inequities in primate societies before they can hope to change human behavior. Because most feminists, and many other anthropologists, have found sociobiological theory itself to be highly sexist, Hrdy's work has been criticized as presenting an unduly bleak and deterministic picture of the lives and behavior of females. Nonetheless, it has challenged traditional views about the primacy of male competitive patterns held by anthropologists, evolutionary biologists and feminists alike, and it is written in a lively accessible style that allows the nonspecialist reader insight into the sociobiological point of view.

Small, Meredith F. (ed.)
  1984   Female Primates, Studies by Women Primatologists. New York: Alan R. Liss.

Somewhat similar to Wasser's book in concept, this edited volume focuses upon an evolutionary approach to the study of female primate behavior. Thirteen chapters, taking the form of research reports and based on original data collected and analyzed by women primatologists, are presented in three major sections: Mothers, Infants and Adolescents; Female Reproductive Strategies; and Patterns of Female Behavior. Although the chapters themselves are of uneven quality, the introduction to the sections, written by established and influential women primatologists, are uniformly valuable in their ability to pull common themes out of the disparate contributions, and more especially in their willingness to address higher-order questions about the behavior and study of female primates. Thelma Rowell speaks directly to the question of whether women primatologists practice primatology differently from men, and Sarah Hrdy presents a cogent summary of the reasons for past androcentrism in primatology, and the major events that have led to the rectification of these biases. Although many of the individual chapters are clearly written, they may prove to be too detailed and specialized to be of great interest to the general anthropology reader, and thus the introductory sections are recommended as being the most useful.

Smuts, Barbara B.
    1985   Sex and Friendship in Baboons. New York: Aldine.

It is widely accepted that mating and kinship interactions form the basis of most primate social bonds, but long-term affiliative relationships between males and females outside these two contexts have been little studied. Such "friendships" are convincingly documented and portrayed in Smuts's book, which is unusual in its attempt to provide a quantitative and evolutionary approach that is neither reductionist nor inaccessible to the average university reader. Statistics are relegated to separate sections at the end of each chapter, and, although challenging, most of the text is a readable account both of baboon behavior and the author's own intellectual odyssey in pursuit of understanding the "essence" of baboon social life. She argues that baboons are sentient animals who pursue cross-sex friendships in a system of reciprocal exchange of social benefits, not necessarily involving directly enhanced reproductive success. This is a somewhat controversial conclusion to both biologists and to those social scientists who would deny nonhuman primates such a degree of self and social awareness. The book is rigorous, it is self-critical, and in large part it achieves the author's goal of portraying the spirit and vitality of the animal and its society.

Strum, Shirley
    1987   Almost Human. New York: Random House.

With many shorter scholarly publications to her credit, Shirley Strum decided to write a popular book on baboons that would convey to expert and public alike her insights into the social lives of these animals. Based on 15 years of fieldwork with one group in particular, "the Pumphouse Gang," the book is primarily the story of how the elaborate social skills and tactics of male baboons obviate the necessity for them to use force and aggression in order to enter and survive in the fundamentally female social world of this species. Strum went into the field armed with the traditional militaristic view of baboon society as a troop centered around combative males, a model extrapolated to all savannah-dwelling primates, especially early hominids. Although she continues to believe that baboons make a good model for early human societies. Strum describes a sophisticated social exchange system in which adolescent and adult males "finesse" their way into the favor of females by offering them friendly gestures and aid in times of conflict, and also by acting on their abilities to observe and predict the reactions of other baboons. Replete with descriptions of individuals followed over many years, and examples of particular incidents that support her theoretical ideas about baboon behavior, Strum's book (like those of Goodall and Smuts) seeks to convey to the reader not just the science of primatology, but also the development of the maturing fieldworker, and the insights into the complex minds of our socially living primate relatives that are achieved through a nonreductionist approach.

Wasser, Samuel K.
    1983   Social Behavior of Female Vertebrates. New York: Academic Press.

The goal of this book is to review a variety of attempts to apply evolutionary theory to the study of female social behavior, and to the study of sex differences in behavior. An edited volume, it is comprised of 13 chapters grouped into 3 major sections (Introduction, Interactions Between the Sexes, and Reproduction, Cooperation and Competition among Females) and covering topics ranging from cuckoldry in ring doves to sociobiological analysis of human female reproductive strategies. The majority of the study reported are on mammalian and avian species. Because of the diversity of topics and species to be covered, it may be difficult for the anthropological reader to absorb, much less access, the wide range of material presented. Thus, the two well-written introductory chapters reviewing sex biases and current trends in behavioral biology are recommended as the most useful chapters for the nonspecialist to read.

Course Component 1

Objectives

To examine the lives and work of selected women scientists, to see how and why they became interested in the study of primates and to analyze their contributions to our knowledge of the behavior and biology of these animals. In particular, how they helped to bring about the changes in theory and practice described in this essay.

Method: presentation, discussion or assignment. The following activities and questions are suggested: (1) Using the documents listed and others that are available to you, and your knowledge of the social and scientific climate of the time, draw up a short "biography" of each scientist. (2) What were the important influences (events, people, ideas, etc.) in their careers? Why were they attracted to primate studies? What was the role of chance? (3) How/what did these women contribute; singly, collectively?
e.g., Singly:

> *Altmann:* methods, focus on female lives
> *Goodall:* long-term, life-cycle studies
> *Hrdy:* critical analysis, introduction of feminist and sociobiological theory
> *Rowell:* questioning of accepted findings and theory
> *Smuts:* concept of friendship, integration of social and biological theories
> *Strum:* long-term studies, challenging of early findings and conclusions, alternatives to
classical dominance theory.

Collectively:

> Methods
> Study of females
> Challenges of 'simple' ideas of social power
> Critique of androcentric theory

(4) Do these women scientists appear to have had any common experiences, aptitudes, influences, reactions etc.? If so, what are they? (5) Is it possible that the different socialization and life experiences of women as opposed to men would give women a "different" approach to science? If so, how might this difference be manifested? (e.g., the asking of different questions, paying attention to different phenomena, a more contextual/integrative approach, empathy with the organism.)

Materials. Popular articles, books and book reviews written by or about the six women scientists listed below and cited in the essay. (n.b.: This list is not exhaustive, nor is it meant to imply a hierarchy or "top six" listing.)

Jeanne Altmann
Altmann, J., 1980. *Baboon Mothers and Infants.* Cambridge: Harvard University Press.
Lancaster, J. B., 1981. Review of *Baboon Mothers and Infants. American Anthropologist* 83:414–415.
Vessey, S. H., 1981. *Baboon Motherhood and Infancy.* Review in *Contemporary Psychology* 26(4):265–266.

Walton, S., 1986. How to Watch Monkeys: Jeanne Altmann Changed the Way Scientists Look at Animals in the Wild. *Science 86* June 1986:23–27.

Film, *Jeanne Altmann and the Amboseli Baboons.* 12 ms. educational program available from Children's Television Network, New York, N.Y. ("3-2-1 Contact," Show #619, from "Mammal's Week").

Jane Goodall

Goodall, Jane, 1986. *The Chimpanzees of Gombe: Patterns of Behaviour.* Cambridge: Belknap Press (Harvard University Press).

Wrangham, R., 1987. Ordinary Chimpanzees. Review of *The Chimpanzees of Gombe, American Journal of Primatology* 13:77–79.

Gardner, B. T., and R. A. Gardner, 1987. Discovering Chimpanzees. Review of *The Chimpanzees of Gombe. Contemporary Psychology* 32(10):850–852.

Simon, S. E., 1985. Jane Goodall: Living with Close Relatives. *American Biology Teacher* 47(5):267–269.

Film, 1984. *Among the Wild Chimpanzees. National Geographic.*

Sarah Blaffer Hrdy

Hrdy, S. B., 1981. *The Woman that Never Evolved.* Cambridge: Harvard University Press.

Hrdy, S. B., 1984. Introduction to Section 2: Female Reproductive Strategies. In M. F. Small (ed.) *Female Primates: Studies by Women Primatologists.* New York: Alan R. Liss Inc., pp. 103–109.

Hrdy, S. B., Autobiographical Note, from R. Bleier, 1986. *Feminist Approaches to Science.* Pergamon Press: Athene Series.

Cheney, D. L., 1982. Females as Strategists. Review of *The Woman that Never Evolved. Science* 215:1090–1091.

Powledge, T. M., 1982. Just-so-stories. Review of *The Woman that Never Evolved. The Nation* May 29:658–670.

Eckholm, E., 1984. New View of Female Primates Assails Stereotypes. *The New York Times* September 18.

Thelma Rowell

Rowell, T. E., 1972. *The Social Behaviour of Monkeys.* Baltimore: Penguin Press.

Rowell, T. E., 1984. Introduction to Section 1: Mothers, Infants, and Adolescents. In M. F. Small (ed.), *Female Primates: Studies by Women Primatologists.* New York: Alan R. Liss, pp. 13–16.

Rowell, T. E., 1988. Monkey Business. Review of *Almost Human.* (S. Strum). *Natural History* 97(1):58–60.

Barbara Smuts

Smuts, B. B., 1985. *Sex and Friendship in Baboons.* New York: Aldine.

Smuts, B. B., 1987. What Are Friends For? *Natural History* 96(2):36–46.

Smuts, B. B., 1987. The Dynamic and Diverse Societies of Primates. *Yearbook of Science and the Future.* Encyclopaedia Brittanica, Inc.

Hall, R. L., 1987. Review of *Sex and Friendship in Baboons. American Journal of Physical Anthropology* 72(1):133–135.

Fedigan, L. M., 1987. Review of *Sex and Friendship in Baboons. American Scientist* 75:535.

Shirley Strum

Strum, S., 1987. *Almost Human: A Journey into the World of Baboons.* New York: Random House.

Schaller, G., 1987. Foreword to *Almost Human. A Journey into the World of Baboons.* New York: Random House.

Rowell, T. E., 1988. Monkey Business. Review of *Almost Human. Natural History* 97(1):58–60.

1988. From the Apes, a Message of Hope. *U.S. News and World Report* January 25, 1988.

Film, *The Pump-House Gang. The World of Survival.*

Course Component 2: Measuring Social Dominance

Objectives

1. To observe, describe and analyze nonverbal dominance/power relations in a social group.

2. To construct and interpret a dominance hierarchy using standardized measures of dominance and/or submission.

3. To describe and discuss the difficulties encountered in defining, measuring, and interpreting nonverbal measures of social dominance.

Identifying and Measuring Dominance Behaviors

Methods

1. Select an observable, stable, social group of nonhuman primates (if possible.) However, other social animals, wild (e.g., a zoo group) or domesticated, or even a preschool play group would be suitable.

2. Learn to identify the individuals in your group.

3. Observe the whole group, noting behaviors and interactions that appear to you to demonstrate the application of social power. Describe these in your own words.

4. Define behavioral or interactional categories based on regular, measurable incidents in your observations.

5. Use these categories to record the behavior of chosen individuals over equivalent periods of time.

6. Compare equal time samples for different individuals, sexes, and age groups.

7. What conclusions or hypotheses can you advance about the power relations in the group?

8. What were the difficulties you encountered (in observing, identifying behaviors, measuring, interpreting, etc.)?

9. Compare your behaviors (your ethogram) with those to be used in constructing a dominance hierarchy or other ethograms available in the literature.

10. How does a unit of behavior relate to a sequence of behavior: what are the advantages of "units" of behavior (measurement, analysis, etc.) and their disadvantages (definition, measure, interpretation, etc.)?

Materials

1. Zoos—primates and other social animals.

2. Research Centers—primates.

3. Dog breeders—individuals with several dogs.

4. Horse breeders—stables.

5. Farms—groups of domestic animals.

6. Daycare Centers or Kindergartens—nonverbal play groups.

7. Research Methods for Studying Animal Behavior in a Zoo Setting (Recommended). A videotape jointly produced by the Minnesota Zoo, Apple Valley, Minnesota, and the Washington Park Zoo, Portland, Oregon (Videocassette 100 minutes, 2 tapes, plus 10 tests, examples of ethograms, bibliographies of research methodology and checksheets used for scoring the sample methods.) Available from the Minnesota Zoo, Education Department, Apple Valley, MN 55124.

8. Lehner, P. N. *Handbook of Ethological Methods.*

Suggested Behaviors to Use in the Construction of Dominance Hierarchies for Primate Social Groups.

A. Aggressive Behaviors.
1. Stare—fixed gaze.
2. Lid—eyebrows raised and forehead retracted upwards to expose eyelids.
3. Open-mouth gape—lower jaw is dropped and the chin is thrust forward while the mouth is held in an open O shape with the lids covering most of the teeth.
4. Head bob—head is moved rapidly up and down with the face expressing numbers 1, 2, or 3.
5. Slap—the ground of other substrate (e.g., branches, cage bars) is slapped with the hand.
6. Lunge—a plunge forward toward an opponent followed by a quick retreat.
7. Cuff—the opponent is hit with the flat of the hand.
8. Pinch/Grab—to take hold of another's body and squeeze to the point of causing noticeable pain.
9. Bite—to seize another with the teeth.
10. Chase—to pursue another with accompanying signals (e.g., numbers 1–9).
11. Displace/Supplant—one individual moves directly toward another who immediately moves out of the former's way. Frequently, the supplanter will stand or sit down in the exact location that the supplantee has just vacated.

B. Submissive Behaviors
1. Grimace/Grin—facial expression in which the lips are retracted from the clenched teeth.
2. Avoid/Run Away—an individual notices another in its path or coming in its direction and changes its movement pattern to avoid an encounter.
3. Scream—a loud, shrill vocalization indicating distress.
4. Crouch—a stooped posture in which the limbs are drawn in close to the body (also known as cringing or cowering).

Constructing a Dominance Hierarchy

Methods

1. Choose one or more of the aggressive behaviors from the list (e.g., supplant). It is also possible to choose one of the submissive behaviors, in which case you would construct a "subordinance hierarchy." Try to choose a behavior you find to be frequent and easy to distinguish, and that usually occurs between just two individuals without the intervention of others.

2. Draw a matrix listing each relevant member of the group across the top of the page, and in the same order down the left hand side of the page (see Figure 1).

3. Each time that you observe one individual of your group to direct the chosen behavior, or signal, unequivocably toward a second, record the interaction in the correct cell of your matrix.

4. Observe the group long enough to record several such interactions between each pair of group members.

Figure 1.
Example of a Dominance Matrix
Original Order

	RECEIVER					
DIRECTOR	**A**	**B**	**C**	**D**	**E**	**F**
A		~~IIII~~	II	~~IIII~~ II	III	II
B				III	IIII	~~IIII~~
C	I	III		~~IIII~~ III	~~IIII~~	III
D					I	I
E		I		~~IIII~~		III
F				IIII		

Figure 2.
Example of a Dominance Matrix
Final Order

	RECEIVER					
DIRECTOR	**A**	**C**	**B**	**E**	**F**	**D**
A		**2**	**5**	**3**	**2**	**7**
C	**1**		**3**	**5**	**3**	**8**
B				**4**	**5**	**3**
E			**1**		**3**	**5**
F						**4**
D				**1**	**1**	

5. Once you have sufficient observations, rearrange the order of your group members so that as many entries as possible are in the upper-righthand half of the matrix. The order

that results in the minimum number of entries on the lefthand side of the diagonal represents a dominance hierarchy (see Figure 2).

6. Discuss the problems you encounter in applying this method of determining dominance hierarchies. For example:

Do all of your recorded interactions occur between just two individuals, or do other group members participate and join in?

Is there a clear "winner" and "loser" in the interactions you recorded, or does one individual threaten only to be counterthreatened by the second?

Is the direction of aggressive signals always the same between two individuals, or do *reversals* occur in which a normally subordinate individual directs aggressive signals at a dominant?

Is the relationship between all pairs/dyads asymmetrical or are there two individuals who direct equal (or very similar) numbers of aggressive behaviors at each other? If so, these two cannot be ranked one above the other, and the hierarchy in your group is not linear.

Are all relationships transitive? That is, if A dominates B, and B dominates C, then A must also dominate C. If not, then the hierarchy in your group is not linear.

3

Incorporating Gender into Archaeology Courses

Janet D. Spector
University of Minnesota

Mary K. Whelan
University of Iowa

When feminist scholarship emerged in the late 1960s as part of the "academic wing" of the contemporary women's movement, people began asking questions about the characteristics and life experiences of men and women not only in the modern world but also in the remote past. They wondered about the origins of male dominance and female subordination, they wondered if there had ever been societies characterized by egalitarian relations between men and women, and they wondered if women at all times and places, past and present, shared certain social "fates" because of their sex. These were not simply academic questions for the people who raised them. They hoped that by studying the past they might learn something about the origins and development of our own gender configurations, and in turn, that this new knowledge of the past might illuminate the present and shape the future. Many turned to archaeology thinking that this field was likely to have such information about the lives of men and women in the past.

Questions about gender are not unlike others commonly addressed by anthropological archaeologists in their investigations of cultures existing prior to the time of written records. Lewis Binford, in an extremely influential paper published in 1962, argued that all categories of cultural behavior have material and spatial dimensions that are visible archaeologically, and in recent years a number of archaeologists have provided support for his assertion by demonstrating the archaeological accessibility of seemingly elusive subjects like social organization, prestige, and ideology (Binford 1962; Deetz 1977; Hodder 1982; McGhee 1977; Miller and Tilley 1984).

Although most archaeologists believe that the material record preserved at archaeological sites can be deciphered (like ancient and fragmentary texts) revealing aspects of prehistoric social life, gender has not yet been among the subjects selected for systematic study. In 1984, Conkey and Spector reviewed the status of scholarship on gender in archaeology. They described the situation in this way:

There is virtually no systematic work on the archaeological study of gender. . . . We know of no archaeological work in which an author explicitly claims that we can *know* about gender in the past as observed through the archaeological record who then proceeds to demonstrate that knowledge, or to describe *how* we can know.

This does not mean that archaeologists have not said anything about gender . . . in past human life. In spite of the absence of serious methodological or theoretical discourse on the subject, the archaeological literature is not silent on the subject of gender. Rather it is permeated with assumptions, assertions, and statements of "fact" about gender. This is a serious problem. [1984:2; emphasis in original]

Unfortunately, this description continues to accurately describe the general state of archaeology, although the situation is changing. Several promising articles have been published recently (Gibbs 1987; Marshall 1985) and a number of unpublished papers are circulating and should be in print soon.

This situation posed some very real challenges for us in designing a curriculum guide. Since there is as yet no body of literature that is both informed by recent feminist scholarship and also uses archaeological data and research strategies to study gender, we could not create our module utilizing current archaeological studies of prehistoric men and women. Instead we chose to organize this module around three areas of importance in the field of gender and archaeology. These include: (1) a feminist critique of archaeology that exposes androcentric and ethnocentric biases (this is one topic on which there is some archaeological literature), (2) the definition of appropriate concepts and methods for the archaeological study of gender, and (3) the generation of new interpretations or alternative scenarios about the past prompted by placing gender at the center of the analysis of major trends in prehistory.

The Problem of Gender Bias in Archaeology

For much of its history archaeology, like most other social sciences, has been androcentric in practice and in thought (see Conkey and Spector 1984 for review). The production and distribution of knowledge (through research, publication, and teaching) has been largely dominated by white, Western, middle-class men. This sociological fact has had an impact on the character of the knowledge produced. Feminist critics across the disciplines have shown that until very recently the experiences and perspectives of women have been peripheralized, trivialized, or ignored by researchers. They have also demonstrated that studies of "Man," purporting to be gender inclusive, are all too often actually gender specific, focusing disproportionate attention on the interests, values, beliefs, accomplishments, and social lives of men, as if men somehow "represented" the species. The concepts "Man" and "Mankind" used in such studies are exclusive rather than universal categories; they are partial and so is the scholarship that is based on this perspective (Minnich 1982:7).

In many fields, including social and cultural anthropology, the recognition of androcentric bias stimulated a tremendous amount of new research. Some work focused explicitly on women to provide more balanced renderings of human society (Bourguignon 1980; Matthiasson 1974; Murphy and Murphy 1974). Other scholars revised or replaced cultural generalizations or theoretical formulations shown to be inadequate or invalid because of gender bias (Leacock 1978; Quinn 1977; Reiter 1975; Rogers 1978; Sacks 1979). Still others conducted research designed to understand how gender "works" and varies historically and cross-culturally (Atkinson 1982; MacCormack and Strathern 1980; Ortner and Whitehead 1981; Williams 1986). Unfortunately, archaeology has lagged behind in its recognition that androcentric bias troubles our study of human prehistory, and the field has not yet contributed to the creation of new perspectives about gender. Without realizing it, archaeologists have tended to project numerous ethnocentric notions about men and women derived from our own culture onto the analysis of other groups. While few archaeologists focus directly on gender as a subject of study, many nonetheless make assertions or incorporate assumptions about the activities, capabilities, social roles, and relative positions of men and women into their studies of other topics, rarely identifying the sources of their notions or attempting to confirm or validate them. They often add another layer to the problem of bias by "gendering" specific sorts of artifacts based on their stereotypic notions about men and women (e.g., men are linked to projectile points, women to pottery).

Not surprisingly, these images of gender arrangements in the past bear a striking resemblance to the present, thus tending to reinforce our own gender beliefs and practices. This uncritical projection of aspects of our 20th-century Western gender system back into the remote past implies that gender configurations are unchanging and immutable, built into the species like erect posture or large brain size. Current anthropological studies prove this to be untrue; gender relations, like other cultural constructions, are highly variable and continue to change over time. The persistence of these stereotypes in archaeology says more about our own culture than about those we attempt to describe and understand.

Current introductory textbooks in human evolution and archaeology provide an interesting measure of the discipline's attitudes toward women and gender. We reviewed several new editions of texts often used in introductory courses to see how gender was presented to students (Campbell 1985; Fagan 1986; Jolly and Plog 1986; Jurmain et al. 1987). Our review suggests that the first step toward incorporating gender into introductory courses will of necessity be the exposure and discussion of gender bias in the textbooks (see Classroom Exercise 1).

For many students, the perspective presented in their introductory classes may be the only exposure they will have to archaeological research and reconstructions of prehistoric lifeways. These courses (or the surveys of prehistory included in more general introductions to anthropology) are important because they disseminate knowledge that is not usually covered by other disciplines. Unlike much of anthropology, which at times overlaps with history, sociology, psychology, and other social sciences or humanities, the information presented in courses on human biocultural evolution and prehistory is uniquely the responsibility of anthropology. We cannot, therefore, assume that biases unconsciously conveyed in an introductory class will be challenged in other undergraduate coursework.

We were interested to see how the new scholarship on women and gender in sociocultural anthropology and related fields had influenced current editions of introductory archaeology texts. Several trends were clear. First, in nearly all cases gender neutral language had replaced the ubiquitous "man" and "mankind" formerly used to refer to humans in general. While this does indicate an encouraging awareness about issues of sexism and gender bias, this "solution" creates a new problem: the apparent invisibility of gender. While formerly only women were invisible, now both sexes are missing, as if prehistory was populated with nameless, faceless, and now genderless "people." Further, while it is true that the word "people" is preferable to "man," we must face the reality of our own culture and recognize that if gender is left unspecified, most students will assume the subject is male. In many texts this assumption is reinforced through illustrations and photographs. For example, though toolmakers are now typically referred to as "they" and not "he," the people shown using and making tools in text illustrations are typically men, not women. The "man the toolmaker" notion is still gender specific in image if not in word.

The apparent invisibility of gender in the texts was also reflected in book indices. We searched for references to gender, sex, women, or men and found coverage restricted to the most predictable contexts like reproduction, estrus, family life, and the division of labor. Authors seemed to avoid addressing issues of gender directly (perhaps for fear of criticism), rarely raising subjects like changing technology, patterns of subsistence or settlement from the perspective of the prehistoric men and women who actually experienced them.

This gender invisibility was more apparent than real, however. Implicit notions about gender occurred frequently, and students reading the texts would be subjected to numerous, unexamined assertions about gender buried in the authors' discussions of other topics. The most striking example of this was in reconstructions of prehistoric social organization. As is true generally in the archaeological literature, these texts often drew upon contemporary Western gender stereotypes to describe men's and women's social positions and roles in societies from 3.4 million years ago up to the more recent past. All of the texts suggested that male-headed, nuclear family organization was the norm in the past, just as it is in the Western world today. The texts also portrayed a rigid and universal sexual division of labor: men were the hunters while women, tethered to home bases by pregnancy and children, gathered plants.

Unfortunately, this presentation of the division of labor by sex was often compounded by another androcentric problem: the differential attention to and valuing of presumed male versus female activities. In our survey we consistently found that male-associated hunting tasks were celebrated as milestones of human evolution and reported in detail while female-associated gathering was given limited attention. In one text, for instance, hunting was discussed on at least 28 occasions in the course of about 70 pages; gathering, in the same text, was discussed twice in less than 3 pages (Campbell 1985). While this was an extreme case, all of the texts we examined displayed an unequal treatment of activities presumed to be gender linked. The overall effect, regardless of the authors' intentions, was to convey the idea that men evolved by hunting while women tagged along gathering and giving birth.

In sum then, the "Man the Hunter" vision of evolution still dominates texts, although often in more muted versions than earlier editions. This theory, because of its obvious sex bias, was one of the first to be challenged by feminist critics (Slocum 1975; Tanner and Zihlman 1976; Zihlman 1978, 1981; Zihlman and Tanner 1978). We did find that some authors at least questioned the validity of this theory and tried to present alternative schemes reducing the significance of hunting, though not the division of labor it supposedly required (e.g., Jolly and Plog 1986). Interestingly, however, the text authors failed to give students a sense of the nature of this debate, or the issues that led to the feminist critiques. More importantly, students were not directed to the numerous articles written on the subject (see Dahlberg 1981; Fedigan 1986; Tanner 1981; Tanner and Zihlman 1976; Zihlman and Tanner 1978). In fact, most authors ignored the issue of gender bias and faulted the "Man the Hunter" model on other grounds.

In the remaining sections of this module we provide concepts and examples to help instructors effectively incorporate gender into their introductory courses and challenge some of the androcentric and ethnocentric ideas embedded in current archaeological writings. Despite the lack of published studies explicitly addressing gender in prehistory, we can raise a number of questions and propose alternative interpretations. The very act of raising the new issues and scenarios allows us to begin to transform our perspectives about the past.

Developing Concepts and Methods for an Archaeology of Gender

A central concern in the archaeology of gender is determining which aspects of gender are expressed materially and spatially at the sites people in the past created and used. All archaeologists assume there are "knowable" correlations between specific material things and spaces on the one hand, and particular activities, behaviors, and beliefs on the other. Without such an assumption we could not hope to learn anything about the past (see Schiffer 1976). We assume that information about gender *is* encoded or reflected in the material remains and their spatial arrangements preserved at sites, but we need new concepts and methods specifically designed to help us decode site materials in terms of gender.

We can draw on the work of researchers outside of archaeology to help us conceptualize gender in its material and nonmaterial dimensions (see Atkinson 1982; Etienne and Leacock 1980; Kessler and McKenna 1978; Martin and Voorhies 1975; Ortner and Whitehead 1981b; Reiter 1975; Rosaldo and Lamphere 1974). Like feminist scholars in other fields, we consider gender to be a cultural rather than a biological phenomenon. In that light it is important to distinguish between sex and gender. Sex refers to genetically determined physical traits differentiating males from females. When anthropologists "sex" skeletal remains they do so by observing certain *universal* features on the bones associated with biological femaleness and maleness. However, when archaeologists examine the placement or positioning of skeletons or materials intentionally buried with them, they are observing culturally determined and *variable* aspects of gender systems expressed in mortuary contexts. It is crucial to keep the biological universals of sex distinct from the culturally variable features of gender. As sociocultural anthropologists have pointed out:

> What gender is, what men and women are, what sorts of relations do or should obtain between them—all of these notions do not simply reflect or elaborate upon biological "givens," but are largely products of social and cultural processes. The very emphasis on the biological factor *within* different cultural traditions is variable; some cultures claim that male-female differences are almost entirely biologically grounded, whereas others give biological differences, or supposed biological differences, very little emphasis. [Ortner and Whitehead 1981b:1; emphasis in original]

Although researchers vary in their theoretical and disciplinary orientations to the subject, most conceptualize gender as a multifaceted social phenomenon with several components including gender role, gender identity, gender attribution, and gender ideology (Kessler and McKenna 1978; Ortner and Whitehead 1981a; also see Scott 1986). A fundamental problem for archaeologists interested in gender is to determine which of these are amenable to direct archaeological investigation and which are archaeologically inaccessible. The following definitions are useful for beginning to think about this issue (see Classroom Exercise 2).

● *Gender Role* describes what men and women actually do—their activity patterns, social relations and behaviors—in specific cultural settings.

● *Gender Identity* concerns an individual's own feeling of whether he or she is a woman or man (or other) regardless of genetic makeup.

● *Gender Attribution* refers to the biological, social and/or material criteria people of a particular social group use to identify others as males, females, or any other culturally defined gender category (e.g., berdache, transsexual). The attribution may or may not conform to an individual's own sense of gender or the initial gender assignment made at birth by those observing the newborn's external genitals or chromosomes.

● *Gender Ideology* encompasses the meanings of male, female, masculine, feminine, sex, and reproduction in any given culture. These might include prescriptions and sanctions

for appropriate male and female behavior or cultural rationalizations and explanations for social and political relationships between males and females.

In delineating these aspects of gender it is important to recognize that they vary from
culture to culture and that they may vary independently. Two cultures may resemble each
other in terms of the actual activities men and women perform (gender role) but differ dramatically in terms of the value attached to the tasks (gender ideology). In one culture, certain
tasks or objects may constitute primary criteria for identifying an individual as male or female
(gender attribution; see Whitehead 1981) while in another group those same tasks or objects
may not be intrinsically gendered. It is also essential to bear in mind that different elements
of a gender system may change independently or at different rates. For example, a change in
gender roles does not necessarily imply corresponding changes in beliefs about men's and
women's work capabilities or power relationships.

All of these aspects of variability complicate efforts to generalize about gender within
prehistoric hunter-gatherer, horticultural, pastoral, or urban societies. While social groups
within each of these categories may share certain features of technological, economic, settlement or social organization, they may differ dramatically along the axis of gender, and their
response to changes might well depend on their gender system. The question is, how can we
learn about any of this from the material remains preserved at archaeological sites?

Conceptualizing gender as something that is culturally constructed, culturally distinctive, and culturally variable has important implications for developing methods for studying
gender archaeologically. Specifically, it helps us frame questions about the material dimensions of gender. How are material things—tools, clothing, ornaments, or the decorative motifs placed on certain artifacts—used to signify differences between men and women? What
are the differences between "male" and "female" activity areas or living spaces? How does
the system of allocating different tasks to men, women, or children affect the way a community organizes space? Are men and women spatially separated within dwellings, household
compounds, or other parts of the community? How are materials and spatial arrangements
used to socialize children into their proper adult roles and behaviors? What are the visual
symbols of femaleness and maleness? How are status differences expressed and reinforced by
restricting access to valued resources?

Thinking about these gendered questions highlights the centrality of material objects in
actually "constructing" gender and reinforcing gender differences. In fact, gender constructions may actually be "built" with the aid of material objects that mark the gender of individuals using, wearing, or otherwise displaying them. These are more than simple associations. The items and their arrangements in space can operate as visual signs of gender, sym-
bolizing gender distinctions and structuring social relations in the ways they are used and by
whom. The objects or spaces themselves are used to actively construct and perhaps modify
notions of gender because they carry social meaning in addition to their utility as tools, clothing, or ornaments. Some of these material dimensions should be observable underground.

One way to explore the relationships between material and nonmaterial aspects of gender is in known or documented cases where we can learn about gender-specific tasks, behaviors, beliefs, and their material and spatial contexts. Ethnoarchaeological studies of this sort
will provide insights about the ways gender organization affects the formation and structure
of the sites people use and will provide some concrete examples about how materials are involved in cultural constructions of gender. We designed Classroom Exercise 2 to give students
some firsthand experience in ethnoarchaeology, studying some of the material dimensions of
gender in our own culture. Thinking about them in a familiar setting makes it possible to
recognize the various interrelated aspects of gender systems and the possible correlations be-

tween a gender system and the materials that characterize, reflect, and shape that system. Many of the questions we raise in the exercise about the material and spatial manifestations of gender in contemporary America could, with minor modification, be raised for any other group, past or present. Although the answers are culturally specific to the contemporary United States, the questions are cross-culturally applicable. Comparative ethnoarchaeological studies will give us some sense of the range of variations in the modern world and at the same time expand our imagery about possibilities in the past.

There is no reason to assume that articulations between gender and materials are unique or recent in human life. It may even be the case that material distinctions are essential for defining and maintaining gender differences. A fundamental question in an archaeology of gender is to determine when gender differences initially emerged as meaningful in human evolution and how such culturally defined differences varied over time and space depending on local circumstances. These are among the central questions to be raised in the next part of our discussion of the archaeology of gender.

Some Key Questions in a Gendered Prehistory

We envision two complementary lines of inquiry structuring an archaeology of gender. The first centers on the evolutionary development of gender differentiation and on the formation of gender-based hierarchies, subjects so far ignored by archaeologists. The major questions are when and under what circumstances did sex differences become culturally salient and then, how did differences become associated with inequalities in power, status, and prestige. The second broad area of study places gender at the center of analysis of major trends in prehistory including hominization, cultural diversification, and the formation of food-producing societies and urban states. This entails examining the contributions of both men and women within each context and examining the differential impact of new ecological, social, or technological developments on men and women. We expect that once sex differences were elaborated into gender differences in human societies, men and women would have experienced cultural events, innovations, contacts, or conflicts in different ways. This kind of archaeological research will produce major revisions in the way we write prehistory.

In the following pages we provide some examples of possible questions and approaches in each of these areas. Of necessity our sample is limited, but we hope it is sufficient to stimulate discussion and illustrate the enormous potential of bringing gender into the center of analysis in prehistoric studies.

The Evolution of Gender Differences and Stratification

Most studies of human evolution, even those critical of "Man the Hunter" scenarios, assert that a sexual division of labor is intrinsically human and assume that such a division is "the original and most basic form of economic specialization and exchange . . . the most fundamental basis of marriage and the family" (Murdock and Provost 1973:203). Textbooks commonly refer to the sexual division of labor as an "essential" element of human culture that, along with technology and language, differentiates us from other primates (Jolly and Plog 1986:234–235; Jurmain et al. 1987:181; see also Isaac 1978). The logic, if it is made explicit at all, seems to be that sex-linked differences inevitably produced gender-linked divisions. Characteristics related to female reproductive functions including pregnancy, childbearing, and lactation are assumed to explain why women could not and did not procure meat for food or defend themselves from predation and came instead to depend on biologically unencumbered males to provide for them and protect them and their offspring. This kind of explanation sounds familiar and even commonsensical to Western readers because within our cultural traditions female biological characteristics are used to rationalize inequities and explain why women cannot perform certain tasks or hold high offices. But such assumptions are easily challenged by studying the lives of women in ethnographically known foraging societies whose activity and mobility patterns are not constrained by their childbearing or child-rearing functions (see Draper 1975; Estioko-Griffin and Griffin 1981; Leacock 1983).

Feminist critics rightfully challenge the overemphasis on presumed male activities related to hunting and defense, and many try to show the possible evolutionary significance of gathering done by women, but few challenge the basic premise linking sex differences to divisions of labor. Almost all researchers assume that a division of labor by sex was present among our earliest human ancestors. We believe an archaeology of gender must begin by raising questions about the origins of the sexual division of labor rather than assuming its existence as part of the process of becoming human especially since this so often builds gender asymmetry into the species from the start.

Our approach to the evolution of gender differentiation and stratification was inspired by several sociocultural researchers including Gayle Rubin (1975) and Salvatore Cucchiari (1981) whose premises depart significantly from those outlined above. Their innovative work helps frame potential research questions about when and how sex differences became culturally elaborated into gender differences, and how this process might be expressed archaeologically. The distinction we made previously between sex and gender becomes important for this discussion. Rubin argues that

> The division of labor by sex can . . . be seen as a ''taboo'': a taboo against the sameness of men and women, a taboo dividing the sexes into two mutually exclusive categories, a taboo that exacerbates the biological differences between the sexes and thereby *creates* gender. [1975:178; emphasis in original]

The division of labor can also be seen as a taboo against sexual arrangements other than those containing at least one man and one woman, thereby enjoining heterosexual marriage. She goes on

> far from being an expression of natural differences, exclusive gender identity is the suppression of natural similarities. It requires repression: in men, of whatever is the local version of ''feminine traits'' in women, of the local definition of ''masculine'' traits. [1975:180]

Although she does not emphasize the archaeological or evolutionary implications of her arguments, they are apparent and made more explicit in the Cucchiari's work.

Cucchiari's emphasis is the formation of gender hierarchy in human evolution. He creatively asks readers to suspend their commonly held belief that gender defines our ''common humanity with thousands of generations past and future'' (1981:31) and has us envision the possibility of human society without gender. In his view,

> gender as a principle of social organization is historically relative. . . . Like other social organizing principles, such as class, gender made its appearance on the human stage at some point in the past, has since become elaborated in a number of different directions, and will most likely yield the stage to other actors in the future. [1981:31]

He suggests that the earliest human groups were not yet dichotomized into two distinct gender categories. According to Cucchiari, gender is not a salient characteristic until the Upper Paleolithic. He argues that Paleolithic art motifs document the change from a nongendered culture to a gendered society.

Rubin and Cucchiari both suggest a kind of "gender revolution" in prehistory that we think might have been comparable in complexity and variability to the subsequent food producing and urban revolutions. Cucchiari expresses the significance of this proposed evolutionary development cogently:

> The task of constructing a model that not only describes genderless society but accounts for its transformation to gender-stratified society becomes immensely complicated when we realize that such a model must also account for the origin of institutions and principles that depend for their existence on the concept of gender: kinship, marriage, the family, incest taboos, and exclusive heterosexuality. [1981:31]

Admittedly, Cucchiari and Rubin lack expertise in archaeology, and thus the scenarios they construct may be somewhat ill-conceived. Still, this kind of work provides a new starting place for questions about human origins. Instead of assuming that earliest human groups were conscious of and elaborated sex differences into differentially valued, gender-exclusive task groups or gender-structured "families," we prefer treating these as cultural developments like many others that emerged for particular reasons under specifiable conditions. We need to determine what gender differentiation might have accomplished among early human populations and what circumstances might have led to gender stratification. Then we need to think about how these social processes might be expressed archaeologically as people began to use materials to signify and reinforce difference.

If it is true that gender-differentiated societies use materials to symbolize difference and to socialize their young (i.e., to construct gender) we need to ask how genderless societies might look materially. Groups that do not divide people into two (or more) mutually exclusive groups on the basis of sex would not have gender-linked spaces, facilities, objects, or symbols. But as gender difference emerges as an important classification system for artifact-producing humans, this should be expressed in their cultural products. Later, when one's gender determines access to limited resources, this too should be expressed materially in burials, artwork, housing, and other gendered spatial arrangements.

Reevaluating early archaeological assemblages with these ideas in mind might expose the emergence and diversification of human gender systems. Archaeologists surveying the panorama of human evolution generally recognize a trend toward increasing artifact diversity over time. According to Jolly and Plog (1986:282) the earliest tool-manufacturing human groups, regardless of geographic location, used essentially the same generalized stone implements for at least half a million years. In fact, there is very little regional or material diversity until some 100,000 to 40,000 years ago when we see a marked trend toward specialization and variability in Neanderthal contexts. This specialization is commonly thought to represent social as well as technological developments, an idea reinforced by the presence of intentional burial practices at Neanderthal sites, the first clear archaeological sign of religion and ritual. Perhaps evidence of emerging human consciousness about "difference" is encoded in these burials: differences between life and death, between the natural and the supernatural, between one's own social group and outsiders, and between males and females.

Jolly and Plog (1986:316–319) and Fagan (1986:137–138) discuss the significance of Neanderthal burials and mortuary objects as a way to provide glimpses of prehistoric belief systems. Unfortunately, while the authors tell us about the objects buried with skeletons identified as male, both texts fail to mention female-associated artifacts, thus missing the opportunity to analyze what may be the first concrete archaeological expressions of gender differentiation. Were Neanderthal females also buried with grave gods? If so, were these similar to or different from those associated with males? Were male and female burial positions similar or different? Did these people treat adults and children in the same way at death? Consideration of the burials with such questions in mind could reveal patterns relating to the prevailing gender roles and ideology. Though we may not be able to decipher the more subtle ideas underlying their burial practices, the evidence should tell us whether or not gender differences were recognized in that context (for an example of working with burial materials see Classroom Exercise 3).

Somewhat later in time, at various locations, we begin to find gender-specific information expressed archaeologically in portable art and cave art. A discussion of Paleolithic art is beyond the scope of this article except to mention that gender representations and symbols are numerous and recognizable and this must have social meaning (for a more detailed discussion see Bender 1989). Recently, a number of archaeologists drawing on ethnographically known cases of contemporary foraging groups have begun to examine the relationships between social life—including aspects of gender—and these forms of artistic expression (see Conkey 1984:253–276; Fisher 1979:134–152; Lewis-Williams 1984:225–252). Such research promises to enhance archaeological interpretations but in whatever ways this artwork is ultimately understood, it does seem that well before the emergence of food production or urbanization, gender differentiation had become an important cultural force shaping human social life.

Burials and visual representations of males and females are conspicuous places to look in the archaeological record for evidence of gender differences in activity patterns and social position (see Gibbs 1987). Although we would certainly expect to find local variations in material patterning depending on the culture and the specific contexts in which gender distinctions are important, the observation of dichotomized artifacts, symbols, burial features, buildings, or rooms are possible material indicators of gender configurations.

The next evolutionary question to be raised concerns the transformation of difference into forms of gender-based stratification, that is, differential access to valued resources based on sex. When did culturally selected differences between men and women become associated with differential value, power, and prestige? When did an individual's gender assignment begin to limit or expand their access to power and valued resources? In our discussion of gender stratification and its material expressions we have avoided specifying male or female dominance. While all documented instances of gender stratification involve male dominance and female subordination—theories of matriarchies are generally rejected in anthropology (see Bamberger 1974; Martin and Voorhies 1975 for discussions of this by feminist anthropologists)—our suggestions about possible material indicators of gender asymmetry do not make any presumptions about the nature of the inequality, pending the results of more thorough investigation (see Leacock 1983 for further discussion). Certainly the rise of male dominance and female subordination—a process associated with innumerable and varied material and spatial forms in the modern world—is one of many subjects worthy of archaeological attention although it may not have been the earliest or the only form of gender-based social stratification (see Lerner 1986).

Gender and Prehistory

Recognizing the emergence of gender difference and stratification as evolutionary processes to be explained rather than assumed as universal establishes a new vantage point for revising current understandings of world prehistory in general. Ultimately, we may discover, as feminist historians have, that bringing gender into the center of analysis demands major revisions in the way prehistory is understood. Once women were introduced into historical analyses as social actors and subjects of study, researchers found it necessary to reframe questions and to reconceptualize the ways history was partitioned. Historians discovered that the periods highlighted were often not gender-neutral but were instead gender-specific (see Kelly-Gadol 1977 for further discussion). Are the conventionally used stages of prehistory similarly flawed? Some archaeologists acknowledge the Eurocentrism inherent in divisions such as Stone, Bronze, and Iron Age (Wobst and Keene 1983). These may have an androcentric slant as well, channeling attention to the progressive evolution of presumably male-associated tools or technological developments of interest to male archaeologists, while ignoring other aspects of life that would encompass the experiences of women as well. There is simply not sufficient research at this time to evaluate this possibility. We do know that gender has not been systematically incorporated into prehistoric studies. When it is, we may find it necessary to revise the ways prehistory is partitioned. Although it is premature to speculate about the form such revisions might take, we can illustrate ways to bring gender into the center of the analysis of one major transformation now emphasized in prehistory.

Generally, archaeologists define three major transformations in the prehistoric development of our species: hominization and the diversification of human culture, the emergence of food-producing societies, and the formation of urban states. We have already suggested how views of hominization are radically altered by assuming a genderless rather than a gendered social world for our earliest ancestors. Once we see gender difference as a cultural phenomenon that developed instead of appearing full blown in our earliest ancestors, we are forced to reevaluate related theories about erect posture, tool manufacture, symbolic communication, and food sharing that assume this gendered division.

Once gender difference does become an important cultural device for allocating different tasks to males and females—as mentioned earlier, perhaps no more than 100,000–40,000 years ago—we can examine processes of cultural change and stability as these might have been experienced by both men and women. Regardless of cultural particulars, if men and women perform different economic activities, have different social and political responsibilities, exploit different resources, use different tools, move about their environments along different routes—all possible outcomes of divisions of labor—we can predict that they had different knowledge, skills, values, and interests. Furthermore, depending on the nature of their work, men and women undoubtedly experienced environmental changes differently. They may have had conflicting opinions about the wisdom of proposed changes in settlement, subsistence, or mobility patterns, and they may have experienced contacts with new groups or ideas quite differently. All of these possible gender-based differences derived from divisions of labor should be considered as we study broad evolutionary patterns revealed in the archaeological record, since they would have influenced adaptation and shaped the character of cultural change or stability.

A necessary first step toward more effective gender analysis in prehistory is to increase awareness of the possible sources of variability in men's and women's activity patterns so we can move beyond superficial characterizations of "hunting," "gathering," and "childcare" as if these were monolithic, indivisible entities. In fact, these and many other activities commonly discussed in archaeological literature are composed of many discrete tasks that could be organized in a number of different ways. Any single task has social, spatial, temporal, and material dimensions (Conkey and Spector 1984; Spector 1983). The *social dimension* includes the composition of a task group in terms of age, gender, size, and relationship of members. The *spatial dimension* refers to the environmental and community location of task performance. The *temporal dimension* isolates the season, frequency, and duration of task performance and the *material dimension* identifies all artifacts, structures, facilities, or any other objects associated with task performance. Attention to these variables of task differentiation will permit more complex comparisons of and generalizations about the activity patterns of men and women, emphasizing similarities and differences in their technical knowledge and skills, mobility patterns, use of space, and the general tempo of their lives.

This type of framework provides one useful way of approaching the archaeological record. Traces of differing task patterns should be expressed in the material and spatial organization of the sites where such tasks were performed. An awareness of cross-cultural variations in task differentiation should alert us to the varied responses prehistoric groups might have had to changes in their physical and social environment. If we wish to understand broad adaptational patterns in prehistory, such as the circumstances promoting or inhibiting the shift from food-collecting to food-producing economies or the factors contributing to the formation of urban states, we need to know something about the previously existing activity patterns of men and women.

We can demonstrate some of these points more concretely by looking more closely at the transition from foraging to food production (i.e., the Neolithic Revolution), a major research area in archaeology. The work of Patricia Draper (1975), a cultural anthropologist who compared gender arrangements among foraging and settled agricultural !Kung San groups, is extremely helpful for archaeology because she pays very close attention to relationships between task, material, and spatial patterns in each context and the ramification of these on the social position of men and women.

Draper's central concern is to determine how a shift to food production—a shift experienced by numerous prehistoric groups—affected the status of women. She shows how the egalitarian relationships between men and women quickly deteriorate in sedentary contexts where women's influence and autonomy is drastically reduced. By mapping the locations of men's, women's, and children's activities in the two settings, Draper is able to compare community layout, architecture, and household equipment. She documents the material, spatial, and social formation of a public/domestic dichotomy in the agricultural villages—a gendered division that did not occur in the foraging context. In essence, she clearly illustrates the ways in which materials and spaces are involved in the cultural construction of gender.

Draper noted a combination of factors that seemed to conspire against women, creating marked gender asymmetry. First, she found significant differences in the subsistence contributions and mobility patterns of men and women in the two situations. Among the mobile foragers, both men and women moved about their environment and were absent from camps for about the same amounts of time. Women contributed as much if not more to subsistence than men, and they directly controlled the resources they gathered. In sharp contrast, the sedentary !Kung women contributed far less to subsistence since more and more of their time was taken up with new, more elaborate food preparation and processing of domesticates. More substantial housing and increased material goods and facilities associated with sedentism demanded more labor from the women as well. While women were increasingly limited to a definable domestic sphere, men became peripheral to households spending more of their time outside the village planting crops and tending fields and domestic animals.

The roles of mother, father, man, and woman were dramatically different in the two settings and socialization of children reflected the change. Among the foraging !Kung there was an absence of rigid sex-typing of adult activities. Boys and girls played together in mixed groups with little pressure to conform to strictly defined gender roles. Childcare, which was done by both males and females in the camps, was not an onerous or particularly time-consuming activity given the long birth intervals (about 4 years) between children and the rhythm of adult work patterns. Draper reported that most adults worked no more than 3 days a week, and community members varied the amount of time they were away from camp. At any given time one-third to one-half of the adult population was in camp and could easily supervise their own children as well as those whose parents were away.

The sedentary !Kung were different. Adult gender roles were sharply delineated and differentially valued. Children were apt to be viewed as real or potential workers and gender role socialization was more rigidly structured. Boys were regularly outside the boundaries of the village herding animals in preparation for their adult roles, while girls stayed close to home assisting their mothers with childcare and domestic chores, now clearly associated with women.

Finally—and perhaps most importantly for archaeologists—Draper contrasted the material characteristics and spatial arrangements of the two communities, showing how these affected social relations between men and women (1975:104–108). She noted that in the "small, circular, open and highly intimate" !Kung camps there were cultural sanctions against any form of authoritarianism, against physical expressions of aggression, and against hoarding material goods (1975:104). In the agricultural villages, by contrast, households were further apart and bounded by fences built to keep domestic animals out. This acted to limit interactions between households, increase privacy, and permit a kind of hoarding by those who had accumulated some material wealth, that was neither possible nor tolerated in the bush. Interestingly, men more often than women were defined as the owners of such property.

Gina Kolata (1974) summarizes several studies done among the !Kung that help explain why it is women and not men who became increasingly confined to the domestic sphere among the sedentary !Kung. That research revealed more generally how the shift to sedentary life had profoundly different consequences for men and women. There is a marked increase in fertility and birth rates in the sedentary villages, apparently related to changes in diet and in infant nursing practices. According to Kolata, "The demographic changes taking place among the !Kung are of interest because the sedentary !Kung seem to have lost a natural check on their fertility rates" (1974:933). She reports that the foraging groups have a nutritionally well-balanced diet in terms of calories, vitamins, and minerals in contrast to the sedentary !Kung who consume a great deal of cow's milk and grain and are generally taller and heavier. One of several effects of this dietary shift seems to be that sedentary women begin to menstruate earlier than nomadic women. Among the foragers girls often marry at puberty, about 15.5 years of age, and have their first children at age 19. Since they have no soft foods to feed their babies, they nurse them for 3 or 4 years during which time they rarely conceive. The combination of late menarche and long birth intervals serves to control population size. In contrast, population size is growing rapidly among the sedentary !Kung. These women wean children much earlier, supplementing nursing with processed grains and cow's milk. Researchers suspect that fertility rates may be higher among the sedentary women because their diet affects both the age of menarche and birth intervals (Kolata 1974:934). Investigators have shown that a woman's body fat must be above a certain minimum for the onset of menstruation and for its maintenance after menarche. !Kung foragers are well nourished but thin. Furthermore, when they lactate women need an additional 1000 calories a day. During the 3- to 4-year interval they nurse their children they may have too little body fat to ovulate. The increased body fat of sedentary women combined with their ability to wean children earlier appears to be increasing fertility and birthrates.

These changes occur in an economic and social context where children have increasing value as workers. It seems that women who might under other circumstances employ known birth control methods to limit the number of children they bear choose instead to have more children. Increased family size, when combined with other aspects of sedentary life, seems to seriously circumscribe women's activities, limit their physical mobility, and eventually undermine their autonomy and social position.

Although archaeologists have previously cited demographic variables in discussing both the causes and effects of food production, they have not examined this from the differing perspectives of the men and women involved. The !Kung research highlights the significance of that omission. We do not mean to imply that the !Kung represent a universal pattern for all groups, past and present, who have experienced this transformation. Clearly, the !Kung are living in a 20th-century world heavily influenced by centuries of colonialism. Instead, we use this case because it so vividly portrays the importance of focusing on gender in examining processes of culture change.

Summary and Conclusions

The process of engendering archaeology requires a reorientation of method and theory in future research. It is our hope that work along the lines suggested above will result in the development of a body of scholarship about archaeology and gender that is informed both by recent anthropological studies of gender and by feminist scholarship more generally. The work of introducing gender into archaeology requires that we focus on women in prehistory. The "discovery" of women in prehistory is a necessary, nontrivial, first step in documenting the importance and diversity of women's roles in the past.

How should we go about accomplishing this task? The goal is partially met by simple revisions in language and model building. Gender neutral language, illustrations, and discussions can be used not to mask the existence of males and females, but to problematize the notion of gender. If we do not assume we know whether gender was a salient category or what gender relations were operative in a given archaeological situation, we open up the possibility of research into women's and men's past activities. A balanced treatment of all productive activities is important; presumed male achievement, invention, or activity must not be given priority over presumed women's work. The fact that we do not know with certainty whether gender was connected to any of the milestones in prehistory (e.g., technological innovations, domestication, religious changes, stratification, urbanism, instances of immigration and colonization) is problematic. However, burial data and spatial distribution studies can provide some information on gender roles. In many cases, simply stating hypotheses for further testing will advance the study of gender and archaeology significantly. For example, if women in a region are assumed to have been responsible for gathering plants, then one could hypothesize that the subsequent domestication of plants and farming activities would also have been women's responsibility. Once presented, such a hypothesis and its fundamental assumptions could be tested with additional data.

A conscious effort at writing women's prehistory will help us to initially address the invisibility of women in prehistory. However, this is not an end point, but only a beginning. Joan Wallace Scott has discussed this with reference to history:

> Historians, for example, have until recently pictured their archetypal actor, the universal human agent, as a white male. Although they have assumed that Universal Man stands for all humankind, in fact this representation creates hierarchies and exclusions. Women, blacks, and various others have been either invisible as historical subjects or somehow depicted as less central, less important, than white men. [1987:94]

Once difference, rather than a universal type (Man), is admitted, the question of gender interrelationships becomes a subject for archaeological inquiry. The important step of dismantling the universal category of "Man" leads logically to a study of the interrelations of female and male gender categories. As more information is gathered concerning women in prehistory, the appropriateness of a universal category defined as "Man" is challenged. The dichotomy of universal male :: particular female loses utility since a part can no longer be presented as typical of the whole. Diversity has been introduced and this alters the investigation so that relations between categories that are defined as different becomes the focus. Were the earliest gender relationships symmetrical (that is, egalitarian) or asymmetrical (males dominate? females dominate?)? When and where did gender asymmetry develop, and, more importantly, why?

Once again the question of approaching gender interrelations with archaeological data arises. One obvious starting place is the examination of archaeological evidence of difference (perhaps as seen in significantly different artifact assemblages, e.g., Upper Paleolithic as compared with Mousterian). When did gender become an important category that was marked with different clothing, decoration, and/or artifact styles? In this we assume that outward symbols of difference are created to signify categories of difference and these are used by humans so that appropriate behavior is maintained. Visual recognition of differences in dress, for example, allows individuals to behave according to culturally defined rules. This opens up research possibilities not only into gender distinctions, but other categories of difference as well (race, ethnicity, group membership, or age for example). Once the materials that mark gender (or other) differences are established, one can go on to ask why and under what circumstances differentiation arose? When do marked differences imply hierarchy (stratification, classes, slavery)? These are questions about relations between categories of difference, and as such, they are questions that would not be asked if a universal standard were presented ("Man"). Relational questions involving difference have potentially rich material manifestations and consequently should be highly visible in the archaeological record.

We hope that the preceding discussion illustrating the many ways gender is embedded in and affects various aspects of human social life suggests directions for revising and reconceptualizing other areas of prehistoric studies. Similar approaches considering the interplay of dietary, social, economic, spatial, and material variables could certainly be applied to the study of the emergence and consequences of urbanization. How did men and women experience or contribute to the breakdown of kinship as a central principle organizing social relations? How were men and women affected by the spatial organization of urban centers and cities? The rise of warfare, occupational specialization, and social stratification? How did the spread of state religions affect gender beliefs and practices? How do gender and class articulate with the rise of the state? All of these and many other questions about this transformation can stimulate new gender-focused archaeological research.

References Cited

Atkinson, Jane
  1982 Review Essay: Anthropology. Signs 8(2):236–258.
Bamberger, Joan
  1974 The Myth of Matriarchy: Why Men Rule in Primitive Society. *In* Women, Culture and Society. M. Rosaldo and L. Lamphere, eds. Pp. 263–280. Stanford: Stanford University Press.
Bender, Barbara
  1989 The Roots of Inequality. *In* Domination and Resistance. D. Miller, M. Rowlands, and C. Tilley, eds. Pp. 83–93. London: Unwin Hyman.

Binford, Lewis
1962   Archaeology as Anthropology. American Antiquity 28(2):217–225.
Bourguignon, Erika
1980   A World of Women: Anthropological Studies of Women in the Societies of the World. New York: Praeger.
Campbell, Bernard G.
1985   Humankind Emerging. 4th ed. Boston: Little, Brown.
Conkey, Margaret W.
1984   To Find Ourselves: Art and Social Geography of Prehistoric Hunter Gatherers. *In* Past and Present in Hunter Gatherer Studies. Carmel Schrire, ed. Pp. 253–276. Orlando: Academic Press.
Conkey, Margaret W., and Janet D. Spector
1984   Archaeology and the Study of Gender. Advances in Archaeological Method and Theory 7:1–38.
Cucchiari, Salvatore
1981   The Gender Revolution and the Transition from Bisexual Horde to Patrilocal Band: the Origins of Gender Hierarchy. *In* Sexual Meanings. S. B. Ortner and H. Whitehead, eds. Pp. 31–79. Cambridge:
Dahlberg, Frances, ed.
1981   Woman the Gatherer. New Haven: Yale University Press.
Deetz, James
1977   In Small Things Forgotten. Garden City, N.Y.: Doubleday.
Draper, Patricia
1975   !Kung Women: Contrasts in Sexual Egalitarianism in the Foraging and Sedentary Contexts. *In* Toward an Anthropology of Women. R. Reither, ed. Pp.77–109. New York: Monthly Review Press.
Estioko-Griffin, Agnes, and P. Bion Griffin
1981   Woman the Hunter: The Agta. *In* Woman the Gatherer. Frances Dahlberg, ed. Pp. 121–151. New Haven: Yale University Press.
Etienne, Mona, and Eleanor Leacock, eds.
1980   Women and Colonization: Anthropological Perspectives. New York: Praeger.
Fagan, Brian
1986   People of the Earth. 5th ed. Boston: Little, Brown.
Fedigan, Linda Marie
1986   The Changing Role of Women in Models of Human Evolution. Annual Review of Anthropology 15:25–66.
Fisher, Elizabeth
1979   Woman's Creation: Sexual Evolution and the Shaping of Society. New York: McGraw-Hill.
Gibbs, Liv
1987   Identifying Gender Represtation in the Archaeological Record: A Contextual Study. *In* The Archaeology of Contextual Meanings. Ian Hodder, ed. Pp. 79–89. Cambridge: Cambridge University Press.
Hodder, Ian, ed.
1982   Symbolic and Structural Archaeology. Cambridge: Cambridge University Press.
Isaac, Glynn
1978   The Food-Sharing Behavior of Protohuman Hominids. Scientific American 238:90–108.
Jolly, Clifford, and Fred Plog
1986   Physical Anthropology and Archaeology. 3d ed. New York: Knopf.
Jurmain, Robert, Harry Nelson, and William A. Turnbaugh
1987   Understanding Physical Anthropology and Archeology. 3d ed. St. Paul, Minn.: West Publishing.
Kelly-Gadol, Joan
1977   Did Women Have a Renaissance? *In* Becoming Visible: Women in European History. Renate Bridenthal and Claudia Koonz, eds. Pp. 137–164. Boston: Houghton Mifflin.

Kessler, Suzanne, and Wendy McKenna
 1978   Gender: An Ethnomethodological Approach. Chicago: University of Chicago Press.
Kolata, Gina
 1974   !Kung Hunter-gatherers: Feminism, Diet, and Birth Control. Science 185:932–934.
Leacock, Eleanor B.
 1978   Women's Status in Egalitarian Society: Implications for Social Evolution. Current Anthropology 19(2):247–254.
 1983   Interpreting the Origins of Gender Inequality: Conceptual and Historical Problems. Dialectical Anthropology 7:263–284.
Lerner, Gerda
 1986   The Creation of Patriarchy. New York: Oxford University Press.
Lewis-Williams, J. David
 1984   Ideological Continuities in Prehistoric Southern Africa: The Evidence of Rock Art. *In* Past and Present in Hunter Gatherer Studies. Carmel Schrire, ed. Pp. 225–252. Orlando: Academic Press.
MacCormack, Carol, and Marilyn Strathern, eds.
 1980   Nature, Culture and Gender. Cambridge: Cambridge University Press.
Marshall, Yvonne
 1985   Who Made the Lapita Pots? A Case Study in Gender Archaeology. The Journal of The Polynesian Society 94(3):205–233.
Martin, M. Kay, and Barbara Voorhies
 1975   Female of the Species. New York: Columbia University Press.
Matthiasson, Carolyn, ed.
 1974   Many Sisters: Women in Cross-cultural Perspective. New York: The Free Press.
McGhee, Robert
 1977   Ivory for the Sea Woman: the Symbolic Attributes of a Prehistoric Technology. Canadian Journal of Archaeology 1:141–149.
Miller, Daniel, and Christopher Tilley, eds.
 1984   Ideology, Power and Prehistory. Cambridge: Cambridge University Press.
Minnich, Elizabeth
 1982   A Devastating Conceptual Error: How Can We *Not* Be Feminist Scholars? Change Magazine April:7–9.
Murdock, George, and Caterina Provost
 1973   Factors in the Division of Labor By Sex: A Cross-Cultural Analysis. Ethnology 12:203–225.
Murphy, Yolanda, and Robert Murphy
 1974   Women of the Forest. New York: Columbia University Press.
Ortner, Sherry, and Harriet Whitehead
 1981a   Sexual Meanings: The Cultural Construction of Gender and Sexuality. Cambridge: Cambridge University Press.
 1981b   Introduction: Accounting for Sexual Meanings. *In* Sexual Meanings. S. Ortner and H. Whitehead, eds. Cambridge: Pp. 1–27. Cambridge University Press.
Quinn, Naomi
 1977   Anthropological Studies on Female Status. Annual Review of Anthropology 6:181–225.
Reiter, Rayna Rapp, ed.
 1975   Toward an Anthropology of Women. New York: Monthly Review Press.
Rogers, Susan C.
 1978   Women's Place: A Critical Review of Anthropological Theory. Comparative Studies in Society and History 20(1):123–162.
Rosaldo, Michele, and Louise Lamphere, eds.
 1974   Women, Culture and Society. Stanford: Stanford University Press.
Rubin, Gayle
 1975   The Traffic in Women: Notes on the 'Political Economy' of Sex. *In* Toward an Anthropology of Women. Rayna Reiter, ed. Pp. 157–210. New York: Monthly Review Press.

Sacks, Karen
    1979   Sisters and Wives: The Past and Future of Sexual Equality. Westport, Conn.: Greenwood
        Press.
Schiffer, Michael
    1976   Behavioral Archaeology. New York: Academic Press.
Scott, Joan Wallace
    1986   Gender: A Useful Category of Historical Analysis. The American Historical Review
        91(5):1053–1075.
    1987   History and Difference. Daedalus 116(4):93–118.
Slocum, Sally
    1975   Woman the Gatherer: Male Bias in Anthropology. *In* Toward an Anthropology of Women.
        Rayna Reiter, ed. Pp. 36–50. New York: Monthly Review Press.
Spector, Janet
    1983   Male/Female Task differentiation Among the Hidatsa: Toward the Development of an Ar-
        chaeological Approach to the Study of Gender. *In* The Hidden Half: Studies of Plains Indian
        Women. P. Albers and B. Medicine, eds. Pp. 77–99. Washington: University Press of America.
Tanner, Nancy Makepeace
    1981   On Becoming Human. Cambridge: Cambridge University Press.
Tanner, Nancy M., and Adrienne L. Zihlman
    1976   Women in Evolution, Part I: Innovation and Selection in Human Origins. Signs 1:585–608.
Welbourn, Alice
    1984   Endo Ceramics and Power Strategies. *In* Ideology, Power and Prehistory. D. Miller and C.
        Tilley, eds. Pp. 17–24. Cambridge: Cambridge University Press.
Whitehead, Harriet
    1981   The Bow and the Burden Strap: A New Look at Institutionalized Homosexuality in Native
        North America. *In* Sexual Meanings: The Cultural Construction of Gender and Sexuality. Sherry
        Ortner and Harriet Whitehead, eds. Pp.80–115. Cambridge: Cambridge University Press.
Williams, Walter
    1986   The Spirit and the Flesh: Sexual Diversity in American Indian Culture. Boston: Beacon Press.
Wobst, H. Martin, and Arthur S. Keene
    1983   Archaeological Explanation as Political Economy. *In* The Socio-Politics of Archaeology. J.
        M. Gero, D. M. Lacy, and M. L. Blakey, eds. Pp. 79–89. Department of Anthropology Research
        Report 23, University of Massachusetts, Amherst.
Zihlman, Adrienne L.
    1978   Women in Evolution, Part II: Subsistence and Social Organization Among Early Hominids.
        Signs 4:4–20.
    1981   Women as Shapers of the Human Adaptation. *In* Woman the Gatherer. Frances Dahlberg, ed.
        Pp. 75–120. New Haven: Yale University Press.
Zihlman, Adrienne L., and Nancy M. Tanner
    1978   Gathering and the Hominid Adaptation. *In* Female Hierarchies. L. Tiger and H. T. Fowler,
        eds. Pp. 163–194. Chicago: Beresford.

Classroom Exercises in the Archaeology of Gender

The preceding essay should orient instructors to the various ways gender can be incorporated into lectures and discussions in introductory archaeology courses or sections of other
courses surveying world prehistory. The exercises below provide some concrete ideas for actual classroom activities and assignments designed to provide students with some direct experience in working with concepts, methods and issues central to archaeological studies of
gender. We tried to present the exercises so that instructors can use them—with minor modification and instructions tailored to meet their particular class objectives and expectations—
as class handouts or models for individual or group projects.

Classroom Exercise 1   Critically Reading Introductory Texts

Note to the Instructor: In the preceding essay we discussed problems of gender bias in archaeological literature emphasizing androcentric and ethnocentric portrayals in introductory texts or androcentrism. As a way to encourage students to sharpen their critical skills, we suggest that they read text chapters or major sections in their text with the following questions in mind. This exercise might be used to structure some portion of class discussion time or it could be used for a written assignment.

1. Does the author give equal attention to the roles, activities, and experiences of women and men in discussing prehistoric lifeways and developments? Be sure to consider the photos and illustrations as well as narrative.

2. In what particular contexts is the author explicitly gender-specific? Go through sections of the text and identify the number of times the author refers to males and females and describe the subjects or contexts "linked to" males versus females in this way? Again, be sure to consider visual materials in the text along with the narrative.

3. When the author describes and discusses *human* characteristics, skills, capabilities, activities, etc. are the generalizations valid or appropriate for both men and women or are they implicitly gender-specific? Be sure to provide specific examples to support your ideas.

4. What gender-specific characteristics, traits, attitudes, aptitudes, etc. does the author explicitly or implicitly assume to be universal, that is, true for all human groups at all time periods? Of these, which do you think are more likely to be *culturally* specific? How could you "test" your ideas?

5. Given the specific features of gender bias discovered in the text, what alternative "scenarios" can you propose to replace androcentric portrayals, that is, how would you revise androcentric or ethnocentric sections of the text? What suggestions can you offer to more explicitly incorporate gender into the text?

Classroom Exercise 2   Material Expressions of Gender in the United States: A Case Study in Ethnoarchaeology

Part 1   *Relationships Between Material and Nonmaterial Dimensions of Gender*

Note to the Instructor: In our discussion of gender as an analytical category, we identified several different aspects of gender including gender role, identity, attribution, and ideology. We also suggested that materials and spatial arrangements are essential ingredients in the cultural construction of gender in any given cultural context. One way to better grasp this idea is to explore the relationships between the material and nonmaterial aspects of gender in known or documented cases. The exercise below should help familiarize people with key concepts in studying gender archaeologically.

In discussing these questions, students should be alerted to areas of potential variation and difference in gender arrangements within American society. For each question they might look for variability in terms of class, ethnicity, geographic region, etc.

1. What daily tasks are typically performed by men versus women in our culture? For each task list any specific materials (tools, equipment, structures, or facilities) associated with these gender-specific tasks? [gender roles]

● Which of the materials seem "diagnostic" or typical of the task? that is, they are not used for any other tasks?

2. What kinds of buildings or rooms in domestic and public buildings are associated with men vs. women or boys versus girls?

● Do both men and women use these spaces or are they sex-segregated? [gender ideology and gender role]

3. What ornaments, clothing, weapons, or symbols in our culture are gender-linked or thought of as male or female?

● When you observe people from a distance, what objects signal their gender? How would you know from dress, jewelry, size or color of things that individuals are male or female? [gender attribution]

4. What consumer goods (look at advertisements) are designed primarily for women versus men and how can you tell? [gender ideology]

5. What specific social occasions or contexts are gender-segregated in our culture? What characterizes these contexts? [gender role, attribution, ideology]

6. What material things are associated with political power or high social status in our culture? Do men and women have equal access to these valued resources? [gender ideology]

7. Many would argue that our culture is male dominated; that women are subordinate to men. Are there any material indicators of this gender asymmetry? [gender ideology]

8. How do children learn about appropriate gender behavior through materials in our culture? (e.g., toys, gifts, rooms, restrictions about movement through space, etc.) [gender ideology]

9. Develop an inventory or list of the gender-specific spaces and things you've identified in the questions above. Compare and contrast men's and women's spaces, objects, and facilities in terms of material of manufacture; size, shape, color, or design elements of various classes, kinds of objects (like clothing, jewelry, equipment, etc.).

Describe any material or spatial patterns that seem to characterize male and female spaces or things in our culture?

Part 2   Mapping Gender

To get another, even more archaeological sense of our gender arrangements, select a "gender-specific site" (e.g., a woman's bedroom, a man's dorm room, a bathroom used only by women, a men's locker or club room, an outdoor area used exclusively by one gender, etc.). Follow these instructions to create maps of these sites.

1. Use graph paper for mapping sites "to scale" and use pencil so mistakes can be easily corrected.

2. Maps should be drawn in "planview" as if the mapper is hovering directly above the site looking straight down. This kind of map is used in archaeology to illustrate the horizontal spatial relationships of various objects, structures, and stationary facilities found at a site.

3. For spatial orientation, indicate North with a small arrow pointing to the top of the map.

4. Select a *scale* for the map. Any map is a miniature representation of reality. A scale is needed to show correct spatial relationships and proportions of objects at sites. The scale used in part depends on the size of a site and the level of detail one hopes to show.

To select a scale first measure or estimate the length and width of the site. Then look at the graph paper divisions and determine how many grid divisions could be used to represent one foot. Using that scale outline the boundaries of the site. Be sure to indicate the scale on the map so others could "read it" (e.g., 5 grid squares—1 foot).

5. Once a scale has been established and the boundaries of the site plotted, map in all the objects (excluding people) that can be graphically shown in their correct spatial orientation and size. Start by mapping large objects and major site features (door openings, dressers, trees, plumbing fixtures, stove, etc., etc.). Then place smaller items on the map.

6. REMEMBER—things are shown as they would look from above. If it is difficult to identify some objects visually they can be labeled on the map by letter or number and described on a separate artifact inventory (see below). The inventory should explain your system and listing these items using a "key", for example, "a" = 3 magazines on a table; "b" = 12 glasses in a cupboard; "c" = 6 sweat socks on the floor of the closet, etc., etc.

Analyzing the maps in terms of gender. Once the maps and inventories are completed, people should exchange them for analysis to determine if, on the basis of materials and spatial arrangements, they can correctly determine the gender of site occupants or places at the site associated with boys/men or girls/women. After studying the maps, people should address the following questions:

● Are there any objects or specific site characteristics that consistently signal the gender of the occupants regardless of the type of site?

● Are any of these made of imperishable materials so that they might actually survive in the archaeological record?

● Would a person from another culture, unfamiliar with our gender system, be able to tell that two different groups of people used the sites and that the difference between the groups was based on their gender rather than their ethnicity or class or activities undertaken there?

● Can you imagine how different any of your sites would look if they were used by *both* men and women?

Classroom Exercise 3   Gender Analysis of Burials

Note to the Instructor: We suggested in the essay that burial sites are likely to be good sources of archaeological information about gender arrangements because we can often determine the "sex" of skeletal remains based upon certain universal, genetically determined characteristics on bones associated with biological maleness and femaleness. If skeletal remains can be "sexed" we can then compare positioning of skeletons, distribution of grave goods or other features associated with males and females to interpret culturally specific aspects of their gender system as these are expressed in mortuary contexts. Remember, this may or may not "reflect" gender specific beliefs or practices in everyday life.

In the following exercise students are asked to work with some simulated site material to learn about some of the prospects and problems of interpreting gender from burial remains. We have provided summary information from a hypothetical "Maritime Archaic" burial site. Maritime Archaic culture was a middle and late Archaic cultural manifestation found from Maine to Labrador between 5000 B.C. and 1000 B.C. As the name implies, the economic orientation of these people emphasized harvesting marine resources including fish, seals, walrus, sea birds as well as terrestrial resources such as caribou and deer. Ground slate artifacts abound and burial sites have indicated elaborate mortuary rituals. (For further information see Fitzhugh 1978; McGhee 1975; Sanger 1973; and Tuck 1976.)

Archaeologists typically view Maritime Archaic people as "egalitarian" but the elaborate burials indicate a high degree of *achieved* status. Further, juvenile burials often contain large quantities of mortuary offerings, suggesting that either the status assignments were more complex than we envision or that burial offerings do not simply reflect an individual's lifetime accomplishments. Our questions emphasize possible differences between males and females in social position, role, or value as these can be observed through burial practices in this population.

Students should familiarize themselves with the attached summary information below (see Table 1) before addressing the questions.

1. Examine the number of burials in each of the three categories: female, indeterminate, male. What sex ratio is present (female:male)? What age ratio is present (adult:juvenile)? How might this sample size and composition affect our ability to generalize about gender arrangements in this culture?

2. Study the artifact assemblage and sort items into "meaningful" categories by presumed use or function (e.g., weapons, cooking tools, eating utensils, tools used to process resources, personal ornaments, items of dress, etc., etc.) Try out several ways to "sort" items until you feel satisfied with one or experiment with several to see which is most useful for addressing the questions below.

● Examine the artifact "types" and their associations by sex *and* age. Are there "significant" associations of artifact types with men versus women? Adults versus juveniles?

● Based on your associations what inferences or generalizations can you make about gender roles or activity patterns of men and women in this population? Differences between adults and youths?

3. Working with this material assemblage how would you determine measures of social "status?" (e.g., number of items per burial? presence or absence of certain items? material of manufacture of certain items?). Apply your measures of status to male, female, and juvenile skeletal remains. Based on your examination what inferences or generalizations can you offer about differences in social position of women, men, and youths in this population?

Try out different measures. What are the complexities of identifying social status based on this type of burial information?

Table 1. Summary of Grave Goods and Associations by Sex and Age

Item	Total	Female	Male	Juvenile
Iron pyrite	17	12 (71%)	4 (24%)	1 (6%)
Quartz cobble/pebble	1847	1020 (55%)	541 (29%)	286 (15%)
Quartz crystal	165	34 (21%)	11 (7%)	120 (73%)
Crystal/mineral/other rocks	109	14 (13%)	80 (73%)	15 (14%)
Shell beads	2387	479 (20%)	1008 (42%)	900 (38%)
Pendant/amulet	84	32 (38%)	25 (30%)	27 (32%)
Bone whistles	29	3 (10%)	9 (31%)	17 (59%)
Unmodified animal bone	606	280 (47%)	255 (42%)	71 (12%)
Shell with red ochre	11	6 (55%)	4 (36%)	1 (9%)
Worked whalebone	3		3 (100%)	
Worked bone	60	46 (77%)	10 (17%)	4 (7%)
Worked antler	20	10 (50%)	5 (25%)	5 (25%)
Beaver incisor (gravers)	165	26 (16%)	94 (57%)	45 (27%)
Bone needle	27	5 (19%)	6 (22%)	16 (59%)
Awl	13	3 (23%)	4 (31%)	6 (46%)
Bone scraper	4	2 (50%)	1 (25%)	1 (25%)
Bone knife	4	1 (25%)	2 (50%)	1 (25%)
Slate knife	1			1 (100%)
Bone dagger	18	5 (28%)	2 (11%)	11 (61%)
Bone foreshaft	21	2 (10%)	10 (48%)	9 (43%)
Harpoon	47	6 (13%)	24 (51%)	17 (36%)
Bone lance	6	2 (33%)	2 (33%)	2 (33%)
Bone point	35	8 (23%)	15 (43%)	12 (34%)
Slate point	23	6 (26%)	7 (30%)	10 (43%)
Slate bayonnet	22	4 (18%)	9 (41%)	9 (41%)
Bone bayonnet	10	5 (50%)		5 (50%)
Stone biface	3	2 (66%)	1 (33%)	
Leister (fishing)	3	2 (66%)		1 (33%)
Gouge	11	5 (45%)	3 (27%)	3 (27%)
Chisel	2	1 (50%)		1 (50%)
Axe	13	6 (46%)	1 (8%)	6 (46%)
Adze	12	4 (33%)	1 (8%)	7 (58%)
Plummet	4	2 (50%)		2 (50%)
Whetsone	5	2 (40%)	2 (40%)	1 (20%)
Ground slate	9	8 (89%)		1 (11%)
Flake	24	1 (4%)	15 (63%)	8 (33%)

4. We have identified four dimensions of gender: gender role, identity, attribution, and ideology. Which of these seem most and least "visible" or accessible archaeologically given your analysis of these burial data?

5. If you were to study remains from a habitation site created by this same population, how would you use the insights from your burial analysis to test hypotheses, supplement information, or further investigate gender? Would you be able to tell male versus female activity areas? Male versus female tools? Ornaments? Symbols? Explain.

Summary Information on Artifacts and Burials From a Hypothetical Maritime Archaic Site

The information below was taken from reports about actual Maritime Archaic burials. For the purposes of this exercise, age divisions have been simplified. The categories given include adult female, adult male, and juvenile (younger than 18 years of age).

There were a total of 80 burials: 20 female, 22 male, 38 juvenile.

The average number of grave goods per female = 120

The average number of grave goods per male = 107

The average number of grave goods per adult (both sexes) = 109

The average number of grave goods per juvenile (both sexes) = 41

The 80 skeletons were divided among 50 graves as follows:

single burials = 30
double burials = 11
triple burials = 4
quad burials = 4

There was no pattern in the multiple burials, although adult/juvenile combinations were slightly more common than adult/adult combinations.

All of the unmodified animal remains were most likely ritual possessions (totem symbols, medicine bag contents, shamanistic items, etc.). These consisted primarily of bird elements (beaks, skulls, wings); small mammal remains (martin skulls, otter jaws, muskrat long bones); and mammal elements (seal claws, bear incisors, deer and caribou antler fragments). No pattern of difference could be seen that covaried in terms of sex. This suggests that if these were status items, they relate to achieved positions.

Burial Bibliography

Fitzhugh, William W.
    1978   Maritime Archaic Cultures of the Central and Northern Labrador Coast. Arctic Anthropology
    15(2):61–95.

McGhee, Robert
 1975   An Archaic Sequence from the Strait of Belle Isle, Labrador. National Museum of Man, Mercury Series, No. 34. Ottawa.
Sanger, David
 1973   Cow Point: an Archaic Cemetery in New Brunswick. National Museum of Man, Mercury Series, No. 12. Ottawa.
Tuck, James
 1976   Ancient People of Port au Choix. Newfoundland Social and Economic Studies No. 17. Institute of Social and Economic Research, Memorial University of Newfoundland.

Gender and Archaeology Annotated Bibliography

In compiling this annotated bibliography we were reminded that the self-conscious and feminist study of gender is still a new approach in archaeology. Unlike the other subfields of anthropology—where there are now numerous publications to refer to—there are few published archaeological studies explicitly informed by the new scholarship on gender. The current published literature mainly falls into two categories: works by archaeologists who do not take into consideration the feminist scholarship on gender, and, works by feminist anthropologists who do not take into consideration the methods and data base of archaeology. We knew of relatively few works that were both written by archaeologists and utilized the new scholarship on gender. In the hopes that we might discover additional published sources we wrote to more than fifty archaeologists asking for references on gender and archaeology. The responses were few and comments ranged from "Good Luck!" to "You mean there ARE some references?". The lack of feminist literature on archaeology and gender is not an illusion but a sad truth. Fortunately, that seems to be changing. Several books about women in prehistory are either planned or in press. Further, a number of sessions on gender and archaeology have been organized at various national meetings (e.g., 1987 American Anthropological Association meeting, 1988 Society for American Archaeology meeting, 1988 Society for Historical Archaeology meeting, 1989 Joint Archaeological Congress). As more archaeologists become interested in the topic, the bibliographic references can only grow.

The works listed below represent conscious selections on our part. Our search included major anthropological and archaeological journals and books likely to be available in American colleges and universities. We did not search the literature from classics, classical archaeology, Near Eastern studies or history, however. Although these fields may contain useful sources, an exhaustive search was beyond our means and expertise. Instead we concentrated on materials by anthropologically trained archaeologists and by sociocultural anthropologists. We divided the references we found useful into two parts. The first part is an annotated bibliography including materials that meet four specific criteria:

1. The works all deal directly with archaeology, either in theory or in practice.

2. The works directly address gender as it is recoverable and interpretable in an archaeological context.

3. The works are relevant to topics covered in introductory archaeology courses.

4. They are published in English, and located in journals or books that are likely to be found in most college or university libraries.

In practice, the first bibliography contains works by archaeologists utilizing at least some of the new scholarship on women.

The second bibliography is not annotated, and covers primarily ethnohistoric sources, usually written by sociocultural anthropologists. In this bibliography we paid special attention to references concerning gender relations in foraging societies, gender relations and the rise of the state, the rise of gender inequality and the beginnings of stratified societies, and the impact of colonization on gender systems. These are topics frequently covered in introductory courses and concern cultures often discussed in some detail (e.g., Egypt, Sumer, Andean Peru). Although archaeological evidence is often not directly used by the authors from this second bibliography, the works still contain valuable information for instructors who are teaching introductory courses in prehistory. Consequently, the materials we included in the second bibliography meet slightly different criteria:

1. The works directly address gender in an ethnohistoric or historic context.

2. The works are relevant to topics covered in introductory archaeology courses.

3. They are published in English, and located in journals or books that are likely to be found in most college or university libraries.

The sources listed here are valuable, but may be somewhat more difficult to use in an introductory course since they do not explicitly focus on the material or spatial dimensions of culture. However, since each author emphasized gender, particularly in the context of changing cultural processes, we felt these reference materials were important.

We intentionally left out material that was primarily concerned with hominid evolution or biological anthropology. These sources are addressed in other modules. Similarly, we have omitted much of the feminist scholarship in sociocultural anthropology and history although it is of use in informing archaeologists about gender cross-culturally. Again, much of this material is presented in other curriculum modules. Finally, we have not included works that deal with archaeology and gender, but do so from gender-biased or ethnocentric perspective.

Bibliography I

Barstow, Ann
    1978   The Uses of Neolithic Archaeology for Women's History: James Mellaart's Work on the Neolithic Goddess at Catal Huyuk. Feminist Studies 4(3):7–18.

    This article, by a religious historian, attempts a reinterpretation of the archaeological material from Catal Huyuk, the Anatolian site that includes remains from some of the earliest urban settlements in the Turkish Neolithic. Based on personal conversations with James Mellaart (the archaeologist who excavated Catal Huyuk) as well as published material from the site, Barstow argues that decorative motifs in the decentralized religious shrines and domestic structures indicate a widespread female religious cult in which women were fully active as equals with men. Barstow further argues that women had independent control of certain economic resources (notably, agricultural produce) which provided them with power and autonomy. Barstow is at pains to distinguish the religious and economic base at Catal Huyuk from later patriarchal forms developed in the Near East (e.g., Sumer). The article is useful in that emphasis is placed on a new interpretation of standard archaeological materials (architecture, decorative symbols, spatial arrangements), and a convincing interpretation of past religious and economic life is presented. This article might be suitable for classroom reading in conjunction with one of Mellaart's works.

Bender, Barbara
    1989   The Roots of Inequality. *In* Domination and Resistance. D. Miller, M. Rowlands, and C. Tilley, eds. Pp. 83–93. London: Unwin Hyman.

Bender tackles the interesting issue of the development of sociopolitical complexity. She argues that domestication need not be seen as a necessary precondition for complexity, which she defines as "institutionalized social inequality." Instead, the author suggests that instances of hunter-gatherer inequality should be examined, and she uses Upper Paleolithic archaeological material from Western Europe as an example. Using changes in the position and types of cave art over time, Bender argues that difference is highlighted and then controlled. She speculates that ritual became more complex and larger social groups were involved, but access to ritual knowledge was no longer open. Instead, men at this time were assuming a gendered role as hunters who controlled social reproduction and so, by extension, women's gendered roles. Also included in this article is a clear and insightful discussion of the "Man the Hunter" and "Woman the Gatherer" question. Bender dismisses both of these models as ethnocentric and emphasizes the flexibility of hominid (and later *Homo*) social constructions.

Braithwaite, Mary
  1982 Decoration as Ritual Symbol: A Theoretical Proposal and an Ethnographic Study in southern Sudan. *In* Symbolic and Structural Archaeology. I. Hodder, ed. Pp. 80–88. Cambridge: Cambridge University Press.

This is an ethnoarchaeological article in which Braithwaite describes the complex ways in which decorated objects (pottery in particular) are used in contemporary Azande culture. The author argues that decorated objects are frequently utilized in situations where the separate male and female spheres coincide (as when food moves from raw to cooked state for example). The decoration is necessary as a means of symbolically mediating and highlighting these spheres. For example, the Azande use decorated pottery to demarcate situations in which food and drink go between men and women. Gender relations are highly structured and male::female are opposed as structural categories. This article, while culturally specific, is an interesting example of the importance of decorated pottery in expressing cultural values.

Conkey, Margaret, and Janet Spector
  1984 Archaeology and the Study of Gender. Advances in Archaeological Method and Theory 7:1–38.

This article reviews the ways in which gender has been treated by archaeologists. The authors argue that while archaeological studies explicitly focusing on gender have been lacking, the literature abounds with ethnocentric and androcentric work that assumes gender relations in the past were similar to idealized Western gender relations in the 20th century. They find this to be the case in paleoanthropology and archaeology, and link this to the continuation of the "Man the Hunter" myth. Conkey and Spector end by advocating a critical reevaluation of the assumptions that underlie much of the past and present work on the division of labor, male and female tasks, and gender relations and status in prehistory.

Cucchiari, Salvatore
  1981 The Gender Revolution and the Transition from Bisexual Horde to Patrilocal Band: the Origins of Gender Hierarchy. *In* Sexual Meanings. S. Ortner and H. Whitehead, eds. Pp. 31–79. Cambridge: Cambridge University Press.

In this provocative work Cucchiari, a sociocultural anthropologist, asks us to envision a genderless society. Tasks (primarily foraging and child tending) are divided by interest only, and kinship structures are absent. Cucchiari speculates that this situation existed into the Middle Paleolithic before the exchange of children between groups brought about an increase in the status and awareness of the female role in reproduction. Kinship systems developed next as did a female ceremonial cult (exemplified by the Upper Paleolithic "Venus" figurines). Cucchiari argues that the exchange of children was used as a model for a later exchange of women, and that this led to gender inequality and ultimately to male dominance. Although his ideas are at times problematic, Cucchiari does utilize archaeological data and interestingly suggests that changes in Paleolithic material culture and cave art reflects changes in the social and gender systems of Paleolithic cultures.

Gero, Joan M.
    1985   Socio-Politics and the Woman-at-Home Ideology. American Antiquity 50(2):342–350.

This article concerns the production of archaeological knowledge, and as such is a valuable contribution to the gender and archaeology literature. Drawing on critical theory, Gero states that a view of archaeology as objective, value-neutral science is inaccurate. Rather, Gero asks that we examine how archaeological knowledge is structured and constrained by the ideology of American culture. She demonstrates one facet of this proposal by examining the patterns of project type (field-based versus laboratory/analytical) and funding (illustrated with data from NSF grants) that correlate with male and female archaeologists. Gero argues that female archaeologists are less likely to be funded and more likely to carry out nonfield research than male archaeologists, and she concludes that this is consistent with an American gender ideology that stereotypes women's work as "home based" and men's work as field related.

Gibbs, Liv
    1987   Identifying Gender Representation in the Archaeological Record: A Contextual Study. *In* The
            Archaeology of Contextual Meanings. Ian Hodder, ed. Pp. 79–89. Cambridge: Cambridge University Press.

Gibbs begins by commenting on the absence of systematic studies of gender in archaeology, and the need to move past ethnocentric and androcentric constructions of past gender relations. She notes that gender constructions are often materially rich in representation, and should therefore be highly visible in the archaeological record. The majority of the article is an example of how an analysis of gender relations might be carried out using burial material, hoards, rock carvings and settlement data from Mesolithic to Bronze Age sites in N.E. Zealand, Denmark. Using multiple lines of evidence Gibbs argues that gender roles changed from male = warfare and agriculture and female = pottery? and domestic activities to a late Bronze Age association of female = agriculture and domestic activities and males = personal appearance and decoration.

Hodder, Ian
    1984   Burials, Houses, Women and Men in the European Neolithic. *In* Ideology, Power and Pre-
            history. D. Miller and C. Tilley, eds. Pp. 51–68. Cambridge: Cambridge University Press.

In this innovative and thoughtful analysis, Hodder investigates prehistoric gender relations as part of a larger pattern of social and ideological strategies. He compares central and western European tombs (form and function) with central European longhouses of the 4th and 5th millennia B.C. Noting eight points of similarity he argues that the later tombs represent a structural transformation of the longhouses. In order to explain why this should have been so, Hodder discusses the functions of longhouses. These, he argues, were in use at a time when labor was scarce and thus women's position was that of reproducer of a scarce commodity. The domestic (female) sphere became the arena for expressing and negotiating tension surrounding control of offspring. Since the tombs show such similar forms, Hodder suggests that they had similar social functions as well. Specifically, he asserts that later in the Neolithic land was the limiting resource, rather than labor. This relieved the tensions among women, men, and lineages for access to laborers, but shifted the competition to access to land. Lineages used tombs to assert their claims to territory and to legitimize these in a supernatural (mortuary) context.

Marshall, Yvonne
    1985   Who Made the Lapita Pots? A Case Study in Gender Archaeology. Journal of the Polynesian
            Society 94:205–233.

Lapita refers to both a style of decorated pottery and a culture resident throughout Oceania between the 1st and 2nd millennia B.C. Marshall suggests that gender roles and the division of labor by sex should be foremost among research topics, as new questions concerning the social organization of Lapita society are asked. She limits her consideration of division of labor to the question of pottery manufacture.

Her review of the ethnographic literature on ceramic production in Oceania revealed that women were more commonly potters in communities on small islands or along coastal margins. Shared duties and male pottery making roles occurred more frequently at inland locations on larger islands. Marshall then noted several similarities between ethnographically known instances of female pottery manufacture and Lapita pottery (including function and trade status). Generalizing from these observations, the author concludes that women were producing Lapita pottery and she ends by discussing the implications of female Lapita pottery for long-distance trade, colonization, culture change and the decline of Lapita pottery.

Spector, Janet D.
   1982   Male/Female Task Differentiation Among the Hidatsa: Toward the Development of an Archeological Approach to the Study of Gender. *In* The Hidden Half. B. Medicine and P. Albers, eds. Pp. 77–99. Washington, D.C.: University Press of America.

This article is primarily methodological, providing a framework of structured questions that researchers with historic and ethnographic documentation can ask in order to study the spatial and material expressions of gender. Spector demonstrates her new approach, called Task Differentiation, using ethnohistoric data for the Hidatsa. Each task is categorized in terms of its social dimension (who performs it), spatial dimension (location), temporal dimension (frequency, duration and season), and material dimension (artifacts and structures). With systematically collected data of this sort, investigators should be able to interpret the gender implications of materials at archaeological sites. For example, Spector shows that among the Hidatsa, activities were highly segregated and she argues that this implies separate spheres of power: women controlled subsistence and construction tasks, while men controlled hunting and warfare.

Welbourn, Alice
   1984   Endo Ceramics and Power Strategies. *In* Ideology, Power and Prehistory. D. Miller and C. Tilley, eds. Pp. 17–24. Cambridge: Cambridge University Press.

In this ethnoarchaeological piece, Welbourn discusses the ceramic vessel types and functions used by Endo people of Kenya. Welbourn provides an interesting structural analysis, demonstrating the equations between ceramics and people, men and women, sacred and profane, and culture and nature. In so doing she illustrates the richness of meaning that pottery form and use has for the Endo. Much of this meaning revolves around male and female spheres of power in the society, as well as the importance of ceramics in life-cycle rituals. Decoration on pottery vessels used in some contexts parallels decoration on Endo men and women, while other vessels (particularly those used by both sexes and all ages) do not follow human decorative patterns. Ceramics both separate the genders and mediate between them. Welbourn supports her structural analysis by examining the uses of broken pots and raw clay (that is, unformed pots). She finds their functions to be consistent with the structural patterns she elucidated for whole vessels.

Bibliography II

Albers, Patricia, and Beatrice Medicine, eds.
   1983   The Hidden Half: Studies of Plains Indian Women. New York: University Press of America.
Etienne, Mona, and Eleanor Leacock, eds.
   1980   Women and Colonization: Anthropological Perspectives. New York: Praeger.
Gailey, Christine Ward
   1985   The State of the State in Anthropology. Dialectical Anthropology 9(1–4):65–89.
Leacock, Eleanor
   1978   Women's Status in Egalitarian Society: Implications for Social Evolution. Current Anthropology 19:247–275.

1983　Interpreting the Origins of Gender Inequality: Conceptual and Historical Problems. Dialectical Anthropology 7:263–284.

Muller, Vianna
1977　The Formation of the State and the Oppression of Women: A Case Study in England and Wales and Some Theoretical Considerations. Review of Radical Political Economics 9(3):7–21.
1985　Origins of Class and Gender Hierarchy in Northwest Europe. Dialectical Anthropology 10:93–105.

Nash, June
1978　The Aztecs and the Ideology of Male Dominance. Signs 4(2):349–362.

Ortner, Sherry
1978　The Virgin and the State. Feminist Studies 4(3):19–35.

Rapp, Rayna
1978　Gender and Class: an Archaeology of Knowledge Concerning the Origin of the State. Dialectical Anthropology 2(4):309–316.

Reiter, Rayna Rapp
1977　The Search for Origins: Unraveling the Threads of Gender Hierarchy. Critique of Anthropology 3(9–10):5–24.

Rohrlich-Leavitt, Ruby
1978　Women in Transition: Crete and Sumer. In Becoming Visible: Women in European History. R. Bridenthal and C. Koonz, eds. Pp. 36–59. Boston: Houghton Mifflin.
1980　State Formation in Sumer and the Subjugation of Women. Feminist Studies 6(1):76–102.

Rothenberg, Diane
1976　Erosion of Power—an Economic Basis for the Selective Conservatism of Seneca Women in the 19th Century. Western Canadian Journal of Anthropology 6(3):106–122.

Silverblatt, Irene
1978　Andean Women in Inca Society. Feminist Studies 4(3):37–61.
1987　Moon, Sun, and Witches: Gender Ideologies and Class in Inca and Colonial Peru. Princeton: Princeton University Press.

Van Allen, Judith
1971　'Sitting on a Man': Colonialism and the Lost Political Institutions of Igbo Women. Canadian Journal of African Studies 6:165–181.

Zagarell, Allen
1986　Trade, Women, Class, and Society in Ancient Western Asia. Current Anthropology 27(5):415–430.

4

Women in Biosocial Perspective

Jane B. Lancaster
University of New Mexico

Orientation

This module is written from the belief that many, very important dimensions of human behavior and biology can best be understood from the perspective of evolutionary biology. This is especially true of human reproduction, an area of biology and behavior closely linked to evolutionary measures of fitness. Just as we recognize that humans have evolved distinctive patterns of bipedalism, feeding, tool using, intelligence, and social groupings, so too we see that evolutionary processes have left a mark on human reproduction in terms of patterns of reproductive maturation, sexuality, fertility, birth, lactation, and parental investment in children.

Two important concepts are central to a perspective drawn from evolutionary biology. The first is the concept of *the environment of adaptation*. The environment of adaptation simply refers to the conditions under which particular patterns of behavior and biology evolved. This is a crucial concept in thinking about human beings because we know that our own evolutionary history has been very rapid and that there have been major, fundamental changes in the context of human experience in recent history. In some senses humans should be thought of as hunter-gatherers (a lifestyle in which we spent 99% of our history) now living under an incredible variety of conditions in terms of nutrition, disease, life course parameters, social density and organization, and level and distribution of resources. Many of the examples in this module will discuss what happens to the evolved reproductive biology of a hunter-gatherer woman when it is played out in modern settings.

The second basic concept drawn from evolutionary biology is that *the reproductive interests and strategies of males and females are not identical*. The biological and behavioral adaptations of male and female can best be understood not as fundamentally complementary and linked in nature but as separate sets that serve the reproductive interests of each sex. This module focuses on the biosocial adaptations found in women that further their fertility and the successful rearing of children. It emphasizes that species do not evolve as single units, but rather the separate adaptations of the sexes must be understood. In other words, here we are not interested in the evolutionary history of the human species, but rather that of women. This perspective also emphasizes active female involvement in the unfolding of her reproductive career in terms of the timing and distribution of her reproductive effort in the life course, the decision whether or not to invest in particular offspring, and the choice of sexual partners. In other words, female choice and the facultative adjustment of female reproductive strategies are seen as an integral part of the human nature of women, selected not by virtue of being the female half of a mated monogamous pair but as being an individual woman reproducing in competition with others to rear her offspring successfully.

Introduction

Recent research on the biology and behavior of women has developed a new perspective on the impact of evolutionary processes on the human nature of women. It provides a fresh set of evolutionary scenarios for the behavioral evolution of women, emphasizing shifts in reproductive biology and behavioral strategies that are adaptations to particular specializations characterizing the human species. Such human reproductive characteristics include (1) the unusually high levels of sustained parental investment in individual children over many years of development, (2) the multiple dependency of weaned juveniles of differing ages on provisioning by their parents, (3) a female fertility closely linked to fat storage and the distribution of resources in the environment, (4) situationally dependent female sexuality, (5) the development of high levels of sexual dimorphism in fat storage but relatively low levels in stature and muscularity, and (6) the wide variation in family formation strategies and human family profiles based on facultative adjustments to the distribution of resources used to rear offspring. All are seen as active outcomes of natural selection—a crucial part of the human adaptational package that emphasizes high levels of parental investment in offspring that can be conditionally altered according to circumstances.

The focus of this module is the impact of human female reproductive, parental investment and family formation strategies on women's evolutionary biology and behavior. It will emphasize the overarching need of female mammals in general and women in particular to acquire resources necessary to bear and rear offspring. These resources include a wide variety of necessities for humans, such as food, housing, safety, and social support. The single most significant biological reality for women during most of human evolutionary history has been the demands of their dependent young that include virtually continuous lactation during the reproductive years. The impact of the special needs of the dependency of multiple children of differing ages and of human lactation has shaped both women's reproductive biology and the parental investment and family formation strategies they pursue. The burden of nearly continuous lactation throughout the reproductive years is so significant for women that it impacts on the timing of fertility and reproduction in the life course and the biology of pregnancy, lactation, fat deposition, and birth spacing. Women have an evolved reproductive biology that is unusually sensitive to the availability of social and physical resources and that adjusts facultatively according to differing distribution, abundance, and predictability of resources.

Female Reproductive Strategies and Environmental Resources

With regard to the reproductive strategies of female mammals, evolutionary theory predicts that, since females bear the very heavy biological burden of gestation, birth, and lactation, they should naturally link their reproductive behavior to the availability of resources to carry the fertilized egg to the status of an independent adult capable of reproduction (Hrdy and Williams 1983; Lancaster 1985). The investment necessary to transform a zygote into an adult is especially heavy for human women, since human children are large, develop slowly, and in many societies need access to specialized resource bases (such as bride wealth, dowry, a homestead, or regular employment) in order to begin reproduction themselves. Hence women face an even heavier burden than other female mammals in their need for reproductive resources. We find that, in such elemental human behavioral patterns as the division of labor, family formation strategies, and parental investment patterns, women are active decision makers in optimizing their access to resources and their ability to produce healthy, competitive offspring.

The Division of Labor and Human Parental Investment Patterns

The evolutionary history of human beings differentiates humans from their close relatives in terms of both reproductive and parental investment patterns. Although the exact evolutionary history of the division of labor is still under dispute in terms of context, timing, and phylogenetic status, there is no disagreement that sometime in human history males and females differentiated their food-getting behavior in ways that allowed males to specialize in getting resources from high on the food chain—an endeavor that was both unpredictable and risky (Lancaster and Lancaster 1983). In contrast, females specialized in acquiring high-quality plant foods (the reproductive and energy storage organs of plants)—an endeavor that is more predictable and relatively low in risk. This specialization of the two sexes in acquiring energy from different levels of the food chain proved to be of great advantage in that female gathering in the short run could underwrite the unpredictable nature of male hunting.

This underwriting of risk not only benefitted both male and female adults but it also was associated with another basic human behavior pattern—the feeding of juveniles; that is, offspring who are weaned but not yet reproductively mature (Lancaster [in press]). Humans are the only species in which not only nursing infants but juveniles as well are freed from responsibility for feeding themselves. Nonhuman primates do not have nutritionally dependent juveniles—at best a monkey or ape mother will permit her juvenile to share her feeding territory and social status or tolerate its scrounging nearby while she feeds. The nutritional independence of juvenile nonhuman primates and group-hunting carnivores comes at a high price—between 70% and 90% of those born never reach adulthood largely because of starvation and attendant disease around weaning (Lancaster and Lancaster 1983). In contrast, among humans regardless of the simplicity of their economy, on average 50% or more of children born reach reproductive age. The evolutionary success of this behavioral complex of the division of labor, food-sharing, and the feeding of juveniles is testified by the doubling of the juvenile phase of the human life course to ten years compared to approximately a five-year period of juvenility typical of the great apes. The length of infancy is similar among the great apes and human hunter-gatherers: about three to four years is the usual period of lactation and birth-spacing interval between two surviving siblings. In the course of human evolution the postponement of maturation to full adulthood and the lengthening of offspring dependency occurred because of a doubling of the juvenile phase, the most perilous point of the life course for group-hunting carnivores and nonhuman primates (Lancaster [in press]). For most mammals the juvenile phase is truly a selection funnel into which many enter but few pass through. Human male and female collaboration in the feeding of juveniles has led to a species-specific profile of the family that includes (at a minimum), at least one male, one female, a nursing infant, and a series of juveniles at different stages of development but all nutritionally dependent on adults. The division of labor and the collaborative feeding of juveniles by adults is a uniquely human evolutionary package that is supported by the role often played by the males as husband-father. It essentially permits a youngster to linger in what for mammals are the perilous juvenile years while it develops the social and foraging skills to function as a highly competitive adult (Johnston 1982). The expansion of the juvenile phase of the life course during human evolution was bought at the price of greatly increased investment in offspring from both parents.

The "Loss of Estrus" or Situationally Dependent Receptivity

Past scenarios for the evolution of the human family and patterns of human female sexuality have focused on a phenomenon that has been variously labeled as loss of estrus, continuous female receptivity, or concealed ovulation (Hrdy [in press]). Such labels imply the existence of an ancestress, either ape or protohuman, who limited her sexuality to the days around ovulation, refused males during parts of the cycle when she was not ovulating and during gestation and lactation, and advertised impending ovulation with either prominent sexual swellings or other attractive behavioral or pheromonal displays. Such scenarios focused on the hiding of ovulation as part of a package in the evolution of the human family, either as a concession to reduce the cost of mate guarding for a male willing to give aid to a female in the rearing of her offspring, as an out-and-out trade of meat for sex, or as a devious ploy to keep a male monogamously mated because he would have to attend a female during most of her reproductive cycle since he could not detect when she might ovulate.

As diverse as these scenarios are, they all depend on two fundamental beliefs; that humans are evolved to form monogamous unions and that, in order to do so, women had to lose estrus so as to hide the timing of ovulation. In spite of the obvious variability in the cross-cultural record in human family-formation patterns, including polygyny, monogamy, and polyandry, and the generally accepted preference for polygyny among most nonwestern societies, such scenarios were reasonably plausible before the in-depth study of primates in their natural habitats. Now it is clear that the baboon-chimpanzee pattern of female sexuality with unambiguous advertising of sexual receptivity and impending ovulation is a specialized adaptation associated with multi-male breeding systems. The other apes (gibbon, siamang, gorilla, and orangutan) do not have this pattern of sexuality, and in all probability the chimpanzee pattern is secondarily evolved. Among the higher primates estrus behavior and assertive female libido tend to be associated with the female having a number of male sexual partners around a single ovulation. All of these males are likely later to be tolerant or even solicitous of the infant conceived. In surveying the specific anatomical and behavioral qualities of human sexuality, Hrdy (in press) characterizes humans as mildly sexually dimorphic in stature and muscularity (about 5–12%) and as having small testes and a large penis in the male, and sexual receptivity in the female that is situationally dependent. Viewed against a backdrop of higher primate patterns (Hrdy and Whitten 1987), this complex suggests early human ancestors who lived in one-male, mildly polygynous groups in which a male did not have to continuously engage in male/male competition (either in terms of physical prowess or in volume of sperm), but in which a female might have to compete with other females for male support and attention. The story of the evolution of the human family can no longer be seen as simply hinging on the establishment of a monogamous pairbond based on meat sharing and the loss of estrus.

Lactation and Human Female Fertility

In spite of the fact that the evolution of the human family has committed males to high levels of male parental investment, especially in the collaborative feeding of juveniles, human females still bear very heavy costs in the care and feeding of their infants. In fact, the single most significant biological reality for most women during most of human history and during the course of most of their adult lives may have been the biology of lactation (Anderson 1983; Harrell 1981; Huss-Ashmore 1980; Lancaster 1985). In traditional societies where marriage is almost universal and where reproducing women rarely contracept and spacing between births is maintained by lactational infertility (Short 1987), lactation should be recognized as a nearly continuous biological state of adult women until after menopause (see Case Study 1).

The further significance of lactation is underscored by Brown's (1970) classic analysis of the division of labor in the cross-cultural record. The underlying characteristics of the tasks assumed by women are their compatibility with lactation—they must be low in risk, performed relatively close to home, easily interrupted, and must not require rapt concentration. No other differentials between the sexes, such as variations in strength, stamina, emotional characteristics, or cognitive aptitudes, appear significant in task allocation in the cross-cultural record. Child care responsibilities have often produced major constraints on what women do in human society (see, for example, Hurtado et al. 1985; Lee 1979), not because of inherent sex differences in aptitude as much as because of the basic mammalian sexual dimorphism in the ability to lactate. Trends associated with modernization, such as reduction in the percentage of women who reproduce, in the numbers of children born to each woman, and in length of breast feeding, have reduced and will continue to reduce the differences between men and women in the roles they play in human society.

Until the onset of high fat and high sugar diets associated with modernization, a major challenge to women has been how to maintain adequate levels of lactation virtually continuously over their reproductive careers without draining caloric and nutrient reserves and depleting their health and the ability to work productively in the feeding of juvenile offspring (Prentice and Whitehead 1987; see Case Study 1). This need for nutrients and energy to support lactation as well as the feeding of weaned juveniles is exacerbated by the unusual growth pattern of the human brain (Dobbing 1974; Sacher and Staffeldt 1974). Unlike those of our close relatives, human infants are born with brains less than 25% of their adult size. Most mammals with single births have more than 75% of adult brain size at birth. This means that the human brain, which is clearly our most important organ of adaptation and which grows slowly over the four years following birth, is at great risk to insult from fluctuating environments. Human females have evolved a very complex and specialized program of growth, fat deposition, and fertility establishment that helps to shield the human infant from environmental perturbations in food supply. Access to and storage of energy resources is so important to a woman's reproduction that it interacts with the timing of completed growth, menarche, and the establishment of regular ovulatory cycles, as well as the development of the fetus. In fact, energy storage is so significant in women that sexual dimorphism in fat location and amount is greater than dimorphism in stature and muscularity (Hall 1985, Stini 1985).

Environmental Resources and Healthy Infertility

As evolutionary biologists we might predict that women should have a reproductive biology that is exquisitely attuned to offspring viability and to the availability of resources in both the physical and social environment since human children require the most extensive and expensive pattern of parental investment of any species yet described (see Case Study 2). This sensitivity is found at both biological and psychological levels. At the biological level Surbey (1987), Stini (1985), Lancaster (1985), and others have noted mechanisms that assay and monitor fat storage and current nutritional status in comparison to past nutrition for the processes of implantation, gestation, birth and lactation. In analyzing infertility, miscarriage and premature delivery in women, Wasser and Isenberg (1986) note an evolved pattern of "healthy infertility" that allows the individual to assess physiologically and emotionally present conditions relative to past. For example, they note that regardless of level, episodes of acute stress are more powerful than chronic stress in provoking miscarriages since a high level of acute stress is more easily measured against past experience. Similarly, acute weight loss is more suppressive of fertility than low amounts of body fat *per se*. Such assessments include unconscious and conscious response to shifts in an individual woman's access to environmental resources and social support systems for the establishment and maintenance of pregnancy and lactation. These abilities essentially provide biological and psychological bases for a woman to cut her losses at any point along the line if the resource base necessary to support reproduction suddenly collapses.

Facultative Adjustments in Human Family-formation Strategies

The reproductive biology of women presents itself as an adapted complex of context-sensitive traits at both the biological and the social-behavioral levels. This complex has evolved to support a highly invested, slowly developing offspring that is nutritionally dependent on adults for many years and born into a sibship of multiple young of different ages, needs, and capacities. Human parents must make decisions at many points about how to invest in offspring over the course of a long maturation during which social and physical resources may fluctuate radically (Lancaster and Lancaster 1987).

Just as the reproductive biology of women has evolved to make phenotypic shifts according to resource availability, so too have human family formation and parental investment strategies. There is no single evolved pattern of family formation or parental investment; rather, evolution has led humans to a pattern of phenotypic plasticity and behavioral variation. The flexible nature of such responses leads to a variety of reproductive programs, as is illustrated in the figure comparing idealized reproductive careers of women in a hunting-gathering and an industrial society, (Figure 1). Neither pattern is more natural than the other: rather, they represent two extremes in a range of variation in biological and behavioral responses present in women.

A similar range of variability can be found in human family-formation patterns, including monogamy, polygyny, single parenthood, and polyandry (Betzig, Borgerhoff Mulder, and Turke 1988). These various patterns of family formation and mating have different costs and benefits for participant members; that is, there are separate, nonidentical tradeoffs for male and female members of each unit (Hill and Kaplan 1988, Irons 1983). These patterns may be viewed as adaptations to variability in social and physical resources between societies and within stratified societies. For example, Boone (1986) and Dickemann (1979, 1981) document a reproductive strategy affecting daughters in the upper portions of stratified, agrarian societies that includes a complex of cultural traits: (1) dowry competition by the parents of daughters to gain access to quality grooms controlling resources needed to underwrite the daughters' successful reproduction, (2) female infanticide or spinsterhood in upper-class fam-

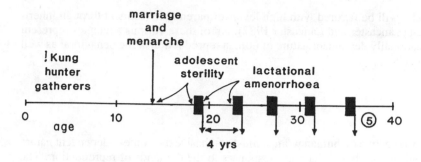

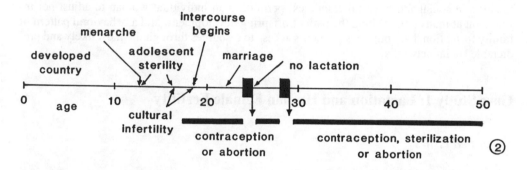

Figure 1. Comparison of patterns of women's fertility in two different societies: a hunter-gatherer and modern, industrial (from Lancaster 1986:18, after Short 1978).

ilies to reduce the number of daughters to be dowered so as not to impoverish the family estate and reduce the ability of their brothers to gain wives, (3) the closeting of women in the home away from stranger males, and (4) a high value placed on bridal virginity and wifely chastity to raise male confidence in paternity for the select grooms who can offer high levels of male parental investment. In the cross-cultural record, societies with such a fixation on control of female sexuality are also ones where there are great differences among men in power and resources, and the intensity with which families protect their daughters' honor is directly correlated with their social status. Often women of the lower classes have much more personal freedom that high-born ladies who are virtual prisoners of their, and later of their husbands', families.

The current historic shift in both modernized and nonindustrial countries toward the formation of single-parent, female-headed households and patterns of behavioral polyandry may be seen not as the result of a breakdown in social and cultural traditions but as an adaptation to a modern world in which males with sufficient and predictable ability to give parental investment are scarce (Lancaster 1989). Under other conditions in which the resource bases necessary to found families are not divisible, such as a small farm, parents may pursue reproductive strategies that differentiate investment among their various offspring on the basis of sex and birth order and produce some children bound for celibacy, such as monks or spinsters; others bound for risky reproduction without a guaranteed resource base, such as adventurer sons who must seek a reproductive estate in the military or through migration; and still other designated heirs who will be favored with high levels of parental investment through inheritance and education (Lancaster and Lancaster 1987). All of these various strategies represent the plastic and situationally dependent nature of human reproduction at the behavioral as well as the biological levels.

Summary

A biosocial perspective on human women must emphasize the context-dependent nature of both their biological and their behavioral responses to the demands of reproduction. The evolutionary history of human female reproductive strategies has increased phenotypic and behavioral plasticity in ways that will optimize a woman's ability to access the resources necessary to produce and rear her children. These include a reproductive biology closely linked to shifts in social and physical resources, permitting an individual woman to adjust her investment at many points along the path of offspring development, and a behavioral pattern of family formation that optimizes women's access to resources through the most likely and predictable social networks.

Case Study 1: Lactation and Human Female Fertility

Suggested Issues

> Fertility and lactation
> Secular trend in age of menarche
> Lactation and child spacing
> Reproductive life courses of hunter-gatherer, agricultural, and industrial societies
> Anorexia and athletes' amenorrhea
> Lactation and the growth of the human brain

> Menstruation has indeed become an iatrogenic disorder of civilised communities. . . . If we were to adopt a back-to-Nature argument, the logical contraceptive to develop would be one that allowed the woman to spend the greater part of her reproductive life in a state akin to lactational amenorrhoea, but without the inconvenience of unwanted lactation. . . . This might allow the ovaries, the breasts and the uterus to spend most of their reproductive lives asleep, instead of constantly on the *qui vive* for a pregnancy that seldom comes. [Short 1978:24, 25]

When the life course of the human female is viewed from the perspective of parenthood, its major features clearly support a uniquely human pattern of high levels of long-term parental investment and the dependency of multiple young of differing ages. Most modern cultures present poor models for the female life course during most of human history because of their wide range of variation in women's activities, health, nutrition, numbers of children born and reared, and the use of techniques to alter the fertility (see Beyene 1989 for contrasting life courses of Greek and Mayan women). A real understanding of the evolutionary pressures lying behind women's reproductive biology must start with a reconstruction of how it unfolds in the forager context in which it evolved: a lifestyle representing fully 99% of human history. Such a model, based on data drawn from the few remaining hunter-gatherers of today, is fraught with distortions and confounds but, nevertheless, has already provided us with some important insights into major evolutionary novelties in the reproductive lives of modern women. Short (1976, 1984, 1987) sketches the most striking aspects of the reproductive lives of women foragers. They include a number of features leading to low fertility without contraception: a long period of adolescent subfertility following late menarche, late age for first birth, a pattern of nearly continuous nursing during the day, many years of lactation for each infant, low frequency of menstrual cycling during the life course, and early menopause. Figure 1 illustrates the contrasting patterns of the reproductive life course of women living in a hunter-gatherer and an industrial society. Whereas a hunter-gatherer woman can expect to produce five children, experience nearly 15 years of lactational amenorrhea (breast feeding that suppresses fecundity) and just under four years each of pregnancy and menstrual cycling, an urbanized woman experiencing two pregnancies with little or no breast feeding is likely to spend over 35 years in menstrual cycling—a ninefold increase. The generality of this world-wide shift from the biological state of lactational amenorrhea to menstrual cycling for women in modern, urbanized societies has been confirmed in the cross-cultural record (Harrell 1981). When the carcinogenic potential of estrogen is considered, it is no wonder that Short (1978) refers to menstruation as an iatrogenic (culturally imposed) disorder of modern life.

Short (1976) discusses another significant novelty in the reproductive lives of modern women: an advance of the age of menarche (first menstrual cycling) for whole populations of women so that mean age of menarche is 12½ rather than 16 or so years as in traditional societies. This advance in age of menarche is associated with a much earlier attainment of adult stature and of adult patterns of female fat deposition. Short reviews the milestones in human pubertal events (see Figure 2). For girls, the first external sign of puberty is the development of the breast bud. This is an odd and noteworthy feature of human development, and one that is likely to go unnoticed without comparative data. The typical primate female will not begin to develop breasts until the later stages of her first pregnancy. The breasts of the human female are made conspicuous and stable with deposits of fat, in contrast to other primates whose breasts experience an increase in glandular tissue that resorbs again after weaning if another pregnancy does not follow. This early development of breasts is due to extreme sensitivity of human breast tissue to very low levels of estrogen early in puberty. The deposition of fat on the breasts, thighs and buttocks during human adolescence is a unique feature of human sexual dimorphism that constitutes a continuous advertisement of an ability to lactate long before fertility is established.

It is also worth noting that menarche (first menstruation) is a relatively late event in the sequence of human pubertal changes, but that it still usually precedes the establishment of regular patterns of ovulation by several years. This is remarkable because for many mammals first estrus is associated with ovulation. For such species as sheep and rats, the positive feedback mechanism between the hypothalamus and the ovary that regulates ovulation is mature at birth, not years after puberty; so that for these species, puberty equals instant fertility. For women, menarche itself is preceded by most of the essential features of physical development indicating adult status; the adolescent growth spurt and the attainment of near-adult values for weight and stature and the growth of breasts and pubic hair (Lancaster 1985, 1986). This delay in the establishment of fertility until after the completion of growth in stature and weight is not typical of most primates. On average, rhesus monkeys have attained only 30% of adult size when they have their first estrous cycles. One might speculate that the unusual demands placed on human females for high levels of long-term parental investment based on experience in the social and physical environment has led to a delay in the maturation of the system regulating fertility until growth is completed and energy is stored in fat reserves but not in the system regulating the onset of sexual behavior. Such a program of development ensures that

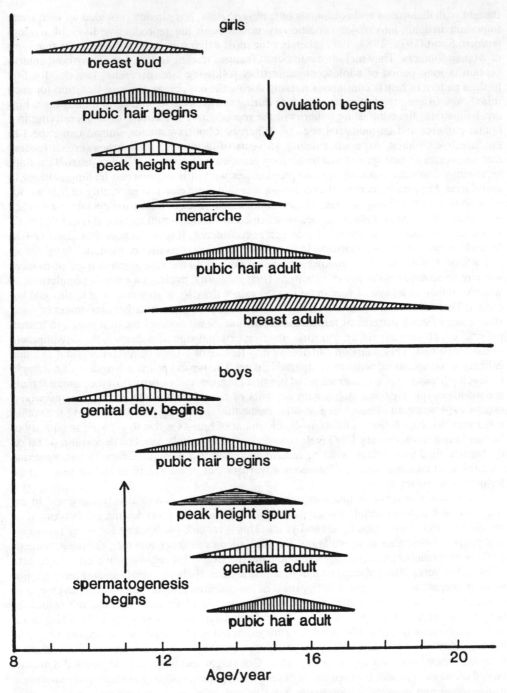

Figure 2. The sequence of pubertal events in boys and girls in modern Western societies, indicating a major contrast between the sexes in the timing of fertility compared to other growth parameters (from Lancaster 1986:20).

young women are unlikely to become pregnant while they are still in adolescent growth so that they will not compete biologically for energy with their first developing fetus and nursing infant.

A crucial factor in the fertility of women relates to levels of fat storage. Frisch (1988) proposes that women will not ovulate unless an adequate store of fat has been deposited: about 22% of body weight or around 150,000 calories, enough to permit a women to lactate for a year without having to increase her prepregnancy caloric intake. The appeal of this hypothesis is that it explains the historic trend in earlier age of menarche (a drop in mean age of menarche of about four years over the past 150 years in developed countries from age 16½ to 12½) and also a probable loss in modern society of a long period of adolescent subfertility. Sedentism combined with high levels of both protein and caloric intake lead to early growth in stature and deposition of fat in young girls and "fool" the body into early reproductive maturation long before cognitive and social maturity are reached.

More recent research (Prentice and Prentice 1988; Prentice and Whitehead 1987) suggests that the amount of fat storage *per se* is less important than whether a woman is in energy balance or losing weight. Their research indicates that women suffer lower daily energy stress from gestation and lactation than do other mammals but only because of a remarkable set of adaptations that reduces the daily nutritional cost to a minimum even though the long duration of gestation and lactation demand a large total investment. These adaptations include a program of female growth and reproductive development that minimizes overlap between the tasks of maturation and reproduction, a sex-typical pattern of fat deposition that provides women with energy reserves to be drawn on in periods of nutritional stress, and a series of physiological adaptations that allow for a reduction in both activity and metabolic rates so that less energy is necessary for basic maintenance when a woman is pregnant or lactating. Viewed in this light, anorexia with loss of menstrual cycling and amenorrhea in athletes under intensive training is not surprising (Frisch 1988; Surbey 1987). Cessation of fertility when energy reserves are being rapidly drained or when caloric intake is immediately expended through physical exertion is an integral part of the reproductive program of women.

Recent research has identified sexual dimorphism not only in the total amount of fat deposited in men and women but also in its location (Huss-Ashmore 1980; Lancaster 1985; Stini 1985). Female fat is deposited on the hips, thighs, breasts, and buttocks under the influence of estrogens whereas male fat is deposited in the form of a "beer belly" under the influence of androgens. Female fat is not just a passive organ for the storage of energy, it also produces a very potent form of the hormone estrogen even after menopause (Frisch 1988). When corrections are made for the smaller body size of the human female, women are indeed a great deal fatter than calculations of average sex differences would indicate. Approximately 15% of body weight of the young adult male, compared to about 26% of the young female, is in fat. When body segments corrected for frame size are compared, women are 40% larger than men for the buttocks segment alone. If fat deposits advertise healthy systemic function and the ability to nurse infants, then it is not surprising that reproductive fat in women is differentially deposited compared to men, localized for more dramatic display, and closely linked to the development of other secondary sex characteristics. Their location outside the trunk cavity and muscle system may also be linked to differences in the biological activity of such fat in the production of estrogen.

There is evidence to suggest that the evolutionary history of human female fat reserves, human patterns of lactation, and the growth of the human brain are closely linked (Huss-Ashmore 1980; Lancaster 195; Prentice and Whitehead 1987). The constituents of human milk are ideally suited to nurture the growth of the human infant's brain but not for rapid growth of its body, which contrasts with many mammals in which the brain is nearly full-grown at birth and the early months of lactation are devoted to rapid somatic growth. At birth the brain of a rhesus monkey infant is about 68% of adult size; chimpanzee 45%, and human 23% (see Figure 3). The human infant's brain grows very rapidly after birth and reaches 45% of adult size by 6–7 months of age, but it is not until the end of the fourth year that it attains nearly 95% of adult volume. In reviewing the most critical and vulnerable periods of human brain growth, Dobbing (1974) focuses on the last three months of fetal life and the first post-natal year as crucial. The vulnerable nature of brain growth for such a long period after birth may explain one recently described feature of maternal weight gain during pregnancy. Winick (1981) notes that fat storage in preparation for lactation is so important that, if a pregnant woman is inadequately nourished, energy stored away in maternal fat will take precedence over fetal growth during the later stage of pregnancy. Winick recommends that women should gain at least 25 pounds during pregnancy to ensure that the fetus will not have to compete for energy with maternal fat storage processes.

In summary, the timing of growth and development and of the onset of reproduction within the life cycle have always been under heavy pressure from natural selection. The result of this pressure is a special program for each species that provides a range of variation appropriate to conditions ranging from optimal to suboptimal habitat. The evolved pattern for human females for most of human evolutionary history as foragers is one of slow growth during a prolonged period of juvenile dependency followed by a rapid completion of growth in stature before menarche. Menarche is followed by several years of sexual activity with very low probability of pregnancy, during which a young women might gain experience about her social and physical environment before undertaking the demands of motherhood. During this period of adolescent subfertility, a substantial store of body fat would be deposited in the human female at the same time that her male peer uses energy surpluses to grow greater stature

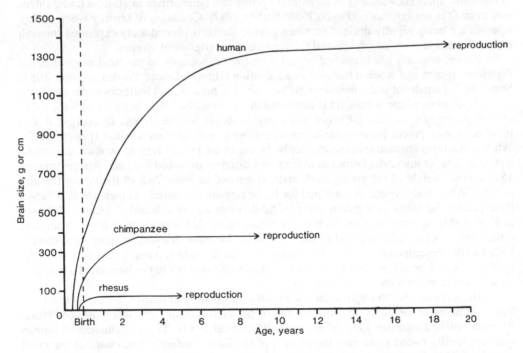

Figure 3: Growth of the brain in humans, chimpanzees and rhesus monkeys (from Lancaster 1986:30).

and lean muscle tissue. This differential in male and female growth patterns leads to the major element of human dimorphism in secondary sex characters: fat storage. The evolutionary pressure for the development of such an unusual degree of dimorphism in nutrient reserves is the unique nutritional demands of the developing human brain, which grows from 23% to 95% of its total size in the first four years of life.

Since the reproductive development of the human female is closely linked to the completion of growth in stature and the storage of energy in body fat, changes in modern life styles have advanced the mean age of menarche and the development of reproductive biology much like the advanced ripening of a hothouse tomato. Unfortunately, other systems involving the brain and cognitive and social maturation are no longer in synchrony with the maturation of human reproductive biology. Novelties in human reproductive biology experienced by modern women include a host of changes associated with new patterns of diet, growth, activity patterns and energy expenditure, and infant feeding. They include major contrasts with hunter-gatherer women: a menarche on average four years earlier, a ninefold increase in menstrual cycling and exposure to estrogens during the reproductive years, perhaps a later age of menopause, a reduction of lactation to only 3–6 months per infant, a reduction of birth spacing from four years to two or less, and a reduction of total number of infants born to only two.

Case Study 2: Healthy Infertility and Taking Losses

Suggested Issues

> Reproductive suppression model
> Parental investment from conception to adulthood
> Mother-infant attachment
> Reproduction and environmental resources (social and physical)
> Psychosocial stress

The Reproductive Suppression Model argues that reproduction should be terminated when eventual failure is *highly likely,* or when present conditions for reproduction are sufficiently poor relative to the future that the benefits of improved probability of reproductive success from delaying until those better times offsets the time and/or physiological costs of the suppression itself. Females who suppress their reproduction at such times will have a higher lifetime reproductive success than those who do not because such tactics conserve their time, energy, and general reproductive condition for those conception that are most likely to succeed. In this way, physiological mechanisms that happen to terminate reproduction under such conditions will gain greater representation in the population by residing in those offspring born under the best conditions for survival, enabling them to utilize and pass on these traits once again. While early suppressions will tend to be favored and are indeed most common, this depends on the predictability of reproductive conditions, which is not always perfect. Thus suppression should be expected relatively late in reproduction as well. [Wasser and Isenberg 1986:155]

Human children are the costliest of offspring for mammalian parents to rear in terms of the total amount of parental nurturance necessary because of the many years over which the children are sustained. We might predict that humans, of all mammals, should be exquisitely sensitive to the availability of reproductive resources in the environment, both physical and social, and because of the long years of investment per child, should be able to continuously monitor fluctuations in support systems. The ability to suppress reproduction in response to cues reflecting environmental harshness or poor physical condition in the parent or offspring is widely known in mammals. Reproductive suppression of this type should not be seen as reproductive failure but rather as a *filtering system* that is highly evolved and has been long in place. Such a filter should include the ability to terminate investment as soon as conditions suggest the unlikelihood of success, thereby guarding against the cost of additional wasted investment. For a slowly developing species committed to singleton births, as are humans, the opportunity costs of failed parental investment are unusually high. According to Wasser and Isenberg (1986), women should have the ability to defer investment, "take their losses," or alter the level of investment at many different points along the reproductive process from conception to implantation, gestation, and birth, and even through lactation and investment during the juvenile years.

There is much evidence to support this hypothesis. Humans are especially susceptible to early reproductive loss compared to other mammals (Short 1979; Wasser and Isenberg 1986). Conception, implantation, and early embryonic development are exceedingly vulnerable in humans: according to Wasser and Isenberg, in modern societies more than 78% of all conceptions spontaneously abort, 1.3% of all births result in neonatal mortality, and 7% of all live births are premature or of low birth weight (i.e., births that would have been near failures or direct losses during most of human history). Ovulatory or implantational failure may be even greater than all these combined; in fact, 15% of all couples are labeled as infertile, being unable to conceive after one year of unprotected intercourse. Much of this suppression appears to be associated with poor condition of either the mother of the conceptus. For example, during the Dutch famine in 1944–45 there were very low rates of pregnancy and successful gestation although fetuses conceived before the famine continued gestation, drawing on maternal reserves to the point of being born with normal body length but very lean. Similarly, fetal abnormalities predict loss. In fetuses spontaneously aborted during the first trimester, more than 60% can be identified with gross genetic abnormalities (Short 1979).

Although poor condition of mother or fetus is highly predictive of reproductive suppression, loss during pregnancy is also very likely under conditions of poor environmental support, both economic and social (Katz and Katz 1987; Newman 1987). Psychosocial stress may be just as important as poor condition in the mother or conceptus, and its significance is a measure of the fact that parental investment in human children is not simply dependent on maternal capacity alone but also depends on a support network being in place over a long period of time. Identified risk factors for reproductive loss, low birth weight, and premature delivery all suggest poor contextual conditions for reproduction, such as a very young mother, socioeconomic stress, social isolation, stressed social networks, an unidentified father, and death of the father during the pregnancy (Newman 1987; Wasser and Barash 1983; Wasser and Isenberg 1986).

There is evidence from the cross-cultural record that humans frequently reassess offspring viability in the days immediately after birth, and many cultures will cease investment in deformed or low birth weight infants (including twins) and in infants without a father (Hausfater and Hrdy 1984; Scheper-Hughes 1987; Scrimshaw 1984). The viability of an infant cannot be fully assessed at birth, however, since that would mean predicting 16 or more years ahead as to whether the infant will be able to (1) survive and grow into a fit adult and (2) gain access to the resources necessary for reproduction. Under these conditions in which parents cannot readily predict the future, they may withhold full commitment until events unfold. For example, Scheper-Hughes (1985) describes conditions in urban slums in Brazil where mothers delay emotional attachment and even full maternal care until it is clear that the child is hardy enough to survive infancy. For these women, "mother-love" with its associated emotions of cradling, nurturing, and protecting is not established during a critical period right after birth when she nurses her newborn child but as long as many months later after the child demonstrates that it will survive. In fact, some forms of neglect may sometimes be seen as "deferred infanticide" as found in many societies in which parents differentially invest in the hardy child or perhaps the favored sex as their ability to invest in their offspring fluctuates from year to year (Johansson 1984). Miller (1987) and Scrimshaw (1984) point to a widely distributed pattern in the Third World where increased rates of neglect and an attendant lower survivorship of daughters comes in the wake of governmental sanctions against female infanticide. The Western cultural model of maternal care that includes a natural ''mother-love,'' rapid bonding between mother and infant after birth and especially during early lactation, and parental care that saturates offspring with affection and resources, is based on a particular set of circumstances in which increments of parental care above a minimum really can make a difference in child survivorship and development (Harpending, Draper, and Pennington [in press]; Pennington and Harpending 1988). In many other cultures, where childhood mortality is little affected by parental behavior, as in societies with high rates of child mortality from infectious disease and a contaminated environment, parents may appear neglectful or indifferent by Western standards because they do not practice parental care strategies that maximize the probability that individual children survive but rather will rear the maximum number of surviving offspring that they can.

This perspective on human reproduction that emphasizes healthy infertility and a model of reproductive suppression raises questions about how modern societies can best respond to such ''pathologies'' as infertility, failure of mother-infant attachment, and child neglect. The most common response is to try to suppress the symptom as quickly and cheaply as possible: give the infertile woman a fertility pill leading to multiple ovulations or implant a number of fertilized eggs, often leading to a multiple pregnancy; enrich the first 48 hours after birth by giving a young, unwed mother extra opportunities to nurse and cuddle her infant in the hope that she will be bonded to it when she takes it alone into a world without social support or resources to raise it; outlaw female infanticide without considering what parents of daughters will do when they do not have the resources to dower them for marriage. Difficulties in human parental investment and attachment to children with poor life expectations are predictable from a reproductive suppression model derived from evolutionary biology. To say that human parental investment is variable according to parental assessment of the life chances of each child does not condone parental abandonment, neglect, or abuse of children. Rather, it points attention to the causes of variability in behavior rather than toward simple attempts to suppress the symptoms. Suppressing the symptoms cannot be a cure when the causes are based on quite realistic assessments of viability and competitiveness of the offspring, especially with regard to the availability of social and physical supports to rear them. Quick and low cost ''fixes'' cannot work because they are competing against a highly evolved and long in-place system protecting human parents from investing in children with predictable, poor outcomes. *The only real ''cures'' will come when modern societies address the basic causes—the difficulties experienced by parents in rearing children in a world with unequal access to highly limited resources.*

Because of the exceedingly high cost and long-term investment necessary to rear a human child, human parents and especially women have evolved an ability to assess both consciously and unconsciously shifts in environmental resources and social support systems needed for the establishment and maintenance of pregnancy and lactation. This evolved system essentially provides both a biological and a psychological basis for a woman to take her losses at many points along the track of investment in a single offspring if the resource base necessary to support reproduction suddenly collapses. For humans, successful maternal performance depends on a solid support platform including both social and economic resources.

References Cited

Anderson, P.
  1983   The Reproductive Role of the Human Breast. Current Anthropology 24:25–46.
Beyene, Yewoubdar
  1989   From Menarche to Menopause: Reproductive Lives of Peasant Women in Two Cultures. Albany: SUNY Press.
Betzig, L., M. Borgerhoff Mulder, and P. Turke, eds.
  1988   Human Reproductive Behaviour: A Darwinian Perspective. New York: Cambridge University Press.
Boone, J. L. III
  1986   Parental Investment and Elite Family Structure in Preindustrial States: A Case Study of Late Medieval-Early Modern Portuguese Genealogies. American Anthropologist 88:859–878.
Brown, J. K.
  1970   A Note on the Division of Labor by Sex. American Anthropologist 72:1073–1078.
Dickemann, M.
  1979   Female Infanticide, Reproductive Strategies and Social Stratification. A Preliminary Model. *In* Evolutionary Biology and Human Social Behavior. N. Chagnon and W. Irons, eds. Pp. 321–367. N. Scituate, MA: Duxbury.
  1981   Paternal Confidence and Dowry Competition: A Biocultural Analysis of Purdah. *In* Natural Selection and Social Behavior. R. Alexander and D. Tinkle, eds. Pp. 417–438. New York: Chiron.
Dobbing, J.
  1974   The Later Development of the Brain and Its Vulnerability. *In* Scientific Foundations Of Paediatrics. J. A. Davis and J. Dobbing, eds. Pp. 565–577. Philadelphia: W. B. Sanders.
Frisch, Rose E.
  1988   Fatness and Fertility. Scientific American 258:88–95.
Hall, R. L., ed.
  1985   Sexual Dimorphism in *Homo sapiens*. New York: Praeger.
Harpending, H., P. Draper, and R. Pennington
  In press   Cultural Evolution, Parental Care, and Mortality. *In* Health and Disease of Populations in Transition. G. J. Armelagos and A. C. Swedlund, eds. South Hadley, MA: Bergin and Garvey.
Harrell, B. B.
  1981   Lactation and Menstruation in Cultural Perspective. American Anthropologist 83:796–823.
Hausfater, G., and S. B. Hrdy, eds.
  1984   Infanticide: Comparative and Evolutionary Perspectives. New York: Aldine.
Hill, K., and H. Kaplan
  1988   Tradeoffs in Male and Female Reproductive Strategies among the Ache, Parts 1 and 2. *In* Human Reproductive Behaviour: A Darwinian Perspective. L. Betzig, M. Borgerhoff Mulder, and P. Turke, eds. New York: Cambridge University Press.
Hrdy, S. B.
  In press   The Absence of Estrus in *Homo sapiens*. *In* The Origins of Humanness. A. Brooks, ed. Washington, D.C.: Smithsonian Institution Press.
Hrdy, S. B., and P. L. Whitten
  1987   Patterning of Sexual Activity. *In* Primate Societies. B. Smuts, D. Cheney, R. Seyfarth, R. Wrangham, and T. Struhsaker, eds. Pp. 370–384. Chicago: University of Chicago Press.
Hrdy, S. B., and G. C. Williams
  1983   Behavioral Biology and the Double Standard. *In* Social Behavior of Female Vertebrates. S. Wasser, ed. Pp. 3–17. New York: Academic Press.
Hurtado, A. M., K. Hawkes, K. Hill and H. Kaplan
  1985   Female Subsistence Strategies among Ache Hunter-Gatherers of Eastern Paraguay. Human Ecology 13:1–28.
Huss-Ashmore, R.
  1980   Fat and Fertility: Demographic Implications of Differential Fat Storage. Yearbook of Physical Anthropology 23:65–91.

Irons, W.
  1983   Human Female Reproductive Strategies.'' *In* Social Behavior of Female Vertebrates. S. Wasser, ed. Pp. 169–213. New York: Academic Press.
Johansson, S. R.
  1984   Deferred Infanticide: Excess Female Mortality During Childhood. *In* Infanticide: Comparative and Evolutionary Perspectives. G. Hausfater and S. Hrdy, eds. Pp. 463–485. New York: Aldine.
Johnston, T. D.
  1982   Selective Costs and Benefits in the Evolution of Learning. Advances in the Study of Behavior 12:65–106.
Katz, S. S., and S. H. Katz
  1987   An Evaluation of Traditional Therapy for Barrenness. Medical Anthropology Quarterly 1:394–403.
Lancaster, J. B.
  1985   Evolutionary Perspectives on Sex Differences in the Higher Primates. *In* Gender and the Life Course. A. S. Rossi, ed. Pp. 3–27. New York: Aldine de Gruyter.
  1986   Human Adolescence and Reproduction: An Evolutionary Perspective. *In* School-Age Pregnancy and Parenthood: Biosocial Dimensions. J. Lancaster and B. Hamburg, eds. Pp. 17–37. New York: Aldine de Gruyter.
  1989   Evolutionary Perspectives on Single-Parenthood. *In* Sociobiology and the Social Sciences. R. B. Bell, ed. Lubbock: Texas Tech University Press.
  In press   Parental Investment and the Evolution of the Juvenile Phase of the Life Course. *In* The Origins of Humanness. A. Brooks, ed. Washington, D.C.: Smithsonian Institution Press.
Lancaster, J. B., and C. S. Lancaster
  1983   Parental Investment: The Hominid Adaptation. *In* How Humans Adapt: A Biocultural Odyssey. D. J. Ortner, ed. Pp. 33–65. Washington, D.C.: Smithsonian Institution Press.
  1987   The Watershed: Change in Parental-Investment and Family-Formation Strategies in the Course of Human Evolution. *In* Parenting Across the Life Span: Biosocial Dimensions. J. Lancaster, J. Altmann, A. Rossi, and L. Sherrod, eds. Pp. 187–205. New York: Aldine de Gruyter.
Lee, R. B.
  1979   The !Kung San: Men, Women, and Work in a Foraging Society. Cambridge: Cambridge University Press.
Miller, B. D.
  1987   Female Infanticide and Child Neglect in Rural North India. *In* Child Survival. N. Scheper-Hughes, ed. Pp. 95–112. Boston: D. Reidel.
Newman, L. F.
  1987   Fitness and Survival. *In* Child Survival. N. Scheper-Hughes, ed. Pp. 135–144. Boston: D. Reidel.
Pennington, R., and H. Harpending
  1988   Fitness and Fertility Among Kalahari !Kung. American Journal of Physical Anthropology 77:303–319.
Prentice, A., and A. Prentice
  1988   Reproduction Against the Odds. New Scientist (April 14):42–46.
Prentice, A. M., and R. G. Whitehead
  1987   The Energetics of Human Reproduction. Symposium, Zoological Society of London 57:275–304.
Sacher, G. A., and E. F. Staffeldt
  1974   Relation of Gestation Time and Brain Weight of Placental Mammals: Implications for the Theory of Vertebrate Growth. American Naturalist 105:593–615.
Scheper-Hughes, N.
  1985   Culture, Scarcity and Maternal Thinking: Maternal Detachment and Infant Survival in a Brazilian Shantytown. Ethos 13:291–317.
  1987   Child Survival. Boston: D. Reidel.

Scrimshaw, S.
    1984   Infanticide in Human Populations: Societal and Individual Concerns. Pages 439–487. *In* In-
        fanticide: Comparative and Evolutionary Perspectives. G. Hausfater and S. Hrdy, eds. Pp. 439–
        487. New York: Aldine de Gruyter.
Short, R. V.
    1976   The Evolution of Human Reproduction. Proceedings, Royal Society, Series B., 19:3–24.
    1978   Healthy Infertility. Upsala Journal of Medical Science, Supplement 22:23–26.
    1979   When a Conception Fails to Become a Pregnancy. Maternal Recognition of Pregnancy, CIBA
        Foundation Series 64:377–394.
    1984   Breast Feeding. Scientific American 250:35–41.
    1987   The Biological Basis for the Contraceptive Effects of Breast Feeding. International Journal of
        Gynaecology and Obstetrics Supplement 25:207–217.
Stini, W. A.
    1985   Sexual Dimorphism and Nutrient Reserves. Pages 391–419. *In* Sexual Dimorphism in *Homo
        sapiens*. R. Hall, ed. Pp. 391–419. New York: Praeger.
Surbey, M. K.
    1987   Anorexia Nervosa, Amenorrhea, and Adaptation. Ethology and Sociobiology 8(3S):47–62.
Wasser, S. K., and D. P. Barash
    1983   Reproductive Suppression among Female Mammals: Implications for Biomedicine and Sexual
        Selection Theory. Quarterly Review of Biology 58:513–538.
Wasser, S. K., and D. Y. Isenberg
    1986   Reproductive Failure among Women: Pathology or Adaptation? Journal of Psychosomatic
        Obstetrics and Gynaecology 5:153–175.
Winick, M.
    1981   Food and the Fetus. Natural History 90:76–81.

Women in Biosocial Perspective: Resources for Classroom Use

Films

N!ai, The Story of a !Kung Woman: John Marshall, Adrienne Miesmer, Sue Marshall Cabezas
(1980 color, 59 min). Available through Documentary Educational Resources, 5 Bridge Street, Water-
town, MA 02172. Formats: 16 mm film, ¾″ video.

In 1950 N!ai was a child roaming the African bush with a small band of hunter-gatherers. Today
she lives with 800 people on a government settlement. From filming spanning 28 years with the !Kung
San, Marshall has produced an intimate portrait on the personal and reproductive history of a hunter-
gatherer woman and of a vanishing way of life as well as !Nai's own evaluation of the changes wrought
by government. The film gives numerous examples of the autonomy of these hunter-gatherer women in
their sexual and reproductive lives and the control of resources they have personally gained.

Masai Women. M. Lewellyn-Davies, (color, 52 min.). Available through Thomas Howe Associates, 1-1226 Homer Street, Vancouver, BC V6B 2Y8, Canada. Formats: 16 mm film, ¾″ video.

The film explores the role of women, young and old, among the Masai of Kenya, a polygynous
pastoral society in which cattle are the main source of sustenance and wealth and children are the measure of success and happiness for both men and women. The film gives rich documentation of the lives
of women whose access to resources to sustain life and reproduction is strictly through significant males:
father, husband, and son.

Annotated References

Popular Scientific Articles Suitable for Undergraduate Reading Supplements

Frisch, R. E.
  1988   Fatness and Fertility. Scientific American 258:88–95.

  A recent overview of Frisch's controversial theory of a critical fatness level (stored energy) as crucial to the establishment and maintainance of women's fertility.

Hrdy, S. B.
  1988   Daughters or Sons. Natural History 97:63–81.

  Overview of differential investment in sons and daughters by parents across the animal kingdom. Good reading to stimulate class discussion about whether differential investment by sex is practiced in our society, in what ways and with what outcomes.

Prentice, A., and A. Prentice
  1988   Reproduction Against the Odds. New Scientist (April 14):42–46.

  Summary of research on fertility in a tribal village in Africa. This research carefully teases apart the effects of nutrition, work, and breast feeding on maternal fertility. Shows how maternal biology adapts to low levels of nutrition and still maintains fertility.

Short, R. V.
  1984   Breast Feeding. Scientific American 250:35–41.

  Short summarizes the evidence for breast feeding as a natural contraceptive for much of human history. He discusses how patterns of breast feeding typical of tribal and hunter-gatherer societies in which nursing bouts are brief (4–5 minutes) but frequent (2–3 times/hour) lead to the suppression of ovulation and long spacing between births.

Winick, M.
  1981   Food and the Fetus. Natural History 90:76–81.

  Discusses the human adaptation for maternal fat storage during pregnancy, which is so important in women that it takes precedence over fetal growth during the last trimester if nutrition is restricted.

Books

Shostak, M.
  1983   Nisa: The Life and Words of a !Kung Woman. New York: Vintage. Paperback.

  Engrossing life history of a hunter-gatherer woman often told in her own words. The author interlaces chapters on the anthropological knowledge about particular life course events common to women in !Kung society and then allows us to see how life unfolded for Nisa and how she felt about it.

Scientific Articles for Lecture Supplements

Hrdy, S. B.
  In press   The Absence of Estrus in *Homo sapiens. In* A. Brooks, ed. The Origins of Humanness. Washington, D.C.: Smithsonian Institution Press.

Review of the theories about the evolution of "continuous female receptivity, loss of estrus, and hidden ovulation" so dear to the heart of armchair theorists. Hrdy compares these scenarios against a backdrop of nonhuman primate reproductive behavior, shows how narrow and ethnocentric past theories have been, and suggests a new model for our protohuman ancestors' sexual behavior.

Irons, W.
   1983   Human Female Reproductive Strategies. *In* Social Behavior of Female Vertebrates. S. Wasser, ed. Pp. 169–213. New York: Academic Press.

Excellent overview of the reproductive strategies of women in three different societies: The Plateau Tonga, Tiwi, Pastoral Yomut. Irons shows how women form social and reproductive alliances that enhance their access to reproductive resources.

Lancaster, J. B.
   1985   Evolutionary Perspectives on Sex Differences in the Higher Primates. *In* Gender and the Life Course. A. S. Rossi, ed. Pp. 3–27. New York: Aldine de Gruyter.

Review of the biology of sex differences in relation to human evolution especially with regard to specialized adaptations in human reproductive biology, such as sex differences in stature, maturational programs, and fat patterning.

   In press   Parental Investment and the Evolution of the Juvenile Phase of the Life Course. *In* The Origins of Humanness. A. Brooks, ed. Washington, D.C.: Smithsonian Institution Press.

Presents an evolutionary scenario for the evolution of human parental investment patterns based on the feeding of juveniles and the doubling of the juvenile period in the life course.

Lancaster, J. B., and C. S. Lancaster
   1987   The Watershed: Change in Parental-Investment and Family-Formation Strategies in the Course of Human Evolution. *In* Parenting Across the Life Span: Biosocial Dimensions. J. Lancaster, J. Altmann, A. Rossi and L. Sherrod, eds. Pp. 187–205. New York: Aldine de Gruyter.

Review of the major shifts in the form of family formation and parental investment strategies comparing low density and high density human societies. One of the most significant of these changes is the shift from rearing healthy children to adulthood to continued investment after puberty to guarantee access to a competitive marriage market for each child.

Prentice, A. M., and R. G. Whitehead
   1987   The Energetics of Human Reproduction. Symposium, Zoological Society of London 57:275–304.

Latest and most complete review of the energetic costs of pregnancy and lactation of humans and how they differ from other mammals. Interesting discussion of how women can maintain high fertility in cultures where food is limited and female labor demanding.

Scrimshaw, S.
   1984   Infanticide in Human Populations: Societal and Individual Concerns. *In* Infanticide: Comparative and Evolutionary Perspectives. G. Hausfater and S. Hrdy, eds. Pp. 439–487. New York: Aldine de Gruyter.

Overview of the cross-cultural record of infanticide. Humans are the only species known for which infanticide is more often practiced by parents than by nonparents. Good discussion of the conditions associated with this behavior.

Short, R. V.
   1976   The Evolution of Human Reproduction. Proceedings, Royal Society, Series B 19:3–24.

Major overview of the shifts in the reproductive life course of women over human history, looking especially at fertility, the timing of menarche and menopause, the impact of breast feeding on fertility, and the 15-fold increase in menstrual cycling.

1987   The Biological Basis for the Contraceptive Effects of Breast Feeding. International Journal of Gynaecology and Obstetrics Supplement 25:207–217.

Scientific review of the mechanisms by which certain patterns of breast feeding may be contraceptive and promote birth spacing.

Surbey, M. K.
1987   Anorexia Nervosa, Amenorrhea, and Adaptation. Ethology and Sociobiology 8(3S):47–62.

Interesting discussion about a lack of fit between evolved biological adaptations and modern life. Complements the material presented in Short (1976).

Wasser, S. K., and D. Y. Isenberg
1986   Reproductive Failure among Women: Pathology or Adaptation? Journal of Psychosomatic Obstetrics and Gynaecology 5:153–175.

Presentation of the reproductive suppression hypothesis to explain reproductive failure and infertility in women.

5

Gender and the Anthropology Curriculum: Aboriginal Australia

Victoria K. Burbank
University of California, Davis

This module focuses on women anthropologists' work on women and the question of status in Aboriginal Australian society. Given the low research priority of women's issues in the recent past and the personal immediacy of these issues, it is not surprising to find that women anthropologists predominate in feminist studies. In their work, men are often just shadows on the page. Aboriginal Australia, however, is in varying degrees a sex-segregated society. In my experience, the exclusion of men from consideration reflects as much a socially created inability to work with men as a sense of making up for lost time in the ethnography of women. It is to be hoped that as more men make the challenges of feminist and gender issues central to their research concerns, a greater balance and greater understanding of sex and gender in Aboriginal society will be achieved. I have never used status as a framework for my own research in Australia, preferring to discover what Aboriginal women perceive to be the issues in their lives. In preparing this review it was clear, however, that the question of status must serve as its focus as it predominated in the majority of works on women and gender. It was also clear that research along these lines has raised a number of significant issues in Australian ethnography. Perhaps more important, although many issues remain to be resolved, these early efforts have cleared away the baggage of conventional wisdom about women's place in society, freeing researchers to seek out new directions—as is represented by the recent shift in focus from women's status to gender relations.

Overview: Feminists' Studies and Gender Analysis in Aboriginal Australia

In this review, I emphasize two aspects of women's roles in Aboriginal Australia: women's place in Aboriginal religion and women's economic role as hunters and gatherers. Paradoxically, the position of women in Aboriginal society has long been a conjecture of Australian ethnographers although, until the 1970s, little anthropological attention focused on the concrete details of women's day-to-day lives. When women have been portrayed as more than barely animate objects, they have usually been described as inferior beings controlled by Aboriginal men:

> Even here the women's work appears to be much more exacting. . . . Such work is the most repulsive . . . and is carried on only under strong compulsion. Compulsion is therefore, as we saw, the chief basis of this division of labour, and it may be said in the Australian aboriginal society the economic fact of the division of labour is rooted in a sociological status— viz., the compulsion of the weaker sex by the 'brutal' half of society. . . . From its compulsory character it follows that the distribution of economic function does not correspond to true co-operation, but that the relation of a husband to wife is in its economic aspect, that of a master to its slave. [Malinowski 1963:287–288].

> The first principle of age-grading, the sexual bifurcation by which women are excluded from participation in the totemic mysteries, immediately limits the female behaviours in the society and tends to simplify their personalities. The man's social personality, on the contrary, becomes more complex by his participation in the various elaborate age-graded rituals. There seems to be considerable evidence for a relationship between this and a man's comparatively complex technical behaviour and a woman's more simple type . . . it is one of the theses of this book that a man's social value is correspondingly more important and his place in the rituals is partly due to and expresses this fact. . . . [Warner 1969:6–7]

> Bern attempts to place polygyny in the broader framework of men's control of women's labour power. . . . This control is elaborated in the structure of religion, whose reproductive themes define mature men as the controllers of both women and the natural environment, and of the process of production . . . women are deprived of political equality and economic autonomy throughout their lives. [Hiatt 1985:44; see Bern 1979]

A reading of remarks like these from mainstream ethnography helps put into perspective why feminist scholarship has focused on an examination of Aboriginal women's lives and a questioning of assumptions about women's status in Aboriginal society. Most of this work is also set in a remembered, reconstructed hunting and gathering society, for the comparative implications of the question of status require that Aboriginal society be a truly independent case. Yet all ethnographic examples are based on Aboriginal groups touched and transformed by Western culture to some degree.[1]

The question of status, that is, the relative power, authority, and autonomy of Aboriginal men and women in "traditional" society, has brought to the fore a number of significant aspects of Aboriginal gender relations including the two that serve as a focus for this brief review: the high degree of male reliance on female production and the notable degree of sex-segregation in the ritual sphere. Treatments of these facets of gender relations take two different analytical paths. Some theorists see women's economic role as associated with the high degree of autonomy they enjoy in Aboriginal society. Others conceptualize women's ritual exclusion with the depths of their subjugation. Following a discussion of these perspectives, two curriculum examples are presented. The first of these, "Women's Ceremonies: Love Magic or Religion?" might be incorporated into lectures on religion or sexuality. The second, "The 'Good Hunters' of the Blyth," should be appropriate for discussions of foraging economies, the division of labor, family demography, or social change.

Women and Subsistence

In her study of women of the Kimberleys, the first comprehensive anthropological study of Aboriginal women, Phyllis Kaberry (1939) provides a picture that flatly contradicts writers

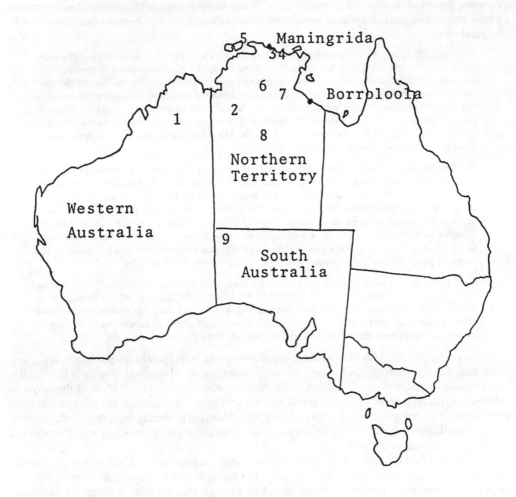

Key

1. The Kimberleys—site of Phyllis Kaberry's fieldwork
2. Area of Catherine Berndt's study of women's changing ceremonies
3. Maningrida—site of Annette Hamilton's northern study
4. The Anbarra of the Blyth River—site of Betty Meehan's work
5. The Tiwi of Melville Island—studied by Jane Goodale
6. Goinjimbi—site of Gillian Cowlishaw's fieldwork
7. Francesca Merlan's site near Elliot
8. The Kaytej of Warrabri—studied by Diane Bell
9. The Yangkundjara and Pitjantjara of Everard Park—site of Annette Hamilton's southern study

Figure 1. Approximate Locations of Field Sites Discussed in this Module.

like Malinowski. Kaberry asserts that women's labor is compulsory only in the sense that it is vital for existence (Kaberry 1939:24). As foragers, the autonomy of Aboriginal women would seem to be complete. They are taught by women, work in the company of other women, and alone decide when and where to pursue their economic tasks (Kaberry 1939:18, 23). If a man may attack a wife for insufficient provisions, so may a woman attack a "lazy" or "unfortunate" hunter (Kaberry 1939:25–26, 76). A woman feeds her husband and children, but a man cannot otherwise dispose of her gathered product (Kaberry 1939:31). The man in turn supplies meat to his wife, and a married woman can expect to eat better than her unmarried sister (Kaberry 1939:36, 101). If Aboriginal woman provides the greater portion of food, this reflects the greater certainty of her quest, not male coercion (Kaberry 1939:25, 36). The advantage a man may have in physical contests with his wife may be overshadowed by his economic dependence on her. Should she pack up her belongings and move to another camp, the economic hardship soon "brings the man to his senses" (Kaberry 1939:142–143). It is Aboriginal women's indispensable economic role and its associated power that underlies her "privileges," "good treatment," and "justice" in the household (Kaberry 1939:36, 143, 165, 271).

Writing more recently, Catherine Berndt and Diane Bell have come to similar conclusions (Bell 1983:45, 50, 55; Berndt 1974;76, 1981:193). Bell, for example, speaking of Central Desert women, sees their economic role as an essential part of their "power base." But not all Australianists take this view of Aboriginal women's subsistence role.

For Gillian Cowlishaw the autonomy of Aboriginal women's economic role indicates only the limits of male domination (Cowlishaw 1979:373; 1978:270). On the basis of her fieldwork in Southern Arnhem Land and an extensive review of the literature, Cowlishaw observes that the economic autonomy of Aboriginal women operates only within "quite narrow limits" (Cowlishaw 1982b:497). While it is true that they can choose when and where to forage, they are obliged to provide food for certain kinsmen, particularly husbands, fathers, and sons (Cowlishaw 1982b:496). Kinship, she says, simply obscures the economic exploitation of women by men (Cowlishaw 1982b:496). Men also have obligations to women, but contribute less, on a less regular basis (Cowlishaw 1982b:496–497). Women, for example, provide food when men are performing ritual activities, whereas men neither provide food during women's rituals nor when they themselves are ritually active (Cowlishaw 1979:378; 1982b:503, 504).

According to Annette Hamilton, women are autonomous producers, but it is because of this, along with their reproductive capacities, that women are "subject to control and manipulation by men, as objects of value" (Hamilton 1975:170). However, in the area of the Western Desert where Hamilton worked, the organization of women's labor both promoted and limited the dominance of men (Hamilton 1980–81). Here, as elsewhere on the continent, women's labor supported men's ceremonial life; the appropriation of women's product, particularly ground grass-seed cakes, provided men with the leisure time necessary to stage their rituals, "which in turn intensified the dominance of men in the culture" (Hamilton 1980–81:13–15). Grass seed is prepared on stone grindstones. Though scarce, these objects are too heavy to transport easily, so they were left in specific locations as the property of uterine kinswomen who alone might use them (Hamilton 1980–81:8). Given the need for the "extractive efficiency" of women, it was in men's interests to reside with their wives' families where the women had access to a grindstone (Hamilton 1980–81:9–10). Hence, argues Hamilton, the organization of women's labor "acted as a kind of perpetual opposition to the men's desires to promote patrilocal residence" and the consolidation of their dominant position in the society (Hamilton 1980–81:4, 10).

Women and Religion

A number of Australianists assert that the dominant position of senior Aboriginal men is maintained by their control of an ideology that is accepted by males and females alike (see, for example, Bern 1979; Cowlishaw 1979:383; Hiatt 1975, 1985; Keen 1982; Rose 1968; White 1974, 1975). Isobel White, for example, has suggested that the sexual fantasies contained in Central Australian myths represent neither patterns for action nor cautionary tales. Rather "the violence of sexual relations" in them can be viewed as "a reflection of the sexual values of a male-dominated society" (White 1975:137–138; but cf. Hamilton 1984). Some years earlier, W. L. Warner, observing the predominance of men in the religious celebrations of northeast Arnhem Land, wrote:

> The superordinate male group made sacred through the ritual initiation of its individual members into the sacred group . . . subordinates the female group which is unified by virtue of exclusion from the ceremonies and of ritual uncleanliness. [Warner 1937:394, quoted in Kaberry 1939:221]

Kaberry, however, began the challenge to this kind of generalization. It does not, she said, characterize relations between the men and women of the Kimberleys. Instead she suggested that both men and women are sacred and profane depending on the context in which they are viewed (Kaberry 1939:277). Both are the uninitiated with respect to the other's secret rituals (Kaberry 1939:221). Women's unity comes not from their shared exclusion and ritual impurity, but rather from shared interests and economic roles. She further suggests that the segregation of the sexes, so apparent in daily life, may have carried over into the religious domain, resulting in a ritual division of labor where each sex continues to pursue its own interests apart from the other (Kaberry 1939:183–184). Men's rituals, for example, include male circumcision, subincision, and ceremonies for endowing men with "strength and success in male pursuits"; women's rituals include the preparation of prepubescent girls for marriage and the manipulation of sexual relationships (Kaberry 1939:236, 254, 276).

Bell again makes a similar argument about Central Australian women. Ritual, she contends, is a "barometer of male-female relations for it provides . . . an arena in which the values of the society are writ large" (Bell 1983:248). Women's power, she argues, is derived from their relationship to the land, to the associated authority of the Dreamtime, and their autonomy as "independent economic producers" (Bell 1983:45, 50, 59). Neither sex "can enjoy unrivalled supremacy," for the other "has recourse to certain checks and balances" (Bell 1983:182). This is illustrated by women's participation in male initiation ceremonies, ceremonies that have, incidentally, been described by another observer as "male dominance rites" (Hiatt 1978:14, in Cowlishaw 1979:383). In the circumcision ceremonies of Central Australia, men celebrate their role of spiritual procreation, and women celebrate their importance as nurturers (Bell 1983:206, 225). Women's participation is not, in Bell's view, auxiliary; rather, they make "young men" in their distinctively female way (Bell 1983:210, 226). For example, circumcision and the nomination of a mother-in-law for the initiate are two key events in the ceremony. The former is the domain of the men, the latter, that of women (Bell 1983:207). As the circumcisor, chosen by the men, is also the future father-in-law of the initiate, the women's choice becomes public before that of the men and may thus possibly influence it (Bell 1980:257).

The grass-seed grinders of the Western Desert described by Annette Hamilton were not only autonomous producers, they were also the possessors of an autonomous and flourishing ritual life. Here both men's and women's ceremonies were based on the same body of mythology; though only women knew their myths and men theirs, the stories of each gender were myths only half-told (Hamilton 1980–81:15–16; 1981a:78). Men, consequently, held women's secret life in some regard (Hamilton 1980–81:15–16). Hamilton suggests that the presence of such cults "must always indicate a position of power for women in terms . . . of their own self-image" (Hamilton 1981a:78). She also says that women's secret ritual life "provides a venue in which solidarity in opposition to men's wishes can be constructed and expressed" (Hamilton 1980–81:17). It is, according to Hamilton, thanks to their secret life that these Western Desert women have successfully opposed polygyny (Hamilton 1980–81:17).

Hamilton, who has worked both in the Western Desert and in north central Arnhem Land, agrees with Cowlishaw insofar as she says that "women's power is greatest when they have least to do with men, and is least when they enter the field where men dominate explicitly, most clearly in the men's ritual life" (Hamilton 1981a:74). However, she points to the significance of regional variation in Aboriginal Australia and contrasts the ritual position of women in Arnhem Land and that of women in the more central regions (Hamilton 1981a:75–77). The former group have no secret cults like women of the Western Desert and appear to have been "incorporated to a much greater extent into the men's ritual life" (Hamilton 1981a:79). Without their own cults they have little to counter the ideology of male superiority expressed in the male-centered ceremonies (Hamilton 1980–81:17; 1981a:79).

Discussion and Conclusion

Feminist studies and the ethnography of gender in Aboriginal Australia indicate that in the hunting and gathering economy, woman's economic role was indispensable. This body of work also suggests that women were, by and large, autonomous producers. Its authors would not, however, all agree with ethnographers such as Kaberry and Bell, who have concluded that this autonomous production is associated with women's autonomy as social beings. Similarly, not all would agree that the sex-segregation of Aboriginal ritual life merely reflects the sexual division of labor in Aboriginal society and the development of two separate but equal groups. For ethnographers such as Cowlishaw and Hamilton, Aboriginal religion bears a message of male superiority that is attended to by men and women alike.

Francesca Merlan has observed that whether Aboriginal women's economic role is described as autonomous or exploited depends on the level of analysis. While the former view is based on a focus on women's daily activities, the latter is based on a picture of women's labor embedded in the larger context of gender relations (Merlan 1988). Cowlishaw and Hamilton have clearly looked at Aboriginal women's subsistence role in terms of the larger picture and have found both the ends and means of women's exploitation in male ritual life. Yet their conclusions about gender relations in Aboriginal Australia differ. For Gillian Cowlishaw (1979), male domination is the *sine qua non* of Aboriginal society; areas of female autonomy indicate only the limits of male control. Hamilton, on the other hand, is less sure. As she says, "this relationship between super- and sub-ordinate, between the strong and the less strong, is never a simple one" (Hamilton 1981a:84; see also Kaberry 1939:271, 275–276, and Myers 1986:248).

It can be seen from this discussion that the question of status has been pivotal in the development of feminist studies and gender analysis in Australian Aboriginal ethnography. The question of women's status, the relative power, authority, and autonomy of Aboriginal men and women, is derived from our concerns and our perceptions of the relations between men and women in our own society (Lamphere 1986; Merlan 1988; Rosaldo 1980:391–393).

As a research framework it has undoubtedly obscured some facets of women's lives and relationships; facets that are beginning to emerge as our questions change and our understanding of the seemingly complex and paradoxical relations between Aboriginal men and women advances. Its concern with a way of life that no longer exists, often even in the experience and memory of informants, probably means that such debates as those discussed in this overview may never be resolved. Nevertheless, the issue of status relations has fostered considerable research, which has provided us with a picture of women and their lives previously absent in the ethnography of the area, thereby enlarging our understanding of this area.

Curricular Example Number One: Women's Ceremonies—Love Magic or Religion?

This example illustrates how the perspective of ethnographers and the words they use to describe what they see can diminish or elevate any human activity. The specific focus here is on women's ritual and its importance in Aboriginal society.

Complex and subtle, Aboriginal religion has long been regarded as the center of Aboriginal life and the key to understanding the culture of its practitioners (Charlesworth et al. 1984:5–6). Recently, it has become apparent that women's exclusion from this central domain of cultural life (Warner 1969) is an illusion, the result of inadequate or misinterpreted information. Women's religious participation ranges from the island-dwelling Tiwi, where men and women are initiated together, to Northern Arnhem Land, where women play an important but auxiliary role in male ceremonies, to Central Australia, where women's ceremonies are separate, "secret and dangerous to men" (Bell 1984:295–296; Hamilton 1981a:78–79). Even so, women's religious activity has frequently been derogated, as in the now often quoted words of Kenneth Maddock:

> Men's cults express broad, cohesive and impersonal themes, such as the fertility and continuity of nature, the regularity of society and the creation of the world. Women's cults are centered on narrow, divisive and personal interests, such as making love magic and reacting to physiological crises. [Maddock 1972:155]

Generally called *yilpinji (yirbindji), jawalju (yawulyu),* or *jarrada (tjarada, djarada),* so called "love magic" ceremonies are indeed widespread in Aboriginal Australia. Phyllis Kaberry provides us with one of the first descriptions of a *yirbindji:*

> The spectacle was a dramatic and vivid one. It took place in the brilliant sunlight, against a background of red sandstone. . . . The women themselves were greased with fat till their skins glistened; bold designs in charcoal, red ochre, and clay were drawn on their bodies, so that they seemed the living incarnation of the landscape. . . .
>
> The preparation took about two hours, for the painting was no mere preliminary, but an essential part of the whole corroboree and much of the success depended on it. . . .
>
> Summed up briefly, the songs refer to the painting, the other forms of bodily decoration, and to the male and female genitals. . . . The lover is pictured as sitting in the camp. He thinks of the girl and trembles with sexual excitement. The woman then "sings" his penis, so that it will grow long. . . . The boy cries for the girl, and his penis grows so long that it falls to the ground like an umbilical cord. The girl trembles with desire and goes to him. He opens her legs and sees her clitoris. . . . The woman "sings" her own genitals, and the man ejaculates. . . .

The singers, who were sitting before the cleared space, began . . . the dancers ran out in a line from the bushes where they had been hidden, beckoning with their arms as though to summon their lovers. . . . After a song had been repeated several times there was a pause until the leader signalled for the next. In this dance they carried fighting-sticks and boomerangs, swinging them from side to side. . . . For the next dance . . . the performers shuffled forward with their hands held before them. . . . After this there was a rest; the red headbands were tied on and the women beckoned with their arms once more. . . . Then the rhythm quickened for the last song . . . the women of opposite moieties faced each other, grasping one another's shoulders, jumping backwards and forwards, and finally simulated intercourse. [Kaberry 1939:259–265][2]

In spite of Kaberry's stress on Aboriginal woman's sacred role in society, she describes the intent of these ceremonies as "magic" and observes that in several of the groups that performed them, the ceremony seemed to "fall outside the ordinary totemic complex," unlike the women's rites for menstruation, puberty, and birth. She notes, however, that in other groups similar rituals are described as sacred or of the Dreaming (Kaberry 1939:266–267). These ceremonies (only recently celebrated in the Kimberleys but with greater historical depth in other parts of Australia) provided women with their only opportunity for "collective and recreative" ritual apart from men. Women, according to Kaberry, participated in the rituals because they wished to obtain a lover or to maintain the sexual interest of a husband. This form of "women's business" was described to her as "poison" and *wa:dji,* that is as "wrong" vis-à-vis marriage rules, and the women "seemed to delight in the illicit character of the dance." Kaberry interpreted the rites as a "safety valve; a means of mitigating the dissatisfaction of the younger women" in a society where marriages were arranged "irrespective of mutual desire" (Kaberry 1939:241, 253, 255–259, 267).

In Kaberry's analysis we undoubtedly have the basis for a characterization of women's cults as "narrow, personal, and divisive"—a magical rather than religious endeavor. Such a characterization, however, ignores more recent studies of women's ceremonial activity.

Catherine Berndt, for example, paints a very different picture of women's secret ceremonies in the Victoria River District (adjacent to the Kimberley area where Kaberry worked), the Northern Territory, and Western Australia. She notes that "love magic" is often an aspect of women's ceremonies, and that indeed this aspect is emphasized by some of the participants, but the ceremonies also contain other features. These include "healing the sick or wounded; stopping quarrels, 'quietening' a man who is having too many extramarital affairs; or attempting to strengthen or restore a man's affection for his wife, or bring him (or the singer's father, or brother) home safely from a journey. In addition, some women . . . stress the religious, or sacred, or Dreaming aspect of the ceremonies" (Berndt 1965:242–243).

A similar argument has been made by Diane Bell, who has been particularly emphatic in her rejection of the label "love magic." Love, she says, is a "poor translation" for what is really "emotional management" (Bell 1981, 1983:162). The word *magic* carries pejorative connotations that reinforce the interpretation of women's rites as deviant, narrow, and personal. On the contrary, *yilpinji* "concerns the whole of Aboriginal society" and "is underwritten by the Dreamtime Law" (Bell 1981, 1983:176–177). For the Kaititj of Central Australia, these rites are used to establish marriages that are "deemed legitimate by society," "force a wayward husband to return, remind a wife of her duty to family and country, or even repulse the unwanted advances of a spouse or lover" (Bell 1981, 1983:173).

Berndt also places the sexual focus in these rituals in its cultural context. She observes, for example, that

The *tjarada* and *jawalju* place some stress on erotic aspects, in conformity with the concept . . . that the relationship between the sexes is of vital importance in the maintenance of both human and animal life, and the reproduction of the various natural species. It is a basic element of human life, and fundamental to the religious concepts of this area. [Berndt 1950:70]

Francesca Merlan (1986a, 1988) takes this argument a step further through her interpretation of Aboriginal sexuality as social instrument. She begins by observing that female maturation is "subject to cultural manipulation." While women may act to transform girls into women, men are more often reported to do so, and their means of doing so are usually sexual in nature. For example, Goodale notes that the Tiwi consider sexual intercourse "the direct and only cause of breast formation, growth of pubic and axillary hair, menarche, and subsequent menstrual periods" (Goodale 1971:45; see also Hamilton 1981b:19). Women's sexuality may also be used instrumentally in Aboriginal society. For example, sexual intercourse may be offered as expiation for an offense (Merlan 1986a, 1987, 1988). In the context of Aboriginal ritual life, Merlan suggests that emotions are managed through the medium of sexuality (Merlan 1987:15). For example, two major themes in a *jarrada* that took place recently near Elliot in the Northern Territory were attractiveness and making men "settle down." Participation in the ceremony renders the woman "irresistible" to the object of her desires. The attractiveness of the woman leads to the man's sexual desire and dependence on her and hence to his eventual domestication (Merlan 1987:16, 18). Sexuality, through ritual manipulation, becomes power. That is, it is not as a subjugated woman with no other recourse, but as a woman with knowledge of and control of the sacred, that Aboriginal woman uses sexuality (as may Aboriginal man) to gain her ends (Merlan 1988).

It is apparent from this brief discussion that whether the label "magic" or "religion" is applied to a specific practice or belief depends as much on the perspective of the observer as on the practice or belief in question. There are many possible reasons for the disparity between Kaberry's description of love rituals and those that followed. It may be, as Berndt has suggested, that in the contact situation the relevance of the Dreaming is diminished and the emphasis shifts, in this case from the sacred to the erotic (Berndt 1950:72). Deborah Rose (personal communication) has suggested that women's business must be looked at within the larger social, political, and historical context. For example, she suggests that at the time of Kaberry's work, women of the Kimberleys may have been finding their sexuality to be problematic, or at least emblematic of the disturbance brought by Europeans to their land. Possibly these women, like those elsewhere (see for example, Berndt and Berndt 1987), were both compelled to provide sex to the white intruders and bear the brunt of Aboriginal male hostility for doing so. Thus their focus on love magic, rather than representing a concern with mere dalliance, might be seen as a major political preoccupation. Or, as Bell has said, as a young single woman, Kaberry may not have been informed of the larger significance of what she saw and heard (Bell 1983:232). Or this may be yet another dimension of the variation in women's lives found across the continent (Hamilton 1981a). It is also apparent that in the context of Australian ethnography, the word *magic* has been associated with discussions that derogate and diminish the religious roles of Aboriginal women. It is thanks to observers who have searched beyond the stereotypes that we are beginning to glimpse this fascinating realm.

Resources for Classroom Use

Readings.   See Bibliography for entries on Bell (1983), Charlesworth et al. (1984), and Rose (1985).

Films for the Classroom: The House-Opening.   Narrated by a woman of Aurukun, this film covers the opening of her house following her husband's death. This is a ceremony in which both men and women take part, and this film illustrates the sometimes separate, sometimes complementary roles of men and women in ritual. To order, contact the Berkeley Media Service, University of California, Berkeley.

Questions for Class Discussion. How might naive Western observers interpret the women's ceremony described by Phyllis Kaberry? What information about Aboriginal society and culture would they need in order to experience this ceremony as its participants do? Develop a hypothesis about how Aboriginal women's concepts of sexuality and power might resolve the dichotomy between ''love magic'' and ''religion.''

Curricular Example Number Two: The "Good Hunters" of the Blyth

This example illustrates the duality of women's productive role and the potential conflicts between subsistence activities and reproductive efforts. It also suggests that these dilemmas may vary with variation in family demography.

There is widespread agreement that Aboriginal women were the primary food producers in the hunting and gathering economy of precontact Australia (see, for example, Bell 1983:54–55; Cowlishaw 1979:220; Hamilton 1975:71; Hiatt 1974:10; Peterson 1974:22 [but cf. Altman 1984:185–187]). Ethnographers, however, have usually followed the "flour frontier," arriving only after cattlemen, missionaries, and government agents had made their mark, to find the local Aborigines mustering cattle or receiving welfare checks.

Women's productive labor seems to have been particularly affected by the introduction of Western foods. Even when Aborigines return to live on their land, as many groups have in recent years, introduced carbohydrates continue to replace those once provided largely by Aboriginal women (Altman 1984; Meehan 1982). Men continue to hunt, but women do not gather vegetable foods to the extent it is believed they once did. There may be several reasons for this. Men may now hunt the feral cattle, pigs, and buffalo introduced by whites (Altman 1984:183). But these new prey deplete vegetable products that women once gathered (Berndt 1981:160). Shotguns and rifles increased male hunting efficiency, but metal digging sticks make little difference in women's gathering ability (Altman 1984:183). Finally, introduced carbohydrates are relatively "cheap, storeable and readily available," whereas store-bought meat is "expensive" and "highly perishable" (Altman 1984:183).

But Aboriginal women have never just gathered vegetables. The fact that women's products often include significant amounts of protein has not gone unnoted (see, for example, Bell 1983:55; Goodale 1971:154; Hamilton 1980–81:11). Today, for example, Anbarra men provide the "fish, birds and mammals, women the goannas [large lizards], freshwater turtles and shellfish" (Meehan 1982:149). The Anbarra returned to live on their land on the northern coast of Arnhem Land by the mouth of the Blyth River some 15 years after they first settled at Maningrida. Finding this group to be a "fully functioning hunting and gathering society," Betty Meehan and her colleague Rhys Jones spent a year observing the economic activity of this group; Jones concentrated on male activities, Meehan on those of women and girls (Meehan 1977a, 1977b, 1982).[3]

Shellfish are an important food source for the Anbarra. Although shellfish contributed 17% of the monthly energy intake at most, Meehan argues that this food is critical to Anbarra well-being. It is a dependable food source, "potentially available year round" and as such is a "constant source of fresh protein" (Meehan 1982:159). As Meehan points out, "it is the amount of protein . . . that each person gets each day that really regulates the health of its members'' (1982:140). It is a low-risk, high-yield activity (a woman can gather 2000 kcal of shellfish in about two hours), that permits more "opportunistic" high-risk foraging strategies. Shellfishing is also an activity that can be undertaken by almost anybody, including old people and young children, heavily pregnant women, and women with young children in their care (Meehan 1977b:524–527, 1982:159–160).

Everyone collects shellfish. Nevertheless, this activity "is a woman's occupation *par excellence*" (Meehan 1982:119). For example, women and girls collected 85% of *Tapes hiantina,* a bivalve that is greatly relished and that accounted for 61% of the total weight of all shellfish collected in the observation year (Meehan 1977a:363, 1982:72, 160). Children who accompany their mothers to the shell beds are not in danger, nor do they interfere with their mothers' gathering activities to the same extent that they do when women are after goanna or yams. Still, women attempt to leave their children with a caretaker in camp when they go to collect shellfish. They may, for example, pretend that their departure is only a brief one to urinate or gather water or wood (Meehan 1982:82). A possible reason for this reluctance is apparent in a comparison of the average weights of *Tapes hiantina* gathered per trip by mature (age 31–50) and younger (age 21–30) women. The older group had significantly greater hauls (Meehan 1982:131–132).

A woman who is productive, skillful, and enthusiastic in her search for goanna, yams, or shellfish is a *djindjana magun-gun,* a "good hunter." But, according to Meehan, even a potentially good hunter is "hampered" by dependent children (Meehan 1982:132). For example, the mother of a newborn may not gather at all until her child is 6 to 9 months of age. A gatherer with older but still dependent children may not only have a load of shellfish to carry but also a child or two (Meehan 1982:83, 96, 135–136).

The Anbarra say that they are having "too many" children now, more than they had before the Europeans came (Meehan 1982:137, 139; see also Hamilton 1975:176, 1981b:119–129; Cowlishaw 1981, 1982a; Reid and Gurruwiwi 1979:6–7).[4] The extent to which the increasing numbers of children interfere with women's productive activities are suggested by Meehan's calculation of the number of yams women would have had to dig before Western carbohydrates were introduced to the group. She found that for at least one month her "figures, requiring women to dig for yams on 28 out of the 30 days in the month, are totally unrealistic in terms of Anbarra foraging styles." A change in the population structure, however, would make the task more feasible. "For example, if there were three less children in the . . . population but three more women, then each woman would have had to gather yams on 20 out of the 30 days" (Meehan 1982:150).[5]

Contact with Westerners and their goods has probably meant that the good hunters of the Blyth no longer need to exert themselves to the extent they once did in the past. But it has also meant that they are less able to do so.

Resources for Classroom Use

Readings.   See entries in Bibliography for Goodale (1971) and Meehan (1982).

Questions for Class Discussion.   Discuss the advantages and disadvantages Anbarra women might experience now that they can purchase rather than gather carbohydrates. What aspects of collecting shellfish are compatible with childcare? What aspects are not? How might the changes in women's productive roles affect relations between Anbarra men and women?

Notes

Acknowledgments. For their comments and assistance I want to thank Catherine Berndt, James Chisholm, Louise Lamphere, Janice Reid, David Riches, Deborah Rose, Warren Shapiro, Isobel White, and the reviewers of the Gender in the Anthropology Curriculum Project.

1. For discussions of the difficulties of assessing the degree and direction of such changes on the status and condition of women see Berndt (1981), Cowlishaw (1986), and Merlan (1985).

2. Several authors have noted that homosexual features are present in women's love rituals. According to Berndt (1965:265) songs in *djarada/ilbindji* and *jawalju* may be "used to attract a person of the same sex." According to Marie Reay (1970:165, 169–170) the motives for holding a *yawalyu* at Borroloola included the desire to obtain other women as lovers. Kaberry (1939:257) mentions that homosexual features were present in the *yirbindji*. Speaking of the *wuljankura* of Central Australia, Roheim (1933:226) says that "the women rub each other's clitoris with their legs, singing of the bell-bird who will fetch their lovers." He also briefly describes the homosexual practices of unmarried girls (Roheim 1933:238).

3. Other quantitative studies are to be found in McCarthy and McArthur (1960) and Altman (1987). More descriptive accounts are to be found in Kaberry (1939:17–24), Gould (1969:5–21), and Goodale (1971:151–176).

4. The increasing family size in Aboriginal populations may be due to a number of factors. These include the suppression of infanticide, the introduction of processed foods leading to earlier weaning and the resumption of ovulation, and medical provisions leading to a reduction in child mortality (see, for example, Reid and Gurruwiwi 1979:6).

5. According to Meehan's calculations this task would be even more feasible if the yam yield was increased (e.g., from about 5 kg to 10 kg per woman, per day) and the caloric requirement decreased (e.g., from 2400 kcal to 2000 kcal per person, per day) (Meehan 1982:150).

Bibliography

Please note: This bibliography includes both the references cited in the text and additional background reading. As the latter are not discussed in the essay or curriculum examples they are briefly annotated.

Altman, J.
   1984   Hunter-Gatherer Subsistence Production in Arnhem Land: The Original Affluence Hypothesis Re-Examined. Mankind 14:179–190.
   1987   Hunter-Gatherers Today: An Aboriginal Economy in North Australia. Canberra: Australian Institute of Aboriginal Studies.
Barwick, D.
   1974   And the Lubras are Ladies Now. *In* Woman's Role in Aboriginal Society. F. Gale, ed. Pp. 51–63. Canberra: Australian Institute of Aboriginal Studies. A discussion of changes in gender relations that accompanied the resettlement of Victorian Aborigines on mission and government stations in the late 1800s.
Bell, D.
   1980   Desert Politics: Choices in the "Marriage Market." *In* Women and Colonization: Anthropological Perspectives. M. Etienne and E. Leacock, eds. Pp. 239–269. New York: Praeger.
   1981   Women's Business is Hard Work: Central Australian Aboriginal Women's Love Rituals. Signs 7:318–337.

1982   Women's Changing Role in Health Maintenance in a Central Australian Community. *In* Body, Land and Spirit: Health and Healing in Aboriginal Society. J. Reid, ed. Pp. 197–224. St. Lucia, Queensland: University of Queensland Press. The present role of Kaititj women as nurturers and healers is contrasted to that of the past.

1983   Daughters of the Dreaming. Sydney: McPhee Gribble/George Allen and Unwin. In chapters 3 and 4, Bell describes Kaytej (Kaititj) women's ritual life and the themes of land, love, and health that motivate it.

1984   Women and Aboriginal Religion: Introduction. *In* Religion in Aboriginal Australia: An Anthology. M. Charlesworth, H. Morphy, D. Bell, and K. Maddock, eds. Pp. 295–303. St. Lucia, Queensland: University of Queensland Press.

1987.   The Politics of Separation. *In* Dealing with Inequality. M. Strathern, ed. Pp. 112–129. Cambridge: Cambridge University Press. A discussion of changing gender and spatial relations in Central Australia. The autonomy of women in foraging society becomes exclusion from the mainstream of power and politics in the contemporary situation.

Bern, J.
1979   Ideology and Domination: Toward a Reconstruction of Australian Aboriginal Social Formation. Oceania 50:118–132.

Berndt, C.
1950   Women's Changing Ceremonies in Northern Australia. Paris: Musee de l'Homme.

1965   Women and the Secret Life. *In* Aboriginal Man in Australia. R. Berndt and C. Berndt, eds. Pp. 236–282. Sydney: Angus and Robertson.

1974   Digging Sticks and Spears, or, The Two-Sex Model. *In* Woman's Role in Aboriginal Society. F. Gale, ed. Pp. 64–84. Canberra: Australian Institute of Aboriginal Studies.

1981   Interpretation and "Facts" in Aboriginal Australia. *In* Woman the Gatherer. F. Dahlberg, ed. Pp. 153–203. New Haven: Yale University Press.

Berndt, R., and C. Berndt
1987   End of an Era: Aboriginal Labour in the Northern Territory. Canberra: Australian Institute of Aboriginal Studies.

Bowdler, S.
1978   Hook, Line and Dilly Bag: An Interpretation of an Australian Coastal Shell Midden. Mankind 10:248–258. A discussion, based on historical and ethnographic sources, of women's fishing and shellfishing activities and the distribution of food resources between men and women.

Burbank, V.
1987   Premarital Sex Norms: Cultural Interpretations in an Australian Aboriginal Community. Ethos 15:226–234. A discussion of female adolescents' sexual behavior in one Aboriginal community and how it currently affects marriage politics.

1988   Aboriginal Adolescence: Maidenhood in an Australian Community. New Brunswick: Rutgers University Press. This discussion of changing marriage practices focuses on adolescent girls and on what they say about men, sexuality, and marriage.

Charlesworth, M., H. Morphy, D. Bell, and K. Maddock
1984   Religion in Aboriginal Australia: An Anthology. St. Lucia, Queensland: University of Queensland Press. A section on women and religion includes selected excerpts of works on women's religious participation in Aboriginal Australia by Bell, Berndt, Goodale, and Kaberry.

Collmann, J.
1979   Women, Children, and the Significance of the Domestic Group to Urban Aborigines in Central Australia. Ethnology 18:379–397. A description of how the domestic economy of Aboriginal groups in Central Australia has been transformed by the collision of Aboriginal goals and Australian bureaucracy, and the resulting changes in gender relations, family organization, and women's place within it.

Cowlishaw, G.
1978   Infanticide in Aboriginal Australia. Oceania 48:262–283.

1979   Women's Realm: A Study of Socialization, Sexuality and Reproduction among Australian Aborigines. Ph.D. dissertation, Department of Anthropology, University of Sydney.

1981 The Determinants of Fertility among Australian Aborigines. Mankind 13:37–55.

1982a Family Planning: A Post-Contact Problem. *In* Body, Land and Spirit: Health and Healing in Aboriginal Society. J. Reid, ed. Pp. 31–48. St. Lucia, Queensland: University of Queensland Press.

1982b Socialization and Subordination among Australian Aborigines. Man 17:492–507.

1986 Broken Promises: Aboriginal Traditions. Paper presented at Australian Institute of Aboriginal Studies Seminar: Hierarchical and Egalitarian Tendencies in Traditional Aboriginal Society.

Glowczewski, B.

1983 Death, Women, and "Value Production": The Circulation of Hair Strings among the Walpiri of the Central Australian Desert. Ethnology 22:225–239. Gender relations are examined via an analysis of hair string presentations between men and women.

Goodale, J.

1971 Tiwi Wives. Seattle: University of Washington Press. A very readable ethnography from the perspective of a woman working with women. Chapter 6 includes a discussion of the Tiwi division of labor and women's hunting activities.

1982 Production and Reproduction of Key Resources among the Tiwi of North Australia . *In* Resource Managers: North American and Australian Hunter-Gatherers. N. Williams and E. Hunn, eds. Pp. 197–210. Washington, D.C.: American Association for the Advancement of Science. Here the sexual division of labor in resource maintenance is examined and related to the Tiwi's view of a world divided into masculine and feminine domains.

Gould, R.

1969 Yiwara: Foragers of the Australian Desert. New York: Charles Scribner's Sons.

Hamilton, A.

1974 The Role of Women in Aboriginal Marriage Arrangements. *In* Woman's Role in Aboriginal Society. F. Gale, ed. Pp. 28–35. Canberra: Australian Institute of Aboriginal Studies. Gidgingali women's views of their role in marriage bestowal. Male ideals do not reflect female perspectives on marriage arrangements.

1975 Aboriginal Women: The Means of Production. *In* The Other Half: Women in Australian Society. J. Mercer, ed. Pp. 167–179. Harmondsworth: Penguin.

1980–81 Dual Social Systems: Technology, Labour and Women's Secret Rites in the Eastern Western Desert of Australia. Oceania 51:4–19.

1981a A Complex Strategical Situation: Gender and Power in Aboriginal Australia. *In* Australian Women: Feminist Perspectives. N. Grieve and P. Grimshaw, eds. Pp. 69–85. Melbourne: Oxford University Press.

1981b Nature and Nurture: Aboriginal Child-Rearing in North-Central Arnhem Land. Canberra: Australian Institute of Aboriginal Studies.

1984 Knowledge and Misrecognition: Mythology and Gender in Aboriginal Australia. Unpublished paper.

Hart, C., A. Pilling, and J. Goodale

1988 The Tiwi of Northern Australia. New York: Holt, Rinehart and Winston. This revision now includes the observations and insights of Jane Goodale. See Goodale (1971) above.

Hiatt, B.

1974 Woman the Gatherer. *In* Woman's Role in Aboriginal Society. F. Gale, ed. Pp. 4–15. Canberra: Australian Institute of Aboriginal Studies.

Hiatt, L.

1975 Swallowing and Regurgitation in Australian Myth and Rite. *In* Australian Aboriginal Mythology. L. Hiatt, ed. Pp. 143–162. Canberra: Australian Institute of Aboriginal Studies.

1978 The Ideological Functions of Aboriginal Religion. Paper presented at the International Conference on Hunters and Gatherers, Paris.

1985 Maidens, Males and Marx: Some Contrasts in the Work of Frederick Rose and Claude Meillassoux. Oceania 56:34–46.

Kaberry, P.

1939 Aboriginal Woman: Sacred and Profane. New York: Gordon Press.

Keen, I.
  1982   How Some Murngin Men Marry Ten Wives: The Marital Implications of Matrilateral Cross-Cousin Structures. Man 18:620–642.
Kennedy, M.
  1985   Born a Half-Caste. Canberra: Australian Institute of Aboriginal Studies. An Aboriginal woman's story of her life as a ward on Palm Island and as a woman in white Australia working on cattle stations.
Lamphere, L.
  1986   Feminism and Anthropology: The Struggle to Reshape Our Thinking about Gender. Paper prepared for Indiana University, Women's Studies Program Tenth Anniversary Volume, June 1985.
Maddock, K.
  1972   The Australian Aborigines: A Portrait of Their Society. Ringwood, Victoria: Pelican.
Malinowski, B.
  1963   The Family among the Australian Aborigines: A Sociological Study. New York: Schocken Books.
McCarthy, D., and M. McArthur
  1960   The Food Quest and the Time Factor in Aboriginal Economic Life. *In* Records of the American-Australian Scientific Expedition, vol 2. C. Mountford, ed. Pp. 145–194. Melbourne: Melbourne University Press.
Meehan, B.
  1977a   Hunters by the Seashore. Journal of Human Evolution 66:363–370.
  1977b   Man Does Not Live by Calories Alone: The Role of Shellfish in a Coastal Cuisine. *In* Sunda and Sahul: Prehistoric Studies in Southeast Asia, Melanesia and Australia. J. Allen, J. Golson, and R. Jones, eds. Pp. 493–531. New York: Academic Press.
  1982   From Shell Bed to Shell Midden. Canberra: Australian Institute of Aboriginal Studies. Pp. 31–37 contain an account of the seasonal movements and activities of the Anbarra. Chapter 7 provides details of shellfish collection and cooking. This volume also contains some interesting photos of shellfish collection.
Merlan, F.
  1985   Review of *Daughters of the Dreaming* by Diane Bell. Oceania 55:225–229.
  1986   Australian Aboriginal Conception Beliefs Revisited. Man 21:474–493.
  1987   Aspects of Ritual and Gender Relations in Aboriginal Australia. Unpublished paper.
  1988   Gender in Aboriginal Social Life: A Review. *In* Social Anthropology and Australian Aboriginal Studies: A Contemporary Overview. R. Berndt and R. Tonkinson, eds. Pp. 15–72. Canberra: Aboriginal Studies Press.
Munn, N.
  1973   Walbiri Iconography: Graphic Representation and Cultural Symbolism in a Central Australian Society. Ithaca: Cornell University Press. This study of Walbiri graphic representations includes discussions of *yawalyu* designs, their origins and functions and women's story telling and accompanying sand graphics.
Myers, F.
  1986   Pintupi Country, Pintupi Self: Sentiment, Place, and Politics among Western Desert Aborigines. Washington, D.C.: Smithsonian Institution Press.
Peterson, N.
  1974   The Importance of Women in Determining the Composition of Residential Groups in Aboriginal Australia. *In* Woman's Role in Aboriginal Society. F. Gale, ed. Pp. 16–27. Canberra: Australian Institute of Aboriginal Studies.
Reay, M.
  1970   A Decision as Narrative. *In* Australian Aboriginal Anthropology: Modern Studies in the Social Anthropology of the Australian Aborigines. R. Berndt, ed. Pp. 164–173. Nedlands, Western Australia: University of Western Australia Press.

Reid, J., and M. Gurruwiwi
  1979   Attitudes toward Family Planning among the Women of a Northern Australian Aboriginal Community. Medical Journal of Australia Special Supplement 1:5–7.
Roheim, G.
  1933   Women and their Life in Central Australia. Journal of the Royal Anthropological Institute of Great Britain and Ireland 63:207–265.
Rosaldo, M.
  1980   The Use and Abuse of Anthropology. Signs 5:389–417.
Rose, D.
  1985   Healing the Dreaming: Social and Cultural Management of a Sacred Site in the Victoria River District. Unpublished paper. A very readable case study about Yarralin women's successful attempt to repair and preserve a women's sacred site. For copies, write to Deborah Rose, Australian Institute of Aboriginal Studies, P.O. Box 553, Canberra, A.C.T. 2601, Australia.
Rose, F.
  1968   Australian Marriage, Land-Owning Groups, and Initiations. In Man the Hunter. R. Lee and I. DeVore, eds. Pp. 200–208. Chicago: Aldine.
Sanson, B.
  1978   Sex, Age and Social Control in Mobs of the Darwin Hinterland. In Sex and Age as Principles of Social Differentiation. J. La Fontaine, ed. London: Academic Press. This paper describes marriage, other aspects of gender relations, and female solidarity in a Darwin fringe camp.
Warner, W.
  1937   A Black Civilization: A Study of an Australian Tribe. New York: Harper.
  1969   A Black Civilization: A Study of an Australian Tribe. Revised Edition. Gloucester, Massachusetts: Peter Smith.
White, I.
  1974   Aboriginal Women's Status: A Paradox Resolved. In Women's Role in Aboriginal Society. F. Gale, ed. Pp. 36–49. Canberra: Australian Institute of Aboriginal Studies.
  1975   Sexual Conquest and Submission in the Myths of Central Australia. In Australian Aboriginal Mythology. L. Hiatt, ed. Pp. 123–142. Canberra: Australian Institute of Aboriginal Studies.
White, I., D. Barwick, and B. Meehan
  1985   Fighters and Singers: The Lives of Some Australian Aboriginal Women. Sydney: George Allen and Unwin. Includes biographical and autobiographical sketches of Aboriginal women and discussions of the relationships between anthropologists and the women they come to know in the field.

Note: To order books from the Australian Institute of Aboriginal Studies, write to Publications Assistant, AIAS, P.O. Box 553, Canberra, A.C.T. 2601, Australia.

6

From Illusion to Illumination: Anthropological Studies of American Indian Women

Patricia C. Albers
University of Utah

Popular images of the American Indian embody stereotypic themes that have displayed remarkable persistence through time. As typically found in novels, film, and other mass media, American Indians have been portrayed in two contradictory ways: as humanity in a state of primordial innocence and as human nature in a state of anarchy. The female component of this imagery has been cast in the opposition of the revered "princess" and the defiled "squaw," or it has been posed in the contrast between an omnipotent "mother earth" and a downtrodden "beast of burden." In either case, she is a symbolic illusion drawn from models of womanhood that are essentially European in origin, and as such, she dramatizes moral and societal dilemmas not of her own creation (Albers 1983a; Albers and James 1987; Allen 1986; Green 1975, 1980; Wittstock 1980). Even when popular representations (Niethammer 1977; Terrell and Terrell 1974) pretend to have some ethnographic validity, they continue to reproduce an image of American Indian women that is frozen in the time frame of a mythical ethnographic present. Native women are pictured as unchanging—clinging to a traditional way of life that exists outside the vicissitudes of history. It is the highly mythologized figures of Pocahontas and Sacajawea that draw public attention (Green 1975; Lurie 1972). This kind of stereotypic image making continues, despite an informed body of research and writing on American Indian women by anthropologists and other scholars.

Anthropological interest in American Indian women began more than a century ago, largely as a result of writings on the Iroquois where the high status of females stimulated much discussion and debate about women's changing position in human evolution (Beauchamp 1889; Carr 1887; Morgan 1962, 1963). Beyond the Iroquois, much of the early ethnographic literature on American Indian women was an extension of the material culture emphasis that dominated the research of American anthropologists. No matter how meager the data on other aspects of their lives, the one area where there was an abundance of information was on their work in technology and art (Mason 1894). During the first half of the 20th century, the ethnographic record on American Indian women increased not only in its scope but in its attention to detail as well. This was a consequence of the fact that most anthropologists trained in North America before 1960 had at least one field experience in an American Indian community. Several of these anthropologists were women, some of whom gave special attention to the lives of females in the communities they studied. The efforts of early ethnographers to document various aspects of women's lives must be acknowledged, for it is in large part through their work that a younger generation of scholars has been able to study the ethnographic record in the light of recent developments in feminist scholarship.

Since the feminist movement in the 1970s, there has been a renewed interest in studying the experiences of American Indian women. Much of the older and newer research has been reviewed in three sources (Bataille and Sands 1984; Green 1983; Medicine 1978) that contain extensive annotated bibliographies, and in a variety of essays that focus on specific culture areas or ethnic groups, including the Northeast (Kidwell 1979), Plains (Liberty 1979; Weist 1980), California (E. Wallace 1978), and Navajo (Frisbie 1982). The existing literature on American Indian women covers a variety of societies and subjects, but most of it consists of autobiography and descriptive ethnography that lack an explicit theoretical and interpretive focus.

Only some of the newer studies on American Indian women have been influenced by current developments in feminist scholarship. One body of recent feminist writing includes revisionist studies that review and critique conventional treatments in historical and ethnographic sources (Bataille and Sands 1984; Green 1980, 1983; Kehoe 1983; Knack 1988; Leacock 1980; Schneider 1983; Weist 1980, 1983). Among other things, these works have shown how Euro-American observers imposed their own biases on interpretations of native women. More specifically, they have shown how scholarly and popular discourse has been filled with contradictory forms of representation. For any given American Indian society, evidence can be found that supports both the idea of female power/autonomy and the notion of female subordination/dependence, even in the work of the same ethnographer (cf. Judith Brown's discussion [1975:237–239] of Morgan's writings on the Iroquois). There is no question that much of the contradiction can be traced to the differing assumptions of the observers. Yet, it is also clear that some of the disagreement reveals considerable variation and change in the lives of American Indian women over time and place.

The other major body of feminist literature is problem oriented, and it is influenced primarily by two different approaches: cultural constructionism and historical materialism. The cultural constructionists, on the one hand, are interested in how American Indian cultures have marked, conceptualized, and privileged their gender categories in such areas as labor, sexuality, and ritual. Most constructionist writings draw on conventional ethnographic sources that contain rich material on cultural symbolism but have little time depth. The historical materialists, on the other hand, are concerned with how the lives of American Indian women changed under the impact of Euro-American colonization. The data base of the historical materialists is largely documentary, including the writings of explorers, traders, and other early observers of American Indian life. Although the ethnohistorical record is diachronic, reliable data arc limited largely to aspects of native economy and politics. Since the work of anthropologists who follow these theoretical approaches is seminal to issues at the cutting edge of feminist scholarship and at the forefront of American Indian ethnography, it serves as a focal point for further discussion.

The Cultural Construction of Gender

The institutionalization of the *berdache* status in North American Indian societies has been a popular subject in introductory anthropology texts. Historically, at least, it served as one of many institutions to illustrate the idea of cultural relativism as it applied to understanding how ''abnormality'' is dealt with in human societies. Notwithstanding its ethnocentric biases, conventional interpretation obscured rather than revealed the cultural dimensions that gave the *berdache* status form and meaning. In contrast to earlier views (Devereux 1937; Hoebel 1960; Kroeber 1940), where the *berdache* was described in a language of isolation and deviance, feminist studies (Blackwood 1984; Callender and Kochems 1983; Martin and Voorhies 1975; Medicine 1983; Whitehead 1981; Williams 1986) see the *berdache* and other transformative statuses as an integral part of the entire cultural canvas on which gender is painted and differentiated in American Indian communities. Although feminist interpretations differ, they share an overriding interest in understanding the ways gender is culturally marked and privileged. By embedding the study of gender in wider ideological and social formations, these and other cultural constructionist studies (DeMallie 1983; Kehoe 1970, 1973, 1976; Powers 1986; Schlegel 1977, 1979) have shown not only how the concept of gender differs cross-culturally but also how the symbols that are salient to gender categories vary as well.

Gender, Role, and Identity

As Kay Martin and Barbara Voorhies (1975:88–107) argue, folk classifications of gender are variable and not limited to models built around the notion of two mutually exclusive sexes. One of the conclusions to be drawn from their work and other recent writings (Blackwood 1984; Whitehead 1981) is that the cultural construction of gender is not a simple or direct reflection of anatomical sex differences. This is especially true in native North America, where there is good documentation of gender variance in role and identity. Most of this literature deals with the institutionalized position of the *berdache*—a status where men take on the occupations, dress, and demeanor of women (Callender and Kochems 1983; Jacobs 1968; Martin and Voorhies 1975; Miller 1982; Thayer 1980; Whitehead 1981; Williams 1986). Some of the writings also consider cases involving transformative gender identities among females, but only two articles (Blackwood 1984; Medicine 1983) have concentrated on women.

The name, *berdache,* is a generic word that is used to identify a variety of institutionalized roles involving changes in the gender status of men, even though its historic etymology has no relationship with conventional usage in the ethnographic literature (Callender and Kochems 1983; Jacobs 1968). This term has been applied to women as well, but some scholars (Blackwood 1984) have argued for the adoption of a generic label that is sex neutral (e.g., cross-gender) or specific to women, as in Walter Williams' (1986:233–234) recent use of the expression ''Amazon.'' Part of the problem with generic names is that their accepted meaning is too specific to encompass the variable ways in which gender was conceptualized and classified in historic American Indian societies. In some societies, such as the Navajo, there was a third-gender category into which both women and men who changed their gender identity were tracked (Martin and Voorhies 1975:89–92). In others, including the Mohave, there were cross-gender categories and separate statuses for female and male gender transformers (Blackwood 1984:29–32). Finally, there were societies such as the Lakota in which the system of gender classification was bifurcated, but in which there was a spectrum of institutionalized roles that represented a mixing or merging of opposite sex attributes in either a woman or a man (DeMallie 1983; Medicine 1983).

No matter how gender transformation was classified and conceptualized, it displayed tremendous variation in native North America. American Indian gender transformers could play the role of the opposite sex all of the time or some of the time. They could dress the part always, sometimes, or not at all. They could be heterosexual, homosexual, or bisexual in their choice of sex partners, and they could marry or remain single. Finally, they might have specialized ritual and/or occupational roles unique to their position or not (cf. Callender and Kochems [1983] for a thorough review of this variation).

Also varied were the ways in which gender change was recognized and sanctioned in American Indian communities. In most of the reported cases, the potentiality for change was recognized by the self-initiated preferences of a child for certain kinds of opposite sex activities and appearances, and/or in the arrival of dreams and visions which supernaturally sanctioned the transformation in the child's gender identity as an adult (Callender and Kochems 1983; Whitehead 1981; Williams 1986). In other cases, however, the role was not entirely self-initiated but was influenced by the expectations of others. Among the Kaska, girls were raised as males when their fathers had no sons (Honigmann 1954:129–130). The Lakota and Piegan often socialized women in manly ways because of a favored child status (Medicine 1983:272).

Even though historic American Indian societies varied in how they conceptualized and incorporated gender transformation into the social fabric of their communities, they recognized that anatomical sex and gender identity were not identical. With some exceptions (e.g., Pima), they not only permitted but also institutionalized changes in gender status. The institutionalization of transformative gender statuses has been reported historically in 113 American Indian societies (Callender and Kochems 1983), with 33 of these having a special position for female gender transformers (Blackwood 1984:29). As a result of pressures from their European colonizers, however, the attitudes of some American Indians toward gender transformation changed and became less tolerant over time. Nevertheless, American Indian female and male gender transformers still exist, and in some communities, they continue to lead lives that conform to their acquired gender status rather than their anatomical sex (Williams 1986:131–232). The existence of gender variation in the roles and behavior of women as well as men has led to much theorizing about why this variance has been accepted and institutionalized in American Indian communities.

Personhood, Production, and Prestige

Basic to recent interpretations of gender variance by feminist scholars (Blackwood 1984; Medicine 1983; Whitehead 1981) is their focus on notions of "personhood" in historic American Indian societies. Of particular importance is the widespread autonomy accorded to individuals in the expression of their personal identity as defined by such things as the work they perform, the sacred roles they play, and the social statuses they occupy. Ideas of individual freedom are found in permissive childrearing practices, in interactive patterns expressing noninterference, and in beliefs that respect the integrity of every person's unique character (Lee 1959; Lurie 1972). The possibility of, and tolerance for, variance in gender identity is clearly an extension of American Indian notions of autonomous personhood.

Taking this argument further, one feminist anthropologist, Harriet Whitehead (1981), has attempted to explain the widespread institutionalization of gender transformation by examining the kinds of criteria American Indians used historically to mark and differentiate gender. According to Whitehead (1981:82–84, 95–97), unlike European societies, anatomical sex and sex object preference were not salient markers of gender. Homosexuality, for example, could exist for both females and males without signifying a change in their gender identity (Whitehead 1981:83). Instead, Whitehead (1981:99–109) argues that the cutting edge of gender identity in American Indian societies was the kind of secular/sacred work people performed. Although acknowledging that gender was defined by a constellation of characteristics, she argues that occupational roles were the most salient markers in gender differentiation, and that they were at the core of symbolic imagery sanctioning gender transformations in dreams, visions, and myths.

Paradoxically, even though productive labor was a critical symbolic marker of gender, the occupational turf of women and men was not rigorously defended in many American Indian societies (Blackwood 1984:33; Buffalohead 1983:238–243; Whitehead 1981:103–109). Among the foraging and highly egalitarian populations of the Great Basin, many of the tasks customarily performed by women and men were readily interchangeable as situations demanded (Friedl 1975:34–36). Even among societies of the Great Plains, where occupational segregation was more rigidly defined, women and men crossed their respective labor boundaries on a circumstantial basis. In addition, women as well as men could become competent in certain tasks associated with the opposite sex without becoming stigmatized or losing their gender identity (Medicine 1983; Schneider 1983; Weist 1980). Although there were cultural differences in the manner and degree in which various occupational domains were crossed by women and men, these were rarely closed. The kinds of institutionalized boundaries that would have prohibited people from taking on the productive role of the opposite sex did not exist in most American Indian societies (Whitehead 1981:105).

Just as important as the openness of occupational boundaries was the relative equality of prestige accorded to people who excelled in their work. Several recent articles (Albers and Medicine 1983; Brown 1975; Buffalohead 1983; Conte 1982; Grumet 1980; Kehoe 1976; L. Klein 1980; Nowak 1979; Rothenberg 1980) have documented how American Indian women followed independent avenues to prestige, power, and wealth in their communities. Since females in many American Indian societies had the liberty to dispose of their property and the fruits of their own labor as they saw fit, the excellence of their productive work benefited them directly (Whitehead 1981:104). Among such widely separated groups as the Ojibway (Buffalohead 1983), Paiute (Knack 1988), Blackfoot (Kehoe 1976), Iroquois (Brown 1975), Hopi (Schlegel 1977), and Tlingit (L. Klein 1980), the work customarily performed by women could be a source of prestige and wealth for those who pursued it. Not only could men gain reknown for their achievements in the domain of female work, but women could also derive prestige for their participation in activities usually performed by males. Thus, when women excelled in warfare, they achieved the same kinds of prestige as their male warrior counterparts (Landes 1968:69; Medicine 1983:174). Importantly, when people achieved prestige through channels most often utilized by the opposite sex, it was not perceived as a threat to established notions of femininity or masculinity (L. Spindler and G. Spindler 1979:36–37; Whitehead 1981:104–109).

While it is clear that the sexual division of labor was flexible and that the productive labor of both sexes offered avenues to prestige and wealth, it is not obvious whether these conditions, while necessary, were sufficient to bring about the institutionalization of transformative gender statuses in various American Indian societies. Indeed, as the work of Evelyn Blackwood (1984) suggests, the crux of the matter may lie elsewhere and be embedded in the kinds of social formations that reproduced historic American Indian societies on a daily and generational basis.

Relationship, Reproduction, and Ritual

Notwithstanding the value placed on personal autonomy, no historic American Indian society was a congerie of independently functioning and self-actualizing individuals. Individual freedom was always defined in its relationship to social responsibility. In theory and in practice, the two represented opposite sides of the same coin. The freedom of individuals to achieve and excel was never realized or acknowledged unless at some level it was linked to the well-being of some wider community (Lee 1959).

Symbolically and in everyday life, the relationship between American Indian women and men tended toward complementarity (Blackwood 1984; Leacock 1978), though Harriet Whitehead (1981) maintains that these relationships were hierarchical. Prior to extensive colonization, complementarity appears to have marked the character of relationships between women and men among the Iroquois (Nowak 1979), the Tlingit (L. Klein 1980), the Navajo (Hamamsy 1957), Hopi (Schlegel 1977), Montagnais (Leacock 1980), Shawnee (Howard 1981), and Ojibwa (Buffalohead 1983) as well as among native societies in California (E. Wallace 1978) and the Great Basin (Knack 1988). In other cases, as among the Blackfoot (Kehoe 1976; A. Klein 1983a), complementarity was an intrinsic part of the sex role plan on an ideological level although the conditions under which this group was living after contact often prevented it from being fully realized in everyday life. Yet, even in those situations where the ideological plan as well as social reality revealed a basic asymmetry, as among the Papago (Sanday 1981:41–45; Underhill 1979) and Lakota (Powers 1986), women were not a disenfranchised and socially unproductive class.

Comparatively speaking, American Indian women had considerable input in the decisions underlying spouse selection and divorce (Blackwood 1984). Among groups such as the Hopi (Schlegel 1977), Paiute (Knack 1980), Navajo (Reichard 1928), Iroquois (Nowak 1979), Santee Dakota (Landes 1968), Blackfoot (Kehoe 1976), and Ojibwa (Buffalohead 1983), marriage rested ideally on a bond created through mutual consensus and respect, not the dominance of one spouse and the subordination of the other. In these societies, a man could not freely appropriate the products of his wife's labor without her consent. Nor did males control the reproductive power of women. Women were active in arranging marriage for their daughters and sons, they could easily dissolve their own marriages. Even among the Lakota, where there were elaborate restrictions on female sexuality, the meaning of practices such as the use of chastity belts was not to maintain virginity for the honor and sexual pleasures of men but rather to increase the fertility of women (Powers 1986:71–73).

As would be expected, women experienced the greatest marital freedoms in societies with uterine patterns of descent and residence (Schlegel 1972). In societies with agnatic systems, there were more restrictions but women were rarely powerless in the decisions surrounding their marital fate (Kidwell 1979; Weist 1980). Evelyn Blackwood (1984:33–34) argues that much of the freedom experienced by American Indian women was a consequence of the fact that the institution of marriage was not heavily invested. Property exchanges at marriage were not extensive and involved only limited obligations between the intermarrying families. In this context, she maintains that a daughter's marriage was not needed in maintaining family rank. Women who were social males, and I would add men who were socially female, could contribute to the well-being of their kin groups through their own productive labors and through marriages to people of the same sex whose children from other unions could be adopted (Blackwood 1984:34). Thus, marriage and marital status were not pivotal markers of gender identity.

Although American Indian societies clearly supported the notion that most of what women and men could do was not restricted by their anatomical sex, they recognized that the human condition is not permeable when it comes to the role that women and men play in sexual reproduction. Procreative sexuality did differentiate women from men, and the one area where there were rigid gender boundaries was in the ritual domain that maintained and ensured the life force and power of the community. Whether sex segregation in ritual was accomplished by women and men occupying different roles in the same ceremony or by performing separate ceremonies, these were the situations where gender boundaries were inviolable (Howard 1981:191–342; Kehoe 1970, 1973, 1976; Nelson 1976). Symbolically and ritually, women were seen as possessing a unique generative power that could be ritually released for the good of the community as in the Sun Dance of the Lakota (Powers 1986) and Blackfoot (Kehoe 1976) or in girls' puberty ceremonies among the Navajo (Frisbie 1967) and Apache (Farrer 1980).

At the time of menstruation and parturition, this power was perceived as inimical to other powers, including but not restricted to those generated by men. It was not viewed as defiling or degrading, however (Buckley 1982; Devereux 1950; Powers 1980). It was ritualized and handled in much the same way as other liminal life-giving/life-taking powers (Milicic 1986). Yet, it could be denied (or made barren) when females transformed their gender identity in manly ways (Blackwood 1984:32), and/or among some groups, when they entered a special, supernaturally sanctioned status that permitted sexual promiscuity (Medicine 1983:272).

Although anatomy per se and sex object preference may have been inconsequential in American Indian gender classification and identity, procreative sexuality did differentiate women from men. It also separated transformed gender identities from nontransformed ones. It was in the symbolic negation of procreation that gender transformation was conceptualized. Gender transformers occupied a liminal status in which the reproductive power of their own sex was denied. Nothing symbolizes this idea of barrenness more poignantly than in the Lakota image of the Double-Woman, who determined the engendered destinies of both women and men. A dead fetus hangs from the rope that ties the Double-Woman together (DeMallie 1983:247). Because gender transformers combined male and female characteristics, some anthropologists have argued that they represented a mediating category which symbolically unified the opposition of femaleness and maleness (DeMallie 1983; Thayer 1980). It can also be argued, however, that they were more like the clown or contrary, whose power was generated in the dialectical negation of their own procreative role (Miller 1982).

No matter what kinds of ritual symbolism were attached to gender transformation, American Indian societies were societies in which production was a production of use values (or simple exchange values), and production that was socially useful was also reproduction in a daily and generational sense (Leacock 1978). Since the forces and relations of production were not widely separated from those of reproduction, it is not surprising that the sexual division of labor and procreation were wedded metaphorically in constructions of gender (cf. Mary Black's discussion [1984] of Hopi corn metaphors). When the two stood in a paradoxical relationship, as was the case with gender transformers, the persons who embodied the contradiction were not denied a place in society. With few exceptions, they were incorporated into the social nexus in meaningful and valued ways. This incorporation was possible not only because it was supernaturally sanctioned and beyond human intervention, but because everything in the state of being male and female, except for procreation, was potentially open and interchangeable.

Since there was not an invidious distinction between what was "male identified" versus "female identified," neither sex inevitably lost or gained status as a result of changing their gender identity completely or taking on certain characteristics of the opposite sex (Blackwood 1984). In the final analysis, it can be argued that gender was not a heavily loaded concept— represented by fixed, tightly integrated and/or hierarchically ranked markers. It was not a superordinate status that tracked and classified people in immutable and narrow ways. Instead, it was a fluid entity whose saliency was variably expressed and grounded in the characteristics of social formations that were kin ordered and largely egalitarian. It was these kinds of social formations that provided the foundation for tolerating and even nurturing transformative gender statuses and other autonomous expressions of personhood.

Women and Colonization

Notwithstanding the fact that much of the ethnographic record represents the lives of American Indian women in a "pristine" and stable state, no interpretation of their historic experience can proceed without a solid understanding of the impact of European colonization on the New World. To its credit, much of the feminist research on the status and role of American Indian women takes it as a matter of course that interpretation must proceed within a solidly documented ethnohistorical framework. In contrast to acculturation studies (Downs 1972; McElroy 1975, 1979; L. Spindler 1962) that look at the consequences of contact as revealed in changing personality and value orientations, most feminist studies focus attention on the political and economic conditions which transformed the lives of American Indian women under colonization, and they draw on dependency theory and related historical materialist perspectives.

What the results of recent research indicate is that colonization has not impacted American Indian women in uniform ways. The data suggest that women's status may have risen among certain groups during early periods of contact (Rothenberg 1980), whereas it declined among others (A. Klein 1983a; Leacock 1980; Perry 1979). Women's base of power was eroded after the formation of reservations in some areas (Albers 1983b; Poole 1986; Rothenberg 1980), while it did not change substantially in others (Hamamsy 1957; L. Klein 1980). In some communities women have expanded their political and economic influence since the 1960s (Albers 1985; Lynch 1986; Powers 1986), although in others it appears to remain quite limited (Weaver 1972). Finally, it is apparent that even within the same population, change has been experienced by women in different ways (Hamamsy 1957; L. Spindler 1962). This kind of diversity defies easy generalization, but it does provide a rich and variable data base in which to identify some of the historical forces that have had an impact on the changing status and role of American Indian women (cf. Etienne and Leacock [1980:1–24] for a good theoretical overview of this subject).

Labor, Kinship, and Politics under Mercantile Expansion: 1500–1850

The period between 1500 and 1850 roughly corresponds with the era of mercantile expansion in North America. It was a time during which most native populations were organized around what Eric Wolf (1982:88–100) calls a "kin-ordered mode of production," but with tremendous variation in the specifics of organization. They included band level foragers (e.g., Paiute, Piegan, Ojibwa), lineage based horticulturalists (e.g., Iroquois, Hopi, Shawnee) and quasi-chiefdoms (e.g., Natchez) (cf. Alice Kehoe's [1981] excellent text on American Indians for a general overview). Within the panoply of divergent kinship orders and subsistence economies, there was considerable variation in what Peggy Sanday (1981) has called "sex role plans." The historic literature offers a wealth of general and particular information on the diversity of these plans in situations where American Indian populations were not only removed from the direct impact of colonization but also where they stood in the path of European trade and settlement.

Changes in native life that altered the role and status of women were a product of a complex set of relationships which included: (1) the distinctive and historically developed characteristics of their own social formations; and (2) the particular and changing associations native populations maintained with their colonizers. On the side of native social formations, preexisting patterns of descent, residence, and the division of labor determined whether the status of women would be enhanced, maintained, or diminished by the colonizing experience. On the side of colonizing relationships, new forms of economic appropriation, the appearance of epidemic disease, and the pressures of Christian missionary activity all played a part in altering the roles of American Indian women. Many forces impacted the changing position of American Indian women under colonization, but the evidence suggests that some of the most profound changes were a consequence of the degree to which native economic activity became specialized and dependent on mercantile markets. More specifically, the data indicate that where local populations evolved specialized economies dependent on European markets, and where female work was subsumed under a labor process dominated by men, the status of women declined. In situations where a dependency on these markets was secondary, or where it did not alter existing social formations, the status of women remained stable and in a few situations may have been enhanced. This can be illustrated by contrasting several case examples from different regions of North America.

The best historical documentation on the changing position of American Indian women comes from the Iroquois. During the early years of contact (c. 1540–1640), the ethnohistoric record presents a picture of a society where women occupied strategic positions in their households and where they wielded considerable economic influence (Trigger 1978). Judith Brown (1975) has argued that much of their early power can be traced to a division of labor, where women not only produced most of the food but where they also controlled its distribution within and outside of their households. The social formation, in which this production was embedded and in which property rights were determined, was organized around a series of matrilineal descent groups or *ohwachira*. Under the supervision of matrons, who were selected from among the membership of a matrilineage, women organized and managed the cooperative groups that worked in the fields, and they had custodial rights over the lands under cultivation as well (Brown 1975:243–250).

Where production, residence, and descent are centered around uterine kin groups, women often occupy a strategic position in the activities of their families and communities (Schlegel 1972). While this kind of social organization provides a necessary foundation for female autonomy and influence, it is not sufficient to explain the considerable power Iroquois women exercised from the late 17th to the mid-18th centuries. The character of this power has been described in a variety of different sources (Brown 1975; Hewitt 1932; Nowak 1979; Randle 1951; Richards 1957; Rothenberg 1976, 1980; Synderman 1948; Tooker 1984; Trigger 1978). Among other things, it included the right of women to select the men who would represent their matrilineages as *sachems* (leaders) in public councils and the right to remove them when they failed to represent a kin group's interests. As Barbara Nowak (1979:97) argues, it was their institutionalized functions in moderating the powers of men that gave women such a high status among the Iroquois, and it was these functions which increased in historic times.

The rise of women's status accompanied the growing involvement of the Iroquois in the European fur trade. The fur-bearing animals, whose peltries were exchanged for trade goods, were depleted in the Iroquois' home territory not long after direct trade was established with Europeans. As a result, the Iroquois had to acquire peltries from the lands of their neighbors through trading, trapping, or thieving. All of these strategies were followed, but the ones that came to dominate Iroquois procurement practices until the 18th century were raiding and warfare. From 1630 to 1701, the Iroquois were engulfed in a series of bitter wars that were waged over access to peltries and fur-bearing land. One consequence of this was that an increasing proportion of male productive labor was devoted to war and other activities that supported Iroquois dependency on the fur trade. As men spent less time in the food quest, the importance of female contributions to subsistence increased. Female subsistence work became a vital component of Iroquois involvement in the fur trade because it supplied men with the provisions they needed to sustain their own specialized labor activities (Nowak 1979:97; Rothenberg 1980:70). Females also played an important role in trading. Records from the early 18th century indicate that men often turned their furs over to women because females were considered shrewder traders, and one account book reveals that 20% of the Iroquois who traded at a post in Albany were women (Norton 1974:28, 35). In general, the ethnohistoric data indicate that the conditions of the fur trade intensified women's control over basic resources.

Another interpretation is that the power of Iroquois women turned on their role in the adoption of war captives. Warfare coupled with epidemic disease took a major toll in the lives of Iroquois men, and the loss of this manpower was recouped by adopting outside males into the community (Synderman 1948:13–10). Since women held an important place in societal provisioning, they played an active role in deciding which captives would be killed or adopted (Hewitt 1932:480; Richards 1957:36–38; Synderman 1948:79). The role that Iroquois women played in replenishing societal manpower through adoption and other means cannot be ignored in explanations of their rising status, and it is surprising that this explanation has been given only passing notice in feminist writings on the Iroquois.

Added to the decline in the male population, there is the fact that warfare and trapping required young men to travel long distances and spend time away from home. Some scholars (Sanday 1973; A. Wallace 1947) have suggested that the extended absence of Iroquois men from their communities created a political vacuum which was filled by women. This is probably the most widely accepted explanation of the rise in female power among the Iroquois, but it is not entirely sufficient because a pattern of extended male absence continued in Iroquois communities long after the political influence of women was eroded (Rothenberg 1980).

Putting the various explanations together, it can be argued that under the conditions of colonization, which contributed to labor intensification, population decline and male absence, the stability of the Iroquois nation and its villages was maintained by a historically developed social formation that organized political continuity and succession through the ties of mothers/daughters and sisters/brothers (cf. Sacks [1982] for an enlightening theoretical discussion of the implications of descent on the politics of gender). As women played a more important economic role under the fur trade, they were in an increasingly powerful position to exercise autonomy and to extend authority beyond their households and matrilineages. Women provided the productive and reproductive ballast, as it were, to reformulate Iroquois political structure in such a way that it could ensure continuity through the female line when the lives and contributions of its men were subject to uncertainty.

Whatever explanations have been offered for the rising status of women among the Iroquois, it is clear that a complex set of interacting conditions were involved in this change. Although the position of Iroquois women was high, it was not exceptional. As Robert Grumet's (1980) research indicates, women were also highly influential among the neighboring Coastal Algonkian. Like the Iroquois, descent and residence were organized around matrilineal descent groups where women occupied strategic positions in the management of land and in the production and distribution of food. Coastal Algonkian women were traders who bartered surplus food and furs for European goods, and they were peace leaders in their own right. Among the Coastal Algonkian, women's base of power does not appear to have been related to any pattern of extended male absence, although it may have been affected by attritions in the size of the male population as a result of disease and warfare. Instead, it appears to have rested directly on female activities that supported the Coastal Algonkians' early dependence on European trade.

Whether women's production in horticulture articulated directly with the European trade or indirectly by supporting the specialized work of men, it appears to have been critical in maintaining or enhancing female autonomy and power. This is confirmed by data from other regions of North America as well. In the Northern Plains, where the status of women among the buffalo-hunting nomads declined, it does not appear to have been substantially eroded among the horticultural villagers. The horticultural activity of women among the Hidatsa and Mandan, for example, not only supported subsistence but it was also a basic component in the trade these villagers maintained with Europeans and neighboring Indian populations. The distribution of corn and other horticultural products inside their villages and beyond was under the control of women (Weist 1980:272). In the Southwest, Hopi women also appear to have retained a strong position under colonization, but their strength resided not in the fact that they were horticultural producers, but that they owned the land on which their husbands produced the crops which they then distributed within and outside the household (Ford 1983:716; Schlegel 1977). Unlike many other populations in the Southwest, the Hopi were relatively isolated and do not appear to have become greatly involved in a commercial trade with Europeans until the mid-19th century.

Among the Iroquois, Coastal Algonkian, Hidatsa-Mandan, and Hopi, production by women and their custodial rights to land and resources were embedded in systems that were organized around matrilineal or uterine principles. Females maintained control over their own sectors of production in the early years of contact. Even in situations where populations developed a specialized sphere of production aimed at European markets, female productive activity was not supplanted nor was it subordinated by a labor domain under male control. Importantly, women retained their spheres of economic independence and in some situations were able to utilize this autonomy to build institutionalized positions of power beyond their households.

This stands in marked contrast to what happened to women among the foraging societies of the Northern Plains, where female power was eroded as a result of a growing dependence on mercantile trade (A. Klein 1983a, 1983b; O. Lewis 1942; Liberty 1979, 1982; Weist 1980). Prior to the European trade and the acquisition of horses in the mid-18th century, the hunting of buffalo among Plains Indian nomads was oriented to consumption and simple exchange with their horticultural neighbors. Buffalo hunting was a communal effort in which both men and women were involved, and everyone who participated in the hunt received a share of the product. After the arrival of horses, which were secured initially through trade and later by raiding, the buffalo hunt became an equestrian activity in which women played no direct role, and as a result, women were removed from a strategic position in the productive process (A. Klein 1983b:153). In the late 18th century, when a commercial market in meat and hides developed, buffalo hunting became a form of surplus production. In order to maintain access to European commodities, an increasing amount of male labor time was spent in hunting buffalo, raiding for horses (both a means of production and a commodity in exchange), and fighting over access to hunting grounds and trade routes. In contrast to the Iroquois, a substantial and direct investment of female labor was required to maintain Plains Indian dependency on mercantile markets. Hides had to be tanned and meat processed into pemmican in order for their commodity value to be realized, and both activities were labor intensive. Among other things, this created a situation where females became workers in a highly specialized production process over which men had ultimate control. As a result, the means of wealth accumulation and prestige were increasingly in the hands of men (A. Klein 1983b:156–158).

Beyond its impact on the division of labor, mercantile expansion brought about significant changes in other areas of Plains Indian social organization. Men needed many wives to process the hides and meats they procured, and polygamous marriages increased as a result (O. Lewis 1942; Weist 1980). In addition, there was a shift toward agnatic patterns of residence, especially among bands who lived on the borders of contested hunting lands and who were most directly involved in warfare with neighboring groups (Moore 1988). Finally, there was a growth in all-male sodalities that played a pivotal role in the affairs of the interband councils. Many of the governing powers once invested in kin groups now became the formal or informal prerogative of the solidarities. As the political and economic role of these groups increased, the kinship avenues through which females asserted their influence became strategically less important (A. Klein 1983b:158–164). Once males controlled production and community decision making, they also exercised increasing power over the destiny of households and the reproduction of their members. In fact, it was the nomadic groups who were most involved in hide production that placed the greatest restrictions on female sexuality (Weist 1980:258–259).

The decline in female status was not uniform, however. There were variations among Northern Plains societies in the relative influence of women. Although the Dakota (Santee or Eastern Sioux) and the Lakota (Teton or Western Sioux) shared a common ethnic background, they became differentiated, ethnically and socially, as a result of the impact of mercantile capitalism. The Lakota were heavily involved in the hide and horse traffic of the High Plains, but the Dakota who lived in the Low Plains were not. The Dakota's dependence on mercantile markets was based on the fur trade. Unlike their relatives further west, Dakota productive activities were much less specialized, and they followed an annual round that shifted between labor activities dominated by women (e.g., maple sugar harvesting in spring) and by men (e.g., deer hunting in fall). The composition of residence groups was situationally determined and organized around the sex who was most important in the subsistence task at hand. Polygamy was not widespread and all-male sodalities were absent or weakly developed. Women had autonomy over their own productive activities, they had a say in their marital destiny, and there were institutionalized channels through which they could influence community decision making (Landes 1968). Following many of the standard criteria that are used to judge female status (Sanday 1981), the position of women among the Dakota was higher than it was among their Lakota kin.

Yet, even among the Lakota and other buffalo-hunting nomads of the high plains, there were institutionalized areas where women did retain a base of power and influence. Mary Jane Schneider (1983) has documented how women achieved wealth and prestige in their own right through their artistic efforts, Beatrice Medicine (1983) has shown how women could use male avenues of raiding and warfare to gain reknown, and Alice Kehoe (1970, 1973, 1976, 1983) and Marla Powers (1980, 1986) have described how women exercised important ritual powers. On balance, the Plains Indian literature indicates that while the influence of women became more circumscribed, females were not powerless and maintained autonomy in many areas of production and social life after the expansion of mercantile markets.

The Subarctic is another region where the status of women declined as a direct result of the growing presence of European commerce. Writings by Eleanor Leacock (1980, 1981) and Karen Anderson (1985) on the Montagnais, Richard Perry's work (1977, 1979) on the Northern Athapaskan, and Sylvia Van Kirk's book (1980) on the Canadian fur trade describe some of the impacts of mercantilism on women's lives. Comparing ethnohistorical documents on the Dogrib, Yellowknife, and Chipewyan, Perry (1979) identifies a direct connection between a group's involvement in the fur trade and the declining status of women. As in the Plains, variations in the changing status of Subarctic Indian women appear to be linked to the degree to which local populations developed specialized, fur-trade economies. Among the Montagnais and Chipewyan, female autonomy and labor activity were subordinated by productive and social changes organized around the growing economic dominance of beaver trapping. In contrast, women's base of power was not completely eroded among foraging groups like the western Ojibwa of Minnesota. Here local economic activity remained diversified and only partially dependent on fur trapping, and as Priscilla Buffalohead's (1983) study suggests, women continued to retain autonomy and exercise influence in many different areas of native life. Similarly, much of the evidence on the Inuit of the Arctic (Agar 1980; Matthiasson 1979) suggests that their involvement in the fur trade was secondary, and it did not alter a preexisting division of labor where women exercised controls over their own work and its product.

It is also the case that mercantile markets did not fundamentally change the forces and relations of indigenous production among some Northwest Coast groups (Littlefield 1988). Evidence on the Tlingit indicates that women played an important role not only in production but also in trade. As Laura Klein (1980:89–98) points out, women managed the wealth and trade in traditional Tlingit society—a role they continued to play in commercial dealings with Europeans (L. Klein 1980:89–98). They were also the ones who supervised the accumulation of potlatch gifts used in ceremonies to validate inherited names and privileges that went to women as well as men. Indeed, women sometimes assumed names associated with chiefly positions (L. Klein 1980:94).

Finally, women's status remained stable among the egalitarian, foraging societies of the Great Basin, where gathering was more important than hunting. The persistence of female autonomy in this region was a consequence of many things, including the continued importance of women's role in food production. Pinyon nuts gathered by women were not only a major food staple, but they were also one of the few native commodities that Great Basin peoples could trade with whites. During the mid-19th century, when most Great Basin populations began to have direct contact with whites, they were incorporated into the systems of their colonizers through various kinds of labor servitude. Women as well as men worked in the mining and agricultural settlements of local whites (Knack 1988). In addition, among some groups, women entered the cash economy through their basketry work. By the beginning of the 20th century, a number of the well-known basketmakers among the Washo had white patrons who supported these females and their families (Fowler and Dawson 1986:730–734). Able to contribute directly, and in some cases substantially, to the provisioning of their families, Great Basin Indian women did not lose their autonomy within their households and communities (Knack 1980, 1988).

If any generalizations can be made about the changing status of American Indian women under the rise of mercantilism, two stand out: (1) that American Indian women had considerable autonomy and influence within their households and communities, and that this was related to the controls they exercised over production and property; and (2) that when production and the fruits of female work were subsumed under labor processes dominated by men, the status of women declined. In many historic American Indian communities, there was not a pronounced separation between the strategic interests of women and men. Female-male relationships tended toward complementarity (Leacock 1978). When European markets shifted a group's economic activity toward a surplus production of commodities dominated by male labor activity, a schism appeared in the interests of women and men. However, it was only when this division also led to a subordination of female labor that women lost power and influence, and this is clearly what happened among the foragers of the Northern Plains. By contrast, even though the fur trade precipitated a widening cleavage in female-male interests among horticulturalists in the Northeast, women were not disenfranchised because they continued to maintain an active involvement in their own sectors of production.

The State, Property, and Household under Capitalism: 1850 to the Present

The years after 1850 coincide with the eras of capitalist agricultural and industrial expansion. In the early period, before 1910, native populations were being resettled on reservations and reserves. With some exceptions, the beginning of reservation settlement marked the end of whatever independence American Indians may have retained under mercantilism and the destruction of a way of life based on foraging and/or horticulture. It was a time of radical change for many American Indians, and it was a period in which the lives of women were altered in profound ways as well (cf. Joseph Jorgenson [1978] for a good political economic overview and analysis of this era).

What the modern data suggest is that, today as in the past, the experiences of American Indian women under colonization have not been uniform, and that their relative status is the result of a complex interplay between the historically developed patterns of relationship prevailing in their own settlements and the changing conditions of the capitalist states in which these communities have become embedded. In modern times, women's lives have been affected by many different forces, but it has been the intervention of various state and church Indian policies that have had some of the most significant impacts on their experience. As these policies have changed over time, they have played a varied and often contradictory role in influencing female status. Several contrasting case examples illustrate this process.

Once again, the example of the Iroquois provides a good point of departure. After the American Revolution, the Iroquois League collapsed, and the Iroquois' position in the fur trade was destroyed. Unable to maintain economic and political independence, they were forced to open their lands to white settlement. The sale of lands and the execution of treaties took place largely outside the legitimate authority structure of *sachems* and their matrilineal descent groups. Under the domination of Canada and the United States, land rights that remained in Iroquois hands were now under the control of men as a form of private property (Nowak 1979:99).

During the years of transition, roughly 1790 to 1820, new forms of production, lumbering and agriculture, were introduced. Among the Seneca, a member nation of the Iroquois, a division of labor emerged where men logged and raised animal fodder crops while women learned white domestic crafts and grew vegetables for consumption and exchange (Rothenberg 1980:78). This transition was accompanied by a number of other changes in female-male relations many of which were sanctioned in the revitalization movement of Handsome Lake (Nowak 1979:100; Rothenberg 1980:78–79). As Anthony Wallace (1969:281) put it, Handsome Lake codified the shift in the "Seneca economic system from a male-hunting-and-female-horticulture to a male-farming-female-housekeeping pattern." Elsewhere a parallel transition was under way, and except at Onondaga and Tonawanda, it was accompanied by the destruction of the traditional hereditary council and its matrilineal support groups. In their place, elected or appointed councils emerged in which women had little or no input. In fact, among the Seneca, women did not obtain the right to vote until 1964 and the right to hold political office until 1966 (Nowak 1979:101; Rothenberg 1980:81). Notwithstanding an erosion of their community-wide powers, women continued to exercise autonomy in their own work and in marriage. While women lacked formal positions in the new political structures, they continued to exercise informal influence (Rothenberg 1980:79–81).

A decline in female power after the formation of reservations is also documented for the Dakota (Albers 1983b, 1985), Lakota (Bysiewicz and Van de Mark 1977), and Wichita (Poole 1988). In these cases, the combined impact of church and state policies transformed communal property relations into private ones, and in so doing, transferred the means of production in farming (e.g., tools, land, knowledge) from women to men. This, in turn, brought about changes in family structure, and in the role of women in their households and communities. Among other things, these policies encouraged an agnatic bias in residence and kin networks, and they supported a division of labor where men became the "breadwinners" and women the "homemakers." Many of the religious ceremonies in which Dakota women once held a vital and equal place (e.g., the *Wakan Wacipi* or Medicine Dance) disappeared and were replaced by Christian and Native American Church rituals where females occupied a subordinate position (Albers 1983b:191). (A similar shift in ceremonial involvement has also been reported for the Menominee [L. Spindler and G. Spindler 1979:36–38] during the reservation era.)

In the case of the Dakota and Lakota, at least, the early decline in the status of women was reversed as a result of changes in state policies after 1950. Instead of supporting family farming and ranching, the new government initiatives encouraged males to become wage laborers and women and children to become dependents of working men or the state. Although employment favored men and provided males with higher wages, jobs were few in number and erratic in duration. In a situation where most males were unable to provide a living wage for themselves, much less a family, the contributions of women from wage work, petty commodity production and welfare assistance became increasingly important in domestic provisioning. As the economic contributions of Dakota and Lakota women rose in relation to men, female autonomy and influence within the household and community also increased. Not only are there more female-headed households today, but an increasing number of extended family networks are organized around uterine ties (Albers 1983b, 1985; Maynard 1979). This change, in turn, has placed women in strategic positions to mobilize and support the extended kin networks that organize community-wide political and ceremonial activity (Albers 1983b; Albers and Medicine 1983; Medicine 1987; Powers 1986).

In some respects, modern Dakota and Lakota females are like the Iroquois women of the early 18th century. Not only do they control basic resources upon which their own household and extended families depend, but they also use these resources to advance family interests in politics and ritual. The increased power of women does not mean that they dominate, but it does mean that there is an increasing parity in their relations with men. In a cultural context where all individual resources are shared but controlled autonomously, and in a social situation where male resources are more erratic than those of women, it is not surprising to find that the daily and generational reproduction of the community is increasingly organized around ties through women.

Unlike the Iroquois, Dakota, and Lakota, the Navajo were able to maintain some of the essential features of their indigenous economy and social organization well into the 20th century. Before reservation settlement, the Navajo were a matrilineal, sheepherding society with a marginal dependence on horticulture and hunting. In traditional Navajo society, women held a central role in production, and they had important property rights as well (Reichard 1928). Until the 1950s, the strategic position of Navajo women in their households and "outfits" persisted in those areas where a domestic-based, sheepherding economy continued, but it was eroded in places where large-scale, commercially oriented cattle or sheep economies were introduced. In both situations, as described by Lila Hamamsy (1957), the means of production shifted increasingly into the hands of men and the status of women declined.

Since the 1950s, sheepherding has remained the hub of a domestic economy that is also dependent on wage labor and welfare assistance. Many in the older generation still live in rural areas and engage in sheepherding, but a growing proportion of younger adults have moved to towns and cities to seek employment. Even though extended families are geographically dispersed and divided into rural/urban sectors, their members are mutually dependent on one another—sharing the resources that come from rural subsistence activity and urban employment (Shepardson 1982). Research by various scholars (Conte 1982; Lamphere 1974, 1975, 1977) has demonstrated that the power of Navajo women is a consequence not only of their economic autonomy but also of their strategic positions in kin-based networks that organize production and reproduction. As Christine Conte's (1982) recent study shows, where sheepherding continues to sustain the domestic economy, Navajo women have considerable influence within extended kin networks. Where Navajo families are dependent on wage labor and/or public assistance, by contrast, many of the kinship avenues through which women exert influence have been eroded as revealed in the work of Ann Metcalf (1979, 1982) on urban Navajo women. In the absence of kin support, these women not only face greater economic uncertainty, but they lack the kinds of social ties that can protect and advance their interests as well.

The persistence of female autonomy in households and domestic groups has also been reported for the Paiute and Tlingit. In both groups, women have played a central role in the provisioning of their families through petty commodity production, wage labor and/or government assistance (L. Klein 1976, 1980; Knack 1980, 1988; Lynch 1986). Among other things, female access to strategic resources has served to consolidate their influence within domestic groups, and this, in turn, has allowed them to expand their power base in community-wide politics. Robert Lynch (1986) has written a detailed case study of this process in one Northern Paiute community, and he has also documented some of the obstacles female leaders have faced in relation to local Bureau of Indian Affairs' officials who favor male leadership. In relation to the Tlingit, Laura Klein (1976:163–167) argues that public leadership has never been sex typed, and as a result, Tlingit women have not had to overcome sex-biased obstacles to assume positions of influence in their kin groups or communities.

If information on the Arctic and Subarctic (Agar 1980; Briggs 1974; Cruikshank 1971; Fiske 1988; McElroy 1979) are added, a compelling picture emerges which indicates: (1) that notwithstanding the impact of church and state policies to the contrary, indigenous and long-standing patterns of female autonomy within domestic groups have persisted into the modern era; (2) that the strong position of women in kin-based networks extends into "public" ceremonial and political domains as well; and (3) that Indian women face profound contradictions vis-à-vis a base of empowerment within their own communities and in relation to the larger societies in which they live.

With respect to the third point, many of today's American Indian women maintain autonomy in their households in relation to their work, property, marital fate, and childbearing decisions. Women are also actively involved in community work and politics aimed at improving the lives of their people: they are tribal administrators and council members as well as leaders of national organizations. In their various leadership roles, women carry influence that is built not only on long-standing traditions which respect the work and autonomy of women, but also on a concrete foundation of female experience and organizing within households, extended kinship networks, and community groups. It is also related to the fact that politics in most contemporary Indian communities are centered around basic reproductive issues—improving jobs, housing, education, and health care as well as protecting community rights in land, water, and mineral resources that can provide for an improved standard of living (Albers 1983b; Chruikshank 1971; Lurie 1972; Lynch 1986; OHOYO 1981; Powers 1986:141–181).

This kind of situation, however, poses a profound contradiction for American Indian women who live in a world dominated by historical traditions based on sexual, class, and racial hierarchy. In the workplace, in government institutions, and in places of public recreation, they are often judged by conceptual models and treated in relationships that deny their autonomy and denigrate their status (Wittsock 1980:207–228). Among other things, American Indian women must combat ideologies of male domination which have been a fundamental feature of the colonizing society that rules them and which have penetrated their own worldviews through the teachings of missionaries, educators, and the media (Allen 1986; OHOYO 1981). In their day-to-day experiences, they must confront the effects of inadequate employment, health care, and educational opportunities. Since most of them live in communities with some of the highest rates of poverty in the United States and Canada, they have experienced many of the consequences of being poor, including being victims of alcohol-related abuse. This abuse is not, nor has it ever been condoned, and it is a major focus of some of the current political struggles American Indian women are waging in their own communities (Powers 1986:173–178).

The work of Louise Spindler (1962) on the Menominee demonstrated that even within the same culture women experienced the impact of colonization in different ways. Consistent with data from the Navajo, her research showed that women in traditional-oriented groups had a higher status than those living among more acculturated groups. This is also supported by research on the Iroquois (Randle 1951; Weaver 1972). A recent study (Albers and Breen 1987) of 1980 census data on American Indians confirms that there is wide variation in the position of American Indian women as revealed by various economic indicators. One of the most significant findings of this research is that the differential income and labor force participation rates of women are higher in reservation than off-reservation settings, and that they are highest in places where Indian employment is dominated by a segregated, Indian preference labor market.

In the final analysis, the status of contemporary American Indian women is paradoxical. This paradox can be explained, in part, by the fact that American Indians have been excluded from a viable place in their national economies, and as a result, a set of material as well as structural conditions have been generated that put women and men in a unique kind of relationship to each other (Jamieson 1981). It is not a relationship built on interests that are divided between the reproductive functions of women and the productive roles of men. Everyone is involved in reproductive strategies that allow people to survive in the absence of work which can provide a living wage. In this situation, the dualism historically associated with capitalism does not divide itself hierarchically along male-female lines in the same way that it does in American and Canadian society at large (Albers 1985:128).

Curriculum Implications

Twenty years ago, introductory anthropology texts drew heavily on the cultural experiences of American Indians for examples and illustration. Today, however, the use of ethnographic materials on North America has decreased significantly. In the works of Felix and Roger Keesing, for example, the 1966 text written by Felix Keesing contained nearly 150 pages devoted to American Indians, while the 1971 coauthored version and the later 1981 text authored by Roger Keesing contained less than 40 pages each on this population. The declining attention given to American Indians in introductory anthropology texts reflects, in part, a shift in the geographic areas anthropologists have been studying in recent years. Much of the newer research appearing in introductory texts comes from areas (e.g., Highland New Guinea) that appeal to the discipline's traditional focus on the "exotic" and that speak directly to topical issues that have been a part of anthropology's intellectual heritage. Salient aspects of contemporary American Indian life, such as the conditions of structural unemployment, do not fit these historical trends.

If American Indians as a population have become less visible in introductory anthropology curricula, then American Indian women have become nonentities. With very few exceptions, American Indian women are not mentioned at all in texts appearing since 1975. Among other things, this absence appears to be related, to two factors. On the one hand, when the subject of gender is raised, it is usually in the context of male-dominated societies (e.g., Yanamamo) rather than ones where, comparatively speaking, females exercised some autonomy and power (e.g., Iroquois). And on the other hand, it has been related to the relative invisibility of American Indian women in much of the ethnographic record. In the Plains area, for instance, state of the art research still focuses on a male universe of hunting and warfare, and women remain largely hidden in descriptive and analytical models of Indian life in this region. While the situation is changing as revealed by the literature reviewed in this essay, much of the newer research on women has not been incorporated into "mainstream" work in anthropology.

Without a balanced and well-integrated treatment of the position of females in American Indian societies, textbooks and other publications destined for general audiences indirectly perpetuate the popular stereotypes from which the public interprets the "reality" and "authenticity" of women's lives. No matter how material on American Indian women is finally integrated into an introductory course curriculum, it needs to be there. Since American Indians are a major part of the ethnic heritage of the United States and Canada, aspects of their historic and modern experience should be included in the curriculum of anthropology courses taught in these two countries. Unless students take specialized courses in minority studies, they are not likely to learn anything about American Indians in courses outside of anthropology.

Curriculum Modules and Source Materials

Manly Hearts and Changing Ones:
Female Gender Variance in American Indian Societies

Objectives. The materials in this module illustrate a number of points: (1) that the character and meaning of gender in American Indian societies has been misrepresented by the imposition of gender constructs that are European in origin (2) that gender roles display tremendous plasticity in American Indian societies, and (3) that American Indian concepts of gender are not associated with invidious and hierarchically ranked distinctions. These points in turn provide evidence that ideas about gender are culturally constructed, and that gender needs to be conceptualized in terms of a fluid continuum of identities rather than differentiated in a fixed and dichotomous way.

Lecture Summary. Ever since the time when explorers, missionaries, and traders were the primary chroniclers of American Indian life, popular descriptions of American Indian women have been marked by stereotypes. Whether described in the mode of a "princess," "earth mother," "squaw," or "beast of burden," their identities have been cast in gender models that are dichotomous and European in origin.

In contrast to the societies of the Euro-Americans who observed and wrote about them, the division of labor in most American Indian societies was flexible. Even though there was a customary division of labor along sex lines, most occupational boundaries were permeable—allowing either women or men to do the work of the opposite sex. Women not only carried out occupations customarily associated with members of their own sex, including gardening, gathering, basketmaking, and hide tanning, but they also pursued a wide range of activities that were more often undertaken by men. Beyond the occasional or specialized instance where women did work associated with men, there were females who became proficient in male-oriented tasks or who took on other manly ways. These women could be talented warriors or hunters. They could be skillful acquisitors of wealth and prestige using masculine avenues to advance their interests, and they could also be assertive in other manly ways including their role as a sexual partner. Even though such women took on features of masculine behavior, as these were culturally defined, they still remained identified as females. Among the Piegan, women with masculine ways were called *Ninawaki* or "Manly Hearts," and they represented one of several culturally accepted roles for women (Lewis 1941). There were also North American Indian women who completely trasnformed their gender and became identified socially and culturally as males. Such were the *Hwame* of the Mohave. These women not only took on manly tasks and behaved in masculine ways, but they assumed the marital and parental status of a male. Indeed, among some American Indian populations, gender transformers were believed to be exceptional people who did their work better than the people of the sex with whom they identified.

How female role variance was expressed differed from one society to another, but in many, the potentiality for gender change was recognized by the child's self-initiated interests in certain activities, and/or in the arrival of dreams and visions which supernaturally ordained a child's transformed gender identity (Callender and Kochems 1983; Whitehead 1981). Among the Lakota, as one example, the women called *Witkowinyan,* or "Crazy Woman," were sexually promiscuous. In a society with a sexual double-standard, the women who dreamed of the Thunder Beings were allowed sexual freedoms open to men but not to other women (Medicine 1983:272). In other reported cases, women identified with a masculine role because they were trained in manly pursuits. Among the Ojibwa, fathers sometimes raised their daughters as men when they had no sons (Landes 1971).

No matter how individual women became manly in their roles and behavior, their changes in identity were not stigmatized in many American Indian communities. One of the major questions anthropologists have tried to answer is why gender variance and role transformation were accepted and institutionalized. There are three major ways anthropologists have attempted to answer this.

1. At the foundation of most answers is the fact that American Indian communities accorded all forms of "personhood" with autonomy and respect. The right to express one's unique individuality is revealed in many areas, but it is especially evident in the area of labor where women and men were permitted to work and achieve in occupational domains identified with the opposite sex. Equally important is the fact that women had independent avenues to prestige, power, and wealth in their communities. Where a female occupation was a source of publicly recognized achievement, it was not denigrated because it was work customarily performed by women.

2. In comparison to many areas of the world, the relationships between American Indian women and men tended toward complementarity. Marriage rested on respect and consensual exchange, not on the dominance of one spouse and the subordination of the other. As Elizabeth Blackwood (1984:33–34) argues, marriage was not heavily invested with wealth, and it was not the primary institution for the maintenance of family rank. Thus, a family did not lose their status if a daughter abandoned a conventional gender role in marriage. In this context,

homosexuality was not seen as threatening to the family or the fabric of society, nor was it a critical component in identifying a person's gender identity.

3. Procreative sexuality did differentiate women from men, however, and the one area where there were rigid gender boundaries was in the ritual domain that ensured the life force and the continuity of the community. Here, as in everyday life, both the feminine and masculine domains were vital and a source of power and prestige. Symbolically, gender transformers occupied a liminal status, and their ritual power was derived from their mediating or, as some argue, their contrary position in society.

Since "femaleness" and "maleness" were not marked by invidious kinds of hierarchical discrimination, women and men did not lose or gain status as a result of changing their gender identity completely or taking on characteristics of the opposite sex. Gender concepts were open and flexible, and they were linked to the particular kinds of kin-ordered, social formations under which many American Indians lived. These formations provided not only a foundation for the emergence of transformative gender statuses but also one for tolerating them as well.

The practice of American Indian women taking on characteristics of the opposite sex— a possibility also open to men in the status that anthropologists identify with the name *berdarche*—demonstrates not only the plasticity of human behavior but it also raises questions about the ways in which gender is conceptualized in human societies. In North American Indian societies, gender was classified in variable ways. In some, such as the Navajo, there was a third-gender category into which the women and men who changed their gender identity were tracked. In others, including the Mohave, there were cross-gender categories and separate statuses for female and male gender transformers. Finally, there were societies such as the Lakota in which the system of gender classification was bifurcated, but in which there was a spectrum of institutionalized roles that represented a mixing or merger of opposite sex attributes in either a women or a man. The existence of variable systems of gender classification reveals that anatomical sex and gender identity are not inevitably linked to each other, and that culture plays an important role in how concepts of gender are constructed and marked.

Discussion Questions. (1) Why are popular characterizations of American Indian women more European than native American in origin? (2) How was gender flexibly defined in American Indian societies? (3) What are some of the conditions in American Indian societies that contributed to an acceptance of people who transformed their gender identities? (4) How are systems of gender classification variable, and what does this tell us about where ideas of gender come from? (5) Why are gender identities not a direct reflection of anatomical sex differences? (6) Is gender becoming more flexibly defined in contemporary American society, and if so, how might this influence societal tolerance for individuals who take on characteristics of the opposite sex?

Classroom Exercise. Ask students to make two columns one headed by the label "female" and the other "male," then ask them to list attributes (i.e., aspects of work, behavior, and dress) commonly associated with each gender category. Once the lists have been compiled, examine each attribute and determine whether it is inevitably associated with the gender under which it is listed. Since most of the attributes are not likely to be exclusive, the situations and cases where a member of one sex works, dresses and acts in a way associated with the other need to be defined. Students should also think about whether this kind of crossing is common, whether people who take on attributes of the opposite sex are stigmatized, and whether gender is really as loaded and fixed as their columns imply. If gender markers are more flexible and less dichotomous in people's lived experience, then how can they be conceptualized in a way that better fits actual practice? This simple exercise can be used to introduce the American Indian case material that examplifies a situation where markers of gender are permeable, or it could follow and encourage students to reflect upon their own gender constructions in the light of data from other cultures.

Background Literature.   With a few exceptions, many of the most interesting interpretive articles on female identity, role variance, and gender transformation in native North America are written at a level that is beyond most introductory students and should only be used as background sources by an instructor.

The literature on popular Euro-American images of American Indian gender constructs contains a variety of useful works (Albers 1983a; Albers and James 1987; Allen 1986; Green 1975, 1980; Kehoe 1983; Leacock 1980; Weist 1983; Wittstock 1980). Of these, three deserve further mention.

● Eleanor Leacock (1980) in "Montagnais Women and the Jesuit Program for Colonization," documents how the biases of Jesuits not only influenced what they wrote about Indian women, but also how they shaped the attitudes of native men toward women.

● Alice Kehoe's (1983), "The Shackles of Tradition," is an excellent analysis of conventional epistemology in anthropology and its impact on the way in which American Indian women's lives have been analyzed.

● Katherine Weist's article (1983), "Beasts of Burden and Menial Slaves: Nineteenth Century Observations of Northern Plains Indian Women," offers a critical assessment of ethnocentric biases found in historical sources used in the analysis of female roles and status.

Writings on gender variance and transformation in native North America include several excellent sources (Blackwood 1984; Callender and Kochems 1983; Medicine 1983; Miller 1982; Thayer 1980; Whitehead 1981; Williams 1986). The most extensive material on women is found in the following:

● Harriet Whitehead's (1981), "The Bow and the Burden Strap: A New Look at Institutionalized Homosexuality in Native North America," is a provocative article that follows a constructionist approach. Basically, it argues that occupation was an elementary marker of gender in American Indian societies, and that it was basic to the identification and institutionalization of gender transformative statuses as well.

● Charles Callender and Lee Kochem (1983) provide the most comprehensive comparative review of the literature on gender transformation in their article "The North American Berdache." Many useful commentaries by other anthropologists are found in the "Reply Section" that accompanies this article.

● Evelyn Blackwood's (1984) article, "Sexuality and Gender in Certain Native American Tribes: The Case of Cross-Gender Females," offers the most complete and exhaustive coverage of female gender transformation. It also contains an original and insightful analysis of how the social formations of many American Indian societies may have contributed to the institutionalization of gender transformative statuses for women.

There are other studies of interest for case materials in lectures or for student reading. Mary Jane Schneider's (1983) encyclopedic study of Plains Indian women's work is an excellent source of information not only on the permeability of occupational boundaries but also on the prestige women derived from their work. Nancy Parezo's (1982) study of sandpainting among the Navajo gives evidence of female participation in an activity usually defined as male, and Terry Reynolds's (1986) study of Acoma demonstrates the creative and economic beliefs women derive from pottery making. Alice Kehoe's (1970) study of Plains Indian ceremonial intercourse, Ann Nelson's (1976) article on female ritual sodalities, Charlotte Frisbie (1969) and Claire Farrer's (1980) works on girls' puberty ceremonies, and the writings of Marla Powers (1980) and Thomas Buckley (1982) on menstruation demonstrate the ritual importance of women in releasing or transferring vitalistic powers necessary to the reproduction of society.

Student Reading. Good ethnographic cases of gender transformation for classroom and/or instructor use come from sources on the Navajo (Hill 1935), Lowland Yuman (Blackwood 1984; Devereux 1937), Piegan (Lewis 1941), and Lakota (DeMallie 1983). Summaries of this case material in readings accessible to students are found in two sources:

● Beatrice Medicine's (1983) work, "Warrior Women"—Sex Role Alternatives for Plains Indian Women" provides an informative overview of variations in female identity. She argues that instead of interpreting female behavior in terms of a fixed, modal personality profile, it needs to be understood in terms of a continuum of varied and shifting roles.

● Kay Martin and Barbara Voorhies' (1975:84–107) chapter, "Supernumerary Sexes," contains an excellent overview of transformative gender statuses worldwide with supportive documentation from several American Indian societies. The authors also include a very useful schematic diagram (p. 89) for illustrating variations in gender classification.

Also of interest for student reading are some articles which support recent theories about female role variance, the interchangeability of female-male occupations, and the prestige of female sacred/secular activities.

● Nancy Lurie's (1972), engaging essay "Indian Women: A Legacy of Freedom," locates its interpretation of female freedoms in the autonomy commonly accorded to all forms of personhood in American Indian societies.

● Priscilla Buffalohead's (1983) article, "Farmers, Warriors and Traders: A Fresh Look at Ojibway Women," is a well-written description of the range of roles women pursued in the historic times, and it is accompanied by an excellent selection of historic photographs.

● Alice Kehoe's (1976) study, "Old Woman Had Great Power," is an absorbing treatment of the range of sacred and secular powers women held in Blackfoot society, and it tempers some of the interpretations of other scholars who imply that Plains Indian women were subordinate and powerless.

Films. There are no films that deal with the specific topic of gender transformation, although there are several that cover subjects which can illuminate aspects of female role variance and the prestige accorded to women in American Indian communities.

Pataky, Veronica. 1966 *The Washo*. Western Artists Corporation.

This movie is helpful in illustrating the prestige given to female productive and reproductive activity. Although much of the filming of a girl's puberty rite was staged in this
movie, it does bring to light the fact that women and their work are valued and that not
all societies see menstruation as degrading or defiling.

Nauman, Jane. 1985 *Lakota Quillwork: Art and Legend*. Santa Fe, N.M.: Onewest Media.
Drawing on symbolic imagery associated with the Double-Woman figure in Lakota
myth, this film provides a good historical and contemporary look at the role of women
as creative artists and preservers of cultural tradition in a Plains Indian society.

University of California. 1962 *Basketry of the Pomo* (Series, Three Parts); 1963 *Pomo Sha-
man* and 1964 *Dream Dances of the Kashia Pomo*. Berkeley: University of California Extension Media Center.
Taken together, these three films illustrate different aspects of female creativity and
prestige in American Indian societies. Two of them are particularly important in highlighting aspects of female involvement in ritual, and the last one also shows how women
can be innovators in culture change.

Autonomous People in a World of Dependency: The Changing Lives of American Indian Women

In teaching about the colonizing experience of American Indian women, the best way
to approach the subject is through the case study method. This module is divided into two
parts. The first involves a controlled comparison of two ethnographic cases where women's
status changed in response to their societies' growing dependency on mercantile trade. The
second part compares several different ethnographic examples of the growing leadership role
of American Indian women in modern times. Both parts of this module have been developed
to illustrate how differences in indigenous social formations and in subsequent colonial relationships impacted the role and status of women in variable ways (see Figure 1 for locations
of North American Indian societies).

Part 1—Women, Work, and Colonization: The Case of the Iroquois and Lakota

In the early stages of colonization, the role and status of American Indian women was
influenced by what kinds of relationships their local communities maintained with colonizing
groups, and how these relations affected the indigenous social formations that organized female productive and reproductive activity. In this regard, the Iroquois and the Lakota are
interesting to compare not only because they are well known but also because they represent
opposing positions on a continuum of female power and autonomy. The Iroquois, on the one
hand, have drawn public attention for their reputed status as a matriarchical society, and the
experience of women has been drawn on extensively to support various matriarchical theories
of human evolution (cf. Bamberger [1974] and Webster [1975] for critical discussions of these
theories). The Lakota, on the other hand, are well known for their role in the Indian wars of
the late 19th century, and as a consequence, they have been widely popularized in the cultural
productions of the media. If students have any image of the American Indian, it is usually
based on a Hollywood stereotype of an equestrian, buffalo-hunting, tipi-dwelling Plains Indian warrior (cf. Albers [1983a] and Weist [1983] for discussions of popular images of Plains
Indian women).

Objectives.   The Iroquois and Lakota can be used as contrasting cases for a number of
different purposes: (1) as an example (Iroquois) of a society where women held considerable

Figure 1. Locations of Selected North American Indian Societies.

influence in institutionalized settings beyond the domestic group, and opposingly as one (Lakota) in which female avenues to power and privilege were restricted, (2) as a comparison of the workings of a social formation with unilineal descent (Iroquois) and one with a cognatic band structure (Lakota), (3) as an illustration of how the "public" domain is embedded in the workings of domestic kin groups (Iroquois) versus a situation where voluntary associations dominate "public" discourse (Lakota), and (4) as a contrast between a society where women's status increased and one where it decreased in the early stages of mercantile dependency.

Lecture Summary. (Iroquois)—Located in the Northeast region of North America, the Iroquois have become well known for the tremendous power women held in this society.

Some scholars have claimed that the Iroquois were a matriarchy in which women were the dominant political force, but this was not the case. Iroquois females did play a major political role that balanced the powers of men. Indeed, it can be said that they were the equals of men, and that as a group they probably had more influence in their society than women among any other population in recorded history. The core features of female autonomy and power in Iroquois society existed well before contact and can be identified with aspects of a division of labor in which female horticulture and male hunting were organized within a matrilineal social formation. Matrilineality and horticultural production, while favorable to the status of women worldwide, do not necessarily give women a strong base of power beyond their households and descent groups. This has led scholars to look for other "causal" forces to explain the attenuated position of women in Iroquois politics from the mid-17th to the mid-18th centuries.

1. The first type of explanation is centered on the factors of production and the increasing importance of female work in food provisioning as men turned toward specialized labor activities to support Iroquois dependence on the fur trade. That women held economic power is unquestionable, and it is indicated, among other things, in the right of women to withhold or give the food upon which male participation in raids, councils, and ceremonies depended (Nowak 1979:97). Also important are the facts that Iroquois women participated in the trade with Europeans, and that they were the "keepers" of the wampum belts used in negotiating trade and peace (Randle 1951:272). In many respects, women were the "bankers" of Iroquois society.

2. The rise of female power occurred at a time when the male population was in decline as a result of war and epidemic disease. In order to maintain their viability as a population, the Iroquois adopted some of their war captives and women played a critical role in this process. After all, women were the ones who had to feed, clothe, and shelter the captives, to provide them protective custody, and to socially incorporate them into their matrilineages. Given their powerful economic base, women were in a strategic position to control critical aspects of reproduction (daily and generational) in Iroquois communities as well.

3. Finally, there is the fact that much of the activity of younger men in warfare and trapping required extended absences from their homes. This kind of situation clearly intensified female autonomy in their local villages, but it is not sufficient to account for the rise in the power of Iroquois women as some scholars imply.

In the final analysis, the key to the expansion of Iroquois women's institutionalized power lay in the workings of a matrilineal social formation in which the relations of production were organized in such a way as to invest women with considerable control over the subsistence resources upon which the Iroquois' involvement and success in the fur trade was dependent. Although the decline in, and absence of, men extended the range of female influence, it took place within a social formation where women were already empowered.

(Lakota)—In the early 19th century, the Lakota (Teton or Western Sioux) occupied a large territory which extended from the Mississippi River in Minnesota to the Powder River in Wyoming. In contrast to the Iroquois, the Lakota and other equestian, buffalo hunting nomads of the High Plains have been described as societies in which women were subordinate and powerless. Beyond the fact that Lakota women lacked institutionalized leadership positions in public councils, their autonomy within the household and their freedom over their own reproductive future was restricted. In addition, they lived in a situation where male production in hunting and raiding was dominant, and where female activities supported the productive efforts of men in a direct way. Like the Iroquois, the division of labor among the

Lakota was highly segregated. But unlike the Iroquois, it was one in which segregation took place primarily within a single production process. Men procured the animals whose hides and meat women processed. The status of women among the Lakota and other nomadic groups in the High Plains, as it was described in the early 19th century, was also historically specific and the result of a growing dependence on mercantile trade.

1. Changes in hunting techniques brought about with the introduction of the horse led to the removal of women from a primary productive role. It should be noted that by contrast, the Lakota's close relatives the Dakota, who lived in eastern Minnesota, had few horses, and they still hunted afoot using older style surround procedures. In communal buffalo drives, women still played an active role, and they held positions of authority in the distribution of the meat (Landes 1968:165).

2. The Lakota and other Northern Plains societies developed a complex and highly specialized division of labor around a surplus productive process in which buffalo meat and hide were central commodities in the European trade. In this trade men hunted the buffalo whose hides and meat women processed, and men also controlled the trade of these commodities in European markets. As the market demand for buffalo increased, men needed more wives to process the buffalo they hunted and polygamy increased as a result.

3. Over time competition increased over access to trade routes and to territories where buffalo were plentiful. A rise in warfare, in turn, led to the growth of military sodalities and leadership/prestige systems based on military achievements. By the early 19th century, it was the all-male military sodalities and councils that exerted the strongest influence over the workings of society.

As men gained preemptive control over strategic resources and as the power invested in all-male sodalities and councils increased, the kinship avenues through which women exercised power became strategically less important. This led to an erosion of female influence not only in the workings of community-wide institutions but also in the day-to-day activities of households. Notwithstanding an overall decline in their autonomy, there were institutionalized areas where Lakota women retained influence. Women achieved prestige and influence through their artistic efforts and specialized roles in ritual, and some even used male avenues of raiding and warfare to gain acclaim.

Questions for Discussion. (1) If both Iroquois and Lakota women were active in production, why is it that the status of women was higher among the Iroquois? (2) Why did women's place in domestic groups give Iroqouis women influence but deny Lakota women access to power? (3) What were the conditions in Iroquois society that brought about a rise in women's power after contact, and what features led to a decline among the Lakota?

Exercise. Select one or more ethnohistorical documents that describe the role and status of women in a Northeastern and/or Plains Indian society. Have students read these documents and analyze them in terms of how author bias colors an understanding of women's roles and status. In doing so, students might be asked to consider the following: (1) What are the biases? (2) Where do they come from? and (3) Can factual information be found in the source and separated from the author's leaps of imagination? Possible documents for classroom use and a critical interpretation of these sources can be found in articles by Alice Kehoe (1983), Katherine Weist (1983), Judith Brown (1975), and Eleanor Leacock (1980).

Background Literature. There are several sources (Brown 1975; Hewitt 1932; Nowak 1979; Randle 1951; Richards 1957, 1974; Rothenberg 1976, 1980; Tooker 1984; Trigger

1978; Wallace 1948) that provide good background information on the Iroquois and the changing position of women in this society. Of these,

● Judith Brown's (1975) work, "Iroquois Women: An Ethnohistoric Note," is the best overall description of women's status in early historic times.

● Barbara Nowak's (1979), "Women's Roles and Status in a Changing Iroquois Society" offers the most detailed summary of primary sources on Iroquois women, and it presents an interesting analysis of how changing property relations led to a decline in women's status.

● Diane Rothenberg's (1980) well-written and thoughtful article, "Mothers of the Nation: Seneca Resistance to Quaker Intervention," provides a provocative analysis of changes in the status of Iroquois women from the 17th to 20th centuries. In particular, it shows how the policies and actions of Quaker missionaries influenced fundamental changes in the division of labor and in domestic and community organization. It is good for student reading as well.

Other studies (Anderson 1985; Buffalohead 1983; Gonzalez 1982; Grumet 1980; Kidwell 1979; Leacock 1980) provide an extended empirical base for comparing women's colonizing experiences in neighboring Indian societies.

● Robert Grumet's (1980) work, "Sunksquaws, Shamans, and Tradeswomen: Middle Atlantic Coastal Alongkian Women During the 17th and 18th Centuries," is a meticulously researched ethnohistorical piece that describes the role and status of Coastal Algonkian women during the colonial era. It gives important information on female autonomy and power in other matrilineal societies that nicely complements the better documented case of the Iroquois.

There are several studies (DeMallie 1983; Hassrick 1964; Landes 1968; Mirsky 1961; Powers 1986) that provide detailed information on women's role and status among the Lakota and Dakota in historic times. In addition, there is:

● Alan Klein's (1983b) article, "The Political Economy of Gender: A 19th Century Plains Indian Case Study." Drawing on information from selected societies in the Northern Plains, this study documents how the introduction of horses and mercantile markets transformed the role of women in production and their status within wider social formations. Another article (1983a) by the same author provides further documentation on this topic.

● Katherine Weist's (1980) essay, "Plains Indian Women: An Assessment," is a comprehensive, comparative review of ethnohistorical and ethnographic sources on women in different Plains Indian societies. Of special interest is the information it provides on the contrasting position of women in foraging and horticultural societies.

There are also a variety of other sources (Kehoe 1970, 1973; Liberty 1979, Schneider 1983; Spector 1983) that offer general comparative discussions of women's roles in the historic Plains.

Student Reading. For the Iroquois, Diane Rothenberg's (1980) study is by far the best written and most provocative account of the changing experiences of Iroquois women under colonization, and it nicely complements Anthony Wallace's (1969) popular historical ethnography on the Seneca. For the Lakota, there are two good sources: Raymond DeMallie's (1983) essay, "Male and Female in Traditional Lakota Culture," is a good summary treatment of sex roles based on ethnographic sources; and Marla Powers (1986) book, *Oglala Women*, covers one group of Lakota women in historic and modern times. In addition:

●Margot Liberty's (1982) article, "Hell Came with Horses," is a nicely written, popular treatment of the impact of the horse and the hide traffic on women's lives in the Northern Plains. It is very appropriate for student reading, and it nicely complements the writings of Alan Klein (1983a, 1983b) on the same subject.

Film. There are no films on the prereservation Iroquois or any Plains tribes that adequately cover women's lives. There is an excellent movie, however, on the Lenape who were neighbors of the Iroquois and shared many cultural practices with them, including matrilineal descent and institutionalized leadership positions for women.

Bock, William Sauts Netamuxwe. 1983 *The Four Seasons in Lenape Indian Life*. New York: Spoken Arts, Inc.
This film traces Lenape life and history through the stories of Old Elm Bark Woman, and in doing so, it presents a balanced treatment of the experiences of women and men under colonization.

Part II—"Doctors, Lawyers, and Indian Chiefs": Contemporary Female Leaders

Throughout North America, American Indian women have assumed a variety of different appointed and elected leadership positions since the 1960s. These include women like Wilma Mankiller, leader of the Cherokee tribe in Oklahoma, and Ada Deer, a former congressional lobbyist who was instrumental in the passage of the Tribal Restoration Act. Today, the involvement of American Indian women in a wide range of occupational professions and their active participation in politics makes them highly visible at the local and tribal, as well as national, level. A major question, therefore, is what has catapulted women into the forefront of American Indian life and politics? Since this question has not been raised in any single work, the answer must be constructed through an examination of various ethnographic cases that discuss women's involvement in professional work and politics.

Objectives. The cases discussed here illustrate situations where (1) women's access to strategic resources has been an important component of their autonomy, (2) where domestic group organization plays a significant role in women's empowerment, and (3) where the status of women in domestic settings is linked to their leadership positions in community-wide work and politics.

Lecture Summary. After American Indians were settled on reservations in the United States further changes took place in the status of women. Among some groups like the Iroquois, Dakota, and Lakota whatever autonomy women may have had was eroded by the policies of various state and church agencies. These populations were encouraged to become private-property holding, nuclear family farmers or ranchers, and in the process, women were denied equal access to the resources upon which their family's livelihood depended. Government and church policies influenced other changes as well, including an increasing agnatic bias in residence, kin support networks, political leadership, and religious institutions (i.e., Native American Church, Handsome Lake Religion). Some native populations, however, escaped the full impact of early federal policies. For a wide variety of reasons, groups like the

Tlingit and Navajo were able to continue certain traditional economic activities well into the 20th century. Even though a dependence on a market economy increased among all of these groups, there was not a pronounced difference between women and men in their access to resources. Among all of these groups, female autonomy within domestic groups was never eroded in any substantial way, and they continued to use their domestic power base as a vehicle for building wider community alliances in ceremony and politics.

By the mid-20th century, however, the decline in women's status among groups like the Dakota and Lakota was reversed as a result of changes in federal policy. Instead of supporting a model based on family farming or ranching, new policy directives encouraged males to become employed breadwinners and women and children to become dependents of working men or the state. Most males were unable to support a family and a nonworking spouse through wage labor, however. Consequently, the contributions of women from wage work and other income-producing activities became increasingly important. As the incomes of Dakota and Lakota women rose in relation to those of men, female autonomy and influence within domestic groups also increased. Today, women play a central role in the extended kin networks that organize community-wide ceremonial activity and an increasing number have been elected to political office or appointed to administrative positions in tribal government.

The critical place of women in households and domestic groups and its relationship to their involvement in modern politics is also revealed in other cases. Paiute and Tlingit women, for example, play a central role in the provisioning of their families through petty commodity production, wage labor and/or government assistance. Among other things, their access to strategic resources has served to consolidate their influence within contemporary domestic groups. Women in both of these groups have also used their domestic power base to expand their roles in community-wide politics.

In the final analysis, the emergence of a strong female leadership in many of today's American Indian communities can be attributed to a number of factors including:

1. Recent federal policy changes (i.e., Indian Self-Determination Act) in the United States have relaxed government controls over many areas of local politics. Tribal governments have more power to manage their own affairs, including the right to make decisions about who holds elected and appointed offices. This, coupled with the national influence of the women's rights movement, has created a climate that is more open to female leadership.

2. Equally important is the continuing, and in some cases, growing access of American Indian women to strategic resources from subsistence production, petty commodity work, wage labor and/or government assistance. This access, coupled with a traditional and long-standing respect for female work and property rights, has given women autonomy and influence within their households and kin groups. From their base of power within domestic groupings, women have been able to effectively mobilize ceremonial and political support in community-wide networks.

3. Finally, there is the fact that many forms of work and leadership are not sex-typed in a fixed and narrow way. Generally speaking, American Indian women have not been stigmatized for working outside the home or for getting educations that qualify them for professional jobs. Among groups like the Tlingit, gender is not a barrier to leadership. Other conditions being equal, women have as much of a chance as men to seek elected and appointed offices.

Questions for Discussion. (1) Why did women's autonomy decrease among the Dakota/Lakota and Iroquois and why was it not eroded among the Tlingit, Paiute, and Navajo in the early reservation era? (2) Why is women's empowerment in domestic groups important to their leadership in community-wide institutions? and (3) What conditions in the past three decades have led to an increasing involvement of women in the leadership of their communities?

Background Literature. There are a variety of sources that deal with the changing position of women in the 20th century and several which present timely data on the lives of women since the 1960s. Sources on the Dakota/Lakota include several works (Albers 1983b, 1985; Albers and Medicine 1983; Bysiewicz and Van de Mark 1977; Maynard 1979; Medicine 1987; Powers 1986). There are numerous studies (Conte 1982; Downs 1972; Frisbie 1967, 1982; Hamamsy 1957; Joe 1982; Lamphere 1974, 1975, 1977; Leighton 1982; Metcalf 1979, 1982; Reichard 1928; Roessel 1981; Shepardson 1982) on Navajo women, and also a few works on neighboring groups in the Southwest (Reynolds 1986; Schlegel 1975, 1977, 1979). Northern and Southern Paiute women have been the focus of a few writings (Knack 1980, 1988; Lynch 1986), and the history of Tlingit women has been a subject in two articles by Laura Klein (1976, 1980). Most of the literature (Nowak 1979; Randle 1951; Rothenberg 1976, 1980) on modern Iroquois women covers their situation in the years before 1960, and although these sources provide in-depth coverage of changes in women's lives during the early reservation era, none of them contain timely information on their present day conditions. In addition, a variety of works have been written on the Arctic (Agar 1980; Briggs 1974; Matthiasson 1979; McElroy 1975, 1979) and Subarctic (Cruikshank 1971, 1975; Fiske 1988). Among these studies, several deserve further mention because they provide a strong interpretive focus for understanding the conditions that contribute to women's status and leadership in contemporary settings.

● Patricia Albers's (1983b) study, "Sioux Women in Transition: A Study of Their Changing Status in Domestic and Capitalist Sectors of Production," offers an explicit theoretical framework for understanding change in the lives of Dakota women from the late 19th century to the present, and it relates this directly to shifts in federal policy. Another article (1985) examines the same case but in terms of its relation to the experiences of women among other ethnic minorities.

● Laura Klein's (1980) "Contending with Colonization: Tlingit Men and Women in Change," is the only exhaustive source on the changing position of women in a Northwest Coast group. It demonstrates how women in Tlingit society have maintained autonomy and power from precontact times to the present, and how they have continuously reformulated their roles in the face of economic change.

●Kathleen Jamieson's article (1981), "Sisters Under the Skin: An Exploration of the Implications of Feminist Materialist Perspective Research," demonstrates that the historic and modern roles of women in Canadian Indian societies were socially productive, and that as a result, their social position within native communities contrasts markedly with the status of white women in Canadian society at large.

Student Readings. The following articles not only provide good background information but they are also accessible to students:

● Robert Lynch's (1986), "Women in Northern Paiute Politics," provides the best coverage of female leadership in tribal politics for any contemporary population, and it also offers an interesting analysis of how women have achieved their power in opposition to the interests of local Bureau of Indian Affairs officials.

● Julie Cruikshank's (1971) work, "Native Women in the North: An Expanding Role," is an accessible account of women's expanding involvement in the work and politics of Sub-arctic populations.

● Laura Klein's (1976) article, "She's One of Us You Know: The Public Life of Tlingit Women," is a good and also accessible account of women's participation in community-wide work and politics. Of special interest are the insights it offers on the lack of sex bias in the professional and political aspirations of the Tlingit.

● Christine Conte's (1982) article, "Ladies, Livestock, Land and Lucre: Women's Net-works and Social Status on the Western Navajo Reservation" is an excellent analysis of the different ways women activate kinship ties to control resources and to enhance their status in rural, domestic settings.

● Marla Powers' (1986) book, *Oglala Women,* includes several chapters devoted to the contemporary lives of one group of Lakota women, and it contains many interesting insights on their varied struggles to improve the living conditions of their people.

● Patricia Albers and Beatrice Medicine's (1983) essay, "The Role of Sioux Women in the Production of Ceremonial Objects: The Case of the Star Quilt," shows how Lakota and Dakota women adopted an Anglo-American art form to use as a ceremonial object in native ritual. In doing so, the article also reveals the prestige this work provides women, and how it influences their role in ceremonial giveaways.

In addition, there are many autobiographical contributions which, except for very recent ones, have been thoroughly reviewed in Gretchen Bataille and Kathleen Sands's book, *American Indian Women: Telling Their Lives,* and the reader is referred to this work for further information.

Films.   There are many films on American Indians that cover aspects of women's contemporary lives. Many of these films concentrate on the technical features of women's crafts-work but not on the role of women as craft producers. In addition, most of them have been filmed in the outdated genre of "Encyclopedia Britannica" films (further information on most of these films can be found in an excellent and recently published annotated bibliography [Bataille and Silet 1985] on American Indians in film). Beyond the woman as craftworker films, there are only a few films that provide insights into the lives of contemporary Indian women. These include:

Borden, John. 1984 *Seasons of the Navajo.* Washington, D.C.: PBS Video
    This is a good depiction of Navajo domestic life which is centered on sheepherding, and
    it presents a balanced picture of female and male roles.

Freedman, Joel. 1988 *Broken Treaty at Battle Mountain.* New York: Cinnamon Productions
    Focusing on the Western Shoshone struggle over land rights in Nevada, this film reveals
    the active participation of women in local level politics.

McCrea, Graydon. 1983 *Summer of Loucheux: A Portrait of a Northern Indian Family.*
Franklin Lakes, N.J.: Tamarack Films
    In providing a well-balanced view of an Indian family's day-to-day lives, this film offers
    an interesting portrayal of the changing position of women.

References Cited

Agar, Lynn Price
  1980   The Economic Role of Women in Alaskan Society. *In* A World of Women. E. Bourguignon, ed. Pp. 305–318. New York: Praeger Press.
Albers, Patricia
  1983a   Introduction: New Perspectives on Plains Indian Women. *In* The Hidden Half: Studies of Plains Indian Women. P. Albers and B. Medicine, eds. Pp. 1–15. Lanham Park, Md.: University Press of America.
  1983b   Sioux Women in Transition: A Study of Their Changing Status in Domestic and Capitalist Sectors of Production. *In* The Hidden Half: Studies of Plains Indian Women. P. Albers and B. Medicine, eds. Pp. 175–234. Lanham Park, Md.: University Press of America.
  1985   Autonomy and Dependency in the Lives of Dakota Women: A Study in Historical Change. Review of Radical Political Economics 17:109–134.
Albers, Patricia, and Nancy Breen
  1987   Deciphering the Census for Trends in the Status of American Indian Women. Unpublished paper presented at the annual meetings of the American Social Science Association, Chicago.
Albers, Patricia, and William James
  1987   Illusion and Illumination: Visual Images of American Indian Women in the West. *In* The Women's West. S. Armitage and B. Jamison, eds. Pp. 51–71. Norman: University of Oklahoma Press.
Albers, Patricia, and Beatrice Medicine
  1983   The Role of Sioux Women in the Production of Ceremonial Objects: The Case of the Star Quilt. *In* The Hidden Half: Studies of Plains Indian Women. P. Albers and B. Medicine. eds. Pp. 123–142. Lanham Park, Md.: University Press of America.
Allen, Paula Gunn
  1986   The Sacred Hoop: Recovering the Feminine in American Indian Traditions. Boston: Beacon Press.
Anderson, Karen
  1985   Commodity Exchange and Subordination: Montagnais-Nascapi and Hopi Women, 1600–1650. Signs 11:48–62.
Bamberger, Joan
  1974   The Myth of Matriarchy: Why Men Rule in Primitive Societies. *In* Women, Culture and Society. M. Rosaldo and L. Lamphere, eds. Pp. 263–280. Stanford: Stanford University Press.
Bataille, Gretchen and Kathleen Sands
  1984   American Indian Women: Telling Their Lives. Lincoln: University of Nebraska Press.
Bataille, Gretchen and Charles Silet
  1985   Images of American Indians on Film: An Annotated Bibliography. Garland Reference Library of Social Science Vol. 307. New York: Garland Publishing Company.
Beauchamp, William
  1889   Iroquois Women. Journal of American Folklore 13:81–90.
Black, Mary
  1984   Maidens and Mothers: An Analysis of Hopi Corn Metaphors. Ethnology 23:279–288.
Blackwood, Evelyn
  1984   Sexuality and Gender in Certain Native American Tribes: The Case of Cross-Gender Females. Signs: Journal of Women in Society and Culture 10:27–42.
Briggs, Jean L.
  1974   Eskimo Women: Makers of Men. *In* Many Sisters: Women in Cross-Cultural Perspective. C. J. Matthiasson, ed. Pp. 261–304. New York: Free Press.
Brown, Judith K.
  1975   Iroquois Women: An Ethnohistoric Note. *In* Toward an Anthropology of Women. R. Reiter, ed. Pp. 235–251. New York: Monthly Review Press.
Buckley, Thomas
  1982   Menstruation and the Power of Yurok Women: Methods in Cultural Reconstruction. American Ethnologist 32:37–56.

Buffalohead, Priscilla
    1983   Farmers, Warriors and Traders: A Fresh Look at Ojibway Women. Minnesota History
        48:236–244.
Bysiewicz, Shirley, and Ruth Van de Mark
    1977   The Legal Status of Dakota Women. American Indian Law Review 3:255–312.
Callender, Charles, and Lee M. Kochems
    1983   The North American Berdache. Current Anthropology 24:443–470.
Carr, Lucien
    1887   On the Social and Political Position of Women Among the Huron-Iroquois Tribes. Harvard
        University Peabody Museum of Archaeology and Ethnology Report 16:207–232.
Conte, Christine
    1982   Ladies, Livestock, Land and Lucre: Women's Networks and Social Status on the Western
        Navajo Reservation. American Indian Quarterly 6:105–124.
Cruikshank, Julie
    1971   Native Women in the North: An Expanding Role. North/Nord 18:1–7.
    1975   Becoming a Woman in Athapaskan Society: Changing Traditions on the Upper Yukon River.
        Western Canadian Journal of Anthropology 5:1–14.
DeMallie, Raymond
    1983   Male and Female in Traditional Lakota Culture. In The Hidden Half: Studies of Plains Indian
        Women. P. Albers and B. Medicine, eds. Pp. 237–267. Lanham Park, Md.: University Press of
        America.
Devereux, George
    1937   Institutionalized Homosexuality of the Mohave Indians. Human Biology 9:498–527.
    1950   The Psychology of Feminine Genital Bleeding. International Journal of Psychoanalysis
        31:237–257.
Downs, James
    1972   The Cowboy and the Lady: Models as a Determinant of the Rate of Acculturation Among the
        Pinon Navajo. In Native Americans Today. H. Bahr et al., eds. Pp. 275–290. New York: Harper
        & Row.
Etienne, Mona, and Eleanor Leacock
    1980   Introduction. In Women and Colonization. M. Etienne and E. Leacock, eds. Pp. 1–25. New
        York: Praeger.
Farrer, Claire
    1980   Mescalero Apache Girl's Puberty Ceremonies. In Southwest Indian Ritual Drama. C. Frisbie,
        ed. Pp. 127–136. Albuquerque: University of New Mexico Press.
Fiske, Jo-Anne
    1988   Fishing Is Women's Business: Changing Economic Roles of Carrier Women and Men. In
        Native People, Native Lands. B. Cox, ed. Pp. 186–198. Ottawa: Carlton University Press.
Ford, Richard
    1983   Inter-Indian Exchange in the Southwest. In Southwest Vol. 10: The Handbook of American
        Indians. A. Ortiz, ed. Pp. 711–722. Washington, D.C.: Smithsonian Institution.
Fowler, Catherine, and Lawrence Dawson
    1986   Ethnographic Basketry. In Great Basin. Vol. 11: Handbook of American Indians, W. D'A-
        zevado, ed. Pp. 705–737. Washington, D.C.: Smithsonian Institution.
Friedl, Ernestine
    1975   Women and Men: An Anthropologist's View. New York: Holt, Rinehart & Winston.
Frisbie, Charlotte
    1967   Kinaalda: A Study of the Navajo Girl's Puberty Ceremony. Middletown, Ohio: Wesleyan
        University Press.
    1982   Traditional Navajo Women: Ethnographic and Life History Portrayals. American Indian
        Quarterly 6:11–42.
Gonzalez, Elice
    1982   An Ethnohistorical Analysis of Micmac Male and Female Economic Roles. Ethnohistory
        29:117–129.

Green, Rayna
  1975   The Pocahontas Perplex: The Image of Indian Women in American Culture. The Massachusetts Review 16:698–714.
  1980   Native American Women. Signs: Journal of Women in Society and Culture 7:248–267.
  1983   Native American Women: A Contextual Bibliography. Bloomington: University of Indiana
  Press.
Grumet, Robert
  1980   Sunksquaws, Shamans, and Tradeswomen: Middle Atlantic Coastal Algonkian Women During the 17th and 18th Centuries. *In* Women and Colonization. M. Etienne and L. Leacock, eds.
  Pp. 43–62. New York: Praeger.
Hamamsy, Lila
  1957   The Role of Women in a Changing Navajo Society. American Anthropologist 59:101–111.
Hassrick, Royal
  1964   The Sioux: Life and Customs of a Warrior Society. Norman: University of Oklahoma Press.
Hewitt, J. N. B.
  1932   Status of Women in Iroquois Polity Before 1784. Smithsonian Annual Report for 1932. Pp.
  475–488. Washington, D.C.: Government Printing Office.
Hill, Willard
  1935   The Status of the Hermaphrodite and Transvestite in Navajo Culture. American Anthropologist 37:273–279.
Hoebel, Adamson E.
  1960   The Cheyennes: Indians of the Great Plains. New York: Holt, Rinehart & Winston.
Honigmann, John
  1954   The Kaska Indians: An Ethnographic Reconstruction. Yale University Publications in Anthropology, no. 51. New Haven, Conn.: Yale University Press.
Howard, James
  1981   Shawnee: The Ceremonialism of a Native American Tribe and its Cultural Background. Ath-
  ens: Ohio University Press.
Jacobs, Sue-Ellen
  1968   Berdache: A Brief Review of the Literature. Colorado Anthropologist 1:25–40.
Jamieson, Kathleen
  1981   Sisters Under the Skin: An Exploration of the Implication of Feminist Materialist Perspective
  Research. Canadian Ethnic Studies 13:130–143.
Joe, Jennie
  1982   Cultural Influences on Navajo Mothers with Disabled Children. American Indian Quarterly
  6:170–190.
Jorgenson, Joseph
  1978   A Century of Political Economic Effects on American Indian Society, 1880–1980. Journal of
  Ethnic Studies 6:1–82.
Keesing, Felix
  1966   Cultural Anthropology: The Science of Custom. New York: Holt, Rinehart & Winston.
Keesing, Felix, and Roger Keesing
  1971   New Perspectives in Cultural Anthropology. New York: Holt, Rinehart & Winston.
Keesing, Roger
  1981   Cultural Anthropology: A Contemporary Perspective. New York: Holt, Rinehart & Winston.
Kehoe, Alice
  1970   The Function of Ceremonial Sexual Intercourse Among the Northern Plains Indians. Plains
  Anthropologist 15:99–103.
  1973   The Metonymic Pole and Social Roles. Journal of Anthropological Research 29:266–274.
  1976   Old Woman Had Great Power. Western Canadian Journal of Anthropology 6:68–76.
  1981   North American Indians: A Comprehensive Account. Englewood Cliffs, N.J.: Prentice-Hall.
  1983   The Shackles of Tradition. *In* The Hidden Half: Studies of Plains Indian Women. P. Albers
  and B. Medicine, eds. Pp. 53–76. Lanham Park, Md.: University Press of America.

Kidwell, Clara Sue
    1979   The Power of Women in Three American Indian Societies. Journal of Ethnic Studies 6:113–121.
Klein, Alan
    1983a   The Plains Truth: The Impact of Colonialism on Indian Women. Dialectical Anthropology 7:299–313.
    1983b   The Political-Economy of Gender: A 19th Century Plains Indian Case Study. *In* The Hidden Half: Studies of Plains Indian Women. P Albers and B. Medicine, eds. Pp. 143–174. Lanham Park, Md.: University Press of America.
Klein, Laura
    1976   She's One of Us You Know: The Public Life of Tlingit Women. Western Canadian Journal of Anthropology 6:164–183.
    1980   Contending with Colonization: Tlingit Men and Women in Change. *In* Women and Colonization. M. Etienne and E. Leacock, eds. Pp. 88–108. New York: Praeger.
Knack, Martha
    1980   Life Is with People: Household Organization of the Contemporary Southern Paiute Indians. Ballena Press Anthropological Papers 19. Socorro, N.M.
    1988   Newspaper Accounts of Indian Women in Southern Nevada Mining Towns, 1870–1900. The Journal of California and Great Basin Anthropology 8:83–98.
Kroeber, Alfred
    1940   Psychosis or Social Sanction. *In* The Nature of Culture. A. Kroeber, ed. Pp. 310–319. Chicago: University of Chicago Press.
Lamphere, Louise
    1974   Strategies, Cooperation, and Conflict Among Women in Domestic Groups. *In* Women, Culture and Society. M. Rosaldo and L. Lamphere, eds. Pp. 97–112. Stanford: Stanford University Press.
    1975   Women and Domestic Power: Political and Economic Strategies in Domestic Groups. *In* Being Female: Reproduction, Power and Change. D. Raphael, ed. Pp. 117–130. The Hague: Mouton.
    1977   To Run After Them. Tucson: University of Arizona Press.
Landes, Ruth
    1968   The Mystic Lake Sioux. Madison: University of Wisconsin Press.
    1971   The Ojibwa Woman. New York: Norton.
Leacock, Eleanor
    1978   Women's Status in Egalitarian Society: Implications of Social Evolution. Current Anthropology 19:247–276.
    1980   Montagnais Women and the Jesuit Program for Colonization. *In* Women and Colonization. M. Etienne and L. Leacock, eds. Pp. 25–42. New York: Praeger.
    1981   Myths of Male Dominance. New York: Monthly Review Press.
Lee, Dorothy
    1959   Freedom and Culture. New York: Prentice-Hall.
Leighton, Dorothea
    1982   As I Knew Them: Navajo Women in 1940. American Indian Quarterly 6:43–51.
Lewis, Oscar
    1941   The Manly-Hearted Women Among the South Piegan. American Anthropologist 43:173–187.
    1942   The Effects of White Contact upon Blackfoot Culture. American Ethnological Society Monographs No. 6. Seattle: University of Washington Press.
Liberty, Margot
    1979   Plains Indian Women Through Time. *In* Lifeways of Intermontane and Plains Montana Indians. L. Davis, ed. Museum of the Rockies Occasional Papers No. 1. Bozman, Mont.
    1982   Hell Came With Horses: Plains Indian Women in the Equestrian Era. Montana: The Magazine of Western History 32:10–20.
Littlefield, Loraine
    1988   Women Traders in the Maritime Trade. *In* Native People, Native Lands. B. Cox, ed. Pp. 173–185. Ottawa: Carleton University Press.

Lurie, Nancy
    1972   Indian Women: A Legacy of Freedom. *In* Look to the Mountaintop. Robert Iacopi, ed. Pp. 29–36. San Jose, Calif.: Gousha Publications.
Lynch, Robert
    1986   Women in Northern Paiute Politics. Signs 11:253–266.
Martin, Kay, and Barbara Voorhies
    1975   Female of the Species. New York: Columbia University Press.
Mason, Otis
    1894   Woman's Share in Primitive Culture. New York: Appleton.
Matthiasson, John
    1979   Northern Baffin Island Women in Three Cultural Periods. *In* Sex Roles in Changing Cultures. Occasional Papers in Anthropology, 1. A. McElroy and C. Matthiasson, eds. Pp. 61–73. Buffalo: Department of Anthropology, State University of New York at Buffalo.
Maynard, Eileen
    1979   Changing Sex-Roles and Family Structure Among the Oglala Sioux. *In* Sex Roles in Changing Cultures. Occasional Papers in Anthropology, 1. A. McElroy and C Matthiasson, eds. Pp. 11–20. Buffalo: Department of Anthropology, State University of New York at Buffalo.
McElroy, Ann
    1975   Canadian Arctic Modernization and Change in Female Inuit Role Identification. American Ethnologist 2:662–686.
    1979   The Negotiation of Sex-Role Identity in Eastern Arctic Culture Change. *In* Sex Roles in Changing Cultures. Occasional Papers in Anthropology, 1. A. McElroy and C. Matthiasson, eds. Pp. 49–60. Buffalo: Department of Anthropology, State University of New York at Buffalo.
Medicine, Beatrice
    1978   The Native American Woman: A Perspective. Austin, Texas: National Educational Laboratory Publishers.
    1983   Warrior Women: Sex Role Alternatives for Plains Indian Women. *In* The Hidden Half: Studies of Plains Indian Women. P. Albers and B. Medicine, eds. Pp. 267–280. Lanham Park, Md.: University Press of America.
    1987   Indian Women and the Renaissance of Traditional Religion. *In* Sioux Indian Religion: Tradition and Innovation. R. DeMallie and D. Parks, eds. Pp. 159–171. Norman: University of Oklahoma Press.
Metcalf, Ann
    1979   Reservation Born—City Bred: Native American Women and Children in the City. *In* Sex Roles in Changing Cultures. Occasional Papers in Anthropology, 1. A. McElroy and C. Matthiasson, eds. Pp. 21–34. Buffalo: Department of Anthropology, State University of New York at Buffalo.
    1982   Life Is Harder Here: The Case of the Urban Navajo Woman. American Indian Quarterly 6:72–89.
Milicic, Bojka
    1986   Menstruants, Mothers, Mourners and Murderers: A Cross-Cultural Study of the Relationship Between Taboos of Menstruation, Childbirth, Mourning and Manslaying. Unpublished M.A. thesis, University of Utah.
Miller, Jay
    1982   People, Berdaches and Left-Handed Bears. Journal of Anthropological Research 38:274–287.
Mirsky, Jeanette
    1961   The Dakota. *In* Cooperation and Competition among Primitive Peoples. M. Mead, ed. Pp. 382–427. Boston: Beacon Press.
Moore, John
    1988   The Cheyenne Nation: A Social and Demographic History. Lincoln: University of Nebraska Press.
Morgan, Lewis Henry
    1962   League of the Iroquois. New York: Corinth Books.
    1963   Ancient Society. Cleveland: World Publishing.

Nelson, Ann
    1976   Women in Groups: Women's Ritual Sodalities in Native North America. The Western Ca-
    nadian Journal of Anthropology 6:29–67.
Niethammer, Carolyn
    1977   Daughters of the Earth: The Lives and Legends of American Indian Women. New York: Col-
    lier Books.
Norton, Thomas
    1974   The Fur Trade in Colonial New York 1686–1776. Madison: University of Wisconsin Press.
Nowak, Barbara
    1979   Women's Roles and Status in a Changing Iroquois Society. *In* Sex Roles in Changing Cul-
    tures. Occasional Papers in Anthropology, 1. A. McElroy and C. Matthiasson, eds. Pp. 95–111.
    Buffalo: Department of Anthropology, State University of New York at Buffalo.
OHOYO, Inc.
    1981   Words of Today's American Indian Women. Wichita Falls, Texas: Ohoyo Resource Center.
Parezo, Nancy
    1982   Sex Roles in Craft Production. American Indian Quarterly 6:125–148.
Perry, Richard
    1977   Variations on the Female Referent in Athabaskan Cultures. Journal of Anthropological Re-
    search 33:99–119.
    1979   The Fur Trade and the Status of Women in the Western Subarctic. Ethnohistory 26:363–376.
Poole, Carolyn
    1988   Reservation Policy and the Economic Position of Wichita Women. Great Plains Quarterly
    8:158–171.
Powers, Marla
    1980   Menstruation and Reproduction: An Oglala Case. Signs: The Journal of Women in Society
    and Culture.
    1986   Oglala Women. Chicago: University of Chicago Press.
Randle, Martha C.
    1951   Iroquois Women, Then and Now. *In* Bureau of American Ethnology Bulletin 149. W. Fenton,
    Ed. Anthropology Papers, Symposium on Local Diversity in Iroquois Culture 8:167–180.
Reichard, Gladys
    1928   Social Life of the Navajo Indians, with Some Attention to Minor Ceremonies. New York:
    Columbia University Press.
Reynolds, Terry R.
    1986   Women, Poetry, and Economics at Acoma Pueblo. *In* New Mexico Women: Intercultural Per-
    spectives. J. Jensen and D. Miller, eds. Pp. 279–300. Albuquerque, University of New Mexico
    Press.
Richards, Cara
    1957   Matriarchy or Mistake: The Role of Iroquois Women Through Time. *In* Cultural Stability and
    Culture Change. V. Ray, ed. Proceedings of the Annual Meeting of the American Ethnological
    Society, Seattle.
    1974   Onondaga Women: Among the Liberated. *In* Many Sisters: Women in Cross-Cultural Per-
    spective. C. Matthiasson, ed. Pp. 401–420. New York: Free Press.
Roessel, Ruth
    1981   Women in Navajo Society. Rough Rock, Ariz.: Navajo Resource Center.
Rothenberg, Diane
    1976   Erosion of Power: An Economic Basis for the Selective Conservatism of Seneca Women in
    the Nineteenth Century. Western Canadian Journal of Anthropology 6:106–122.
    1980   The Mothers of the Nation: Seneca Resistance to Quaker Intervention. *In* Women and Colo-
    nization. M. Etienne and E. Leacock, eds. Pp. 63–87. New York: Praeger.
Sacks, Karen
    1982   Sisters and Wives: The Past and Future of Sexual Equality. Urbana: University of Illinois
    Press.

Sanday, Peggy
    1973   Toward a Theory on the Status of Women. American Anthropologist 75:1682–1700.
    1981   Female Power and Male Dominance: On the Origins of Sexual Inequality. New York: Cambridge University Press.
Schlegel, Alice
    1972   Male Dominance and Female Autonomy: Domestic Authority in Matrilineal Societies. New Haven, Conn.: Human Relations Area Files Press.
    1973   The Adolescent Socialization of the Hopi Girl. Ethnology 12:449–462.
    1975   Three Styles of Domestic Authority: A Cross-Cultural Study. *In* Being Female: Reproduction, Power and Change. D. Raphael, ed. Pp. 165–176. The Hague: Mouton.
    1977   Male and Female in Hopi Thought and Action. *In* Sexual Stratification: A Cross-Cultural View. A. Schlegel, ed. Pp. 245–269. New York: Columbia University Press.
    1979   Sexual Antagonism Among the Sexually Egalitarian Hopi. Ethos 7:124–141.
Schneider, Mary Jane
    1983   Women's Work: An Examination of Women's Roles in Plains Indian Arts and Crafts. *In* The Hidden Half: Studies of Plains Indian Women. P. Albers and B. Medicine, eds. Pp. 101–122. Lanham Park, Md.: University Press of America.
Shepardson, Mary
    1982   The Status of Navajo Women. American Indian Quarterly 6:149–169.
Spector, Janet
    1983   Male/Female Task Differentiation Among the Hidatsa: Toward the Development of an Archeological Approach to the Study of Gender. *In* The Hidden Half: Studies of Plains Indian Women. P. Albers and B. Medicine, eds. Pp. 77–99. Lanham, Md.: University Press of America.
Spindler, Louise
    1962   Menomini Women and Culture Change. Memoirs of the American Anthropological Association 91:14–20.
Spindler, Louise, and George Spindler
    1979   Changing Women in Men's Worlds. *In* Sex Roles in Changing Cultures. Occasional Papers in Anthropology, 1. A. McElroy and C. Matthiasson, eds. Pp. 35–48. Buffalo: Department of Anthropology, State University of New York at Buffalo.
Synderman, George
    1948   Behind the Tree of Peace. Philadelphia: University of Pennsylvania.
Terrell, John Upton, and Donna M. Terrell
    1974   Indian Women of the Western Morning. Garden City, N.Y.: Doubleday.
Thayer, James
    1980   The Berdache of the Northern Plains: A Socioreligious Perspective. Journal of Anthropological Research 36:287–293.
Trigger, Bruce
    1978   Iroquoian Matriliny. Pennsylvania Archaeologist 48:55–66.
Underhill, Ruth M.
    1979   Papago Woman. New York: Holt, Rinehart & Winston.
Van Kirk, Sylvia
    1980   "Many Tender Ties": Women in Fur-Trade Society in Western Canada, 1670–1870. Norman: University of Oklahoma Press.
Wallace, Anthony
    1947   Women, Land and Society. Pennsylvania Archaeologist 17:1–35.
    1969   The Death and Rebirth of the Seneca. New York: Vintage Press.
Wallace, Edith
    1978   Sexual Status and Role Differences. *In* California, Vol. 8: Handbook of North American Indians. R. Heizer, ed. Pp. 683–689. Washington, D.C.: Smithsonian Institution.
Weaver, Sally
    1972   Medicine and Politics among the Grand River Iroquois. National Museum of Man, Publications in Ethnology 4. Ottawa.

Webster, Paula
    1975   Matriarchy: A Vision of Power. *In* Towards an Anthropology of Women. R. Reiter, ed. Pp.
        141–156. New York: Monthly Review Press.
Weist, Katherine
    1980   Plains Indian Women: An Assessment. *In* Anthropology on the Great Plains: The State of the
        Art. W. R. Wood and M. Liberty, eds. Pp. 255–272. Lincoln: University of Nebraska Press.
    1983   Beasts of Burden and Menial Slaves. *In* The Hidden Half: Studies of Plains Indian Women.
        P. Albers and B. Medicine, eds. Pp. 29–52. Lanham Park, Md.: University Press of America.
Whitehead, Harriet
    1981   The Bow and the Burden Strap: A New Look at Institutionalized Homosexuality in Native
        North America. *In* Sexual Meanings: The Cultural Construction of Gender and Sexuality. S. Ortner
        and H. Whitehead, eds. Pp. 80–115. New York: Cambridge University Press.
Williams, Walter
    1986   The Spirit and the Flesh: Sexual Diversity in American Indian Culture. Boston: Beacon Press.
Wittstock, Laura
    1980   Native American Women: Twilight of a Long Maidenhood. *In* Comparative Perspectives of
        Third World Women. B. Lindsay, ed. Pp. 207–228. New York: Praeger.
Wolf, Eric
    1982   Europe and the People without History. Berkeley: University of California Press.

7

Anthropological Scholarship on Gender in the English-speaking Caribbean

A. Lynn Bolles
University of Maryland, College Park

Deborah D'Amico-Samuels
Culturelinc Corporation

This essay delineates the substantive and theoretical foci of anthropological and other relevant research on women in the English-speaking Caribbean. Limitations of space, as well as the complexities of comparisons across lines of history, culture, and language within the region, make it impossible to do justice to the entire Caribbean region in this orienting essay. The focus on particular countries within the West Indies, most notably Jamaica, is the result of the historical concentration of research in those places, as well as of the authors' own research experiences. Fortunately, the current plethora of research, especially that by Caribbean scholars, promises to balance our picture of women in the region in the near future.

The historical roots of contemporary work on gender lie in the decades following the rebellions and protests of West Indian women and men during the 1930s. Profound anger over working conditions, grinding poverty, and political powerlessness during this period led not only to the formation of trade unions and political parties, but also to scholarly investigations concerning socioeconomic conditions in the West Indies. In 1938, a Royal Commission was appointed by the British Parliament to survey the region and to make recommendations based on their work. The report of this commission emphasized the disorganization of West Indian family life, and cited as problems patterns of childbearing and rearing and sexual relationships.

This report contained the seeds of much of the research done on this region over the next 35 years. The high incidence of childbearing outside of legally sanctioned unions became a factor that both had to be explained and was used to explain the poverty in which the majority of black and poor West Indians lived. The role of women in West Indian societies was defined as matriarchal, while men were seen as irresponsible and/or peripheral to families. The more overt race, class, and gender bias of the Royal Commission gave way over time to anthropological theories that recognized regional cultural norms regarding kinship and/or the overarching realities of racism, poverty, and the effects of slavery and colonialism. However, the structure and cycles of family life, and the roles of men and women within these, were inextricably linked to socioeconomic conditions in the region, and theories regarding West Indian family life were thus seen as politically charged and of practical importance.

Despite the centrality of women-related *issues* (such as matrifocality, female-headed households, and fertility patterns) to Caribbean social and cultural anthropological research, *women per se* were missing from the analysis. That is, while describing forms of family and household structures and to some degree social class, social scientists ignored the roles that women play in culture and society and the relations of gender as they affect social structures; these issues were extracted from, or were invisible in, the rigorous debate. Therefore, prior to the rise of feminist scholarship, much and nothing had been said about women of the English-speaking Caribbean and gender relations in those cultures and societies.

Fortunately, this is no longer the case. A profusion of women-focused research emanates from the campuses of the University of the West Indies (UWI) and the Institute of Social and Economic Research (ISER), thanks to the development of a women's studies program on all campuses and to the Women in the Caribbean Project of ISER, a three-year study carried out by a multidisciplinary research team from the Eastern Caribbean branch of the UWI system. In addition, a number of North American women anthropologists have made substantial contributions to the study of Caribbean women in culture and society.

The women-focused research of the past 15 years is of two interconnecting categories: some feminist scholars have focused on the role and status of women in culture and society, while others have focused on women and household structures. These studies direct their attention to the interrelationships among women, men, children, work, and family. They place complex systems of domestic activities and production within a framework of political economy. As Christine Barrow, an anthropologist based in Barbados, notes: "anthropologists have brought women to the forefront of their studies, allowed them to speak, and given precedence to their own perceptions of themselves and the world around them" (1986b:1).

This essay focuses on three interrelated themes: (1) the historical development of the assumed European "norm" regarding gender and family versus the Afro-Caribbean role of women; (2) a discussion of recent research on women's role and status; and (3) an examination of work done on the political economy of women and their households. This emphasis on the position of women within West Indian political economy follows from the fact that much of the research done in the region has approached the themes delineated above from the perspective of the practical and political realities of a region plagued by poverty. For example, work done by scholars at the University of the West Indies is expected to provide necessary input for policy concerning women and development. This essay, then, has comparatively little to say about women and religion, or ritual, or on the more interpretive aspects of gender relations. Hopefully, gender-focused research in the region will begin to make the connections between the more elusive aspects of the sociocultural construction of gender and development concerns.

Background: European "Norm"/Black Reality— "Equal under the Whip"

The Caribbean region has experienced two of the most extreme forms of exploitation known in human societies—slavery and colonialism (Sutton and Makiesky-Barrow 1981:469). The resulting oppression brought together two cultural systems—West African and European—which through the process of creolization gave rise to particular complex social formations. Overall, Caribbean societies are highly stratified by race, class, and ethnicity, and by gender inequality. How this came to be has its baseline in the days of slavery, which forged future patterns of social relations in the region.

Much of the social science literature, from the 1930s to the early 1970s, stresses the differences that appear between aspects of culture that are perceived as "European" (read white or light-skinned, and/or upper- or middle-class) and as the social "norm" on the one hand; and the cultural systems of the West Indian majority on the other. Over four centuries of European colonization resulted in the sociopolitical hegemony of the upper classes and the accompanying derision of the cultures of the masses. Light skin color and/or middle-class status approximated the socially approved "norm," while the African cultural patterns and dark skins of the black majority were sources of disparagement.

Detailed investigation by anthropologists eventually challenged the notion that Afro-Caribbean families represented disorganized and/or pathological adaptations to the conditions of slavery. Such a view resulted from looking at female-headed households in the Caribbean through Euro-American eyes. For example, the model of a family as two adults of the same generation, but different sexes, who are the biological parents of children with whom they live rests in part on a gender division of labor requiring a male breadwinner and a female homemaker, and also on the belief that conjugal relations are more important than consanguineal ones. The West Indian family differs from this not only in reality but in beliefs about what a family is and what is appropriate for its members to do. Anthropologists learned that in order to understand both the economic support of households and children, as well as domestic responsibilities (such as laundry and meal preparation) and child care, they could not assume that the boundaries of a dwelling defined a family and what it does. Often, eating, sleeping, financial support, and childrearing were shared among a network of male and female relatives and neighbors.

The focus of our attention here is the positive nature of these cultural patterns of Afro-Caribbean people; specifically, how their West African heritage influenced women's position in culture and society during Caribbean culture building. How did these new cultural forms provide the basis for future generations of Black Caribbean women? From the very beginning of slavery, both men and women labored side by side in the sugar cane fields. In some cases, other production-related jobs on sugar estates were designated specifically to men or women. However, for the majority who labored in gangs, only age and health differentiated one slave from another. In most areas of the Caribbean, especially in the early days, men outnumbered women (e.g., in 1789 in Jamaica, the ratio was 2:1 [Mair 1977:5]). However, after the abolition of the slave trade in 1807, to maintain the numbers of slaves needed for labor, women became important persons as breeders of slave infants for the biological reproduction of labor. The enslaved woman who bore six children became a "privileged person" by law. Such a clear recognition of the black woman's vital role as mother indirectly helped to keep alive her awareness of herself as a woman. And, as Jamaican historian Lucille Mair notes: "it is essentially such awareness of oneself as a human being which makes the individual refuse to be reduced to the level of a non-human being, in the way that slavery attempted." West African traditions of production, kinship, and family also supported the positive valuation of motherhood and the "equality" fostered by the estate labor force.

In African "sending" societies, women were not either agriculturalists/producers *or* mothers, but *both*. The complexities of West Indian plantation life distorted this heritage while ironically reinforcing it; many mothers felt the deep cruelty of bringing children into slavery and resisted the master's encouragement to do so, preferring abortion to the "privileges" accorded mothers. The use of women as laborers in the fields beside men also revealed biases of color and gender; the majority of black women were field slaves in Jamaica, and the majority of field slaves were black women. Although men and women labored equally in the field gangs, the chances of a female doing any other task was slim. Being a nurse or midwife, which were among the few possibilities open to black women, was not usually granted any form of remuneration or social value by the slave masters.

Within the community of slaves, the African influence in the creole Caribbean social order was strong. In the slave quarters, the division of domestic labor may have been quite sex-segregated, but each person's labor had value for the individual, one's neighbors and one's kin, rather than for the master, as was the case with labor in the cane fields. Moreover, here, in contrast to the patriarchal tradition in Europe, where women's status was derived from a spouse or father, women of African descent achieved status within their households and communities as individuals in their own right. Motherhood in this context is shorthand for procreation, childrearing, kinship, family, and women's central role in all of these activities. As Mintz states, "West Africa and the Afro-Caribbean, . . . have demonstrated a version of equality in some population sectors that European societies, with their quite basic view of *women as property,* neither understand nor accept" (1981:532).

The confluence of the "European"- and African-based systems reinforced black women's economic and maternal capacities and ultimately shaped the overall gender division of labor among the enslaved. However, because of the stratification of these societies, the African-based systems remained distinguishable from what the European colonists promoted as the "norm." During the post–emancipation period, options for the freed black depended on his or her society. In Barbados, land was extremely limited, therefore the economic system of sugar production merely shifted from one fueled by slave labor to one serviced by an agricultural proletariat. However, there were countries where land unsuitable for sugar cane was available, such as Jamaica, St. Lucia, and Guyana. There, the rise of a black peasantry took many forms, but was a predominent social characteristic and an alternative to sugar cane plantation labor. In the same moment, the social stratification of these societies was solidified, with the majority of blacks forming the bottom of the hierarchy, the colored population assuming the middle status, and the white plantocracy and European colonists occupying the apex. Depending on the society and the size of the ethnic population, indentured East Indians were placed at the bottom level, while Christian Syrians and Lebanese, Shepardic Jews, and Chinese made inroads toward the middle class and became buffers between the small white ruling class and the black masses.

Along with social stratification came increasing levels of sexual inequality. The domination of European constructs of gender-appropriate role, status, and proper place in society can be seen in turn of the century laws and policies throughout the region. For example, mass marriage campaigns attempted to convince West Indians to transform consensual or common law relationships into patriarchal legal marriages, and enlisted churches, schools, the press, radio, and welfare agencies in this effort. Economic opportunities during this time were controlled by those who perceived the masses of black women as without skills, pools of cheap human labor power, and always available for exploitation. So, then (as now) the political, economic, and social elites excluded most black women from access to expertise and status (Mathurin-Mair 1977:3). Throughout the region, domestic service continues to be the occupation of most Afro-Caribbean women.

Early debates about the black Caribbean family raised questions regarding whether or not the Western family form—legalized marriage and a nuclear household—represented the aspiration of all families, particularly those who couldn't afford it. Some argued that a single value system was shared by all classes and colors in these societies, but that the poor found it necessary to wait years before they could pay the costs of a wedding and home construction. Others maintained that the Caribbean family resulted in part from a West African cultural heritage in which the mother-child unit was separate from the father in patrilineal polygynous kin systems and autonomous in matrilineal ones. More recent research shows that, like all people, folk in the Caribbean are often caught between conflicting notions of what they want, and are also responding to economic conditions beyond their immediate control.

The Role and Status of Black Caribbean Women

While prefeminist scholars focused on the male's inability to meet Western concepts of "father," anthropologists and regional scholars working in the '70s and '80s have looked more closely at women, what they do and under what conditions. In their article on Barbados, Sutton and Makiesky-Barrow (1981) focus on one rural community where both did field-work—10 to 12 years apart. They discuss the historical background and the contemporary community in terms of five issues: (1) participation of both sexes in family and nondomestic activities; (2) the relative autonomy of women and men and the mechanisms by which they achieve status and prestige; (3) the significance attached to motherhood and its influence on women's economic dependence and independence; (4) cultural conceptions of sex roles and identities; and (5) effects of recent changes on the balance of power between the sexes (1981:470). Although Sutton and Makiesky-Barrow found some decline in women's auton-omy, as a result of the increasing hegemony of capitalism and its associated divisions between domestic and public life, they did not find the strict replication of sexual inequality in Bar-bados that exists in other "Western" societies. They attribute this to a cultural ideology that gives to both women and men a similar set of positively valued characteristics and abilities, and that identifies parenthood and sex as two highly valued experiences (Sutton and Mak-iesky-Barrow 1981:496). Women's independent access to resources via a kinship system and the economy combine with these beliefs to minimize gender differences and emphasize the effectiveness of the individual, thus accounting for a more equal status between the sexes.

Although some sense of gender equality does exist in West Indian societies, relative to their European and Euro-American counterparts, there is a sharp division in the organization of household labor. Women perform a disproportionate amount of work and usually carry the enormous responsibility of ensuring the survival of family members (Powell 1984:104). Vic-toria Durant-Gonzalez (1982:3) calls this set of activities "the realm of female responsibil-ity." She states that a large proportion of women in the English-speaking Caribbean are "in charge of producing, providing, controlling, or managing the resources essential to meeting daily needs." This concept of female responsibility ranges from a woman "being singly in charge of economic resources and managing a household and its members, to sharing respon-sibilities with a mate and/or relatives, to providing the full range of material and nonmaterial needs of daily life" (1982:3).

Here, we see the reality of the "price" of the inclusive concept of motherhood that obtains in the West Indies. Since most Caribbean women are employed in low-paying, low-skilled, and menial jobs or are unemployed, how can they fulfill all that is expected of them? Here, the ideological support mechanisms found in the African-based traditional role of women in Caribbean societies prove to be invaluable cultural assets. Work, no matter how dead-end, has meaning in terms of how a woman attempts to meet her familial responsibili-ties, and is also an essential part of her self-image and her conception of womanhood. Durant-Gonzalez states that the women interviewed in her sample cited "independence" as a com-ponent in the conceptualization of womanhood. Independence was conceived of as exercising options, making decisions, and establishing a female role as contributor to the household and as a participant in the economic sector. Christine Barrow's work (1986a) analyzes this notion of "independence," which is often used to describe West Indian women and how they carry out their responsibilities. This term has its merits and limitations; it both clarifies and obfuscates reality. Barrow argues that the group of women she worked with in Barbados spoke of independence as a quality based on having one's own source of economic support—from employment, other income-generating activities and, where possible, savings—while at the same time organizing and utilizing support from others. Autonomy implies exercising options while making decisions for oneself and having control over one's own destiny with no strings attached.

Independence, then, is not coterminous with female autonomy. Economic self-sufficiency is far beyond the means of most to whom the term *independent* has been applied. Rather than acting on behalf of a single person, autonomy implies interdependency found among a number of individuals. Autonomy is highly valued, and lifetimes are spent fulfilling obligations to others so as to reinforce that reciprocal support in time of need. Barrow says, "one is considered foolish to refuse support from those who give, especially if they have a culturally prescribed obligation to do so" (1986a:8).

One mechanism used to preserve autonomy is to maintain reciprocal relationships within the networks. Barrow (1986a:9) describes the etiquette of network exchanges as such that "independence" or at least the public image of it, is maintained. Behavior such as direct begging or public donations "violate" that autonomy. The most critical characteristic of successful network management is to avoid total dependence on one source of support, particularly a male partner. If a relationship endures over the years, the male support tends to become secure. However, it can never be fully relied upon, as at any stage of a marital union—visiting, common-law, and points in between—the relationship can be temporarily or completely terminated. Therefore, women's control over their lives functions as a degree of economic autonomy that includes the nature of earning, spending, saving, property ownership, and the sexual division of "money matters." According to Christine Barrow (1986a:11) female autonomy is encouraged from an early age and education is emphasized as the means to get a good job. The major life-long strategy then, to "cut and contrive," involves female networks that assist mothers, sisters, daughters, and "in-laws" (children's father's female relatives) alongside income-generating activities.

The Political Economy of Women, Work, and Households

The economic strategies and cultural mechanisms employed by the majority of Caribbean women to fulfill their roles as mother and provider are the substance of the next category of recent women-focused anthropological studies. Some anthropologists and other social scientists researching women have looked beyond women in their communities (cf. Sutton and Makiesky-Barrow), placing women, men, children, and households in a wide framework of political economy. Examples of this type of research are Deborah D'Amico-Samuels' (1986) research on the impact of tourism on women, work, and family, Shellee Colen's (1986) New York-based study of women migrants, and A. Lynn Bolles' examination of economic crises and working-class households (1986).

In her study, "You Can't Get Me Out of the Race: Women and Economic Development in Negril, Jamaica," Debby D'Amico-Samuels carefully documents the interplay of historical cultural precedents of gender relations and the changing relations of production and reproduction in a fishing, coconut-processing village that was transformed into a tourist resort. She describes the transformation of women's economic activities from subsistence agriculturalists and coconut oil "higglers" (petty traders) to cottage owners, managers, and workers, and from sugar cane plantation labor, produce higglering, and unemployment to craft and food vending with a tourist clientele. Affecting these changes were the influence of local politics, class, and color stratification systems, and the functioning of an economic development model.

One of the features of Negril's tourist sector was the creation of a crafts market for vendors to sell their goods. D'Amico-Samuels compared, by gender of the vendor, what was sold, the rate of profit, and other business strategies. She found that women vendors had difficulty in separating overhead costs from household necessities. Profit seemed to be identified with what was left over after there was both "enough stock in the shop and enough food in the house." Here again, the other side of the inclusion of provider within the concept of mothering is illuminated. If one of the assets of this concept is that it encourages women to engage in productive activities, it also enmeshes these activities in reproductive responsibilities. "If women's work activities and earnings are more closely tied to household responsibilities than men's, this may mean that women make decisions about time and money differently than do men, and that they must be more mindful of others in making these decisions" (D'Amico-Samuels 1986:238). Thus, while women involved in tourism in different ways saw no conflict between their mothering and familial roles and their work, the former structured the latter, with the result that women in different economic positions were involved in less lucrative work than were men of their class.

Moreover, the involvement of government development policy and practice, the role of foreign investors, and the dependent nature of a tourist economy operated to reduce control of women, especially the poorest women, over many aspects of their work and income. For example, after nearly ten years of struggle over the piece of land on which they had established their market, Negril vendors were relocated on a property owned by the government. Here, many of the domestic activities they had engaged in at the "captured" (illegally seized by squatting) site were now forbidden. Women were now forbidden to do their laundry or cook for their children when business was slow. In response to complaints by tourists and hoteliers, periodic government sweeps resulted in arrests and seizure of the goods of vendors who walked the beaches and roads. The women, however, constantly created new ways of fulfilling the multiple aspects of their roles as workers, mothers, members of kin groups, and providers; they refused to be forced out of the race for survival or the struggle to achieve economic mobility for themselves and their families. By their defiance and determination, they redefined what their market, their profession, and their mothering would be about. They continue to do their laundry, care for their families, and conduct business when and where they must.

Shellee Colen's research (1986) on Caribbean women as private household workers demonstrates how far many of these women must go to maintain their sense of independence and autonomy, within a context of high unemployment at home and work structured by race, gender, and class divisions abroad. Colen shows that women from varying levels of working-class and lower-middle class backgrounds leave St. Vincent and work as private domestics in New York City in order to realize an earning capacity necessary to fulfilling their "realm of female responsibility." Because the economy of a country like St. Vincent places severe economic constraints on both men and women, everyone searches for alternatives. Decisions to seek alternatives are not easily made, but are essential in survival strategies for many Afro-Caribbean women. The short-term goal of these women migrants is to immediately fulfill their duties and obligations to family and dependents—maintaining their spots in the St. Vincent-based domestic networks. The long-term plan is to acquire a way to do this networking in a less problem-filled manner, by becoming a U.S. citizen and sponsoring the migration of dependents to the United States.

Colen vividly describes the price black Caribbean women pay in securing "independence" and "autonomy," and the irony of being forced to leave their children in order to fulfill their mothering role. Colen's more recent work (1987) demonstrates the way in which scholarship on Caribbean women, within the context of a global economy, can become part of a cross-cultural analysis of mothering that is rooted in awareness of the shifting realities of race, class, and gender. In redefining their own role as workers and as mothers, U.S. middle- and upper-class white women look across lines of race and class, rather than across those of gender, to establish a new domestic division of labor. Colen explores what this means for notions of mothering held by both employer and West Indian domestic worker.

In another example of how particular social forces influence women's lives and those of their dependents, the work of A. Lynn Bolles in Jamaica delineates the links between urban working-class Jamaican households and international monopoly capitalism. Regardless of household composition, all urban working-class women and other household members tend to use a variety of economic activities to compensate for the lack of full employment and to guarantee their survival. The economic constraints stem from the political economy of Jamaica, which is in turn determined directly and indirectly by the movement of international capital. The coexistence of the formal and informal economic sectors and the way working-class people utilize those sectors on their own behalf suggests another strategy in which women fulfill their responsibilities to self and others.

An informal economic activity, a "backyard nursery," exemplifies how that sector incorporates a woman's family, neighborhood, and coworker-based social networks for the survival of the individual as well as for the extended household unit. A backyard nursery is the most popular form of daycare among working-class Jamaicans. One woman ran such a nursery in her Kingston home. She had two children of her own; the youngest was a toddler. Previously, this woman worked as a sewing machine operator in an off-shore production plant until she had her last child. When she returned from maternity leave, the factory closed down. In need of an income, the woman told friends that she was taking care of children. Former coworkers, friends, neighbors, and family began to drop off their children on a regular and temporary basis. Although she no longer earns the J$50.00 per week as a garment worker, when her own child-care costs are deducted, her present day-care earnings equal those lost in formal sector employment.

These three examples of recent anthropological studies on women, work, and households provide detail on how the majority of Caribbean women manage and manipulate that which they have control over in response to shrinking economic options. Sustaining and propelling these activities are the ideological supports that women learn as resources in their culture. These patterns of behavior and worldview include a woman's concepts of mother *and* worker as her proper role in society. Women who daily face the need to put food on the table, send children to school, and keep healthy the future generations of the region force us to consider theory and practice regarding development and political economy as no one else can. The daily struggle of Caribbean women to meet the needs of children graphically illustrates the stakes in global and academic debates over what development is and who should control it. At the same time, women's skill and ingenuity in feeding and raising families and wresting a living from economies that exclude them from all but the least rewarding work reveals a reservoir of human potential that is frustrated, rather than engaged, by the current economic policies of the region.

Conclusion

A feminist perspective in the recent anthropological literature on women and gender relations in the English-speaking Caribbean has provided important insights and theoretical contributions to the study of highly stratified, complex societies. It has been standard social science practice since the 1940s to analyze West Indian societies in terms of concepts of race, class, and ethnicity within the constructs of historical process. These theoretical tools as points of departure have greatly enhanced how gender relations and the role of women in culture and society are perceived and examined. The scholarship on West Indian women raises complex questions regarding the nature of status in the kinds of stratified societies in which anthropologists work today; it illuminates the interrelations among gender, race, and class inequalities and provides material crucial to the debate over the nature and direction of contemporary world development. Caribbean feminist scholarship and that of feminist Caribbeanists are truly on the cutting edge of this endeavor and can be a key locus for cross-cultural comparisons.

References Cited

Barrow, Christine
  1986a   Autonomy, Equality and Women in Barbados. Paper presented at the 11th annual Caribbean Studies Association Meeting, Caracas, Venezuela, May.
  1986b   Anthropology, the Family and Women in the Caribbean. Paper presented to the Inaugural seminar, Women's Studies Program, University of the West Indies, St. Augustine, Trinidad.
Bolles, A. Lynn
  1986   Economic Crisis and Female-headed Households in Urban Jamaica. *In* Women and Change in Latin America. J. Nash and Helen Safa, eds. Pp. 65–83. South Hadley, Mass.: Bergin and Garvey.
Colen, Shellee
  1986   With Respect and Feelings: Voices of West Indian Domestic and Child Care Workers in New York City. *In* All American Women: Lines That Divide, Ties That Bind. J. Cole, ed. Pp. 46–70. New York: Free Press.
  1987   Like a Mother to Them: Meanings of Child Care and Motherhood for West Indian Child Care Workers in New York. Paper presented at the American Anthropological Association annual meeting, Chicago.
D'Amico-Samuels, Deborah
  1986   You Can't Get Me out of the Race: Women and Economic Development in Negril, Jamaica, West Indies. Ph.D. dissertation, City University of New York.
Durant-Gonzalez, Victoria
  1982   The Realm of Female Familial Responsibility. *In* Women and the Family. Pp. 1–27. ISER, Barbados: Women in the Caribbean Project.
Mathurin-Mair, Lucille
  1977   Reluctant Matriarchs. Savacou 13:1–6.
Mintz, Sidney
  1981   Economic Role and Cultural Tradition. *In* The Black Woman Cross-Culturally. F. Chioma Steady, ed. Pp. 515–534. Cambridge: Schenkman.
Powell, Dorian
  1984   The Role of Women in the Caribbean. Social and Economic Studies 33(2):97–122.
Sutton, Constance, and Makiesky-Barrow, Susan
  1981   Social Equality and Sexual Status in Barbados. *In* The Black Woman Cross-Culturally. For Chioma Steady, ed. Pp. 469–498. Cambridge: Schenkman.

Curricular Example One: Cross-Cultural and Intra-Cultural Variability of Gender

Instructors can use either or both of these exercises to encourage student understanding about gender, specifically using West Indian material.

Aim: to use material on West Indian women to raise questions about the cross-cultural variability of gender roles, and the difficulties of evaluating the status of women in different societies.

Readings (see annotated bibliography for complete references)

Bennett Justus, Joyce: "Women's Role in West Indian Society"; Sutton, C., and Makiesky-Barrow, S.: "Social Equality and Sexual Status in Barbados"; Marshall Paule: *Brown Girl, Brownstones.*

Assignment

Divide the class into three groups of students, and have each group read one of the above selections. Alternatively, just the articles by Bennett Justus and Sutton/Makiesky-Barrow can be assigned and two groups can do the exercise below. The reading by Marshall is considerably longer, and less explicit in its portrayal of roles and status, but makes for rewarding reading and a more personalized view of conflicting ideas regarding gender roles and status within the family. Make each group aware of the focus of the exercise below so that they can take appropriate notes on the readings.

Exercise

Have each group meet during class time (for a very large class, subgroups may be necessary) for half an hour. Instruct each group to prepare the following lists based on their reading:

1. List the kinds of things girls and women are expected to *do* in the society which the author is describing;

2. List the kinds of qualities and characteristics which women are expected to develop and display in this society;

3. List the reasons the author offers for why girls and women are expected to behave in these ways.

After these lists have been compiled, ask for a recorder to put them on the board. Invite a general discussion of the following questions:

1. Do all of the authors seem to agree on the appropriate gender roles for West Indian women? If not, how do they differ? Can the lists be combined into a composite picture of West Indian expectations for female behavior?

2. Have the class collaborate in constructing parallel lists for gender roles and expectations as they experience them. Record their list on the board beside those for West Indian women.

3. Can a general statement be made regarding women's status among West Indians as compared to women's status in the students' own society? How do they think status should be evaluated—should women be compared with women in other societies, or with men in their own? Across class groups and ethnic/racial categories? Can a composite set of expectations for women be devised which would give women more choices than they have in either place?

Film

Sweet Sugar Rage. This discussion can be greatly enhanced by having the class view this film, and raising the question of the various arenas (work, family, unions, church) in which women's role and status is evaluated, reinforced and/or challenged. The film also makes evident the work of Jamaican women to direct change in their position in society.

Aim: To understand the interrelationships among different forms of inequality and different aspects of individual identity; specifically, the ways in which gender affects and is affected by race and class in the experiences of West Indian women.

Readings

Colen, Shellee: "With Respect and Feelings—Voices of West Indian Domestic and Child Care Workers in New York City"; Cliff, Michelle: *Abeng,* or Hodge, Merle: *Crick Crack Monkey;* Moses, Yolanda: "Female Status, the Family and Male Dominance in a West Indian Community."

Assignment

Divide the class into three groups, and assign each one of the above readings. (In the case of the novels, *Abeng* and *Crick Crack Monkey,* you may want to choose a particular incident and assign only that part of the novel. Alternatively, if a monograph is usually assigned, semi-autobiographical novels such as *Abeng, Crick Crack Monkey* and *Brown Girl Brownstones* in Example One may be ways of allowing people to speak for themselves, as opposed to being described by an anthropologist.)

Exercise

1. Have each group complete a list of the main *differences* and *similarities* the author describes as existing between women of different colors, and/or classes and/or nationalities. Have a recorder from each group put the lists on the board, and have another student from each group verbally describe one incident or research finding that illustrates the differences and/or similarities among women that are emphasized in their assignment.

2. Have students divide into pairs and briefly interview each other regarding their own race, class, and gender positions. Have them ask each other to describe an incident in their lives that made them especially aware of one or more of these classifications. Do they experience one of these aspects as more meaningful to their own identity than others? As shaping outsiders' attitudes and behaviors toward them more than others? As affecting their lives and life chances more significantly? How or why?

3. Have each student write a paragraph or two on their understanding of gender, class, and race and how it has been affected by their reading and discussions with their classmates.

Curricular Example Two: Women, Family and Household

(Lecture Summary; see detail in essay)

Much of the recent work done by anthropologists working in the Caribbean, as well as much of the work done by the women's studies groups at the University of the West Indies campuses and departments, implicitly or explicitly confronts the earlier social science literature on the region, and its obsession with family structure. This confrontation has yielded much that is of interest to instructors of the introductory anthropology course. Notions of family and of gender-appropriate roles often go hand in hand. However, to move students beyond a "circus side show" response to family variation, material is needed that can be linked to changes in U.S. society and can demonstrate the ways in which other cultures make distinctions among elements of gender and family which students are accustomed to thinking of as indivisible. It is hoped that the Caribbean concept of family presented below, especially the notion of mothering it includes, will do this for students.

Feminist scholarship on the Caribbean rounds out the exhaustive literature on family structure in the region by adding the dimension of gender to the class, race, cultural, and historical aspects of kinship considered by social scientists in the early part of this century. What the anthropologists working in the region prior to the interest in gender were trying to explain was the fact that so many households were headed by women, and that so many children were born outside of marriage. Massiah notes that, for the region as a whole, about 32% of households are headed by women; the highest proportion of these households is found in Guyana [47%], while the lowest occurrence is in St. Kitts [22%] (1982).

Although anthropologists have disagreed vehemently over explanations for female-headed households in the Caribbean, a number of common features of Caribbean families have been described. A life cycle approach reveals that, although at any given time, there are many households headed by women, most women and men eventually marry and stay married. Both women and men appear to pass through three stages of relationships, not necessarily with the same individuals. Visiting relationships constitute the first stage. A man visits a woman living at her parents' home, or later at a home of her own. Sweetheart, common law or live-in relationships follow in the cycle. Eventually, a couple who have lived together for many years and borne children together decide to legally marry. This pattern has been observed primarily among black Caribbean populations, and among the poor and working class.

Detailed investigation by anthropologists eventually challenged the notion that such families represented disorganized and/or pathological adaptations to conditions of slavery. Such a view results from looking at female-headed households in the Caribbean through Euro-American eyes. The Caribbean family differs from this in practice and in beliefs. Anthropologists learned that in order to understand both economic support of households and domestic responsibilities, they could not assume that the boundaries of a dwelling defined a family and what it does. Moreover, the assumption that the biological father should or does bear the brunt of breadwinning is not borne out in Caribbean family systems. Indeed, a combination of beliefs about gender resulting from an ever-changing blend of a West African cultural heritage, European beliefs, legal definitions of family and inheritance, and economic and political pressures have made it unlikely that the male/biological parent/breadwinner roles will be fulfilled by the same person. There is a deeply entrenched expectation that women will work not only at domestic chores and childrearing but also at income-earning activities; in fact, this is an integral part of what it means to mother in the Caribbean. Because incomes for most women are inadequate to support households, assistance from kin and neighbors is sought and reciprocated. The necessity of working for women means that children often spend some of their early years in the extended care of relatives; for example, sometimes those in rural areas care for children of mothers who migrate to the cities or even to other countries in search of work. (Consideration of these issues—what constitutes the boundaries of a family, who does what jobs considered family work and the issue of the relationship of biological parenting to child rearing—can be linked to current US experiences such as "surrogate parenting," problems of inadequate day care, the rise in the number of women in the work force, the difficulties of getting men to pay child support, the changes in living standard experienced by parents of each gender following divorce, etc.)

While prefeminist research focused on the male's inability to meet Western concepts of "father," anthropologists and regional scholars working in the '70s and '80s have looked more closely at what women do and think. They have also been sensitive to the context of underdevelopment and the way in which exploitation by multinational corporations, the IMF, and policies of industrialized nations have impacted on women in their struggles to fulfill the Caribbean notion of "mother." Their work has yielded an understanding of Caribbean families that includes gender as a factor in shaping families and a sense of how this has changed historically.

What has emerged from this literature is a view of the family and of gender roles that tries to answer the question of why women, who have lower rates of employment, a narrower range of job options and lower incomes in both the formal and informal sector, are increasingly the primary support of children during much of their lifetimes. Although in the Caribbean, gender role expectations, cultural models of family, bilateral inheritance and contributions from kin and "baby fathers" (biological fathers) enable a woman to minimally support a household, the initial excitement of Western feminists over the lack of polarization between motherhood and working has given way to the sobering realization that women's dual responsibilities toward children are most often undertaken in conditions of poverty and limited choices. As women in the United States are discovering, working outside the home does not automatically empower women.

This does not mean that Caribbean men contribute little to households in which they have children, to children residing in the households in which they themselves live, or to the households of their mothers and sisters. It does mean that they have more of a choice about when and how much to contribute than women do. This choice applies not only to money, but to time invested in child care and maintenance of the household necessary to that care. This basic gender inequality is not unique to the Caribbean, but the regional context provides women with the ideology to develop their own sources of support through work and social relations, thus rendering them less dependent on a spouse than women in the ideal Euro-American model described above.

However, race, class, and regional dynamics, given the role of the Caribbean in international capitalist development, combine with gender inequality in the household and the job market to ensure that women have a difficult time of it. For example, it is increasingly the case throughout the region that ties to a land base that can support a cohesive and extended kin group have grown weaker. Wage labor is harder to find, and income from the informal sector is precarious as well. At the same time, prices for many basic goods and services have risen astronomically due to conditions created by the rising costs of debt service.

Students can be challenged to find differences and parallels between black Caribbean family systems and families in our own society. It can be pointed out that many women in the

United States, bereft of a history of reliance on extended kin and having only recently begun to "network," have learned a lesson Caribbean women have known for centuries—the exhausting meaning of combining work inside and outside the home. The rise in divorce rates and the observed decline in the standard of living for women and children, placed alongside the Caribbean material, prompts the question of whether, where women earn income as individuals they will be called upon to support children in the absence of male willingness or ability to do so. What does the expectation that women will and should work mean for families in the context of low wages and a narrow range of jobs for women, without a policy for day care, without changes in expectations for male parenting? What can we learn from the flexibility of Caribbean family systems that can make changes in our own society more bearable?

Annotated Bibliography: Anthropological and Scholarly Materials

Chioma Steady, Filomina, ed.
    1981   The Black Woman Cross-Culturally. Cambridge, Mass.: Schenkman.

    This anthology is one of the best sources on the issues that emerge from the anthropological literature on Caribbean women specifically and on black women in general. The section devoted to the Caribbean contains several articles which are listed and briefly described below:

Bennett Justus, Joyce
    1981   Women's Role in West Indian Society.

    Bennett Justus focuses on socialization by gender within the family, and thus rounds out a literature that tends to locate causality at the structural level. The usefulness of this article for the introductory anthropology teacher is that it answers questions students in such courses often raise (i.e., those of a psychological nature). The author draws on Chodorow's concepts to explain how boys and girls learn behaviors and ideology appropriate to Caribbean gender systems.

Bilby, Kenneth, and Filomina Chioma Steady
    1981   Black Women and Survival: A Maroon Case.

    The authors consider some of the key questions concerning Caribbean women, within the context of Maroon (runaway slave and escaped African) communities historically. Thus, they raise the issue of the adaptive advantage of matrifocality among groups organized to fight for survival. The very existence of Maroon communities during slavery is a surprise for many introductory anthropology students, and raises for them new dimensions of the complex roles of women and men in slave societies.

Mintz, Sidney
    1981   Economic Role and Cultural Tradition.

    Long a proponent of the uniqueness of Caribbean and West African perspectives on gender, Mintz here clearly states how he views the economic roles of Caribbean market women as contributing to a degree of female autonomy not yet achieved by Western societies. The article also reviews explanations for the economic independence of women in the region.

Moses, Yolanda
    1981   Female Status, the Family and Male Dominance in a West Indian Community.

    Moses analyzes the relationship between women's economic contributions to households and their status, teasing out the contradictions among money, responsibility, power, and ideology that this relationship suggests. Two features of the article make it valuable for understanding the complexity of the questions the author raises: first, Moses compares women of different classes; second, she discusses the tension between the ideology of male dominance and the reality of female responsibilities.

Sutton, Constance, and Susan Makiesky-Barrow
  1981 Social Inequality and Sexual Status in Barbados.

In their consideration of the status of women in Barbados, the authors discuss the effect of plantation slavery and incorporation into the world capitalist system on beliefs and behaviors related to gender. They conclude that the status of women in the household and in the local community is based on their access to independent sources of income through work and kin networks, their centrality to the kinship system and a cultural ideology that positively values similar characteristics in both men and women.

Solien Gonzalez, Nancie
  1981 Household and Family in the Caribbean: Some Definitions and Concepts.

This is a reprint of a classic in Caribbean anthropology, and is the quickest way to grasp the literature that the scholarship on women attempts to redress.

Colen, Shellee
  1986 With Respect and Feelings: Voice of West Indian Domestic and Child Care Workers in New York City. *In* All American Women: Lines That Divide, Ties That Bind. Johnetta Cole, ed. Pp. 46–70. New York: Free Press.

Colen's article focuses on the feelings and analyses of West Indian immigrant women concerning their employers and the conditions under which they work. Especially valuable for the quotes from women themselves, which describe their relationships with the families for whom they work, as well as with their own kin.

Clarke, Edith
  1966 My Mother Who Fathered Me. London: Allen and Unwin.

First published in 1957, Clarke's book is recommended for those interested in going deeper into the prefeminist anthropology of the region. The introduction to the book, by M. G. Smith, succinctly reviews this literature, and Clarke's material actually contains a wealth of information on women, embedded in discussions of family structure.

Massiah, Jocelyn
  1982 Women Who Head Households. *In* Women and the Family. Pp. 62–130. Barbados: WAND of ISER, U.W.I.

Good compilation of data about female-headed households throughout the Caribbean.

Rubenstein, Hymie
  1987 Coping with Poverty: Adaptive Strategies in a Caribbean Village. Boulder: Westview.

Rubenstein's discussion of domestic life in St. Vincent is rich in detail, and provides new and careful distinctions among kin roles and kin terms which bear on discussions of Caribbean families and gender roles.

Whitehead, Tony
  1986 Breakdown, Resolution and Coherence: The Fieldwork Experiences of a Big, Brown, Pretty-Talking Man in a West Indian Community. *In* Self, Sex, and Gender in Cross-Cultural Fieldwork. Tony L. Whitehead and Mary E. Conway, eds. Urbana: University of Illinois Press.

Whitehead uses his own field experience to analyze norms governing behavior by gender, color, and class. Thanks to the author's candor, this article offers an understanding of Caribbean gender ideology and its meaning for an individual, as well as a valuable and rare account of the ways in which cross-cultural fieldwork is affected by the gender of the researcher.

Women in the Caribbean Project
  1982 Women and the Family. Institute of Social and Economic Research, University of the West Indies, Cave Hill, Barbados.

Part of the publication series of the Women in the Caribbean Project (WICP), this volume focuses on the meaning that the culturally assigned role of women in families has for their status, their well-being, and their autonomy.

An overview of the articles in this collection is provided by Hermione McKenzie, a Caribbean sociologist long concerned with gender. Entitled "Introduction: Women and the Family in Caribbean Society," her article gives a critical and synthetic assessment of the contributions to the volume, as well as in-depth discussion of women's status from a regional perspective.

Also of interest in this collection is Victoria Durant-Gonzalez's article, "The Realm of Female Familial Responsibility," which tackles the question of the meaning of female economic as well as domestic and childrearing responsibilities for women. Because its conclusion is considerably less sanguine than that of other anthropologists who address this issue, this article serves as a provocative counterpart to the work of Mintz, Sutton and Makiesky-Barrow and others.

The other volume by the Women in the Caribbean project which specifically addresses the issues raised most often by anthropologists working in the region is the one entitled *Women and Work*. A useful overview is contained in the article by Patricia Anderson, entitled "Introduction: Women, Work and Development in the Caribbean." Anderson explains the region-specific model that the Project developed to measure the status of women in the region.

Volumes by the WICP can be ordered from Caribbean Books, P.O. Box H, Parkersburg, Iowa 50665 (or phone 319/346-2048). Selected articles from all of the work of the Women in the Carribean Project are contained in two special issues of the journal. *Social and Economic Studies*, volume 35, Numbers 2 and 3, June and September 1986, Jocelyn Massiah, editor. (This journal is published by the Institute for Social and Economic Research, University of the West Indies). The special value of these works is that the perspective on women and gender issues is that of indigenous social scientists who live and work in the Caribbean.

For those interested in pursuing Caribbean gender research, the unpublished dissertations below are recommended. Those in the New York metropolitan area can read most of these at the Research Institute for the Study of Man [sic!]. 162 East 78 Street, N.Y. Those done at universities in the United States can be purchased from University Microfilms.

Bolles, A. Lynn
    1981   The Impact of Working-Class Women's Employment on Household Organization in Kingston, Jamaica. Unpublished Ph.D. dissertation, Department of Anthropology, Rutgers University.
D'Amico-Samuels, Deborah
    1986   You Can't Get Me Out of the Race: Women and Economic Development in Negril, Jamaica. Unpublished Ph.D. dissertation, Department of Anthropology, City University of New York.
Mair, Lucille Mathurine
    1974   A Historical Study of Women in Jamaica, 1655–1844. Unpublished Ph.D. dissertation, Department of History, University of the West Indies at Mona, Kingston, Jamaica.
Reddock, Rhoda
    1984   Women, Labour and Struggle in Twentieth Century Trinidad and Tobago, 1898–1960. Unpublished Ph.D. dissertation, University of Amsterdam.
Whitehead, Tony L.
    1976   Men, Family and Family Planning: Male Role Perception and Performance in a Jamaica Sugartown. Unpublished Ph.D. dissertation, Department of Anthropology, University of Pittsburgh.

Other Resources for Students

Novels. Unfortunately, many works by Caribbean writers are difficult to get, either in libraries or bookstores. This is particularly true of works by women. However, Heinemann Educational Books, Inc. (4 Front Street, Exeter, New Hampshire 03833) publishes a paperback Caribbean Writers series, which includes some of the works listed below:

Hodge, Inerle
    1970   Crick Crack, Monkey.

Hodge offers a rare view of the conflicts between middle-class religion and lifestyle and "yard" (poor and working-class) life, seen through the eyes of a young Trinidadian girl. The novel offers a good sense of what color, class and gender in Caribbean society can mean to an individual.

Marshall, Paul
    1959   Brown Girl, Brownstones.

Recently reissued by the Feminist Press (New York), this novel is widely available. Marshall describes a mother-daughter struggle that encompasses the issues of gender from the divergent perspectives of an immigrant from Barbados working as a domestic/factory worker and her American-born daughter. Young undergraduates seem to identify with the generation gap issues raised, while students who are themselves immigrants identify with both mother and daughter. The novel raises issues of the culturally specific Caribbean notions of gender as they clash with U.S. versions of women's roles.

Michelle, Cliff
    1984   Abeng. Trumansburg, N.Y.: Crossings Press.

Abeng is about the intellectual coming of age of a middle-class, very light-skinned girl, and it explores the issues of class, color, and gender through her friendship with a dark-skinned, impoverished girl of her own age.

Short Articles and Collections

Mair, Lucille Mathurin
    1975   The Rebel Woman in the British West Indies during Slavery. Institute of Jamaica. (Available through Caribbean Books, P.O. Box H, Perkersburg, Iowa 50665; (phone 319/346-2048).

This booklet, complete with illustrations, renders an exciting and inspiring account of the role of women in resisting slavery.

Savacou 13

This special issue of the Caribbean artists movement was devoted to women's issues. The Introduction by Hermione McKenzie and the article, "Reluctant Matriarchs" by Lucille Mathurin have become classics and raise questions regarding the status of Caribbean women from a critical and regional perspective. Available through Caribbean books (see above).

Women's International Resource Exchange (WIRE)
    1987   Women in the Rebel Tradition: The English-Speaking Caribbean. WIRE, 2700 Broadway, New York, N.Y. 10025 ($4).

Contains short and timely articles on women in Jamaica, Grenada, and Trinidad, which address such issues as violence against women, the rights of domestic workers, and women in culture and politics. The volume includes articles by domestic workers, political leaders, and social scientists, as well as selections by poets, and a description of Sistren, a Jamaican women's theatre group.

Films

Sweet Sugar Rage

This film illustrates the process of consciousness-raising theatre as developed by Sistren, a working-class women's theatre group from Jamaica. What is unique and exciting about this film is that it both makes clear the harsh conditions under which women live and work *and* what is being done to change these conditions in a creative way. Note: the film is in Jamaican creole and may not be easily understood in spots. Available from Third World Newsreel, 335 West 38 Street, New York, N.Y. 10010; 212/947-9277.

Smile Orange

Available from commercial video rental outlets in some places, this film is a spoof of the tourist industry from the perspective of Jamaican male workers. Although both the Jamaican and tourist women are stereotypic portrayals, these provide material for discussing the race and class dimensions of gender relations.

8

Gender Relations in Sub-Saharan Africa

Betty Potash

Since the 1970s gender relations and their transformation have been an important theme in research on Sub-Saharan Africa.[1] Available data have brought into focus the lives of African women and contributed to theories of gender relations. For anthropologists, such research poses particular challenges. Insofar as women and men have been shown to participate differently in the economic, social, political, and religious life of their societies, we cannot continue to describe institutions as if they were gender neutral when they are not. Rather, an understanding of social organization and social process requires new conceptualizations that use gender as an integral theme of analysis, not as a marginal category. By focusing on participatory patterns and the diverse interests and strategies of women and men we obtain a more realistic picture. Furthermore, since the allocation of rights and responsibilities among men and women has implications for their relationship to one another and to their society, such analyses hold promise for improving our understanding of gender systems.

In this chapter I examine some of the topics typically covered in an introductory course from a gender perspective based on data on Sub-Saharan Africa. Aspects of economic, social and political organization, and religion are discussed, as well as the cultural construction of gender. Limitations of space and the particular focus of this chapter have necessitated omitting some important issues. Two omissions require particular comment. Although women in development is an important topic in African research, and African data. Were extensively used both in Ester Boserup's pioneering work (1970) which showed the negative impact development has had on women, and in its subsequent critique by Beneria and Sen (1981), this topic is not covered here (for recent coverage, see Bujra 1986, Nelson 1981, and Stichter and Parpart 1988). An equally difficult omission concerns foraging societies such as the !Kung and Mbuti, which are usually discussed in introductory courses. Evolutionary theories of the emergence of gender hierarchy frequently contrast the egalitarianism of foragers with the situation in more stratified systems. Since foragers present contrastive cases to many features characterizing food producers they must either be treated topically as exceptions to trends or dealt with as a separate unit. In view of the fact that African foragers are well known to anthropologists, I have decided not to review this material here. Readers unfamiliar with this literature should consult Draper (1975), Friedl (1975), Leacock and Lee (1982), Lee (1979), Shostak (1983) and the film *N!ai: The Story of a !Kung Woman*.

Theories of Gender Hierarchy and Gender Perspectives in Ethnography

The literature on Sub-Saharan African can be conveniently grouped into theoretical works dealing with gender hierarchy and ethnographic accounts, many of which use transactional and actor-oriented approaches to challenge orthodox interpretations. A central issue for feminist theory is the extent to which male dominance is found cross-culturally, and the processes associated with the development of gender hierarchy. Interpretive problems abound. The variant patterns of control women and men exercise in different spheres of activity do not easily translate into concepts of dominance and subordination (Schlegel 1977). The manner in which local cultures and capitalist penetration interact to affect the situation of men and women does not reduce to an issue of male dominance. Finally, while dominance remains an important focus for research, there are many other important questions we can ask about the complex relationships between women and men and their society. Among Africanist scholars who come from a wide variety of disciplines, some anthropologists have taken a broad view of the complexity of gender relations (Amadiume 1987; Guyer 1986; Kettel 1986; Llewelyn-Davies 1981; MacCormack 1980); but anthropology has certainly been affected by the centrality of this theme in feminist discourse (Obbo 1980; Oboler 1985; O'Laughlin 1974; Pellow 1977).

Many Africanist researchers argue that women's position has generally declined as a result of the colonial and capitalist encounter (Bujra 1986; Etienne and Leacock 1980; Henn 1984, 1988; Robertson 1987; Robertson and Berger 1986; Stamp 1986; Stichter and Parpart 1988; Strobel 1982), although there are exceptions to this trend (Guyer 1984a; Vellenga 1986). A critical question is the nature of the precolonial system. Is gender hierarchy attributable to European contact, or did such hierarchies exist prior to colonialism? What types of historical data are needed to understand precolonial systems, their diversity, and the transformations that occurred in this period? Are processes of postcolonial societal transformation uniform or diverse, and how determining are political and economic policies? Throughout this chapter I present data that touch on, but do not resolve, these issues.

The conceptual models that are most used in African gender studies focus on the connections between the political economy and gender relations. An emphasis on underdevelopment as a process, concepts drawn from dependency theory and world systems approaches, and Marxist and neo-Marxist models are found to varying degrees. By contrast, symbolic structuralism, studies of the cultural construction of gender, and of the relationship between sex, gender roles, and sexual behavior, including homosexuality, are less well represented. Currently popular emphases on emergent, counterhegemonic, and subordinate forms of consciousness and discourse tend to submerge gender issues, focusing largely on politically and economically disadvantaged groups (Ranger 1986), although there are exceptions (Coplan 1987). Some schema, such as Michelle Rosaldo's (1974) domestic-public dichotomy, associated respectively with women and men, or Sherry Ortner's (1974) and Ortner and Whitehead's reformulation and expansion (1981) that links nature and culture, self-interest versus societal interest and prestige differences to this hierarchy, are not well supported by data on precolonial African political systems and on women's involvement in anticolonial protest movements.

The two major paradigms that have been developed in relationship to African materials are those of Claude Meillassoux (1981) and Karen Sacks (1982). Both claim to be Marxist, but differ totally in their interpretations. Meillassoux has been particularly popular with some Marxist feminists who see women's reproductive roles as the locus of their oppression. Combining a Marxist interest in the extraction of labor and goods with a view of marriage which owes much to Lévi-Strauss, Meillassoux argues that through their control over marriage, senior men control the labor and produce of women and juniors under lineage modes of production. As we shall see below, there are variations in the manner by which marriages are actually arranged and differences in the extent to which men control women's productivity.

In contrast to French Marxist approaches, Karen Sacks's version of Marxism is related to cultural evolution and belongs to that school of thought best known through the work of Eleanor Leacock. Arguing against any universal male dominance, Sacks sees class formation and the development of the state as major factors in the subordination of women. In nonclass societies, which include foraging societies with communal modes of production in which women and men are equal, and food-producing systems with corporate kin modes of production where women in their role as sisters are equal in their own kin group and have rights to the means of production, there is no dominance. With the emergence of classes and the state, equality is lost and women become subordinate wives. Although this paradigm usefully directs our attention to the diversity among African societies and raises important questions about the relationship of classes and the state to gender, there are problems concerning the nature and extent of women's rights as sisters in prestate food-producing systems, which I address below.

A different approach to the study of gender relations, and one more commonly employed in ethnographic research, focuses less on theories of dominance and deals more with how women and men as social actors use systems to achieve ends. In contrast to more deterministic models, such praxis approaches emphasize human resourcefulness while recognizing systemic limitations, and suggest that women and men are not merely passive victims of political and economic trends, but utilize both customary and new possibilities. A more dynamic view of social systems and their internal contradictions emerges, with greater attention given to ethnohistorical and ethnographic particulars. These studies also serve as correctives to the normative, sociocentric, and androcentric orientations of some of the classic literature.

A collection of essays on widows in Africa, for example, shows that widows are not passive pawns in male transactions governing widow inheritance. Rather than being automatically absorbed in leviratic or other arrangements, widows make choices from the options available to them, which vary in different places. In some cases widows refuse such relationships; in others men may be reluctant to take over widows. The levirate is sometimes a cultural ideal rather than a statistical reality, and where practiced it often differs from initial marriage. Widows, for example, generally support themselves, have more autonomy than wives, and may reside separately from their husband's successor, heading their own households and managing their own affairs. In some places they enter new marriages or return to their own kin. By examining the strategies and interests of women and men and the factors affecting their decisions, it becomes evident that neither alliance nor descent theories of marriage, which presuppose shared corporate interests and normative behavior, are adequate to account for the complex range of actual relationships and choices (Potash 1986a).

Other ethnographic accounts using an actor-oriented approach examine the manner in which women seek to further political and economic interests (Bledsoe 1980; Etienne 1979, 1986; Hay 1976; MacCormack née Hoffer 1974, 1983; Oboler 1985; Schildkrout 1978; Vellenga 1986), describe the strategies women employ in modern urban settings (Bujra 1975; B. Lewis 1977; MacGaffey 1986, 1988; Nelson 1979, 1987; Obbo 1980; Parpart 1986, 1988; White 1988), show how the desire to maintain consanguineal ties and/or ties to children affect marriage and residential choices (Abu 1983; Etienne 1986; Landberg 1986; Schildkrout 1986), and examine factors affecting marital stability (Potash 1978).

Ethnohistorical perspectives have similarly modified our understanding of many institutions, showing how these have been transformed over time. Guyer (1986), tracing two centuries of Beti (Cameroon) history, demonstrates that polygyny and widow inheritance expanded with the development of commerce and the increased political and economic value of women, and then declined as the economy shifted to cocoa cultivation. Chanock (1982) and Wright (1982) show how customary marriage law was created during the colonial period in response to men's fears about the growing independence of women. In Robertson and Klein's (1983) collection of essays on female slavery, a number of accounts describe how the increase in female slaves affected kinship politics, enabling men to avoid matrilineal and affinal claims by taking slave wives. The position of free wives may also have been undermined. Amadiume (1987), Awe (1977), Kettel (1986), and others examine women's precolonial political roles that disappeared under the impact of colonialism and Christianity. These and other works challenge the lack of attention to process of the classic literature.

Other theoretical and ideological approaches such as symbolic structuralism (Comaroff 1985) and reflexive studies are also found in the literature, but to a lesser degree. Mariam Slater's *African Odyssey* (1976) anticipates by several years the current wave of interest in reflexive anthropology. Other works in this genre include the pseudonymous Manda Cesara's (1982) account of her fieldwork from a feminist perspective and the classic accounts of Laura Bohannon, which are widely used in introductory courses (Bohannon 1966; Bowen 1964).

A different approach is that of Ifi Amadiume (1987) who uses the sex-gender distinction as her major analytic framework. Noting that members of either sex could fill male gender roles, she critcizes earlier anthropological interpretations of Igbo society for failing to appreciate the sex-gender distinction that she attributes to racism and ethnocentrism. Contemporary feminist scholars are similarly taken to task for their arrogance in assuming the universality of Western constructs and issues. In a work that uses cultural and historical rather than materialist or actor-strategist analysis, Amadiume contrasts the rigidity of Western models with the flexibility of the Igbo gender system where daughters could fill male (sons) roles and could be husbands without being considered "masculine" or losing their femininity. Before Christian influence, successful women and men used wealth both to take titles and to acquire wives. Female assertiveness was expressed in the actions of different women's groups, which included groups of lineage daughters, of lineage wives, and a community-wide Women's Council under the leadership of titled women.

Having sketched in a broadbrush manner the contemporary theoretical issues that have dominated the anthropological discourse on African women, I turn now to indicate some of the ways that socioeconomic and cultural factors affect the varying positions of women and men in Africa. My objective is to show how material gathered from gender studies enriches our understanding of social process, providing important correctives to key concepts, with implications well beyond Africa. I begin with an examination of gender issues in economic organization, a topic that has received perhaps the most attention in recent research on Africa.

Economic Organization

One of the major issues—both in the economic history of Africa and in Western attempts to understand African women's economic activities in the present—arises from a misconception. In the West, husbands and wives often pool incomes to fund a range of household activities. By contrast, husbands and wives in Africa generally have separate incomes which they do not pool, and they individually underwrite different household activities, with women generally responsible for feeding and clothing their own children. The imposition of a Western model—whether by concept or by colonial and postcolonial economic policy—has had profound implications for African women.

The monetization of African economies has generally required women to add income-earning activities to meet their traditional obligations without their access to the means to do so. Men, on the other hand, have generally been favored in access to cash-earning opportunities on the assumption that men's earnings would contribute to a common household fund to support other household members. As a consequence, women need men's cash contributions, which are not always forthcoming, leading to increased marital tension. Nonetheless, while these features are generally true, there is wide variation. In this section, I examine three major themes in the gendered division of labor in Africa. First, I review the patterns of women's productive activities across the continent. Next, I note the specific features of the monetization of African economies, and finally I examine the distinctive effects on women of rural to urban migration. To highlight the variability of these features, I cite the specific strategies women have deployed throughout West Africa's "Cocoa Belt."

Although patterns of productive organization vary, the overall importance of women's economic activities is evident from a United Nations study which estimates that women supply 70% of the labor in food production, 60% in marketing, 50% in animal husbandry, and 100% in food processing (UNECA/FAO 1974). In the late precolonial period, most African economies were based on subsistence cultivation, although a number of pastoralist systems were present, as well as some foraging societies whose characteristics are similar to those reported for other regions of the world. Patterns of productive organization varied. Baumann, in a 1928 study, mapped the sexual division of labor for 140 societies and identified areas of female farming, male farming, and mixed systems. Men were generally responsible for clearing. In the Eastern, Southeastern, and Central parts of the continent, there was and continues to be a high incidence of female farming (Clark 1980; Potash 1985; Stamp 1986; Wilson 1982); in some parts of West Africa, men cultivate, although women help with harvesting and processing (Afonja 1986). In other places, both men and women cultivate, either jointly (Muller 1986), independently, with women and men responsible for different crops (Guyer 1984a, Ottenberg 1959), or both (Netting 1969); while a pattern of compound-based communal farming under the control of the senior male head is found in the West African savannah (Hemmings-Gapihan 1982; Meillassoux 1981; SEDES study reported in Guyer 1984b).

In contrast to Meillassoux's assertion that senior men control the produce of women, in most societies women and men have independent control over their productivity and the uses to which this is put. The most widespread pattern is one in which women provide the major portion of the food supply and feed themselves and their children through cultivation. Each wife has her own granary and independently controls her food supply, a pattern that is also found in some systems where men are involved in cultivation, such as Tonga (Colson 1951). Control over food and its preparation has practical and symbolic importance: it is a source of pride, it gives women some degree of economic security and lessens dependence on men, it provides a moral basis for claims to children's support in old age, and withholding food by refusing to cook for a husband is one of the few sanctions a woman has over her husband's behavior.

If we examine the perceptions of contemporary African women, it is evident that they see themselves as working for their own and their children's benefit, not for their husbands. It seems probable that earlier generations of African women held similar views. Although a woman may have contributed to her husband's accumulation of wealth and status, in practice men seldom exercised direct control over wives' productive activities and could not appropriate their produce in many places, even where there were ideologies of male ownership (Clark 1980; Hay 1976; Oboler 1985; Potash 1985). In systems of female farming, men contributed particular types of produce from hunting, herding, and fishing, and met social obligations, including bridewealth payments, through control over prestige resources; but there was no tradition of men being the sole or even the primary provider for the household. Women in such societies, in addition to providing for their children, may have made small contributions to their own or their husband's kin group activities and provided assistance to their parents, but such social expenditures were often quite limited and depended on available resources.

In those systems where men produced the bulk of the food supply or made important contributions to subsistence, women were sometimes able to use some of their produce, crafts, or earnings from trade for social and personal, as well as domestic expenditures (Amadiume 1987; Etienne 1980; Hemmings-Gapihan 1982; Netting 1969; Ottenberg 1959). In communal compound systems of the savannah, members are fed from the produce of communal fields controlled by the compound head. Women and men also have private plots whose produce they can use for their own purposes (SEDES study reported in Guyer 1984b). Gulma women in Burkina Faso until recent times raised groundnuts that they traded, using the proceeds to purchase raw cotton which they spun into thread and gave to kin to weave. The cloth was used by women to contribute to the bridewealth of sons and nephews and to trade for cattle and salt (Hemmings-Gapihan 1982). In Kano, Nigeria, where Muslim husbands are entirely responsible for food provision, Hausa women use their income from trade to contribute to sons' bridewealth, and particularly to the dowries of daughters, to buy clothing for themselves and their children, give gifts to female friends and relatives, and buy luxury items such as jewelry (Schildkrout 1983).

These patterns of income control contradict Meillassoux's assertion that senior men control the produce of women and juniors. Such arrangements are certainly reported for some places, as in Meillassoux's study of the Guro of Ivory Coast, but they are not universal. Indeed, although Hemmings-Gapihan does not relate her material to Meillassoux's work, the data she presents on Gulma (and material on the Senufo and other groups, as well) raise important historical questions about West African savannah systems. Until quite recently when junior men became involved in cash-earning activities, Gulma women were not much involved in food production after the early years of marriage. The reduced availability of sons' labor necessitated their involvement, giving household heads control over women's productivity and bringing about a decline in women's independent economic activities. Since high labor migration by young men has characterized much of the savannah region, one wonders what impact migration may have had on contemporary patterns of productive organization.

This is not to suggest that women in the precolonial period were free of male controls or necessarily had economic positions equal to those of men. Researchers differ in their interpretations of women's position. Some emphasize the exploitative character of women's family support responsibilities; others stress the value of women's work, their competence, and their relative economic independence. But the direct appropriation of women's labor and produce is only reported in a few places and may be associated with the expansion of long-distance trade, the need to provision caravans, and the emergence of powerful men and women who had to feed retainers. Such trade is clearly connected to the expansion of Beti (Cameroon) polygyny in the 19th century, when powerful men accumulated hundreds of wives and widows whom they used as a labor force to feed clients (Guyer 1984a, 1986). In some areas of Africa, female slaves were used in similar fashion to feed caravans (Harms 1983; Robertson and Klein 1983).

The precolonial pattern of separate incomes for women and men has not served African women well in contemporary society. The monetization of the economy has transformed reciprocal exchanges of goods and services into cash transactions. But access to cash is limited, particularly in rural areas where most women reside. Factory goods have replaced local crafts, reducing incomes for some and requiring additional expenditures for others. Where women bear major support responsibilities, they have had to add income-earning activities to subsistence cultivation in order to meet such obligations. In those areas where men formerly were responsible for the provision of food, their involvement in earning cash frequently reduces their contribution or converts it into a monetary payment which women need to supplement in order to feed their families (Abu 1983; Bukh 1979).

New bases of prestige and increased family conflicts are other developments associated with monetization. Although men in precolonial societies often controlled such prestige sectors of the economy as pastoralism and hunting, a man's status also depended on his ability to manage domestic affairs, attract dependents, and have numerous wives and offspring, activities in which he was heavily dependent on women, whether or not their contribution was formally recognized. Today, wealth is measured in cash that is acquired independently of women, and women's subsistence activities are often accorded little recognition.

The importance of cash is also associated with increased marital conflicts over the inadequacy of men's contributions in many places (Stamp 1975–76). Men typically have a broad range of extradomestic obligations whose claims they must balance against the needs of wives and offspring (Potash 1985). Parents, and particularly mothers, have a strong claim on a man's resources that may take precedence over those of his own family of procreation. Other obligations include contributions to the bridewealth of kinsmen, help in educating younger siblings, expenditures for funerals and other rituals, contributions to community associations and self-help projects, and in matrilineal systems, the support of sisters and sisters' children. Men often have greater access to cash and more discretionary use of income than women, and may use their funds to enhance status, take additional wives, purchase clothing and luxuries, entertain friends, and support girlfriends. In polygynous households a man is expected to equalize contributions among wives. Since unemployment is high and wages and income from cash crops low, the amount of assistance women receive is often quite minimal. Sometimes husbands send nothing.

African women frequently complain about husbands' neglect and accuse men of spending their earnings on beer and prostitutes, yet husbands and wives do not generally know each others' incomes. In the absence of studies of male expenditure patterns, it is not possible to determine what proportion of income goes to wives, mothers, and other kin and what is actually spent on living expenses and luxuries.

Rural Economic Transformation

Colonial economic policies and unfavorable terms of incorporation into a global economy have markedly affected all African societies with local variations in coping strategies. Colonial policies sought to promote the production of export crops and/or to create a migrant labor force by involving men through taxation, labor conscription, and forced cultivation. Women were expected to cultivate food (Hay 1976; Henn 1984; Klein 1980; Wilson 1982). Postindependence development programs have continued the pattern. Extension services, farm credit, and training in economically productive activities are generally geared to men who are presumed to be the family providers. Cooperative marketing associations typically include men as members who receive the payments, even where it is women who do the work. Development programs for women emphasize home economics or craft production.[2]

Despite policies that favor men in the acquisition of new skills and income-earning activities, there are varied local responses (Dey 1981; Weil 1986). Senufo women (Ivory Coast) adopted cash cropping while men continue to cultivate the grain staples and also obtain income from carving and cattle sales (SEDES study cited in Guyer 1984b). In some places, women work on cash crops but men control the income. Women's reactions differ. There are cases of women withdrawing their labor if men keep the proceeds and fail to provide adequately for wives and children (Brain 1976). Akan wives (Ghana) expect to be rewarded for work on their husband's cocoa farm with the gift of a farm or other compensation. If this is not forthcoming, women leave (Okali 1983). Divorcées and widows sometimes use government agencies to press claims for compensation as "employees" of their "employer" husbands who have not given them farms or other payment (Vellenga 1986). A different tactic is used by Kikuyu (Kenya) women who channel cash crop earnings into self-help groups to prevent husbands from appropriating funds. Even though such activities may not generate profits they sageguard income (Stamp 1975–76, 1986). While these strategies are only found in some places and are variably effective, they do show women's resistance.

Another common pattern is one where women cultivate food crops while men are involved in labor migration or cash cropping (Brown 1980; LeVine 1966; Potash 1980, 1985; Richards 1940). While widespread, the impact of migration varies with the age and marital status of the migrant, the length of time away, and the economic and social organization of the sending community. In some parts of Africa where female farming predominates, the introduction of the plow replaced men's contribution in digging fields and freed them to migrate. The clearing of new lands ceased, first as a result of colonial policies that prevented territorial expansion and village mobility, and later due to land shortages. Reduced land yields and the need to earn cash is responsible for the increase in women's work in these places rather than the need to replace male labor (Potash 1980, 1985). In other regions, women have sometimes had to increase their food production and/or take over men's tasks in cultivation as their husbands or sons became involved in export crop production or migration (Bukh 1979; Guyer 1984a; Hemmings-Gapihan 1982; Henn 1984; Richards 1940). Whatever the pattern, women's work loads are considerable and have probably increased since precolonial times.

The West African Cocoa Belt is one of many areas in which detailed comparisons can be made to show the complexity of socioeconomic transformation. Although cocoa farming was introduced as an activity for men during colonial period, there are variations in the extent to which cocoa was adopted and/or displaced other activities, culturally distinct patterns of productive organization, differences in the degree of women's involvement, and varied social and economic correlates. Reactions to fluctuations in world market prices are also diverse. These differences relate to the nature of precolonial social systems, cultural practices, and coping strategies.

Sima Afonja's (1986) comparison of three Yoruba (Nigeria) communities is a case in point. In Ile-Ife, where women's income was based on the processing and marketing of food raised by men, the shift to cocoa cultivation has impoverished women. There is little food to market. Patrilineal inheritance of land excludes women from owning cocoa farms, while the development of tenant farming obviates the need for women's labor. In Ondo, by contrast, cognatic inheritance rules and an early development of land sales rather than tenancy enables some women to become owners of cocoa farms, while others are able to obtain income from work in cocoa production. Finally, Abeokuta never became a center of cocoa cultivation. Both women and men had an early involvement in long-distance trade, first in slaves and later in legitimate goods, which is lucrative. Cocoa is less attractive and the land is not so suitable; thus cash crop cultivation did not take root.

Further to the west, among the matrilineal Akan of Ghana another pattern emerges in which some women become independent cocoa producers in addition to working on their husbands' farms. Wives receive gifts of some of the farms they help their husbands to develop. They also purchase farms with income earned from food sales, and sometimes receive gifts from fathers and matrilineal kin. Finally, colonial changes in marriage and inheritance laws entitled women married under the Ordinance Act to a share of their husband's estate. Women in the cocoa belt, and widows in particular, fared better than women in urban settings when world cocoa prices remained high (Vellenga 1983, 1986).

Some of the most complex transformations associated with cocoa cultivation are found among the Beti of Cameroon. Where men's wealth and power had formerly depended on clients, wives, and widows, the shift to a cocoa economy was accompanied by a decline in both large-scale polygyny and the inheritance of widows, and an increase in the value placed on land and patrilineal descent. Cultural practices associated with the gender division of labor contribute to male involvement in cocoa. Customarily, men cultivated forest plots from an upright position, using different tools than women who worked on open fields from a bent position. As men became involved in cocoa, the proportion of women's food crops needed for subsistence increased. As in other societies, men have greater access to cash. However, recent changes in market conditions have reduced the income disparity. A growing market for food has been created with the expansion of the nearby capital; at the same time, cocoa prices have declined. Women are able to take advantage of these new opportunities; men are not. Gender specific patterns of cropping limit men's ability to cultivate such marketable food (Guyer 1984a, 1986).

Changing market conditions, and declining cocoa prices have had a different sequence of impacts on the Ewe community of Ghana studied by Jette Bukh (1979). Here, too, men took up cocoa farming while women intensified food production. As cocoa prices declined, men found it necessary to migrate in search of income. Initially, women accompanied their husbands. However, as the Ghanaian economy collapsed women returned to the rural area to resume subsistence cultivation. Men remained in town but remittances declined, leading to the dissolution of marriages. Women seee little point in being tied to an absent husband who does not provide. Today, there is a high incidence of unmarried women who head their own households and who are poor.

The vulnerability of African economies to world commodity prices, the attempts to cope, and the social and economic consequences of relying on cash crop production or labor migration are evident from these and other studies. But the underdeveloped character of African economies and their articulation with the world capitalist system provides few opportunities to develop successful alternative strategies (Bujra 1986).

While monetization of Africa's economies has had a profound impact on women and men, so has their migration to urban areas. During the colonial period, permanent urbanization was not envisioned for the newly created colonial cites in East, Central, and Southern Africa, and women were generally discouraged from migrating. Limited job opportunities and housing, low wage structures which prevented men from supporting families, and legal and administrative barriers such as the Pass Laws of South Africa or the registration requirements for "femmes libres" in the Congo served to restrict women's movement (Southall 1961; Wilson 1982). Local resistance to women's migration was also encountered. The Luo Union in colonial Kenya, for example, rounded up single women in town and sent them home is disgrace. Studies of the creation and codification of Native Law shows how men's concerns about female migration and its perceived threat to marital stability influenced the development of legal codes of marriage and divorce (Chanock 1982; Wright 1982). Despite these pressures, some women did migrate in search of wealth, independence, or both and earned their living through the informal economy: the sale of sexual and domestic services, beer brewing, selling cooked food, and petty trade. Janet Bujra (1975) and Luise White (1988) recount the early history and resourcefulness of women migrants to Nairobi who supported kin and acquired houses through the sale of sexual services. Nicci Nelson provides data on contemporary beer brewers (1979) and prostitutes (1987) and Francille Wilson discusses the situation in Zaire

(1982). In a few places where authorities wished to attract labor or stabilize the work force, as on the Zambian copperbelt, women's migration was encouraged (Parpart 1986, 1988).

A different pattern obtained in the old precolonial cities of West Africa that had an indigenous female population which was augmented by migration (Southall 1961). Sex ratio differences were less pronounced and women could engage in customary economic and social roles. But changes in the colonial economy also impaired women's economic situation in some places. Robertson (1984) traces the changing economic activities of Ga women in Accra, Ghana, showing how the introduction of motorized fishing boats and the formation of state corporations that monopolized the distribution of fish affected their incomes. Since women had formerly acquired fish from their husbands which they then sold locally, and long distance, these developments deprived them of a lucrative source of income. Now they are forced to engage in petty trade, which yields little. Since husbands do not provide support, women are poor.

Since independence, women's migration to urban centers has increased. However, employment opportunities are more limited to women than for men and even informal sector opportunities are declining in some places. Women use a variety of survival strategies, ranging from trade and informal sector activities (MacGaffey 1986, 1988; Nelson 1979, 1987; Sudarkasa 1973) to modern sector jobs (Schuster 1979, 1981) and/or partial reliance on men for support (Lewis 1977; Mandeville 1979; Pellow 1977).

Although more women have moved into urban areas since independence, the majority of African women are still rural. Gender differentiated migration patterns are widespread, resulting in family separation. The limited employment opportunities for women and the low wages of many men, which are inadequate for family support, are often cited as explanations for women's greater concentration in rural areas (Boserup 1970). However, it is important to recognize that neither these conditions nor the structure of the capitalist economy which vests reproductive costs in rural households (Meillassoux 1981) are adequate to account for women's willingness to remain in the countryside. Marriage and land systems are also implicated, and women's perception of their own interests require articulation. I found in Kenya that married Luo women are concerned with providing for their families and safeguarding land rights for themselves and their children; they are reluctant to depend on husbands for support, fearing polygyny, co-wife favoritism, and neglect. Thus, women who accompany husbands to town during the early years of marriage usually return after the birth of one or two children. Even urban women in modern sector employment, those with good informal sector earnings, or women whose husband's income is adequate to support them in town, still want rural security. Luo women insist on having a house built for them and lands allocated even if they live in town.

Although husbands seldom object to rural women's cash-earning activities, which are generally spent on household needs, the situation regarding urban women is more complex. These are questions about the extent to which urban women are more independent (Little 1973; Obbo 1980; Oppong 1974; Pellow 1977; Schuster 1979, 1982) and variations in the extent to which men in different cities are threatened by or accepting of urban wives working. In some East and Central African cities such as Lusaka, men are ambivalent. They regard nonworking housewives as parasites who live off their husbands. At the same time, they object to wives coming into contact with strangers (Schuster 1982). Luo men in Nairobi fear the independence of women and seek to control their incomes (Parkin 1978). Some women do succeed in attaining freedom from male control by resource acquisition (Obbo 1980, 1986).

In many West African cities, by contrast, men seem more accepting of women's earnings, but women are sometimes increasingly dependent on them if male incomes are greater (Oppong 1974, Pellow 1977). However, even in West Africa there is resentment and ambivalence regarding successful women in some places. Ghanaian traders are regularly accused by government officials and in the press of hoarding and profiteering. Nigerians call successful women "cash madams." Nigerian businesswomen who do not come from prominent families with influential connections are widely thought to use "bottom power" to obtain lucrative contracts. The stereotypical association of wealth with sex is also found in Kenya. In addition to "sugar daddies" there are "sugar mommies," women who are suspected of attracting young men through their wealth and generosity. Other instances of the scapegoating of women are reported by Wipper (1972).

Some of the complexity of attitudes and differences between cultures can be illustrated by a conversation that I had in Lagos, Nigeria, with Yoruba friends. They were interested in my Kenyan research and wanted to know how Kenyan and American marriages compared. I told them about joint bank accounts, which I described as a mechanism for shared savings in the United States, in contrast to Kenya where they are a means by which men control women's income. In Nairobi, although wives regularly hide funds from their husbands, they may be required to deposit their salaries into joint accounts for which men hold the only passbooks. My Yoruba friends, all highly educated professional women, expressed sympathy for the Kenyan wife but would not believe that Americans really had joint accounts. They were certain that this was a sham and that husbands and wives kept their real incomes secret and separate. If not, the naïveté of American women would surely leave them without resources since husbands were bound to withdraw money for girlfriends or new wives. My Yoruba friends would never let their husbands know their earnings.

Independent income control and the reluctance of women to rely on husbands' support is reported in many places. Even in high-income households where the husband's salary may cover the larger portion of expenses and where he is in a position to support his wife, there are conflicts over household contributions. Many women prefer to work and have their own independent incomes. In a study of elite couples in Ghana, Oppong (1974) found only a few women who were willing to stay at home.

Social Organization

Recent ethnographic research has provided a rich body of data on women's patterns of participation in marriage, family, and kin relations and the connections between participatory patterns, interests, and power. Although there are no comparative syntheses on many of these issues, it is possible to extrapolate from the literature a number of themes that provide insight into social organization and gender relations. The complex interplay of intergenerational, conjugal, and consanguineal ties is particularly revealing.

In many African societies the most important economic and emotional ties for women and men are intergenerational, not conjugal. For women it is children; for men, parents. Women depend on children for both emotional support and security in old age. Particularly in some polygynous systems, women may be reluctant to rely on husbands who may take additional wives whom they favor.[3] A number of studies show how the desire to maintain ties to children affects decisions about divorce, remarriage, and residence (Etienne 1986; Landberg 1986; Schildkrout 1986) and may stabilize even unsatisfactory marriages where women would lose custodial rights over children (Potash 1978).[4] In some places women leave their husbands when mature sons establish their own households in order to live with offspring (Klima 1970). Terminal separation is also practiced in some matrilineal and cognatic systems where women return to their natal kin to accompany children, further their own interests, or secure their children's property and political rights (Fortes 1950; Goody 1962, 1973; Turner 1957). Maternal-child links, own or adopted, may also provide a woman with a following of dependents who can be an important source of her political power and office holding, as among the Baule of the Ivory Coast (Etienne 1979, 1986).

For men, too, conjugal interests may be secondary to intergenerational ties but their links are to the parental generation. Although men receive economic assistance from children in old age, a man's most important emotional attachment and strongest obligation is often to his mother. He may be expected to build a house for her and provide economic assistance, obligations that outweigh those to wives and children. Christian and Western influence conflict with these ideals, sometimes causing strain.

Kin group ties are also important to women in many places. A number of studies, particularly Karen Sacks's (1982) work, document the uses women make of kinship and the manner in which rights in natal groups provide them with alternatives to marriage. Such ties are important for labor assistance, access to land, and support in marital disputes. Some women diviners and curers are possessed by ancestral spirits of their kin group (Ngubane 1977). In some places women participate in the political and judicial decisions of their natal group, a practice facilitated by local endogamy or residential propinquity (Amadiume 1987; Sudarkasa 1981).

To illustrate the importance of these relationships I will examine how women use these ties to further their own interests. Examples will be restricted to economic rights and their social implications. Since these patterns have implications for marital relationships, students might find comparisons with American, including African-American, family and kinship systems interesting with respect to conjugal expectations and the degree of independence/isolation accorded the nuclear family. Although African and African-American families are differently structured, a similar emphasis is placed on extended family and intergenerational ties (Stack 1974; Sudarkasa 1980), while the occurrence of fosterage arrangements in both suggests different ideas about parental and kin claims to children (Goody 1982). In Africa, as here, formal education, geographic and social mobility, and housing arrangements reduce the amount of assistance available from children and kin, increasing women's vulnerability. Descent group organization, residence, and other aspects of social structure should also be examined from a gender perspective. Emphasis could be placed on the varied positions of women in their natal groups and the connections between natal group rights and interests, residential choices, and the different degrees of dependence on marriage.

Labor Assistance, Kinship, and the Interdependence of Generations

The importance of kinship relations for African men has long been recognized. Access to productive resources, support in disputes, assistance with bridewealth, help in emergencies, links to ancestors and a host of other reciprocal rights and obligations are well documented. By contrast, the manner in which women use kinship connections is underresearched, although more studies are now becoming available.

Kinship seems to me to be a major means by which women mobilize labor assistance for both domestic and productive activities. The conflict between productive and reproductive roles characteristic of industrialized Western societies may not have been common in Africa until recent times, since women could call on a variety of kin for help. Preliminary research suggests that the links which are used are primarily intergenerational, although younger siblings assist in some places. Such assistance is particularly important at two stages: during a woman's childbearing years and in old age. The various claims women have over specified categories of relatives such as brother's children, husband's sister's children or daughter-in-law have usually been interpreted in the literature as mechanisms for strengthening kinship bonds, for training a child, or as oddities of particular kinship and marriage systems. They have practical significance as well.

The introduction of formal education and new employment possibilities reduces the availability of such aid in many places, as do new housing arrangements in urban settings. For the affluent, the use of servants is replacing kin-based assistance, with important implications for social stratification. Although reliance on servants is readily apparent to any researcher in urban Africa, only a few studies note this dependence (Oppong 1974; Stichter 1986) and serious research on servants is limited (Sanjek n.d.). The other source of nonkin assistance is apprenticeship systems, which are particularly widespread in West Africa (Goody 1982) and the less formalized use of kin and nonkin to train children in new skills (Brydon 1979).[5]

The most common source of help for younger women are their own children or other children within the compound. Enid Schildkrout (1978, 1983) shows how purdah secluded Hausa women in Kano, Nigeria, depend on children to trade for them. In contrast to many regions of Africa where women are supportive of children's education, Hausa women are resistant since they can only engage in income earning activities with children's help. Even more common than trade is the aid children offer in the domestic arena. It is a commonplace that children help collect water and fuel, tend younger children, and assist with cooking. Frequently they also assist with farm tasks and/or collecting vegetables (Nukunyu 1969; Oboler 1985; Ominde 1970; Richards 1939). Luo mothers who do not have children old enough bring an unmarried sister into the home as a nursemaid who also provides domestic help. Some practices, such as having a younger sister or other relative ceremonially accompany a bride to her new home or a new mother on her return to her husband may also have labor assistance implications although the data are scant on the actual activities that are performed. In many places, women or their husbands have claims on specified categories of junior kin (Etienne 1979; Goody 1973, 1982; Krige 1974; Lallemand 1977). In West Africa, these patterns are particularly widespread and are described as fosterage (Goody 1982) or adoption (Etienne 1979).

Kin-based assistance is not limited to children. In a number of groups, particularly in Ghana, a woman's mother may be an important source of aid. Unpublished data from a pilot study I undertook in 1972 among the Ewe of Ghana suggest that women's trade activities depend on the type of domestic assistance that is available to them. Where women have mothers in residence, or where their own children are older, they are able to engage in more lucrative long-distance trade. If only younger children are in the home or if no assistance is available, women generally limit their activities to the local market or the verandah. In Accra and other places in Ghana where mothers and daughters sometimes live in the same household, such assistance does not require fosterage (Pellow 1977). Where mothers are not resident, women send children to their grandmothers for rearing, thereby freeing themselves to engage in productive activities (Oppong 1974; Pellow 1977). Among the Swahili in Tanzania divorced and widowed women also leave children with mothers or female uterine kin when they enter new marriages or spend time traveling between marriages (Landberg 1986). Lynne Brydon (1979) describes the transformation of Ewe fosterage patterns in response to changing conditions. Where children were once given to older childless relatives to provide the elderly with help, the pattern changed to one of sending children to absent members outside the home community in order that they be trained in new skills while providing domestic assistance. As formal education replaced the importance of such training, fosterage took another form. Today it is primarily women living away from home who send young children to be fostered by their grandmothers in order to free themselves to work.

It is not only women of childbearing years who rely on juniors for help; older women do so as well. Sons and daughters-in-law are of particular importance in many societies; daughters help if they reside in the same community. The importance of such ties for older women is evident in a number of studies of widows which indicate that their decisions about remarriage, residence, and leviratic relationships are often determined by their desire to maintain links with sons and sometimes daughters in order to be assured of support in old age (Landberg 1986; Muller 1986; Potash 1986c; Schildkrout 1986). In some groups woman-woman marriage provides a mechanism by which a barren woman can acquire rights over sons and/or daughters-in-law (Krige 1974), although such marriages serve a variety of purposes (Amadiume 1987; Krige 1974; Obbo 1976; Oboler 1980; O'Brien 1977).

Daughters-in-law are particularly important sources of labor in some places. A Lovedu (South African) woman without sons may still claim her brother's daughter as a daughter-in-law in order to obtain assistance. In such situations, the woman's daughter becomes a female husband but it is the intergenerational, not the conjugal tie that is important (Krige 1974). Elsewhere, I describe the importance of daughters-in-law among the Luo where a son's wife begins her marriage farming and cooking under her mother-in-law's supervision, a widespread pattern in Africa. Although wives of older sons are eventually given their own land, the wife of the youngest continues working for her mother-in-law throughout the older woman's life. Mothers-in-law have control over farming and cooking decisions, although this is negotiable, and also have considerable say over the rearing of grandchildren (Potash 1985). In many societies there is a marked change from the young, sometimes shy bride, to the competent matron and the matriarch of the compound.

As we noted above, many of these patterns of labor assistance have been subject to change under modern conditions. Older women, too, are experiencing a decline in the help that was formerly available. In some places urban migration removes sons and sometimes daughters-in-law from the community (Lallemand 1977; Potash 1986c). In other areas, adult children who formerly assisted become involved in more lucrative cash activities, reducing their help (Hemmings-Gapihan 1982). Older women may receive monetary assistance from absent sons but unless this is substantial, enabling them to hire help, they may find themselves in difficult situations. The woman without sons and daughters-in-law is in particularly dire straits in some places (Lallemand 1977; Muller 1986).

Property Rights, Kinship, and Marriage

Although anthropology texts usually distinguish usufructory rights from private property and sometimes discuss the relationship between private property and class formation, gender issues are inadequately treated. In most African societies, women only have access to land and housing either through marriage or through membership in a descent group. Although not determining, these patterns structure the options available to women and have implications for marital stability and the distribution of domestic power.

Karen Sacks (1982) has called our attention to the importance of women's rights in their natal community, for which she uses the term *sister* as a convenient shorthand. She suggests that sisterhood confers important rights in all African societies except where processes of state formation or class formation have destroyed these rights. Although women's positions in their natal groups vary,[6] and the ethnographic literature does not support Sacks's contention that such rights are universal in stateless systems, where women have the right to return to their kinsmen they have alternatives to marriage and are able to exercise some leverage in conjugal relationships.

Natal group rights are particularly pronounced in some matrilineal and cognatic descent systems where women and children are valued assets, adding to the growth of a community and contributing to a brother's influence and power. Where headmanships and chieftainships depend on a following, the support of a sister and her children may be crucial. Brothers may give sisters priority over wives. In such situations affinal and natal kin compete for a woman's residence and loyalty, thereby enhancing her power and position. Among the Baule of the Ivory Coast, women themselves may obtain headships (Etienne 1986). In other places, ties may be among female uterine kin rather than between sisters and brothers (Landberg 1986; Poewe 1981). A wide range of sources documents some of these patterns (Abu 1983; Cesara 1982; Etienne 1986; Fortes 1950; Goody 1962; 1973; Landberg 1986; Mitchell 1956; Poewe 1981; Turner 1957; Vellenga 1986).

In some areas with patrilineal and/or cognatic descent, women may obtain access to land and housing through natal ties, although they have more limited rights. They cannot transmit such rights to their children, who must either remain in their father's community or eventually return, sometimes accompanied by their mother (Gulliver 1964; Oboler 1986). Since women do not contribute to the growth of such communities through their children, they are more likely to be regarded as dependents than assets and may have little influence or power. Specific attitudes vary. In Burkina Faso, Mossi widows, although accepted and treated with respect as "sisters," are suspect because their affines do not wish them to remain (Lallemand 1977). Hausa brothers in Kano help support sisters but pressure them to remarry (Schildkrout 1986), while in Tanzania Barabaig women must live alone without their children in their brother's compound and cannot remarry since additional dowry is not available (Klima 1970). In such situations, although women have alternatives to unsatisfactory marriages or to remaining as widows in their husbands' community, their positions may be marginal.

There are also societies where women have no claims on their natal kin or are afforded refuge only in extreme cases (Muller 1986; Potash 1978, 1986c). Such women are entirely dependent on marriage for access to land and housing which they need to support themselves and their children. They may find it necessary to maintain even unsatisfactory marriages in order to retain land rights. Elsewhere I have shown how such systems not only stabilize marriage, but also affect the balance of power in conjugal relationships (Potash 1978). Since women have nowhere to go in cases of marital dissolution and may lose rights to children as well, they have less negotiating power. Husbands have power over wives who must accommodate themselves to marriage and can only use indirect or nonconfrontational strategies to evade control; wives have no comparable control over husbands. In some places the high rate of marital stability partly reflects such limited options.

In the past, land rights obtained by women on marriage were secure, particularly in societies where women could return to their husbands' community even after a lengthy separation (Oboler 1985, 1986; Potash 1978; Whyte 1979). However, the transformation from usufruct to private property, while variable in its effects, may be undermining women's claims in some places. Few women receive titles to land and some analysts predict that women will lose customary rights as sons or affines sell holdings (Okeyo 1980). There is scattered evidence that this is already happening in some places (Potash 1986a), although hard data on land concentration and the impact of land tenure changes are difficult to come by (Shipton 1988). Kenyan newspapers report incidents of widows being driven from the land. In Burkina Faso, a Widows and Orphans Association was formed in 1977 to help such women. I have also been told of the formation of widows' associations in Zaire and southeastern Nigeria, but I have no further details. In contrast to the negative impact privatization has had in some places, in others women have been able to purchase land from earnings (Afonja 1986; Vellenga 1983, 1986). In both situations patterns of conjugal and affinal relations are much affected.

Important as property systems are in structuring options, they should not be regarded as determining. The personalities and resourcefulness of women (Obbo 1980, 1986), attitudes toward marriage and divorce, and the prospects for remarriage for women who desire husbands and/or children are also important. In some places such prospects are limited or nonexistent for both widowed and divorced women (Klima 1970; Oboler 1986; Potash 1978, 1986c; Whyte 1979). In others there are no barriers, thereby giving women greater freedom to terminate unsatisfactory unions (Goody 1962; Landberg 1986; Salamone 1986; Verdon 1982). In the Jos Plateau region of Nigeria, for example, multiple marriages for women are common, either sequentially or in polyandrous arrangements. Although women depend on marriage for land, their ability to move from one husband to another gives them considerable power since wives are highly valued (Muller 1969, 1986; Netting 1969; Sangree 1969).

Differences between initial and subsequent marriages following divorce or death raise important questions about alliance theories of marriage and the durability and significance of affinal ties. There are important variations in the ways in which such marriages are arranged. Moreover, the duration and benefits of such marital alliances are not uniform across societies (Potash 1986b). In many places, even if women have little control over first marriages, they have considerable say over subsequent spouses (Landberg 1986; Muller 1986). The Swahili pattern of preferential endogamous first marriages within a cognatic descent group, followed by divorce and remarriage is one example. In later marriages women exercise free choice. They often select up-country migrants who have less control over wives, enabling women to devote more time to cooperative activities with female uterine kin (Landberg 1986). In some places women also exercise choice in first marriages (Etienne 1986; Salamone 1986). Such patterns suggest that contrary to Meillassoux's contention, senior men do not necessarily control marriage. Senior women may also influence or even determine marriages. In Liberia and Sierra Leone, female heads of the Sande or women's secret society control Kpelle, Sherbro, and Mende marriages, which gives them considerable power (Bledsoe 1980; MacCormack 1979); Lovedu women exercise claims on brothers' daughters as daughters-in-law who provide them with labor assistance (Krige 1974); and women as well as men act as go-betweens in arranging Luo marriages (Potash 1978). The consent of mothers as well as fathers is often required.

Space does not permit more than a brief mention of many of the other issues addressed in recent research. Individual monographs provide an ever-growing body of data on marriage relationships, attitudes toward marriage, the meaning of marriage for women and strategies women employ to obtain domestic power or evade husbands' control (Abu 1983; Bledsoe 1980; Cesara 1982; Etienne 1983; Harrell-Bond 1975; Kettel 1986; Muller 1969, 1986; Netting 1969; Obbo 1976, 1986; Poewe 1981; Potash 1978; Whyte 1979). The transformation of marriage systems in relationship to colonial changes in marriage laws, missionary activities and new ideologies, and socioeconomic transformation are other topics of interest (Bukh 1979; Chanock 1982; Etienne 1983; Guyer 1986; Obbo 1980; Oppong 1974; Poewe 1978; Robertson 1984; Schuster 1979; Smock 1977; Vellenga 1983, 1986; Verdon 1982; Wright 1982). A number of comparative studies are also available which incorporate gender perspectives in dealing with household and community organization (Guyer 1981), female husbands (Krige 1974), matrilineal systems (Poewe 1981), and widows (Potash 1986b). Finally, there are a number of studies of women's political rights in both their natal and marital communities that I address below.

Political Organization

The manner in which we conceptualize politics affects our understanding of women's involvement. An earlier generation of anthropologists who sought to find in acephalous societies functions analogous to those performed by the state, focused on the community as the locus of political behavior, defining politics as those activities that extended beyond the household or domestic group. Thus Fortes (1953, 1969) distinguished the politico-jural from the domestic domain. M. G. Smith, Barth, and other transactional analysts broadened this definition to encompass all behavior, considering politics to be an analytic aspect of action rather than an empirical sphere of activity. In this broad sense, virtually all studies of women's status are by definition political studies insofar as they deal with power. However, the emphasis on community persists in many studies of politics and gender. It is involvement in community decisions that is taken as evidence of women's political participation.

Rosaldo (1974), for example, saw women's confinement to the domestic domain and man's near monopoloy of the public sphere as the key to male dominance universally, although she later modified her views. Although societies differ in the extent to which such spheres are distinct, she argued, and women in some places obtain power through manipulation, by taking on masculine political roles and by the formation of separate women's groups, the public domain remains the arena of politics and power. A growing body of literature is now available on female office holders (Aidoo 1981; Awe 1977; Bay 1983; Bledsoe 1980, 1984; MacCormack née Hoffer 1974, 1979, 1983; Okonjo 1976, 1983), women's organizations (Amadiume 1987; Ardener 1973; Bledsoe 1984; Kettel 1986; Klima 1970; MacCormack 1979; Okonjo 1976, 1983; Van Allen 1972, 1976; Wipper 1984), and women's involvement in anticolonial protest movements (Mba 1982; O'Barr 1984; Urdang 1984; Van Allen 1976; Wells 1983). A number of biographical studies of politically prominent women are also available. These studies written by historians and political scientists as well as anthropologists are bringing to light neglected political roles of women.

However, a number of important conceptual issues remain unaddressed. How valid is the political-domestic dichotomy, particularly for stateless societies? To what extent are community politics responses to colonially created structures of government? How do unorganized women and women who are not office holders participate in political life and influence affairs? Whose interests are represented by female office holders and women's groups? In many precolonial stateless societies the unit of political action was not the community but the domestic group or its subdivisions, acting alone or in combination with others. Such actions had implications for the persistence and growth of communities and for the maintenance of law and order. But prior to colonialism there were no community institutions of governance, as such, and no community decision making in many places. Even in some states, as Sudarkasa (1981) shows for West Africa, domestic groups or compounds continue to have important political roles, being represented on town or ward councils and acting in disputes as a court of first resort.

Although not a focus of study, a variety of evidence suggests that women as well as men are involved in domestic politics, but the extent of participation and influence are not ascertainable from available data. A few examples will suffice. The fission of households and lineages in patrilineal systems often follow matricentric lines, and rivalry between co-wives can be a precipitant to separation. In some places, mothers accompany and/or support sons who seek to establish households independent of their fathers (Klima 1970). The ease with which new communities are formed or allegiances altered shows the autonomy of domestic groups. A variety of kinship links of both the husband and wife are used as a basis of community affiliation, particularly in some cognatic and matrilineal systems (Colson 1951, 1962, Etienne 1986; Kopytoff 1977; Mitchell 1956; Turner 1957), and in times of emergency or community ostracism. Where village headmanships or chiefdoms are found, the ability of a leader to attract and retain followers is a key to power. In some places women as well as men can become chiefs (Etienne 1986; MacCormack née Hoffer 1974, 1983). In others, the support of women and their children is crucial (Mitchell 1956; Turner 1957). Mitchell shows how men desirous of becoming headmen of their own village must convince their sisters to leave their maternal uncle by demonstrating greater ability to protect their sister's interests. Turner shows how brothers compete with husbands to attract women and their children.

The imposition of colonial rule markedly changed these structures, reducing the autonomy and mobility of domestic groups and shifting the locus of political activity from transactions within and between domestic groups to the community, district, or state. Native Authority systems were imposed and native courts vied with other institutions for resolving disputes. Both land shortages and the requirements of administrative recognition affected the ability to found new communities.

Women were particularly affected since colonial authorities only recognized men as leaders. In some societies where women had led councils or community organizations which operated to protect their interests in the precolonial period, these disappeared. In Tanzania Klima (1970) found such a council still operating among the Barabaig in the 1950s, but only the name remained among the Tugen in neighboring Kenya (Kettel 1986). Among the Igbo of Nigeria, missionary influence and colonial policy ended women's title taking and modified the political role of women's councils. Through such groups women had mobilized to protect their interests and influence community affairs. Igbo women formerly gathered at the household of a male offender, singing derisive songs and roughing him up when "making war" or "sitting on a man" (Van Allen 1972). The *Anlu* of the Kom of Cameroon is a similar institution (Ardener 1973). Interpretations differ on the extent to which the Sande or women's secret society of West Africa expresses female solidarity. MacCormack (1979, 1980) sees this institution as protecting women's interests; Bledsoe (1984) finds that Sande leaders, who are aristocratic women, use the organization to promote their own interests and that of the men to whom they are attached. Amadiume (1987) dealing with a different system, suggests that organizations of Igbo lineage daughters and lineage wives did not have identical interests; daughters had authority over wives.

In state systems of government, female office holding either disappeared or was sharply reduced. Office holding had taken various forms in precolonial times with positions in some places reserved to represent women, while female office holders in other places represented varied interests. A common pattern in Africa was the institution of the Queen Mother or King's Sister who was regarded as the king's counterpart, albeit with lesser authority. She frequently had her own court, heard cases, and sat on councils, and her concurrence was necessary in many matters. In some cases the Queen Mother was seen as protecting the ruler's interests; in others, the interests of the people or of the royal lineage against possible excesses of the king. In a number of chiefdoms there were some offices which were gender neutral and could be held by women or men (Etienne 1986; MacCormack née Hoffer 1974). There were also a number of positions reserved for women. In Dahomey wives, slaves and sisters of the king were office holders acting as a check on their male counterparts in order to protect the king's interests (Bay 1983). The Iyalode of the Yoruba, by contrast, was a woman whose role was to represent women (Awe 1977). Okonjo (1976) describes the dual sex systems of the Igbo community of Onitsha, Nigeria, where a female ruler and council paralleled the king and his council but were concerned with women's affairs.

Despite the loss of female office holding and the changing political order, colonialism did not necessarily end women's participation in public affairs. A number of women's anti-colonial movements are recorded (Mba 1982; O'Barr 1984; Urdang 1984; Van Allen 1976; Wells 1983). Some analysts link such movements to the precolonial traditions of women's activism (Mba 1982; Okonjo 1976, 1983), but it is not clear that such traditions existed in all places where protest movements occurred. Other analysts see a real decline or disappearance of women's political power (Amadiume 1987).

In contemporary Africa one finds women office holders both elected and appointed at the national level. In addition, there are national women's organizations, and in many governments national women's bureaus have been established, sometimes under United Nations' pressure. However, the extent of women's influence on national policies is unclear. In some countries such as Nigeria, analysts see the development of women's branches of national parties as co-opting women, whose interests cease to be served (Mba 1982). In other countries such as Tanzania, these organizations do seek to promote women's interests but are not always successful (O'Barr 1984). National women's groups, often composed of elite and/or educated women, may not always reflect the issues of concern to nonelites (Amadiume 1987; Vellenga 1986; Wipper 1975), a problem with which Americans are certainly familiar.

Perhaps it would be useful analytically to distinguish women's interests from women's rights. In many places nonelite women organize in community self-help groups, trade associations, and credit unions either through their own efforts or under the aegis of development planners and others to promote their interests. These often center on income-generating activities, nursery schools, children's education, nutrition and health, local dispensaries and other matters of local interest. Some groups are effective, other short-lived (Stamp 1975–76, 1986; Strobel 1979; Wachtel 1975; Wipper 1984). The competing demands on women's time, limited financial returns, internal power struggles and corruption, and poor results are some of the factors that lead to the dissolution of such organizations. National groups, particularly those composed of elite women, are sometimes supportive of such activities, but often focus on legal issues such as marriage and inheritance laws, equal rights and opportunities for women, and other matters of interest to them. Occasionally such groups are primarily vehicles for expressing high status. The extent to which nonelites are concerned with such matters, however, is uncertain (Amadiume 1987; Vellenga 1986; Wipper 1975).

A major problem in understanding both the contemporary political scene and earlier periods is the paucity and nature of the available data. Although one can identify women's political involvement, the data are too scattered to generalize adequately.

Religion and Ideology

Recognition has generally been given in the literature to women's as well as men's participation in African religious life. Among the many possible citations from classic works we find studies of female initiation rites (Richards 1956), discussions of gender symbolism (Turner 1967, 1969), accounts of spirit possession and divination among women and men (Beattie and Middleton 1969, I. M. Lewis 1966, 1971), descriptions of witchcraft beliefs (Middleton and Winter 1963), and discussions of women's and men's participation in new African religions (Sundkler 1961). Recent studies generally add to the body of ethnographic data and sometimes offer correctives to customary interpretations of religious practices.

In many African societies, sacrifices at both the community or kin group and household level are performed by men who represent the group to the ancestors or spirits. Women, how-

ever, may have independent contact with ancestral and other spirits whose powers they channel for divination and curing. Among the Zulu of South Africa, diviners are women who are
possessed by spirits of their patrilineage (Ngubane 1977); among the Sisala in Ghana, both
women and men divine but only men obtain leadership roles in the divination cult (Mendosa
1979). In both systems clients include men and women. In the Great Lakes area of East Africa
there were a number of possession cults led by women, at least one of which, the Nyabingi
cult, at various times in the precolonial and early colonial period served as a center for political
resistance (Berger 1976, 1981; Robins 1979). In some places there are women's ritual associations such as the West African Sande secret society (Bellman 1979; Bledsoe 1980, 1984;
MacCormack 1979, 1980), or healing cults with female leadership (I. M. Lewis 1971, Spring
1978). Some analysts see such groups as promoting solidarity among women (MacCormack
1979, 1980; Spring 1978); others emphasize the hierarchical aspects and show how powerful
women use the group to consolidate their position (Bellman 1979; Bledsoe 1984).

Other studies use symbolic approaches (Comaroff 1985; Llewelyn-Davies 1981;
MacCormack 1980). Alma Gottlieb (1982), for example, tries to understand why menstruating women are prohibited from entering the forest among the Beng of the Ivory Coast. She
takes as her starting point the explanations given by the Beng themselves. The commonly
made association between menstruation, pollution, and the low status of women is questioned
in a complex analysis that examines activities considered polluting to the earth, as well as
activities barred to menstruating women. Beng distinguish two types of fertility, human fertility and that of the earth, which must be kept separate. Thus, sexual activity is barred in the
forest, people must bathe to "wash off sex" before entering fields in the morning and to wash
off the earth at night, and women cannot cook for their husbands or enter the fields while
menstruating, as all of these activities bring two types of fertility into contact. By contrast,
there is no prohibition on sexual activity during menstruation since these boundaries are not
violated. Neither women nor menstruation are polluting as such. Harriet Ngubane's (1977)
account of Zulu (South Africa) medicine also includes interpretations of symbolism. Of particular interest for this paper is her description of women who are seen to straddle this world
and the world of the spirits as diviners, mothers of birth, and mothers of death who act as
chief mourners and are involved in burial. Although birth and death are seen as polluting,
divination is pure.

Anita Spring's (1978) discussion of healing takes a different approach. Arguing that
most anthropological studies ignore the reality of women's illness, she criticizes social conflict interpretations of spirit possession and analyses which see possession as a mechanism by
which women can express frustration, gain attention, and acquire goods in a "war between
the sexes" (Beattie and Middleton 1969; I. M. Lewis 1966, 1971). Berger (1976) also criticizes such analyses in East Africa. Spring finds a high incidence of dysmenorrhea and fevers
caused by bilharziasis, gonorrhea, and other bacterial diseases which may affect fertility.
Moreover, 21.3% of Luvale women in Zambia who have completed their reproductive years
are childless, and 53.8% of women between ages 30 and 34 and 58.8% of women between
35 and 39 are subfecund. Taking anthropologists to task, Spring states, "Frequently, when
possession rituals occur for a woman experiencing 'reproductive disorders,' her problem is
said by the anthropologist to be 'social conflicts,' which inhere in her status as a woman in a
male-controlled society. . . . Not only are women's concerns seen as negative complaints,
'reproductive disorders,' rather than positive affirmations, 'I want to have children,' but
women themselves are seen as 'conflict producers' who disrupt the order of the male universe
with fictitious complaints.' She goes on to note the solidarity aspects of cults and points out
that Luvale ritual, which often involves seclusion for a few months to a year, may actually

improve the chances of keeping a child alive because of increased attention to health, nutritional changes, and isolation from the spread of infectious disease.

Healing is a widely reported activity in the new religions of Africa. In her introduction, and in several papers in the volume she edited, Bennetta Jules-Rosette (1979) notes that such activities and other expressive roles are frequently, but not invariably, the province of women, while men tend to control formal decision-making structures and occupy leadership roles. This appears to be the case even in movements initially led or founded by women. Much of the recent research on African religion deals with such new movements, with a particular emphasis on the manner in which they restructure symbols and give meaning to experience. Ranger (1986) in a review of this literature, which unfortunately makes no mention of gender, notes the shift in emphasis from studies which treated independent churches as anticolonial protest movements to a broader view of protest which encompasses the full range of disaffection in contemporary African societies.

Although such analyses situate religious developments in a broader socioeconomic and political context, insofar as studies typically deal with only one or two of the churches in a community, many questions remain. If new religions restructure meanings and provide coping mechanisms in a transformed and transforming political and economic scene, how do nonmembers, who presumably experience the same dislocations, regard contemporary life? In many communities today there are several competing religions, each of which attracts only a minority of the local population, although they may be part of larger regional movements. Comaroff's (1985) figures on the Southern Africa Tshidi are a case in point. Out of a district population of 45,000, only 1000 are members of African Independent churches, 3750 are Zionists, and 6000 are affiliated with international Western church denominations. Her study, which examines the manner in which Tshidi transformed colonial images into a counterculture, is based on a study of two congregations, each with a membership of approximately 100. To what extent are the conceptual restructurings of these or other congregations representative of the community as a whole? Which meanings are shared and which are unique to these groups? To what extent do women and men share these meanings?

Karla Poewe (1978) in a study comparing Jehovah's Witnesses and Seventh-Day Adventists uses a gender perspective. She examines the appeal of Jehovah's Witnesses to enterprising men in a society governed by matrilineal ideology with strong ties among women. Differences in the retention of members by these denominations are analyzed in relationship to both organizational structures and beliefs. In the less formal Adventist congregations women sometimes leave the church or depart from its teachings when these conflict with customary practices and ideas concerning marriage. Beliefs in the imminence of Armageddon and a more separatist social structure enable Witnesses to better retain members.

Islam is even more widespread than Christianity in Africa and is growing. A number of studies are available on women in Islamic societies (Barkow 1972; A. Cohen 1969; R. Cohen 1971; Coles n.d.; Landberg 1986; Pittin 1983; Smith 1955; Schildkrout 1983, 1986; Strobel 1979). Although comparative syntheses are not yet available these works suggest considerable variation in Islamic practices which relate to cultural differences.

Cultural Constructs of Gender

In contrast to New Guinea and other places where extensive work has been done on the cultural construction of gender, Africanists have largely ignored this issue. Issues that might usefully be pursued in an introductory course are derived from data gathered for other purposes. One issue is the relationship between biological sex and gender. The widespread oc-currence of female husbands, which is reported for over 30 African societies, indicates their separability. Krige (1974) and O'Brien (1977) review some of this literature. Other studies include Amadiume (1987), Obbo (1976), and Oboler (1980). In some places female husbands may simultaneously be wives in other relationships. Sexual relationships between female hus-band and wife are specifically denied in most studies. It is sociological rather than biological factors that determine roles.

Sexual behavior, by contrast, appears to have little to do with gender identity. However, homosexuality has not been extensively researched. I am aware of only two studies: a con-temporary account of Mombasa (Shepherd 1987) and a study based largely on oral history dealing with institutionalized practices no longer extant (Evans-Pritchard 1970). There are also occasional references in the literature to homosexuality (Schapera 1941) and transvestism (Besmer 1983; I. M. Lewis 1971). These studies strongly suggest that sexual expression does not affect gender roles. Shepherd's study of Mombasa (Kenya) shows a linkage between so-cial position and lesbian and homosexual relationships. High status women who wish to avoid a marriage may establish a lesbian relationship with a lower status woman, providing her with wealth and support. Young low status men frequently enter into homosexual relations with wealthier older men. In both situations women and men participate in groups and activities appropriate to their sex and status, and neither feminine nor masculine identities are lost.

In precolonial times Azande warriors in bachelor companies living in barracks at court commonly took boy wives. Such wives socially acted as women, eating separately from men and performing domestic functions, as well as engaging in homosexual activities. As they grew older, they in turn became warriors, taking boy wives until such time as they married. Thus, homosexual activities and gender roles were associated with life cycle stages rather than with biologically based identities. Although these relationships were socially accepted, les-bianism, while practiced, met disapproval. Azande men attributed lesbianism to husbands' neglect in polygynous households. Such relationships were often disguised as ordinary friend-ships. In former times they were widely practiced by daughters and sisters of the nobility (Evans-Pritchard 1970). Lesbianism is also reported in Botswana. Schapera (1941) claims that such relationships are not ''genuine homosexual affairs'' involving the total exclusion of men, but rather are resorted to by neglected wives to obtain sexual satisfaction. Although the extent of sexual preference may be understated in these studies, such preferences do not lead to the assumption of distinct social roles and identities, a factor that may partially account for the invisibility of homosexuality in Africa.

Behaviors associated with gender roles are not fixed. Marked changes in rights, respon-sibilities, and behavioral expectations are linked to life-cycle changes, which are sometimes but not invariably connected with aging (Beidelman 1980; La Fontaine 1978). Women may change from a shy bride to an assertive mother safeguarding the rights of her children, to a domineering mother-in-law. In some places, postmenopausal women are described as becom-ing social men. Older women are sometimes thought to have considerable spiritual power and may be feared in some societies, as among the Yoruba whose Gelede ritual expresses both fear and respect (Drewal and Drewal 1983). In some places, the more rigid biology-linked behavioral expectations of the West do not apply. Amadiume (1987) notes how assertiveness was expected of Igbo women and men before Christianity. Both sexes used title taking and the acquisition of wives to express success. The discontinuities in men's behavior are equally striking. In many pastoral societies and societies with age sets, there is a marked transition from the brave, impetuous, wild warrior to the pacific, restrained, judicious elder (Llewelyn-Davies 1981; Spencer 1965). Such transitions raise questions about the meaning of masculin-ity and femininity and the purported fixity of biology-linked behaviors.

Conclusion

In this orienting essay I have attempted to show the importance of integrating gender perspectives into the introductory curriculum. A broad range of topics has been examined in this chapter showing the importance of women's participation in economic, social, political, and ritual life and the differential impact societal transformation and incorporation into a global economy has had on women and men. The text and the citations to the literature should enable readers to find sufficient source material to prepare units for classroom presentation. I do not expect that any instructor would wish to use all of the material presented here. Rather, the issue is one of conceptualization. Our understanding of cultural meanings, social organization, and social process and the manner in which we analyze institutions shifts when we incorporate a gender perspective. Whatever the topic, we need to ask how women and men are involved and what are the implications of such involvement.

The preparation of teaching modules on gender is somewhat at variance with the theme of this chapter, which has focused on the need to integrate such perspectives throughout the curriculum. The module on the cultural construction of gender could stand alone or could be used as part of a broader discussion dealing with cultural and biological underpinnings of behavior. These data could also be incorporated into discussions of social organization. The other module deals with some of the issues considered in the section on economic transformation. To help students better understand contemporary global events and the importance of cultural and historical insights, some portion of the discussion could be devoted to an analysis of an event currently in the news, drawing on appropriate references in this chapter for background material on whatever aspects of socioeconomic transformation are involved. Table 1 is a summary of ethnic groups and their location; Figure 1 is a map of Africa.

Notes

1. Although anthropologists have contributed greatly to this research, much work in recent years has been done by scholars from a variety of disciplines whose work will also be cited here.

2. The emphasis on home economics serves a number of political agendas. Insofar as donors of foreign aid such as the United States are concerned with fostering a climate of investment safety and stability, congressional and international mandates to do something for women can be met by such programs without threatening economic and political power structures. Local power holders support such programs for similar reasons, and they appeal to women who are concerned with improving the health and life chances of their families. Finally, departments of home economics in Western universities benefit from additional students and grants at a time when enrollments are dropping as Western women seek other opportunities. Unfortunately this emphasis is not an adequate substitute for programs that empower women or provide them with income earning opportunities.

3. Attitudes toward polgyny vary within and between societies. In many places co-wife jealousy is endemic and cooperation limited. The Luo (Kenya) term for co-wife, *nyieka*, translates as my partner in jealousy. The Hausa (Nigeria) term for co-wife, *Kishiya*, literally means jealousy. In other places co-wives cooperate in trade and economic affairs (MacCormack 1983) and women may also take wives for themselves or their husbands (Amadiume 1987). Under this arrangement, the woman taking a wife benefits from control over her labor, which allows for the accumulation of wealth and frees the wife taker from some domestic duties.

4. There are systems where children are regularly fostered and marital stability is not increased (Goody 1962; Lallemand 1977; Landberg 1986).

Table 1. Ethnic Groups Cited in the Text and Their National Location

Akan	Ghana
Azande	Sudan
Barabaig	Tanzania
Baule	Ivory Coast
Beng	Ivory Coast
Beti	Cameroon
Dahomey	Benin
Ewe	Ghana
Ga	Ghana
Gulma	Burkina Faso
Guro	Ivory Coast
Hausa	Nigeria
Igbo	Nigeria
Kikuyu	Kenya
Kom	Cameroon
Kpelle	Liberia
!Kung	Botswana and Namibia
Lovedu	South Africa
Luo	Kenya
Luvale	Zambia
Maasai	Kenya and Tanzania
Mbuti	Zaire
Mende	Sierra Leone
Mossi	Burkina Faso
Nandi	Kenya
Senufo	Ivory Coast
Sherbro	Sierra Leone
Sisala	Ghana
Swahili	Kenya and Tanzania
Tonga	Zambia
Tshidi	Botswana and South Africa
Tswana	Botswana and South Africa
Tugen	Kenya
Yoruba	Nigeria
Zulu	South Africa

5. Men, too, may rely on kin and servants for assistance. This is particularly true for unmarried men residing outside their home community.

6. The different positions of women in their natal groups is symbolically shown in funeral arrangements. Igbo women cannot be buried in their husband's home but must be returned to their own kin. Lineage daughters bring the body home. If a woman has been mistreated they refuse to remove the corpse. The husband and his kin must pay a fine (Amadiume 1987). Among the Luo, however, a woman has no right to be buried in her father's home. Her grave is in her husband's compound. Should a woman die while visiting her natal kin she must be buried outside the homestead gate.

7. Given the importance of such symbolic approaches in contemporary anthropology and the implications of Comaroff's analysis (1985) for interpreting the political situation in South Africa some comment on this work is in order. Interpreting marginal separatist churches and their reformulation of meanings as representative of Tshidi resistance to the South African political scene is misleading. These groups are quite small—2 congregations of 100 people each out of a population of 45,000. How do the re-

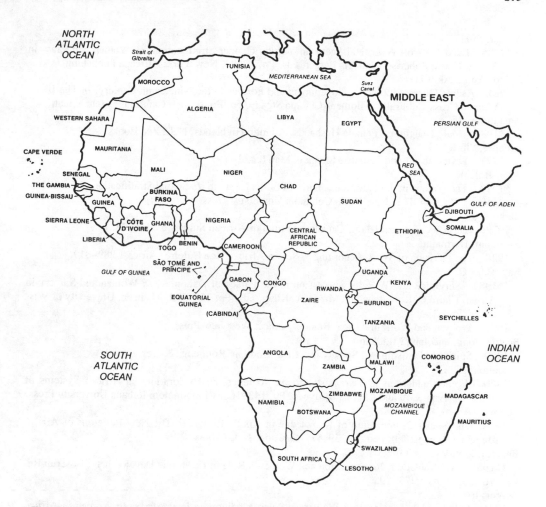

Figure 1. Map of Africa [Reprinted from *Global Studies: Africa*, 3d edition, by permission of the Dushkin Publishers Group, Inc., Guilford, Connecticut].

maining Tshidi express their resistance? What meanings do they give to the contemporary economic and political scene and how do their meanings relate to their political action?

References Cited

*Particularly useful for introductory courses. Could also be assigned to students.

**Important background material for instructors which is too complex or long for most beginning students.

Abu, Katherine
    *1983   The Separateness of Spouses: Conjugal Resources in an Ashanti Town. *In* Female and Male in West Africa. Christine Oppong, ed. Pp. 156–169. London: Allen & Unwin.

Afonja, Simi
    *1986   Land Control: A Critical Factor in Yoruba Gender Stratification. *In* Women and Class in
        Africa. Claire Robertson and Iris Berger, eds. Pp. 78–92. New York: Africana Publishing.
Aidoo, Agnes Akosua
    1981   Asante Queen Mothers in Government and Politics in the Nineteenth Century. *In* The Black
        Woman Cross-Culturally. Filomena Chioma Steady, ed. Pp. 65–79. Cambridge: Schenkman.
Amadiume, Ifi
    **1987   Male Daughters, Female Husbands. Atlantic Highlands, N.J.: Zed Books.
Ardener, Shirley G.
    *1973   Sexual Insult and Female Militancy. Man 8:422–440.
Awe, Bolanle
    *1977   The Iyalode in the Traditional Yoruba Political System. *In* Sexual Stratification. Alice Schle-
        gel, ed. Pp. 144–161. New York: Columbia University Press.
Barkow, J.
    1972   Hausa Women and Islam. Canadian Journal of African Studies 6:317–328.
Baumann, Hermann
    1928   The Division of Work According to Sex in African Hoe Culture. Africa 1:289–319.
Bay, Edna C.
    **1982   Servitude and Worldly Succession in the Palace of Dahomey. *In* Women and Slavery in
        Africa. Claire C. Robertson and Martin A. Klein, eds. Pp. 340–369. Madison: University of Wis-
        consin Press.
    1983   Women and Work in Africa. Boulder, Colo.: Westview Press.
Beattie, John, and John Middleton
    1969   Spirit Mediumship and Society in Africa. London: Routledge & Kegan Paul.
Beidelman, T. O.
    1980   Women and Men in Two East African Societies. *In* Explorations in African Systems of
        Thought. Ivan Karp and Charles Bird, eds. Pp. 143–165. Bloomington: Indiana University Press.
Bellman, Beryll
    1979   The Social Organization of Knowledge in Kpelle Ritual. *In* The New Religions of Africa.
        Bennetta Jules-Rosette, ed. Pp. 39–57. Norwood, N.J.: Ablex.
Beneria, Lourdes, and Gita Sen
    **1981   Accumulation, Reproduction and Women's Role in Economic Development: Boserup Re-
        visited. Signs 7:279–298.
Berger, Iris
    1976   Rebels or Status-Seekers? Women as Spirit Mediums in East Africa. *In* Women in Africa.
        Nancy J. Hafkin and Edna G. Bay, eds. Pp. 157–182. Stanford: Stanford University Press.
    1981   Religion and Resistance. Tervuren: Musee Royale de l'Afrique Centrale.
Besmer, Fremont C.
    1983   Horses, Musicians and Gods: The Hausa Cult of Possession Trance. Zaria, Nigeria: Ahmadu
        Bello University Press.
Bledsoe, Caroline
    **1980   Women and Marriage in Kpelle Society. Stanford: Stanford University Press
    **1984   The Political Use of Sande Ideology and Symbolism. American Ethnologist 11:455–473.
Bohannon, Laura
    *1966   Shakespeare in the Bush. Natural History 75:28–33.
Bowen, Eleanor Smith
    *1964   Return to Laughter. Garden City, N.Y.: Doubleday.
Boserup, Ester
    **1970   Women's Role in Economic Development. New York: St. Martin's Press.
Brain, James L.
    *1976   Less Than Second-Class: Women in Rural Settlement Schemes in Tanzania. *In* Women in
        Africa. Nancy J. Hafkin and Edna G. Bay, eds. Pp. 265–284. Stanford: Stanford University Press.

Brown, Barbara B.
   1980   Women, Migrant Labor and Social Change in Botswana. Working Papers in African Studies, 41. Boston: Boston University.
Brydon, Lynne
   1979   Women at Work: Some Changes in Family Structure at Amedzofe-Avatime, Ghana. Africa 49:97–107.
Bujra, Janet
   *1975   Women Enterpreneurs of Early Nairobi. Canadian Journal of African Studies 9:213–234.
   **1986   Urging Women to Redouble Their Efforts . . . Class, Gender and Capitalist Transformation in Africa. *In* Women and Class in Africa. Claire Robertson and Iris Berger, eds. Pp. 117–141. New York: Africana Publishing.
Bukh, Jette
   *1979   The Village Woman in Ghana. Uppsala: Scandinavian Institute of African Studies.
Cesara, Manda
   1982   Reflections of a Woman Anthropologist: No Hiding Place. New York: Academic Press.
Chanock, Martin
   1982   Making Customary Law: Men, Women and Courts in Colonial Northern Rhodesia. *In* African Women and the Law: Historical Perspectives. Margaret Jean Hay and Marcia Wright, eds. Pp. 53–68. Boston: Boston University Papers on Africa.
Clark, Carolyn
   *1980   Land and Food, Women and Power in Nineteenth Century Kikuyu, Africa 50:357–370.
Cohen, Abner
   1969   Custom and Politics in Urban Africa. Berkeley: University of California Press.
Cohen, Ronald
   1971   Dominance and Defiance. Anthropological Studies, 6. Washington, D.C.: American Anthropological Association.
Coles, Catherine M.
   n.d.   Hausa Women's Work in a Declining Urban Economy: Kaduna, Nigeria, 1980–1985. Unpublished MS.
Colson, Elizabeth
   1951   The Plateau Tonga of Northern Rhodesia. *In* Seven Tribes of British Central Africa. Elizabeth Colson and Max Gluckman, eds. Pp. 94–164. Manchester: Manchester University Press.
   1962   Residence and Village Stability among Plateau Tonga. *In* The Plateau Tonga of Northern Rhodesia: Social and Religious Studies. Pp. 172–207. Manchester: Manchester University Press.
Comaroff, Jean
   1985   Body of Power, Spirit of Resistance. Chicago: University of Chicago Press.
Coplan, David B.
   1987   Eloquent Knowledge: Lesotho Migrants' Songs and the Anthropology of Experience. American Ethnologist 14:413–434.
Dey, Jennie
   1981   Gambian Women: Unequal Partners in Rice Development Projects? *In* African Women in the Development Process. Nici Nelson, ed. Pp. 109–123. Totowa, N.J.: Frank Cass.
Draper, Patricia
   **1975   !Kung Women: Contrasts in Sexual Egalitarianism in Foraging and Sedentary Contexts. *In* Toward an Anthropology of Women. Reyna Reiter, ed. Pp. 77–109. New York: Monthly Review Press.
Drewal, Henry John, and Margaret Thompson Drewal
   1983   Gelede: Art and Female Power among the Yoruba. Bloomington: Indiana University Press.
Etienne, Mona
   *1979   The Case for Social Maternity: Adoption of Children by Urban Baule Women. Dialectical Anthropology 4:237–243.
   *1980   Women and Men, Cloth and Colonization: The Transformation of Production-Distribution Relations among the Baule. *In* Women and Colonization. Mona Etienne and Eleanor Leacock, eds. Pp. 214–239. New York: J. F. Bergin, Publishers.

1983   Gender Relations and Conjugality among the Baule. *In* Female and Male in West Africa. Christine Oppong, ed. Pp. 303–320. London: Allen & Unwin.

**1986   Contradictions, Constraints and Choices: Widow Remarriage among the Baule of Ivory Coast. *In* Widows in African Societies. Betty Potash, ed. Pp. 241–283. Stanford: Stanford University Press.

Etienne, Mona, and Eleanor Leacock, eds.
1980   Women and Colonization. New York: J. F. Bergin, Publishers.

Evans-Pritchard, E. E.
1970   Sexual Inversion among the Azande. American Anthropologist 72:1428–1434.

Fortes, Meyer
1950   Kinship and Marriage among the Ashanti. *In* African Systems of Kinship and Marriage. A. R. Radcliffe-Brown and Daryll Forde, eds. Pp. 252–285. Oxford: Oxford University Press.
1953   The Structure of Unilineal Descent Groups. American Anthropologist 55:17–41.
1969   Kinship and the Social Order. Chicago: Aldine.

Friedl, Ernestine
1975   Women and Men: An Anthropologist's View. New York: Holt, Rinehart, & Winston.

Goody, Esther
1962   Conjugal Separation and Divorce among the Gonja of Northern Ghana. *In* Marriage in Tribal Societies. Meyer Fortes, ed. Pp. 14–55. Cambridge: Cambridge University Press.
1973   Contexts of Kinship. Cambridge: Cambridge University Press.
**1982   Parenthood and Social Reproduction: Fosterage and Occupational Roles in West Africa. Cambridge: Cambridge University Press.

Gottlieb, Alma
*1982   Symbolism of Menstruation among the Beng. Africa 52:34–48.

Gulliver, Philip
1964   The Arusha Family. *In* The Family Estate in Africa. Robert F. Gray and Philip Gulliver, eds. Pp. 197–231. Boston: Boston University Press.

Guyer, Jane I.
**1981   Household and Community in African Studies. African Studies Review 24:87–139.
**1984a   Family and Farm in Southern Cameroon. African Research Studies No. 15. Boston: Boston University.
*1984b   Women in the Rural Economy: Contemporary Variations. *In* African Women South of the Sahara. Margaret Jean Hay and Sharon Stichter, eds. Pp. 19–33. New York: Longman.
**1986   Beti Widow Inheritance and Marriage Law: A Social History. *In* Widows in African Societies. Betty Potash, ed. Pp. 193–220. Stanford: Stanford University Press.

Hafkin, Nancy J., and Edna G. Bay
1976   Women in Africa. Stanford: Stanford University Press.

Harms, Robert
1983   Sustaining the System: Trading Towns along the Middle Zaire. *In* Women and Slavery in Africa. Claire C. Robertson and Martin A. Klein, eds. Pp. 95–111. Madison: University of Wisconsin.

Harrell-Bond, B. E.
1975   Modern Marriage in Sierra Leone. The Hague: Mouton.

Hay, Margaret Jean
*1976   Luo Women and Economic Change During the Colonial Period. *In* Women in Africa. Nancy J. Hafkin and Edna G. Bay, eds. Pp. 87–111. Stanford: Stanford University Press.

Hay, Margaret Jean, and Sharon Stichter
*1984   African Women South of the Sahara. New York: Longman.

Hemmings-Gapihan, Grace S.
*1982   International Development and the Evolution of Women's Economic Roles: A Case Study from Northern Gulma, Upper Volta. *In* Women and Work in Africa. Edna G. Bay, ed. Pp. 171–191. Boulder: Westview Press.

Henn, Jeanne K.
  1984   Women in the Rural Economy: Past, Present and Future. *In* African Women South of the Sahara. Margaret Jean Hay and Sharon Stichter, eds. Pp. 1–19. New York: Longman.
  1988   The Material Basis of Sexism: A Mode of Production Analysis. *In* Patriarchy and Class: African Women in the Home and the Workforce. Sharon B. Stichter and Jane L. Parpart, eds. Pp. 27–59. Boulder: Westview Press.
Hoffer, Carol P. [also see MacCormack]
  *1974   Madam Yoko: Ruler of the Kpa Mende Confederacy. *In* Women, Culture and Society. Michelle Rosaldo and Louise Lamphere, eds. Pp. 173–189. Stanford: Stanford University Press.
Jules-Rosette, Bennetta
  1979   The New Religions of Africa. Norwood, N.J.: Ablex.
Kettel, Bonnie
  *1986   The Commoditization of Women in Tugen (Kenya) Social Organization. *In* Women and Class in Africa. Claire Robertson and Iris Berger, eds. Pp. 47–62. New York: Africana Publishing.
Klein, Martin A.
  1980   Introduction. *In* Peasants in African Societies: Historical and Contemporary Perspectives. Pp. 9–45. Beverly Hills: Sage Publications.
Klima, George J.
  1970   The Barabaig. New York: Holt, Rinehart & Winston.
Kopytoff, Igor
  1977   Matrilineality, Residence and Residential Zones. American Ethnologist 4:539–559.
Krige, Eileen Jensen
  *1974   Women-Marriage, With Special Reference to the Lovedu: Its Significance for the Definition of Marriage. Africa 44:11–37.
La Fontaine, J. S.
  1978   Introduction. *In* Sex and Age as Principles of Social Differentiation. Pp. 1–21. New York: Academic Press.
Lallemand, Suzanne
  1977   Une Famille Mossi. Paris: Recherches Voltaiques, 17.
Landberg, Pamela
  *1986   Widows and Divorced Women in Swahili Society. *In* Widows in African Societies. Betty Potash, ed. Pp. 107–131. Stanford: Stanford University Press.
Lappe, Frances Moore, and Joseph Collins
  *1989   Why Can't People Feed Themselves. *In* Annual Editions in Anthropology. Pp. 220–225. Guilford, Conn.: Dushkin Press. [Originally *in* Food First: Beyond the Myth of Scarcity. New York: Random House, 1977]
Leacock, Eleanor, and Richard Lee
  1982   Politics and History in Band Societies. New York: Cambridge University Press.
Lee, Richard
  **1979   The !Kung San: Men, Women and Work in a Foraging Society. New York: Cambridge University Press.
Lewis, Barbara
  1977   Economic Activities and Marriage among Ivoirian Urban Women. *In* Sexual Stratification. Alice Schlegel, ed. Pp. 161–192. New York: Columbia University Pres.
Lewis, I. M.
  1966   Spirit Possession and Deprivation Cults. Man (ns) 1:307–309.
  1971   Ecstatic Religion. Harmondsworth: Penguin Books.
Little, Kenneth
  1973   African Women in Towns. New York: Cambridge University Press.
Llewelyn-Davies, Melissa
  *1981   Women, Warriors and Patriarchs. *In* Sexual Meanings. Sherry B. Ortner and Harriet Whitehead, eds. Pp. 330–358. New York: Cambridge University Press.

MacCormack, Carol P.
  **1979   Sande: The Public Face of a Secret Society. *In* The New Religions of Africa. Bennetta Jules-Rosette, ed. Pp. 27–39. Norwood, N.J.: Ablex.
  **1980   From Proto-Social to Adult: A Sherbro Transformation. *In* Nature, Culture and Gender. Carol P. MacCormack and Marilyn Strathern, eds. Pp. 95–119. New York: Cambridge University Press.
  1983   Slaves, Slave Owners and Slave Holders: Sherbro Coast and Hinterland. *In* Women and Slavery in Africa. Claire C. Robertson and Martin A. Klein, eds. Pp. 271–295. Madison: University of Wisconsin Press.
MacGaffey, Janet
  1986   Women and Class Formation in a Dependent Economy: Kisangani Enterpreneurs. *In* Women and Class in Africa. Claire Robertson and Iris Berger, eds. Pp. 161–178. New York: Africana Publishing.
  1988   Evading Male Control: Women in the Second Economy in Zaire. *In* Patriarchy and Class: African Women in the Home and the Workforce. Sharon B. Stichter and Jane L. Parpart, eds. Pp. 161–177. Boulder: Westview Press.
Mandeville, Elizabeth
  1979   Poverty, Work and the Financing of Single Women in Kampala. Africa 49:42–52.
Mba, Nina
  1982   Nigerian Women Mobilized: Women's Political Activity in Southern Nigeria, 1900–1965. Research Series, 48. Berkeley: Institute of International Studies, University of California.
Meillassoux, Claude
  **1981   Maidens, Meal and Money. New York: Cambridge University Press.
Mendosa, Eugene L.
  1979   The Position of Women in the Sisala Divination Cult. *In* The New Religions of Africa. Bennetta Jules-Rosette, ed. Pp. 57–67. Norwood, N.J.: Ablex.
Middleton, John, and E. H. Winter
  1963   Witchcraft and Sorcery in East Africa. New York: Praeger.
Mitchell, J. Clyde
  **1956   The Yao Village. Manchester: Manchester University Press.
Muller, Jean-Claude
  **1969   Preferential Marriage among the Rukuba of Benue-Plateau State, Nigeria. American Anthropologist 71:1057–1062.
  1986   Where to Live? Widows' Choices among the Rukuba. *In* Widows in African Societies. Betty Potash, ed. Pp. 175–193. Stanford: Stanford University Press.
Nelson, Nici
  *1979   Women Must Help Each Other: The Operation of Personal Networks among Buzaa Beer Brewers in Mathare Valley, Kenya. *In* Women United, Women Divided. Patricia Caplan and Janet Bujra, eds. Pp. 77–98. Bloomington: Indiana University Press.
  1981   African Women in the Development Process. Totowa, N.J.: Frank Cass.
  1987   Selling Her Kiosk: Kikuyu Notions of Sexuality and Sex for Sale in Mathare Valley, Kenya. *In* The Cultural Construction of Sexuality. Pat Caplan, ed. Pp. 217–240. London: Tavistock.
Netting, Robert McCormack
  **1969   Women's Weapons: The Politics of Domesticity among the Kofyar. American Anthropologist 71:1037–1046.
Ngubane, Harriet
  1977   Body and Mind in Zulu Medicine. New York: Acadenic Press.
Nukunyu, G. K.
  1969   Kinship and Marriage among the Anlo Ewe. New York: Humanities Press.
O'Barr, Jean
  *1984   African Women in Politics. *In* African Women South of the Sahara. Margaret Jean Hay and Sharon Stichter, eds. Pp. 140–156. New York: Longman.

Obbo, Christine
  1976   Dominant Ideology and Female Options: Three East African Case Studies. Africa 46:371–389.
  **1980   African Women: Their Struggle for Economic Independence. London: Zed Press.
  1986   Some East African Widows. *In* Widows in African Societies. Betty Potash, ed. Pp. 84–107. Stanford: Stanford University Press.
Oboler, Regina Smith
  *1980   Is the Female Husband a Man?: Woman/Woman Marriage among the Nandi of Kenya, Ethnology 19:69–88.
  **1985   Women, Power and Economic Change: The Nandi of Kenya. Stanford: Stanford University Press.
  1986   Nandi Widows. *In* Widows in African Societies. Betty Potash, ed. Pp. 66–84. Stanford: Stanford University Press.
O'Brien, Denise
  1977   Female Husbands in Southern Bantu Societies. *In* Sexual Stratification. Alice Schlegel, ed. Pp. 109–127. New York: Columbia University Press.
Okali, Christine
  **1983   Kinship and Cocoa Farming in Ghana. *In* Female and Male in West Africa. Christine Oppong, ed. Pp. 169–179. London: Allen & Unwin.
Okeyo, Achola Pala
  1980   Daughters of the Lakes and Rivers. *In* Women and Colonization. Mona Etienne and Eleanor Leacock, eds. Pp. 186–213. New York: J. F. Bergin, Publishers.
Okonjo, Kamene
  *1976   The Dual Sex Political System in Operation: Igbo Women and Community Politics in Midwestern Nigeria. *In* Women in Africa. Nancy J. Hafkin and Edna G. Bay, eds. Pp. 45–58. Stanford: Stanford University Press.
  1983   Sex Roles in Nigerian Politics. *In* Female and Male in West Africa. Christine Oppong, ed. Pp. 211–223. London: Allen & Unwin.
O'Laughlin, Bridget
  1974   Mediation of Contradiction: Why Mbum Women Do Not Eat Chicken. *In* Women, Culture and Society. Michelle Rosaldo and Louise Lamphere, eds. Pp. 301–318. Stanford: Stanford University Press.
Ominde, Simeon H.
  1970   The Luo Girl from Infancy to Marriage. London: MacMillan.
Oppong, Christine
  **1974   Marriage among a Matrilineal Elite. Cambridge: Cambridge University Press.
Ortner, Sherry B.
  1974   Is Female to Male as Nature Is to Culture? *In* Women, Culture and Society. Michelle Rosaldo and Louise Lamphere, eds. Pp. 67–89. Stanford: Stanford University Press.
Ortner, Sherry B., and Harriet Whitehead
  1981   Introduction. *In* Sexual Meanings. Pp. 1–27. New York: Cambridge University Press.
Ottenberg, Phoebe
  1959   The Changing Economic Position of Women among the Afikpo Ibo. *In* Continuity and Change in African Cultures. William R. Bascom and Melville J. Herskovits, eds. Pp. 205–224. Chicago: University of Chicago Press.
Parkin, David
  1978   The Cultural Definition of Political Response. New York: Academic Press.
Parpart, Jane L.
  *1986   Class and Gender on the Copperbelt: Women in Northern Rhodesian Copper Mining Communities, 1926–1964. *In* Women and Class in Africa. Claire Robertson and Iris Berger, eds. Pp. 141–161. New York: Africana Publishing.
  1988   Sexuality and Power on the Zambian Copperbelt: 1926–1964. *In* Patriarchy and Class: African Women in the Home and the Workforce. Sharon B. Stichter and Jane L. Parpart, eds. Pp. 139–161. Boulder: Westview Press.

Pellow, Deborah
    1977   Women in Accra. Algonac, Mich.: Reference Publications Inc.
Pittin, Renee
    1983   Houses of Women: A Focus on Alternative Life-Styles in Katsina City. *In* Female and Male
        in West Africa. Christine Oppong, ed. Pp. 291–303. Winchester, Mass.: Allen & Unwin.
Poewe, Karla
    **1978   Religion, Matriliny and Change: Jehovah's Witnesses and Seventh-Day Adventists. Amer-
        ican Ethnologist 5:303–322.
    1981   Matrilineal Ideology: Male-Female Dynamics in Luapula, Zambia. London: Academic Press.
Potash, Betty
    *1978   Some Aspects of Marital Stability in a Rural Luo Community. Africa 48:380–397.
    1980   The Impact of Labor Migration and Monetization: Analyzing Social and Economic Transfor-
        mation in a Karachuonyo Community. Unpublished paper presented at African Studies Association
        Meetings.
    *1985   Female Farmers, Mothers-in-law and Extension Agents: Development Planning and a Rural
        Luo Community. Working Papers in International Development, 90. East Lansing, Mich.: Mich-
        igan State University.
    **1986a   Widows in African Societies: Choices and Constraints. Stanford: Stanford University
        Press.
    1986b   Introduction. *In* Widows in African Societies. Betty Potash, ed. Pp. 1–44. Stanford: Stanford
        University Press.
    1986c   Wives of the Grave: Widows in a Luo Community. *In* Widows in African Societies. Betty
        Potash, ed. Pp. 45–66. Stanford: Stanford University Press.
Ranger, Terence
    1986   Religious Movements and Politics in Sub-Saharan Africa. African Studies Review 29:1–70.
Richards, Audrey
    1939   Land, Labour and Diet in Northern Rhodesia. Oxford: Oxford University Press.
    **1940   Bemba Marriage and Present Economic Conditions. Rhodes Livingston Papers, 4. Man-
        chester: University of Manchester Press.
    **1956   Chisungu: A Girl's Initiation Ceremony among the Bemba of Northern Rhodesia. New
        York: Grove Press.
Robertson, Claire
    **1984   Sharing the Same Bowl: Women and Class in Accra, Ghana. Bloomington: Indian Univer-
        sity Press.
    1987   Developing Economic Awareness: Changing Perspectives in Studies of African Women,
        1976–1985. Feminist Studies 13:97–136.
Robertson, Claire, and Iris Berger
    1986   Women and Class in Africa. New York: Africana Publishing.
Robertson, Claire C., and Martin A. Klein
    **1983   Women and Slavery in Africa. Madison: University of Wisconsin Press.
Robins, Catherine
    1979   Conversion, Life Crises, and Stability among Women in the East African Revival. *In* The New
        Religions of Africa. Bennetta Jules-Rosette, ed. Pp. 185–203. Norwood, N.J.: Ablex.
Rosaldo, Michelle
    1974   Women, Culture and Society: A Theoretical Overview. *In* Women, Culture and Society.
        Michelle Rosaldo and Louise Lamphere, eds. Pp. 17–43. Stanford: Stanford University Press.
Sacks, Karen
    **1982   Sisters and Wives. Westport, Conn.: Greenwood.
Salamone, Frank A.
    1986   Will She or Won't She? Choice and Dukawa Widows. *In* Widows in African Societies. Betty
        Potash, ed. Pp. 153–175. Stanford: Stanford University Press.
Sangree, Walter
    1969   Going Home to Mother: Traditional Marriage among the Irigwe of Benue-Plateau State, Ni-
        geria. American Anthropologist 71:1046–1057.

Sanjek, Roger
n.d.   Maid Servants and Market Women's Apprentices in Adabraka. Unpublished MS.
Schapera, Isaac
1941   Married Life in an African Tribe. New York: Sheridan House.
Schildkrout, Enid
*1978   Age and Gender in Hausa Societies: Socio-Economic Roles of Children in Urban Kano. *In*
Sex and Age as Principles of Social Organization. J. S. La Fontaine, ed. Pp. 109–137. New York:
Academic Press.
1983   Dependence and Autonomy: The Economic Activities of Secluded Hausa Women in Kano.
In Female and Male in West Africa. Christine Oppong, ed. Pp. 107–127. Winchester, Mass.: Allen
& Unwin.
1986   Widows in Hausa Society: Ritual Phase or Social Status? *In* Widows in African Societies.
Betty Potash, ed. Pp. 131–153. Stanford: Stanford University Press.
Schlegel, Alice
1977   Sexual Stratification. New York: Columbia University Press.
Schuster, Ilsa
**1979   New Women of Lusaka. Palo Alto: Mayfield Publishing.
1981   Perspectives in Development: The Problem of Nurses and Nursing in Zambia. *In* African
Women in the Development Process. Nici Nelson, ed. Pp. 77–98. Totowa, N.J.: Frank Cass.
*1982   Marginal Lives: Conflict and Contradiction in the Position of Female Traders in Lusaka,
Zambia. *In* Women and Work in Africa. Edna G. Bay, ed. Pp. 105–127. Boulder: Westview Press.
Shepherd, Gill
*1987   Rank, Gender and Homosexuality: Mombasa as a Key to Understanding Sexual Options. *In*
The Cultural Construction of Sexuality. Pat Caplan, ed. Pp. 240–271. London: Tavistock.
Shipton, Parker
1988   The Kenyan Land Tenure Reform: Misunderstandings in the Public Creation of Private Property. *In* Land and Society in Contemporary Africa. R. E. Downs and S. P. Reyna, eds. Pp. 91–
135. Hanover, N.H.: University Press of New England.
Shostak, Marjorie
*1983   Nisa: The Life and Words of a !Kung Woman. New York: Vintage Books.
Slater, Mariam K.
1976   African Odyssey. Garden City: Doubleday.
Smith, Mary
*1955   Baba of Karo. New York: Philosophical Library.
Smock, Audrey Chapman
1977   The Impact of Modernization on Women's Position in the Family in Ghana. *In* Sexual Stratification. Alice Schlegel, ed. Pp. 192–215. New York: Columbia University Press.
Southall, Aiden
1961   Social Change in Modern Africa. New York: Oxford University Press.
Spencer, Paul
1965   The Samburu. London: Routledge & Kegan Paul.
Spring, Anita
**1978   Epidemiology and Spirit Possession among the Luvale of Zambia. *In* Women in Ritual and
Symbolic Roles. Judith Hoch-Smith and Anita Spring, eds. Pp. 165–191. New York: Plenum
Press.
Stack, Carol
1974   All Our Kin. New York: Harper & Row.
Stamp, Patricia
*1975–76   Perceptions of Change and Economic Strategy among Kikuyu Women of Mitero, Kenya.
Rural Africana 29:19–43.
1986   Kikuyu Women's Self-Help Groups. *In* Women and Class in Africa. Claire Robertson and
Iris Berger, eds. Pp. 27–47. New York: Africana Publishing.

Stichter, Sharon
    1986   Women, Employment and the Family in Nairobi: The Impact of Capitalist Development in
        Kenya. Working Papers in African Studies, 121. Boston: Boston University.
Stichter, Sharon, and Jane L. Parpart
    1988   Patriarchy and Class: African Women in the Home and the Workforce. Boulder: Westview
        Press.
Strobel, Margaret
    **1979   Muslim Women in Mombasa: 1890–1975. New Haven: Yale University Press.
    1982   Review Essay: African Women. Signs 7:109–131.
Sudarkasa, Niara
    **1973   Where Women Work. Ann Arbor: University of Michigan Museum of Anthropology.
    1980   African and Afro-American Family Structure. Black Scholar 2(8):37–60.
    *1981   Female Employment and Family Organization in West Africa. In The Black Woman Cross-
        Culturally. Filomina Chioma Steady, ed. Pp. 49–65. Cambridge, Mass.: Schenkman Publishing.
Sundkler, B. G. M.
    1961   Bantu Prophets in South Africa. London: Oxford University Press.
Turner, Victor
    1957   Schism and Continuity in An African Society. Manchester: Manchester University Press.
    1967   The Forest of Symbols. Ithaca: Cornell University Press.
    1969   The Ritual Process. Chicago: Aldine.
United Nations Economic Commission for Africa
    1974   The Data Base for Discussion on the Interrelations between the Integration of Women in De-
        velopment, Their Situation and Population Factors in Africa. E/CN.14/SE/37.
Urdang, Stephanie
    *1984   Women in Contemporary National Liberation Movements. In African Women South of the
        Sahara. Margaret Jean Hay and Sharon Stichter, eds. Pp. 156–170. New York: Longman.
Van Allen, Judith
    *1972   Sitting on a Man: Colonialism and the Lost Political Institutions of Igbo Women. Canadian
        Journal of African Studies 6:165–181.
    1976   'Aba Riots' or 'Igbo Women's War'? Ideology, Stratification and the Invisibility of Women.
        In Women in Africa. Nancy J. Hafkin and Edna G. Bay, eds. Pp. 59–85. Stanford: Stanford Uni-
        versity Press.
Vellenga, Dorothy Dee
    1983   Who Is a Wife? Legal Expressions of Heterosexual Conflict in Ghana. In Female and Male in
        West Africa. Christine Oppong, ed. Pp. 144–156. London: Allen & Unwin.
    **1986   The Widow among the Matrilineal Akan of Southern Ghana. In Widows in African Soci-
        eties. Betty Potash, ed. Pp. 220–241. Stanford: Stanford University Press.
Verdon, Michel
    1982   Divorce in Abutia. Africa 52:48–67.
Wachtel, Eleanor
    *1975   A Farm of One's Own: The Rural Orientation of Women's Group Enterprises in Nakuru,
        Kenya. Rural Africana 29:69–80.
Weil, Peter
    1986   Agricultural Intensification and Fertility in the Gambia (West Africa). In Culture and Repro-
        duction: An Anthropological Critique of Demographic Transition Theory. W. Penn Handwerker,
        ed. Pp. 294–321. Boulder: Westview Press.
Wells, Julia C.
    **1983   Why Women Rebel: A Comparative Study of South African Women's Resistance Move-
        ments in Bloomfontein (1913) and Johannesburg (1958). Journal of Southern African Studies
        10:55–70.
White, Luise
    1988   Domestic Labor in a Colonial City: Prostitution in Nairobi, 1900–1952. In Patriarchy and
        Class: African Women in the Home and the Workforce. Sharon B. Stichter and Jane L. Parpart,
        eds. Pp. 139–161. Boulder: Westview Press.

Whyte, Susan Reynolds
   1979   Wives and Co-Wives in Marachi, Kenya. Folk 21–22:133–147.
Wilson, Francille Rusan
   **1982   Reinventing the Past and Circumscribing the Future: *Authenticité* and the Negative Image
      of Women's Work in Zaire. *In* Women and Work in Africa. Edna G. Bay, ed. Pp. 153–171. Boul-
      der: Westview Press.
Wipper, Audrey
   1972   African Women, Fashion and Scapegoating. Canadian Journal of African Studies 6:329–349.
   1975   The Maendeleo ya Wanawake Organization: The Co-optation of Leadership, African Studies
      Review 18:97–120.
   *1984   Women's Voluntary Associations. *In* African Women South of the Sahara. Margaret Jean
      Hay and Sharon Stichter, eds. Pp. 59–87. New York: Longman.
Wright, Marcia
   1982   Justice, Women and the Social Order in Abercorn, Northeastern Rhodesia, 1897–1903. *In*
      African Women and the Law: Historical Perspectives. Margaret Jean Hay and Marcia Wright, eds.
      Pp. 33–51. Papers on Africa. Boston: Boston University.

Teaching Modules

**These readings may be too complex or too long for students in most introductory courses. Instructors should use their own judgment. They could serve as a basis for lectures, or where length is the issue selective chapters could be assigned.

Module 1: The Impact of Socioeconomic Transformation on Women and Gender Relations

Readings

Afonja, Simi
   1986   Land Control: A Critical Factor in Yoruba Gender Stratification. *In* Women and Class in Af-
      rica. Claire Robertson and Iris Berger, eds. Pp. 156–169. New York: Africana Press.

Contrasts the response of three Yoruba communities to the introduction of cocoa, showing how differences in descent and inheritance, land sales, and tenancy relate to the varying impact of cocoa on women's economic situation.

Beneria, Lourdes, and Gita Sen
   **1981   Accumulation, Reproduction and Women's Role in Economic Development: Boserup Re-
      visited. Signs 7:279–298.

Provides a Marxist theoretical insight into Boserup's study which showed how development had harmed women. The focus is on processes of capital accumulation and women's reproductive roles rather than unequal education. Questions whether modernization theory can benefit women given the nature of articulation with a capitalist economic system.

Brain, James L.
   1976   Less Than Second-Class: Women in Rural Resettlement Schemes in Tanzania. *In* Women in
      Africa. Nancy J. Hafkin and Edna G. Bay, eds. Pp. 265–284. Stanford: Stanford University Press.

Shows how the organization of resettlement schemes gives men control over income while women do much of the work, leading women to withdraw their labor.

Bujra, Janet
  **1986 Urging Women to Redouble their Efforts . . . Class, Gender and Capitalist Transformation
    in Africa. *In* Women and Class in Africa. Claire Robertson and Iris Berger, eds. Pp. 117–141. New
    York: Africana Publishing.

  A theoretical review from a Marxist perspective on the impact of capitalist penetration on gender
and class in Africa. Shows how capitalist penetration has not drawn women into wage labor but has
channeled their efforts into petty commodity production and petty trade.

Bukh, Jette
  1979 The Village Woman in Ghana. Uppsala: Scandinavian Institute of African Studies.

  Describes the impoverishment of women and the dissolution of marriage resulting from the adoption of cocoa, declining cocoa prices, labor migration, and the collapse of the Ghanaian economy.

Guyer, Jane
  **1986 Beti Widow Inheritance and Marriage Law: A Social History. *In* Widows in African Soci-
    eties. Betty Potash, ed. Pp. 193–220. Stanford: Stanford University Press.

  Shows the complex relationship between changes in the political economy and features of social
organization with a particular emphasis on polygyny and widow inheritance. Describes the expansion
of plural marriage in response to increased trade and its decline as the economy shifted to cocoa cultivation.

Hemmings-Gapihan, Grace S.
  1982 International Development and the Evolution of Women's Economic Roles: A Case Study
    from Northern Gulma, Upper Volta. *In* Women and Work in Africa. Edna G. Bay, ed. Pp. 171–
    191. Boulder: Westview Press.

  Shows how famine relief offered new cash-earning opportunities for young men, leading to a decline in their participation in farming and an intensification of women's work in food production.
Women have less time to devote to their own activities and are less able to participate in socially important exchanges.

Lappe, Frances Moore, and Joseph Collins
  1989 Why Can't People Feed Themselves? *In* Annual Editions in Anthropology. Pp. 220–225.
    Guildford, Conn.: Dushkin Publishing. [Originally *in* Food First: Beyond the Myth of Scarcity.
    New York: Random House, 1977]

  Shows how colonial policies of cash cropping, labor migration, and land policies have created the
present situation of food shortage.

Potash, Betty
  1985 Female Farmers, Mothers-in-law and Extension Agents: Development Planning and a Rural
    Luo Community. Working Papers in International Development, 90. East Lansing, Mich.: Mich-
    igan State University.

  Describes the social organization of female farming, the importance of mothers-in-law in farming
decisions, and the organization of agricultural extension services which are directed to men. Shows how
extension policy cannot work because it requires precisely those inputs in short supply for women: cash
for seed and fertilizer and labor for additional weeding.

Vellenga, Dorothy Dee
  1986 The Widow among the Matrilineal Akan of Southern Ghana. *In* Widows in African Societies.
    Betty Potash, ed. Stanford: Stanford University Press.

  Shows the impact of the introduction of cocoa and colonial changes in marriage and inheritance
laws. Contrasts the situation of widows, wives, and divorced women in cocoa belt areas and notes how

widows are relatively advantaged through their acquisition of cocoa farms in comparison with widows in other regions of Ghana.

Issues to be Examined

Aim: To show how development activities and patterns of incorporation into a global capitalist economy have affected women and gender relations.

1. A number of readings show how development policies that are implicitly based on Western assumptions about men's productive roles and family support responsibilities unwittingly hurt or neglect women. Consider the implications in Kenya of directing agricultural services to men when it is the Luo women who do the farming (Potash). Discuss women's response to men's control over income in Tanzanian resettlement schemes (Brain). Why is it important for development planners to understand gender differences in productive activities and family support roles?

2. Beneria and Sen and Bujra show the negative impact that capitalist penetration and processes of incorporation into a global economy has had on African people. Using Afonja, Bukh, Guyer, and Vellenga compare the impact of cash cropping on women and the manner in which this modified gender relations. Contrast the different patterns of women's involvement in cocoa cultivation, the implications of such patterns for marriage relationships and forms of marriage, and the impact of the collapse in world cocoa prices. Were all of these developments harmful to women (compare Guyer and Vellenga with Bukh and Afonja)? What does dependency on world cocoa prices suggest about the creation of underdevelopment (a process) in contrast to undeveloped? Is there a convergence of results despite local differences in processes of transformation? What limits do macro-economic systems places on options?

3. A number of factors relate to the increase in woman's work including land shortages and reduced yields (Lappe and Collins and Potash), monetization (Hemmings-Gapihan and Potash), reduced availability of husband or children's labor due to labor migration or cash cropping (Bukh, Hemmings-Gapihan, Guyer) or school attendance (Potash). Discuss these issues. For example,

- Compare the impact of labor migration on women's work among the Gulma where women have had to replace sons' labor, among the Ewe where husbands are not available, and among the Luo where men had not been much involved in farming precolonially.

- Consider the implications of these processes for food shortages in Africa. Distinguish natural from man-made disasters; drought from famine.

4. Take an event currently in the news (e.g., a U.N. discussion on economic development or trade, a World Bank policy or protests about new government economic policies in response to the World Bank, famine relief, or discussions of foreign aid). Using insights on processes of socioeconomic transformation and culture, have students interpret this event. Show how anthropological insights are useful for understanding foreign policy and political events. Emphasize why things may appear differently to Third World peoples given their history and experiences.

Module 2: Cultural Constructions of Gender: Biological Sex, Social Roles, and Sexuality

Note: This unit would be strengthened by a comparative perspective using material from New Guinea and on American Indians.

Readings

Amadiume, Ifi
**1987   Male Daughters, Female Husbands. Atlantic Highlands, N.J.: Zed Press.

Shows the flexibility of the Igbo gender system in which women could fill male roles. Notes how assertiveness was not restricted to men and describes how both women and men took titles and acquired wives as a mark of wealth and success. Wives, in turn, helped husbands accumulate wealth and freed female husbands from domestic work.

Ardener, Shirley G.
1973   Sexual Insult and Female Militancy. Man 8:422–440.

Describes women's use of sexual insults in conflicts with Kom men when they seek to protect their interests.

Evans-Pritchard, E. E.
1970   Sexual Inversion among the Azande. American Anthropologist 72:1428–1434.

Describes former patterns of institutionalized homosexuality among warriors and ongoing lesbianism among Azande.

Gottlieb, Alma
1982   Symbolism of Menstruation among the Beng. Africa 52:34–48.

Shows how menstruation is not regarded as polluting per se but links menstrual taboos to Beng distinctions between human fertility and the fertility of the earth.

Krige, Eileen Jensen
1974   Woman-Marriage, with Special Reference to the Lovedu: Its Significance for the Definition of Marriage. Africa 44:11–37.

Shows the importance of daughters-in-law to Lovedu women and shows how women can claim a brother's daughter in marriage even if they have no son.

Llewelyn-Davies, Melissa
1981   Women, Warriors and Patriarchs. In Sexual Meanings. Sherry B. Ortner and Harriet Whitehead, eds. Pp. 330–358. New York: Cambridge University Press.

Describes age-related changes in masculine behavior, shows how warriors, not women, are associated with the wild, and describes Maasai beliefs about the cultural creation of women's fertility.

MacCormack, Carol P.
**1980   From Proto-Social to Adult: A Sherbro Transformation. In Nature, Culture and Gender. Carol P. MacCormack and Marilyn Strathern, eds. Pp.95–119. New York: Cambridge University Press.

Critiques Lévi-Strauss's formulation and shows how initiation rather than gender is involved in nature/culture distinctions among the Sherbro.

Oboler, Regina Smith
1980   Is the Female Husband a Man?: Woman/Woman Marriage among the Nandi of Kenya. Ethnology 19:69–88.

Shows the relationship between female-female marriage and women's need for heirs to inherit their house-property.

Shepherd, Gill
1987   Rank, Gender and Homosexuality: Mombasa as a Key to Understanding Sexual Options. In The Cultural Construction of Sexuality. Pat Caplan, ed. Pp. 240–271. London: Tavistock.

Shows how homosexual and lesbian relationships relate to social status, not gender, linking high and low status men and women. Notes that such relationships have no effects on the retention of masculine and feminine identities or on participation in relevant gender groups and activities.

Van Allen, Judith
1972 Sitting on a Man: Colonialism and the Lost Political Institutions of Igbo Women. Canadian Journal of African Studies 6:165–181.

Describes women's assertiveness in protecting themselves against male misbehavior, noting their use of sexual referents and physical actions in the precolonial period.

Issues to Be Examined

Aim: To show how gender is culturally constructed and to distinguish between biological sex, gender roles, and sexual behavior.

1. Have students read either van Allen or Ardener. Would such militant behavior with sexual innuendos be acceptable for American women? For American men? What does this say about how cultures shape different behavioral expectations in accordance with gender images? What is masculine and what is feminine?

2. Examine the similarities in Igbo women's and men's manner of expressing success by taking titles and wives (Amadiume). Do American men and women have the same or gender differentiated means of expressing wealth and accomplishment?

3. What does the existence of female husbands indicate about the separation of gender roles and biology? What social factors account for woman-woman marriage? What does this institution say about the social nature of marriage? Consider the different uses of female-female marriage described by Krige, Amadiume, Oboler, e.g., to acquire rights over daughters-in-law, to obtain the labor of wives, to have an heir to one's husband's estate, to acquire ties to children, etc.

4. How is menstruation perceived among the Beng? Why is it not regarded as polluting? What advantages do women enjoy during their menstruation? What does this indicate about cultural differences in perceptions of female biology?

5. Does homosexual expression necessarily affect gender identity? In Mombasa and elsewhere in Africa these issues are not linked. Compare this with the United States.

6. To what extent are gender linked behaviors fixed? To what extent are they expected to change over the life cycle? Consider Llewelyn-Davies and MacCormack. Instructors might also wish to see Drewal and Drewal, cited in the bibliography. Consider the importance of rites of passage in signaling changed expectations. Do American ideas about masculinity and femininity show similar life-cycle changes?

9

Gender Studies in Latin America

June Nash
City College, City University of New York

In the process of drawing women, as investigators and subjects, into the discourse of the social sciences, a new, multivocalic model of society is being forged. Women's presence in the expanded scientific discourse not only changes the nature of the investigators' relationship to their subject matter—the goal of gender studies, according to Marilyn Strathern (1987)—it subverts existing paradigms (Nash 1976). When the first objective is achieved, the paradigmatic shift is a necessary consequence.

My task here is to consider the degree to which research focusing on women has altered the relationship of social scientists to field research in Latin America, and in turn how research that takes women into account has changed our view of Latin American societies and cultures. The research generated has set off a paradigmatic shift that subverts our notions of gender relations, class, hierarchy, revolution, and social transformation. Taking women's work and responsibilities into account has forced us to turn from the worksite in formal economic enterprises to the sites of reproduction to comprehend the most dynamic arenas for change.

The progress that has been made in the past two decades has assured recognition of the growing field of feminist scholarship on Latin America (Nash and Safa 1986). I shall summarize some of the contributions made by feminist scholarship in the following areas: (1) the origin of sexual hierarchy in preconquest empires and the impact of colonization of ranked and nonranked societies; (2) women's contributions in domestic production and the interplay of social reproduction, production for the market, and biological reproduction; and (3) the newly emergent international division of labor, with its sharp reversal of gender levels of employment in multinational corporations and the growing informal sector. These and other contributions to the anthropology of Latin America have, for the most part, escaped textbook inclusion, despite the fact that they have fundamentally changed our thinking about society, the economy and the polity in Latin America.

The Origin of Sexual Hierarchy and the Impact of Colonization

The Victorian assumption of the universal ascendancy of men throughout the world was underwritten by many anthropologists who uncritically assigned women to subordinate status in the societies and cultures of the world. Evans Pritchard (1965, cited in Etienne and Leacock 1980) confirmed this Victorian assumption in his memorial lecture to the women students of Bedford College, given in honor of the feminist founder of the college. This view was revitalized in the introduction to a volume edited by Rosaldo and Lamphere (1974) that marked the advent of a female-oriented perspective. The editors also affirmed the universal separation of public and private spheres and the Aristotelian opposition of females identified with nature and males identified with culture.

Implicit in the universalizing of these phenomena is the biological basis for female subordination, although the editors of *Women, Culture and Society* (Rosaldo and Lamphere 1974) were careful to insist on the cultural conditions that led to it. Eleanor Leacock was among the major theorists who attacked the view that hierarchical gender relations were universal. She argued that this view ignored the historical and ethnographic evidence to the contrary. Comparative evidence for the impact of colonization in establishing gender hierarchy in the Americas is contained in an article she coauthored with Nash (Leacock and Nash 1977) and in the anthology she edited with Etienne (Etienne and Leacock 1980). Articles by Nash (1980) and Silverblatt (1980) contained in that volume show how the gender-structures of meaning permeated the emergent power hierarchy in the social and supernatural order in the high civilizations of Middle America and the Andes. Aztec cosmology projects a gender-structured supernatural world that changed from androgenous progenitors and paired male-female deities of natural forces to male deities at the apex of a polytheistic religion glorifying conquest (Nash 1978). The Inca projected a cosmovision that included male and female powers related to the sun and moon, but as Silverblatt (1987) shows, the priority of male inheritors of the sun deity was emerging at the time of the conquest. With the advent of colonization, upper-class indigenous women were, for a brief time, incorporated in the upper echelons of colonial society as wives and mistresses. But as the mestizo race they mothered increased in numbers and threatened the prerogatives of *criollos* (children born of Spanish parents in the New World), women of all classes in the central plateau of Mexico and in the Andes lost the advantages they experienced in the early years of conquest and found themselves reduced in their autonomy and control even in the subsistence sector.

These reanalyses of Spanish accounts of the preconquest and colonial periods establish the historical basis for the origins of male dominance. They suggest how gender hierarchy is related to state formation and indicate how ideologies regarding male and female characteristics, by projecting gender hierarchy into the supernatural world, condone male superordination.

The conquest and colonization by the Spaniards had a different impact on state societies such as the Inca and Aztec and nonranked horticultural and hunting gathering societies. The greatest contrast in the social structures of these societies can be seen in the status of women. While there are many similarities in the way gender relations were structured in the case of the high civilizations of Middle and South America, there is great diversity among the Amazonian peoples, the coastal tribes of Chile and Argentina and those of the Pampas that can still be discerned today.

Using these ethnographic cases selectively, some scholars support the thesis of universal subordination of women. The assumption is that if these groups represent the primeval past, and if they exhibit gender hierarchy, then women's subordination is a universal human condition. Certain lowland tribes of the Amazon, where male dominance seemed to characterize gender relations, were chosen as the prototype for indigenous groups that lacked political hierarchies. The Yanomamo, or "fierce people" as Napoleon Chagnon (1968) called them, were the favored textbook subjects, since they seemed to act out the stereotypes of male dominance and subordination of women by "uncivilized" or "primitive" people. Judith

Shapiro (1976) recognizes the sexual hierarchy present among the Yanomamo, but she emphasizes the ritual and ceremonial life that continually reaffirms it. This is no "natural" or biological given, but an explicit male monopoly of sacred and ceremonial life.

Ellen Basso's (1973) study of the Kalapalo Indians of Central Brazil provides a study of people with similar origins who demonstrate far less gender hierarchy. Basso explores the basis for both female and male leadership, finding that the *Anetaw,* or village patrons, include women as well as men who act as mediators between village and household group. Although men have exclusive control over the powerful trumpets through which communication with spirits is achieved, women are not entirely deprived of this venue. Women who have been cured by shamans can sponsor feasts, commanding the labor of kin to contribute food. They acquire prestige in this role just as the male trumpet players, and on their deathbed they are allowed to view the trumpets. A woman's brother becomes her best support and defender against a domineering husband. Since their children are preferred marriage mates, a strong sibling set of two generations provides an important basis for cooperation and support that often becomes the basis for chieftans to emerge as powerful leaders. Basso's study, by involving women as well as men in her investigation, reveals the mediated power relations in which male dominance in one arena is modified by women's control in another.

The historical basis for fostering aggressive behavior is well documented in Shelton Davis's *Victims of the Miracle* (1977). Conflict and the readiness to engage in battle is not a cultural given but a historically generated adaptation. The Kalapalo may, indeed, reveal greater cooperative and egalitarian relations because they have been more removed from the encroachment of pillaging colonists. This factor, completely ignored in Chagnon's monograph, is shown in Buenaventura-Posso and Brown's (1980) study of the Bari of the Amazonian jungle area of Colombia. Descriptions of peaceful, egalitarian relationships were conspicuously present in ethnographic descriptions from the earliest colonial contacts until the recent introduction of capitalist enterprises. Bari women engage in ceremonial rites and play the flutes explicitly proscribed for women in areas where male dominance prevails (Basso 1973; Murphy and Murphy 1985). They undertake most tasks along with men, and where they have predominant participation, as in spinning and weaving, their contribution to the family and society is structured in such a way that leadership is ephemeral, changing from day to day as the social groups that occupies the large communal houses reorganizes itself for daily tasks. Spanish accounts throughout the conquest and colonial period remark on the resistance of the Bari to military or even missionary intrusion, and are consistent in their comments on the egalitarian nature of the society.

The importance of a gendered perspective is dramatically underscored in the ethnographies of Yolanda and Robert Murphy (1960; 1985). In their first field trip in 1952, Yolanda and Robert collected data on the Mundurucu that led to Robert's monograph *Headhunter's Heritage* (Murphy 1960). Our view of the fierce "headhunters of the forest" is transformed as we read about Borai gently disengaging herself from the eight-month-old baby she is suckling. Moving away from the "dispassionate scientist's view" (Murphy and Murphy 1985:73) that characterized the earlier monograph (Murphy 1960) the Murphys candidly assess the changes in their perspective. The men's house is a focus for their discussion. In a paper that Robert Murphy published in 1959, the separate male house symbolized the site for constructing and affirming men's dominant position in the society. In their dual perspective achieved after a quarter century, the Murphy's analyze the ambiguity inherent in the exclusive domain of men as a site to guard themselves against women and to overcompensate for their own sense of weakness.

Even a single well-recorded case of egalitarian gender relations such as that of Buenaventura-Posso and Brown discredits the thesis of universality of male supremacy. The

Etienne and Leacock volume is replete with other cases of preconquest societies that lacked gender hierarchy until they were forced or persuaded to adopt practices and beliefs that underwrite male dominance hierarchies.

Women's Contribution in the Domestic and Informal Economy

The persistence of women in the subsistence sector of Latin American societies defies the assumptions contained in both Marxist and developmental models of Latin American society, that these activities would gradually disappear with the increasing penetration of capitalism. Dalla Costa (1972) was among the early feminist scholars who theorized about the interdependence of capitalist exploitation and women's oppression, maintaining that the unpaid labor of women in the home keeps the costs of reproducing the labor force low. Elizabeth Jelin (1976) elaborated this point for Latin America, showing that the low price for paid domestic labor as well as unpaid services of wives extend the oppression of women and expand the potential of capital accumulation. The production of commodities by semisubsistence peasant agriculturalists further subsidizes the industrialization policies promoted by many Latin American countries. Price controls on these products have forced Andean people in household production to bear the burden of inflation (Babb 1982). Women's handicraft products in weaving, pottery, and knitting have won a place in national and international markets that is beginning to overcome some of the values disparaging women's work in the indigenous economy (Littlefield 1979).

Comparing Latin American, European and other societies, Norman Long (1984) indicates the cultural priorities that have preserved the domestic modes of production. By keeping the costs of reproducing the labor force at a minimum, subsistence activities carried out in the household have subsidized workers in capitalist enterprises. But beyond these economic criteria, domestic production, usually in the charge of women, satisfies deeply rooted patterns of behavior that have preserved cultural lifeways along with human lives that would otherwise be threatened by the vicissitudes of capitalist production (Annis 1987).

The persistence of craft production, despite the penetration of capitalist production, reveals the many adaptations women make in changing economic settings even while pursuing traditional arts. Buechler (1986) shows the strategies women have devised to gain entry into the market with their craft production even while fulfilling domestic roles. She underlines the importance of recognizing the specific historical context of capitalist penetration and local resistance to the destruction of the economy. Distinct modes of production within a social formation provide the stage but do not determine the actions of men and women.

The devaluation of the subsistence sector of production by most economic analysts is due to lack of data about nonmarket activities as well as to the general devaluation of women's work. A conference sponsored by the Ford Foundation in Rio de Janeiro in 1978 addressed the problem of data gathering at its source: the census enumerations of activity rates. Neuma Aguiar (1986) points out two biases in research: (1) the inadequacy of categories used in most census surveys, and (2) the failure to capture nonmarket inputs. Both failures reflect male biases in the census bureaucracies that define the categories in use. As a result, existing stereotypes related to designation of "household head" become reified in data.

The limited perspective in data-gathering agencies can be overcome with the following recommendations made at the Rio de Janeiro conference and summarized by the organizer, Neuma Aguiar (1986). First, both in terms of a chronology for comparative research and its importance, is the need for ethnographic studies to complement survey research. Unless on-the-ground studies are carried out to determine what in fact is being done by women and men in different economic settings, the questions asked by census takers will not capture the range and diversity of female and male activities. The primary tenet of ethnographic studies is the framing of questions in relation to observed regularities. Census takers and those who rely on their findings construct questionnaires that reify their assumptions about society. One of these has been that women do not work in subsistence farming, but only "help" in periods of plant- ing or harvesting. As a result, they ask questions only about the "household head," assumed to be a male, and prefer males as respondents. Even if women are asked what they do, they might reaffirm the men's statements. In those cultures where women are categorically en- joined from doing men's work, particularly that which involves using "men's" tools such as the hoe and plow, one must develop the research tactics of a detective to catch them in the act. Such is the case with Maya women of traditional communities in Chiapas, Mexico, who, if they are left without menfolk to do the work of their fields and do not have money to hire help, sneak out to work in the fields (Nash 1970).

In the crisis years of the 1980s women worked openly with men, especially in the town- ships of Chenalho and Oxchuc, where limited land and high interest costs for farm credit forced men to resort to work on the plantations even more frequently. When Indians engage in wage work for agroindustrial enterprises, cultural prohibitions are relaxed. Guatemalan Maya women migrate to the coast to work in agroindustry; these inhibitions are relaxed as women work alongside men in the coffee and cotton harvests (Bossen 1984).

The wide variety of economic activities undertaken by women in the domestic mode of production illustrates the social construction of gender roles. The only universal feature is the complementarity of gender-defined roles and the resulting interdependence of the sexes. The increasing range and variety of male roles in urban areas undercuts the more balanced sym- metry of this interdependence, as we shall see below.

It is precisely because women's roles in production are conditioned by their reproduc- tive roles that we learn more about the contradictions inherent in capitalism. Lourdes Beneria and Gita Sen (1981:160) clarify this relationship between the processes of accumulation and changes in women's work: "The tendency of capitalist accumulation is to separate direct pro- ducers from the means of production and to make their conditions of survival more insecure and contingent."

Heleieth Saffioti was one of the first Latin American scholars to relate the conditions of women's employment to presumptions about their domestic responsibilities. In her book, *Women in Class Society* (1969), she shows the feminine side of the reserve labor force. High rates of labor participation by women in the 19th century changed as capital-intensive pro- duction eliminated many of the jobs done by women. Yet with all the changes in levels of wage labor activity, women continue to have the double burden of domestic work both as housewives and servants. The low-paid services of women in the home subsidizes a low-paid work force, keeping down the costs of reproduction, as Elizabeth Jelin demonstrated (1976).

Older forms of patriarchy that persisted in peasant households on haciendas were broken down with the spread of capitalist agriculture but were often replaced with new forms. In Peru, as Deere (1977) has shown, the impoverishment of female-headed households reduces their autonomy, and many women must resort to extended household residence with their parents. Deere shows that prior to the land reform of 1969, these peasants maximized domestic ac- cumulation of capital by increasing the number of children available as workers on the lands of the lord. With the succession of commodity production and wage work, the value of both child and female labor is reduced without the compensating access to new opportunities that men enjoy. Bolivian women have experienced a similar decline in activity rates in rural agriculture as the services required of them on the old landed estates were nullified by passage of the land reform act in the 1950s (Sautu 1981).

Changing rates of participation of women in the work force reflect both the changing demand for labor and the relative efficiency of data collection. In Bolivia, where women had always maintained high activity rates in agriculture prior to the 1952 land reform, they are no longer forced to work in fields of the large landholders. The lower rates of participation recorded in recent censuses may reflect the failure of the census enumerators to account for nonmarket activities. In Bolivia, as elsewhere, it is well recognized that "the whole peasant family participates in the cultivation of the land . . . [and] women also assume the task of selling the farm produce in the local market'' (Sautu 1981:157).

Subsistence agriculture, where it survives, has not fully been evaluated as to its contributions to reproduction of the labor force. However, studies that provide a data base for a fundamental reevaluation are now available and must be incorporated in aggregate analyses at national and international levels. Three volumes of articles edited by Leon de Leal and Deere (1980; 1982a; 1982b) span the local, regional, national, and international levels of economic integration, bringing to bear data on the economic, social, and cultural conditions in which women act to reproduce the society. Their analysis of the sexual division of labor in Colombia and Peru (Deere and Leon de Leal 1985) demonstrates the value of careful observation combined with a developed theoretical position that takes women into account. Differences in land holding and wealth among the peasantry of the Andes results in very different levels of participation of women in agricultural work.

Variation in the level of commercial activity also defines the possibilities for women gaining income outside the domestic sphere, as Bourque and Warren (1981) show in their comparison of women in a rural village and market town. Mutual dependence in a complementary division of labor reinforces the social structures within which men and women play their roles (Bourque and Warren 1981). This may result, as Isabell (1978) notes in the Andes, in a parallel dyadic structure that is not comprehensive using conventional political power models.

The importance of the multiplicity of economic activities carried out by women in meeting domestic needs is rarely conceptualized as an opportunity cost for female wage employment, since the realm of economic behavior relates only to labor in market terms. Marianne Schmink (1986) poses this problem of the conflicting demands put on women in the wage-earning market and the domestic economy. She shows that household mediation of the resources and income generated in the domestic context merits serious study because of the light it sheds on the articulation of productive and reproductive spheres.

Although economic determinism characterizes much of the analysis of gender relations, ethnographic case studies show the importance of cultural factors such as the patterning of class positions, marital relationships, and the varying strength of kinship networks that reciprocally contribute to and are reinforced by economic differences. Schmink (1986) and Bolles (1986) show how the dialectic of gender relations informs and shapes the larger dialectic of class formation in the process of capitalist penetration. In Jamaica, Bolles shows that households formed by permanent unions are able to reinforce income generation. Similarly Schmink indicates how relative degrees of poverty in Bello Horizonte, Brazil, are attributed in part to the inability to utilize available workers in the household. The economic status of the family influences, and in turn is influenced by, the composition of its membership.

The spread of import-substitution industrialization after World War II resulted in the preferred employment of men in capital-intensive industries (Ortego de Figueroa 1976; Sautu 1981; Vasquez de Miranda 1977). The loss of value for child labor that could no longer be integrated into farm production and the concomitant increase in the "cost" of raising children create a trend in the direction of smaller families that, according to Frances Rothstein (1986) can be seen in Mexico today. This parallels earlier trends in industrialized countries, but in Mexico the overall impact is far less than in advanced industrial countries. Safa's (1984) comparison of New Jersey and Sao Paulo garment workers illustrates this contrast in perceived benefits of raising children. We shall illustrate the dialectic of production and reproduction in case studies from industrializing and industrialized areas.

Women in the New International Division of Labor

Third World countries are experiencing an unprecedented expansion of capitalist institutions in rural and urban areas. Analytical modes for the insertion of women in production vary from the Marxist "reserve labor pool" to that of the segmented labor market. Saffioti's (1969) study of women in capitalist production analyzes women's labor as a reserve maintaining itself in "outmoded" modes of production. This labor is commanded by the dominant mode of production when demand for labor increases. In their marginally utilized roles, women bear the brunt of economic fluctuation as the first to be fired and the lowest paid. More recent researcsh shows that, while women are drawn into labor markets in periods of high demand, their lower labor costs make them a more attractive source of labor during economic crises.

Brazil is a crucial arena in which to explore the contradictions in women's positions resulting from the uneven expansion of capitalism. Saffioti (1986) shows this in her comparison of women in two garment factories representing different levels of technological application. She concludes that women are consistently losers with technological innovation since their control over jobs that demand craft skills, and even the job itself, is lost as automation proceeds.

Another level of uneven development in Brazil is analyzed by Aguiar (1984) in her comparative study of women in a plantation system, a government irrigation project, and an industrial capitalist enterprise. Differential access to the housing and food resources supplied as payment in kind in the first two of these enterprises exacerbated the marginality of the women engaged in production. Men were given house lots and the wages for the labor of the entire family. Widowed and divorced women were thus cut out of the community as well as out of the work force in the plantation. Social workers in the government-controlled project tried to discourage women from working in agriculture, in contrast to plantation settings where women were superexploited. The transnational textile firm that Aguiar studied paid higher wages but offered less stable employment. Women workers suffered even more than male workers from fluctuations, since they could not cultivate community ties in this setting because of the constant moves conditioned by short employment periods. This negated an important strategy that often compensates for women's vulnerability in the labor market.

Uneven development is also found in Latin American countries that have not experienced the remarkable growth of Brazil. Women have shown a great deal of flexibility in adapting to economic changes that expelled them from the agricultural domestic economy. Laurel Bossen (1984) and Florence Babb (1986) describe how women in a wide variety of economic contexts in Guatemala and Peru supplement household income with petty commodity production. Class position modifies the impact of capitalist transformations. In Guatemala, upper-class women in the capital have more autonomy and control over resources than proletarianized women in the sugar plantation, even though the penetration of capitalist institutions is greater in the former setting. Bossen (1984:320) concludes that "both structurally and culturally, capitalism has brought about a redivision of labor which has relatively penalized women.'' Young (1978) found a similar transformation in Oaxaca as women lost their handicraft production with the introduction of factory-made goods.

The dynamic interplay between women's economic contribution and the way it is perceived and negotiated in social interaction is illuminated by Susan Bourque and Kay Warren's (1981) comparison of two highland Peruvian communities. In Mayobamba, a potato-growing, cattle-and sheep-herding community, the tradition of communal works with a core of adult male family heads excludes women from taking advantage of communal resources such as irrigation. With an increase in the number of cash transactions in this agricultural village, women's control of domestic resources is weakened. However, when we turn to Chiuchin, some 2000 feet lower and more involved in trade networks with Lima, the cash economy opens new opportunities for women to enter capitalist exchange systems. Although their husbands still have the greater contact and opportunities to advance economically through truck transportation, women have more opportunity to maintain their position in the household and community than women at a higher altitude. In this comparison, we can see that while capitalist exchanges disturb the complementarity that is noted in highland society, they may also provide compensating opportunities as women gain entry in the new system.

Segmentation of the labor force in Third World countries is clearly related to different modes of production, yet sectors of the labor force that enter into the different modes of production are often integrated within the family (Nash 1982). It is in this context that we can appreciate the crucial importance of women's roles in articulating distinct modes of production. Women's economic objectives often differ from those of men, who may welcome wage work in commercial agriculture, since it is they who try to preserve the subsistence cultivation that permits survival of their children (Rubbo 1975). Women engaged in piecework and putting out systems in their homes weave together the production schedules of highly capitalized and mechanized enterprise with their familial chores in the home, as Judith-Marie Buechler demonstrates in her article on Bolivian artisans (1986). In their trading activities, women are the mediators in bringing commodities produced on the world market to women who produce handicraft items for that market. As managers of household expenditures, they convert men's wages earned in capitalized enterprises into use values for household consumption. This task has become increasingly more difficult, as forced labor migrations and the increase in female-headed households break traditional redistribution channels in the family.

Disaggregation of employment data by sex and class sets into relief the differential effects of the penetration of capitalist enterprises in Latin America. In a comparison of the countries in the southern cone of South America, Ruth Sautu (1981) shows that there is an increase in countries with an expanding tertiary sector, creating a demand for women in clerical and service occupations, at the same time that there is a decrease in the activity rates of lower-class women. Urban educated women in Argentina are responding to the increasing demand for women in finance, commerce, and government at the same time that women are losing jobs in industry. Archetti and Stolen (1978) demonstrate the enormous differences in the situation of women in Argentina over time and in different modes of production, thus demonstrating the untenability of the thesis of the universal subordination of women in that context.

The importance of an approach focusing on women is even more apparent in the analysis of the global integration of capital. In the recent expansion of industry across national boundaries, the ''comparative advantages of women's disadvantages,'' in Lourdes Arizpe and Josefina Aranda's (1981) felicitous phrasing, become more explicit. Their disadvantaged position in the labor markets of the less developed countries and their greater availability give them a preferential status in the multinational corporations' search for cheap labor.

Feminist studies sharpen the historically specific contexts that condition women's entry into the labor force. Whereas women's labor appeared to be a reserve when the ideology of patriarchy characterized their commitment to domestic labor as primary, their labor has always been an essential part of specific labor markets. With the integration of production at a global level, women have become the preferred labor force. The growing unemployment of men and the superemployment of women in regions with export processing zones changes the dynamic of exploitation of women in the labor market in the household (Fernandez-Kelly 1983; Nash and Fernandez-Kelly 1984).

Studies of the aggregate figures on employment reveal the highly segmented labor force participation by gender. Increases in the number of women employed in the wage labor force continue to reflect the greater concentration of women in the service section, where 67.2% of Latin American women were employed (International Labor Office 1980). Brazil, like other more industrialized Latin American countries, showed a rise in women employed in manufacturing, exceeding that of male employment during the 1970s, when there was a 181% growth in manufacturing. The increase in their participation rates from 13.6% to 29.6% in 1976, reversed earlier trends showing declining or stabilized rates of employment in industry (Schmink 1986). In Mexico, women's participation in the wage labor force rose from 240,000 in 1930 when they were 4.5% of the work force, to 2,892,000 in 1974 when they constituted 19.1% of the work force (de Leonardo 1976). In the years following, their rate of participation increased as they were employed in the bottom level of the labor force.

The high rates of female participation in the labor force have raised questions about the motivations to work and what it means about the changing nature of the family. Patricia Fernandez-Kelly (1983) points out that, although the newer electronic shops prefer young unmarried women because it is assumed that they do not have family responsibilities and that they will soon leave the labor force, these young women are in fact often the principal support of their parents and siblings under working age. She found that one in three families is headed by a woman, and that in 1982, three out of four women provided the only means of support for their families in the border garment industries she studied (1983:4). Despite the large share of household expenses borne by women working in the *maquiladoras* (assembly industries), they still do most of the housework: the average working day of these women was 15 hours (1983:137).

The other question concerning women's work in industry is whether it improves the status of women in the wider society. Summing up the evidence from studies of Latin American industrialization in the 1980s, Susan Tiano (1986) defines the major debate as one revolving around two opposed theses. The first is that integration of women into the political and economic life of the nation is ensured by their entry into industrial production. The second is that women are marginalized by their entry into industrial production. The majority of the writers she reviewed indicated that industrialization and modernization benefit only a few middle-class women, while the majority of production workers, especially in the electronics *maquilas,* have only a limited working span. Women contribute to the full proletarianization of men in their families, often underwriting the costs of men's training and education for more secure jobs, allowing them the free time to pursue further education or attend union meetings. Only one author (Rosen 1982) maintained that industrialization increases gender equality by absorbing women in the labor force and by diffusing liberal, egalitarian ideology.

The runaway shops raise the level of competition among workers to an international level, as Safa contends (1981:433). These industries in flight from high wage areas are ever ready to depart if labor starts to make demands in their new sites. Their preference for women workers is, in fact, built into their mobility, since it is assumed that young women are only temporary members of the work force.

With the new international division of labor brought to Latin American countries by multinational corporations operating in free trade zones, women are the preferred labor force for low-skilled assembly jobs. These trends may now be reversed as men seek government backing to demand jobs in the *maquiladoras*. Arnulfo Castro Munire, President of the Association of Maquiladoras, was quoted by Richard J. Meislin, a reporter for the *New York Times* (March 19, 1984; Section D) as saying, "We had become a matriarchy. It had ruptured the social equilibrium." A deliberate effort is now being made in Ciudad Juarez to hire men, and Castro reported that one-third of the workers are male. Up to the present time, only 10% of the shops are organized, and even organized shops tend to be conciliatory in an area of high unemployment. Future research will show whether an increase in the proportions of male workers assumed to have a greater commitment to permanent employment will result in pressures for greater job stability.

An important facet of the international movement of investments is the fluctuation in the exchange rate for currency. The steady devaluation of the Mexican peso has made labor costs increasingly attractive to American business. An assembly line worker now earns $28 for a 45-hour week. Differential currency exchanges also stimulate migration within Latin America. Margalit Berlin (1984) has shown that, because of the favorable exchange rates in Colombia for Venezuelan currency, Colombian women are willing to work in Venezuelan factories paying too low a wage to attract natives. Migration from labor-exporting countries such as Bolivia, Colombia, Ecuador, and Peru can be expected to continue, both in direct migration to the United States and to the more industrialized countries of South America (Sassen-Koob 1984). The uneven development of Latin American countries and regions in the period of import substitution from the end of World War II to the end of the 1960s can be expected to intensify these movements in the 1980s.

Those who feel most poignantly the effects of the integration of production on a global level are the migrants. Women differ from men in their assessment of the new social and cultural setting. As Patricia Pessar (1986) shows, women from the Dominican Republic often prefer to remain in the United States because of the enhanced appreciation of their role in the household. Their work outside the home enables them to make a greater economic contribution to the household expenses than they could expect in their home country. Contrary to expectations, women's work heightens their self-esteem as wives and mothers, affording them an opportunity to participate as equals and thus actualize these roles more fully. Like Dominican migrant women, Columbian women maintain close ties with their families in Colombia even when they intend to stay. Their familial lives influence their decisions to work and to remain in the United States or return to Colombia just as in the case of Dominican women (Berlin 1984).

These personal accounts of migrants remind us that the structural parameters derived from aggregate data must eventually be interpreted in terms of the decisions made by human beings who have the illusion, if not the experience, of autonomous control over their lives. Structuralist premises are good for postmortems. They can rarely predict what people will do in response to changes in their environment or even what any individual will opt to do. Feminist studies have favored the more personalized and intimate portrayal of women in all the roles they occupy.

While development literature has drawn attention to the growing gap between rich and poor nations, scholarship focusing on women shows that women's share has diminished at a greater rate (Buvinic et al. 1983). Always the predominant population in the "informal economy" (Arizpe 1977), women are found in increasing numbers in the poorly remunerated ranks of the self-employed. When there are no adult males in the household, women are even more likely to have recourse to the informal economy (Bolles 1986).

Once considered a transitional phenomenon in the development process, the informal economy is increasingly recognized as a structural feature of peripheral accumulation (Portes and Walton 1981). The two major occupations available for women migrating from rural areas to the cities of Latin America are domestic service and street selling (Bunster, Chaney and Young 1985; Rubbo and Taussig 1978). Women with children prefer the latter since it allows them greater autonomy, and as children grow they can be an asset in selling (Arizpe 1977). Bunster, Chaney and Young (1985) have shown that women enter the informal economy as a means of maintaining their children and themselves in work that allows them greater flexibility.

Studies by feminist scholars such as these raise our awareness of the importance of the informal economy ensuring survival of increasing numbers of the urban poor. Women who have paid attention to the activities of women in the barriadas of the great metropolitan areas of Latin America are more likely to recognize the highly organized collective activities in which they struggle for basic needs such as water, electricity, police protection and schools. Perlman (1976) and Peattie (1976) reject the view of the barrio dwellers as "marginalized" (Nun et al. 1968; Quijano 1971). As central figures in these struggles, women have gained a basis for political leadership in the current crisis. Prates (n.d.) shows this in Uruguay, de Oliveira (n.d.) in Mexico, Nash (1988) in Bolivia, and Andreas (n.d.) and Radcliffe (n.d.) in Peru.

The debt crisis looming in Third World as well as First World countries is sharpening the disparities in income level as jobs in the formal sector diminish and men are cast into the informal sector along with women. In order to pay the debt, many countries are using more than 50% of the income from exports. Taxes are being imposed for the first time on subsistence sector producers. Industry fostered during the rapid development from the 1950s to the 1970s has stagnated along with the restriction on credit and imports. As workers are laid off from industrial jobs as the economic crisis deepens, the class struggle is moving from the sites of production to neighborhoods and the streets.

Women are prominent in the political mobilization against economic conditions imposed by the International Monetary Fund for debt repayment. In their role as housewives, women are more alert to the threat to life imposed by those countries that have conformed to these conditions. Hundreds of women in the Bolivian tin mining communities have joined miners laid off in the nationalized mines to oppose the government's policies. When the march of thousands of people was blocked by the army from entering La Paz and staging mass protests, women set up pickets of hunger strikers in the capital city and in the mining centers. Their protest continues as the government has continued to restructure the economy in favor of foreign interests usurping the few profitable mines (Nash 1988).

Peruvian women have been equally militant in protesting the massive layoffs in industries and fisheries. Carol Andreas (1986) has shown the devastation of the Peruvian economy in the 1980s and the forceful opposition of workers in factories and fish processing plants throughout the country. Their struggles demonstrate the courage and conviction of women fighting the government's policy of orienting economic and political life to the international market without consideration of the threat to survival (Andreas 1986:77). Women in highland communities from which many men have migrated in search of wage employment in cities are independently organizing to preserve their position in the subsistence economy.

The restructuring of Mexico's economy in the decade of the debt crisis has forced much of the industrial production in garment work and assembly operations into an underground economy of home work where women are more intensively exploited than ever. Jose Antonio Alonso (1979, 1984) documented the trends in the garment trade in suburbs of Mexico City in the 1970s as small shops unable to compete with the multinational corporations in the capital turned to home workers who bear the risks but little of the profits in the new industrial patterns. Lourdes Beneria and Martha Roldan (1987) have summarized the massive changes brought about in Mexico's industries affecting the survival of families and analyzed it in relation to international labor markets. They reveal the personal, social and cultural dynamics of the restructured labor market that challenge theories of class based on economic determinism. Their study reveals the continuous feedback between class and gender construction along a number of dimensions, showing how gender subordination is reinforced in the workplace and in the home (Beneria and Roldan 1987:102).

Conclusions

Research that has taken women into account has brought a multidimensional analysis to the study of Latin American society. When women are considered as an integral part of historical transformations, the dynamics of social, cultural, ideological, and political developments are taken into account. Government policies that ignore these many facets of social change are doomed to failure.

Most of the work in this new perspective has concentrated on women's roles in the work force. Studies of gender relations in the Amazonian River basin and tributary area are an exception in their exploration of the psychological and social characteristics of gender segmentation. More studies of upper- and middle-class women, female organizations, and legal studies of women's status in the family and society are needed, but the significant gains that have been made need to be incorporated in textbook and course presentations of Latin American society.

References Cited

Aguiar, Neuma
  1984   Household, Community, National and Multinational Industrial Development. *In* Women and the International Development of Labor. June Nash and Maria Fernandez Kelly, eds. Pp. 117–137. Albany: State University of New York Press.
  1986   Research Guidelines: How to Study Women's Work in Latin America. *In* Women and Change in Latin America. J. Nash and H. Safa, eds. Pp. 22–34. South Hadley, Mass.: Bergin and Garvey.
Alonso, Jose A.
  1979   The Domestic Seamstresses of Netzahualcoyotl: A Case Study of Feminine Overexploitation in a Marginal Urban Area. Ph.D. dissertation, Department of Sociology, New York University.
  1984   The Domestic Clothing Workers in the Mexican Metropolis and Their Relations to Dependent Capitalism. *In* Women, Men, and the International Division of Labor. J. Nash and M. Patricia Fernandez-Kelly, eds. Pp. 161–172. Albany: State University of New York Press.
Andreas, Carol
  1986   The Barriada as Locus of Revolutionarende Peru. Resources for Feminist Research on Social Issues of Feminism and the State Process 15(1):5–17.
  n.d.   People's Kitchens and Revolutionary Organizing in Lima, Peru. Unpublished MS.
Annis, Sheldon
  1987   God and Production in Guatemala. Austin: University of Texas Press.
Archetti, Eduardo, and Kristo Anne Stolen
  1978   Economia domestica estrátegias de herencia y acumulación de capital: La Situación de la Mujer en Norte de Santa Fé, Argentina. America Indigena 38:383–403.

Arizpe, Lourdes
  1977   Women in the Informal Labor Sector: The Case of Mexico City. Signs 3(1):25–37.
Arizpe, Lourdes, and Josefina Aranda
  1981   The "Comparative Advantage" of Women's Disadvantages: Women Workers in the Straw-
    berry Export Business in Mexico. Signs 7:453–473.
Babb, Florence
  1982   Economic Crisis and the Assault on Marketers in Peru. *Women in Development*. Working
    Papers. East Lansing: Michigan State University.
  1986   Producers and Reproducers: Andean Marketwomen in the Economy. *In* Women and Change
    in Latin America. J. Nash and H. Safa, eds. Pp. 53–64. South Hadley, Mass.: Bergin and Garvey.
Basso, Ellen B.
  1973   *The Kalapalo Indians of Central Brazil*. New York: Holt, Rinehart and Winston.
Beneria, Lourdes, and Gita Sen
  1981   Accumulation, Reproduction, and Women's Role in Economic Development. Feminist Stud-
    ies 8(1):157–176.
Beneria, Lourdes, and Martha Roldan
  1987   The Crossroads of Class and Gender. Industrial Homework, Subcontracting and Household
    Dynamics in Mexico City. Chicago: University of Chicago Press.
Berlin, Margalit
  1984   The Formation of an Ethnic Group: Colombian Female Workers in Venezuela. pp. 257–270.
    In Women and Change in Latin America. J. Nash and H. Safa, eds. Pp. 257–270. South Hadley,
    Mass.: Bergin and Garvey.
Bolles, Lynn
  1986   Female-Headed Households in Urban Jamaica. *In* Women and Change in Latin America. J.
    Nash and H. Safa, eds. South Hadley, Mass.: Bergin and Garvey.
Bossen, Laurel
  1984   The Redivision of Labor. Albany: State University of New York Press.
Bourque, Susan C., and Kay Barbara Warren
  1981   Women of the Andes: Patriarchy and Social Change in Two Peruvian Villages. Ann Arbor:
    University of Michigan Press.
Buechler, Judith-Maria
  1986   Women in Petty Commodity Production in La Paz, Bolivia. *In* Women and Change in Latin
    America. J. Nash and H. Safa, eds. Pp. 165–189. South Hadley, Mass.: Bergin and Garvey.
Buenaventura-Posso, Elisa, and Susan E. Brown
  1980   Forced Transition from Egalitarianism to Male Dominance: The Bari of Colombia. *In* Women
    and Colonization. Mona Etienne and Eleanor Leacock, eds. Pp. 109–133. New York: Monthly
    Review Press.
Bunster, Ximena, Elsa Chaney, and Ellen Young
  1985   Sellers and Servants. Working Women in Lima, Peru. New York: Praeger.
Buvenic, Myra, Margaret A. Lycette, and Paul McGreevey
  1983   Women and Poverty in the Third World. Baltimore: Johns Hopkins Press.
Chagnon, Napoleon
  1968   Yanomamo: The Fierce People. New York: Holt, Rinehart and Winston.
Dalla Costa, Mariarase
  1972   Women and the Subversion of Community. *In* The Power of Women and the Subversion of
    Community. M. Dalla Costa and S. James. Bristol, England: Fall Wall Press.
Davis, Shelton
  1977   Victims of the Miracle. Development and the Indians of Brazil. New York: Cambridge Uni-
    versity Press.
Deere, Carmen Diana
  1977   Changing Social Relations of Production and Peruvian Peasant Women's Work. Latin Amer-
    ican Perspectives 4:48–69.

Deere, Carmin Diana, and Magdalena Leon de Leal
  1985   Peasant Production, Proletarianization, and the Sexual Division of Labor in the Andes. *In* Women and Development: The Sexual Division of Labor in Rural Societies. L. Beneria, ed. Pp. 675–693. New York: Praeger.
Etienne, Mona and Eleanor Leacock, eds.
  1980   Women and Colonization. Anthropological Perspectives. South Hadley, Mass.: Bergin and Garvey.
Evans-Pritchard, E. E.
  1965   The Position of Women in Primitive Societies and in Our Own. *In* The Position of Women in Primitive Societies and Other Essays in Social Anthropology. London: Faber and Faber.
Fernandez-Kelly, M. Patricia
  1983   For We are Sold, I and My People. Albany: State University of New York Press.
International Labor Office
  1980   Women in World Development. Geneva: United Nations.
Isabell, Billie Jean
  1978   To Defend Ourselves: Ecology and Ritual in an Andean Village. Austin: University of Texas Press.
Jelin, Elizabeth
  1976   The Bahiana in the Labor Force in Salvador, Brazil. *In* Women and Change in Latin America. June Nash and Helen Safa, eds. Pp. 129–146. South Hadley, Mass.: Bergin and Garvey.
Leacock, Eleanor, and June Nash
  1977   Ideology of Sex: Archetypes and Stereotypes. Annals of the New York Academy of Sciences 275.
de Leonardo, Margarita
  1976   Mexico. *In* La Mujer: Explotacion, Lucha, Liberacion. Clara Eugenia Aranda, et al., eds. Pp. 1–58. Mexico: Editorial Nuestro Tiempo.
Leon de Leal, Magdalena, and Carmen Diana Deere
  1980   Mujer y Capitalismo Agrario. Bogota: Associacion Colombiana para el Estudio de la Poblacion.
  1982a   Las Trabajadoras del Agro: Debate sobre la Mujer en America Latina y el Caribe. Vol. 2. Bogota: Associacion Colombiana para el Estudio de la Poblacion.
  1982b   Sociedad, Subordinacion y Feminismo: Debate sobre la Mujer en America Latina y el Caribe. Vol. 3 Bogota: Associacion Colombiana para el Estudio de la Poblacion.
Littlefield, Alice
  1979   The Expansion of Capitalist Relations of Production in Peasant Crafts. Journal of Peasant Studies 6(4):471–488.
Long, Norman, ed.
  1984   Family and Work in Rural Societies: Perspectives on Non-wage Labour. London: Tavistock.
Murphy, Robert
  1959   Social Structure and Sex Antagonism. Southwestern Journal of Anthropology 15(1):89–98.
  1960   Headhunter's Heritage. Social and Economic Change among the Mundurucu Indians. Berkeley: University of California Press.
Murphy, Yolanda, and Robert Murphy
  1985   Women of the Forest. New York: Columbia University Press.
Nash, June
  1970   In the Eyes of the Ancestors: Belief and Behavior in a Maya Community. New Haven: Yale University Press.
  1976   A Critique of Social Science Models in Latin America. *In* Women and Change in Latin America. June Nash and Helen Safa, eds. Pp. 1–24. South Hadley, Mass.: Bergin and Garvey.
  1978   The Aztecs and the Ideology of Male Dominance. Signs 4(2):349–362.
  1980   Aztec Women: The Transition from Status to Class in Empire and Colony. *In* Women and Colonization: Anthropological Perspectives. Mona Etienne and Eleanor Leacock, eds. Pp. 134–148. South Hadley, Mass.: Bergin and Garvey.

1982   Implications of Technological Change for Household Level and Rural Development. *In* Technological Change and Rural Development in Developing Countries. Peter M. Weil and J. Elterich, eds. Pp. 429–476. Newark, Del.: University of Delaware Press.
1988   The Mobilization of Women in the Bolivian Debt Crisis. Women and Work. Los Angeles: Sage.
Nash, June, and M. Patricia Fernandez-Kelly
1984   Women, Men and the International Division of Labor. Albany: State University of New York Press.
Nash, June, and Helen Safa, eds.
1986   Women and Change in Latin America. South Hadley, Mass.: Bergin and Garvey.
Nun, Jose, Miguel Murnas, and Juan Carlos Marin
1968   La Marginalidad en Argentina: Informe Preliminar. Mimeo., Torcuato di Tello Centro de Investigacion.
de Oliveira, Criancina
n.d.   Empleo Feminino en Mexico en Tiempo de Expansión y Recesión Economica: Tendencias Recientes. Paper presented at the December 1987 meeting of DAWNE.
Ortego de Figueroa, Teresa
1976   A Critical Analysis of Latin American Programs to Integrate Women in Development. *In* Women and World Development. Irene Tinker and Michele Bo Bramsen, eds. Washington, DC: Overseas Development Council.
Peattie, Lisa
1976   "Tertiarization" and Urban Poverty in Latin America. *In* Urbanization and Inequality. Wayne A. Cornelius and Felicity M. Trueblood, eds. Pp. 109–123. Gainesville: University of Florida Press.
Perlman, Janice
1976   The Myth of Marginality: Urban Politics and Poverty in Rio de Janeiro. Berkeley: University of California Press.
Pessar, Patricia
1986   The Role of Gender in Dominican Settlement in the United States. *In* Women and Change in Latin America. J. Nash and H. Safa, eds. Pp. 272–292. South Hadley, Mass.: Bergin and Garvey.
Portes, Alejandro, and John Walton
1981   Labor, Class and the International System. New York: Academic Press.
Prates, Suzana
n.d.   Participacion Laboral Femenina en el Proceso del Crisis. Paper presented at the December 1987 meeting of DAWNE in La Paz, Bolivia.
Quijano, Anibal
1971   Nationalism and Capitalism in Peru. A Study in Neoimperialism. Helen R. Lane, translator. New York: Monthly Review Press.
Radcliffe, Sarah
n.d.   "Asi es una Mujer del Pueblo": Los Nuevos Grupos de Mujeres y el Gobierno de APRA, Peru 1985–1987. Paper presented at March 1988 meeting of Latin American Studies Association in New Orleans.
Rosaldo, Michele Zimbalist, and Louise Lamphere, eds.
1974   Women, Culture, and Society. Stanford: Stanford University Press.
Rosen, Bernard C.
1982   Industrial Connection: Achievement and the Family in Developing Societies. New York: Aldine.
Rothstein, Frances
1986   Capitalist Industrialization and the Increasing Cost of Children. *In* Women and Change in Latin America. J. Nash and H. Safa, eds. Pp. 37–52. South Hadley, Mass.: Bergin and Garvey.
Rubbo, Anna
1975   The Spread of Capitalism in Rural Colombia: Effects on Poor Women. *In* Toward an Anthropology of Women. Pp. 333–358. New York: Monthly Review Press.

Rubbo, Anna, and Michael Taussig
1978 Up off Their Knees: Servanthood in Southwest Colombia. *In* Female Servants and Economic Development. Pp. 5–29. Ann Arbor: University of Michigan Occasional Papers in Women's Studies, No. 1.
Safa, Helen
1981 Runaway Shops and Female Employment: The Search for Cheap Labor. Signs 7(2):418–433.
1984 Women, Production and Reproduction in Industrial Capitalism: A Comparison of Brazil and U.S. Factory Workers. *In* Women and the International Development of Labor. June Nash and Maria Fernandez Kelly, eds. Albany: State University of New York Press.
Saffiotti, Heleieth Iara Bongiovani
1969 Women in Class Society. New York: Monthly Review Press.
1976 Relationships of Sex and Social Class in Brazil. *In* Women and Change in Latin America. June Nash and Helen Safa, eds. Pp. 147–159. South Hadley, Mass.: Bergin and Garvey.
Sassen-Koob, Saskia
1984 Labor Migration and the New Industrial Division of Labor. *In* Women, Men and the International Division of Labor. J. Nash and M. Patricia Fernandez-Kelly, eds. Pp. 173–204. Albany: State University of New York Press.
Sautu, Ruth
1981 The Female Labor Force in Argentina, Bolivia and Paraguay. Latin American Research Review 16:152–159.
Shapiro, Judith
1976 Sexual Hierarchy among the Yanomama. *In* Women and Change in Latin America. J. Nash and H. Safa, eds. Pp. 86–101. South Hadley, Mass.: Bergin and Garvey.
Silverblatt, Irene
1980 "The universe has turned inside out . . . There is no justice for us here": Andean Women under Spanish Rule. *In* Woman and Colonization: Anthropological Perspectives. Mona Etienne and Eleanor Leacock, eds. Pp. 149–185. South Hadley, Mass.: Bergin and Garvey.
1987 Moon, Sun, and Witches. Gender Ideologies and Class in Inca and Colonial Peru. Princeton: Princeton University Press.
Strathern, Marilyn
1987 An Awkward Relationship: The Case of Feminism and Anthropology. Signs 12(2):276–292.
Tiano, Susan
1986 Women and Industrial Development in Latin America. Latin American Research Review 21(3):157–170.
Young, Kate
1978 Modes of Appropriation and the Sexual Division of Labor: Case Study from Oaxaca, Mexico. *In* Feminism and Materialism. A. Kuhn and A. M. Wolpe, London: Routledge and Kegan Paul.

Resources for Classroom Use

Anthologies

Veneria, Lourdes, and Martha Roldan
1987 The Crossroads of Class and Gender: Industrial Homework, Subcontracting, and Household Dynamics in Mexico City. Chicago: University of Chicago Press.

This anthology contains articles on women in Mexico, bearing on women and production.

Nash, June, and Helen Safa, eds.
1986 Women and Change in Latin America. South Hadley, Mass.: Bergin and Garvey.

This anthology includes 17 articles on women in Latin American countries. Most articles are directed toward showing how taking gender issues into account changes our perception of the social structure. Major focus is on women in the workplace.

References: Basic Statistics on Women

Chaney, Elsa
  1984   Women of the World: Latin America and the Caribbean. Washington, D.C.: Bureau of the Census.

  Excellent summary of pertinent data on women, demography, employment, etc.

Monographs

Bourque, Susan and Kay Warren
  1981   Women of the Andes. Ann Arbor: University of Michigan Press.

  Comparison of a highland Indian community and a provincial town, showing the way in which women are integrated into the regional economy and their adaptive strategies for survival.

Murphy, Yolanda, and Robert Murphy
  1974   Women of the Forest. New York: Columbia University Press.

  Origin myths of this society relate the theft by men of sacred trumpets from women. The uneasy sex hierarchy suggests the social construction of male dominance in this jungle society.

Films

  The Double Day, Ellen Ladd, Producer and Director, 54 minutes. Distributed by Cinema Guild.
  I Spent My Life in the Mines, June Nash, Producer and Director, Roy Loe, filmmaker. 45 minutes; distributes by Cinema Guild.
  The Faces of Change: Andean Women, Hugh Smith, Producer and Director, 19 minutes. Distributed by University of California, Berkeley

Autobiographies

Barrios de Chungara, Domitilla
  n.d.   Let Me Speak. The Autobiography of a Bolivian Mining Woman. Moema Vieser, editor. New York: Monthly Review Press.
Burgos-Debray, E., ed.
  1984   I, Rigoberta Menchu: An Indian Woman in Guatemala. New York: Monthly Review Press.
Friedlander, Judith
  1981   Being Indian in Hueyapan. A Study of Forced Identity in Contemporary Mexico. New York: St. Martin's Press.
Nash, June
  n.d.   Class Consciousness and World View of a Bolivian Mining Woman. *In* A Dialogue on Third World Women: Learning Through Humanities. Washington, D.C.: D.C. Community Humanities Council.

First Assignment

  Each student should choose an autobiography to be read in conjunction with showings of the film related to the culture of the subject. Domitilla Barrios de Chungara and Basilia's autobiographies can be related to the film, "I Spent My Life in the Mines," based on the life history of a Bolivian mining family. Burgos-Debray's edition of the autobiography can be read with the film, "The Mountain Trembles," in which she appears. Students can be assigned to write an essay relating the woman's life experiences to the culture and society in which she was socialized, showing how gender influenced her life choices. Particular attention should be paid to the development of consciousness in life experience. What is the intersection of class, ethnicity, and gender in the life experience?

Students should read *Women of the Andes* and view the film by Hugh Smith, "Faces of Change," the section on Andean Women. They should then write an essay discussing women's roles in agriculture and their perception of their contribution. How does this change when women go to the city? How have the land reform and cooperatives affected women's participation?

Second Assignment

Students should read Robert Murphy's 1960 monograph, *Headhunter's Heritage: Social and Economic Change among the Mundurucu* and Yolanda and Robert Murphy's 1974 (reprinted 1985) *Women of the Forest* to assess the changing paradigm for interpreting gender hierarchy. The frank appraisal of the Murphys in assessing their own relation to the fieldwork and their past publications makes this an extremely valuable exercise. Students should write an essay on changing methodology and theory regarding gender as exemplified in these monographs. The importance of a dual perspective can be explored in this excellent case study.

Third Assignment

Students should read Napoleon Chagnon's *Yanomamo: The Fierce People* and Ellen B. Basso's *The Kalapalo Indians of Central Brazil,* assessing the contrasts in views of similar Brazilian Amazonian cultures. Methodological differences, contrasts in the way each ethnographer related to subjects, and the interpretation of evidence can be analyzed by the students in an essay comparing the two monographs. The real structures of subordination existing in Yanamamo society analyzed by Judith Shapiro (1976) can be assessed in contrast to the ideological configurations regarding gender roles that figure in myths and rituals.

10

The Politics of Gender in the Middle East

Sondra Hale
University of California, Los Angeles

This module is designed to help teachers of introductory anthropology courses integrate into their courses material on Middle Eastern women. While all of the geographical regions with which this book deals are fraught with problems beyond the exclusion of women or distorted data on women (i.e., all of them have a considerable literature which is, at best, ethnocentric), the literature on the Middle East[1] is particularly problematic. I propose that the literature on the Middle East has women and gender arrangements at the core of its ethnocentrism, and that the concept of gender is highly charged and politicized precisely because Western social scientists and Western-trained scholars of the Middle East have given an "Orientalist" (Said 1978) interpretation to data on Middle Eastern women. Likewise, some Middle Easterners, partially in response to Western writings, have also, if differentially, politicized gender relationships.[2]

The politics within the Middle East, the position of the Middle East in world politics, and even the dynamics between U.S. and Middle Eastern scholars[3] make this a very difficult subject matter to teach. Moreover, the Middle East is staggeringly diverse in modes of economy, culture, ethnicity, race, language, class, ideology, *and* religion. The intersection of class, ethnicity, and religion, for example, is a dynamic that confounds our scholarship a great deal. The ways in which indigenous religions, economies, and cultures have interacted with British (and many other) imperialisms further compound analyses. Inevitably, then, gender relationships and how they were/are affected by forms of colonialism and neocolonialism are highly regionally, culturally, and economically diverse.[4] Recent analyses of these complexities in their relationship to the networks of everyday life are changing the face of regional studies and, therefore, the field of anthropology.

Until very recently scholarship on the Middle East treated women as if they were encapsulated in defined and bounded groups or categories (e.g., households, lineages, tribes, ethnic or sectarian groups). Often, male researchers left the data-collection on women to their spouses[5] or failed to gather such data altogether. The politics of knowledge in the Middle East exaggerated this situation. Because of the ways in which we perceived the "seclusion" of women, male scholars were able to rationalize the exclusion of women in much of their analysis.

It has partially been the historicist/Arabist/Islamicist legacy[6] of Middle East studies that, until recently, impeded the development of women's studies in the region and virtually relegated feminist studies to a backseat. Anthropologist Suad Joseph explains that

> Functionalism, Orientalism, sexism, and certain feminist approaches have enforced one another in depicting Middle Eastern women as confined to their kin, tribal, ethnic, class, or national boundaries; as isolated from men; and as passive actors in the public domain. [Joseph 1983:2]

Joseph further contends that anthropological models, dominated by functionalism (exemplified by Coon's "ethnic mosaic" [1958]) and reinforced by pluralism, looked to "an ethnic division of labor in which interethnic relationships occur only in the marketplace" (1983:2). Furthermore, "perhaps in no area of the world have western gender biases more emphatically polarized male and female images than in Middle Eastern Studies" (1983:3).

Studies of Middle Eastern women have also suffered from an overreliance on various dichotomies, which can at best be seen as heuristic devices, but are often reified: honor/shame, patron/client, and public/private. Added to this dichotomous thinking has been an overemphasis on Islam as a cultural (superstructural) determinant, a process discussed more thoroughly below. All of these theoretical, ideological, and methodological elements above have "confined the consideration of Middle Eastern women to a limited discussion of veils, honor and shame, kinship, cousin right, polygyny, and Islam" (Joseph 1983:3).

Central Research Issues—Problematics

The overemphasis on Islam as a cultural determinant of Middle Eastern women's behavior and status is a special problem in the literature. Furthermore, there is a dubious link that historical writings about Islam have made with sexuality. Anthropologist David Waines has argued that from the 17th century and earlier, Europeans wrote of a lascivious Islam, which has embedded within it a repugnant sexual morality. To these early observers the tyrannical nature of "oriental" society was reflected in ruler over subject and man's wanton possession of woman as object—the secluded, mysterious, erotic Muslim woman (1982:643–644). Into the 1980s there is still a significant body of literature that "assumes *a priori* the existence of a universal Islam which mysteriously moulds behaviour 'from above'" (Waines 1982:652).

Another problem is that Islamic law, *sharia*, has promoted a great deal of uniformity throughout the Islamic world. Thus, since gender relationships are rather strictly formalized in the *Qur'an*, in the *hadiths*, and in *sharia;* and since these religious and legal doctrines are seen by many Muslims as eternal and universal; and since women are unequal under these theological and legal doctrines, women are seen as enduring a universal and uniform state of subjugation. The new literature has the task of helping us recognize diversity, variability, and historical and political dynamics: "Only if we understand clearly the specificities of Middle Eastern states, classes, and ideological formations can we apprehend the necessary context for evaluating women's place in politics today" (Joseph 1986:7).

Many of these research problematics can be seen in anthropological research on the veil. There are few, if any, other regions of the world where one element in the culture still symbolizes so much to scholars and observers as does the veil in the Muslim Middle East. It is used as a symbol by nationalist apologists and by Middle Eastern and Western feminists alike.

It conjures up the exotic, the erotic, the process of seclusion, the *harem*,[7] marginalization, modesty,[8] honor and shame, social distance, gender segregation, and, of course, the subordination of women. Middle Eastern feminists themselves, especially those who were trained by foreign missionaries or who were taught in Europe or in schools staffed by Europeans, often were influenced to treat the veil as a symbol of their oppression. An example is a 1928 essay by Nazirah Zein Ed-Din, ''Removing the Veil and Veiling'' (al-Hibri 1982). The tradition continues today whether or not the authors differ greatly in their views, whether or not they are Euroamerican or indigenous, male or female, whether or not they subscribe to the salience of the veil or see it as a weak variable.[9] The image of the veil is so pervasive that Middle Eastern anthropologist David Waines suggests that

> The act of cultural observation and understanding is like drawing back a veil in order to grasp the meaning of cues and symbols of other cultures, rather than imposing meaning upon such symbols from behind the seclusion of one's own cultural veil. For too long the western observer, accustomed to gaze through a veil darkly, has accepted formless shadows as tangible objects of reality. [1982:643]

The fact is that veiling or not veiling, the type or occasion, the category of person veiling (e.g., class, region, type of occupation, urban or rural), and the politics of it (as in Iran) are exciting variables all too rarely analyzed. Whether or not donning the veil is for the purpose of enacting seclusion (social distance from men), making a statement about sexuality (social control), or affirming Islam (modest dress for women and men), or it is for fashion or national dress (sometimes as an abrogation of Western style and values, as in Iran), or simply because it is deemed more practical or economical than other modes of dress (e.g., encourages use of local material rather than the purchase of imported goods)—the reasons for veiling are seldom explored. Besides, the word *veil* is used indiscriminantly to describe variations that extend from a ''moderate'' *hejab* (modest Islamic dress), which might be a longer skirt and sleeves with a head scarf, to more thorough coverall gowns (covering from head to foot, including gloves, with only the eyes showing), to a wrap-around, to a simple filmy covering for the face.

These are variable modes of dress internationally and intranationally, among classes, urban or rural, according to religion, sect, or ethnicity. Most significantly, these are often *individual* variables. In the film, ''The Veiled Revolution'' (Elizabeth Fernea), Egyptian women explain their voluntary adoption of modest Islamic dress (which varies appreciably in the film) in terms of their differing degrees of compliance to the faith, will power, determination, and other factors.

For a century in Sudan most Northern Muslim women have worn a loose, wrap-around, filmy gown referred to as the *tobe,* which they wear in public or around male strangers in private. Although some women used to cover their faces with a piece of the *tobe,* the common Western reference to this dress as ''veiling'' is a distortion. The reasons women state for wearing the *tobe* are as varied as the reasons listed above, and in recent years many have stopped wearing it. Now the *tobe* is often little more than the modest ''national dress'' of a large portion of the population, and for some middle-class women in the urban area the outfit for ceremonial occasions. For some (i.e., a small Islamic fundamentalist minority), the *tobe* has been replaced by the *hejab* (''Islamic dress''), which varies in severity. Reasons given for wearing the *hejab* are individual, ranging from a vague ''for religious reasons'' to ''it's cheaper and more accessible than the *tobe,*'' which consists of eleven yards of expensive imported cotton. The *tobe* is now seen by many as more ''progressive'' or ''modern,'' with some Sudanese resenting the imported idea of the *hejab.* One seldom hears that either the *tobe* or *hejab* is for the purpose of ''hiding'' or ''secluding'' women, nor that they function to inhibit sexuality. What are mentioned are "self-respect," "modesty," and "protection from leering men" (strangers). Always the voluntary nature is stressed. Clearly uses of and attitudes toward the *tobe* and *hejab* have changed historically and differ demographically; furthermore, individual choice magnifies both variation and compounds analysis.[10]

Another cultural trait that some researchers use to symbolize the status of women in the Middle East is female circumcision, which is frequently referred to as "female genital mutilation," charged language posing as "clinical." The hysteria that has accompanied the "discovery" by Westerners of this custom, which has its most extensive use in Sudan, has further veiled, if you will, our ability to carry out valid research in the area. The fact that we have mistakenly associated this custom with Islam, thereby generalizing for the entire Middle East, further stereotypes the women of the area and inextricably links Islam with issues of sexuality and subordination.[11]

In 1966 a germinal collection of articles on honor and shame in Mediterranean societies established this dichotomy as an appropriate framework for analyzing many aspects of Middle Eastern and Mediterranean societies (Peristiany).[12] Interpretations of gender relations were thereafter frequently framed in terms of the passive ideals of chastity, virginity, and femininity for women; whereas for men there were the more active concepts of valor, machismo, revenge, manliness, and brotherhood. In many ways the dichotomy of honor and shame interfaces with Islam, sex, gender and subordination. When we investigate the theoretical and empirical research on the Mediterranean and Middle East, we see that the code of honor and shame is assumed to be the dominant value system in small, face-to-face communities. Below, in Course Component Number Two, I present Forouz Jowkar's lively challenge to the conventional approaches to "honor/shame" (1986).

Trends in Feminist Scholarship

Against this backdrop I want to present what I perceive to be the trends in newer writings about women in the Middle East.[13] The literature has moved from (1) the nearly total exclusion of women (marked in the anthropology of the Middle East because of the spatial separation of women and their presumed inaccessibility to male—or even female—anthropologists, to (2) the presenting of women only as members of particular categories (e.g., tribes, kin groups, especially families, and the like) creating, therefore, another kind of invisibility, to (3) cultural relativist studies of women, to (4) studies of the oppression of women—by feminists and nonfeminists,[14] to (5) studies of the ways in which women are changing the face of the society (e.g., by entering the work force, through the devaluation of domestic labor, through their influencing of the national polity, and through their participation in social movements). Since the early 1980s, there has been a new trend—the new descriptive ethnography—which will be discussed below.[15]

The first anthology in English of Middle Eastern women writing about their lives, *Middle Eastern Muslim Women Speak* (edited by Elizabeth Fernea and Basima Qattan Bezirgan [1977]), was more a compendium than a theoretical treatment of this complex subject. The next year Lois Beck and Nikki Keddie's *Women in the Muslim World* (1978), an anthology focusing on ethnographic and sociological studies, inaugurated new research perspectives on Middle Eastern women. Beck and Keddie cautioned against a too-simplistic view of the impact of Islam on women:

> The question is not why traditional Islamic culture has been more discriminatory toward women than other major cultures . . . the real question, which contains policy implications

for population control, improved child rearing, educational development and economic change, is why Islamic society has been more conservative in its maintenance of old laws and traditions in this area than have other societies. [Beck and Keddie 1978:27]

This book was followed by a plethora of works on women, making it timely for anthropologist Amal Rassam, herself a pioneer in the study of Middle Eastern women (e.g., under Vinogradov 1974), to publish an article which envisioned the formation of an emerging theoretical framework. "Towards a Theoretical Framework for the Study of Women in the Arab World" (1982a) departs rather dramatically from the literature's dependence on studies of the seclusion of women, veiling, cousin marriage, and female circumcision. Rassam argues that there are three important dimensions to analyzing women's lives: the social organization of power, the ideological and institutional means of controlling women's sexuality, and the sexual division of labor in the society. "From this perspective, the family/household becomes the logical focus for analysis as it is the arena where these three areas intersect. . . . As such, the family/household may be considered as a system of structured cross-sexual relationships underwritten by a specific Arabo-Islamic ideology" (1982a:127).

The organizational questions Rassam asks in this 1982 article presage much in the anthropological work that was to come: (1) What is the prevalent ideology with regard to the nature of sexuality in the Arab world? (2) How is gender identity constructed? (3) What are the normative patterns of interaction among members of the household? (4) How is labor organized within the household? (5) What is the role of the state in promoting and effecting changes in the area of women's status (1982a:128)? While referring to the Muslim world as one characterized by extreme sexual asymmetry (1982a:121), Rassam argues for a position that came to characterize feminist work in the late 1980s; she calls for a perspective that views both women and men as being equally integral to the functioning of the system as a whole (1982a:122).

Fernea's 1987 presidential address to the Middle Eastern Studies Association focused on the ways that research on women and gender has affected Middle Eastern studies, especially by challenging the distinction between public and private (e.g., Nelson 1974). Formerly scholars could see their studies as falling into either/or, thus justifying studying only one of the spheres. Usually it was the public domain that was acknowledged, allowing most to give relatively little importance to the private domain.

In the 1970s, men and women began to ask a basic question. In this public/private formulation, were we not ignoring the most important area of the society itself—the area where public and private coincided, the area where many of the major decisions about politics, economics, education, birth control were made, that area where men and women's lives meshed—the area of the family? [Fernea 1987:4]

A second example of the impact of women's studies on Middle Eastern Studies is in the area of religion. An added dimension to that field is research on Sufi sisterhoods or women's auxiliaries, which changed the study of religious brotherhoods, thus changing the perception of Sufism and modifying Islamic studies (Fernea 1987:5). A third example is the reintroduction of oral tradition as a viable means of literary expression and, in the case of Lila Abu-Lughod (1987), an ethnographic method for exploring gender relations (see Course Component Number Two).[16]

By 1985 there was at least one major new anthropologically oriented anthology published, *Women and the Family in the Middle East: New Voices of Change*, edited by Fernea. This book represents several new approaches. First, the editor chose to focus on one institution, the family,[17] and each contributor focused primarily on one society—i.e., greater tendency toward cultural specificity. We also see an increase in the percentage of "indigenous" contributors to the compendium, in this case some 75% of 33 contributions. Finally, the editor opted to present the themes of the collection as much through fiction and poetry as through anthropology proper.

It would be foolhardy to condense the variety of approaches to the study of Middle Eastern women to any one model; clearly, the writing is not unified. There are still a number of Middle Easternists who are writing within the philosophical framework of cultural relativism (e.g., Wikan 1982; Fernea 1985, but especially in her ethnographic films [see annotated bibliography]); those who are writing more apologetically (e.g., al-Hibri 1982); and those who are writing within a feminist universal framework in an attempt to deal with the subordination of women (e.g., Nawal El-Saadawi 1980; Fatna Sabbah [pseud.] 1984; Amal Rassam 1982; Juliette Minces 1978, 1982; Germaine Tillion 1983; as well as some of my own work, e.g., Hale 1986, 1987a, and forthcoming). In addition, some feminists from the Middle East are attempting to find the grounds for female emancipation embedded in the *Qur'an*, the *hadiths*, and *sharia*. Sociologist Fatima Mernissi, a well-respected and influential scholar (e.g., 1975), is investigating these original texts in an effort to turn traditional interpretations of these on their heads (1986). Conversely, writing under a pseudonym, another indigenous social scientist, Fatna Sabbah, in *Woman in the Muslim Unconscious* (1984), examines two main discourses, the religious erotic discourse and the orthodox discourse. In raising the question of "Why are silence, immobility, and obedience the key criteria of female beauty in . . . Muslim society?" (1984:3), she sees the female body presented as the product of male pleasure in the religious erotic discourse and the female body as the product of male sacred power in the orthodox discourse. Her concluding chapter on female beauty as a mirror of the male condition is a feminist *tour de force*.

Two other important but divergent emerging themes in the recent anthropological literature are the integration of gender and politics (universalistic), on the one hand, and the "new ethnography" (greater cultural specificity), on the other. Perhaps in no one publication is the former more present than in *MERIP Middle East Report*, the foremost American Left publication on the Middle East. The MERIP Collective has consistently examined issues relevant to women factory and migrant workers, and about the sexual division of labor. (The theme of women as political activists is dealt with in Course Component Number One.)

In general, even among feminists doing research on the Middle East, voices of women themselves have not been well represented. Most researchers speak *for* women. As Soha Abdel Kader argues in a review of research on women in the Middle East, "Instead of arguing whether Islam is beneficial or detrimental to women's roles, it might be best to study what aspects of religion women practice, and what aspects of it they think is of importance to their lives" (Abdel Kader 1984:160). Thus, feminist anthropologists have often *forgotten* their feminism and its process when writing on the Middle East.

The five ethnographies used most extensively for this module and included in the annotated bibliography or in Course Component Number Two (Abu-Lughod 1987; Altorki 1986; Dorsky 1986; Makhlouf 1979; Wikan 1982), span nine years and represent, in themselves, from Makhlouf (1979) to Abu-Lughod (1987), a movement away from speaking *for* women (in Makhlouf's case, however, it is from a male poet's voice) to women speaking for themselves. These works demonstrate a growing sophistication in their use of the personal as expression of the values and ideologies of the society. Women are beginning to emerge as real—individuals and as members of both kin and extra-kin social groups.

With these ethnographies teachers will be able to integrate into their syllabi and texts different concepts of household management; varied mechanisms and strategies for negotiating around ideologies; complex individual responses to religion, from everyday observances to ideological thought; gender dynamics as symbolized by seclusion and the veil; ideas around kinship; and information on female bonding. Other works used in Course Component Number One lead us to strikingly different ideas about the political/public roles of Middle Eastern women. The research on women is contributing to the emancipation of the field from Orientalism.

Course Component 1

Women as Political Actors

Introductory anthropology courses often include sections on political hierarchies and processes, class stratification, and on resistance strategies, including participation in social movements. In the past these have featured males as political actors. Recent research on Middle Eastern women enables us to integrate material on women into these segments of a course. A valuable (and student-accessible) resource is a special issue of *MERIP (Middle East Report)* on *Women and Politics in the Middle East* (1986). Suad Joseph introduces the issue with an overview on "Women and Politics in the Middle East." Historian Judith Tucker examines the interesting case of "Insurrectionary Women: Women and the State in 19th-Century Egypt." In the same issue three anthropologists document the political roles and participation of Iranian (Hegland), Palestinian (Peteet), and Sudanese (Hale) women.

The authors present their subject matter with reference to different levels and types of political activity—not merely or primarily the cliched "private" domain, with women exerting only informal political power through men. Rather, women are involved in the same kinds of political activity as men, not restricted to power gained only through gossip or political songs.[18]

In her introduction Suad Joseph analyzes the differing ways that women have been mobilized in the Middle East, and she shows how this has been interpreted by women themselves, by men, and by the state. She maintains that "women become a subject of mobilization, targets of political action programs, a mass to be welded into citizens or political followers" (Joseph 1986:3–4). She asks if the nature of women's political participation differs if it is initiated by the state (as in Turkey and Iraq), by nationalist movements (as Peteet presents in her article on Palestinians), by Communist parties (my Sudan article) or by spontaneous revolt (as we see in Tucker's Egyptian study or Hegland's study of Iran). Joseph, Tucker, Peteet, and Hegland analyze women in the contest for citizenry, as political actors, and as the nexus of the relationship among feminism, nationalism, class and state.

My own article, "Wing of the Patriarch" (Hale 1986), explores the potential for the uses of "traditional" culture to mobilize women against their oppression as women. In referring to the *zaar* (commonly referred to as a "spirit-possession cult" or ritual) as a "prefigurative political form," the protest ceremony is given *political* and social meanings, not just ritualistic, symbolic, or psychoanalytical meanings (e.g., Kennedy 1967). In this 1986 article and in another (1987b), I interpret the *zaar* as a potentially political gathering that is an occasion for group therapy and for consciousness-raising, self-help, healing through collective action, and emotional solidarity. "It is experiential, subjective, egalitarian, and affective. The *zaar* is a mode of ending the self-subordination of women by forcing men, if only temporarily, to submit to women's demands" (1987b:123–124). Such a political interpretation of women's everyday networks, rituals, and "traditional" cultural activities enables one to interpret women's "private," "informal," and/or "secluded" activities as or in relation to the "public," "formal" arena associated with "male politics."

Very recent anthropological literature presents the individual woman as political actor in the Middle East, albeit the woman as *leader* or *hero*. In analyzing the relationship between feminist movements and social transformation, anthropologist Cynthia Nelson "rediscovered" Egyptian feminist Doria Shafik, an activist who from 1945 to 1957 worked for the full political rights of women (Nelson 1986:16). Shafik founded the first post–World War II feminist journal published in Arabic, *Bint al-Nil* (Daughter of the Nile), and later formed a political party under the same name. In 1948 she organized a demonstration to seize Parliament by women (Nelson 1986:22)! She campaigned all her life, organizing others, but also engaging in individual acts of defiance and resistance. Nelson points out that, until she discovered Shafik, the feminist political activism of Egyptian women was blanked out between Huda Shaarawi, often seen as Egypt's first feminist activist, and Jihan Sadat, wife of Egypt's president, who lobbied at a Parliamentary level for women's rights, or Nawal El-Saddawi, the 1970s' and 1980s' activist doctor/intellectual (e.g., 1972, 1980) and novelist (e.g., 1983), who was jailed by Sadat.[19]

Even more traditional sources can be mined for evidence of women's political experience. Anthropologist Sawsan El-Messiri's 1977 article, "The Changing Role of the Futuwwa in the Social Structure of Cairo," contains a startling sliver of data on woman-as-leader. She analyzes the role of the *futuwwa* (pl. *futuwwat*), a word that denotes a strong, bold *man*, but also carries the connotation of a religious or outlaw orientation. She says, "By definition the *futuwwat* are young men, yet among them were several *futuwwa* women, such as . . . 'Aziza al-Fahla of al-Migharbilin" (1977:237). These neighborhood bosses or protectors sought to be known in their neighborhoods as paragons of the virtues that Caireens would like to claim as their own. These qualities are reflected in the nicknames of some of the better-known *futuwwat*, such as *al-fahl al-kabir* (the big animal), *zalat* (the stone), *al-Husan* (the horse). In other words, the *futuwwat* are physically imposing (1977:243). El-Messiri reproduces a description of 'Aziza al-Fahla from the memoirs of Mahmud al-Miligi:

> I saw 'Aziza al-Fahla who was at the top of all the *futuwwat* of al-Migharbilin. A giant lady who possessed extraordinary strength. Around her arms were tons of gold (i.e., bracelets). One blow from her hand was enough to knock any man to the ground. A blow with her head would split a stone. She was married to a man called *al-fahl al-kabir*, the big animal. He used to support his wife in any quarrel, but this was rare because 'Aziza was always capable of gaining victory alone. By becoming one of 'Aziza's follower [*sic*], I learned my first lesson in *fatwana* (i.e., the brave deeds of the *futuwwat*). [El-Messiri 1977:243]

Course Component 2

By using only a few works, teachers of introductory anthropology may enhance their courses by incorporating materials on Middle Eastern women that deal with Islam, sexuality, seclusion, veiling, and concepts of honor and shame, without committing the sins of our fathers and mothers. One excellent example is a work by Lila Abu-Lughod (1987), *Veiled Sentiments: Honor, Modesty, and Poetry in a Bedouin Society*. This book offers teachers of anthropology a way to teach about the veil and seclusion with a heightened sensitivity. It is also a rare chance to see *men* from women's eyes—an effective classroom reversal strategy. The study, which won the Stirling Award in Psychological Anthropology in 1984, is based on research carried out over the two years that she was living among Awlad 'Ali Bedouin women of Egypt. She shows, primarily through women's love poems, that although the women are segregated from men and oriented toward other women, they develop deep affective bonds with men. "For the Awlad ʿAli Bedouins, the bonds of womanhood that integrate the world of women have much to do with shared suffering and longing for those outside their community" (1985:657)—thus the study integrates men and women in the same society—and presents views by women about men.[20]

Shunning the usual simplistic notions around honor and shame, Abu-Lughod gives a highly complex explanation of *hasham:*

> Those who are coerced into obeying [social rules] are scorned, but those who voluntarily defer are honorable. To understand the nature, meaning, and implications of voluntary deference we must explore the concept of *hasham*. Perhaps one of the most complex concepts in Bedouin culture, it lies at the heart of ideas of the individual in society. . . . In its broadest sense it means propriety. [1987:105]

Such a complex concept allows her to give us a more complex explanation for veiling:

> The best test of the validity of this interpretation of *hasham*—that denial of sexuality is equated with deference—is its power to explain the pattern of women's veiling. Bedouins consider veiling synonymous with *hasham*. . . . Symbolizing sexual shame as it hides it, veiling constitutes the most visible act of modest deference. [1987:159]

As mentioned earlier in the text, veiling is usually interpreted as a symbol of female subordination—a view that runs contrary to some recent and respected works, such as this one. The veil can be seen simply as (and is often considered by most Middle Eastern women to be) a statement about modest deference, which men may display as well. Or, it may be seen as a mode of communication (i.e., that the woman is beautiful, modest, and honorable). It is also a major visible symbol of marital status in many areas, as in Oman. From Omani material we can learn that "the *burqa* [veil] beautifies in a spiritual sense. . . . "The woman becomes beautiful because the *burqa* is beautiful, a treasured ornament. A woman's beauty is enhanced all the more by wearing it (Wikan 1982:101). Such rationalizations of veiling, although open to challenges, are effective in presenting the concept to undergraduates.

Abu-Lughod makes it clear that among the Awlad ʿAli Bedouin poetry is not the only medium through which people express their experiences in everyday life. But they do use it to express special sentiments. It is a distinct discourse on personal life. Abu-Lughod uses women's poetry to present discourses on loss, pride, death, honor, love, star-crossed love, arranged marriage, divorce, polygyny, and the like. Her research in a highly segregated society allows us to reconsider ideas about seclusion (that there are positive aspects), the subordination of women (that it may not be the woman's self-image), female associations and bonding (which give them strength and raise self-esteem), and gender relationships in a Middle Eastern context (that these can be expressed passionately). Abu-Lughod not only explodes misconceptions about male/female relationships in the Egyptian Bedouin context, her work also puts the honor/shame dichotomy within a cultural relativist framework.

The code of honor and shame, closely associated with ideas around seclusion/segregation/veiling, is assumed to be the dominant value system in small, face-to-face communities. We can often observe that the system establishes systems of hierarchy along the measures of social ideals such as wealth and sexuality; that relations of class and social honor may not agree theoretically or empirically; that in urban localities, in particular, sexual double standards are prevalent; that no religious doctrine/dogma by itself can account for the origin of sexual double standards; that the honor/shame ideology is in close relationship to the physical segregation of the sexual division of labor and that they reinforce each other; that the dominant sexual ideology demands from women a self-definition as virgins and mothers; that sexual modesty is seen to preserve the social order, though "from an anthropological perspective the adaptiveness is contingent upon the ecological, economic, and political imperatives of the area, and is the ideological reflection of the domestic division of labor" (Jowkar 1986:51).

Even if we look upon the concepts of honor and shame as adaptive mechanisms for changing, and even if we propose empirically based processes of complementarity of the public and private spheres, these can only mask an inherent structural inequality of gender relationships. Jowkar's universalistic approach to the subordinating aspects of an honor/shame value system exemplifies some of the rather forceful positions of a number of indigenous feminist anthropologists (1986),[21] offsetting Abu-Lughod's cultural relativism. Both these approaches can be useful in an undergraduate class: the veil, as it symbolizes honor and shame, is not an "irrational" imperative linked to male domination, but is an aspect of material culture that points to the structural inequality of gender relationships.

Select Annotated Bibliography

The New Ethnography: Cultural Specificity vs. Universalistic Models

Below are data from four selected ethnographies, three of which were written by indigenous anthropologists.[22] These ethnographies remind us of the gaps in our research, mainly urban studies of middle-class or even upper-class women. They also represent some of the regions where anthropological research can be carried out more easily in the sense of governmental acceptance of fieldworkers—Egypt, Yemen Arab Republic, and Oman. As a perusal of the bibliography reveals, we are missing studies of such crucial areas as Iraq and Syria.

Another strand connects these studies: the process of going back to the drawing board, not in the sense of restudying and replicating, but in the sense of painstakingly describing the "other half" of the world of Middle Easterners.

1. *Changing Veils: Women and Modernization in North Yemen* by Carla Makhlouf (1979) is the earliest study I deal with. It is deceptively simple in its portrayal of Yemeni women, but it also represents a tradition we have quickly left behind.

Makhlouf's study is of 40 mostly upper-class women in the city of Sanaʿa (in the same vein as Altorki, who is discussed below). She divides the work into chapter headings that are not very informative; it is the subheadings that reveal the structure and ideology of her work: Politico-Religious Idcology; Women's Separate Sphere; The Veil: Social Reality and Symbolism; Woman's Power in Society; Ritual and Symbolism; The Yemeni Women's Association; Some Notes on Television; From Kinship to Friendship; The Desertion of Tradition; A "Pluralized" Society; On Crises; Critical Experiences: Disruption and Redirection; Commuters and Outsiders; and Redefining Women.

Makhlouf uses the voice of a male Yemeni poet Muhammad al-Sharafi to express women's ideals around veiling and seclusion. This is in sharp contrast to Abu-Lughod (1987), who is discussed above, and creates the results we might expect: apologetics; romanticization of the veil; sexualizing or eroticizing of the veil; interpretation of veiling as play between the sexes (i.e., enticement, mystery, conspiracy); and seclusion and veiling as a ritualized mating dance. Yet, there is sometimes more to it than that. She quotes Al-Sharafi:

> What is a woman's worth,
> Who did not break a chain
> Destroy a prison
> Tear all veils. [1979:94]

Makhlouf also falls into the cliched dichotomy of "traditional" and "modern," although she presents it as a dialectic. Her most interesting material concerns the creation of cultural images and values, with special reference to sex-roles and how these are changing.

2. *Women in Saudi Arabia: Ideology and Behavior among the Elite* by Soraya Altorki (1986) is another example of work by an indigenous anthropologist. She looks at the ideology and behavior of three generations of elite women of Jiddah, Saudi Arabia.

Typical of the "new ethnography," she relies less on theory and abstraction than on description and cultural specificity. Also, the new Middle Eastern ethnographies are relying on investigations of domestic groups through the eyes of the women themselves and on the personal relationships of researcher to researched.

Altorki found that being an "indigenous anthropologist" had its problems: "I soon discovered . . . that although I was raised in a Saudi Arabian family, my long years of residence abroad had made me somewhat of a stranger in my own culture" (1986:2).[23] Altorki's analyses of her fieldwork would enhance the fieldwork sections in the anthropology curriculum, especially in raising questions around "foreign" and "indigenous" anthropologists.

There are many advantages for the instructor of anthropology in looking at the world of women. It allows us recess from the traditional dichotomies of "modern" and "traditional," especially in terms of how we generally see Middle Eastern societies. By looking at the behavior and everyday workings of domestic groups, we can more clearly see the mechanisms that women use to negotiate gender power relations and social reality.

Altorki analyzes such key institutions and concepts as *wafa'*, which she defines as "the pattern of social visits between women and the resultant ties of mutual support and assistance. It also refers to gifts and favors exchanged between friends (male and female)" (1986:170), in order to analyze intra-gender and inter-gender relationships. Anthropological theories around gift exchange can be augmented by Altorki's work.

In terms of the "honor/shame" dichotomy discussed in the text, Altorki's study adds complexity, other dimensions, and a more *personal* look at the model in the sense of what it looks like to actors on the ground. She presents us with the concepts of shame/sin (*'ayb/dhanb*) and anger/contentment *(ghadab/rida')* and attempts to show us how women use a series of strategies to manipulate or negotiate gender relationships.

Every aspect of Jiddah elite society has its flipside, and everything is changing. So, although Altorki uses some of the traditional institutions we have always used to analyze women's spheres (i.e., kinship and marriage), she is constantly analyzing the dynamics, contrasting ideology and social reality in the process.

Our views of Saudi society, perhaps more than any other in the world, have suffered from grave ethnocentric analyses, especially with regard to the role of women. U.S. popular culture in the form of such television movies as "Death of a Princess" have distorted the reality of Saudi society and gender relations. Altorki shows that both men and women have modified key concepts of social control "to accommodate their incipient independence from parental control and from obligations to a wide network of kin" (1986:161). Thus, although the ideology stresses (1) male dominance, (2) women's subordination and seclusion, (3) children's absolute obedience to parents, (4) solicitous attention to kinship groups, (5) veiling of women, (6) attribution of rationality to men and emotionalism to women, (7) arranged marriages, and (8) property inheritance that favors males (1986:149–150), Altorki, not only shows adaptation, but resistance strategies that alter the process.

By presenting firsthand ethnographic description, Altorki destroys a number of ethnocentric myths about Arabian gender relations. The cultural specificity has, then, universal implications. Ironically, for as "firsthand" and descriptive as it is, the study seems devoid of real people.

3. *Behind the Veil in Arabia: Women in Oman* by Unni Wikan (1982) has become one of the more controversial works within the "new ethnographies" because it again raises the specter of "cultural relativism." Amal Rassam, an "indigenous feminist anthropologist," questions Wikan for her position that "the Sohari woman's experience of herself rather than my experience of her" (Wikan 1982:5) is what she is trying to understand. Let me quote Rassam:

> She adopts a "neutral" posture with regards to the condition of Omani women. She also argues that Omani women are not subjugated but are proud and active participants in their own culture. . . . [at this point Rassam quotes some of Wikan's abysmal statistics on Omani female participation in education.] One wonders why illiteracy, ignorance and disease should be accepted as organic components of any cultural tradition . . . how does illiteracy, isolation and ignorance affect women's experience of themselves? [Rassams 1982:586]

Wikan gives us a cultural relativist position on the veil, disguised as the view from inside (i.e., Omani women's view). An entire chapter is devoted to the *burqa* (facial mask). Anthropology instructors who want to offset American ethnocentrism around veiling may want to read such expressions as "It is not that we wear *burqa* because it is shameful to go without it, but because it is beautiful to go with it" (1982:88). Wikan tells us an Omani woman wears the *burqa* "to communicate to the world her sense of being a beautiful, modest, and honorable woman. . . . Could there be a more unequivocal way of telling [societal ideology] the Sohari woman that her relationship to her husband is a unique one" (1982:88)? Wikan insists that the *burqa* is not inherently suppressive but "is experienced as much more an integral and cherished part of the woman's self" (1982:106).

Wikan's study is very similar to Middle Eastern ethnographies of an earlier period in anthropology—except that this time the women are made visible. Based on eight months of fieldwork, she describes in some detail gender identity in the town of Soha, using social visiting, networking, household affairs, neighborhood and family relations, and the values and ideologies that shape women's lives.

4. *Women of ʿAmran: A Middle Eastern Ethnographic Study* by Susan Dorsky (1986) is very much within the genre of what I have termed "the new ethnography" of Middle Eastern women. It is a descriptive, highly detailed, very personalized, and not very abstract or theoretical portrait of women's lives in North Yemen. Unlike Altorki or Wikan, she begins with an introductory chapter that places the work within an epistemological context, with special reference to the literature on male/female differences. However, these ideas are basically dropped after the initial chapter, and the work thereafter is oiled by descriptions of everyday affairs (e.g., childrearing practices, marriage negotiations, marital relations) and then sections on friendship and on family ties based on marriage and descent. This format should be familiar enough to teachers of anthropology that integrating this material into the curriculum will not constitute a radical restructuring.

Dorsky does, however, present her subject matter, not unlike the poetry of Abu-Lughod's Bedouin subjects discussed above, from various women's perspectives, mainly in the form of fables. These are highly useful for presenting emic or insider views. Also, the best portion of the work is her portrayal of female solidarity, the bonding among women neighbors and friends—not just the kin that we might expect. The challenge to male authority through solidarity is an element sorely missing in most of the anthropology curriculum.

Some of the other scholars also publishing more culturally specific monographs (i.e., ethnographies by women anthropologists sensitive to gender issues) are Vanessa Maher, *Women and Property in Morocco: The Changing Relation to the Process of Social Stratification in the Middle Atlas* (1974); Daisy Dwyer, *Images and Self-Images: Male and Female in Morocco* (1978); Susan Davis, *Patience and Power: Women's Lives in a Moroccan Village* (1982); and Christine Eickelman, *Women and Community in Oman* (1984). Although there are many other works that have made valuable contributions to the anthropological study of women (some of which were discussed in the text), there is not space to summarize or annotate most of them.

Selected Works from Allied Fields

There are also the major contributions of scholars from fields outside anthropology who have influenced the field of Middle Eastern women's studies (e.g., Nikki Keddie [1972, 1973, 1979, and with Beck 1978]); religious studies scholars John Esposito (1981) and Valerie Hoffman-Ladd (1987); Moroccan sociologist Fatima Mernissi (e.g., 1975, 1977, 1982, 1986); political scientist Eliz Sanaserian (1982); Linda Soffan (1980); Azar Tabari (pseud.) (1982, with Nahid Yehaneh; 1986); literature specialist turned social critic Leila Ahmed (1982a, 1982b, 1987); historians Judith Tucker (1985, 1986) and Afaf Marsot (1978); and sociologists Nadia H. Youssef (1976, 1978) and Soha Abdel Kader (1984, 1987). Political scientist Mervat Hatem is writing some of the most intellectually stimulating and ideologically provocative feminist works that we have seen recently (e.g., 1986a, 1986b).[24] One of the best and most recent review articles on the relationship of gender and Islam is by historian Margot Badran, "Islam, Patriarchy, and Feminism in the Middle East" (1986).

Anthologies on Middle Eastern Women

It was Fernea and Basima Qattan Bezirgan who edited the first anthology in English of Middle Eastern women writing about their lives. *Middle Eastern Women Speak* (1977) included a traditional section, with verses from the Qur'an, an early lament by a poet of early Islam, a biographical sketch of Aisha, wife of Mohamed; a section on change with women's voices from songs and lullabies to memoirs, interviews, and biographical sketches; a last section on change, which includes more resistance literature. Regions included are Andalusia (rarely covered), Afghanistan, Tunisia, Egypt, Morocco, Turkey, Iraq, Algeria, Jordan, Lebanon, and Iran.

In terms of the anthropology of Middle Eastern women, however, it was Lois Beck and Nikki Keddie's *Women in the Muslim World* (1978) that began a new era. The compendium consists of an introduction and 33 articles divided into four parts: General Perspectives on Legal and Socioeconomic Change; Historical Perspectives; Case Studies: Nomads, Villages, Town and City Dwellers; and Ideology, Religion, and Ritual. There are 18 anthropologists represented in the volume: Aswad, Beck, Chatty, Schaefer (Davis), Dwyer, Fischer, Friedl, J. Gulick, M. Gulick, Joseph, Maher, El-Messiri, Morsy, Pastner, Peters, Pillsbury, Rosen, Tapper; and a number of sociologists—Minces, Youssef, Vieille, and Del Vecchio Good.[25]

Some ten Middle Eastern regions are included, and the major themes and issues around which the editors organized the collection include family and gender roles, the impact of capitalism and wage labor on household economy, the relationship between male dominance and Islam, and the implications of women's participation in the wage-labor market.

Women and the Family in the Middle East, edited by E. Fernea (1985), is another attempt by the editor to have Middle Eastern women speak for themselves and to mix anthropology with literature, while dealing with the themes of family; health and education; war, politics, and revolution; religion and law; work; and identity. Two themes emerge: the Middle East's waning interest in looking to the West for social models, and the tendency by Middle Eastern writers to give us interpretations that are more characterized by gender integration (i.e., the idea that women and men are part of a unified social life).

Selected Works of Fiction and Documentary or Feature Films

There are a number of literary and visual works which in their understanding of cultural processes often transcend ethnographic works. Such a work is Ali Ghalem's *A Wife for My Son* (1984), a moving portrait of an Algerian family caught in tradition and poverty and the young woman who is the nexus of it. Illuminated in the novel are ideas around kinship and family, marriage and sexuality, gender relations inside and outside the family, problems of Third World labor migration to European cities, female solidarity, and women's emancipation.

There is also the authenticity of Alifa Rifaat's stories, *Distant View of a Minaret,* the "feminism" of a traditional woman (1983). There are the novels of Nawal El-Saadawi (e.g., 1983) or Etel Adnan (1982), and the considerable poetry of Middle Eastern women. Literary criticism of Middle Eastern novels and short stories can be revealing of material on women. For example, Mona Takieddine-Amyuni gives us many insights into the images of Arab women in the works of Mahfouz and Tayeb Salih (1985). Oral histories or individual testimonies have revealed in highly personal ways the aspirations, suppressed feelings, and ideas about one's role in society: Nayra Atiya's *Khul-Khaal: Five Egyptian Women Tell Their Stories* (1982) and Henry Munson's *The House of Si Abd Allah: The Oral History of a Moroccan Family* (1984).

A pioneering work that stands alone in the 1960s and is still very useful for our students is Fernea's barely fictionalized *Guests of the Sheik* (1965), comparable and probably more authentic even than Laura Bohannan's *Return to Laughter.* By focusing on the everyday lives of village women, Fernea illuminated women's domestic power and analyzed kin and friendship networks. This cultural relativist work is now a "classic" in cultural specificity and, if read sensitively, serves as a corrective to most of the literature on seclusion and harems. Fernea's early 1980s' ethnographic films, "A Veiled Revolution" (veiling and its meaning in Egypt), "Some Women of Marrakech" (contrasts honor and shame and public and private, and discusses the role of women in the family and society and the function of marriage), and "The Price of Change" (women working for change or in public life in Egypt: a village birth control dispenser and adviser; urban sewing and literacy teacher; parliamentary representative; and a factory worker), are invaluable visual depictions. Another, "Women Under Siege," I have not seen; these may all be ordered from the University of Texas Film Library. There are other worthy ethnographic films. For example, I have not yet seen the well-reviewed film by Fadwa El-Guindi, "El Sebou', Egyptian Birth Ritual." But Fernea's four films are interesting because they represent a *body* of work.

There are European feature films that present powerful themes, such as revolution and the roles of women (e.g., "The Battle of Algiers"); the exploitation of rural workers by colonialists and neocolonialists and these workers' protests (e.g., "Ramparts of Clay"); the problematics of ethnic relations under colonialism (e.g., "The Olive Trees of Justice"); and many others made by Middle Eastern filmmakers that delineate, often as a subplot, the position of women in the fabric of the society (e.g., "A Wedding in Galilee").

Notes

Acknowledgments. My various fieldtrips to the Middle East were funded in part by Fulbright-Hays, American Research Center in Egypt, American Association of University Women, and the National Endowment for the Humanities. Archival research for this module was partially carried out at the University of California, Los Angeles, while I have been an Affiliated Scholar, Center for the Study of Women, 1987–88. The Center partially funded my 1988 field trip.

1. The term *Middle East* is itself problematic. Anthropologist Dale Eickelman's concept of the "Middle East" relies on "the presence throughout the area of key cultural symbols and their variants and . . . shared historical circumstances [that justify] that this region can . . . be considered as a single sociocultural area" (1981:4). While remaining critical of the term, he maintains that it is the best available and that one simply has to acknowledge its limitations and avoid glossing over the extensive differences, variations, and contradictions. Edward Said in *Orientalism* would have us recognize the orientalist and eurocentric aspect of the term (1978).

2. See, for example, Yusuf (1965).

3. Until recently there seemed to be little dialogue between Western feminists and Middle Easternists (not, of course, mutually exclusive categories), and now there is considerable tension. It is my contention that the friction that has developed especially recently in Middle Eastern women's studies may be a result of the existence of a greater number of indigenous anthropologists who are working in women's studies than might be the case in other regions. These are scholars with their own brand of "feminisms" and a certain resentment of the ethnocentrism of aspects of Western feminist ideologies. There are also questions raised about Western appropriation of Middle Eastern culture in the form of scholarly research and publication. See, for example, Leila Ahmed's review (1987) of Margot Badran's translation and editing of Huda Shaarawi's *Harem Years* (1987).

4. Although for heuristic purposes I have treated the Middle East as one area, I have tried to avoid treating it as a monolith (see Note 1). To use Sudan as just one Middle Eastern example, there may be as many as 582 ethnic groups and 110 separate languages (Sudan 1958). The country is often classified as Arab, but this is really a misnomer; one of the most culturally significant groups in the North, the Nubians, although Muslim, is not Arab. Even using the term *Muslim* can be misleading, as much of the Southern Sudan is not Muslim, and there are pockets of Christians in the North and South. As one might imagine, the culture histories are very complex, especially the Islamic histories and the histories of the Arabicization processes. There are also dozens of sects and brotherhoods *(turuq),* many of which are highly politicized. Such complexity is typical of Middle Eastern countries. In order to make the essay more manageable, I have focused on the *Muslim* Middle East.

5. For example, Hildred and Clifford Geertz, Margaret and John Gulick, Elizabeth and Robert Fernea, Mary Hoogland [Hegland] and Eric Hoogland, Christine and Dale Eickelman, etc.

6. When I think of Middle Eastern studies as "conservative," my reference point is a field dominated, until recently, by historians of antiquity, ancient art historians, classical linguistic/language specialists (especially Arabists), and Islamicists—or the "Orientalists" proper. Studying contemporary society and politics, for example, has never been prestigious.

7. See Leila Ahmed's discussion of "Western Ethnocentrism and Perceptions of the Harem" (1982b).

8. For a discussion of modesty see Antoun (1968) and a reply by Abu Zahra (1970). See also Hoffman-Ladd's "Polemics on the Modesty and Segregation of Women in Contemporary Egypt" (1987).

9. Some recent examples are *Veil of Shame* (Accad 1978); "Through a Veil Darkly" (Waines 1982); "Unveiling Arab Women" [review essay] (Rassam 1982b); "To Veil or Not to Veil" (Betteridge 1983); *Changing Veils* (Makhlouf 1979); *Beyond the Veil* (Mernissi 1975); *Behind the Veil in Arabia* (Wikan 1982); "Lifting the Veil" [review essay] (Hatem 1985); *Veiled Sentiments* (L. Abu-Lughod 1987); the film by Elizabeth Fernea, "The Veiled Revolution," and many others. By implication, the title of one of the most famous pieces by a Middle Easternist, *The Hidden Face of Eve*, refers to veiling (El-Saadawi 1980). El-Saadawi's works deal with a number of these themes, which I have referred to as problematic. The work just mentioned deals with female circumcision through the eyes of an indigenous (Muslim) feminist and nationalist. Her first major work on the subject of women *(Women and Sex)* was published in Arabic in 1972 in Beirut, after she had been subjected to censorship in Egypt. I was in Cairo just after the book was published and was able to experience the "shock waves" in a society not used to women (or anyone) discussing sexuality so frankly. It is interesting to compare it to Abdel Wahab Bouhdiba's *La Sexualité en Islam* (1975). See Jon Anderson's "Social Structure and the Veil" (1982) for a fairly typical contemporary treatment of the function of the veil.

10. This is not to deny that forms of dress, such as the veil, can be used to subordinate women or may symbolize that subordination. There may also be elements of coercion and force, as in Iran and Saudi Arabia. In these situations and in others, veiling may be a statement by men about women, made through mandatory women's dress.

11. See Nawal El-Saadawi's *The Hidden Face of Eve* (1980). Readers and teachers interested in female circumcision in Sudan can consult literature by Sudanese doctors, one of whom is a sociologically sophisticated feminist (Toubia 1985). American feminist medical anthropologist Ellen Gruenbaum also attempts to place the custom in a context that reduces its sensationalist quality and makes a contribution to our understanding of "Reproductive Ritual and Social Reproduction" (1988). Both Toubia and Gruenbaum place female circumcision in its historical, political, and material context, while not shirking its relationship to female subordination. Another work by a Sudanese woman doctor, Asma El Dareer, is useful from the medical point-of-view, but lacks a sociological analysis (1982). For other interesting interpretations of the practice in Sudan, see Hayes (1975) and Boddy (1982). Even though in the bibliography I have entered enlightened works on the subject of circumcision, as a caveat, I would recommend that, even if an instructor consults these works, dealing with the custom in the introductory anthropology curriculum demands a highly informed and sensitized teacher.

Sociologist Mervat Hatem, in reviewing three works for *The Women's Review of Books,* includes Ann Cloudsley's *Women of Omdurman: Life, Love and the Cult of Virginity* (1985), a study of Sudanese women, and refers to this book as a "good example of the Objectionable Orientalist approach which presents Middle Eastern women as an 'alien' and 'exotic' group that is 'separate' and 'different' from the rest of us" (1985).

12. Obviously the honor/shame motif is salient in the writings on Mediterranean societies. See, for example, Schneider (1981) and Gilmore (1982). It is significant, however, that the honor/shame motif disappears from the scene in a relatively new anthology on *Women of the Mediterranean* (Gadant 1986).

13. It is important to stress here that I am dealing with sources in English only, with only occasional references to major works in Arabic or French. It goes without saying that there are a number of works in these two languages; fortunately some of the major ones are being translated (e.g., El-Saadawi [1980] and Tillion [1983 (1966)]).

14. These trends are sometimes contemporaneous, especially numbers 3 and 4.

15. In terms of trends, it is significant that the recent ex-President of the Middle East Studies Association, Elizabeth Fernea, is a leading feminist Middle Easternist anthropologist (e.g., 1965, 1970, 1976, 1985; and Fernea and Bezirgan 1977), and that in more recent years anthropologists have begun to assert themselves in an organization that had traditionally been dominated by the ancient historians, classicists, and "Orientalists."

16. In a 1985 work, *Daughters of Yemen*, Mishael Maswari Caspi has translated the poetry of Yemenite Jews, revealing many of the same modes of expression and ideas as the Abu-Lughod work.

17. Earlier in the text I had criticized the literature on Middle Eastern women for an overemphasis on the family. Fernea's collection, however, is a departure in that she tried, for the most part, to present us with interpretations of the family from Middle Easterners themselves.

18. Although Mary Hegland does refer to the fact that "the roles of Aliabad [Iran] women in community politics retained their indirect, protected, supportive and secondary character even after their participation in the revolution" (1986:46), her analysis puts women squarely in the political realm.

19. Historian Margot Badran has translated and introduced Huda Shaarawi's memoirs, *Harem Years: The Memoirs of an Egyptian Feminist* (1987), which was reviewed by Leila Ahmed (1987). See above Notes for more information on El-Saadawi's publications.

20. *Guests of the Sheik* (Fernea 1965) does the same using fiction.

21. A recent article by an Educational Studies professor at the Free University of Iran, Rokhsareh S. Shoaee, dispels any notion we might have that Muslim women are passive in national politics. Her study of Iranian women who are members or supporters of the Mujahidin-e Khalq is a direct challenge to the notion that Islam, women, and national political activity are incompatible elements (1987).

22. "Indigenous" only in the sense of being Middle Eastern, part Middle Eastern, or having Middle Eastern parents, not necessarily referring to currently living in or within that region, ethnic group, or class.

23. Altorki has written more extensively on this theme in a work she coedited with Camillia El-Solh (1988). Hussein Fahim has also edited a collection of works on indigenous anthropology, including an article by Altorki (Fahim 1982).

24. There are other scattered works of a sociological nature (e.g., a UNESCO collection, *Social Science Research and Women in the Arab World*, with an introduction by Amal Rassam [1984]); sociologist Janet Abu-Lughod's new essay on "The Islamic City" (1987) has an unusual and stimulating section on gender segregation; Mai Ghoussoub's 1987 "Feminism—or the Eternal Masculine—in the Arab World" gives a New Left perspective on the subject. There have also appeared several interdisciplinary anthologies on Muslim women (e.g., Smith 1980; al-Hibri 1982; Utas 1983; and Hussain 1984). Bibliographies of works on Middle Eastern women which are still useful are Gulick and Gulick (1973) and Al-Qazzaz (1977).

25. These articles are not included in References Cited unless they were cited elsewhere in the text.

References Cited

Abdel Kader, Soha
    1984   A Survey of Trends in Social Sciences Research on Women in the Arab Region, 1960–1980.
        In Social Science Research and Women in the Arab World. Pp. 139–175. London: UNESCO,
        Frances Pinter.
    1987   Egyptian Women in a Changing Society, 1899–1986. Boulder, Colorado: Lynne Rienner.
Abu-Lughod, Janet
    1987   The Islamic City—Historic Myth, Islamic Essence, and Contemporary Relevance. International Journal of Middle East Studies 19:155–176.
Abu-Lughod, Lila
    1985   A Community of Secrets: The Separate World of Bedouin Women. Signs 10(4):637–657.
    1987   Veiled Sentiments: Honor and Poetry in a Bedouin Society. Berkeley: University of California
        Press.

Abu-Zahra, M.
   1970   On the Modesty of Women in Arab Muslim Villages: A Reply [to Antoun]. American An-
      thropologist 72:1079–1092.
Accad, Evelyne
   1978   Veil of Shame: The Role of Women in the Contemporary Fiction of North Africa and the Arab
      World. Sherbrooke: Naaman.
Adnan, Etel
   1982   Sitt Marie-Rose: A Novel. Sausalito, California: Post-Apollo Press.
Ahmed, Leila
   1982a   Feminism and Feminist Movements in the Middle East. *In* Women and Islam. Azizah al-
      Hibri, ed. Pp. 153–168. Oxford: Pergamon.
   1982b   Western Ethnocentrism and Perceptions of the Harem. Feminist Studies 8(3):521–534.
   1987   Women of Egypt [review essay]. Women's Review of Books 5(2):7–8.
Al-Hibri, Azizah, ed.
   1982   Women in Islam. Oxford: Pergamon.
Al-Qazzaz, Ayad
   1977   Women in the Middle East and North Africa. An Annotated Bibliography. Austin: Center for
      Middle Eastern Studies, University of Texas.
Altorki, Soraya
   1986   Women in Saudi Arabia: Ideology and Behavior among the Elite. New York: Columbia Uni-
      versity Press.
Altorki, S., and C. El-Solh, eds.
   1988   Arab Women in the Field: Studying Your Own Society. Syracuse: Syracuse University Press.
Anderson, Jon
   1982   Social Structure and the Veil: Comportment and the Composition of Interaction in Afghani-
      stan. Anthropos 77:397–442.
Antoun, Richard
   1968   On the Modesty of Women in Arab Muslim Villages: A Study in the Accommodation of Tra-
      ditions. American Anthropologist 70(4):671–697.
Atiya, Nayra
   1982   Khul-Khaal: Five Egyptian Women Tell Their Stories. Syracuse: Syracuse University Press.
Badran, Margot
   1986   Islam, Patriarchy, and Feminism in the Middle East. Trends in History 4(1):49–71.
Beck, Lois, and Nikki Keddie, eds.
   1978   Women in the Muslim World. Cambridge: Harvard University Press.
Betteridge, Anne
   1983   To Veil or Not to Veil: A Matter of Protest or Policy. *In* Women and Revolution in Iran. G.
      Nashat, ed. Boulder, Colorado: Westview Press.
Boddy, Janice
   1982   Womb as Oasis: The Symbolic Context of Pharaonic Circumcision in Rural Northern Sudan.
      American Ethnologist 9(4):682–698.
Bouhdiba, Abdel Wahab
   1975   La Sexualité en Islam. Paris: Presses Universitaires de France.
Caspi, Mishael Maswari, trans.
   1985   Daughters of Yemen. Berkeley: University of California Press.
Cloudsley, Anne
   1985   Women of Omdurman: Life, Love and the Cult of Virginity. New York: St. Martin's Press.
Coon, Carleton S.
   1958   Caravan: The Story of the Middle East. New York: Holt, Rinehart and Winston [1951].
Davis, Susan
   1982   Patience and Power: Women's Lives in a Moroccan Village. New York: Schenkman.
Dorsky, Susan
   1986   Women of ʿAmran: A Middle Eastern Ethnographic Study. Salt Lake City, Utah: University
      of Utah.

Dwyer, Daisy
    1978   Images and Self-Images: Male and Female in Morocco. New York: Columbia University
        Press.
Ed-Din, Nazirah Zein
    1982   Removing the Veil and Veiling. Salah-Dine Hammoud, trans. *In* Women and Islam. Azizah
        al-Hibri, ed. Pp. 221–226. New York: Pergamon [1928].
Eickelman, Christine
    1984   Women and Community in Oman. New York: New York University Press.
Eickelman, Dale
    1981   The Middle East: An Anthropological Approach. Englewood Cliffs, N.J.: Prentice-Hall.
El Dareer, Asma
    1982   Woman, Why Do You Weep? Circumcision and Its Consequences. London: Zed.
El-Messiri, Nawal
    1977   The Changing Role of the Futuwwa in the Social Structure of Cairo. *In* Patrons and Clients.
        E. Gellner and J. Waterbury, eds. Pp. 239–253. London: Duckworth.
El Saadawi, Nawal
    1972   Woman and Sex [in Arabic]. Beirut.
    1980   The Hidden Face of Eve. Sherif Hetata, trans. London: Zed.
    1983   Woman at Point Zero. London: Zed [1975].
Esposito, John
    1981   Women in Muslim Family Law. Syracuse: Syracuse University Press.
Fahim, Hussein, ed.
    1982   Indigenous Anthropology in Non-Western Countries. Durham, N.C.: Carolina Academic
        Press.
Fernea, Elizabeth
    1965   Guests of the Sheik: An Ethnography of an Iraqi Village. Garden City, N.Y.: Doubleday An-
        chor.
    1970   A View of the Nile. New York: Doubleday.
    1976   A Street in Marrakech: A Personal Encounter with the Lives of Moroccan Women. Garden
        City, New York: Doubleday.
    1987   Presidential Address, 1986. Middle East Studies Association Bulletin 21(1):1–7.
Fernea, Elizabeth, ed.
    1985   Women and the Family in the Middle East. Austin: University of Texas Press.
Fernea, Elizabeth, and Basima Qattan Bezirgan, eds.
    1977   Middle Eastern Muslim Women Speak. Austin: University of Texas Press.
Gadant, Monique, ed.
    1986   Women of the Mediterranean. A. M. Berrett, trans. London: Zed [1984].
Gellner, Ernest, and John Waterbury, eds.
    1977   Patrons and Clients in Mediterranean Societies. London: Duckworth.
Ghalem, Ali
    1984   A Wife for My Son. London: Zed.
Ghoussoub, Mai
    1987   Feminism—or the Eternal Masculine—in the Arab World. New Left Review 161:3–19.
Gilmore, David
    1982   Anthropology of the Mediterranean Area. Annual Review of Anthropology 11:175–205.
Gruenbaum, Ellen
    1988   Reproductive Ritual and Social Reproduction: Female Circumcision in Sudan. *In* Economy
        and Class in Sudan. Norman O'Neill and Jay O'Brien, eds. Pp. 308–325. London: Gower.
Gulick, John, and Margaret Gulick
    1973   An Annotated Bibliography of Resources Concerned with Women in the Modern Muslim
        Middle East. Princeton: Princeton University Program in Near Eastern Studies.
Hale, Sondra
    1983   Women and Work in Sudan: What Is Alienated Labor? Proceedings, Conference on Women
        and Work in the Third World. Berkeley: Center for the Study, Education and Advancement of
        Women, University of California.

1986   The Wing of the Patriarch: Sudanese Women and Revolutionary Parties. MERIP Middle East Report 16(1):25–30.

1987a   The State of the Art of Feminist Anthropology of the Middle East. Paper for the 85th Annual Meeting, American Anthropological Association, Philadelphia, December 1987.

1987b   Women's Culture/Men's Culture: Gender, Separation, and Space in Africa and North America. American Behavioral Scientist 31(1):115–134.

Forthcoming   Transforming Culture or Fostering Second-Hand Consciousness? Women's Front Organizations and Revolutionary Parties—the Sudan Case. *In* Women and Arab Society: Old Boundaries, New Frontiers. Judith Tucker, ed.

Hatem, Mervat
1985   Lifting the Veil [review essay]. Women's Review of Books 2(10):13–14.
1986a   The Enduring Alliance of Nationalism and Patriarchy in Muslim Personal Status Laws: The Case of Modern Egypt. Feminist Studies 6(1):19–41.
1986b   Sexuality and Gender in Segregated Patriarchal Systems: The Case of Eighteenth- and Nineteenth-Century Egypt 12(1):251–274.

Hayes, Rose
1975   Female Genital Mutilation, Fertility Control, Women's Role and the Patrilineage in Modern Sudan. American Ethnologist 2(4):617–633.

Hegland, Mary
1986   Political Roles of Iranian Village Women. MERIP Middle East Report 16(1):14–19, 46.

Hoffman-Ladd, Valerie
1987   Polemics on the Modesty and Segregation of Women in Contemporary Egypt. International Journal of Middle East Studies 19(1):23–50.

Hussain, Freda, ed.
1984   Muslim Women. New York: St. Martin's.

Joseph, Suad
1982   The Family as Security and Bondage: A Political Strategy of the Lebanese Urban Working Class. *In* Towards a Political Economy of Urbanization in Third World Countries. Helen Safa, ed. Pp. 151–171. New Delhi: Oxford University Press.
1983   Working Class Women's Networks in a Sectarian State: A Political Paradox. American Ethnologist 10(1):1–22.
1986   Women and Politics in the Middle East [introduction]. MERIP Middle East Report 16(1):3–7.

Jowkar, Forouz
1986   Honor and Shame: A Feminist View from Within. Feminist Issues 6(1):45–65.

Keddie, Nikki, ed.
1972   Scholars, Saints and Sufis. Berkeley: University of California Press.
1973   Is There a Middle East? International Journal of Middle East Studies 4:255–271.
1979   Problems in the Study of Middle Eastern Women. International Journal of Middle East Studies 10:225–240.

Kennedy, John
1967   Nubian Zar Ceremonies as Psychotherapy. Human Organization 26(4):185–194.

Maher, Vanessa
1974   Women and Property in Morocco: The Changing Relation to the Process of Social Stratification in the Middle Atlas. Cambridge: Cambridge University Press.

Makhlouf, Carla
1979   Changing Veils: Women and Modernization in North Yemen. Austin: University of Texas Press.

Marsot, Afaf Lutfi al-Sayyid
1978   The Revolutionary Gentlewoman in Egypt. *In* Women in the Muslim World. Lois Beck and Nikki Keddie, eds. Cambridge: Harvard University Press.

MERIP Middle East Report
1986   Women and Politics in the Middle East 16(1).

Mernissi, Fatima
    1975   Beyond the Veil: Male-Female Dynamics in a Modern Muslim Society. Cambridge: Cambridge University Press.
    1977   Women, Saints, and Sanctuaries. Signs 3(1):101–112.
    1982   Virginity and Patriarchy. Women's Studies International Forum 5(2):183–193.
    1986   Misogynist Hadith: Reporting or Fabricating Religious Literature? Why Aicha's Corrections Were Omitted. Paper for Conference on Women and Arab Society: Old Boundaries, New Frontiers. Washington, D.C.: Georgetown University, April 10–11, 1986.
Minces, Juliette
    1978   Women in Algeria. *In* Women in the Muslim World. Lois Beck and Nikki Keddie, eds. Pp. 159–171. Cambridge: Harvard University Press.
    1982   House of Obedience: Women in Arab Society. London: Zed.
Munson, Henry
    1984   The House of Si Abd Allah: The Oral History of a Moroccan Family. New Haven: Yale University Press.
Nelson, Cynthia
    1974   Public and Private Politics: Women in the Middle Eastern World. American Ethnologist 1:551–553, 560.
    1986   The Voices of Doria Shafik: Feminist Consciousness in Egypt, 1940–1960. Feminist Issues 6(2):15–31.
Peristiany, J. G., ed.
    1966   Honour and Shame: The Values of Mediterranean Society. Chicago: University of Chicago Press.
Peteet, Julie
    1986   No Going Back: Women and the Palestinian Movement. MERIP Middle East Report 16(1):20–24.
Rassam, Amal [also see Vinogradov]
    1980   Women and Domestic Power in Morocco. International Journal of Middle Eastern Studies 12:171–179.
    1982a   Towards a Theoretical Framework for the Study of Women in the Arab World. Cultures 8(3):121–137.
    1982b   Unveiling Arab Women [review essay]. The Middle East Journal 36(4):583–587.
    1984   Introduction: Arab Women: The Status of Research in the Social Sciences and the Status of Women. *In* Social Science Research and Women in the Arab World. Pp. 1–13. UNESCO. London: Frances Pinter.
Rifaat, Alifa
    1983   Distant View of a Minaret and Other Stories. London: Quartet.
Sabbah, Fatna (pseud.)
    1984   Woman in the Muslim Unconscious. New York: Pergamon Press.
Said, Edward
    1978   Orientalism. New York: Pantheon.
Sanaserian, Eliz
    1982   The Women's Rights Movement in Iran: Mutiny, Appeasement, and Repression from 1900 to Khomeini. New York: Praeger.
Schneider, Jane
    1971   Of Vigilance and Virgins: Honour, Shame and Access to Resources in the Mediterranean Societies. Ethnology 10:1–24.
Shaarawi, Huda
    1987   Harem Years: The Memoirs of an Egyptian Feminist (1879–1924). Margot Badran, trans. and ed. New York: Feminist Press.
Shoaee, Rokhsareh S.
    1987   The Mujahid Women of Iran: Reconciling "Culture" and "Gender." The Middle East Journal 41(4):519–537.

Smith, Jane, ed.
    1980   Women in Contemporary Muslim Societies. Lewisburg: Bucknell University Press.
Soffan, Linda Usra
    1980   The Women of the United Arab Emirates. London: Croom Helm.
Sudan (Ministry of Social Affairs)
    1958   First Population Census of the Sudan, 1955–56. Khartoum.
Tabari, Azar (pseud.)
    1986   The Women's Movement in Iran: A Hopeful Prognosis. Feminist Studies 12(2):343–360.
Tabari, Azar, and Nahid Yehaneh, eds.
    1982   In the Shadow of Islam: The Women's Movement in Iran. London: Zed.
Takieddine-Amyuni, Mona
    1985   Images of Arab Women in *Midaq Alley* by Naguib Mahfouz, and *Seasons of Migration to the North* by Tayeb Salih. International Journal of Middle East Studies 17(1):25–36.
Tillion, Germaine
    1983   The Republic of Cousins: Women's Oppression in Mediterranean Society. London: Al Saqi Books [1966].
Toubia, Nahid
    1985   The Social and Political Implications of Female Circumcision. *In* Women and the Family in the Middle East. E. Fernea, ed. Pp. 148–159. Austin: University of Texas Press.
Tucker, Judith
    1985   Women in Nineteenth-Century Egypt. Cambridge: Cambridge University Press.
    1986   Insurrectionary Women: Women and the State in 19th-Century Egypt. MERIP Middle East Report 16(1):9–13.
Utas, Bo, ed.
    1983   Women in Islamic Societies: Social Attitudes and Historical Perspectives. New York: Olive Branch Press.
UNESCO
    1984   Social Science Research and Women in the Arab World. London: Frances Pinter.
Vinogradov, Amal [also see Rassam]
    1974   French Colonialism as Reflected in the Male-Female Interaction in Morocco. Transactions of the New York Academy of Sciences 36:192–199.
Waines, David
    1982   Through a Veil Darkly: The Study of Women in Muslim Societies. Comparative Studies in Society and History 24(4):642–659.
Wikan, Unni
    1982   Behind the Veil in Arabia: Women in Oman. Baltimore: Johns Hopkins University Press.
Youssef, Nadia H.
    1976   Women in the Muslim World. *In* Women in the World. L. B. Iglitzin and Ruth Ross, eds. Pp. 203–217. Santa Barbara: Clio.
    1978   The Status and Fertility Patterns of Muslim Women. *In* Women in the Muslim World. Lois Beck and Nikki Keddie, eds. Pp. 69–99. Cambridge: Harvard University Press.
Yusuf, Shaykh Hajii
    1965   In Defense of the Veil. *In* The Contemporary Middle East. B. Rivlin and J. Syzliowicz, eds. Pp. 335–359. New York: Random House.

11

Women in Hindu Society

Lina M. Fruzzetti
Brown University

India is a country of vast regional, cultural, social, and religious differences. Although Hinduism is the major form of religious ideology, there are many non-Hindu communities in India. These other communities, or minorities, as they are referred to in India, are the Muslims, Jains, Buddhists, Christians, a small Jewish group, and tribals, who have their own separate form of worship. Within Hinduism itself there are many sects that vary the performance of rituals and introduce different manifestations of gods and goddesses into the sacred domain. As the dominant religion in India, however, Hinduism pervades all other groups in Indian society. For this reason alone, this chapter will focus on Hindu women.

Symbolic and cultural approaches, which examine the meaning and symbolism of Hindu gender, are among the most insightful studies of women in India and are the foci of this essay. The emphasis of these theoretical approaches highlights the basis and the source of our understanding of women and the meaning of gender. The chapter also incorporates anthropological studies of Indian women that do not utilize the symbolic approach, though those are not my specialty. In the annotated bibliography one can find a wide range of studies dealing with Hindu women from various methodological and theoretical perspectives.

The serious study of gender in India did not begin until the late 1960s. There are multiple reasons for this, including the emergence of feminism in the West, the growth of interest in comparative studies of women and women's issues in the non-Western settings, and the general development of anthropological method and theory in India. India presented a special situation for the anthropologist. In India, one was presented with the caste system, a system of social organization radically different from any form of social organization found in the West. In order to understand India, the anthropologist was compelled to gain a comprehension of the caste system and its workings. Earlier studies by Indologists, which focused on the philosophical and religious aspects of caste and Hinduism, did not provide the anthropologist with the set of tools necessary to understand the social structure of contemporary India. As anthropologists devised the tools to analyze and understand issues of caste and hierarchy, male and female researchers alike realized the importance of understanding women in Hindu society and the need to examine gender in the study of caste and hierarchy.

This essay will briefly discuss the development of women's studies (which is different from the history of Indian women) as it leads to a more serious consideration of gender issues in anthropology. Present gender studies that concentrate on the areas of kinship, ritual, and caste are outgrowths of these theoretical developments. It is important to have an understanding of these developments and changes even in introductory courses on gender studies in India. This discussion of Hindu women is limited in its consideration of the diversities in cultural practices and meanings of actions in India. Nonetheless, I would argue that issues which revolve around marriage, dowry, and rituals (domestic and temples) transcend some of these cultural and regional differences. The institution and culture of household rituals are performed in most areas of India. Hinduism, the prevailing religion, has a common civilization construct that all believers of the religion uphold. The chapter does not assume or propose a unified cultural interpretation to the rituals of women per se, but demonstrates that a world of women does exist which needs to be interpreted and understood no matter where it is in India (Fruzzetti 1982).

Contemporary literature on Indian women, cultural/symbolic as well as feminist, challenges preexisting works on and interpretations of women in India. This new focus and voice to represent women in their own domain and cultural context has changed the way we understand India and in particular Indian women.

In 1954, H. N. C. Stevenson examined status in the Hindu caste system, initiating a discussion of purity and pollution and its impact on Hindu women (Stevenson 1954). These concerns about female purity/pollution were further examined by K. Gough in her studies of female initiation rites and the definition of marriage among the matrilineal Nayar groups in the state of Kerela. She tied the analysis of initiation rites to larger issues and debates on the definition of marriage and family (Gough 1952, 1955, 1959). Her psychoanalytical explanation showed that the *tali* tying ritual has the dual function of expressing a union between the prepubescent girl with a man outside her lineage and removing the horror of incest from her lineage: in the rite, the girl is symbolically deflowered by a man outside her lineage while her sexuality is renounced by members of her own lineage. In her analysis she associated female defloration with a Nayar male's fear of incest with his own mother since sister and mother are equaled. Gough concluded that "Initiation rites are a symbolic defloration because of the items used in the rituals stressing phallic aspects as well as female fertility" (Gough 1955:87).

The publication of Gough's articles was followed by Yalman's account on the purity of women in the castes of Malabar and Ceylon (Yalman 1963). His analysis of similar rites among the patrilineal Sinhalese groups showed that "filiation through the mother, and the protection of female purity is fundamental to the caste system of Ceylon and Malabar and these principles may have structural implications in other Hindu castes" (Yalman 1963:25). Yalman's article brought into question Gough's Freudian interpretation of woman's purity and triggered research interest into the issues of women's sexuality and its relevance to caste and kinship issues.

Even though today's studies of women in India have some of their origins in the writings of Stevenson, Gough, or Yalman, none of these anthropologists (or their contemporaries) had a primary interest in the study of women. Their primary interest remained the clarification of the caste system, which they undertook using a British structural-functional framework. The advantage of structural-functional over earlier Indologist approaches to Indian society was its emphasis on the social rather than the philosophical and religious components of caste. The disadvantage of these approaches was their dependence on the "observable facts" and their disregard for the underlying ideology that could have contributed to an understanding of the principles of the system itself.

Dumont's work departed from structural-functionalism by approaching the study of caste as a total social fact, and seriously examining the role of ideology in the system (Dumont 1957, 1958, 1959, 1966, 1970). This new approach demonstrated the analytical interconnectedness between culture and society and resulted in a conceptual framework in which social structure was seen as an integral part of culture. In his examinations of caste purity and pollution, Dumont showed that the marital exchange of women between kinship lines maintained descent groups and regenerated caste groups.

Of the early structural-functionalists, Yalman's approach came the closest to Dumont's insights. Yalman proceeded in his analysis of Sinhalese groups by focusing on Dumont's approach to structure and ideology and called for a uniform cultural analysis (Yalman 1963:25). He went on to show that the initiation rites do have social functions (Yalman 1967).

He relates the concerns with woman's sexuality and purity to caste and kinship principles. Furthermore, Yalman is concerned with the social significance of the rites, what they aim at, relate to, and signify in relation to the actions taking place and to the larger concerns of society. [Fruzzetti 1981:13]

For some anthropologists in the 1970s and 80s, this understanding highlighted the importance of scholarly research on women in Indian society and led to a renewal of research in kinship and ritual and the birth of contemporary gender studies. It was now apparent that an analytical treatment of caste and issues of hierarchy could not ignore the domain of women.

Although Stevenson, Gough, Yalman, and Dumont may be considered precursors of modern gender studies in India, they were not the only scholars who provided information on Indian women and their lives during the 1950s and '60s. One of the best studies from this period is M. N. Srinivas's study of the Coorgs of South India which includes an excellent analysis of ritual purity and pollution in relation to women's life-cycle rites. For Srinivas, the discussion of ritual purity and its opposition "are intimately related to permanent features of the social structure like caste and okka" (Srinivas 1965:104). He refers to the pollution resulting from birth and menstruation having the potential to pollute men, caste, and the lineage (okka). Later he shows how these concerns are connected to the village at large and goes on to describe what women in this society do to avoid polluting other members of their lineage (1965:104).

Most of the other information on Indian women from the 1950s and '60s is descriptive. For example, Mandelbaum's Society in India volume two, Part II contains a chapter on Family and Kinship relations. In this chapter, Mandelbaum provides a section on girls and women and describes family roles, children and the bonds of filiation (Mandelbaum 1967, 1970). Other examples include Berreman's accounts of the Hindus of the Himalayas, which briefly mentions the role of women in the social, family, and economic spheres (Berreman 1974), and work by Mayer (1960) and F. G. Bailey (1964, 1966). For an extreme example of the superficial treatment received by women in most pre-1970 studies, see the work of Andre Beteille. In his discussion of change and the caste system, Beteille emphasizes the outward manifestations of change represented by styles of female dress, or what Srinivas coined "sanskritization," as one moves up in status (Beteille 1965:50–51).

Women, Structure, and Ideology: Contemporary Gender Studies

The majority of contemporary gender studies in India have been conducted among urban women. Topics covered in these urban studies include women and the work force (Bhatt 1981;

Kapur 1970, 1974; Mies 1983, 1986), education (Mitra 1979; Rao and Rao 1988), and politics (Awasty 1982; Khan 1979; Mazumdar 1979; Nandy 1988). Of these topics the one which has received the most attention is women in the work force, reflecting a growing concern in India over women's poverty and the lack of opportunities for women in the paid labor force.

In some Indian communities a woman's worth is measured by her ability to provide supplemental income to the household whereas in other communities married and unmarried women are not allowed to work. D. Jain castigates the communities that do not allow their women to work. In one of her essays, written with N. Banerjee, she states that "the cultural inhibition in Bengal, while it presumes to protect the women from the humiliation of working under other people, finds begging and domestic work less 'humiliating' " (Jain and Banerjee 1985:227). N. Banerjee shows that destitute Bengali women who want to work rather than beg have two traditionally accepted options: domestic service and prostitution (1985:227). The two authors question the cultural adulation Bengali women receive from their men, and ask whether the "dignified treatment such as respect and protectiveness meted out to them in public places, the worshipfulness of Bengali men to their women folk" is worth the price that they have to pay (Jain and Banerjee 1985:227). Maria Mies (1983, 1986) analyzes women workers in an agrarian society and describes how development changes the worth of their labor. Furthermore, her research on women's handicraft occupations lays the emphasis on labor and tradition. Her work is driven by questions about why women work and what are the implications of those decisions for women's lives within traditional households. Research such as this is also important because it calls attention to the need for additional research on and criticism of the social and cultural values. Research on women and work does not merely provide ethnographic descriptions of the work but raises theoretical questions about the significance and meaning of women workers, what the new woman achieves or loses as a result of working, and what the challenges to tradition might be (Chaki-Sircar 1984; Dube et al. 1986; Everett 1981; Lessinger 1986).

A related topic that has been the subject of research is women and change. In her studies of urban working women, Kapur tries to show that a working Hindu woman need not totally change her values as a result of her decision to work (1970, 1974). She found that a woman goes to work with the same "patterns of socialization" that are

> considerably influenced by the value system and religious ethos prevalent in a particular time. Thus, a woman's internalized role and status will be determined by the attitudes and behavioral patterns of society toward her and by her own self-image which will be created in her by them. [Kapur 1974:52]

Nonetheless, Kapur also looks at ways that the values of women workers in a modern setting are affected and changed by the work place.

R. S. Khare's (1976) study of the domestic domain of women—the kitchen area, the hearth—addresses the question of cultural change and the effects of these changes on the traditional cultural construction of a wife and mother. The kitchen area and the hearth fall within the domain of women. Women are described as doing daily meticulous chores, caring for children and elders, and attending the household ritualized domain. Khare shows that the "basic Hindu association between kinship, cooking, and marriage continues to hold with the modern to keep the place of the domestic hearth secure" (Khare 1976:254). He demonstrates that women and children in a Hindu family are closely identified with the existence "and the continuation of the domestic hearth and its fire. Continuation of this complex means deciphering and consolidating one's social place in society" (1976:116).

There are a number of other good general survey studies of women and culture change in India. Some of these works focus on changes in family and marriage relations (Hate 1969;

Kapadia 1966; Misra 1984) while others address contemporary topics of concern to women (e.g., rape and bride burning: R. Ghadially 1988: section three). For additional sources on change which address issues much in need of research within India today see D. Jain (1975, 1980), D. Jain and N. Banerjee (1985), and R. Ghadially (1988).

Symbolic and Cultural Approaches: Women and the Sacred Domain

Two interesting anthropological studies of Hindu gods and goddesses that directly relate to Indian women are those of A. Ostor (1980) and L. Babb (1975). The theme of Ostor's ethnography is the festival of the divine sacred couple, Siva and Durga. He explains that the rituals involved in the festival are about the goddess Durga's married life, "her strife with Siva, her problems with children and parents, her petulance, her neglect by Siva" (Ostor 1980:22). The couple reflects the model for human married people. Durga, who is "the faithful and devoted wife, forever complaining about her husband, reproaching him for his infidelities, upbraiding him for his unconventional ways" is idealized and worshiped by married women. According to mythology, Durga went annually to her father's house. Reenacting Durga's journey, many married Indian women perform a yearly ritual. In parts of India where the ritual is observed, married women along with their children and husband return to their paternal households for the festival of the goddess (1980).

Babb's study is more general than Ostor's; he concentrates on an array of Hindu festivals, describing both the benign (Durga) and the malevolent (Kali) aspects of the goddess. He shows that the malevolent, bloodthirsty goddess Kali is not represented in a matrimonial context; Durga, the protectoress and the mother, is the manifestation of the goddess at marriages. Here the author compares the ideal sacred model of the divine pair to the level of humans. He states that

> deities of this kind seem to embody certain key values of Indian civilization. It is as if the imposition of a basic vehicle of social order-marriage on the relationship between god and goddess creates the possibility for the elaboration of divine attributes in accordance with basic order-producing values. [Babb 1975:224]

Anthropologists from the early 1970s on acknowledged the separate treatment of Indian women in their studies (see Barnett 1976; David 1973; Das 1982; Fruzzetti 1981, 1982; Kolenda 1968, 1982a, 1982b; Madan 1982, 1987; Wadley 1975, 1980; Wadley and Jacobson 1986). The cultural context of these studies set them apart from the earlier more descriptive ethnographies. Kinship studies by scholars such as Vatuk, Khare, Madan, and Kolenda that examine kinship in terms of urban India or household rituals have contributed to the understanding of gender in India.

David (1973) and Barnett (1976) drew upon Dumont and Schneider's methodological approach to the study of kinship and introduced the idea of the cultural construction of gender and the person. Their approach called for research on cultural notions of the conception of person and the indigenous meanings of blood and semen. This emphasis has contributed to a more sophisticated understanding of gender in India.

Feminist perspectives and a concern for women's issues changed and problematized our understanding of Indian women, caste, class, culture, and gender symbolism. Caste was found to have other than a functional significance. Class was separated from caste (Beteille), and researchers began to decipher class from caste in studies of women and work and women in urban and rural areas. Women workers were addressed without reference to their low or high caste standing. Economically imposed inequality was addressed as a gender problem and not as an issue of caste purity and pollution. Joan Mencher (1972), Andre Beteille (1965), and G. Berreman (1974) present a changing view of caste, all insisting on the importance (and emergence) of class in India.

While Mencher demystifies caste for the untouchables in India, taking a more rational, economic based, rather than traditional Hindu, interpretation of caste purity/pollution, Moffatt argues that she gives insufficient attention to analyzing the forms of consciousness that are present among the low castes (Moffatt 1979:10–11). The disagreement between Moffatt and anthropologists such as Mencher and Berreman hinges on the former's belief that symbolic approaches which explore cultural meanings of the construction of gender are the important avenue for future research.

Two studies that do just this are Krygier (1982) and Stutchbury (1982). Krygier discusses female purity and its opposition by analyzing the effect of menstrual blood on caste and household kinship relations. Stutchbury compares *sati* (widow burning) to human sacrifice (which took place in parts of India during the 19th century). Death in Hinduism is impure and Stutchbury argues that one way for the Hindus to contain impurity was through the practice of *sati,* where ''the impurity of death pollution which is focused on the widow is removed from the world of men by her immolation,'' (Stutchbury 1982:37). *Sati* and human sacrifice where both tied to gender issues: *Sati* removes impurity due to death and the offering of human sacrifices appeased the female goddess, Kali.

Some of the latest studies of Indian women use symbolic and cultural approaches to illuminate the position and status of women in Indian society (Dhruvarajan 1988; Fruzzetti 1982; Marglin 1985; Wadley 1975). Wadley's research is directed at comprehending the ideal Hindu woman (Wadley 1975; Wadley and Jacobson 1986). Recognizing that a cultural study of women has to consider the importance of religion and its impact on gender, she draws on the analogy of women and Hindu divinity through their daily lives in her ethnography, *Shakti* (Wadley 1975). Wadley claims that religious values are the root of women's dual reality in Indian society: they ''are threatening: their sexuality is destructive to men, whose energy they sap, yet their fertility is needed for bearing their sons'' (Wadley 1980:40). She argues that an understanding

> of the dual character of the Hindu female's essential nature (her *sakti* and *prakriti*) is an essential backdrop for understanding the rules and role models for women in Hindu South Asia. The centrality of the theme of the dual character of the Hindu female in norms and guidelines for proper female behavior, especially in the male-dominated classical texts or folk traditions, is seen most clearly in the role of wife (good, benevolent, dutiful, controlled) and mother (fertile, but dangerous, uncontrolled). [Wadley 1980:29]

Wadley's study is complemented by Marglin's analysis of women temple dancers in terms of auspiciousness and inauspiciousness, purity and pollution (Marglin 1985). Temple dancers *(devadasis)* are considered wives of the god Jagannatha but they are also concubines of the temple priests. As wives, they are deemed auspicious and pure while as concubines, they are considered inauspicious and polluted. The study gives detailed explanations of the concepts and meanings of purity and pollution that affect not merely temple dancers but all women in Indian society. The problem emphasized in this ethnography is common to all women in Indian society: how to maintain purity.

L. Fruzzetti's work analyzes women and the construction of gender through women's marriage and birth rituals. Her ethnographic study challenges previous research work by treating women's rituals as worthy in and of themselves rather than as reflections of larger societal concerns. She details and describes the marriage rites performed by women: rites of welcome and farewell, bathing rites, and rites that enact what a new wife will do in her new household (i.e., the rituals of the kitchen and household deities). Fruzzetti links

> women's rituals to categories of action, to exegeses of rituals, to exchange among persons
> and groups, and ultimately to the domains in which all of these symbols, actions, and persons
> are enhanced with meaning. [Fruzzetti 1982:61]

Her study addresses how the rituals help one to understand what women's sacred performances signify and how women use rituals to orient their world and construct their reality.

Vatuk, although not writing specifically about women in her excellent study of kinship and marriage exchange in urban North India (Vatuk 1972), presents a very good account of women, their world, worries, gossips, kinship tensions, dowry and marriage concerns. Her detailed description of women's morning and afternoon activities in a neighborhood is telling of Vatuk's sensitive understanding of women's needs, values, and the expression of these cultural sentiments. She shows that women, despite being in an urban area, still comply with traditional village norms and behavior (Vatuk 1972; esp. chapters 4 and 5).

A more recent book on women's rituals first explains the subjugation and exploitation of the women by men and then proceeds to question the symbolism and meanings attached to the culture of Indian women (Dhruvarajan 1988). She raises issues that challenge the cultural ideal of the chaste woman. In a way, the study parallels culturally oriented studies where the sacred symbolism of a woman's body (or the significance of gender) is reconstructed. The above ethnographies serve as one body of literature and can be supplemented by readings from two edited volumes (Allen and Mukherjee 1982; Wadley and Jacobson 1986).

New Directions in Indian Women's Studies

The women's movement in India began before India's independence. Women were actively involved as volunteer social workers in the 1920s and '30s. During the nationalist movement, Mahatma Ghandi called on women to do social work for poor and destitute women. Some of these organizations are the subject of two recent studies by Patricia Kaplan (1985) and Joanna Liddle and Joshi Rama (1986). Both analyze women's historical social movements, looking into women's participation in voluntary work, social work, and humanitarian service. The tone of these ethnographies differs from some earlier studies because not only is the contemporary domain of women examined but their place in history is also acknowledged. What is interesting is the relationship of these and similar studies to the growth of a contemporary women's movement in India that incorporates both older women's organizations and the more recent political feminist movements.

Unfortunately, very little is written about the recent social and political developments of women. The best sources for present coverage of these issues are Indian periodicals and films. *Manushi* (of human beings) is a journal that grew out of the concerns and interests of the Stree Adhikar Manch (Forum for the Rights of Women). *Manushi*'s office serves as a meeting place for women and also provides shelter for many distressed women. It combines education about women's issues along with practical assistance for women. As a journal, it has been consistent in publishing articles about different issues that affect women. The journal tends to combine the practical work of women activists with academic research work. This journal is available in many North American universities, as is a book of articles from *Manushi* (Kishwar and Vanita 1984). These articles represent the most articulate feminist interpretations of women in India today.

A very good cross-disciplinary reader for undergraduate students that examines contemporary women's issues of violence, divorce, and rape as well as the media's presentation of them through films and videos is Ghadially's *Women in Indian Society* (1988). For an interesting study on the status of women and education see Mitra (1979).

Conclusion

In the past, studies of Indian women erred when Western anthropologists applied their own cultural concepts (e.g., oppression, subjugation, and exploitation) to infer Indian cultural meaning. Today, the best comparative studies use indigenous concepts for their analytical work. The past decade has been a period during which numerous scholars have written studies on topics that range from the cultural construction of gender to the women's movements, women in the labor market, fertility studies, female infanticide, literacy, and women and rituals. What seems exceptionally fortuitous for Indian studies is the continuation of this serious research on gender, and the impact of this research on comparative woman's studies and on a better understanding of the international women's or feminist movement.

In conclusion, this essay attempts to partially summarize the history of research on women in India. I have tried to show that the study of women came as a result of changes in the methodological approaches to the study of culture and society in India. These new approaches helped anthropologists better understand concepts of purity and pollution, hierarchy and ideology through cultural categories and construction. In turn, this resulted in the acknowledgment that (for a comprehensive understanding of Indian society) detailed studies of women and aspects of their lives were necessary.

Two areas recognized as being important for an understanding of gender in India today are gender/life-cycle rites and the women's movement/feminist question. These two topics will be briefly discussed in the following two instruction modules. Both instruction modules are complemented by this introductory essay.

Life-Cycle Rites and the Construction of Gender

An effective way to study Hindu women is through their rituals. Hindu women in India can be regarded as constituting a separate world, where they are the main actors in everyday activities, from household chores to life-cycle rituals. A separate women's domain exists, a domain that is a culturally constructed realm where women interact with each other. This separate world of and for women with its delineated activities is not an expression of antagonism or sexual imbalance between men and women. An indigenously separate world of women expresses a complex structure where women interact with other women in socially and culturally defined roles as wives, mothers, and sisters. In this area of interaction, rituals of household and life-cycle rites express meanings and symbols appropriate to women and to the construction of gender. Birth, marriage, and death affect men differently than women, but the symbolism emphasizes the complementary nature of men and women. Ritual is the medium and the idiom that women utilize to be separate and yet complementary to men. Thus through life-cycle rituals, one can understand aspects of women in a Hindu society.

Course Issues

Introduction to an Indian Hindu Society: The Household Domain. (Here the main focus is to understand what constitutes the Hindu household, and to work out the concepts, definitions, and terminology used to describe the society.)

1. What constitutes a Hindu household and family?
Readings: Part 11 from Mandelbaum (1970) on the Family and Kinship Relations; or from Vatuk (1972) chapters three and seven, on the household and the neighborhood, organization and networks of women. From Allen and Mukherjee (1982) chapter 1 on the Hindu women.
The structure of the family will in turn offer the student a sense of what women do and where, the organization of the family, and the opportunity to question whether women hold positions of authority and power.

2. The kinship organization of the family. This section will illustrate the significance of the kinship system and organization. The system of relationships, what constitutes kinship, the gender code of conduct, behavior or how it restricts and structures the activities within and outside the household are crucial for an understanding of gender in India.
Readings: From Ostor et al. (1982) articles by Fruzzetti, Ostor, and S. Barnett on the cultural construction of the person in North and South India; or from the same volume the articles by Madan and Carter on the ideology of the person as a householder or hierarchy and the person. From Vatuk (1972) chapter five on family and kinship.

3. The ritual domain: life-cycle rites. Chapters from Fruzzetti (1982, 1981, esp. 1982:chapts. 2 and 3). These chapters cover rituals and the kinship structure and how the two are brought together through life-cycle rites. Chapter 3 is directly tied to marriage rites, explaining the significance of these rites to the construction of gender. Fruzzetti's (1981) analysis of menstrual rites emphasizes constructs of gender and purity; Fruzzetti and Ostor (1976) describe gender symbolism and its construction to marriage rites and the kinship reckoning; or Pocock (1971) where he devotes a section on household rites and sibling relations. Chapter three from Babb (1975) is an explanation of life-cycle rites in rural India. Khare's (1976) chapters six through nine add to the explanation of marriage by adding to a new dimension, the preparation of foods by women in ritualized contexts. One could conclude this section with a novel by Murthy, *Samaskara,* where an untouchable women pollutes a Brahmin priest by her sexual contact with him. (This novel is also the subject of the film *Samaskara.*)

4. The sacred domain and its impact on the ideal model of women is useful because it sets the study of Indian Hindu women within a specific cultural context. Thus the work of Wadley and Jacobson (1975, 1986) as well as Babb (1975), chapter seven: Madan (1987, esp. chapts. 1 and 2, where he describes issues of domesticity, auspiciousness, and purity are extremely helpful in this section. From Allen and Mukherjee (1982), articles by Allen, Krygier, and Stutchbury would be good comparative material and sequel to the above section.

5. A specific case study of a life-cycle rite is crucial. Why is marriage so important for the study of gender in India? Chapters one and four of Fruzzetti (1982) deal with the issues of dowry and sacredness of the marriage rites themselves. The chapters lay out the argument for the importance of marriage among the Hindus and how marriage in turn reflects the purity

of women's statuses. In Vatuk (1972) chapter four, the importance of marriage in the urban context is explained. The pioneering work of Tambiah (1973) on the dowry system and its changes in use and adaptation in Hindu marriages are an addition to the readings here.

Women's Movement and the Feminist Question in India

Recent atrocities such as bride burnings and dowry deaths of women are concerns of both rural and urban Indian women from all classes and castes. Women's outcry against dowry pressures and demands calls into question present aberrations of marriage and dowry practices and points to a need for the government to establish a legal ruling to abet the problem. Hindu ideals of a woman are still observed in India today. The sacraments of marriage are performed for the continuation of the male descent lines, caste principles, and personal completion of one's sacred duties in this life.

Despite the official abolition of the dowry system in 1961, the practice continues under the guise of gifts and prestations. Dowry, called *stridhan* (gifts of the bride), was traditionally for the use of and under the control of the bride. Today, the gifts given by the bride's family at marriage are not under her control. If the bride dies, the gifts remain with her in-laws. Since Hindu laws allows a widower but not a widow to remarry, a widower can remarry and accumulate additional wealth for himself and his household.

There is more cultural pressure for parents to find husbands for their daughters than wives for their sons. This pressure is related to the cultural concepts of purity and pollution of married and unmarried women. In the past, fear of pollution resulted in a girl's marriage being negotiated as soon as she menstruated cycle. Even in modern Indian households, unmarried girls are not welcome and families are pressured to find husbands for their daughters. "Dowries" are still given, but in different forms than in the past. Recently, this giving and taking of gifts at marriage exchanges has undergone cultural aberrations. Newly married girls are pressured by their in-laws to ask their parents for additional cash or goods. Some of these brides are driven to suicide when they are unable to meet the demands of their in-laws while others are either burnt or mysteriously killed. The cultural concepts of an auspicious or blessed married woman is contradicted by the increasing numbers of bride burnings. Although this phenomena is not the norm for newly married women, the frequency is great enough that its occurrence is a concern to women in India.

Feminist and other women's groups in India are trying to challenge this growing problem. Some seek governmental support for the creation of tougher laws to protect women from such atrocities. Others try to educate the society against these practices. This education campaign is done through street plays, the use of popular folk songs, poetry, newspaper articles, and short films. The poetry chides women for the roles they accept for themselves or force their daughters to take. Plays on bride burning attempt to highlight inconsistencies between the ideal and the reality of women's lives, and to emphasize the greed of people today. In short, the use of popular culture medium questions the socialization process of girls. It is obvious to feminists that the increase in bride burnings and dowry deaths parallels the country's unemployment rate and the increased demand for consumer goods in urban and rural areas.

Women's organizations and feminists question the notion of auspiciousness that is connected to the Hindu ideal of a married woman (the images of a docile, self-effacing, selfless woman) if she is not protected by her husband. They question a model that idealizes women when the model itself contributes to the demise of women's status. Both women's organizations and feminists agree that the problem is rooted in the sacred ideology of Hinduism. The purity of women, their adherence to the code of conduct of the male line, and the sacredness and purity of their actions all contribute to the maintenance of the caste system. Change in religion is slow, but what women activists are trying to do is make the public aware of and take measures to address the existing problem. Education and employment of girls is crucial for their safety. Shelter homes for widows and battered wives, homes for girls from destitute families to learn trades, and orphanages are growing in numbers. These varied activities are recognized by male and female scholars, the film industry (both documentary and popular films), playwrights, and novelists.

The Problem: Setting the Parameter to Study Indian Women

1. What is the Indian feminist or women's movement about? How can we understand and distinguish this system from the Western feminist movement?
Here the focus should be on defining cultural concepts and introducing ideas of the sacred, since the construction of gender in India is embedded in Hindu religious ideology. The teacher might first present Western notions of feminism and then try and understand the Indian notions of the same movement within the cultural context of India.

2. *Readings:* Dandekar 1986; Forbes 1981, 1982; Minault 1982; Misra 1979.

3. Show one of two films: *Home and the World,* by S. Ray, or *Devi,* also by S. Ray. The theme in the first film is the emergence of a married upper class woman from the secluded world of women *(purdah)* into the public arena and her attempts to understand the political independence movement. She falls in love with her husband's friend who is influential in her efforts to free herself. The film ends with her becoming a widow. The second film is described in the list of Indian films in this module. Both films help Western students focus on the problem of tradition and its imposition on and power over women and family. Both pictures also present students with an Indian depiction of a woman's world.

Women, Work, and Gender and the Dissolution of the Family

1. The significance of this theoretical topic helps the student put the above issues into perspective through a discussion of the family and women workers. It also assists the student conceptualize what these changes afflicting gender mean.

2. *Readings:* Andiappan 1980; Jacobson 1974; Lebra et al. 1984; Mazumdar 1979; Sharma 1980; Srinivas 1977, 1984; Vatuk 1972; Wadley and Jacobson 1986.

3. *Film: Mahanagar* by S. Ray on the problems of a woman worker in the city of Calcutta. The film is about a traditional family in Calcutta whose daughter-in-law has to find work outside the house because of economic necessity. She works during the day and takes care of the household chores by night. The film is about the conflicts and tensions that develop between a husband and wife as a result of the wife's growing independence resulting from a job outside the home. The film in a subtle way asks if there are any alternatives for women and if so what are the infrastructures for these options?

Contemporary Issues in India: The Gender Question

1. The discussion here should address the success or the failure of the Indian feminist and women's movements. The central issues for discussion are dowry deaths, education, and amniocentesis test, widowhood, female infanticide, and abortion. Here, the teacher can introduce any other contemporary Western women's concerns for comparative purposes.

2. *Readings:* Selection from Jain and Banerjee (1985) on different aspects of women in the labor force. Another useful reader is Ghadially (1988).

There are a few ethnographies about the condition of women in the work force not mentioned earlier in this module that might be useful as companion to the above readers, for example, Miller's (1980, 1981) excellent work on the endangered female sex records valuable demographic information on what women face today in terms of bride burning and shows that this phenomena is but one aspect of a larger problem. Also see Anita Desai's diary of her travels around India meeting and talking with women.

Women's Movement and the Absence of an Ideology

1. Have a discussion on the present feminist movement and the earlier, preindependence women's movements in India. Discuss the inherent contradictions between the feminist and the earlier nationalist women's movement. A few of the issues that can be addressed in this sections are: the role of the family and the state, the aims and goals of the government and its commitment to women.

2. *Readings:* Two excellent accounts of the history of the women's movement in India (Liddle and Rama 1986) or the account of a single movement in South India (Kaplan 1985) would be the best way to introduce this section. Another ethnography is the one by Chaki-Sircar 1984) on the question of working women and the argument she introduces of feminism. Along with this longer study, articles and works of Auer and Gross (1980), Borthwick (1984), Lessinger (1986), Vishwanth (1987), or selections from Kishwar and Vanita (1984).

3. *Films: No more Silent,* directed by Laurette Deschamps or *Sudesha,* directed by Deepa Dhanraj.

Indian Films that Could Be Used for Teaching on Gender Issues in India

Subha/Umbartha, by Jabar Patel
A married woman leaves her husband and child to go and work in a woman's shelter. She returns to find that her husband is ready to marry again. Her first action of leaving the house already breaks the code of behavior for a married woman.

Amma Ariyan, by John Abraham
A powerful film about the Kerela leftist movement that also portrays mothers and the relations to their sons. The mother theme in contemporary setting.

Paroma, by Aparna Sen (one of two women filmmakers in India).

Many Indian middle class intellectuals feel that the film has a misguided message. The film is about a dissatisfied married middle class woman who seeks freedom through sexual emancipation. The film had tremendous effect in Calcutta; men were especially critical of the film and some forbade their wives to see it.

Antarjoli Jatra, by Gautom Ghosh

Based on the novel by Kamol Majumdar, a film about a young girl being married to a very old man waiting to die on the banks of the Ganges. The "chandal" the untouchable and impure caste group that cremate the dead, refused to officiate and protested against the young bride being burned with her husband. The filmmaker instead depicts the beautiful love relations between the chandal and the girl. The film is an attack on Brahmanical traditions.

Tarong, by Kumar Sahni

A film that depicts the disintegration of a rich businessman's household. A laborer's wife forms the bridge between the owner and the laborers.

Phani Amma, by Prema Karnath

A woman widowed at an early age, spends her time in social work and helping other widows.

Rao Saab, by Vijay Mehta

Film about widow remarriage. This time against a colonial setting.

Duniya na maane, by Shantaram

A great classic. A young girl is married to an old man with grown children (her own age). She refuses to consummate the marriage yet she supports the old man to run the family and helps him to fulfill his role as a father. His inability to be a father and control his children was created after his marriage to the young girl. In turn he commits suicide in order to release his young wife but he leaves a confused girl who is seen as a widow even though she never even consummated the marriage.

Charulata, by S. Ray (The Lonely Wife)

Charulata is a married upper class woman who feels neglected by her journalist husband. Her husband's younger brother takes an interest in Charulata's artistic leanings. In the process, the elder brother's wife falls in love with her husband's brother, a troublesome affair in an extended household. The film is a sensitive portrayal of married women's lives and daily problems.

Devi (The Goddess), by S. Ray

The film represents rural life about 100 years ago. A young bride in her in-laws' house tends to the family's ancestral deity, Mother Goddess Kali. She shares the house with her widowed father-in-law, husband's brother, his wife and son. Her own husband is away studying in Calcutta. The father-in-law dreams that the goddess Kali is reincarnated in his daughter-in-law and he, along with the villagers and the priest begin to worship her as the Goddess. The film ends with the wife-goddess questioning the sacredness of the miracle.

Samaskara, by Anantamurti

A film about mortuary rites. It involves a village's dilemma about a low caste prostitute, her dead Brahmin lover and the pure priest whose decision to officiate the rituals brings him in close contact with impurity. The film uses the role of a prostitute to question ritual, purity, and sexuality in one's society.

India Cabaret, by Mira Nair
   A woman filmmaker shows the night life of a city, depicting strippers in a nightclub. The film touches on the question of inconsistencies of idealhood of women and yet shows the flashy side of the city and its abuses of women.

Dadi's Family
   A film of a grandmother in her extended household. She is portrayed as someone who manages the daily household chores amidst tensions, labor and being a "wife of a line" in contrast to a daughter of the "house."

No Longer Silent, by Laurette Deschamps
   Documentary film which exposes problems women are facing in India today. The film focuses on two activist women in New Delhi and through them addresses issues of bride burning, starvation, women's unemployment, women's health and more.

Munni (Little Girl): Childhood and Art in Methila
   A short and pleasant documentary about a little girl, Munni, among the Mithila, a community of artists. Through her eyes one sees the activities of her community, their art, preparations, and the finished work of older women artists.

References Cited

Abdu Lali, Sohaila
   1988   Rape in India: An Empirical Picture. *In* Women in Indian Society. R. Ghadially, ed. New Delhi: Sage Publications.
Allen, Michael, and S. N. Mukherjee, eds.
   1982   Women in India and Nepal. Canberra: Australian National University.
Anant, Suchitra
   1986   Women at Work in India: A Bibliography. New Delhi: Sage Publications.
Andiappan, P.
   1980   Woman and Work: A Comparative Study of Sex Discrimination in Employment in India and the U.S.A. Bombay: Somaiya.
Archer, William G.
   1984   Songs for the Bride: Wedding Rites of Rural India. New York: Columbia University Press.
Awasty, Indira
   1982   Rural Women of India: A Socio-Economic Profile of Jammu Women. New Delhi: D. K. Publishers.
Babb, Lawrence A.
   1970   Marriage and Male Violence. Ethnology 9:137–148.
   1975   The Divine Hierarchy: Popular Hinduism in Central India. New York: Columbia University Press.
   1988   Indigenous Feminism in a Modern Hindu Sect. *In* Women in Indian Society. R. Ghadially, ed. 1988. New Dehli: Sage.
Bailey, F. G.
   1964   Caste and the Economic Frontier. Bombay: Oxford University Press.
   1966   Tribe, Caste and Nation. Manchester: Manchester University Press.

Barnett, S.
    1976   Coconuts and Gold. Contributions to Indian Sociology (N.S.) 10:133–156.
Berreman, Gerald D.
    1974   Hindus of the Himalayas: Ethnography and Change. Berkeley: University of California Press.
Beteille, Andre
    1965   Caste, Class and Power. Berkeley: University of California Press.
Bhatt, E.
    1981   SEWA Women Break Free from Parent Body. Manushi 2(2):13–15.
Borthwick, M.
    1984   The Changing Role of Women in Bengal. Princeton: Princeton University Press.
Carter, T.
    1982   Hierarchy and the Concept of the Person in Western India. *In* Concepts of Person: Kinship,
            Caste and Marriage in India. A. Ostor, L. Fruzzetti, and S. Barnett, eds. Pp. 118–142. Cambridge:
            Harvard University Press.
Chaki-Sircar, Manjusri
    1984   Feminism in a Traditional Society: Women of the Manipur Valley. New Delhi: Vikas Pub-
            lishing House.
Dandekar, Hemalata
    1986   Indian Women's Development: Four Lenses. South Asia Bulletins, (1), Spring: 25–29.
Das, Veena
    1982   Structure and Cognition: Aspects of Hindu Caste and Ritual. New Delhi: Oxford University
            Press.
David, K.
    1973   Until Marriage Do Us Part: A Cultural Account of Jaffna Tamil Categories for Kinsman. Man
            8:521–535.
Dhruvarajan, V.
    1988   Hindu Woman and the Power of Ideology. South Hadley, Mass.: Bergin & Garvey.
Dube, Leela, Eleanor Leacock, and Shirley Ardener, eds.
    1986   Visibility and Power: Essays on Women in Society and Development. New Dehli: Oxford
            University Press.
Dumont, Louis
    1957   Hierarchy and Marriage Alliance in South Indian Kinship. Occasional Paper 12. London:
            Royal Anthropological Institute of Great Britain.
    1959   Pure and Impure. Contributions to Indian Sociology 3:8–39.
    1958   A. M. Hocart on Caste—Religion and Power. Contributions to Indian Sociology 11:45–63.
    1966   Fundamental Problem in the Sociology of Caste. Contributions to Indian Sociology 9:17–37.
    1970   Homo Hierarchicus. Mark Salisbury, trans. Chicago: University of Chicago Press.
Everett, J. Matson
    1981   Women and Social Change in India. New Delhi: Heritage Publishers.
Forbes, Geraldine
    1981   The Indian Women's Movement: A Struggle for Women's Rights of National Liberation? *In*
            G. Minault, ed. The Extended Family: Women and Political Participation in India and Pakistan.
            New Delhi: Canakya Publications.
    1982   Caged Tigers: First Wave Feminists in India. Women's Studies International Forum 5(6):525–
            536.
Fruzzetti, Lina
    1981   Purer than Pure, or the Ritualization of Women's Domain. Journal of the Indian Anthropo-
            logical Society 16:11–18.
    1982   The Gift of the Virgin. New Brunswick: Rutgers University Press.
    1984   Kinship and Ritual in Bengal: Anthropological Essays. New Delhi: South Asian Publisher Pvt.
            Ltd.
Fruzzetti, Lina, and Akos Ostor
    1976   Seed and Earth: A Cultural Analysis of Kinship in a Bengali Town. Contributions to Indian
            Sociology (N.S.) 10:97–132.

Ghadially, R., ed.
  1988   Women in Indian Society. New Delhi: Sage Publications.
Goody, J., and S. J. Tambiah
  1973   Bride Wealth and Dowry. Cambridge: Cambridge University Press.
Gough, Kathleen
  1952   Incest Prohibitions and Rules of Exogamy in Three Matrilineal Groups of Malabar Coast. Internal Archives of Ethnography, Vol. 46, No. I.
  1955   Female Initiation Rites on the Malabar Coast. Journal of the Royal Anthropological Institute 85:45–80.
  1959   The Nayars and the Definition of Marriage. Journal of the Royal Anthropological Institute Vol. 89:523–534.
Gupta, A. R.
  1982   Women in Hindu Society. New Delhi: Jyotsma Prakashan.
Gupta, Giri Raj
  1974   Marriage, Religion and Society. New York: Wiley.
Hate, Chandrakala Anandrao
  1969   Changing Status of Women in Post Independence India. New York: Paragon Book.
Jacobson, Dorianne
  1974   The Women of North and Central India: Goddesses and Wives. *In* Many Sisters: Women in Cross Cultural Perspective. C. J. Matthiasson, ed. Pp. 99–177. New York: Free Press.
Jain, Devaki
  1975   Indian Women. New Delhi: Government of India.
  1980   Women's Quest for Power: Five Indian Case Studies. Ghaziabad: Vikas.
Jain, Devaki, and Nirmala Banerjee, eds.
  1985   Tyranny of the Household. New Delhi: Shakhti Books.
Jung, Anees
  1987   Unveiling India: A Woman's Journey. New Delhi: Penguin Books.
Kapadia, K. M.
  1966   Marriage and Family in India. 3d ed. Madras: Oxford University Press.
Kaplan, Patricia
  1985   Class and Gender in India: Women and Their Organizations in a South Indian City. London: Tavistock Publications.
Kapur, P.
  1970   Marriage and the Working Woman in India. New Delhi: Vikas Publishing.
  1974   The Changing Status of the Working Woman in India. New Delhi: Vikas Publishing.
Khan, Mimtaz Ali
  1979   Status of Rural Women in India: A Study of Karnataka. New Delhi: Uppal.
Khan, M. S., and R. Roy
  1984   Death Dowry. Indian Journal of Social Work 45:303–307.
Khare, R. S.
  1976   The Hindu Hearth and Home. Durham: North Carolina Academic Press.
Kishwar, Madhu, and R. Vanita, eds.
  1984   In Search of Answers: Indian Women's Voices from Manushi. London: Zed Books.
Kolenda, P.
  1968   Region, Caste and Family Structure: A Comparative Study of Indian "Joint" Family. *In* Structure and Change in Indian Society. M. Singer and B. Cohn, eds. Pp. 339–396. Chicago: Aldine.
  1982a   Caste, Cult and Hierarchy. Delhi: Manohar.
  1982b   Widowhood among "Untouchable" Chuhras. *In* Concepts of Person: Kinship, Caste and Marriage in India. A. Ostor, L. Fruzzetti, and S. Barnett, eds. Cambridge: Harvard University Press.
Krygier, Jocelyn
  1982   Caste and Female Pollution. *In* Women in India and Nepal. Michael Allen and S. N. Mukherjee, eds. Pp. 76–104. Canberra: Australian National University.

Lalitha Devi, V.
    1982   Status and Employment of Women in India. New Delhi: B. R. Publishing Corp.
Lebra, Joyce, Joy Paulson, and Jana Everett
    1984   Women and Work in India: Continuity and Change. New Delhi: Promila.
Lessinger, Johanna
    1986   Work and Modesty: The Dilemma of Women Market Traders in South India. Feminist Studies
        12(3):581–600.
Liddle, Joanna, and Joshi Rama
    1986   Daughters of Independence: Gender, Caste and Class in India. London: Zed Books Ltd.
Madan, T. N.
    1982   The Ideology of the Householder among the Kashmiri. *In* Concepts of Person: Kinship, Caste
        and Marriage in India. A. Ostor, L. Fruzzetti, and S. Barnett, eds. Pp. 99–117. Cambridge: Har-
        vard University Press.
    1987   Non-Renunciation: Themes and Interpretations of Hindu Culture. New Delhi: Oxford Uni-
        versity Press.
Mandelbaum, David
    1967   Society in India, Continuity and Change, Vol. I. Berkeley: University of California Press.
Mandelbaum, David
    1970   Society in India, Continuity and Change, Vol. II. Berkeley: University of California Press.
Marglin, Frederique Apffel
    1985   Wives of the God-King: The Rituals of the Devadasis of Puri. New Delhi: Oxford University
        Press.
Marriott, McKim
    1968a   Multiple Reference in Indian Caste Systems. *In* Social Mobility in the Caste System in India.
        James Siverberg, ed. Pp. 103–114. Paris: The Hague/Mouton.
    1968b   Caste Ranking and Food Transaction: A Matrix Analysis. *In* Structure and Change in Indian
        Society. M. Singer and B. S. Cohn, eds. Pp. 133–171. Chicago.
Mathur, K. S.
    1964   Caste and Ritual in a Malwa Village. Calcutta: Asia Publishing.
Mayer, A.
    1960   Caste and Kinship in Central India. London: Routledge.
Mazumdar, Vina, ed.
    1979   Symbols of Power: Studies on the Political Status of Women in India. Bombay: Allied Pub-
        lishers.
Mencher, Joan
    1972   Continuity and Change in an Ex-Untouchable Community of South India, *In* The Untoucha-
        bles in Contemporary India. J. Michael Mahar, ed. Pp. 37–56. Tuscon: University of Arizona
        Press.
    1974   The Caste System Upside Down, or the Not-So-Mysterious East. Current Anthropology
        15:469–493.
Mies, Maria
    1983   The Lace Makers of Narsapur: Indian Housewives Produce for the World Market. London:
        Zed Press.
    1986   Indian Women in Subsistence and Agriculture Labor. Geneva: International Labor Office.
Miller, Barbara
    1980   Female Neglect and the Costs of Marriage in India. Contributions of Indian Sociology
        14(1):95, 129.
    1981   The Endangered Sex: Neglect of Female Children in Rural North India. Ithaca: Cornell Uni-
        versity Press.
Minault, G.
    1982   From Purdah to Politics: The Social Feminism of the All India Women's Organization. *In*
        Separate Worlds: Studies of Purdah in South Asia. Hanna Papenek, and Gail Minault, eds. Pp.
        245–261. Delhi: Chanakya Publications.

Minault, Gail, ed.
  1981   The Extended Family: Women and Political Participation in India and Pakistan. Columbia: South Asia Books.
Misra, T.
  1986   Feminism in a Traditional Society? Economic and Political Weekly 21(43):54–56.
Mitra, A.
  1979   The Status of Women: Literacy and Employment. New Delhi: ICSSR—Programme of Women's Studies II.
Moffatt, Michael
  1979   An Untouchable Community in South India: Structure and Consensus. Princeton: Princeton University Press.
Nandy, Ashis
  1988   Women versus Womanliness in India: An Essay in Social and Political Psychology. *In* Women in Indian Society. R. Ghadially, ed. Pp. 69–80. New Delhi: Sage.
Ostor, Akos
  1980   The Play of Gods: Locality, Ideology Structure, and Time in the Festivals of a Bengali Town. Chicago: University of Chicago Press.
Ostor, A., L. Fruzzetti, and S. Barnett
  1982   Concepts of Person: Kinship, Caste and Marriage in India. Cambridge: Harvard University Press.
Papanek, H., and G. Minault
  1982   Separate Worlds: Studies of Purdah in South Asia. New Delhi: Chanakya Publications.
Paul, Madan C.
  1986   Dowry and Position of Women in India: A Study of Delhi Metropolis. New Delhi: Inter Indian Publishers.
Pocock, David
  1957a   Inclusion and Exclusion: A Process in the Caste System in Gujerat. Southwestern Journal of Anthropology 13:19–31.
  1957b   Hierarchy and Marriage Alliance in South Indian Kinship. Occasional Paper 12. London: Royal Anthropological Institute of Great Britain.
  1971   Kanbi and Patidar: A Study of the Patidar Community in Gujarat. London: Oxford University Press.
Rao, V. V. P., and V. N. Rao
  1988   Sex Role Attitudes of College Students in India. *In* Women in Indian Society. R. Ghadially, ed. Pp. 109–123. New Delhi: Sage Publications.
Roy, Manisha
  1975   Bengali Women. Chicago: University of Chicago Press.
Schneider, David
  1968   American Kinship: A Cultural Account. Englewood Cliffs, N.J.: Prentice-Hall.
Shah, A. M.
  1974   The Household Dimension of the Family in India. Berkeley: University of California Press.
Sharma, Ursula
  1980   Women, Work, and Property in North-West India. Honolulu: University of Hawaii Press.
Singer, Milton
  1968   The Indian Joint Family in Modern Industry. *In* Structure and Change in Indian Society. M. Singer and B. S. Cohn, eds. Pp. 423–452. New York: Wenner-Gren Foundation for Anthropological Research.
  1972   When a Great Tradition Modernizes: An Anthropological Approach to Indian Civilization. New York: Praeger.
Srinivas, M. N.
  1965   Religion and Society Among the Corps of South India. Oxford: Clarendon Press.
  1977   The Changing Position of Women in India. Man 12(3):221–238.
  1984   Some Reflections on Dowry. New Delhi: Oxford University Press.

Stevenson, H. N. C.
    1954   Status Evaluation in the Hindu Caste Systems. Journal of the Royal Anthropological Institute
        84:45–65.
Stutchbury, Elizabeth Leigh
    1982   Blood, Fire, and Mediation: Human Sacrifice and Widow Burning in Nineteenth Century In-
        dia. *In* Women in Indian and Nepal. Michael Allen, and S. N. Mukerjee, eds. Pp. 21–75. Canberra:
        Australian National University.
Tambiah, S.
    1973   Dowry, Bride Wealth and the Property Rights of Women in South Asia. *In* Bride Wealth and
        Dowry. J. Goody and S. J. Tambiah, eds. Pp. 59–169. Cambridge: Cambridge University Press.
Van der Veen, Klass
    1972   I Give Thee my Daughter: A Study of Marriage and Hierarchy among the Analvil Brahmans
        of S. Gujarat. Assen: Van Gorcum.
Vatuk, Sylvia
    1969   A Structural Analysis of the Hindu Kinship Terminology. Contributions to Indian Sociology
        (n.s.) 3:94–115.
    1972   Kinship and Urbanization: White-Collar Migrants in North India. Berkeley: University of Cal-
        ifornia Press.
Vishwanath, L. S.
    1987   Women's Development through Voluntary Effort: Some Issues and Approaches. Indian Jour-
        nal of Social Work 47(3).
Wadley, Susan S.
    1975   Power in the Concept and Structure of Karim Pur Religion. University of Chicago Studies in
        Anthropology: Series in Social, Cultural and Linguistic Anthropology, No. 2. Chicago: Depart-
        ment of Anthropology, University of Chicago.
    1980   Hindu Women's Family and Household Rites in a North Indian Village. Unspoken Worlds:
        Women's Religious Lives in non-Western Cultures. S. Falk, N. Auer, and R. M. Gross, eds. Pp.
        94–109. New York: Harper & Row.
Wadley, Susan S., and D. Jacobson
    1986   Women in India: Two Perspectives. Delhi: Manohar Publications.
Yalman, Nur
    1963   On the Purity of Women in the Castes of Ceylon and Malabar. Journal of Royal Anthropo-
        logical Institute 93:25–58.
    1967   Under the Boo Tree: Studies of Caste, Kinship and Marriage in the Interior of Ceylon. Berke-
        ley: University of California Press.

Two source texts:
Dasgupta, K., ed.
    1976   Women on the Indian Scene: An Annotated Bibliography. New Delhi: Abhirav.
Jahai, Jhirnath
    1985   Women in Changing Society: A Bibliographical Study. Delhi: Mittal Publications.

Annotated Bibliography

Allen, M., and S. N. Mukherjee
    1982   Women in India and Nepal. Canberra: Australian National University.

        A series of articles covering historical and anthropological concerns of women in the two countries.
The articles contrast and compare the women; one of those worthwhile edited volumes on women's
issues.

Babb, Lawrence A.
    1975   The Divine Hierarchy; Popular Hinduism in Central India. New York: Columbia University
        Press.

A general ethnography of a village in India. The author describes the folk as well as Brahmanic festivals. The chapters on life-cycle rites and divine hierarchy does touch on women's (feminine) role in society. A good introductory book on Indian Hindu society.

Banerjee, Nirmala
1985   Women Workers in the Unorganized Sector: The Calcutta Experience. London: Sangam Books Ltd.

The theme of the book is the lower class women in the unorganized sectors of Calcutta. Few books deal with the unorganized sectors and this is an excellent documentation of Calcutta's women workers.

Bhattacharyya, Narendra Nath
1975   Ancient Indian Rituals and Their Social Contents. Delhi: Manohar Book Service.

A book about women's rituals and participation. Women's symbolic and cultural representation are exhibited and played out in the construction of gender.

Borthwick, M.
1984   The Changing Role of Women in Bengal. Princeton: Princeton University Press.

An excellent in-depth historical account of 19th-century women, their coming "out" in public, their fight and the resultant women's movement.

Chaki-Sircar, Manjusri
1984   Feminism in a Traditional Society: Women of the Manipur Valley. New Delhi: Vikas Publishing House.

The author investigates North-east Indian women in a study of a matrilineal group undergoing change. The author equates feminism with matrilineality but fails to demonstrate that clearly. Her main issue in the book is the independence of working women of Manipur, although their social organization does not portray the freedom for women.

Custer, Peter
1986   Women's Role in the Tabhaga Movement. Manushi 6(2):28–33.

A short sociohistorical paper on Bimala Maji role in the Tebhaga movement in the 1940s. The Tebhaga peasant uprising movement was an example of rural resistance and the important political role that women played.

Dhruvarajan, V.
1988   Hindu Women and the Power of Ideology. South Hadley, Mass.: Bergin & Garvey.

A new study which challenges religious and cultural perceptions of Hindu women. She raises issues about women's subjugation in light of powerful patriarchal system.

Dube, Leela, Eleanor Leacock, and Shirley Ardener, eds.
1986   Visibility and Power: Essays on Women in Society and Development. New Delhi: Oxford University Press.

A series of essays organized around the theme of women's reproductive power and the sexual division of labor. The biological and sociocultural aspects of women are examined in light of economic development and its impact on gender relations.

Everett, Jana
1981   Approaches to "Women in Question" in India: From Materialism to Mobilization. Women's Studies International Quarterly 4(2):169–78.

This is a report that looks at the consequences of modernization on women's associations, women and militancy, and the feminist movement in India.

Forbes, Geraldine H.
    1982   Caged Tigers: First Wave Feminists in India. Women's Studies International Forum 5(6):525–
        536.

    Rise of the Indian feminist movement looked at historically. Women's organization at the turn of
the century marks the main theme of the paper.

Freeman, James M.
    1980   The Ladies of Lord Krishna: Rituals of Middle-Aged Women in Eastern-India. *In* Unspoken
        Worlds: Women's Religious Lives in Non-Western Cultures. Falk, S., Nancy Auer and Rita M.
        Gross, eds. Pp. 110–126. New York: Harper & Row.

    Analysis of Krishna and the lure of older women to his worship.

Fruzzetti, Lina, and A. Ostor
    1982   Kinship and Ritual. New Delhi: South Asia Publishers.

    Analysis of birth rituals and gender construction, kinship issues in an Indian rural town.

Fruzzetti, Lina
    1982   The Gift of the Virgin. New Brunswick: Rutgers University Press.

    Analysis of Hindu women's marriage rituals and develops an argument for the cultural construction
of gender. The book deals with women's symbolism and the use of these symbols to reconstruct their
everyday reality.

Ghadially, Rehana, ed.
    1988   Women in Indian Society. New Delhi: Sage Publications.

    A collection of essays ranging from the sacred or cultural ideals of femaleness to stereotyping of
women. The articles on women and violence, women and the media add a new dimension to the study
of Indian women. The last essay raises the question of awareness, women's consciousness in modern
India and what the implications might be for culture.

Gough, K.
    1955   Female Initiation Rites on the Malabar Coast. Journal of the Royal Anthropological Institute
        85:45–80.

    A seminal article on matrilineal women and the rituals of menstruation. The article raises matrili-
neal descent questions, marriage and women's roles and an excellent account of initiation rites.

Gupta, D. P.
    1970   Legalization of Abortion in India. Eastern Anthropologist 32(1):55–57.

    Results of the survey on attitudes toward abortion and its significant impact on women and family.

Inden, Ronald B., and Ralph Nicholas
    1972   A Cultural Analysis of Bengali Kinship. *In* Prelude to Crisis: Bengal and Bengal Studies in
        1970. Peter J. Bertocci, ed. Pp. 91–97. Michigan State University Studies Series, East Lansing.

    An in-depth article relating to constructing a person (man/woman).

Harper, E. B.
    1964   Ritual Pollution as an Integrator of Caste and Religion. *In* Religion in South Asia. E. B. Har-
        per, ed. Pp. 151–197. Berkeley: University of California Press.

An analysis of rituals and ways that these could remove pollution. The articles point to women's potential pollutants.

Jacobson, Dorianne
  1982 Studying the Changing Roles of Women in Rural India. *Signs* 8(1):132–137.

This is a brief account of rural women, their internal conflict and the seclusion of females through the practice of *purdah*. It is a personable account by a woman anthropologist.

Jacobson, Dorianne
  1980 Golden Handprints and Red-Painted Feet: Hindu Childbirth Rituals in Central India. *In* Unspoken Worlds: Women's Religious Lives in Non-Western Cultures. S. Falk, Nancy Auer, and Rita M. Gross, eds. Pp. 71–93. New York: Harper & Row.

Household and life-cycle rites portray the varied articles in the book. Some of the articles, especially Jacobson, speak to that issue.

Jacobson, D.
  1974 The Women of North and Central India: Goddesses and Wives. *In* Many Sisters: Women in Cross-Cultural Perspective. C. J. Matthiasson, ed. Pp. 99–177. New York: Free Press.

From an edited volume, articles looking at women cross-culturally, trying to arrive at general theory and common factors which afflict women.

Jain, Devaki, ed.
  1975 Indian Women. New Delhi: Publications Division, Ministry of Information and Broadcasting, Government of India.

A series of articles on broad general topics of women in private and public domain.

Jain, Devaki, and N. Banerjee, eds.
  1985 Tyranny of the Household: Investigative Essays on Women's Work. New Delhi: Shakti Books.

An excellent volume on a series of articles that analyze the culture of gender through household activities. The articles compare the emerging woman worker to her traditional roles. The basis for the analysis in the essay is done by looking at changes that are taking place in relation to what the alternatives are for women in contemporary India.

Kaimal, Palma, and Diane Jones
  1984 Women in the Arts. *In* Women and Work in India. Joyce Lebra, Joy Paulson, and Jana Everett, eds. New Delhi: Promilla and Co.

The book is a series of articles looking at the concept of women and work. The question of women in the labor force for a wage instead of fulfilling the cultural expectation, is the analysis put forward by some of the authors.

Kaplan, Patricia
  1985 Class and Gender in India: Women and Their Organizations in a South Indian City. London: Tavistock Publications.

An excellent study of women's organizations in South India. The book analyzes women's social work, the culture of working women and housewife. Voluntary association is a midway activity which is culturally accepted for women as a form of unpaid ''work.''

Kishwar, Madhu
  1986 Dowry: To Ensure Her Happiness or to Disinherit Her. Manushi 6(4):2–13.

Article by one of the prominent Indian women. The issue of dowry and its role to inheritance and family structure in terms of unequal distribution of sexual power is the basis of the paper. She concludes that women's status remains low, if dowry practices persist.

Kishwar, M., and R. Vanita, eds.
   1984   In Search of Answers: Indian Women's Voices from Manushi. London: Zed Books.

A series of articles addressing the issue of women, work, and the role of culture. The articles take a feminist approach to the dilemmas and contradictions that afflict women today.

Lebra-Chapman, Joyce
   1986   The Rani of Jhansi: A Study in Female Heroism in India. Honolulu: University of Hawaii Press.

The book is about the legendary Rani Lakshmibai of Jhansi and the part she played in the Great Rebellion of 1857. Her story is told through oral tradition, songs, poetry, and enactment of plays. She is considered to be one of India's heroines. Her fight against the British colonial rule of 1857–58 marks an important phase in gender relations to India's politics. A good historical account of the Rani.

Lessinger, Johanna
   1986   Work and Modesty: The Dilemma of Women Market Traders in South India. Feminist Studies 12(3):581–600.

The petty traders in S. India and the inappropriateness of the work for the women. The cultural conflict between "good" women who tend to the house and "earning" women who work publicly is addressed in the article.

Liddle, Joanna, and Joshi Rama
   1986   Daughters of Independence: Gender, Caste and Class in India. London: Zed Books Ltd.

An account of the history of the women's movement, politically and socially. The theme of the book is the role and relationships between gender and class. The book describes the explorations of upper-class women's activities in the women's movement.

Madan, T. N.
   1987   Non-Renunciation: Themes and Interpretations of Hindu Culture. New Delhi: Oxford University Press.

An excellent recent publication on important issues such as domesticity and detachment, auspiciousness and purity and eroticism. Madan's treatment especially of the first three chapters is useful for an introductory course on gender in India.

Mann, K.
   1987   Tribal Women in a Changing Society. New Delhi: Mittahl.

Tribal women are often neglected in the study of Indian women. This volume examines the Bhil women and the changes that they face as a result of contact with Hinduism and sanskritization.

Marglin, Frederique Apffel
   1985   Wives of the God-King: The Rituals of the Devadasis of Puri. New Delhi: Oxford University Press.

The study is about Devadasis, girls offered to Lord Jagannatha, who are wedded to the god and temple priests. Devadasis devote their life to ritual activities around the Temple of Puri. The book analyzes the relationship between power and ritual purity and the role that women play.

Mies, Maria
    1986   Indian Women in Subsistence and Agriculture Labor. Geneva: International Labor Office.

The impact of agriculture modernization on women is the major subject of the book. Three rural Indian villages are represented in the study and used to document the crucial part which women perform on the farms.

Mies, Maria
    1983   The Lace Makers of Narsapur: Indian Housewives Produce for the World Market. London: Zed Press.

An ethnographic description of women's rural occupation through the handicraft of lace making. These women are seen as supplementing their husband's income. A moving account of the dilemmas which women face, women's exploitation by the traders and women's double work burden is the underlying theme of the book.

Miller, B.
    1981   The Endangered Sex: Neglect of Female Children in Rural North India. Ithaca: Cornell University Press.

The study documents early child negligence because of their sex. Sex discrimination and infanticide by rural women or girls is the topic of the book.

Miller, Barbara
    1980   Female Neglect and the Costs of Marriage in India. Contributions of Indian Sociology 14(1):95, 129.

Issues of gender differences and ways that it manifests itself in marriage is the theme of this excellent paper. Marriage and the demand of dowry by males creates pressure which leads to the high mortality rate of girls.

Mitra, A.
    1979   The Status of Women: Literacy and Employment. Programme of Women's Studies (11). New Delhi: Allied Publishers.

The book addresses the rise of women literacy and questions elitist form of education for rural India.

Mitra, A.
    1979   The Status of Women: Household and Non-household Economic Activity. Bombay: Allied Publisher.

Women's status is measured through their economic earnings.

Mukherjee, Prabhati
    1983   The Image of Women in Hinduism. Women's International Forum 6(4):379.

A brief description of religion and women's roles, the ideal model of women and issues of contemporary Indian legislation.

Nicholas, R.
    1981   The Goddess Sitala and Epidemic Smallpox in Bengal. Journal of Asian Studies 41:21–44.

A good descriptive article on the goddess of small pox, the way that women approach the goddess for cure and assistance. Good article for use in a course on rituals and gender in India.

Searle-Chatterjee, Mary
    1981   Reversible Sex Roles: The Special Case of Benares Sweepers. New York: Pergamon Press.

Stevenson, H. N. C.
    1954   Status Evaluation in the Hindu Caste Systems. Journal of the Royal Anthropological Institute
            84:45–65.

    Excellent article which raises questions of purity/pollution, women's pollution, internal versus ex-
ternal pollution of women.

Stutchbury, Elizabeth Leigh
    1982   Blood, Fire, and Mediation: Human Sacrifice and Widow Burning in Nineteenth Century In-
            dia. *In* Women in India and Nepal. Michael Allen and S. N. Mukherjee, eds. Pp. 21–75. Canberra:
            Australian National University.

    A rich descriptive and analytical article on *sati* and human sacrifice, showing women's status within
the sacred realm.

Van der Veen, Klass
    1972   I Give Thee My Daughter: A Study of Marriage and Hierarchy among the Anavil Brahmans
            of S. Gujarat. Assen: Van Gorcum.

    An ethnography of a high caste community, their elaborate marriage exchanges and the issues of
hierarchy. The author is too preoccupied with explaining hierarchy and hypergamy and misses explaining what the marriage rites achieve in terms of status for women. Nonetheless the book has very interesting sections of marriage discussions and exchanges of women between male descent lines.

Vishwanath, L. S.
    1987   Women's Development through Voluntary Effort: Some Issues and Approaches. Indian Jour-
            nal of Social Work 47(3).

    Paper that discusses ways to organize poor women's voluntary work. Introducing issues of health
care and income generating activities to the unorganized poor women.

Wadley, Susan S.
    1980   Hindu Women's Family and Household Rites in a North Indian Village. *In* Unspoken Worlds:
            Women's Religious Lives in non-Western Cultures. S. Falk, Nancy Auer, Rita M. Gross, and S.
            Falk, eds. Pp. 94–104. New York: Harper & Row.

    Rites which take place at home and are performed by women make up the core of this article.

Wadley, Susan S., and D. Jacobson
    1986   Women in India: Two Perspectives. New Delhi: Manohar Publications.

    The two authors' papers on Indian women which analyze the question of status control of sexuality
and behavior, tradition and religious prescriptions. Their main concern is an understanding of what constitutes sacred women and ideal wife. Jacobson's article is a good descriptive study of women in rural
India.

Wadley, S. S.
    1975   Power in the Concept and Structure of Karim Pur Religion. The University of Chicago Studies
            in Anthropology. Series in Social, Cultural and Linguistic Anthropology, No. 2. Chicago: De-
            partment of Anthropology, University of Chicago.

    A study and exploration of women's rites through special recitations accompanying the rituals.

Wulff, Donna Marie

1985   Images and Roles of Women in Bengali Vaisnava padavali kirtan. *In* Women, Religion and Social Change. Yvonne Yazbeck Haddad and Ellison Banks Findly, eds. Pp. 217–245. Albany: State University of New York Press.

Role of women's participation in religious devotional matters. Change of women's activities and ideas relating to the scared.

12

Center, Periphery, and Hierarchy: Gender in Southeast Asia

Aihwa Ong
University of California, Berkeley

Gender Systems in Southeast Asia

Compared to other parts of the world, Southeast Asian cultures are distinguished by the relatively high position of women. Distinctive cultural features that emphasize complementarity rather than opposition, and authority based on rank rather than gender, challenge our Western ways of thinking about gender inequality. Moreover, the reworkings of these cultural features in the process of social change—the Green Revolution, employment of women in transnational factories, tourist industry, and socialist revolution—provide rich material for theorizing about gender construction, power, and cultural difference.

"Southeast Asia" generally refers to ten countries: Vietnam, Laos, Kampuchea (Cambodia), Thailand, and Burma on the mainland, and Malaysia, Singapore, Brunei, Indonesia, and the Philippines in the insular half. It is a culturally diverse and densely populated region (over 200 million in 1980). Situated at the crossroads of the world's major civilizations, the region shares common characteristics in ecosystems, forms of livelihood, religions, languages, and the reception of foreign influences. This "syncretic" tradition of melding transcultural influences (Buddhism, Hinduism, Islam) with local animist beliefs and practices is evident in everyday life. For instance, Islam adopted since the 15th century, has coexisted with women's active participation in economic and social affairs (Reid 1988, chapter 4). The impact of Western colonialism has had a more diverse effect on women's status.

The interests of Western powers have accounted for our uneven anthropological knowledge about the region. Before the Second World War, British anthropologists conducted research in colonial territories (Burma, Malaya, Singapore). The postwar emergence of American anthropology reflected Western promotion of "economic development" in peasant societies worldwide. In the late 1950s, the Massachusetts Institute of Technology set up the "Mudjokuto Project" in Java, while Cornell University sent its own group to study Thai peasant society. These anthropologists blazed the trail for fieldwork in rural communities in Indonesia, Malaysia, Thailand, and the Philippines. The isolation of Burma and the Indochina conflict closed the door to sustained research in those countries. Such uneven coverage of the region is reflected in the scholarship on gender.

Southeast Asian specialists have long been struck by the relatively high status of women vis-à-vis men, whether among slash-and-burn groups (e.g., Freeman 1970; Leach 1954), wet-rice peasants (Swift 1963), or traders and urban migrants (Djamour 1965). Their "baseline" of comparison seemed to be the gender-stratified systems of East and South Asian societies and European and North American societies. Anthropologists sought to explain this "favorable sexual equality" in bilateral social organization, the sexual division of labor, and weak state control (Burling 1965; Hanks and Hanks 1963; Winzeler 1983).

In the island world, male and female are considered to be descended from the same source. Thus brother-sister, husband-wife pairs, and twins are widely viewed as complementary halves (see, for example, Boon [in press]; Sanday [in press]). This customary *(adat)* emphasis on unity and complementarity in Malay and Indonesian societies modifies the patrilineal bias of Islam. Parents favor sons and daughters equally, rather than preferring sons as in societies that require the payment of dowry (H. Geertz 1961; Swift 1963). Parents often bypass Islamic inheritance laws, which award sons full shares and daughters half-shares. Following *adat*, parents try to bequeath daughters full shares, or favor them over sons in awarding choice holdings (Banks 1983:137–138; Kessler 1977). In mainland Buddhist societies, women also inherit padi fields, houses, and in Burma, agricultural implements (Ebihara 1977; Potter 1977; Spiro 1977).

Marriage customs throw further light on the favorable position of women vis-à-vis men. Malay grooms send bridal gifts and wedding expenses to the bride's parents, and not vice versa as in dowry systems (Banks 1983; Djamour 1965). In mainland peasant societies, for example, the groom also provides bride service (Ebihara 1974; Ngo 1974; Potter 1977). The emphasis on bilateral relations in many communities is carried over to the equitable partition of marital property after divorce. Women usually retain custody of the children (Djamour 1965; H. Geertz 1961; Spiro 1977). In most cases, incompatibility is sufficient grounds for divorce. In Islamic societies, only the husband has the right to pronounce divorce, but a disaffected wife can initiate divorce through a religious judge. In non-Islamic societies like Burma, women initiate divorce proceedings more often than husbands (Spiro 1977:287–288). Compared to Chinese and Indian societies then, divorce is relatively easy to obtain in Southeast Asia. There is usually no disgrace attached to a divorced woman, and she is often viewed as a desirable marriage partner, even by younger men.

Marriages often suffer because of conflict between loyalty to spouse and loyalty to parents (Spiro 1977:277–278). This expresses the tension between the complementarity of male and female and emphasis on seniority/age over gender. In Malay-Indonesian language (Bahasa), for example, seniority, not gender difference, is consistently marked. Authority accrues to persons because of seniority, or rank, not gender. In everyday life, authority is defined according to age-sex categories; for example, unmarried Malay women and men are referred to as "unripe" (i.e., immature persons lacking intellectual capability). However, Islamic influence is seen in the close monitoring of single women (virgins) but not young men. In contrast, married women throughout the region participate actively in economic and social activities. After marriage, the young couple tend to practice ambilocal residence for a short period. They eventually set up a separate household, often near the woman's parents' home. A youngest daughter who takes care of her aged parents stands to inherit the family house.

Muslim women in Southeast Asia contradict the picture that Islam deprives women of economic power and confines them to a "private" sphere. In Kelantan, women handle household money and their own earnings. Unveiled, they have traditionally engaged in rice farming and petty trading. Clive Kessler notes that among the poor fisherfolk, men's dependence on conjugal cooperation for household needs "militates against any marked subordination of women to men" (1977:304). Secondly, women inherit land, which enables them to maintain independent households in polygamous unions and after divorce. Because of their active roles in earning a livelihood, Islamic inheritance and marriage laws have less adverse effects on them, and may even work to their advantage in combining the status of wife with independent householding (Firth 1966).

Similarly, in mainland societies, women help support their families, control the household budget, enjoy freedom of movement, and engage in petty trade (Ebihara 1974; Potter 1977; Pelzer-White 1987). However, in Thailand, Buddhist notions of gender difference stress female inferiority despite the widespread participation of women in all levels of the economy (Khin Thitsa 1980; Kirsh 1983). In pre-revolutionary Vietnam, Confucianism adopted by the upper-class subordinated women, whereas among the peasantry, husband-wife equality was celebrated (Ngo 1974).

It is, however, women's role as mothers that gives them critical influence over the immediate family and in fostering interhousehold relations. Hildred Geertz (1961) uses the term *matrifocality* to describe the influence of the Javanese mother in everyday life. The significance of maternal influence and kin has also been noted among urban Malays (Djamour 1965) and in matrilineal societies. Nancy Tanner (1974) maintains that in Javanese, Atjehnese, and Minankabau societies, the mother-child bond seems culturally valued over the conjugal tie. The mother is "structurally central" in that she has some control over the kin unit's economic resources and is critically involved in kin-related decision-making process.

In many societies (organized according to bilateral or matrilineal principles), women's influence is further strengthened by the coresidence or residential propinquity of kinswomen. Residential clusters of kinswomen increase female solidarity in their communities (Ebihara 1977; Jayawardena 1977; Potter 1977; Siegel 1969; Tanner 1974). Matrifocality and female residential propinquity are among the most overt features which indicate that throughout the region it is not possible to distinguish women's "domestic activities" from their work in the fields, marketing, or social influence (Blanc-Szanton 1972; Dewey 1962; Ebihara 1974; Firth 1966; H. Geertz 1961; Potter 1977).

Common principles of organization—authority based on seniority rather than gender, complementary female and male roles, groom payment of wedding expenses, relative ease of divorce, matrifocality, and residential clusters of kinswomen—are found in their numerous cultural variants throughout Southeast Asia. However, in everyday life, women must actively secure their bases of autonomy. In making a point generalizable to the situation of all Southeast Asian peasant women, Kessler (1977) argues that Kelantanese Malay women's individually acquired income should be seen as a strategy to avoid subjugation by husbands and as the realization of enforced independence, especially following divorce. I found that Malay village women expect their husbands to pay for all family expenses (as required by Islamic law), while saving their own private wealth for contingencies (Ong [in press]; cf. Swift 1963). Thus, Malay women's "relative autonomy" should be seen as the opposite side of their socioeconomic insecurity in relationship to men, and to male prerogatives in forming and breaking marital relations.

Despite such intriguing gender configurations and their expressions in actual practices, the theoretical significance of this Southeast Asian material escaped the attention of American feminists who emerged in the 1970s. Thus, in her theoretical overview, Michele Rosaldo argued that the "public/domestic" dichotomy in everyday life (drawn from a historical phase in Western capitalist development) accounted for women's "universal subordination" (1974:7). Since the 1970s, the struggle for an anthropology of women (later gender) involved feminists doing interpretive anthropology (where culture was treated as a system of symbols to be decoded; see C. Geertz 1972), and those of a Marxist persuasion (whose aim was to theorize the relation between political economy and gender inequality). A fruitful dialogue between these two streams can contribute to new perspectives on gender in Southeast Asia, as well as challenge anthropological theory itself.

In what follows, I will discuss a few key ethnographic examples that show what is distinctive about gender and power in Southeast Asia. These studies fall under four main themes: center-periphery; matriliny; socioeconomic change; and the cultural construction of gender.

Center-Periphery: Distribution of Prestige

A sensible way to begin a discussion of gender in Southeast Asia is a description of basic principles governing local worldviews. As mentioned earlier, the underlying thread in local cosmological systems is an emphasis on unity and complementarity. This worldview distinguishes between the sacred and profane, the powerful and the weak, friends and enemies, along a center-periphery axis (Heine-Geldern 1956; Tambiah 1977). In traditional Southeast Asian kingdoms, authority, moral power, and prestige accrue to those at the center, and low status to those at the periphery. This "galactic polity" (Tambiah 1977) codes cosmological, topographical, and political-economic features of life throughout Southeast Asia. In social relationships, power gravitates to those at the still center, but is depleted in the turbulent periphery (Anderson 1972). Shelly Errington (in press) has suggested that the unity/complementarity and center/periphery schemes produce a "political geography of potency," which in effect maps gender relations in various configurations throughout the region.

In small-scale, slash-and-burn systems of the archipelago, gender is muted, and yet "makes a difference" when it comes to prestige (Atkinson [in press]). Michelle Rosaldo (1980a) first found that among the Ilongots, women and men are considered similar human beings, but their complementary activities—women in the homesteads, men venturing further afield—defined their differential access to moral status. Men's head hunting activities take them beyond the community, enabling them to acquire the knowledge and passion central to moral superiority. This center-periphery principle awards prestige to persons whose activities define the moral dimensions of social life.

Following Rosaldo, Jane Atkinson (in press) investigates gender meanings in relationship to prestige among the Wana, swidden agriculturalists of central Sulawesi. Like the Ilongots, Wana idiom emphasizes human "sameness" of women and men, the complementary nature of their work and of their roles in procreation. Wana also prize experience that lies beyond the everyday farming activities of the homesteads. Atkinson discusses how, in daily life, muted gender distinctions are "inveigled" into a "prestige structure" (Ortner and Whitehead 1981) that values male activities—shamanism, legal authority, and community leadership. These positions of authority derive from having special access to distant realms, and "distance is an aspect of men's, not women's, experience" (Atkinson [in press]). Not all men attain such knowledge, and so the grounds for moral superiority is not explicitly gender-bound. That those who attain such positions are predominantly male "is treated as a fluke of fortune, rather than a categorical process of inclusion and exclusion." Thus Wana women represent the everyman, and individual Wana men attain spiritual rewards as leaders. Wana "men are like women, and something more" (Atkinson [in press]). Tsing (in press) presents a similar gender system among the Meratus of Kalimantan (Borneo).

Gender as concept and practice in egalitarian Southeast Asian societies compels feminists to rethink three sets of assumptions. The above cases challenge Marxist-feminist claims (e.g., Leacock 1972) that gender asymmetry does not exist in egalitarian societies. Secondly, they limit the applicability of the "public/domestic model" of gender asymmetry, which argues that a universal opposition between "domestic" and "public" roles leads to gender asymmetry (Rosaldo 1974:8). The center-periphery principle in Southeast Asia does not make such distinctions in terms of the way the "domestic" fits into the social arena. Women's lack of prestige reflects their lack of access to "spiritual capital" in a political geography based on morality, not economy.

In complex systems like Javanese society, prestige structures place "spiritual potency" (Errington [in press]) at the center rather than the periphery. Moral status is aligned along this axis, expressed in highly stylized speech, and not explicitly in gendered terms. The high-status individual claims "considerable potency" by evincing the greatest restraint and dignity in his speech, manner and daily activity (Keeler [in press]). The wife of such a high-status man is obliged to protect his dignity. "With less status to affront," women are permitted a wider range of styles. They can be dealt with more informally, speak more freely, and express strong emotions (considered "crude"). Less encumbered by status obligations, women can participate, and be effective in, economic and social activities deemed too socially depleting for their husbands (Keller [in press]; cf. Hatley [in press]).

Ward Keeler notes that although Javanese male-female status contrast is not absolute, "it inclines men and women to situate themselves at different places in a hierarchy of statuses, and thereby commits them to different relations with potency and style." This distribution of prestige along a continuum offers the possibility for individuals to engage in gender "switching." Transvestites in both Javanese and Wana societies dramatize the fluidity of gender permitted in these prestige structures.

Matriliny and Islam

Center-periphery principles also underlie matrilineal systems, expressed most clearly in the distribution of moral power and division of labor. Among the Atjehnese in North Sumatra, women take care of families and maintain ancestral rice lands, while men travel (*merantau*) to earn cash incomes and acquire Islamic knowledge (Siegel 1969). Men's travels in the periphery can be a source of honor and of shame. Those making the yearly trip home without money and gifts from the outside world are treated like children by their wives (Siegel 1969, chapter 5). Their claim of superior Islamic status is continually weighed by women in terms of what they can provide for the families.

Minangkabau society in West Sumatra presents an interesting case of how women as a group have held on to high status despite Islamization, colonialism, and incorporation within the nation-state. Kathleen Gough (in Schneider and Gough 1961) maintains that the penetration of market relations into Minangkabau society fragmented matrilineal groups into elementary units, thereby breaking up women's customary influence. This assertion is challenged by Kahn (1976), who argues that Minangkabau matriliny was both altered and preserved (in a "deformed" system) as commercial interest waxed and waned in the colonial and postcolonial era. The failure of a capitalist economy to install itself in Western Sumatra left much of the subsistence system still under the control of matrilineal groups.

Peggy Sanday (in press) offers another view for the survival of matriliny in highland Minangkabau villages. In Minangkabau worldview, senior women and men form a single unit, each having different rights. Status is based on preserving *adat*, not on gender opposition or inequality. Women and men have different but complementary roles in perpetuating adat.

Ancestral lands and houses are inherited along the female line. Senior women teach adat, which is infused with a distinctively feminine quality, emphasizing nuturant and respectful social interactions. Thus women symbolize the moral strength and the source of life itself.

Men's roles are to protect matrilineal control of ancestral property. Young men are required to leave their families and villages in order to seek wider knowledge and experience. Despite Islam and the male-dominated village councils, senior men represent matrilineal interests. This is because men measure their moral worth in terms of their ability to protect matrilineal adat and ancestral property. In other words, matrilineal adat is placed in "a sacred frame of reference" (Sanday [in press]), coexisting in mutual reinforcement with Islam as two equal strands of natural law in Minangkabau society. It remains to be seen whether Sanday's optimistic view of female power in Minangkabau society can be sustained in the most recent wave of Islamic resurgence. However, her analysis shows that attention to indigenous conceptions of gender is critical to the study of kinship systems.

Economic Development and Female Status

The examples cited above show how symbolic analysis can disclose the key principles governing gender constructs and behavior in Southeast Asian societies. However, few interpretive anthropologists deal with what happens to symbolic meanings when the region became incorporated into the "periphery" of global systems centered in Western and Japanese metropoles.

In anthropology, "change" is conceived mainly in terms of the diverse impact of colonialism, capitalism, and the modern nation-state on indigenous cultural systems. The modernization approach suggests that strategies for improving female status in Southeast Asia should be based on increasing women's access to modern education and occupations (Ward 1963). The optimism of this view is tempered by Ester Boserup's (1970) findings that the commercialization of agriculture in ex-colonial countries did not promote the status of indigenous women. However, Boserup is criticized by Marxist feminists who insist that an analysis of changing relations of production must precede any attempt to understand women's role in development. Ann Stoler (1977) rejects Boserup's argument that colonialism reduced women's status as a sex, charging that feminists erred in treating "women as a homogeneous group." Instead, Stoler argues that the "economic determinants of female status" included autonomy (in disposing of the fruits of one's labor) and social power (control over the lives of others, such as by appropriating the products of their labor). In Java, the green revolution exacerbated fundamental differences between women "in their access to and control over productive forces" (1977:89). Double-cropping and government credit enriched landholding families, and the status of the women in this stratum rose as they came to control more land and the distribution of harvesting jobs sought by poor women. Some landholding women parlayed their agricultural earnings into profitable trading activities. Meanwhile, decline in the number of harvesting jobs reduced the earning power and autonomy of landpoor and landless women. Nevertheless, in some ways they were less badly affected than poor men, who did not have traditional access to off-farm work. Stoler thus concludes that capitalist development and class stratification do not necessarily produce sexual dichotomization in which women as a group were more adversely affected than men. In rural Java, women in the privileged class came to acquire more autonomy and social power than poor women and men.

Maila Stivens (1981) also uses a Marxist model to criticize another popular assumption: that capitalism inevitably reduces extended kin relations to isolated, male-dominated nuclear units. Comparing Malay matrilineal society in Negri Sembilan with a Sydney neighborhood in Australia, Stivens argues that the social requirements for reproducing the capitalist system actually encourage a tendency toward the formation of female-centered kin networks. Although older Malay women are excluded from direct participation in wage labor, the capitalist system relies on their unpaid housework to subsidize young working women and men. These female-centered networks, which help reproduce the labor reserve, have had a contradictory effect on women's status: although they keep Malay women subordinated in the capitalist economy, they offer informal economic and moral support, which fosters female solidarity. By thus defining female status solely on the basis of access to economic resources and role in reproducing the capitalist system, both Marxist approaches ignore cultural experience, thereby giving gender construction a rather mechanistic cast.

For Marxist feminists, the intersection of gender and class discloses the historically specific conditioning of sexual inequality in particular situations. An analysis informed by this view tends to focus on modern forms of domination, while reducing local cultures to a role of supporting capitalism and class ideology. There is also a tendency to couch explanations of sexual inequality in functionalist terms derived from mainstream anthropology. In contrast, interpretive anthropologists handle gender as cultural concepts, but they pay little or no attention to its articulation with contemporary structures of power. By alternately focusing on the workings of class or gender as the primary explanatory category of male-female relations in Southeast Asia, these divergent approaches reflect tensions between political economy and interpretive anthropology. I suggest below that a promising direction for understanding gender difference in the contemporary world is one that incorporates insights from both approaches.

Gender, Industrialization, and Nationalism

By the late 1970s, feminists had shifted from using universalizing frameworks (public/domestic model, class analysis) of sexual inequality to more subtle insights into the cultural constructions of gender in historical time. A major contribution of feminism is its destabilization of anthropological frameworks. By insisting that we question the underlying logic of anthropological constructs for Western male biases, feminist perspectives challenge the degree to which Western thinking reflects the lived experiences of peoples who are the subjects of anthropological inquiry. Together with the critique of colonialism, feminist interrogations contribute to the intellectual climate whereby the authority claims of ethnographic writing can be challenged (Clifford 1986).

In Southeast Asian studies, the feminist challenge to the ''naturalness'' of Western sexual categories revives interest in Margaret Mead's evocative description of the patterning of gender difference in Bali (Bateson and Mead 1942). The task of feminist anthropology is now to deconstruct gender as a unitary cultural category (Strathern 1981), and to consider gender as constituted by the intersections of power structures in changing societies. Benefitting from the work of Marxist feminists, Rosaldo suggests an approach in which the concept of self includes a sense of gender, cultural identity, and social class (1980b:400). Secondly, gender was reconsidered as an analytical concept experienced and reproduced through everyday practice (Ortner and Whitehead 1981). In other words, gender is taken as process constituted in the dialectical relationship between meaning and practice, in a historically specific, power-laden context (Ong 1987). A meeting of Marxism and interpretive anthropology occurs in works which attempted to examine how indigenous gender meanings were and are changed, reconstituted and experienced through colonialism, capitalist development and nationalism.

Cristina Blanc-Szanton (in press) presents an interesting case of changing gender concepts among the Ilonggo, Visayas (Philippines) over 400 years of colonialism. Under the Spanish and later the Americans, the Ilonggo selectively incorporated features of Western gender systems forced upon them, while holding on tenaciously to a gender construction that emphasized complementary, not contrastive, gender difference. Again, echoing themes in other island cultures, rank rather than gender was the significant marker. Through their history of Western domination, Ilonggo political leaders (*datu*, as principalia) competed by deploying daughters to attract enterprising men as members of their entourages. European images of deferential and weak women might have suggested the acceptance of female subordination. However, the Ilonggo continue to consider women and men in the same social rank to be of equal standing and social influence.

The analysis of changing gender systems under cultural imperialism is especially urgent as Southeast Asia undergoes the fastest rate of industrialization and tourism in the world. The rapid expansion of the prostitution industry and the export of female workers and brides have led to the widespread degradation of Southeast Asian women locally and overseas. Some preliminary studies of Thai prostitutes suggest complex reformulations of sex images and roles in the transnational context (e.g., Khin Thitsa 1980).

These themes are also explored in my study of Malay women workers in transnational factories based in Malaysian free trade zones (Ong 1987 [in press]). My work discusses the transformation of Malay gender concepts, experiences, and subjectivity through Malay women's participation in transnational factories, consumer culture, and Islamic revivalism. I argue that in Malay village society, fathers and brothers were responsible for guarding the moral purity (virginity) of young unmarried women. This Malay-Muslim gender system was appropriated by modern Japanese factory managers to reinforce male authority and female obedience on the shop floor. Village parents wanted their daughters to earn wages without jeopardizing their moral status, while the factories wished to gain legitimacy for the harsh work conditions imposed on the young women. Citing ''Pan-Asian values,'' corporate policies stressed a ''family system'' whereby Malay women were urged to be loyal and hard-working. In one factory, the manager presented himself as having moral custody over the chastity of his female workers. A similar case where modern factories manipulate indigenous gender values is reported by Celia Mather, who observes that an alliance between the ''Islamic patriarchy'' and industrial management legitimized the exploitation of young Javanese women (1983).

Following Foucault (1980), I describe how power, operating strategically in everyday action and discourse, constituted women as subjects and as objects. Through labor control and corporate discourse, working women were induced to monitor themselves and acquire a new degree of self-awareness. Furthermore, as members of the emergent Malay working class, factory women became the target of public disapproval and a key symbol in the struggle over national culture. Politicians, educators, and Islamic revivalists assailed the new ''immoral'' image of young Malay women in free trade zones. An explosion of sexual discourse and the promulgation of new gender images were new forces in regulating female sexuality. Alternately portrayed as oppressed workers and independent working women, as virtuous Muslims and as pleasure-seekers, Malay women were compelled to define themselves as worker, consumer, or Islamic women. Meanwhile, the government-controlled media promoted a positive image of the housewife (i.e., a status of dependency realized mainly by women in the middle classes). By handling gender formulations as contingent and in flux, I show women acquiescing as well as resisting gender images produced at the intersections of culture, class and state policy. My work suggests that a new direction for the anthropology of gender should include both the transformation of gender systems and of gendered subjectivities in the process of social change.

Feminist Insights and Anthropology

Women in Southeast Asian societies are traditionally viewed as enjoying relatively high status vis-à-vis men. This view stems largely from the fact that both sexes engage in farm activities, and that local worldviews stress gender complementarity and unity. If we take a dynamic view, Southeast Asian societies are especially interesting for illuminating the processes whereby gender is "inveigled" into larger structures of power, both indigenous and foreign. This essay suggests that indigenous values like center-periphery, matrifocality, and the priority of rank over gender—critical in preserving women's economic and social rights and privileges—are increasingly being co-opted or superseded by larger systems of inequality. Changes associated with the green revolution and transnational capitalist production have produced new gender constructions based on class (e.g., the reviled factory woman versus the housewife ideal of the new middle classes). At the same time, the latest wave of Islamic revivalism seeks to produce a structure of control over female sexuality never before encountered in island Southeast Asia.

Recent studies that integrate insights from political economy and symbolic analysis point to an exciting direction for the anthropology of gender. Studies of gender difference must grapple with the interplay of global and local forces, alien and indigenous cultural meanings, social structure and human action in historically specific circumstances. Finally, the recognition that gender is a process mediated by power relations challenges the anthropological concept of culture. The "syncretic" cultural milieus of Southeast Asia provide a fertile ground not only for refining the way we deal with gender, but also cultural difference in a transcultural world.

References Cited

Anderson Benedict
    1972   The Idea of Power in Java. *In* Politics and Culture in Indonesia. C. C. Holt, B. Anderson, and J. Seigel, eds. Ithaca: Cornell University Press.
Atkinson, Jane
    In press   How Gender Makes a Difference in Wana Society. *In* Power and Difference: Gender in Island Southeast Asia. J. Atkinson and S. Errington, eds. Stanford: Stanford University Press.
Banks, David
    1983   Malay Kinship. Philadelphia: Ishi.
Bateson, Gregory, and Margaret Mead
    1942   Balinese Character: A Photographic Essay. Wilbur G. Valentine, ed. Special Publications of the New York Academy of Sciences, Volume 2.
Blanc-Szanton, Cristina Blanc
    1972   A Right to Survive: Subsistence Marketing in a Lowland Philippine Town. University Park: Pennsylvania State University Press, 1972.
    In press   Collision of Cultures: The Predicaments of Gender under Spain, the United States, and National Independence in Lowland Visayans, Philippines. *In* Power and Difference. J. Atkinson and S. Errington, eds. Stanford: Stanford University Press.
Boon, James
    In press   Balinese Twins Times Two: Gender, Birth Order, and Household in Indonesia/Indo-Europe. *In* Power and Difference. J. Atkinson and S. Errington, eds. Stanford: Stanford University Press.
Boserup, Ester
    1970   Women's Role in Economic Development. New York: St. Martin's.

Burling, Robbins
    1965   Hill Farms and Padi Fields: Life in Mainland Southeast Asia. Engelwood Cliffs, N.J.: Pren-
       tice-Hall.
Clifford, James
    1986   On Ethnographic Authority. *In* Writing Culture. J. Clifford and G. Marcus, eds. Berkeley:
       University of California Press.
Dewey, Alice
    1962   Peasant Marketing in Java. New York: Free Press.
Djamour, Judith
    1965   Malay Kinship and Marriage in Singapore. London: Athelone.
Ebihara, May
    1974   Khmer Village Women in Cambodia: A Happy Balance. *In* Many Sisters: Women in Cross-
       cultural Perspective. C. Matthiasson, ed. Pp. 305–347. New York: Free Press.
    1977   Residence Patterns in a Khmer Peasant Village. Annals of the New York Academy of Sciences
       293:51–68.
Errington, Shelly
    In press   Power and Difference. A Theoretical Overview. *In* The Paradox of Gender. J. Atkinson
       and S. Errington, eds. Stanford: Stanford University Press.
Firth, Rosemary
    1966   Housekeeping among Malay Peasants. New York: Humanities Press.
Foucault, Michel
    1980   The History of Sexuality, Volume I. Translated by Robert Hurley. New York: Vintage Books.
Freeman, Derek
    1970   Report on the Iban. London: Athelone.
Geertz, Clifford
    1972   The Interpretation of Cultures. New York: Basic Books.
Geertz, Hildred
    1961   The Javanese Family. New York: Humanities Press.
Hanks, Lucien, and Jane Hanks
    1963   Thailand: Equality between the Sexes. *In* Women in the New Asia. B. Ward, ed. Paris:
       UNESCO.
Hatley, Barbara
    In press   Theatrical Image and Gender Ideology in Java. *In* Power and Difference. J. Atkinson and
       S. Errington, eds. Stanford: Stanford University Press.
Heine-Geldern, Robert
    1956   Conceptions of State and Kingship in Southeast Asia. Cornell University: Southeast Asia Data
       Paper 18.
Jayawardena, Chandra
    1977   Women and Kinship in Acheh Besar, Northern Sumatra. Ethnology 14(1):21–38.
Josselin de Jong, P. E.
    1960   Islam versus Adat in Negri Sembilan (Malaya). Bijdragen 116(1):158–203.
Kahn, Joel
    1976   "Tradition," Matriliny and Change among the Minankabau of Indonesia. Bidjragen
       132(1):64–95.
Keeler, Ward
    In press   Speaking of Gender in Java. *In* Power and Difference. J. Atkinson and S. Errington, eds.
       Stanford: Stanford University Press.
Kessler, Clive
    1977   Conflict and Sovereignty in Kelantanese Malay Spirit Seances. *In* Case Studies in Spirit Pos-
       session. V. Crapanzano and V. Garrison, eds. Pp. 295–331. New York: Wiley.
Khin Thitsa
    1980   Providence and Prostitution: Image and Reality in Buddhist Thailand. London: Change Inter-
       national Reports.

Kirsch, Thomas
    1983   Buddhism, Sex Roles, and the Thai Economy. *In* Women of Southeast Asia. P. van Esterik,
        ed. DeKalb: Northern Illinois University, Center for Southeast Asian Studies, Occasional Paper
        no. 9.
Leach, Edmund
    1959   The Political Systems of Highland Burma. Cambridge: Harvard University Press.
Leacock, Eleanor
    1972   Women's Status in Egalitarian Society: Implications for Social Evolution. *In* The Origins of
        the Family, Private Property, and the State. F. Engels, ed. Pp. 7–67. New York: International
        Publishers.
Nego Vinh Long
    1974   Peasant Women, *In* Vietnamese Women in Society and Revolution, Volume I: The French
        Colonial Period. Pp. 25–40. Cambridge: Vietnam Resource Center.
Ong, Aihwa
    1987   Spirits of Resistance and Capitalist Discipline: Factory Women in Malaysia. Albany: State
        University of New York Press.
    In press   Japanese Factories, Malay Workers: Class and Sexual Metaphors in West Malaysia. *In*
        Power and Difference. J. Atkinson and S. Errington, eds. Stanford: Stanford University Press.
Ortner, Sherry
    1974   Is Female to Male as Nature is to Culture? *In* Women, Culture and Society. M. Rosaldo and
        L. Lamphere, eds. Pp. 67–87. Stanford: Stanford University Press.
Ortner, Sherry, and Harriet Whitehead
    1981   Introduction: Accounting for Sexual Meanings. *In* Sexual Meanings. S. Ortner and A. White-
        head, eds. Pp. 1–27. New York: Cambridge University Press.
Peletz, Michael
    1987   Female Heirship and the Autonomy of Women in Negri Sembilan, West Malaysia. *In* Re-
        search in Economic Anthropology, volume 8. B.Isaac, ed. Pp. 67–107. Greenwich, Conn: JAI
        Press.
Pelzer-White, Christine
    1987   Status, Culture and Gender: Continuity and Change in Women's Position in Rural Vietnam.
        In Women, State, and Ideology. H. Afshar, ed. Pp. 226–234. Albany: State University of New
        York Press.
Potter, Sulamith
    1977   Family Life in a Northern Thai Village. Berkeley: University of California Press.
Reid, Anthony
    1988   Southeast Asia in the Age of Commerce, 1450–1680, Volume 1: The Lands Below the Winds.
        New Haven: Yale University Press.
Rosaldo, Michelle Z.
    1974   Women, Culture and Society: A Theoretical Overview. *In* Women, Culture and Society. M.
        Rosaldo and L. Lamphere, eds. Pp. 17–42. Stanford University Press.
    1980a   Knowledge and Passion: Notions of Self and Social Life. Stanford: Stanford University
        Press.
    1980b   The Use and Abuse of Anthropology: Reflections on Feminism and Cross-cultural Under-
        standing. Signs 5(3):389–417.
Sanday, Peggy
    In press   Matriliny and World View in West Sumatra. *In* Beyond the Second Sex: Essays in the
        Anthropology of Gender. P. Sanday and R. Goodenough, eds. Philadelphia: University of Penn-
        sylvania Press.
Schneider, David, and Kathleen Gough
    1961   Matrilineal Kinship. Berkeley: University of California Press.
Siegel, James
    1969   The Rope of God. Berkeley: University of California Press.

Spiro, Melford E.
   1977   Kinship and Marriage in Burma: A Cultural and Psychodynamic Analysis. Berkeley: University of California Press.
Stivens, Maila
   1981   Women, Kinship and Capitalist Development. *In* Of Marriage and the Market. K. Young, C. Wolkowitz and R. McCullagh, eds. Pp. 112–126. London: CSE Books.
Stoler, Ann
   1977   Class Structure and Female Autonomy in Rural Java. *Signs* 3:74–89.
Strathern, Marilyn
   1981   Culture in a Netbag: The Manufacture of a Subdiscipline in Anthropology. *Man* (n.s.) 16:665–688.
Swift, Michael
   1963   Men and Women in Malay Society. *In* Women in the New Asia. B. Ward, ed. Pp. 268–286. Paris: UNESCO.
Tambiah, S. J.
   1977   The Galactic Polity: The Structure of Traditional Kingdoms in Southeast Asia. Annals of the New York Academy of Sciences, Vol. 293.
Tanner, Nancy
   1974   Matrifocality in Indonesia and Africa and among Black Americans. *In* Women, Culture and Society. M. Rosaldo and L. Lamphere, eds. Pp. 126–159. Stanford: Stanford University Press.
Tsing, Anna
   In press   Gender and Performance in Meratus Dispute Settlement. *In* Power and Difference. J. Atkinson and S. Errington, eds. Stanford: Stanford University Press.
Van Esterik, Penny, ed.
   1983   Women of Southeast Asia. DeKalb: Northern Illinois University, Center for Southeast Asian Studies, Occasional Paper no. 9.
Ward, Barbara, ed.
   1963   Women in New Asia. Paris: UNESCO.
Winzeler, Robert
   1982   Sexual Status in Southeast Asia: Comparative Perspectives of Women, Agriculture and Political Organization. *In* Women of Southeast Asia. P. van Esterik, ed. DeKalb: Northern Illinois University, Center for Southeast Asian Studies, Occasional Paper no. 9.

Course Component 1

Aim: To Understand Women's Status and Matriliny in Minangkabau Societies

Anthropologists have long been fascinated by matrilineal societies because of the high status enjoyed by women as a group. The largest matrilineal societies are the Minangkabau in North Sumatra (Indonesia) and daughter communities in Negri Sembilan (Malaysia). These Islamic matrilineal systems, which have survived intact foreign cultural domination, provide an interesting paradox for kinship and feminist theories. Two major questions are (1) How can a matrilineal system that favors high status for women flourish within an Islamic framework? and (2) How have matrilineal social and cultural forms managed to persist despite their incorporation into national and global economies? [Please consult the bibliographic essay for readings suggested below.]

Exercise 1.   The high moral and economic status of women in Minangkabau society

1. In what ways are Minangkabau women figures of strength and power? What are the complementary roles of men? For an understanding of matrifocality in Minangkabau societies, see Tanner (1974), Jayawardena (1977), Sanday (1988, in press). These women-centered networks now extend beyond village households as Minangkabau women become migrant workers in modern factories (Stivens 1982). Matrifocality and matriliny are strengthened by the tradition of voluntary male out-migration. See Naim (1985); Peletz (1987a).

2. How does the center-periphery model of Minangkabau society challenge the private/public concept, which some feminists (Rosaldo 1974; 1980a) used to explain "universal" female subordination? Secondly, Ortner's (1974) claim that the nature/culture model is a universal construction of sexual inequality is refuted by the Minangkabau conceptions of nature, culture, and gender relations (Sanday 1988, in press).

3. Some anthropologists (e.g., Claude Lévi-Strauss) hypothesize that kinship systems were originally based on the exchange of women by men, with prestige going to the wife-taking group. Can a case be made that in 19th-century Negri Sembilan, matriliny operated as a system for the exchange of men and their labor power? See Peletz (1987b).

Exercise 2.   Social change and the persistence of matriliny in Minangkabau societies.

1. Some anthropologists argue that colonialism has eroded women's customary rights in clan representation (Josselin de Jong 1960; Kahn 1976). Colonial land policy and postcolonial Islamic nationalism have also caused a shift away from matrilineal land rights to private property in Negri Sembilan (Josselin de Jong 1951; Swift 1963).

2. Nevertheless, others argue that on the contrary, matriliny has survived recent historical changes and women's high status has been preserved. See Stivens (1981), Peletz (1987a) and Sanday (in press).

Course Component 2

Aim: To Evaluate the Impact of Transnational Factories on Women's Status and Identity

In recent years, transnational corporations have recruited peasant women in the Third World as an industrial labor reserve. "Free-trade zones" scattered throughout Southeast Asia are the arenas within which a nascent female working class is being made. What are the new modes for controlling female labor? Have female workers acquired new forms of gender and class consciousness?

New Forms of Control and Resistance

1. "Modernization" theorists argue that the status of women increases when they participate in industrial employment (Lim 1983). This view contradicts Boserup's (1970) argument that development marginalizes women's participation in the modern economy. The impact of multinational factories in Southeast Asia suggests a more complex picture. Compare and contrast changes in the status of peasant women when they become workers in multinational factories (Ong [in press]; Mather 1983).

2. Global industries organize workers through the hierarchical division of labor by sex and nationality. In addition, work discipline is ensured in at least two other ways: through the management techniques like time-motion studies (Taylorism), manipulation of work shifts, etc.; and through emotional control, using techniques that define and redefine workers' sexuality and self-perceptions. See Grossman (1978), Ong (1988, in press).

3. In Malaysia and Indonesia, religion and indigenous values have been incorporated into corporate techniques for managing female workers. This management policy combines capitalist and local notions of hierarchy and gender to produce a new gender ideology on the shop floor. See Ong (1987, Part 3), and Mather (1983).

4. Given the pervasive surveillance on and off the shop floor, factory women participate in both covert and overt protests against factory discipline and social criticisms. See Ong (1988, in press).

New Freedoms, Subjectivities and Consciousness

While young women are subjected to new forms of domination in modern factories, they simultaneously gain new freedoms at home. Their earning power produces a degree of autonomy, expressed mainly in consumption and spouse selection, which weakens the authority of kinsmen over them. In Malaysia, this would-be social emancipation is widely perceived as a threat, both to male power in Malay culture and to a government concerned with retaining foreign investments. Ong (in press) maintains that this complex experience of felt oppression and freedom, self-esteem and public censure, produces a profound sense of ambivalence in Malay factory women, as well as the development of new consciousness that is both gender and class-specific. Industrial employment and social surveillance provide the context wherein gender becomes redefined through the dialectic between social control and workers' changing self-perceptions. Ong (1987, Part 3) talks about the formation of a new "class sexuality" among Malay factory women in Malaysia. As sexual difference becomes part of corporate rationale for labor control, its perceived unruly nature attracts public censure and Islamic criticisms. As women workers mediate this reconstitution of their identity, sexuality, and its regulation and expression, becomes an increasingly critical part of women's transformed subjectivities.

Films for Classroom Use

The Global Assembly Line, by Lorraine Gray, with Anne Bohlen and Maria P. F. Kelly (58 minutes, color, 16mm). Video. This is a vivid portrayal of women workers—Filipino, Mexican, and American—working and protesting against employment conditions in transnational factories.

Becoming American, by Ken and Ivory Levine (58 minutes, or 30-minute version, color, 16mm). Video. A chronicle of Hmong refugees from Thailand adjusting to life in Seattle. Both films may be bought or rented from New Day Films, 22 Riverview Drive, Wayne, NJ 07470-3191; (201) 633-0212.

A recent film explores "the multiplicity of identity" of Vietnamese women in Vietnam and in California. It also raises questions about the politics of translation in filmmaking. *Surname Viet Given Name Nam* is produced by Trinh T. Minh-ha (1989, 108 mins, color and b&w, 16mm), and distributed by Women Make Movies, 225 Lafayette St., Suite 212, New York, NY 10012.

Bibliographic Essay

Kinship and Social Organization

See Penny van Esterik's "Introduction," in Penny van Esterik, ed., *Women of Southeast Asia* (DeKalb: Northern Illinois University, Center for Southeast Asian Studies, Occasional Paper no. 9, 1983) for an overview. Also consult Robert Winzeler's article, "Sexual Status in Southeast Asia: Comparative Perspectives of Women, Agriculture and Political Organization," in the same volume, pp. 176–213. The bibliography is useful.

The following studies discuss the prominent roles of Southeast Asian women in the family, economy, and local community. For Malay society, see Michael Swift, "Men and Women in Malay Society," in Barbara Ward, ed., *Women in the New Asia* (Paris: UNESCO, 1963), pp. 268–286, for a good introduction. Classic studies that stress dependence on maternal kin include Judith Djamour, *Malay Kinship and Marriage in Singapore* (London: Athelone Press, 1959), and Rosemary Firth, *Housekeeping among Malay Peasants* (London: Athelone Press, 2d ed., 1966), chapters 2 and 3. For Malay conceptions of kinship and gender, see David Banks, *Malay Kinship* (Philadelphia, ISHI Press, 1983), Chapter 5, and Carol Laderman, *Wives and Midwives* (Berkeley: University of California Press, 1982).

Hildred Geertz introduced the concept of "matrifocality" in *The Javanese Family: A Study of Kinship and Socialization* (New York: Free Press, 1961). This concept is applied to the matrilineal Minangkabau and Atjehnese in Nancy Tanner, "Matrifocality in Indonesia and Africa and among Black Americans," in Michelle Rosaldo and Louise Lamphere, eds., *Women, Culture and Society* (Stanford: Stanford University Press, 1974), pp. 126–159. For another view of relations between Atjehnese women and their husbands and sons, see James Siegel, *The Rope of God* (Berkeley: University of California Press, 1969), Chapter 7. [See also *Matrilineal Societies*, below.]

In mainland societies, women's influence is also expressed through kinship and residential propinquity. See May Ebihara, "Khmer Village Women in Cambodia: A Happy Balance," in C. Matthiasson, ed., *Many Sisters: Women in Cross-cultural Perspective* (New York: Free Press, 1974), pp. 305–347; and "Residence Patterns in a Khmer Peasant Village," in S. Freed, ed., *Anthropology and the Climate of Opinion* (Annals of the New York Academy of Sciences, vol. 293, 1977). Consult also Sulamith Potter, *Family Life in a Northern Thai Village: A Study in the Structural Significance of Women* (Berkeley: University of California Press, 1977), Mi Mi Khaing, *The World of Burmese Women* (London: Zed Press, 1974), and M. E. Spiro, *Kinship and Marriage in Burma* (Berkeley: University of California Press, 1977).

Center and Periphery

For a discussion of the principles of center and periphery (and egalitarianism versus hierarchy), see Michelle Rosaldo, *Knowledge and Passion: Ilongot Notions of Self and Social Lilfe* (Stanford: Stanford University Press, 1980), pp. 229–231. This view is further explored in the collection edited by Jane Atkinson and Shelly Errington, *Power and Difference: Gender in Island Southeast Asia* (Stanford: Stanford University Press, in press). See Shelly Errington's "Power and Difference: A Theoretical Overview." Papers by Jane Atkinson, "How Gender Makes a Difference in Wana Society" and Anna Tsing, "Gender and Performance in Meratus Dispute Settlement" deal with prestige structures in outer island societies. For contrasting constructions of prestige in complex systems, see Ward Keeler, "Speaking of Gender in Java," and Barbara Hatley, "Theatrical Image and Gender Ideology," in the same volume.

On the mainland, small-scale groups also exhibit gender fluidity, again along a center-periphery axis. See Nancy Eberhart, ed., *Gender, Power, and the Construction of the Moral Order: Studies from the Thai Periphery* (Madison: University of Wisconsin Center for Southeast Asian Studies, Monograph Series no. 4, 1988).

Matrilineal Societies

The structural and affective centrality of women in matrilineal society is discussed in Nancy Tanner, "Matrifocality in Indonesia and Africa and among Black Americans," in M. Rosaldo and L. Lamphere, eds., *Women, Culture and Society,* Stanford University Press, pp. 129–159; Chandra Jayawardena, "Women and Kinship in Aceh Besar, North Sumatra," *Ethnology* 14(1):21–38; and Peggy Sanday, "Matriliny and World View in West Sumatra," in P. Sanday and R. Goodenough, eds., *Beyond the Second Sex* (Philadelphia: University of Pennsylvania Press, forthcoming). See also P. Sanday, "The Reproduction of Patriarchy in Feminist Anthropology," in Mary Gergen, ed., *Feminist Thought and the Structure of Knowledge* (New York University Press, 1988), pp. 49–68, which argues that women are central to the prestige hierarchy in Minangkabau society. For male out-migration, see Mochtar Naim, "Implications of Merantau for Social Organization in Minangkabau," in Lynn Thomas and Franz von Benda-Beckmann, eds., *Change and Continuity in Minangkabau* (Ohio University Monographs, Southeast Asia Series, no. 71, 1985), pp. 111–117. Other papers in Part I of this volume deal with the links between kinship and larger organizations in Minangkabau society. Michael Swift's *Malay Peasant Society in Jelebu* (London: Athelone Press, 1965) is the classic study of Minangkabau daughter communities in Negri Sembilan, Malaysia.

Another important theme in matrilineal societies is the impact of Islam, colonialism, and economic development on women's status and power. For the Minangkabau society in Sumatra, see Joel Kahn, " 'Tradition,' Matriliny and Change among the Minangkabau of Indonesia," *Bidjragen* 132, no. 1 (1976):64–95. For social change among the matrilineal Malays in Negri Sembilan, Malaysia, see P. E. de Josselin de Jong, "Islam versus *Adat* in Negri Sembilan (Malaya)," *Bijdragen* 166 (1960):158–203. The most recent studies are by Michael Peletz (1987a and 1987b): "Female Heirship and the Autonomy of Women in Negri Sembilan, West Malaysia," in Barry Isaac, ed., *Research in Economic Anthropology*, vol. 8 (Greenwich, Conn.: JAI Press, 1987) pp. 67–107, and "The Exchange of Men in 19th-Century Negri Sembilan," *American Ethnologist* 14 (1987):449–469; and *A Share of the Harvest* (Berkeley: University of California Press, 1988). For the effects of industrialization on matrilineal kinship, see Maila Stivens, "Women, Kinship and Capitalist Development," in Kate Yong, C. Wolkowitz, and R. McCullagh, eds., *Of Marriage and the Market* (London: CSE Books, 1981) pp. 112–126.

Religion and Gender Constructs

Many anthropologists see religion as a source of ideas that denigrate women. This presents an interesting paradox in Southeast Asian societies, where women play a prominent economic role. A debate over the impact of a presumed Buddhist earthly/spiritual model on Thai gender asymmetry provides an interesting angle to Sherry Ortner's "Is Female to Male as Nature is to Culture?'' in M. Rosaldo and L. Lamphere, eds., *Women, Culture and Society,* op cit., pp. 67–87. Both Thomas Kirsch, ''Text and Context: Buddhist Sex Roles/Culture of Gender Revisited,'' *American Ethnologist* 12(1985):302–320; and Khin Thitsa, *Providence and Prostitution: Image and Reality in Buddhist Thailand* (London: Change International Reports, 1980) argue that Theravada Buddhism views women as bound to earthly desires, and men as more ready to give up such attachments. This image of women as materialist and lustful becomes the rationalization for job stratification (Kirsch), and an ideology of oppression for women (Khin Thitsa). See also P. van Esterick, ''Laywomen in Theravada Buddhism,'' in P. van Esterik, ed., *Women of Southeast Asia,* op cit., pp. 55–78. In contrast, Charles Keyes, ''Mother or Mistress but Never a Monk: Buddhist Notions of Female Gender in Rural Thailand,'' *American Ethnologist* 11 (1984):223–240, maintains that Buddhism confers a ''naturally'' superior status on women as mothers. [See also *Economic Role and Changing Status.*]

For the effects of patrilineal bias in Islam on Malay women, see Carol Laderman, ''Putting Malay Women in their Place,'' in P. van Esterik, *Women in Southeast Asia,* pp. 79–99. New Islamic conceptions of women are discussed in Judith Nagata, *The Reflowering of Malaysian Islam* (Vancouver: University of British Columbia Press, 1984), Chapters 4 and 5; and Aihwa Ong, ''Japanese Factories, Malay Workers: Class and Sexual Metaphors in West Malaysia,'' in J. Atkinson and S. Errington, eds., *Power and Difference,* op cit.

Economic Role and Changing Status

As a cultural complex, Southeast Asia enjoys the singular distinction of widespread participation of women in traditional economies. Women's work in agriculture is discussed by almost all of the studies mentioned in *Kinship and Social Organization* above. The effects of postwar developments on gender roles are summarized in Barbara Ward, ed., *Women in the New Asia: The Changing Social Roles of Men and Women in South and Southeast Asia* (Paris: UNESCO, 1963). Women's importance in marketing is described in Alice Dewey, *Peasant Marketing in Java* (New York: Free Press, 1962), and Rosemary Firth, *Housekeeping among Malay Peasants,* Chapter 7.

The 1970 publication of Ester Boserup's *The Role of Women in Development* (New York: St. Martin's Press) stimulated a reconsideration of the effects of development on the status of Southeast Asian women. Ann Stoler discusses the uneven impact of the green revolution on Javanese peasant women. See her ''Class Structure and Female Autonomy in Rural Java,'' *Signs* 3 (1977):74–89, and ''Rice Harvesting in Kali Loro: A Study of Class and Labor Relations in Java,'' *American Ethnologist* 7 (1977):678–698.

Economic development also stimulated female out-migration and changing role in the wider economy. For Malaysia, see Heather Strange, *Rural Malay Women in Tradition and Transition* (New York: Praeger Publishers, 1981). In Singapore, the results of social engineering is discussed in Aline Wong, ''Planned Development, Social Stratification, and the Sexual Division of Labor in Singapore,'' *Signs* 7 (winter 1981):434–452.

The status of Thai women has been examined in relation to educational policies and the development of an urban service sector. For a view of how women of different class and ethnic groups participate in the economy and redefine work and leisure, see Cristina Blanc-Szanton, ''Gender and Intergenerational Resource Allocations: Thai and Sino-Thai Households in Central Thailand,'' in L. Dube and R. Palriwala, eds., *Structures and Strategies: Women, Work and Family in Asia* (India: Sage, 1989). Susanne Thorbek portrays the lives of female slum dwellers in *Voices from the City: Women of Bangkok,* London: Zed Books, 1987. New ways of evaluating female status is described by Marjorie A. Muecke, "Make Money not Babies: Changing Status Markers of Northern Thai Women," *Asian Survey,* 24 (April 1984):459–470. The growing problem of prostitution linked to female migration has attracted a perhaps disproportionate interest among scholars. See Pasuk Phongpaichit (economist), *From Peasant Girls to Bangkok Masseuses* (Geneva: International Labour Office, 1982). Sociologist Siriporn Skrobanek writes a hard-hitting piece on "Thai Women in the International Sex Trade," *Southeast Asian Chronicle* 81 (1984). A less critical view is presented by Erik Cohen, "Thai Girls and Farang Men: The Edge of Ambiguity," *Annals of Tourism Research* 9 (1982):403–428. [See also *Religion,* above.]

The *Southeast Asia Chronicle* has devoted three issues to the position of Southeast Asian women from a political economic perspective. They are "Changing Role of Southeast Asian Women" (no. 66, February 1979), "Tourism: Selling Southeast Asia" (no. 78, April 1981), and "Beyond Stereotypes: Asian Women in Development" (no. 96, January 1985).

A collection to look over is Lenore Manderson, ed., *Women's Work and Women's Roles: Economics and Everyday Life in Indonesia, Malaysia and Singapore* (Canberra: Australian National University, Development Studies Centre, no. 32, 1983). See articles by Leslie O'Brien and Norma Sullivan for macro-level views on women's economic participation in Malaysia and Indonesia. Linda Connor and Susanna Price argue that modern improvements in public health and in textile manufacturing, respectively, have had marginalizing effects on poor women.

Industrialization and the Remaking of Gender

Besides agricultural development, the 1970s saw the introduction of labor-intensive manufacturing by transnational companies. This export-led industrialization has had profound impact on rural women in Southeast Asia. Many studies have been conducted by nonanthropologists. For an overall perspective on corporate policy and labor use in Southeast Asia, see Linda Y. S. Lim (economist), *Women Workers in Multinational Corporations: The Case of the Electronics Industry in Malaysia and Singapore* (University of Michigan, Occasional Paper no. 9, 1978) and her "Capitalism, Imperialism, and Patriarchy: The Dilemma of Third World Women Workers in Multinational Factories," in June Nash and Patricia Fernandez-Kelly, eds., *Women, Men, and the International Division of Labor* (Albany: State University of New York Press, 1983). For more detailed discussions of corporate control over female workers, read Rachel Grossman (economist), "Women's Place in the Electronic Circuit," *Southeast Asia Chronicle* 66 (1979):2–17. A public health view is given in Vivian Lin, "Productivity First: Japanese Management Methods in Singapore," *Bulletin of Concerned Asian Scholars,* 16 (1984):12–25.

For an ethnographic study, see Aihwa Ong, *Spirits of Resistance and Capitalist Discipline: Factory Women in Malaysia* (Albany: State University of New York Press, 1987). Different interpretations of spirit possession in factories are considered in Susan Ackerman and Raymond Lee, "Communication and Cognitive Pluralism in a Spirit Possession Event in Malaysia," *American Ethnologist* 8 (1981):789–799; and Aihwa Ong, "The Production of Possession: Spirits and the Multinational Corporation in West Malaysia," *American Ethnologist* 15 (1988):28–42.

The impact of industrialization elsewhere in Southeast Asia has barely received scholarly attention. Two exceptions are Celia Mather, "Industrialization in the Tangerang Regency of West Java: Women Workers and the Islamic Patriarchy," *Bulletin of Concerned Asian Scholars* 15 (1983):2–17; and Kathryn Robinson's "Women and Work in an Indonesian Mining Town," in L. Manderson, ed., *Women's Work and Women's Roles*, op. cit., pp. 111–127.

To gain a cross-cultural perspective on the impact of free trade zone employment on Third World women, see Lydia Kung, "Factory Work and Women in Taiwan: Changes in Self-Image and Status," *Signs* 2 (1976):35–58; and Patricia Fernandez-Kelly, "Women in the Marquilidoras," in J. Cole, ed., *Anthropology for the 1990s: Introductory Readings* (New York: Free Press, 1988). A film documentary, "The Global Assembly Line," presents a comparative view of women workers in global factories. [See Films for Classroom Use.]

Women, Politics, and the State

Very little anthropological attention has been paid to women in politics, despite their political prominence in many Southeast Asian countries. The Philippines is one society where women are simultaneously included and excluded from the political process. See Cristina Blanc-Szanton, " 'Big Women' and Politics in a Philippine Fishing Town," in V. H. Sutlive, N. Altshuler, and M. Zamora, eds., *Women and Politics in Twentieth Century Africa and Asia*, Studies in Third World Societies, no. 16 (Williamsburg: Dept. of Anthropology, College of William and Mary, 1981) pp. 123–141. In Malaysia, women play handmaiden roles in political mobilization. See Lenore Manderson, "The Shaping of the Kaum Ibu (Women's Section) of the United Malays National Organization," in Wellesley Editorial Committee, *Women and National Development* (Chicago: University of Chicago Press, 1977). Aihwa Ong discusses the symbolic image of women for nationalism and race in "Changing Malay Families: State Power, Islamic Resurgence and the Body Politic," in Aihwa Ong, ed., *Family Predicaments* (forthcoming).

The impact of socialism on women's status in Indochina has been studied by political scientists: Jayne Werner, "Women, Socialism and the Economy of Wartime North Vietnam, 1960–1975," *Studies in Comparative Communism*, 14 (Summer 1981):165–190; Christine Pelzer-White, "Status, Culture, and Gender: Continuity and Change in Women's Position in Rural Vietnam," in Haleh Afshar, ed., *Women, Work and Ideology in the Third World* (London: Tavistock, 1985), pp. 225–234; and Arlene Eisen, *Women and Revolution in Vietnam* (London: Zed Books, 1984). For a comparative perspective, see Nina Adams (historian), "Women's Weaving Cooperatives in Laos," *Indochina News* (February 1987).

The Politics of Transcultural Representation

An emerging literature considers the politics of ethnographic representations of women in Third World societies. See Aihwa Ong, "Colonialism and Modernity: Feminist Re-Presentations of Women in non-Western Societies," *Inscriptions* 3/4 (1988):79–93; and Anna Tsing, "Temporary Wives," (forthcoming). An allied concern is with the transcultural construction of Southeast Asian women in immigrant contexts. For popular images of Southeast Asian women in the United States, see Ara Wilson, "American Catalogues of Asian Brides," in J. Cole, ed., *Anthropology for the Nineties: Introductory Readings* (New York: Free Press, 1988) pp. 114–125. Southeast Asian female immigrants are also socialized into American middle-class models. See Gail P. Kelly, "The Schooling of Vietnamese Immigrants: Internal Colonialism and its Impact on Women," in Beverly Lindsay, ed., *Comparative Perspectives of Third World Women* (New York: Praeger, 1980), pp. 276–296.

13

Transformations of Gender in Modern China

Ann Anagnost
University of Illinois, Urbana-Champaign

Not long after arriving in central China to do fieldwork in the spring of 1981, I had been given a free ticket to see *New Year's Sacrifice,* a film based on a short story by Lu Xun (Lu Hsun), a writer of the 1920s and 1930s. Lu Xun's story is written as the first-person narrative of a young urbanized intellectual on a visit to his rural hometown. During his stay, he becomes reacquainted with the history of a servant woman crazed by a lifetime of misfortune. She had been widowed twice and her only child had been killed by wolves. Due to her unfortunate past, the woman was regarded as doubly cursed. Not only was she believed to be ill-starred and therefore to blame for the misfortunes of her family; but also her association with death rendered her ritually polluted. A central incident of the story was her employer's insistence that she not handle the ritual objects set out for the New Year's sacrifice. In the film version, the woman's story ends with her dismissal from her employer's house in mid-winter and her death from exposure at the doorstep of the family she had once served.

Lu Xun's focus in the story was on the unreflexive detachment of the narrator (Huters 1984). As an urbanized intellectual, he comments on the "backwardness" of the village to which he returns. Yet despite his alienation, he enjoys a privileged position in the class and gender system underlying the "feudal" ideology that oppressed this poor woman.[1] The movie, however, focuses entirely on the theme of women's oppression in prerevolutionary China. The figure of the unreliable narrator disappears completely and Lu Xun's subtle art is transformed into a representational form conventional to postrevolutionary political culture—"recalling the bitter past to compare the sweet present." As I left the theater, I noticed with surprise that the departing crowd of viewers was composed almost entirely of very elderly women, navigating the walkway in small groups as they hobbled on bound feet. Among them was a younger woman in her 50s. Her graying hair, cut short in a bob, contrasted with the thinning topknots of the older women. Perhaps she was a cadre in charge of ideological work, for, as she circulated among them on her unbound feet, she would run up addressing each in turn, "You remember, how bitter it was!" and dumbly they would nod their assent.

I was struck by this scene. Indeed it gave me a feeling of euphoria to think how radically the lives of women had changed in China since the revolution. As I recounted my emotional response to a male colleague who had been in China longer, he responded with a tale of his own. He had been walking down one of the main avenues of the city to find himself startled by the sight of a woman being beaten by two men. Several dozen observers had gathered to watch the scene but no one appeared likely to intervene. My friend ran off to find a police officer. The officer arrived, made inquiries, and then laughed. This was no affair of his. It was a family matter. The woman had been disobedient. This account, needless to say, instantly deflated my euphoric assumption that things had really changed for women. How could such a public display of male authority go unquestioned? What had happened to the new socialist institutions that were supposed to come to the support of women? Where were the public-spirited mediators from the resident's committee or the women's association?

Women and Revolution

The Chinese woman does not yet exist either, among the masses; but she is begining to want to exist. [Mao Zedong to André Malraux c. 1958 *Anti-mémoires*, cited in Young 1973.]

I have begun with these stories because they represent the paradox faced by feminist scholars of China today. Although things have changed in many ways, the lived reality of women in China is far from the idealized portrayals of gender equality we wanted to believe in the 1960s when representation was more controlled by socialist realist conventions. Until recently, firsthand observations of Chinese society were limited by the whirlwind impressions of official delegations visiting China and the controlled access of Western visitors to conversing freely with ordinary people. With the liberalization of the Deng Xiaoping era, fieldwork by Western social scientists has been possible, but it continues to be tightly controlled by local as well as central political authorities.[2] Despite the limitations imposed on it, recent fieldwork has allowed Western scholars a closer look at the reality of women's lives. Current and future work based on firsthand observation will have a profound impact on our understanding of women and socialism in China.

Despite the importance of these recent developments, a critical reevaluation of gender politics in socialist China did not have to await the opening of China to the West. Since the mid-1970s, a number of studies have used documentary evidence to evaluate the degree to which the Chinese revolution has fulfilled what Western feminists had always assumed to be its radical promise to women.[3] These studies all focus on the issue of how patriarchal structures have been reproduced and even strengthened under socialism. This issue was pioneered by Diamond (1975) who was among the first to question Chinese political rhetoric that attributed the problem of women's subordination to a persistent "feudal-patriarchal" ideology. Dismissing the idea that this persistence was due simply to a slower rate of change in the realm of ideas, she looked instead at how the material organization of rural society, despite its socialist transformation, might be responsible for the reproduction of a preliberation gender ideology. Diamond suggested that the collectivization process itself led to the reconstitution of localized lineages. Although collective units were not designed to conform to preexisting social groupings, in practice they often did so because the underlying network of kin relations reinforced the effectiveness of collective leadership. The most extreme examples of this patrilineal bias were found in single lineage villages or villages in which one or more lineages controlled the local power structure. In these cases, local collective organization often paralleled kinship organization, and the distribution of resources was organized more in terms of kinship loyalties than by a universalizing state ethic.

Among the factors Diamond mentions in her complex argument, perhaps the most significant was the continuing practice of village exogamy and virilocal residence. Rural women have continued to marry out, leaving behind and entering into communities of men tied through bonds of agnatic kinship.[4] As might be expected, these practices complicated the relationship of women to property in their natal villages (Croll 1984). The socialist state had assumed that once private property was collectivized, "feudal ideology" would disappear through education, and no distinction would be made between men and women in their claims on collective resources. However, despite the fact that all members of a collective had an equal claim, resources were allocated, for the most part, on a household basis and thereby came under the jurisdiction of the household head, usually its senior male member. Women lost out when they married away into their husbands' villages, because their natal villages refused to relinquish resources from local control. In cases where uxorilocal marriage, which has been at times mildly promoted by the state, was attempted, the local leadership were often unwilling to share local resources with families that properly "belonged" elsewhere, with the husband's kin. Virilocal residence continues into the present to be the dominant pattern of postmarital residence in the Chinese countryside. A newspaper account from the early 1980s documents the ill treatment of a man who married uxorilocally. His access to collective resources was blocked by his wife's kinsmen who referred to him as a "dog entering the door" *(Chinese Peasant Gazette,* 15 February 1981:7).

Another serious handicap for women was the reluctance of collective leadership to allow them advanced education and training for technical or administrative work. Training women for these posts was perceived by local leaders as a waste, since their skills would be "lost" to their natal communities when they married out to join their husbands' kin elsewhere.[5] This understandably proved a major barrier for women to take significant roles in leadership or to participate in the more skilled and usually better compensated job classifications.[6] This is not to say that women never occupy leadership positions. There is evidence enough in the Chinese press to suggest otherwise, especially in urban work units. But, in the countryside, women continue to be a very small minority of those who occupy positions of authority, within the bureaucratic structure. On the local level, women cadres are found, most typically, in the position of head of the local women's association *(fulian)* and their leadership roles are thus contained within what are considered to be women's concerns.[7]

Diamond's study of how patriarchal structures have come to be reproduced under socialism illustrates a dynamic governing the relationship between the Chinese state and local society that predates the revolution. In its attempt to superimpose a bureaucratic organization on rural society, the state, in pursuing its primary interests of social control and expropriation of revenues, has always had to deal with the tension between administrative units and the ways in which society organizes itself. These tensions have continued unabated with the evolution of a socialist state in China. Although the commune system was originally designed to rationalize production on a large scale, in practice its smaller component units of brigade- and team-level organization proved to be the effective units of accounting and organization of production. As mentioned above, these smaller units often tended to realign their boundaries with social groupings, organized along patrilineal kinship lines or the boundaries of the "natural" community,[8] to encourage production and the delivery of state quotas. Organization that follows the path of least resistance facilitates expropriation of a community's surplus product at the expense of "social control" which, in the expanded goals of the socialist state, would include the restructuring of local society and the revolutionary transformation of "feudal" family relations. Both of these goals were undeniably attained up to a point; however, the question remains as to whether the socialist state's failure to complete the process was a conscious decision in its developmental strategy. Were women, in fact, "sold down the river" by the party to attain quick results in the economic realm?

Since Diamond's study, there have been a number of studies that focus in more detail on the effects of CCP policies which contributed to the reconsolidation of rural patriarchy. Johnson (1983) claims that the party's insistence that the problem of gender inequality was primarily ideological absolved them from looking at its structural basis. The reluctance of the party to deal with the structural issues stemmed from the intrinsic conflict between class and gender as targets for revolutionary change. Once land reform was completed, the reconsolidation of patriarchal structures was assured with the "leadership's recognition of the utility of strong families and rooted communities for its other economic and political goals" (Johnson 1983:219). The great value that the party placed on a strong family order as contributing to rural stability limited the potential of party policies for radical family reform. The party's strategy was instead directed toward "selectively destroying, repressing and reforming, as well as building on, the structure and values of the 'feudal base' it inherited" (1983:220). The result was the placing of women's issues on a relatively low priority, while retaining an ideological commitment to gender equality. The implication was that the natural evolution of socialist society would eliminate the economic bases that contribute to women's subordination in rural society (1983:221).

Andors (1983) argues that women became, in the course of socialist development, a force that could be unleashed in political and economic mobilization. It was assumed that once women fully participated in the work force, the basis of gender inequality would disappear. During periods when a Maoist development strategy was in ascendancy, women were brought into the public arenas of work and politics. However, this participation was based on the premise that true equality could be achieved only by the erasure of sexual difference in the workplace. Much attention was paid to women working in jobs traditionally associated with men—women working on high tension wires, driving tractors, and other high visibility accomplishments. "Iron girl" work teams competed with their male counterparts to prove themselves equal to any task. Although this may have gained a privileged status for a minority of women models, mostly it resulted in women bearing a double burden. They were responsible for household tasks, which continued for the most part to be unvalorized labor, as well as being assigned, outside the household, the more menial and less valued tasks for which lower compensation was justified by a sexual division of labor.[9]

A third study (Stacey 1983) presents a more radical argument that suggests the party offered to peasant males the patriarchal authority once enjoyed by family heads of the preliberation elite as a strategy for enlisting their support. The peasant family economy had been badly damaged by the economic and political crises of the prerevolutionary period. Land reform and the early stages of collectivization ensured its restoration by taking households as the units of distribution and membership in collective organizations. The collectivization of agriculture did expand women's participation in labor but in ways guaranteed not to undermine patriarchal control. Stacey contends that although women's participation in collective labor succeeded in changing the substance of the traditional sexual division of labor, it failed to level a "fundamental challenge to the traditional view that female labor was naturally different from and subordinate to that of men" (1983:208). The most controversial thesis in her study is that the reconstitution of rural patriarchy was in fact a conscious goal of the party, strengthened by popular support, to ensure a stable family order for subsequent development. A more recent study (Wolf 1985) takes issue with Stacey's argument suggesting that although CCP policies may have strengthened rural patriarchy in effect, this outcome was unintended and the result of a revolution dominated by men who failed to question their own sexist assumptions in promoting policy and assigning priorities.

All of these studies attempt to account for the failure of the revolution to deliver on its perceived potential for transforming gender relations in Chinese society. Both class and gender, as the bases for different kinds of oppression, provided the categories through which revolutionary activism was deployed. They were the structuring principles of the struggle process and performance. If the postrevolutionary reality has indeed demonstrated the effective transformation of class relations in the creation of a classless society, or indeed, as became apparent in the political strife of the 1960s, one which had given birth to an inverted status hierarchy, gender appears not to have undergone a parallel transformation or at least not to the same degree.[10] Despite the continuing importance of gender equality in the declared objectives of the party and state, it clearly has remained subordinate to questions of class in the party agenda. As Young (1989) suggests, "women" as a totality is a category that must cross-cut class divisions; and any program designed to improve their status as a group defined entirely by their sex, by definition, comes under attack as bourgeois liberalism in its capacity to weaken class solidarity.

In the economic reforms that have swept China since 1978, the dismantling of the collective economy and the return to the household as the basic unit of production have strengthened further the structures that sustain rural patriarchy. "They reinforce the private aspects of the patriarchal family economy and extend the social and economic domain of male kin and neighborhood-based work groups" (Stacey 1983:271–272). It remains to be seen whether the new economic and spatial mobility of rural households will break down primordial kin-based groupings (as suggested by Johnson 1983:217), or whether lineages will continue to provide the underlying corporate structure for economic enterprises in the emerging free market economy.

On the ideological front, although the problems of women continue as public issues of concern to the state, it is clear that the resolution of these problems continues to be couched in terms of the patriarchal family. State-sponsored educational work in the countryside emphasizes household harmony and the smoothing over of intrafamilial "contradictions" especially in the historically conflictual relations between mothers-in-law and daughters-in-law. Locally organized campaigns target families where this conflict is especially intense for ideological work and local party organizations—such as the youth league and the women's association—converge their efforts on these hapless families to encourage them to reform. Family members are exhorted to "obey the elder, and love the young" *(cunlao aiyou)*. This maxim not only reasserts the hierarchical principles of age and generation but gender as well, when it is used in this context. The "five-good" family campaign *(wuhao jiating)* defines model family status in terms of harmonious relations between parents and children, husbands and wives, mothers-in-law and daughters-in-law, among sisters-in-law, and among brothers (Anagnost 1985:83). This set of family relationships as specified above does not exhaust all possible domestic relationships except in a patriarchal system that under socialism has not only persisted in practice but has done so with the apparent support of the state.

This is not to say that the state's concern for women is not genuine; but the relationship between the ideologies of kinship and the state as they have emerged over the last several centuries are so interwoven that their disarticulation was perhaps never a conscious goal of China's revolution. A possible exception is an elite minority of women caught up in the intellectual ferment of the May Fourth period in the 1920s which explored Western ideas about gender and personhood. Even for elites who espoused family reform as an important goal for China's modernization, this did not necessarily mean the dissolution of the patriarchal family but only a loosening of its oppressive hold on women and youth.

In retrospect this comparatively conservative objective was apparent in the evolution of the party's family policy forged in the context of war as early as the Yenan period (1940s). In Jack Beldon's emotionally charged account of "Goldflower's Story," which was the first exposure of many Western feminists to the possibilities of revolution for women in China, a peasant woman fought for her liberation from an abusive husband and father-in-law. Her struggle received the encouragement and support of the women's association which acted as a powerful advocate on the behalf of women (like Goldflower) to limit the abuses of patriarchal authority but not to effect its complete usurpation. Although Goldflower leaves her husband in the end, the women's association first attempts a reconciliation. Patriarchal authority was not to be displaced but merely held in check for specifically defined abuses. As part of his role as a journalist reporting on communist successes during wartime, Beldon's encounter with Goldflower was not accidental. By the time he gathered her story she had become an experienced activist in promoting the policies of the party. She epitomizes the emergence of a new political subject created by the discursive strategies of the party and deployed in the service of party goals (as described by Barlow 1988:12–13). Her story can be placed in the narrative tradition of "speaking bitterness" *(su ku)* which played such an important role in the inscribing of a mythic history that represented the bitterness of the old society in invidious contrast to the sweet present.[11] "Women," or more specifically, "poor peasant women," became a highly emotionally charged and politicized category, along with "poor peasant" and "landlord" in the discourse and dramaturgy of revolutionary struggle. These categories were given local salience in the classification of local persons into these categories and whose stories made consciousness of oppression more immediate and tangible.[12]

Given the evidence that we can deduce from "Goldflower's Story" that the intent of the party was from the beginning to limit patriarchal authority in rural villages rather than to displace it entirely,[13] the question then becomes to what extent the Chinese revolution has passed into a state of Thermidorian reaction (as Stacey has suggested) or to what extent the radical promise of the Chinese revolution for the transformation of gender relations was in part a projection onto the Chinese experience of Western feminism.[14] Perhaps it is time to review how "Chinese feminism" has been constituted in Western feminist discourse and how this construction has distorted our interpretation of how "women" operated as a category in Chinese political discourse. My discussion of this issue below is heavily indebted to the work of Tani Barlow. Although Barlow is a historian interested in how the issue of gender figured in the emergence of a female consciousness in 20th-century Chinese literature, the implications of her work for anthropologists dealing with gender issues in contemporary Chinese culture are very challenging and important.

In her dissertation, Barlow (1985) questions the underlying assumptions of critiques by Western feminists of the failure of the Chinese revolution to realize its promise to women. Failure may lie not so much with the revolution and what it promised as with the failure of Western feminism itself to define what feminism was in the context of modernizing China. They took what appeared to be feminist issues, beginning with the early 20th-century movements to abolish footbinding, concubinage, and arranged marriage; and constructed with them a Chinese feminism based on Western ideas of individual self-determination (1985:23). These issues, along with others such as the education of women, were, in the context of an emerging Chinese nationalism, not so much signs of a new feminine subjectivity (with the prominent exceptions of some elite women), as they were signs of a "modernity" essential to the definition of a newly emerging national self-image. This confusion on the part of Western feminists, Barlow suggests, is illustrated in the comment by Roxane Witke that "Chinese feminism was the only national feminism to be initiated by men on behalf of their sisters" (1985:23). Western fantasies about a postrevolutionary utopia of gender equality were projected onto "women" as an emerging ideological category in Chinese political discourse. Barlow's critique makes it paramount for us to first to become aware of our own ethnocentric preconceptions about what feminism is before we can understand fully the discursive functioning of women as an ideological category in the Chinese context. In addressing this latter project, Lu Xun's unreliable narrator comes to mind. For him, the "woman question" was clearly symbolic of a much wider malaise that weakened China in the struggle for national autonomy.

In a more recent paper, Barlow remarks that "a chief success of 'Maoism' was its ability to mount discourses that categorized and deployed political subjects in relation to the state/ nation or the *guo*" (1988:1–2). In this sense, she suggests that *funu* ("woman/women") is an invention specific to Chinese socialism that marks a site for the normalization of practices and for the "invasive uses of power."[15] The invention of "woman" as a political category must be seen as part of the larger emergence of a discourse of modernity in 20th-century China, one that helped to empower the socialist state. "Woman" as constructed in this context constituted a novelty within this emerging discourse and must therefore be understood historically.[16] This project is in accord with contemporary feminist theory that would argue that

> the concept "woman" cannot stand as an analytical category in anthropological enquiry, and consequently there can be no analytical meaning in such concepts as "the position of women," the "subordination of women" and "male dominance" when applied universally. [Moore 1988:7]

Likewise, if we accept the above as a basic tenet of feminist methodology, then a similar approach must also be made toward understanding historically situated "feminisms" that may be constructed in quite different ways from our Western conceptions of what feminism means.

Barlow's work suggests that "Chinese 'feminism' lacked the subject of its own discourse" and had to invent it, in part through ideas borrowed from the West (1985:6). But this notion of "woman," as an autonomous entity, a female being, separable from familial roles, had little or no referent in Chinese society outside of a small circle of theorists. The insubstantiality of this notion of "woman" in the abstract as an already constituted interest group precluded a more radical program of family reform. Women, themselves continued to identify with their kin and family roles, and therefore were motivated to restore the integrity of the family that had been rent by decades of economic and political crisis (1985:24–25).

Gender and Hierarchy

Barlow's study of how "woman" came to be constructed as a novel category in a 20th-century discourse of modernity begins with the social determinations of gender in late imperial China (i.e., the Qing Dynasty 1644–1911):

> The late imperial sex-gender system was indeed organized around the priority of agnatic kinship. But the patrilineal, patrilocal kinship world had never been enforced by a strictly binary discourse which polarized "male" and "female," as in the modern West. In fact, rather than forming a central male/female opposition, Qing China drew a spatialized hierarchical grid in which male/female was subordinated to bisexual, marital unity inside the patriline. Kinship discourses and clan regulations positioned all Chinese inside the "natural" hierarchies of *jia* (family), *zu* (lineage), and a myriad pseudo-familist institutions. . . . Regulatory discourse assigned specific *position* to define human beings. Inside the multitude of hierarchical, architectonic, designated places, gender existed neither as *place*, nor, as in the bourgeois West, *essence*, nor as a *symbolic* expression of fecundity or fertility. Gender was rather a single axis among many. [1985:1–2, emphases in original.]

Although the *jia* (family) and *zu* (lineage) differed in many respects, they both shared a common kinship discourse which defined the "natural" hierarchical links between categories of kin along the axes of inside and outside (of the patriline or surname group) and of above and below (parents and children, seniors and juniors) (1985:37). These hierarchical "natural" orders were inscribed in what Barlow calls regulatory discourse that included didactic texts defining proper female deportment and filial duties as well as the imperial examination system which was the major avenue of social mobility for men in the inculcation of Confucian values. Among the most important of these regulatory discourses was the doctrine and practice of the Three Bonds that designated a set of homologous, hierarchical relations:

> Emperor : subject :: father : son :: husband : wife

These three sets of relationships encapsulated the interpenetrating domains of monarchy and patrilineal kinship which, as Barlow argues, subordinated gender to kin categories. The proper ordering of kin relations within the *jia* (family) or *zu* (lineage) provided a metaphor for the ordering of the larger polity. The discourses of monarchical rule and patrilineal kinship worked on each other analogically. "If the monarch was the 'son' of Heaven, the 'husband' was a monarch to his wife, a Heaven to his wife's Earth" (1985:38). The position of the subject within the system was always relative, occupying a superior position in some instances, an inferior one in others.

Barlow's account of late imperial determinations of gender emphasizes the role of relation and position in structuring the hierarchical organization of Chinese society. In other words, gender by itself did not define positions within the structure. It was one principle among many, that combined with kinship, generation, age, and rank to determine a subject's position within the family and in society. She contrasts this relational aspect of gender with Western notions that ascribe gender with a primary determining power to define the person. In pointing to this difference between 19th-century notions of gender in China and in the West, Barlow is not suggesting that women were not subordinate to men, but that the structure of that subordination differed from the West and the way in which it was experienced differed as well because of its submersion in the discourse of kinship and family roles.

In order to understand the role of gender in the interpenetrating discourses of kinship and state and its continuing salience in a postrevolutionary context, we need first to explore gender as a cosmological system embedded in social practice. Central to the Chinese concept of gender is *yin/yang* dualism. *Yin* is usually identified as the female principle and *yang* is its male correlate. These identifications make *yin* and *yang* the obvious signifiers of gender difference. However, the pair has a much wider cosmological significance as one of the central principles of the regular operation of the universe: the bipolarity of nature. The natural world operates as a ceaseless flow of change. Everything exists in a state of constant flux with its opposite which is not only its complement but is necessary to its identity. One cannot exist without the other. Even the most polarized expression of one contains the germ of the other, so that everything is constantly in process, transforming into its opposite. Things in the material world are definable phases in this dynamic interplay. Light and dark, hot and cold, as well as male and female are all manifestations of it.

The dynamism of this principle of bipolarity would lead us to predict that the Chinese construction of gender is more fluid than the Western concept of gender as opposed and discretely defined essences, and so it is. Both men and women as physical beings contain a measure of both *yin* and *yang*, and, indeed, the correct balance between them define well-being and good health. However, women are still undeniably associated with *yin* in ways that men are not. Moreover, they are recognized at times as being more *yin* than at others (as are men, but never to the same degree), especially when they have come into contact with the ritual pollution of birth, death, or menses. For this reason, postmenopausal women, especially if their status in the family had been elevated to that of mother-in-law, often experienced a marked personality change in mid-life from a quiet and reserved manner to one that was more assertive and outgoing. The cessation of menses corresponded to a change in a woman's position within the authority structure of the family from a subordinate position to one where she could exert authority over others (as a mother-in-law).[17]

Yin/yang dualism has a long history in the evolution of a Chinese cosmology. In fact, it may be considered as one of those primordial elements in the earliest developments of a distinctly Chinese worldview. However, despite the fundamental importance of the *yin/yang* bipolarity throughout China's philosophical evolution, its internal relation has not gone unchanged. Indeed, with the rise of a stable centralized state in China during the Han dynasty (206 B.C.–A.D. 220), there appears to have been a major transformation of how the relationship between *yin* and *yang* was conceptualized. *Yin/yang* complementarity became absorbed into an emerging Confucian orthodoxy that emphasized a balanced harmony of hierarchical relationships sustained by an ethics of reciprocal obligations. This emphasis on hierarchy reordered the relationship between *yin* and *yang,* so that *yang* was not only more highly regarded but was also considered to be morally superior to *yin.*

The implications of this change for the reordering of gender relations becomes evident when we see how this hierarchical rearrangement of *yin* and *yang* became grafted onto a theory of human nature in which *yin* was recognized as the source of emotions, and thus "the cause of confusion and evil," whereas *yang* was identified with the rational faculties (Overmyer 1980:158). In moral terms, *yin* was subject to negative feelings of covetousness, while *yang* became paired with the highest of the Confucian virtues, humanity *(ren)* (1980:158). Moreover these associations became tied to the system of hierarchical relations that ordered household and state. *"Yin* is inferior to *yang* as wife is to husband and subject is to ruler" (1980:158). From this it is clear tht despite the characterization of *yin* as the female principle and *yang* as the male principle, these terms have to be understood in a relative rather than an absolute sense. Whereas a man may be *yang* to his wife's *yin* he was *yin* with respect to his superiors in rank. Thus, *yin* and *yang* retained their complementarity in relation to each other, but their hierarchical arrangement was crosscut by other hierarchical principles that ordered human relations along the multiple axes of age, generation, birth order, and status. In this sense, the structuring of relationships could never be reduced exclusively to the principle of gender alone, as became possible in Western gender discourse.

However, despite the relational aspect of *yin/yang* ordering in the hierarchical structures that organized society (so that it was possible in this system for a woman to occupy a superior position to men by virtue of rank, age, or generation), the association of women with *yin* always carried the potential to undermine their positional advantage. Because the *yin*-ness of woman made her subject to rule by emotions, she was incapable of moral cultivation and therefore must be controlled by men, her moral superiors by virtue of their rational will. Therefore, although the status of *yin* and *yang* was defined through relative position in the varied dimensions of social hierarchy, there was also an implicit belief that men and women were not equal in terms of their psychological and intellectual abilities *whatever* their rank. This conceptualization of gender difference was based on a relative polarization of *yin* and *yang* in which women's inferiority could be ascribed to the naturally disruptive qualities of *yin* against which the social order must protect itself.[18] But since *yin/yang* theory started out nonhierarchically there remains a question of whether there is a potential for its hierarchization to be reversed and under what conditions that reversal might be brought about. For instance, the implications of a polarization of *yin* and *yang* in the psychological realm was never thoroughly realized in the metaphysical realm.

> In consequence the role of *yin* was understood at two different levels, with the relationship between metaphysical good and psychological evil never fully clarified. It is significant that at a penultimate level a certain amount of polarized hostility between *yin* and *yang* was granted, even in philosophy. Here *yin* was equated with death and confusion. At the popular level this rift in the metaphysical web was much expanded. [Overmeyer 1980:158]

Barlow cautions that one must be wary of conflating *yin/yang* with the categories of man and woman. To do so would be falling into the trap of our own essentialized notions of gender.[19] However, I would argue that while *yin* and *yang* might have retained their character as interpenetrating realms at the metaphysical level, in practice they became more polarized during specific periods in Chinese history and that this relative polarization did have implications for gender relations during the periods in question.

Barlow's work suggests a contrast between the negative valuation of *yin* late in the 19th century, during which China was experiencing a Han revival, with a more positive valuation in the 16th century during which the widespread urbanization and commercialization of Chinese society contributed to elite dissatisfaction with a rigidly hierarchical family structure (1985:47). A rise in female literacy undermined the premise that women were unteachable or that their potential for literary attainments was any less than men, a discussion that was to reappear in the 20th century but with the added element of Western ideas. This periodization suggests the importance of historicizing any discussion of a Chinese gender system. The meaning and cultural valuation of *yin* and *yang* fluctuated over time. Beyond this historical dimension also lies a social one in the division between elite and popular discourses. As Overmeyer suggested above, the relative polarization between *yin* and *yang* was intensified in the realm of popular religion and expressed in ideas about ritual and feminine pollution (Ahern 1975; Sangren 1987). But even in this realm, diversity ruled. Many secret societies and heterodox religious movements, including the Taipings, vigorously espoused an ideology of gender equality. This diversity reinforces the necessity of placing discussions of Chinese gender clearly within its specific sociohistorical context.

Gender Ideology in the Post-Mao Period

To illustrate a number of the points essayed above, I will take Barlow's very sensitively written account of a Woman's Day celebration in which she herself took part while resident in Shanghai in 1981. This story will illustrate the incommensurability of feminisms East and West, and especially, the subordination of gender to social role. She describes the confrontation between the feminism of Western women invited to the celebration and a Chinese aesthetic of what constitutes appropriate entertainment for such an affair, in this case a *yueju* opera (in which both male and female roles are played by women) called "Beating the Princess." The plot centers on the relationship between a vain and stupid princess who outranks her husband. They have a fight because she refuses to honor her father-in-law at his birthday party because of her higher rank. She runs to her father, the emperor, to complain. He resolves the conflict of ordering principles between rank and gender by promoting his son-in-law to a rank equal with his daughter. The princess promises never to disrespect her husband again (Barlow and Lowe 1987:191). Barlow reports that the Chinese audience viewed this opera as a conflict over rank and not as a story about sexual politics. Indeed, she has a difficult time communicating her discomfort about the incident to a Chinese woman colleague.

> The Chinese audience saw a story primarily about a conflict over rank. In it, two hierarchies collided, giving rise to a situation where rules of propriety were not clear-cut. In the first, the natural law of officialdom and the throne determined that the princess outranked her own husband, and thus was not under any obligation to attend his father's birthday party. The second involved the age hierarchy familiar to all families regardless of rank, which determines that any woman will attend the birthday party of her father-in-law. The resolution of this impasse did indeed involve the humiliation of the princess. But theoretically, a similar story could have been told about a junior son, if, for example, the boy had scorned a poor, elderly woman who happened to be a friend of his own father, or had disrespected virtue or seniority. *This is not to say that junior men hold exactly the same position as junior women.* But in the story we saw, the conflict between rank in political culture and rank in family could not be properly adjudicated until the emperor raised his son-in-law to his daughter's rank. He could not lower her status; and he did not want to order her to obey someone less exalted than herself. The only resolution was to promote the husband, compelling the princess to obey the family hierarchy of her in-laws, and preventing her from being able to revenge herself later on her husband or his father. [Barlow and Lowe 1987:192–193; emphasis added].

Barlow argues that the princess was humiliated not because she was a woman but because she had flagrantly violated the requirements of her social role as a daughter-in-law. In this sense, she abused her rank.

Essential to my interpretation of Barlow's story is the degree to which the opera dramatizes the stereotype that women are assumed to abuse power if not properly subordinated to male supervision. This aspect of the *yin*-ness of women has reasserted itself with a vengeance in the post-Mao period, especially in the criticism of Jiang Qing, Mao's widow, who now personifies the qualities of untamed *yin*—arrogance of power and sexual licentiousness. As an exemplar of the propensity of women to abuse power, she joins the venerable ranks of the Empress Wu (Tang Dynasty) and Cixi (the last empress of the Qing). Jiang Qing has accordingly become a convenient vehicle for indirect criticism of Mao, without anyone having to challenge his charismatic legacy head on. It is as if the *yin* part of his nature, his less rational self, as the instigator of the Cultural Revolution (now referred to as the "ten years of chaos") could be somehow made separate from his more positive image. This "feminization of evil" has now become a pervasive image of the Cultural Revolution period.[20] The irony of this image lies in the fact that the Cultural Revolution, despite its horrors, was the most successful period in the erasure of gender inequality in its assaults on Confucian ideology.

Another measure of how much has changed in the post-Mao era can be read in the degree to which gender is becoming reinscribed with difference. This is readily apparent in the revalorization of feminine self-adornment which is welcomed not only as relief from the dreary, unremitting androgyny of Cultural Revolution dress, but also as a form of liberating self-expression (Honig and Hershatter 1988). Permed hair, bright colors, and cosmetics are the instruments that visibly write this difference. And yet there is also an awareness of where this emphasis on personal adornment and display might lead in terms of objectifying and commodifying women. Honig and Hershatter (1988:49) cite a poetic commentary on the use of the female image in advertising that appeared in the *China Youth News:*

> A rubber tire and a fashionable woman
> Like a horse and a cow in heat, have nothing to do with each other. . . .
> Since "the price is reasonable" and the maker honest.

why have a girl
Make eyes at the customers?

More insidious than this objectification is the reassertion of sexual difference in terms of "essentializing" terms. A recent essay compares male and female students, contrasting the thinking of male students: broad and quick, wide-ranging, independent; with that of female students: narrow, easily distracted, trivial, diligent, meticulous (1988:15–16).[21] Barlow (1985) traces this sexualization of women to the May Fourth period during which the importation of Western concepts emphasized sexuality both as the medium of self-expression and as the essential definition of the person.

Likewise, in the current redefinition of gender roles, a return to the Chinese feminine ideal of the "virtuous wife and good mother" *(xianqi liangmu)* is also in reaction against what are now judged to be Cultural Revolutionary excesses in the erasure of sexual difference, epitomized by what are now referred to as the "fierce-browed female 'daring generals' " (cited in Honig and Hershatter 1988:175).[22] If the post-Mao period marks a return to a Confucian ideal of women's role, it is, at least, phrased in terms of what new criteria should define the "virtuous wife and good mother" for the 1980s. The ideal wife should be "a tender and compassionate partner for her husband, should support him in his work and point out his shortcomings, and, most important, should have knowledge, skills, and ideas of her own" (1988:175). A woman should not submit through blind obedience to her husband but at the same time she is largely responsible for managing the practical and emotional demands of the marital relationship.

Yet another dimension of the post-Mao gender system is the redefinition of woman's role as daughter-in-law within the patrilineal family. In the early postrevolutionary period, an important aspect of the party's assault on "feudal" family values was to support daughters-in-law in their confrontation with abusive mothers-in-law. Problems between mothers-in-law and daughters in-law continue to be an important focus in the post-Mao period. Now, however, it is more likely the daughter-in-law who becomes the focus of reform in her failure to respect and care for her mother-in-law, and even, in extreme cases, in her outright abuse of the older woman. To a certain extent, these problems may indicate the degree to which the feudal authority of mothers-in-law has indeed been smashed by the rapid social change of the socialist period. Today, daughters-in-law are often much more independent, especially if they work outside the home and exert more control over household finances. This appears especially true in urban settings; however, in rural contexts one wonders the degree to which the burden of blame for unharmonious relations between these two family actors is a reassertion of rural patriarchy over young wives as was discussed above in the context of the "five-good" family model. This may be true especially where women's economic contribution to household finances takes the form of unpaid labor in the family enterprise rather than in wages earned in a job outside the family. In either context, whether urban or rural, one would think that this emphasis on daughters-in-law as potentially disruptive agents within the family, is one that would reinvoke the cultural construction of women's *yin* nature as a dangerous and disruptive force that must be guided by the rational will of the state.

Conclusion

Despite these disturbing signs of an intensification of gender inequality in the post-Mao period, the future does not look totally bleak. Honig and Hershatter document the extent to which women's issues are now being discussed in a public discursive domain that has expanded to include formerly unmentionable topics, such as divorce, sexuality, domestic violence, and sexual harassment. They also point to the representation of women models selected for their economic achievements under the current reforms in which their gender is incidental to their value to the state for demonstrating that the policies are working. This new model of women as successful economic actors is similar to the "Iron Girl" model of the Cultural Revolution era in that both were "byproducts of political campaigns that had objectives other than raising the status of women" (1988:31). Honig and Hershatter critique this model as misleading women about their opportunities in the economic sphere. These models for women do not prepare them "for the obstacles they would actually face in school and at work, and did prepare them to blame themselves if they met with failure" (1988:30). But it remains to be seen whether these new models can implement their vision of "a gender-free" world by providing women with subject positions as able economic managers and small-scale entrepreneurs. It is still a case of the state creating categories for its own purposes in promoting its policies, but how these roles come to be embodied in practice might possibly have interesting implications for expanding women's roles in society.

In conclusion, the assessment of Chinese women themselves of how much things have changed must be taken into account. The elderly women who filed out of the movie theater described in the opening paragraphs of this essay may have been only nodding their assent automatically at the prodding of a party activist. But the consciousness of enormous change is present at both ends of the generational continuum. The elderly grandmothers in the film Small Happiness exclaim with an almost scandalized appreciation at the freedom of younger women in Long Bow village today. And in Barlow and Lowe's memoir of their stay in China, they record one Chinese women's assessment of the situation:

> [She] sees the problem as enormously complex and as one of the greatest burdens inherited from the old society. But when she thinks about sexual equality what springs into her mind is her grandmother, the distance separating her from her grandmother is unimaginable. [1987:199]

The experience of Chinese women under socialism is instructive to us all of the enormous complexities of transforming gender ideologies and that there are no easy answers or short cuts to changing gender ideologies by fiat but only a long, slow dialectical process of change.

Notes

Acknowledgments. Earlier versions of this curriculum guide have been read or discussed with Lisa Rofel and Marilyn Young. Special thanks to Tani Barlow for letting me cite her unpublished work and for challenging my ethnocentric biases. Thanks also to numerous anonymous reviewers for the AAA Project on Gender in the Curriculum.

1. Lu Xun's story recounts this woman's being "sold" into a second marriage against her will by her dead husband's family. Her obvious powerlessness to prevent this unwanted marriage was compounded by the ridicule to which she was subjected for failing to protest it enough. By not killing herself, she had acquiesced.

2. In 1981, the official policy limited field research by foreign social science scholars to a maximum of two weeks in their fieldsites, especially those in rural locations. These time restrictions have been loos-

ened considerably since then. Wolf (1985) gives the best account of the frustrations of doing anthropological fieldwork in the PRC and especially of the problems encountered by women scholars.

3. The Communist Party's revolutionary strategy was to mobilize those sectors of the population it identified as oppressed—peasants and workers as victims of the class system, women and youth as victims of feudal family relations. During the revolutionary period, the party organized not only poor peasants' associations but also women's associations in rural villages to provide structural support for the overthrow of class enemies and family tyrants respectively. As I will discuss below, the discourse of revolution created new political subjects by means of the classificatory strategies of the party (see Barlow 1985, 1988).

4. There is some evidence that in some areas at least there was a breakdown in intra-lineage, intra-village marriage taboos, although most of this evidence comes from Guangdong (see for instance Parish and Whyte 1978:171–2). Chan et al. (1984) in their study *Chen Village* cite some instances where women defied the cultural norm against surname exogamy and married other Chens in the same village. There is evidence to suggest that the administrative reorganization of the countryside under socialism has led to an intensified localism that encouraged village endogamy. Virilocality has broken down more completely in urban areas. With the scarcity of housing, young couples reside with either the husband's or wife's parents according to which has more room to accommodate them (Honig and Hershatter 1988:139).

5. This attitude strikingly parallels the prerevolutionary family ideology that having a daughter was like "spilling water on the ground." Any investment in training and educating her would ultimately go to the benefit of her husband's family and his community, and not to her natal village.

6. The film *Small Happiness* (Gordon and Hinton 1984) illustrates a case in which a young woman was able to receive training as a tractor driver only to discover that the feudal attitudes of the community would not permit her to practice her skills. Work as a tractor driver would have required her to cross the boundaries of sexual segregation in the community as these are currently defined and therefore her virtue would be questioned. Not only she, but her husband's family would lose face and so she gave up her claims on a job better compensated than those usually taken by women.

7. For instance, the head of the local women's association is often charged with the responsibility for fertility limitation. Contraception is thereby identified as a "woman's concern." The implications of the present birth policy for women and for the assertion of state power will be explored in the second curriculum example on the "one-child family" policy in the post-Mao period.

8. What is called the "natural" village, in Chinese, refers to communities organized on the basis of patrilineal descent. In my use of this term, I do not mean to imply that this is in fact a natural social grouping, but I am merely following Chinese usage. Indeed, the persistence of patrilineal descent as a principle of social organization in the Chinese countryside is proof of how much the naturalness of such social groupings has never been brought sufficiently into question in the context of planned social change in postrevolutionary China. This has placed serious constraints on the realization of gender equality in rural Chinese society, as will be argued below.

9. There were attempts during socialist high tides to "socialize" housework by providing communal canteens and child care facilities, thus freeing women's labor for the demands of mass collective construction efforts such as those engaged in during the Great Leap Forward (1956–58). The rural canteens did not survive the famines which followed this policy initiative, while child care facilities were more successful in some areas. In urban areas, both canteens and child care are still available in work units that can afford them.

10. Postrevolutionary statuses in Chinese society constituted an inverted hierarchy in which those who enjoyed elite status in preliberation China occupied the lowest rung and workers and poor peasants the highest. See Billeter (1985) and Kraus (1981) for detailed descriptions of the influence of one's "class background" for determining one's status in all aspects of everyday life. Stacey suggests that the empowerment of peasant heads of households, although it was seen as a conservative step in party policy,

was still theorized in terms of an eventual transition to socialism. No such theoretical vision guided the conservative turn in the party's retreat on family reform (Stacey 1983:251).

11. Mythic history and socialist realism are the two dominant modes of representation cultivated in Chinese political culture which lock into each other in the process of "recalling the bitter past to savor the sweet present." "Speaking bitterness" may have been intended originally as a tool to transform consciousness of those oppressed in the old class society, but it later became institutionalized as a history that inscribed the revolution as necessary and inevitable and that could reinvent successive political campaigns focused on class struggle with a similar urgency. This narrative form underlies the cinematic transformation/appropriation of Lu Xun's story described at the beginning of this essay. For classic examples of other "speaking bitterness" texts narrated by women see "The Story of Selling Oneself" and "A Woman Farmhand" in Sidney L. Greenblatt," (ed.) *The People of Taihang.*

12. At the same time, the creation of politicized subjects such as Goldflower gave the party an activist within the household that could press on the more conservative male household heads to comply with party policies, especially during the period of rapid state-engineered change. The female protagonist of the enormously popular film, *Li Shuangshuang,* made in the 1950s during the period of socialist transformation, exemplifies the power and energy of women as political subjects unleased by party mobilization. Audiences loved the tart-tongued female lead and the strategies she employed to get her narrowminded husband to mend his ways.

13. This suggestion may not be entirely fair as Goldflower's story takes place in the context of the civil war in northern China in which a more radical displacement of patriarchy may have been feared as too destabilizing for a political authority under siege.

14. There can be no doubt that the Chinese woman became a powerful image in Western feminist discourse. This is not to derogate the ideological effect of this imaginary construction in the context of Western feminism in that it has helped to rethink gender as ideology embedded in practice thereby problematizing its reproduction and transformation. Ironically, these implications of the relationship between ideology and practice emerged during the Cultural Revolution's campaign against feudal thought (such as in the campaign against the "four olds") which was not specifically directed at the issues of gender.

15. For a demonstration of how "woman" may operate as a category of political discourse that extends the power of the state into society, see the second curriculum example which deals with the one-child family policy in the post-Mao period.

16. One might argue that neither class nor gender are universal categories but social determinations that developed into sinified forms in the context of the Chinese revolution. Class as an abstract term of classification became reworked into a set of categories defining a moral order that was uniquely Chinese and that operated as a status hierarchy in the new society.

17. Wolf (1972) gives a detailed description of a woman's life course and her changing position within the patriarchal family. This change in status marks the transition of the woman from the outside to the inside of the patriline.

18. In the realm of the family, women's disruptive quality was not so much conceptualized as *yin* as identified with her outsider status. Young wives presumably incited their husbands to demand family division and the breakup of the extended family in which brothers and their families lived together with their parents.

19. Barlow, personal communication.

20. I am indebted to Marilyn Young for this felicitous phrase.

21. Rofel (1989) has documented a similar reversion to sex stereotyping in a factory setting as a rationale for job assignments and wage differentials under the post-Mao economic reforms in industry.

22. An important novel about the Cultural Revolution period is Gu Hua's *A Small Town Called Hibiscus* (1984) in which the two principal characters embody oppositional feminine stereotypes: the "good

mother and virtuous wife" who is victimized by a ruthless local Party cadre, a woman who presumably represents Jing Qing herself.

References Cited

Ahern, Emily (Martin)
    1975   The Power and Pollution of Chinese Women. *In* Women in Chinese Society. Margery Wolf and Roxane Witke, eds. Pp. 193–214. Stanford: Stanford University Press.
Anagnost, Ann
    1985   Political Culture and Popular Practice in PostMao China. Unpublished Ph.D. dissertation, University of Michigan.
Andors, Phyllis
    1983   The Unfinished Liberation of Chinese Women, 1949–1980. Bloomington: Indiana University Press.
Barlow, Tani
    1985   The Place of Women in Ding Ling's World: Feminism and the Concept of Gender in Modern China. Unpublished doctoral dissertation, University of California, Davis.
    1988   Theorizing Woman: *Funu, Guojia, Jiating* [Woman/women, Nation, Family]. Unpublished paper delivered at a panel entitled "Reconceptualizing the Chinese State" at the 1988 annual meeting of the American Anthropological Association.
Barlow, Tani, and Donald M. Lowe
    1987   Teaching China's Lost Generation. San Francisco: China Books and Periodicals. [Originally published as Chinese Reflections. New York: Praeger, 1985].
Beldon, Jack
    1970   Goldflower's Story. *In* China Shakes the World. New York: Monthly Review Press.
Billeter, Jean François
    1985   The System of 'Class-Status'. *In* The Scope of State Power in China. Stuart R. Schram, ed. Pp. 127–169. London: School of Oriental and African Studies.
Chan, Anita, et al.
    1984   Chen Village: The Recent History of a Peasant Community in Mao's China. Berkeley: University of California Press.
Croll, Elisabeth
    1984   The Exchange of Women and Property: Marriage in Post-Revolutionary China. *In* Women and Property—Women as Property. Renée Hirschon, ed. Pp. 44–61. New York: St. Martin's Press.
Diamond, Norma
    1975   Collectivization, Kinship, and the Status of Women in Rural China. *In* Toward an Anthropology of Women. Rayna Reiter, ed. Pp. 372–395. New York: Monthly Review Press.
Gordon, Richard and Carma Hinton
    1984   Small Happiness (film). Philadelphia: Long Bow Group.
Greenblatt, Sidney L.
    1976   The People of Taihang. White Plains, N.Y.: International Arts and Sciences Press.
Gu Hua
    1983   A Small Town Called Hibiscus. Beijing: Panda Books.
Honig, Emily, and Gail Hershatter
    1988   Personal Voices: Chinese Women in the 1980s. Stanford: Stanford University Press.
Huters, Theodore
    1984   Blossoms in the Snow: Lu Xun and the Dilemma of Modern Chinese Literature. Modern China 10(1):49–78.
Johnson, Kay Ann
    1983   Women, the Family and Peasant Revolution in China. Chicago: University of Chicago Press.

Kraus, Richard Curt
1981   Class Conflict in Chinese Socialism. New York: Columbia University Press.
Lu, Hsun (Lu Xun)
n.d.   New Year's Sacrifice. Chosen Pages from Lu Hsun. New York: Cameron Associates, Inc. [Reprinted in a number of Lu Hsun collections].
Moore, Henrietta L.
1988   Feminism and Anthropology. Minneapolis: University of Minnesota Press.
Overmyer, Daniel L.
1980   Dualism and Conflict in Chinese Popular Religions. *In* Transitions and Transformations in the History of Religions. Frank E. Reynolds and Theodore M. Ludwig, eds. Leiden.
Parish, William, and Martin Whyte
1978   Village and Family in Contemporary China. Chicago: University of Chicago Press.
Rofel, Lisa
1989   Hegemony and Productivity: Workers in Post-Mao China. *In* Marxism and the Chinese Experience: Issues of Socialism in a Third World Socialist Society. Arif Dirlik and Maurice Meisner, eds. Armonk, N.Y.: M. E. Sharpe.
Sangren, P. Steven
1987   Orthodoxy, Heterodoxy, and the Structure of Value in Chinese Rituals. Modern China 13(1):63–89.
Stacey, Judith
1983   Patriarchy and Socialist Revolution in China. Berkeley: University of California Press.
Wolf, Margery
1972   Women and the Family in Rural Taiwan. Stanford: Stanford University Press.
1985   Revolution Postponed: Women in Contemporary China. Stanford: Stanford University Press.
Young, Marilyn B., ed.
1973   Women in China. Ann Arbor: University of Michigan Center for Chinese Studies.
1989   Chicken Little in China: Some Reflections on Women. *In* Marxism and the Chinese Experience: Issues of Socialism in a Third World Socialist Society. Arif Dirlik and Maurice Meisner, eds., Armonk, N.Y.: M. E. Sharpe. (in press).

Example One
Footbinding: The Bodily Inscription of Gender Difference

Suggested applications: the cultural construction of the person
                                 the bodily inscription of cultural codes

The problem of speaking about practices such as footbinding that may be repugnant to a Western sensibility is how to speak of them without contributing to the construction of a colonial discourse. Spivak points out this difficulty in the context of British colonial discourse on suttee. She articulates the colonial dimension as follows: "White men are saving brown women from brown men" (Spivak 1985:121). In China, the instigators of reform to eradicate the practice of footbinding may have been Chinese, yet to some extent these reformers were elite males influenced by Western education and missionary horror at the practice. While avoiding the Scylla of colonial discourse, one must also avoid the Charybdis of an extreme relativist position which makes anything that fits into the "integral fabric" of a culture justifiable in those terms. One might compare comparable practices that mark bodies in our own culture: face-lifts, liposuction, nose jobs, electrolysis, waxing, anorexia, etc., as a way of equalizing the power relationship in our explanation of alien customs which involve pain or "an improvement of nature" but which always exist in reference to a code.

The act of suffering oneself to be written by the group's law is oddly accompanied by a pleasure, that of being recognized (but one does not know by whom), of becoming an identifiable and legible word in a social language, of being changed into a fragment within an anonymous text, of being inscribed in a symbolic order that has neither owner nor author. [de Certeau 1984:140]

In the film *Small Happiness,* an elderly man known by the women of Long Bow Village as an "old feudal" *(lao fengjian)* gleefully remembers the old days when it was easy to keep one's wife in line by stomping on her bound feet. Few practices were as powerful a symbol of women's subordinate status in traditional China as the tiny crippled feet of women who bear this marking of culture on gender. Originating as a fashion among palace dancers a millennium ago, the practice was promoted by neo-Confucian reformers from the Song Dynasty (A.D. 960–1279) onward as an effective way of ensuring the virtue of women by circumscribing their movement. Footbinding became, as did widow chastity, not only a sign of feminine virtue and respectability but of the moral standing of the community as a whole.[1] Although footbinding was still widespread in many areas of China at the beginning of this century, the practice increasingly came under attack by a Western-influenced, educated elite caught up in the intellectual ferment of the May Fourth Movement (1920s). In the struggle to find China's modern identity, footbinding became an integral part of the "woman question" along with women's education, freedom to marry, and reform of the patriarchal family. Young, urban, educated men returned home to the provinces to tell their mothers to unbind their sisters' feet. Young women began to encourage each other to unbind their own feet despite social and familial disapproval. "Natural foot societies" proliferated often in association with the movement to educate women. The pain of footbinding was regarded as an obstacle to women's education because it disrupted one's ability to concentrate (Ebrey 1981:245). In a newly emerging modernity, footbinding no longer signified respectability but became instead a sign of cultural backwardness.

Although the practice of footbinding may have been limited at first to elite families who could afford to sacrifice the labor power of their women, certainly by the 19th century and most likely earlier, the practice had become widespread among nonelites as well, especially in regions where local practice excluded women from agricultural labor. Hakka women, as members of a quasi-ethnic minority distinct from the surrounding Han Chinese populations, were easily recognized by their regular participation in agricultural work and in their correspondingly unbound feet. Likewise in the tea and silk producing regions of southern China, footbinding was less prevalent in peasant families. In other areas, however, special kneepads were invented to allow even the boundfoot woman to engage in the more back-breaking agricultural tasks, such as transplanting rice, often assigned to women. In the northwest province of Shaanxi where Long Bow village is located, the practice was so popular that large feet were a matter of shame and could seriously harm a woman's marital prospects. Indeed, large feet were such a liability that a woman might choose to bind them again to make them smaller if the first attempt was unsuccessful. If the large-footed woman was able to forget her deficiencies, the taunts of others were quick to remind her of it. "Look at this! The person has not yet arrived and her feet are already here!"[2] The smallness of one's feet therefore became an acutely conscious measure of feminine presentability, and this is important to remember when trying to understand how footbinding could have been a form of oppression that women enacted against themselves. Mothers would bind the feet of their tiny daughters and as they grew older, the daughters themselves would take responsibility for binding their own feet and those of their daughters.

There were varying degrees of severity in the binding, depending on how small a foot was desired. In nonelite families where women were responsible for work in the household, women were merely hobbled, allowing them to move unaided. In more severe cases, the support of a cane or a companion may have been required. Footbinding not only condemned women to a life of relative immobility, but it was a terribly painful process, especially in its initial stages. In binding, the large toe was left free but the rest were folded under and drawn toward the heel as closely as possible. A bandage about ten feet long was applied tightly so that the foot was subjected to ''unremitting pressure'' (Levy 1966:26). Young girls between the ages of 6 to 8 years old had their feet bound, usually by their mothers. Many recall the pain that was so great they couldn't sleep. While subject to sores and putrescence which caused them further suffering, their feet were forced into a succession of progressively smaller shoes until they achieved the desired three inches in length, a process that took about two years.

Bound feet were not just the physical means to restricting women's mobility but were part of a symbolic complex which situated the patriarchal household *(jia)* in the larger social and political order. The principles of hierarchy that organized the household on the basis of age, sex, and generation provided the metaphor that ordered the relationship between loyal subjects and the state. The patriarchal authority of the male head of household resembled the authority of a ruler over his domain. Households were organized around the continuity of male agnates. Therefore, the predominant residence rule upon marriage was that the bride would move to her husband's village.[3] A woman newly married occupied the lowest rung in this system of relationships. Entering her husband's family as a stranger, her loyalty and sense of propriety as yet untried, she was therefore untrustworthy and in need of supervision. She constituted a threat to the reputation of the *jia*. If she were to lose her virtue, she would lose face for the family. As a stranger, her primary loyalties were suspect. She was ''raw'' *(sheng)* and not ''cooked'' *(shu)* which in Chinese conveys the difference between outside and inside, between stranger and familiar, between suspicion and trust.[4]

Confined to the inside, the newly married woman was placed under the supervision of her mother-in-law. Position within the structure of the *jia* created divisions between women. Women's status within the patriarchal family changed as their position within that structure changed. Once a woman had assured continuity for the family by providing it with sons, she then achieved a more authoritative position within the structure as the elder generation. Her achieving this status was entirely dependent on her own reproductive success in producing a ''uterine'' family embedded within the larger patriarchal structure (Wolf 1972). Gender as a principle of organization within the household crosscut the hierarchical placement of age and generation. The three of these together determined the relative position of each woman within the *jia* ensuring that relations between them would be hierarchically ordered within the patrilineal structure.

Binding the feet of women was therefore the physical manifestation of the symbolic importance of women to the inside. Women, especially younger ones, were confined to the home. They were called ''inside persons'' *(neiren)* or ''those of my household'' *(wo jialide)* by men.[5] This seclusion of new wives within the household was not defined by a symbolic opposition of public and private domains, rather it was an indication of a daughter-in-law's stranger status in her husband's family.[6] The elderly women in *Small Happiness* recall the constraints placed on their movement. To leave the house, a daughter-in-law required the permission of her mother-in-law who would pull a long face and give grudging consent only if the younger woman promised not to be long.

The relegation of women to the inside ensured the segregation of the sexes, one of the fundamental principles of the Confucian moral order. Sexual segregation along with hierarchical ordering of relationships assured the maintenance of roles that were the structural basis for the Chinese *jia*. As a woman entered into her successive roles within that structure, first as a daughter-in-law and then as a mother-in-law, her license of movement outside the house may have widened, but her feet permanently bore the marks of confinement that physically limited her movement while, at the same time, signifying her respectability.

Notes

1. See Mann (1987) for a discussion of this aspect of widow chastity. The story "Ah Ao" by Sun Hsi-chen suggests how the interests of the community as a whole in the virtue of its women were expressed. A young woman caught in a premarital relationship is subject to abuse and even death at the hands of the community. Her mother bankrupts herself to give a massive feast to the entire community as a way of buying mercy for her daughter. The feast is not a celebratory occasion but an "eat in" through which the community applies a punitive sanction on the household by exhausting its resources. Even the mother of the girl's partner in sin participates with gusto, illustrating the double standard operative in the moral community. The story strikingly parallels a fantasy based on an incident in her family's mythic history by Maxine Hong Kingston in *The Woman Warrior* (1976). In this story, not only was there an "eat in" but the family home and all its possessions were trashed by the villagers.

2. This is quoted from the film *Small Happiness* (Gordon and Hinton 1984). Most of the elderly women who appear in the film do have bound feet, thus attesting to the prevalence of the practice in the northwest of China. If footbinding correlates highly with the practice of female seclusion, one might speculate whether its prevalence in the northwest might be related to the cultural influence of large communities of Chinese Muslims.

3. Uxorilocal marriage was practiced occasionally in households where there were no sons to continue the family into the next generation. In order to attract a potential son-in-law into a situation that might prove otherwise disadvantageous for him, the wife's family might agree to allow all subsequent male children of the union to bear their father's surname, as long as the first could be designated as the bearer of the mother's surname. However, this sort of arrangement was considered not only demeaning but even unfilial in that it would deprive a man's ancestors of their future descendants. Even so, an arrangement of this kind might have appealed to a man who lacked the material resources to establish a household of his own, especially when the prospective wife's family was considerably better off.

4. See Yang (1989) for the distinction between "raw" and "cooked" and also Barlow (1985) for a discussion of the opposition between inside and outside.

5. Again this is taken from the film *Small Happiness* (Gordon and Hinton 1984). Watson (1986) tells how the relative "namelessness" of the women in the Cantonese village of her study compares forcibly with the accumulation of names by men marking the important transitions in their lives. The namelessness of women suggests that for them personhood is quite differently defined than for men insofar as names in Chinese society are a public acknowledgment of one's unique social identity that is denied to women. In this sense, a naming system is just as much a writing of culture on gender as are the more physically manifested scripts: footbinding, ear piercing, dress and coiffure.

6. Although this strict segregation of the sexes may have been more true of elite households, there were large areas of China where peasant households also observed this practice. This was especially true in the northwest where Long Bow Village is located.

References Cited

Barlow,Tani
      1985   The Place of Women in Ding Ling's World: Feminism and the Concept of Gender in Modern
         China. Unpublished doctoral dissertation, University of California, Davis.

De Certeau, Michel
    1984   The Practice of Everyday Life. Berkeley: University of California Press.
Ebrey, Patricia B.
    1981   The Movement Against Footbinding. Speeches, letters, and association by-laws. *In* Chinese
        Civilization and Society: A Sourcebook. New York: The Free Press.
Gordon, Richard, and Carma Hinton
    1984   Small Happiness (film). Philadelphia: Long Bow Group.
Kingston, Maxine Hong
    1976   The Woman Warrior: Memoirs of a Girlhood Among Ghosts. New York: Knopf.
Levy, Howard S.
    1966   Chinese Footbinding: The History of a Curious Erotic Custom. New York: Walton Rawls.
Mann, Susan
    1987   Widows in the Kinship, Class, and Community Structures of Qing Dynasty China. Journal of
        Asian Studies 46(1):37–56.
Spivak, Gayatri C.
    1985   Can the Subaltern Speak?: Speculations on Widow-Sacrifice. Wedge 7/8:120–130.
Sun Hsi-chen
    1975   Ah Ao. *In* Fragment From a Lost Diary. Naomi Katz and Nancy Milton, eds. Pp. 72–83.
        Boston: Beacon Press. [Reprinted from Living China. Edgar Snow, ed. London: Harrap, 1936.]
Watson, Rubie
    1986   The Named and the Nameless: Gender and Person in Chinese Society. *American Ethnologist*
        13(4):619–631.
Wolf, Margery
    1972   Women and the Family in Rural Taiwan. Stanford: Stanford University Press.
Yang, Mayfair
    1989   The Gift Economy and State Power in China. Journal of Comparative Studies in Society and
        History 31(1) (January):25–54.

Example 2
The Politics of Fertility: China's One-Child Family Policy

Suggested applications: the relationship between production and reproduction
directed change in modernizing states
modernity as a transnational culture

    In the post-Mao period (1976–present), the Chinese leadership has simultaneously pro-
moted two policies that appear incompatible with each other. The "responsibility system in
agriculture" is intended to raise the productivity of peasant agriculture by granting more economic autonomy to the household; while the "one-child family" policy is designed to radically limit the rate of population growth. The contradiction between them lies in the incentive
that the current economic policies give to peasant households to increase their labor power by
having more children. Despite their incompatibility, the objectives of these two policies are
connected in the political rhetoric of the Chinese state. Any gains made in the area of agricultural productivity, the official argument insists, would be offset by an unchecked increase
in population. The state has decided that only a radical policy which limits births to one per
couple will enable the country to attain the economic goals set for the end of this century.
This argument joins the two policies together in a comprehensive plan for economic development.

    While the economic reforms have been welcomed in the countryside, the birth policy
has met with widespread resistance. This is reflected in the strategies for its implementation.

Policy directives, which in China have the force of law, set strict quotas on the number of births for local areas. Couples may apply for official permission to have a child and may often have to wait years for their turn so that these local quotas will not be exceeded. After the birth, they are pressured to sign a one-child pledge card guaranteeing no further births and strict sanctions are placed on families to ensure they fulfill their pledge. If a woman becomes pregnant again despite all of these sanctions and pledges, she is obligated to undergo abortion procedures and she or her husband are strongly encouraged to undergo sterilization or they face severe economic penalties.

Although these procedures are meant to be voluntary, local officials can bring tremendous pressure to bear on couples by means of sanctions and threats to ensure their compliance. Local officials themselves are under heavy pressure from the ''higher ups'' to stay within their birth quotas and meeting these quotas has become an important measure of their political efficacy. Political recognition and promotion is based on ends, not means. Forced sterilizations and abortions, although unlawful, are the measures used by some local officials to ensure that quotas are met. Although the state deplores these abuses of power, it fails to take responsibility for them as the inevitable result of its own policies and practices. It is difficult to measure how widespread are these coercive practices, because the success of the policy is highly exaggerated in many areas. The alternative to coercive measures is for local officials to misreport local birth statistics in response to pressures from above. Coercion and misreporting both attest to the degree to which rural populations have resisted the implementation of the one-child family policy.[1] This resistance is best understood by placing it in the context of the present organization of production in the countryside.

Under the new economic policies instituted since 1978, agriculture has been decollectivized, making the household the primary economic unit in the rural economy. All children have become a valuable resource not only as labor in the newly reconstituted household economy, but male children are even more necessary to ensure the social reproduction of the household, as daughters continue to marry out. Parents who lack male children will not only find themselves short of labor power in their household enterprises in the immediate future, but they also face an insecure old age when they retire from agricultural work with no male offspring to support them and no collective welfare fund to protect them. Their daughters will owe their primary loyalties to their husbands' families and will not be able to offer sufficient aid to their aging parents.

The implications for women of the bind placed on the rural household caught between these conflicting policies has been devastating. Their bodies and reproductive powers have become a contested domain in a power struggle between the state and the patriarchal family which has, ironically, become reconstituted under socialism. Women suffer from this contestation in a most physical way. Although the official policy appears to contain no bias as to which partner should undergo sterilization, the women in the film *Small Happiness* (Gordon and Hinton 1984) tell us that in practice it is mostly women who undergo the procedure. The rationalization is that whatever long-term health effects may result, it is preferred that the ''full labor power'' of men in their prime be spared surgical interventions because of their importance in agricultural work.[2] Concealed pregnancies also expose women to risk when they are pressured into abortions in the third trimester. In terms of both surgical procedures, abortion and sterilization, women become the structural victims of the struggle between the state and the patrilineal family; their bodies bear the brunt of punishment for noncompliance.[3]

Given the tremendous popular resistance that make such measures necessary, why would the state promote such a radical population policy at the same time that it encourages the economic autonomy of the household? The arguments for the one-child policy do not make a convincing case for urgency in terms of a subsistence crisis.[4] The argument for the policy is mostly phrased in terms of the relative degree of development China will be able to achieve by the year 2000. Failure to fulfill the quotas set by the state merely means that certain economic goals may not be achieved by the end of the century. This suggests that the impetus for the policy derives less from demographic or economic imperatives and more from political objectives: the attainment of an arbitrarily defined standard of living according to a plan.[5] Under the one-child policy, the family finds itself caught in an irresolvable contradiction between its own interests as defined in the economic reform and the ultimatum by the state to limit its fertility. The strict insistence that families have one child and one child only increases the importance that first births be male births. In recent years the state has relaxed its policies to a certain extent to allow some rural families to try again if their first baby is a girl, in recognition of the hardships the policy has placed on peasant households (and in the face of tremendous resistance to the policy in the countryside). However, permission for a second birth is difficult to obtain and is supposed to be given only in cases where the household meets certain criteria.

Given these difficulties, the preference for sons is almost universal, and has led to a number of practices that victimize women. As in the case of abuses at the hands of local officials, abuses that derive from the woman's family are also condemned by the state, yet its policies are nonetheless responsible for their appearance. In the context of the one-child family, female infanticide has become a tactic for ensuring that one's only child is male. Although infanticide may be an extreme response to the policy, its increased incidence has caused some alarm that serious sex-ratio imbalances may result in some local areas. The birth of daughters is also often blamed on the mother as women are considered to be responsible for the outcome of a birth. Despite birth policy propaganda that it is the father's contribution that determines the sex of the child, mothers are often blamed for bearing daughters and may find themselves severely punished by their husbands and mothers-in-law.[6] Stories abound in the Chinese press about women who are mentally and physically abused, coerced to divorce, or pushed toward suicide because of their failure to produce a son. Although these cases may be the exceptions rather than the rule, they are recognized by the state as sufficiently widespread to be a cause of concern in its criticism of a "feudal" family ideology.

The following account is an illustration of how the state distances itself from its responsibility for abuses arising from its own policies. The suicide of a young mother was attributed to the maltreatment she had received at the hands of her husband and mother-in-law after her failure to bear a son. The local party committee launched a community-wide investigation of intrafamilial relations to detect other cases where daughters-in-law may be at risk. The result of their survey revealed a number of household statistics that defined the targets for subsequent ideological work: 147 households were designated as "dangerous households" in which tensions due to the birth of daughters had reached the point where violence was imminent, 267 "problem households" had already exceeded their birth quota and had not yet sought sterilization. After a vigorous campaign, it was reported that most of the "dangerous households" had been persuaded into harmony and the "problem households" had undergone sterilization procedures (*Chinese Peasant Gazette*, 29 August 1982). A paternalistic concern for the plight of women on the part of the state becomes the means to turn the screws ever tighter, ensuring total compliance to the very policy that places women at risk. The state places the blame on the persistence of a feudal-patriarchal ideology, not on its own policies. In this way the state attempts to impose the "norm" of the one-child family onto a practical environment in which children are still very much an economic asset while at the same time presuming to protect women and children.[7]

How can we be critical without being judgmental? Do we simply dismiss the coercive aspects of the one-child policy as the draconian measures of a non-Western state, an oriental despotism? Perhaps the answer is to reflect the critique back to an international definition of what modernization is. China has been praised for its success in implementing its birth policy; the designers of the policy have been given prestigious awards by the United Nations in recognition of their achievement. The uncritical praise of China's success on the part of those who support fertility limitation as a strategy for economic development has failed to evaluate its human costs. Population control has become a sign of modernity, a form of "sympathetic magic" meant to evoke the indicators of a postindustrial society without possessing the material basis for such. Should we not recognize the complicity of Western social science discourse in the creation of an international culture that measures development in terms of control? In the case of a birth policy, control is exerted over the very resource, population, which, defined by its excess in relation to an imposed standard of development, has become the accepted indicator of the relative poverty of nations and as such endows such efforts toward its control with no insignificant measure of symbolic capital in the developed world.

Finally, we should perhaps reflect on the symbolic importance China's birth policy has had in our own political culture. China provides us with an anamorphosis, a distorting mirror image of our own ethical dilemma about control over reproduction. For pro-life advocates, it provides a horrific image of to what extremes the legality of abortion might lead. At the same time, it provides those who are pro-choice with an equally horrific image of the dangers of state intervention into reproductive decisions. The appropriation of the forced abortion issue by the pro-life movement has fueled the abortion controversy in this country. But the issue is just as potent a weapon for those who are pro-choice. The question ultimately is over who has the authority and the right to make choices: the state, the patriarchal family, or women as individuals.

Notes

1. The birth policy has been much more successful in urban areas where urban work units have more effective sanctions in their power to allocate housing, educational, and employment opportunities for workers and their children.

2. Yet, in the same film, we learn that men have flocked to new job opportunities opened by the recent economic reforms and women are left to do most of the agricultural tasks. One suspects that a patrilineal bias may be at work here. Wives, after all, are expendable. If the policy were to change at some point in the future, a man can divorce his sterilized wife and try again. This suggestion is supported by the discussion below of marital tensions resulting from the birth policy.

3. The implacement of IUD's is another means through which this discipline is imposed on women's bodies. Official permission for removing IUD's is difficult to obtain regardless of symptomatic counterindications because removal is counter to the birth policy. The devices in use also lack a cord that might otherwise facilitate unofficial removal. This has resulted in the proliferation of back alley practitioners who remove the devices with improvised hooks, leading often to infection and death. The situation is a grim mirror image of the practice of illegal abortions in our own history before abortion was legalized.

4. There is an extensive literature on China's one-child family policy. Croll (1983) discusses the contradictory relationship between the agricultural and birth policies. Wasserstrom (1984) details the various forms of popular resistance against the one-child family policy. Aird (1986) discusses the issues of coerciveness and questions the state's argument for the policy's necessity. See also Croll et al. (1985) for a comprehensive collection of essays, most notably Davin's essay on the impact of the policy in the countryside.

5. It is perhaps no accident that the state has chose to "grasp hold" of reproduction precisely at the moment it has loosened its grip on production. The locus of control, in a state apparatus which defines itself as the leadership of a planned economy, has been repositioned elsewhere. This argument is explored in more detail in Anagnost (1988).

6. This responsibility for the outcome of reproduction is perhaps connected to beliefs surrounding the influence of the mother's activities and diet on the unborn fetus (Furth 1987). A mother-in-law's stake in the reproductive outcome of her daughter-in-law rests on the older woman's interest in the continuity of her "uterine family" into the next generation (Wolf 1984).

7. Social surveys of this sort dramatically illustrate what Foucault (1979) calls "meticulous rituals of power" in which subjects are distributed according to a grid which exposes anomalies in the social body to the panoptic gaze of the state. Power is knowledge because those activities which produce information are in themselves material displays of power. In the case of China, ideological education is a means for the state to represent itself, even when the ostensible objectives of these sorts of activities are illusory, attaining the form but not the substance of form (Anagnost 1988).

References Cited

Aird, John S.
   1986   Coercion in Family Planning: Causes, Methods, and Consequences. *In* Congress of the U.S. Joint Economic Committee, China's Economy Looks Toward the Year 2000 (2 vols.). Washington, D.C.: Government Printing Office.
Anagnost, Ann
   1988   Family Violence and Magical Violence: Woman as Victim in China's One-child Family Policy. Women and Language 11(2):16–22.
Cross, Elisabeth J.
   1983   Production Versus Reproduction: A Threat to China's Development Strategy. World Development 11(6):467–481.
Cross, Elisabeth, Delia Davin, and Penny Kane, eds.
   1985   China's One-Child Family Policy. London: Macmillan.
Davin, Delia
   1985   The Single-child Family Policy in the Countryside. *In* China's One-Child Family Policy. Elisabeth J. Croll et al., eds. Pp. 37–82. London: Macmillan.
Foucault, Michel
   1979   Discipline and Punish. New York: Vintage.
Furth, Charlotte
   1987   Concepts of Pregnancy, Childbirth, and Infancy in Ch'ing Dynasty China. Journal of Asian Studies 46(1):7–36.
Gordon, Richard, and Carma Hinton
   1984   Small Happiness (film). Philadelphia: Long Bow Group.
Wasserstrom, Jeffrey
   1984   Resistance to the One-Child Family. Modern China 10(3):345–374.
Wolf, Margery
   1977   Uterine Families and the Women's Community. *In* Conformity and Conflict: Readings in Cultural Anthropology. James P. Spradley and David W. McCurdy, eds. Pp. 201–208. [Reprinted from Margery Wolf, Women and the Family in Rural Taiwan. Stanford: Stanford University Press, 1972].

Women in China
Teaching Bibliography

Barlow, Tani, and Donald M. Lowe
  1985   *Feminism* and *Sexism* in Chinese Reflections. New York: Praeger. [Reprinted as: Teaching
      China's Lost Generation. San Francisco: China Books and Periodicals, 1987]

  These are chapters in a longer memoir of teaching in China in 1981–82 by two authors who are
sensitive to the issues of cultural interpretation. The chapter entitled "Feminism" has a fascinating account of a Women's Day celebration that describes the cultural gap between Western and Chinese feminisms. See especially the two chapters entitled "Feminism" and "Sexism."

Beldon, Jack
  1970   Goldflower's Story. China Shakes the World. New York: Monthly Review Press.

  This short excerpt from Beldon's account of the war-torn 1940s is a classic reading in Western
discussions of women and revolution in China. It is similar in some respects to the "speaking bitterness"
narratives cited below (Greenblatt 1976), but it also details the process of struggle and the role of the
women's associations in supporting individual women's struggles.

Croll, Elisabeth
  1984   The Exchange of Women and Property: Marriage in Post-Revolutionary China. *In* Women
      and Property—Women as Property. Renée Hirschon, ed. New York: St. Martin's Press.

  In prerevolutionary Chinese society, women's labor, fertility, and person constituted property in
marriage transactions. Accordingly brideprice (or betrothal gift) was considered compensation to the
bride's family, while dowry, although it remained a woman's personal fund, was less obligatory and
served a more symbolic function in maintaining face for the family of the bride. The postrevolutionary
socialist state, in its efforts to improve women's relation to property, assumed that once private property
was collectivized and "feudal" ideology was abolished through education, the problem would resolve
itself. However, the patriarchal family has continued as a viable unit of production and consumption in
the rural collective economy where it derives its wealth from a concentration of labor rather than landed
property. This heightened value for their labor has not necessarily worked to the benefit of women, but
has increased their value in marital exchange which remains under the control of patriarchal authority
and contributes to the resilience of traditional marriage practices under socialism. For a more extended
treatment of marriage in socialist China, see her *Politics of Marriage in Contemporary China* (Cambridge University Press, 1981).

Diamond, Norma
  1975   Collectivization, Kinship, and the Status of Women in Rural China. *In* Toward an Anthro-
      pology of Women. Rayna Reiter, ed. New York: Monthly Review Press.

  Socialism has failed to displace feudal-patriarchal ideology in rural China because the cohesiveness
of patrilineal kin groups lends itself to collective agriculture. Women upon marriage continue to move
from one group of male kinsmen to another. Virilocal marriage reproduces the economic, social and
ideological structures which subordinate women and limit their access to land, educational opportunities
and leadership roles.

Furth, Charlotte
  1987   Concepts of Pregnancy, Childbirth, and Infancy in Ch'ing Dynasty China. Journal of Asian
      Studies 46(4):7–35.

Due to its focus on Chinese theories of fertility and procreation, this article necessarily involves a discussion of gender ideology as it was articulated in late Imperial China and which continues to carry its influence into contemporary popular thought. Furth suggests that reproductive medicine offered a dual model of Confucian gender relations. On the one hand, women were perceived as being physically weak and dependent on a patriarchal social order, while at the same time they were seen as sources of destructive emotions and polluting substance that subverted that order. Women were caught between the images of "negative sexual power and socially acceptable weakness" (9).

Honig, Emily, and Gail Hershatter
1988 Personal Voices: Chinese Women in the 1980s. Stanford: Stanford University Press.

Written by two social historians who have spent considerable time in China in the last several years, this book examines newly emerging areas of public discourse on issues concerning women in the post-Mao era. Taking their data from letters to the editor in women's magazines and in newspapers, the authors discuss the redefinition of moral boundaries in courtship, marriage, and divorce, the reinscription of sexual difference in a newly valorized "femininity" that marks a retreat from the relative androgeny of the Mao years and other issues which provide a fascinating commentary on the changing position of women in the family and the workplace. Each chapter is followed by a sampling of these letters in translation.

Lu Hsun (Lu Xun)
n.d. New Year's Sacrifice. Chosen Pages from Lu Hsun. New York: Cameron Associates, Inc. [Reprinted in a number of Lu Hsun collections]

This short story, one of Lu Hsun's best known, deals with some of the issues discussed in the emergence of Chinese feminism in the early 20th century, including widow remarriage and the objectification of women in marriage exchange.

Watson, James L.
1982 Chinese Kinship Reconsidered: Anthropological Perspectives on Historical Research. China Quarterly 92:589–622.

This state-of-the-art essay reviews recent research on Chinese kinship by both historians and anthropologists. It is exemplary for its historical sensitivity in its discussions of the Chinese lineage and patrilineal family.

Watson, Rubie S.
1986 The Named and the Nameless: Gender and Person in Chinese Society. American Ethnologist 13(4):619–631.

Chinese naming patterns mark gender difference. Only men accumulate a number of names marking important transitions in their lives while women remain relatively nameless. The namelessness of women suggests that for them personhood is quite differently defined than for men insofar as names in Chinese society are a public acknowledgment of one's individuality.

Wolf, Margery
1985 Revolution Postponed: Women in Contemporary China. Stanford: Stanford University Press.

This study of women in the People's Republic of China is one of the few written by an anthropologist and is based on fieldwork research. It unavoidably reflects the constraints placed on social science research by American scholars in the early years following the normalization of relations with the PRC. Indeed, the chapter entitled "Speaking Bitterness" is an unparalleled account of the difficulties encountered in such an endeavor. Especially interesting is Wolf's discussion of how her own difficulties in research were complicated by her identity as a woman and as spouse to a senior male scholar, both of which are interesting reflections of her object of study. Her data suggest that the Chinese revolution has fallen far short of its promises to women. She attributes this failure to socialist China's primarily male leadership and their lack of awareness of their patriarchal biases in promoting policy. The book has chapters on both urban and rural women, on marriage, and on China's controversial birth policy.

Wolf, Margery
    1977   Uterine Families and the Women's Community. *In* Conformity and Conflict: Readings in Cultural Anthropology. James P. Spradley and David W. McCurdy, eds. Pp. 201–208. Boston: Little, Brown.

This short reading excerpted from Margery Wolf's Women and Family in Rural Taiwan (Stanford University Press, 1972) introduces the concept of the uterine family, a concept devised by the anthropologist to describe how the Chinese patrilineal family is experienced by the women who marry in. In contrast to the enduring patriline which includes dead ancestors and unborn descendants in an unbroken line, the uterine family is born anew with each generation. By bearing sons for her husband's patriline, a woman not only provides a secure niche for herself, but also, in her close affective ties with her sons, she is able to gain a measure of power and influence in the household. Rural women also have informal access to power through the women's community which may counter male abuse of power through gossip and the force of public opinion.

Wolf, Margery
    1974   Chinese Women: Old Skills in a New Context. *In* Women, Culture, and Society. M. Zimbalist Rosaldo and Louise Lamphere, eds. Stanford: Stanford University Press.

How did women become such successful activists for revolutionary change when their participation in public affairs was so severely circumscribed in prerevolutionary China? Wolf argues that the skills developed by women in managing interpersonal relations in a male dominated society were the same as those needed by women in their newly acquired roles of leadership after liberation.

Wolf, Margery, and Roxane Witke, eds.
    1975   Women in Chinese Society. Stanford: Stanford University Press.

This collection features a number of papers written by anthropologists. Notable among these are Marjorie Topley's study of marriage resistance sisterhoods in prerevolutionary Guangdong, Margery Wolf's paper on women and suicide, and Emily (Ahern) Martin's paper on female pollution.

Women in China
Resources for Classroom Use

Articles

[Below is a list of shorter readings suitable for an undergraduate course. For annotations, see the accompanying teaching bibliography.]

Barlow, Tani, and Donald M. Lowe
    1985   Feminism and Sexism *In* Chinese Reflections. New York: Praeger. [Reprinted as: Teaching China's Lost Generation. China Books and Periodicals, 1987]
Beldon, Jack
    1970   Goldflower's Story. China Shakes the World. New York: Monthly Review Press.
Diamond, Norma
    1975   Collectivization, Kinship, and the Status of Women in Rural China. *In* Toward an Anthropology of Women. Rayna Reiter, ed. New York: Monthly Review Press.

Lu, Hsun (Lu Xun)
   n.d.   New Year's Sacrifice. Chosen Pages from Lu Hsun. New York: Cameron Associates, Inc.
   [Reprinted in a number of Lu Hsun collections]
Watson, Rubie S.
   1986   The Named and the Nameless: Gender and Person in Chinese Society. American Ethnologist
   13(4):619–631.
Wolf, Margery
   1984   Uterine Families and the Women's Community. *In* Conformity and Conflict: Readings in Cultural Anthropology. James P. Spradley and David W. McCurdy, eds. Boston: Little, Brown.

Books

Wolf, Margery
   1972   Women and the Family in Rural Taiwan. Stanford: Stanford University Press.

Cultural Documentation

Ebrey, Patricia B.
   1981   Chinese Civilization and Society: A Sourcebook. New York: Free Press.

   This collection has a number of primary source materials in translation on women, marriage, and the family throughout Chinese history. The items are presented chronologically but there is a topical index for ease in locating materials. The items concerning the anti-footbinding movement (pp. 245–248) are useful background for example one of this unit. There are also in translation some letters by women in the process of deciding whether or not to unbind their feet during the intellectual ferment of the 1920s, that demonstrate the concerns and difficulties experienced by educated women of that time.

Greenblatt, Sidney L. ed.
   1976   The Story of Selling Oneself and A Woman Farmhand. *In* The People of Taihang. White Plains, N.Y.: International Arts and Sciences Press.

   These two stories exemplify the narratives of ''speaking bitterness'' that were so potent in fueling the revolutionary momentum of land reform and collectivization through their depiction of gender and class oppression.

Honig, Emily, and Gail Hershatter
   1988   Personal Voices: Chinese Women in the 1980s. Stanford: Stanford University Press.

   In addition to its being an excellent introduction to gender issues and current debates within China itself, this book also has a wide range of materials in translation that have been taken from Chinese newspapers and women's magazines. Much of this material is in the form of letters to the editor; and although they appear in an officially controlled context, they give a very clear picture of the present limits to the discussion of alternatives for women in a range of issues.

Films and Videos

Small Happiness. Carma Hinton and Richard Gordon (1984, color, 58 min.) Available through: New Day Films, 22 Riverview Drive, Wayne, N.J. 07470-3191 (201) 633-0212. Formats: 16mm film: purchase $800, rent $90; video (VHS/Beta/3/4") purchase $480, rent $75

   In China, the birth of a son is considered a ''great happiness'' and the birth of a daughter a lesser one, hence the title *Small Happiness*. This award-winning film is about the women of Long Bow Village by a filmmaker with unparalled access to rural China. Carma Hinton is the daughter of William Hinton, author of *Fanshen,* a celebrated eyewitness account of land reform. She was born and raised in China and speaks the language with native fluency. In the film, village women respond to questions posed by an unseen narrator as they carry on their work of husking corn, rolling noodles, washing clothes, and other tasks. This interview format is interspersed with ethnographic clips of life in the village: a bridal pair bowing to the groom's ancestors, women working in the fields and in a brigade sawblade factory.

In less than an hour and with great sensitivity and balance, the film touches on an impressive array of issues which touch on the lives of women. Women of several generations and positions within the village order tell their stories. Older women tell of women's oppression in the old society and marvel at the relative freedom of younger women today. One of these venerable ladies demonstrates the proper way to bind one's feet as she tells of the pain she suffered as a young girl when her own feet were bound. Another explains how her progressive daughter-in-law helped her to stand up against her feudal-minded husband. A woman cadre involved in promoting the stringent one-family policy comments on the difficulty of her work and the tremendous resentment it focuses on her as the agent of this unpopular policy. A young girl tells of a work strike in the local brigade-owned factory in which the employees, all of them young unmarried girls, were successful in their standoff with the factory manager, an older male kinsman, in negotiating some improvement in their appalling work conditions. This film is highly recommended not only as an informative look at women in rural China but also as perhaps the finest ethnographic film about China available today.

China's One-Child Policy. Nova Special. (1985)

This is an excellent documentary on China's population policy. With very little editorial comment, it documents the arguments that the state makes for the policy, the means of implementing it, its unpopularity, and the tactics used in cases highly resistant to the more common means of inducing compliance.

Visual Materials

Levy, Howard S.
1966   Chinese Footbinding: The History of a Curious Erotic Custom. New York: Walton Rawls.

This account of footbinding is by an unreconstructed "orientalist" scholar who tends to exoticise the erotic associations of the custom. However, it does have good background material and a number of useful line drawings and photographs of feet which illustrate the physical effects of footbinding.

14

Gender in the Anthropology
of the United States

Ida Susser
Hunter College
City University of New York

Much of the exciting research on the anthropology of the United States concerns social relations of power. We often use material about the United States in introductory anthropology courses to foster our students' comparative understandings and their ability to reflect critically on their own society. The wealth of new material being developed about women and gender in the United States facilitates the accomplishment of both of these goals.

Anthropological research on the United States necessitates attention to the historical processes that have led to differentiation by class, ethnicity, race, and region as well as gender. It must also be concerned with the state policies, economic circumstances, and social organization which serve to either maintain, break down, or reconfigure class, gender, and racial divisions. While a number of recent ethnographies have addressed these issues, a comprehensive analysis of stratification within the changing economic structure of the contemporary United States has yet to emerge.

Just as the experiences of people in the United States are complex and determined by historical period, background, income, age, the availability and kinds of employment, and state policies, so gender will be manifested differently among different sectors of the population. Gender hierarchies may be maintained by different means among different groups with differing access to resources and different histories of socialization. In other words, without gender as an important category of analysis, we cannot understand U.S. society, but in the absence of a clear analysis of U.S. history and culture, we cannot clearly understand the meaning of gender or the gendering of experience.

Fundamental changes have taken place over this century with respect to the position of women in the U.S. workforce, the experience of family life, and the state regulation of family policy. While black, poor, and immigrant women have participated in paid employment since the 19th century, historically many married women, especially white mothers, have been excluded from many forms of sector paid employment. Since the 1950s, a rapidly increasing proportion of U.S. women have been hired in low paid temporary and part-time jobs. In the

343

1980s, women with children under six have become the most rapidly increasing sector of the workforce.

A transformation in family life is also occurring. Only 27% of households in the United States are now constituted as the normative "nuclear" family (two parents and their children). The number of female-headed households continues to rise throughout the population, and the women who head such households increasingly find themselves in poverty. One in five U.S. children are now being reared below the poverty line. State regulation of public assistance and other forms of supplementary income for households over this period has tended to perpetuate class, race, and gender divisions and has done less than in other industrial countries to alleviate the pauperization of women and children (Abramovitz 1988; Mullings 1987). Other dramatic developments affecting women in the United States in the late 20th century include the availability of contraception and abortion, and the burgeoning of reproductive technology. All of these changes have had differing impacts on women in different sectors of the economy and have highlighted contradictory aspects of women's experiences of sexuality, motherhood, parenting and cultural definitions of gender.

There are three interrelated areas of research where the introduction of gender considerations into U.S. anthropology has been most significant. The first concerns *work*, both paid and unpaid labor. There has been extensive debate over the social and economic significance of housework and women's responsibilities for childcare. In addition, women's disadvantage in the labor market and their generally underpaid and insecure employment have been the subject of both statistical and ethnographic research. These two concerns meet in the analyses of the interaction between paid work experiences, household organization, and links to the wider community and institutional structures (Lamphere 1987; Milkman 1987; Sacks and Remy 1984; Susser 1982; Zavella 1987).

A second important research area is the study of *gender, power, and politics*. Building on the feminist recognition that private life, "the personal," is a political terrain, kinship, domesticity, and gossip, for example, have been considered as part of the process of structuring, maintaining, and challenging power in society. This recognition has led to work that stressed the importance of women's social activities in maintaining group relations and facilitating social movements (Bookman and Morgen 1988; Lamphere 1987; Leonardo 1986; Susser 1982). This research challenges the conception of politics as primarily electoral-related activities by focusing on women's involvement in grassroots community and workplace activism (Bookman and Morgen 1988).

Another dimension of the reevaluation of what is political has been the analysis of the politics of gender socialization and the generation of inequality between the sexes in childhood, adolescent, and young adult experiences (Chodorow 1978; Mitchell 1974). This focus had led to more extensive attention to the life cycle and the political and social importance of ritual life events (such as at the onset of menstruation, marriage, and childbirth). Along with the political analysis of the personal there has emerged within feminist anthropology a broader discussion of sentiments and issues of psychoanalytic significance. Questions concerning the possibly differing social and emotional needs of men and women have been examined. Similarly, the objectification of women has been discussed from both a social and psychoanalytic perspective (Chodorow 1978; Dimen 1986; Gilligan 1982). A reanalysis of sexuality and the cultural dimensions of gender formation has also been developing (Dimen 1986; Oakley 1984; Ross and Rapp 1983).

A third important emphasis of feminist anthropology in the United States has been on *stratification*, specifically the examinations of the intersection of class or race, ethnicity, and gender. In studies of migration, for example, generally focused primarily on ethnicity and race, questions about gender have been emerging. Studies have demonstrated different patterns of male and female migration, differing work opportunities, and gendered strategies for coping with economic hardship. An area for further study concerns the way in which class differences within each ethnic, racial, and migrant population affect the structuring of gender relations (Colen 1985; Dill 1988; Gilkes 1982; Zavella 1987). Work such as this is important as it reveals much about the definition and experience of class in relation to gender in U.S. society. While research in this area is still scanty (reflecting in part an inadequate analysis of class processes), studies of gender provide an important pathway to consider class issues from a fresh dimension.

For example, a comparison of the experiences of poor women on welfare, working class women, and professional women indicates marked contrasts in fertility decisions, employment opportunities, household organization, childrearing options, and involvement in community mobilization. Each of these processes provides a context for the negotiation of gender relations and the undermining or persistence of inequality between men and women. More and more research is aimed at understanding the generation and perpetuation of gender hierarchies within these specific social and historical contexts and the role of the state in perpetuating gender dimensions within social stratification. Particularly for women, the groups outlined, those on public assistance, working wage earners (or their wives), and professional salary earners (or their wives) are not static categories; the descent of women into poverty, precipitated by factors such as childrearing, divorce, job loss, and aging, has to be analyzed in terms of the double jeopardy of gender and class inequality and the impact of state policies in industrial societies (Abramowitz 1988; Mullings 1987; Sidel 1986).

These three conceptual contributions concerning work, politics and stratification have fundamentally altered the contemporary anthropology of the United States and they pose theoretical challenges for anthropology which go beyond the reanalysis of the position of women. A focus on women at work raises the question—how and why does gender affect the workforce, and the experience of work? Why is it not possible simply to do research on workers—their income and their relationship to the workplace, machinery, and their employers? Some theorists, such as Max Weber and Talcott Parsons, argued that the workplace of advanced industrial societies is governed by universalistic values and by economic factors such as costs and wages, none of which would take gender into account. There will be aberrations, such theorists suggest, in which personal relationships take precedence; but on the whole, in principle, economic and universalistic values rule.

However, an analysis of employment patterns in the United States reveals major discrepancies in employment and income among large categories of workers, including women, native Americans, African-Americans and Latino immigrants. An analysis of the income gap between men and women in U.S. society (women consistently earn only about two-thirds of men's income in most occupations) and of the employment experiences of women, leads directly to questions of work history, life cycle, ages of childbearing and rearing, child care policies, and community support systems, and state policies regarding reproduction and family law. In other words, we are led to examine the social organization of the family, and the community as well as the impact of government policies to understand the experience of women in the workplace (Milkman 1987; Sacks and Remy 1984).

These findings lead to the recognition that broader issues of government policy, household and community organization are crucial to the work experience of different immigrant groups and similarly, African-Americans (Mullings 1984; Nash and Kelly 1983; Safa 1983; Sutton and Chaney 1987; Zavella 1987). It becomes clear that the advantages reaped by the white American man in the job market have to be understood in light of the social organization of his household (i.e., gender relations and childrearing, etc.), the community, and the policies of the state (Abramovitz 1988). Thus, one crucial contribution of the analysis of gender to an understanding of stratified industrial society is the recognition of the interdependency of the workplace with kinship and household arrangements, the social organization of the community and societal policies concerning the reproduction of the workforce, the nature of the work (paid and unpaid) and the impact of corporate policies in defining gendered occupations and workforces.

The public/private dichotomy, exemplified in the analytic separation of workplace and the domestic sphere has a long history as a framework in Western social science, including some influential feminist anthropological theory of the mid-1970s. This history partially reflects the confinement of many women to household activities with the emergence of industrialization and the ideological justification which accompanied this. Women were viewed as belonging in the nonmonetary, unpaid, humanistic "private" household sphere, while men entered the instrumental public world, earned money, and participated in political processes.

The idea that the "personal" is political and that individual feelings and experience in dyadic or domestic relationships both reflect and affect hierarchy and power, including the power of the state, leads to a reevaluation of the analytic usefulness of the public/private dichotomy. Once we reject the conceptual separation of public and private, workplace and household, everyday personal events can be seen as reflections and indications of power relations and hierarchy perpetuated also in other arenas, such as the workplace and civil institutions (see Dimen 1986; Hooks 1987). The same hierarchical relationships may be played out and reinforced in the social organization of our schools, social services and governing bodies (Abramovitz 1988; Mullings 1987).

The recognition that the personal is political is integrally related to the broadening of views of the workplace and of specific loci of power. It leads us beyond unions, company management, and formal government institutions to understand the distribution of power within society. This formulation is not found in gender studies alone; for example, social historians, and researchers of contemporary social movements have emphasized the political aspects of people's daily experiences. Anthropologists studying societies other than our own have long emphasized the intertwining of personal events with political processes. It was the foundation for much anthropological criticism of the application of models from political science to non-Western societies. However, gender studies in the United States have emphasized that an analysis of institutional structures of political power alone is no more useful in advanced industrial society than it was in non-Western societies. Thus, the study of power relations with respect to gender forces us to question broad theoretical frameworks such as the public/private dichotomy and the narrow definition of the political, which have been widely accepted by social scientists in the analysis of advanced industrial societies.

U.S. Anthropology

An introductory anthropology course with a section on the contemporary United States generally includes discussions of stratification, work, ethnicity, migration, the structure of the family as a normative model, and the impact of public institutions on daily life. Research on gender has emphasized each of these dimensions. This section will consider the significance of gender in theoretical developments in the areas of family and kinship, migration, and the analysis of social relations of power in the United States.

Kinship and the U.S. Family

The civil rights movement and the urban rebellions that followed combined with the women's movement to introduce class, race, and gender into the analysis of American kinship. Surprising as it may seem, prior to the late 1960s most anthropological accounts of U.S. kinship focused on the family as a unit, and presumed that family to be a heterosexual married couple with several children. Until the mid 1960s the concept of the "broken" family, almost any family which did not conform to this standard, was common.

In 1967, Daniel Patrick Moynihan published his report on "The Tangle of Pathology" among black families in which he argued that the excess of female-headed families resulted from the disruptions of slavery, and was perpetuated through the lack of stable male-headed households in subsequent generations (see Rainwater and Yancey 1967). His argument exaggerated that of Oscar Lewis who claimed that Puerto Rican and Mexican families lived in a "culture of poverty" which was self-perpetuating (Lewis 1959, 1966). During this period, historically inaccurate, "victim-blaming" analysis was rampant because so little had been written or understood about the varieties of American kinship patterns (E. Franklyn Frazier's work is one example of research which did confront issues of class and race concerning the black family [1939]).

Numerous anthropological critiques have appeared that demonstrate the theoretical and empirical fallacies of the Moynihan and Lewis positions. One of the best is an essay by Eleanor Leacock (1971). Lewis himself clarified his ideas and reiterated that he saw the economic constraints of industrial society as paramount in shaping the lives of the poor for both men and women (1968). Historical research documents the fact that slavery was a cruel and devastating experience, in which children, wives, and husbands were sold without regard for family ties, and in which black women were subject to sexual exploitation by white slaveowners and managers. However, after the Civil War, the freed black population generally established stable nuclear families when employment and economic resources permitted (Gutman 1976).

In contrast to the denigration of poor black families implied in the Moynihan report, Carol Stack's *All Our Kin* clearly demonstrated the reciprocal strategies used by black women to maintain families on incomes far below the poverty level. She documents the importance of broad and extensive networks in the survival of the inner city poor. Rather than focusing on the issue of "female-headed households," Stack presents an anthropological analysis of the system of kinship among poor U.S. black families and illuminates the importance of gender-specific reciprocity in this system. Other studies have demonstrated the importance of such kinship networks among poor white women as well, and extended the point to show how reciprocal strategies serve to build a base for community mobilization (Sharff 1987; Susser 1982, 1986a, 1986b; Valentine 1978).

Thus researchers began to identify class-based variations in the U.S. family and to consider the differing importance of kin networks among people from different socioeconomic strata (for example, see Rapp 1987). On the basis of these studies, kinship has come to be seen as one of a number of ways in which class-specific groups in the United States generate the bonds upon which economic and social strategies are based. Sources of community solidarity and mobilization are also developed among neighbors and people involved in child-related activities. As many analysts of U.S. society have pointed out, it is largely women who develop these contacts and mobilize to maintain them through a variety of social processes (Gilkes 1982; Leonardo 1986; Sacks 1984; Susser 1986a; Yanagisako 1977).

Thus, studies focusing on women and urban poverty over the past two decades have demonstrated the centrality of links between women, created by women to develop household and community strategies for coping with and combatting the material and moral injuries inflicted by lack of opportunity and inadequate economic resources. Far from documenting a resignation to a culture of poverty that destroys the lives of its children, such studies portray the daily struggles of men and women to create livable environments (Gilkes 1982; Valentine

1978). These studies are crucial to understanding life among the poor in advanced industrialized society, both because women and their children make up the large majority of those living in poverty and because women are central to the social organization of such communities.

Migration

Research that incorporated gender issues has made striking contributions in studies of migration in the Third World (e.g., Nash and Kelly 1983; Sutton and Chaney 1987). Migration, ethnic mobilization, and assimilation have been persistent concerns in U.S. society for several hundred years. Since the major migration of the Irish accelerated in the 1840s, populations from all parts of the world have been recruited to work in U.S. industry. While the long history of migration with the accompanying discrimination, formation of ethnic communities and varying forms of social and economic integration which occurred in the United States cannot be discussed in detail here, some aspects relating to gender and maintenance of household and community are considered.

From the early 1800s men, women, and children were employed in the New England textile industry. However, since initially men had to be hired away from work on the farms and the labor of young unmarried women was more readily available, the differential in wages between men and women and the classification of jobs by gender was established in the earliest mills. This did not mean that the women passively accepted their position. One of the earliest documented mill strikes occurred among women workers in Pawtucket, Rhode Island, in 1834. The first workers in these mills migrated from New England's rural areas. In some areas, special boarding houses for young women were created in order to facilitate such recruitment. Later on, immigrant women from Ireland, Poland, and other destitute European peasantries replaced the New England workers, but the gender differentiation in pay and the segregation of men's and women's work remained, combined with ethnic discrimination in both pay and job categories (Lamphere 1987).

The nationalities and gender of migrants to the United States over the past hundred years have varied with federal immigration policies, specific work recruitment policies, and the economic and political situation in the varying places from which populations have come. Policies may emphasize families or they may restrict the migration of relatives. Recruiters for work may concentrate on male workers, as in the recruitment of Chinese and later Japanese men to build the transcontinental railroads in the late 1800s. They may concentrate on women workers as in the current hiring of domestic workers from the Caribbean. Each of these migration and employment policies has created specific family and household conditions. Different strategies have been employed by migrants to support households, and hold families together, within these external constraints (see Sutton and Chaney 1987).

Many new issues arose following the U.S. migration policies of the 1960s. Different populations, coming from different economic circumstances and finding different economic niches in the United States employed contrasting strategies. Such strategies and constraints in turn influenced gender relations in the household and within the broader community. Analysis is further complicated by the fact that women's marginality may be perpetuated in the United States not because of a simple persistence of cultural mores, but because living conditions, and especially economic conditions, remain similar. Sweatshops, household production, and domestic work are common options for migrating women, and these forms of work may perpetuate or change their position in the household and their wider political and economic impact depending on many variables.

Migration is of interest in the study of gender relations partly because it separates the various jobs often performed by women, such as childrearing, maintenance of the household, care for the elderly, across different economies and politics. Thus, gender relations are altered in many different aspects. In some cases, broad international kin networks may free women to work and pursue educational goals. More frequently, however, migrant women earn very low wages without benefits or security, and may have to live in two households and maintain both (Colen 1985; Sutton and Chaney 1987). Such situations are worse for undocumented workers, with little recourse against employers and easily vulnerable to economic exploitation and sexual harassment at work. Migration is an increasingly central aspect of U.S. society and gender is an essential consideration in understanding the migration experience, the social organization of migrant communities, and the complex political-economic forces which have shaped national policies regarding migrants.

Social Relations of Power: Class, Race, Ethnicity, and Gender

I have argued that it is important to ask questions about gender, race, class, and ethnicity when teaching or pursuing research on questions having to do with issues such as the family, migration, work, and the like. It is also important to examine the ways that patterns of hierarchy, domination, and oppression are structured in our society, that is, to examine stratification. Much of the new feminist anthropology does just this. For example, there are a number of excellent resources that investigate the ways that race, ethnicity, gender, and class shape work experiences in the United States. Some of this work is particularly interesting because it focuses on both the oppressive nature of the organization of work and the strategies diverse groups of women have used to try to transform the conditions of their lives.

In the past several years there have been several book length studies of women workers that combine ethnographic, historical, and theoretical material to elucidate the lives of diverse groups of working women in the United States. For example, Patricia Zavella's work on Chicana cannery workers (1987), Louise Lamphere's research on immigrant textile workers (1987) and Karen Sacks's study of hospital workers (1987) each document the complex ways that women's work options and experiences are differentiated by race and ethnicity. The examination of women's work cultures, particularly those aspects of work culture that are related to their experiences as women, provides exciting insights about ways that gender can create a bonding (and therefore the basis for an alliance among women) even under conditions where race and ethnicity often divide workers. In these instances family and community events and concerns are introduced into the workplace by women (sharing pictures of family members, life-cycle celebrations such as baby showers, etc.), facilitating social interaction across language barriers as well as across racial and ethnic community boundaries.

Another important resource for the study of working-class women's lives is the collection *Women and the Politics of Empowerment*, edited by Ann Bookman and Sandra Morgen (1988). Case studies in this book document the variety of ways that women mobilize within their communities and their workplaces to better their own lives and those of their families. These strategies range from individual acts of resistance such as "standing up to the missus" by black domestic workers (Dill 1988) to collective action by women factory, hospital, clerical, and street vending workers. The book also explores working-class women's community activism—their neighborhood organizations, coalitions to improve health care and education, their involvements in social service and social change and advocacy groups.

The intersection of race, class, and gender is as significant in community mobilization as in the workplace. In New York City, working-class white women organized block association activities in cooperation with African American women. However, in a variety of settings they found integrated projects undermined by white working-class men who had not been involved in cooperative community work and maintained sharply racist boundaries (Susser 1982). Women organizing for health care in a poor community had to confront divisive issues of class and race among themselves before they could mobilize effectively to keep open a clinic (Morgen 1988). The particular experiences of African American residential segregation and discrimination have led African American women employed as lawyers, nurses, teachers, and social workers to become leaders in their own communities. Cheryl Townsend Gilkes documents the informal nature of such community work and the constant blurring of professional and community concerns that strengthened personal ties and allowed these women to become crucial and important resources for ghetto neighborhoods. Thus, as mentioned earlier, women are at the center of much community organization in the United States and issues of class, race, and ethnic segregation are constantly shaping their efforts at community mobilization.

Just as with work and the creation of communities, the construction of parenthood varies by class, ethnicity, and historical context and there is no one universal way in which U.S. gender is created. The danger of discussions such as Nancy Chodorow's *The Reproduction of Mothering* (1978) or Carol Gilligan's *In a Different Voice* (1982) is that psychological explanations of why women want to be mothers tend to be substituted for historical explanations of how they became "mothers." On the other hand, the processual examinations of gender at work, in the community, and in the household leave unanswered questions as to how women and men themselves reproduce hierarchical and asymmetrical gender relations in their daily lives and the contradictory ways they feel about such experiences. Such gender hierarchies in turn vary by class and ethnicity (see Cole 1985; Dill 1988; Rapp 1987).

Chodorow argues that all children, across different classes and societies, are reared by women and that this poses specific problems for girls in developing a gender identity. She presents a complex argument relating women's socialization in industrial society to the mode of childrearing and suggests that women are not only trained but psychoanalytically prepared for their submissive, relational roles in society. Clearly, as in many feminist works of this kind, the model of women is a middle-class Western model. The contrasts with the emotions and behavior of women from different classes and historical backgrounds are not explored. The single mother household and the historical experiences of African American women who have always worked have generated strong independent women who do not easily fit such claims for the universality of a submissive feminine personality (see Cole 1985; Dill 1988; Gilkes 1982; Stack 1974). Works by Hooks, Dill, Cole, and others serve as important correctives to the Chodorow and Gilligan perspectives in their analysis of the experiences of women from different class and ethnic backgrounds in the United States.

The focus on gender has led to a fundamental reshaping of analyses of U.S. society. While not undermining a focus on production and employment as central to understanding advanced industrial societies, the emphasis on women's experience has reintroduced the influence of the state and shaping of social reproduction into anthropological analysis. Social reproduction, in this sense, is viewed as the means for the reproduction of workers and the maintenance of the structure of advanced industrial society. Thus, it includes not only biological reproduction of workers and sustenance, but the social organization that engenders socialization and training of workers within any particular society. Social reproduction is certainly not restricted to women's work. However, a consideration of women's experience in the household and community has led to a greater focus on issues of social reproduction. A discussion of women's work as care providers leads to better understanding of questions concerning the maintenance of the young, disabled, and elderly in industrial society. Research on migration and gender has provided a more sophisticated understanding also of the distribution of costs of social reproduction across different regions and economies.

In other words, a focus on gender has led to wider recognition of the impact of migration, welfare policies, and reproductive technologies, as well as children, housing, and educational policies, on the social organization of employment, households, and communities in the United States. Relations between men and women at work, in the household, and in the community can be seen as either coping or resistance strategies within this wider context. Thus, questions such as "What is motherhood?", "What is fatherhood?", or concepts of gender hierarchy are worked out by men and women operating within the history of state legislation and the conflicting demands of the workplace and the social reproduction of the workforce. As suggested earlier, the answers to these questions and concepts will vary according to the historical experience (class, race, or ethnicity) of the people involved.

The two modules that follow examine the issues raised above with respect to two widely different areas of study. The first looks at the literature on work and community and draws on examples to demonstrate the important contribution of gender studies in this area. Using the same theoretical concepts outlined above, the second module examines the concept of "motherhood" in U.S. society and the ways in which anthropological studies of gender have contributed to current understanding of the issue.

References Cited

Abramovitz, Mimi
  1988   Regulating the Lives of Women: Social Welfare Policy from Colonial Times to the Present. Boston: South End Press.
Bookman, Ann, and Sandra Morgen
  1988   Women and the Politics of Empowerment. Philadelphia: Temple University Press.
Chavkin, W., ed.
  1984   Double Exposure. New York: Monthly Review Press.
Chodorow, Nancy
  1978   The Reproduction of Mothering: Psychoanalysis and the Sociology of Gender. Berkeley: University of California Press.
Cole, Johnnetta, ed.
  1986   All American Women: Lines that Divide, Ties that Bind. New York: Free Press.
Colen, Shellee
  1986   With Respect and Feelings: Voices of West India Childcare and Domestic Workers in New York City. *In* All American Women: Lines that Divide, Ties that Bind. Johnetta Cole, ed. New York: Free Press.
Davis, Angela
  1983   Women, Race and Class. New York: Random House.
Dill, Bonnie T.
  1988   Making Your Job Good Yourself: Domestic Service and the Construction of Personal Dignity. *In* Women and the Politics of Empowerment. Ann Bookman and Sandra Morgen, eds. Pp. 33–53. Philadelphia: Temple University Press.
Dimen, Muriel
  1986   Surviving Sexual Contradictions: A Startling and Different Look at a Day in the Life of a Contemporary Professional Woman. New York: Macmillan Publishing Co.
Etienne, Mona, and Eleanor Leacock, eds.
  1980   Women and Colonization. New York: J. F. Bergin/Praeer.
Frazier, E. Franklin
  1939   The Negro Family in the United States. Chicago: University of Chicago Press.
Garrison, Vivian, and Carol Weiss
  1987   Dominican Family Networks and United States Immigration Policy: A Case Study. *In* Caribbean Life in New York City: Sociocultural Dimensions. C. Sutton and E. Chaney, eds. Pp. 235–255. New York: Center for Migration Studies.

Gilkes, C.
    1982   Holding Back the Ocean with a Broom. *In* The Black Woman. L. Rodgers-Rose, ed. Pp. 217–
        231. Beverly Hills: Sage.
Gilligan, Carol
    1982   In a Different Voice: Psychological Theory and Women's Development. Cambridge: Harvard
        University Press.
Gutman, Herbert
    1976   The Black Family in Slavery and Freedom 1750–1925. New York: Pantheon.
Hooks, Bell
    1981   Ain't I a Woman: Black Women and Feminism. Boston: South End Press.
    1984   Feminist Theory: From Margin to Center. Boston: South End Press.
Komarovsky, Mirra
    1964   Blue-Collar Marriage. New York: Random House.
Kuhn, Annette, and Anne Marie Wolpe
    1978   Feminism and Materialism: Women and Modes of Production. London: Routledge & Kegan
        Paul.
Lamphere, Louise
    1987   From Working Daughters to Working Mothers: Immigrant Women in a New England Indus-
        trial Community. Ithaca: Cornell University Press.
Leacock, Eleanor, ed.
    1971   The Culture of Poverty: A Critique. New York: Simon & Schuster.
Leonardo, Micaela Di
    1986   The Varieties of Ethnic Experience: Kinship, Class and Gender Among California Italian
        Americans. Ithaca: Cornell University Press.
Lewis, Oscar
    1959   Five Families: Mexican Case Studies in the Culture of Poverty. New York: Basic Books.
    1966   La Vida: A Puerto Rican Family in the Culture of Poverty—San Juan and New York. New
        York: Random House.
    1968   The Culture of Poverty. *In* On Understanding Poverty: Perspectives from the Social Sciences.
        D. P. Moynihan, ed. New York: Basic Books.
Liebow, E.
    1967   Tally's Corner. Boston: Little, Brown.
Lopez, Iris
    1987   Sterilization among Puerto Rican Women in New York City: Public Policy and Social Con-
        straints. *In* Cities of the United States: Studies in Urban Anthropology. L. Mullings, ed. Pp. 269–
        292. New York: Columbia University Press.
Martin, Emily
    1987   The Woman in the Body. New York: Beacon Press.
McCourt, Kathleen
    1977   Working Class Women and Grass Roots Politics. Bloomington: Indiana University Press.
McIntosh, Mary
    1978   The State and the Oppression of Women. *In* Feminism and Materialism: Women and Modes
        of Production. Annette Kuhn and Anna Marie Wolpe, eds. Pp. 254–290. London: Routledge &
        Kegan Paul.
Milkman, Ruth
    1987   Gender at Work: The Dynamics of Job Segregation by Sex during World War II. Chicago:
        University of Illinois Press.
Mitchell, Juliet
    1974   Psychoanalysis and Feminism. New York: Pantheon Books.
Morgen, Sandra
    1988   "It's the Whole Power of the City against Us!": The Development of Political Consciousness
        in a Women's Health Care Coalition. *In* Women and the Politics of Empowerment. A. Bookman
        and S. Morgen, eds. Philadelphia: Temple University Press.

Mullings, Leith
   1984   Minority Women, Work & Heath. *In* Double Exposure. W. Chavkin, ed. New York: Monthly
      Review Press.
Mullings, Leith, ed.
   1987   Cities of the United States: Studies in Urban Anthropology. New York: Columbia University
      Press.
Nash, June, and Marie P. Fernandez-Kelly
   1983   Women, Men and the International Division of Labor. Albany: SUNY Press.
Oakley, Ann
   1984   Taking It Like a Woman. New York: Random House.
Pessar, Patricia
   1987   The Linkage between the Household and Workplace of Dominican Women in the U.S. *In*
      Caribbean Life in New York City: Sociocultural Dimensions. Constance Sutton and Elsa Chaney,
      eds. Pp. 255–278. New York: Center for Migration Studies.
Petchesky, Rosalind
   1984   Abortion and Woman's Choice: The State, Sexuality and Reproductive Freedom. Boston:
      Northeastern University Press.
Rainwater, Lee, and William Yancey, eds.
   1967   The Moynihan Report and the Politics of Controversy. Boston: MIT Press.
Rapp, Rayna
   1987   Urban Kinship in Contemporary America: Families, Classes and Ideology. *In* Cities of the
      United States: Studies in Urban Anthropology. Leith Mullings, ed. Pp. 219–243. New York: Co-
      lumbia University Press.
Ross, Ellen, and Rayna Rapp
   1983   Sex and Society: A Research Note from Social History and Anthropology. *In* Powers of De-
      sire: The Politics of Sexuality. Ann Shitow, Christine Stansell, and Sharon Thompson, eds. Pp.
      51–74. New York: Monthly Review Press.
Rowland, Robyn
   1987   Technology and Motherhood: Reproductive Choice Reconsidered. Signs 12(3):512–528.
Rubin, Lillian
   1976   Worlds of Pain: Life in the Working-Class Family. New York: Basic Books.
Sacks, Karen
   1984   Generations of Working-class Families. *In* My Troubles Are Going to Have Trouble with Me:
      Everyday Trials and Triumphs of Women Workers. Karen Sacks and Dorothy Remy, eds. Pp. 15–
      39. New Brunswick, N.J.: Rutgers University Press.
   1988   Caring By the Hour. Urbana: University of Illinois Press.
Sacks, Karen, and Dorothy Remy, eds.
   1984   My Troubles Are Going to Have Trouble with Me: Everyday Trials and Triumphs of Women
      Workers. New Brunswick, N.J.: Rutgers University Press.
Safa, Helen
   1983   Women, Production and Reproduction in Industrial Capitalism: A Comparison of Brazilian
      and U.S. Factory Workers. *In* Women, Men and the International Division of Labor. June Nash
      and Marie P. Fernandez-Kelly, eds. Pp. 95–117. Albany: SUNY Press.
Schneider, David
   1980   American Kinship: A Cultural Account. Chicago: University of Chicago Press.
Schneider, David, and Raymond Smith
   1973   Class Difference and Sex Roles in American Kinship and Family Structure. Englewood Cliffs,
      N.J.: Prentice-Hall.
Seifer, Nancy
   1976   Nobody Speaks for Me: Self-Portraits of American Working Class Women. New York: Simon
      & Schuster.
Sharff, Jagna
   1987   The Underground Economy of a Poor Neighborhood. *In* Cities of the United States: Studies
      in Urban Anthropology. Leith Mullings, ed. Pp. 19–51. New York: Columbia University Press.

Sidel, Ruth
  1986   Women and Children Last: The Plight of Poor Women in Affluent America. New York: Viking Press.
Singer, Peter, and Reane Wells
  1985   Making Babies: The New Science and Ethics of Conception. New York: Scribners'.
Stack, Carol
  1974   All Our Kin: Strategies for Survival in a Black Community. New York: Harper & Row.
Susser, Ida
  1982   Norman Street: Poverty and Politics in an Urban Neighborhood. New York: Oxford.
  1986a   Political Activity among Working-class Women in a U.S. City. American Ethnologist 13(1):108–117.
  1986b   Work and Reproduction: Sociologic Context. Occupational Medicine: State of the Art Reviews (3):517–530.
Susser, Ida, and John Kreniske
  1987   The Welfare Trap: A Public Policy for Deprivation. *In* Cities of the United States: Studies in Urban Anthropology. Leith Mullings, ed. Pp. 51–71. New York: Columbia University Press.
Sutton, Constance, and Elsa Chaney
  1987   Caribbean Life in New York City: Sociocultural Dimensions. New York: Center for Migration Studies.
Thorne, Barrie
  1981   Rethinking the Family. New York: Longman.
Valentine, Betty Lou
  1978   Hustling and Other Hard Work. New York: Free Press.
Yanigasako, Sylvia
  1977   Women-centered Kin Networks in Urban Bilateral Kinship. American Ethnologist (2):207–226.
Zavella, Patricia
  1987   Women's Work and Chicano Families: Cannery Workers of the Santa Clara Valley. Ithaca: Cornell University Press.
  1988   The Politics of Race and Gender: Organizing Chicana Cannery Workers in Northern California. *In* Women and the Politics of Empowerment. Ann Bookman and Sandra Morgen, eds. Pp. 202–227. Philadelphia: Temple University Press.

Module One: Work, Community, and Household

Some of the topics that can be addressed include the structure of employment in the United States; the common and contrasting experiences and conditions of workers, that is, men and women, white and people of color; culture and behavior in the workplace; the shaping of the family through work; women and workplace organizing; women as community activists; women as the center of kin networks and ritual.

The primary goals of this course segment are to (1) raise issues that are directly related to students' experiences and to (2) introduce material about gender in the United States that will help students put their own particular gender, race, class, and ethnic experiences into perspective as they learn about women whose lives are different from their own. Resources that will help do this include the following:

Films

Metropolitan Avenue (60 min., color) available from New Day films.

Rosie the Riveter (60 min., color) available from New Day films.

Harlan County USA

Babies & Banners

Union Maids

Readings

Bookman, Ann
  1988   Unionization in an Electronics Factory: The Interplay of Gender, Ethnicity and Class. *In*
    Women and the Politics of Empowerment. A. Bookman and Sandra Morgen, eds. Pp. 159–180.
    Philadelphia: Temple University Press.
Bookman, Ann, and Sandra Morgen
  1988   Women and the Politics of Empowerment. Philadelphia: Temple University Press.
Dill, Bonnie T.
  1988   Making Your Job Good Yourself: Domestic Service and the Construction of Personal Dignity.
    In Women and the Politics of Empowerment. A. Bookman and Sandra Morgen, eds. Pp. 33–53.
    Philadelphia: Temple University Press.
Gilkes, C.
  1982   Holding Back the Ocean with a Broom. *In* The Black Woman. L. Rodgers-Rose, ed. Pp. 217–
    231. Beverly Hills: Sage.
Lamphere, Louise
  1987   From Working Daughters to Working Mothers in a New England Industrial Community. Ith-
    aca: Cornell University Press.
Mullings, Leith
  1984   Minority Women, Work and Health. *In* Double Exposure. W. Chavkin, ed. Pp. 121–138.
    New York: Monthly Review Press.
Sacks, Karen, and D. Remy
  1984   My Troubles Are Going to Have Trouble With Me. Specifically: introduction and articles by
    Frankel, Machung, Katz, and Kemnitzer.
Susser, Ida
  1982   Norman Street: Poverty and Politics in an Urban Neighborhood. New York: Oxford.

Using some of the materials annotated above, discuss some of the interconnections between work, household, and community in women's lives. What is important is not just to
have students understand about women and work, women and family, and women and community involvement/activism, but for them to understand how women's structural location
within and between these domains leads to particular kinds of oppression (e.g., the "double
day"); critical problems for social policy in this country (e.g., how to deal with the dramatic
changes in society that follow from women's increasing participation in paid labor); and
modes of resistance by women both within the workplace and in their communities. Based on
an enriched understanding of these issues after class lecture and discussion, you might want
to bring the students back to the particular experiences of women in their families with the
following project:

Project for Students.   Interview three generations of women: someone of their own generation, their mother's generation, and their grandmother's generation.

   Ask questions concerning:
      work experience
      childbirth decisions
      division of labor in the household—childrearing responsibilities, cleaning, cooking,
shopping, etc.

role in kin networks
community involvement
Write an essay comparing the experiences of women in the three generations and relating the differences to changes in U.S. society over the past 30 years (such as changing employment and educational opportunities for men and women, availability of contraception and abortion, child care services, after school programs, and changes in men and women's expectations of one another).

Students should be asked to select women to interview from a variety of class and ethnic backgrounds. This will facilitate comparison of the experiences of immigrant groups, Afro-Americans and other sectors of U.S. society.

Class presentations of the work will allow students to compare and discuss the experiences of the women interviewed and to draw more general conclusions about the historical changes in women's position among different groups in U.S. society.

Module Two: Motherhood in U.S. Society

Topics: Questions of Definition of Motherhood: Biological, Social, Legal

What do "mothers" do, nowadays as opposed to 20 years ago—changing roles and expectations; patterns of childbirth—class and ethnic variations; patterns of childrearing—class and ethnic variations; socialization and expectations of boys and girls—class and ethnic variations; changing expectations/experiences of sexuality for women—contraception, abortion; are women socialized for sociability and kin connectedness from childhood, while men are socialized for achievement and separation? If this is true, is this simply a middle class phenomenon in U.S. society or does it have broader implications? How does the growing phenomenon of single parenting (mostly mothers) affect the experience and definition of motherhood?

Exercise

Essay.   Select a controversy such as the recent debate over surrogate motherhood, or the workforce requirements for mothers on public assistance, parental leaves, or abortion. Outline the two sides of the debate and identify the ways in which opposing positions reflect different and changing definitions of motherhood.

Class Project.   Having analyzed the conceptions and expectations of motherhood present in such debates, and the changing conditions under which parenting is taking place, students could organize a debate in class around one or two of the issues chosen.

Readings

Abramowitz, Mimi
    1988   Regulating the Lives of Women: Social Welfare Policy from Colonial Times to the Present. Boston: South End Press.

Colen, Shellee
    1986   With Respect and Feelings: Voices of West India Childcare and Domestic Workers in New
       York City. *In* All American Women: Lines that Divide, Ties that Bind. Johnnetta Cole, ed. Pp.
       46–70. New York: Free Press.
Dimen, Muriel
    1986   Surviving Sexual Contradictions: A Startling and Different Look at a Day in the Life of a
       Contemporary Professional Woman. New York: Macmillan.
Gilligan, Carol
    1982   In a Different Voice: Psychological Theory and Women's Development. Cambridge: Harvard
       University Press.
Sidel, Ruth
    1986   Women and Children Last: The Plight of Poor Women in Affluent America. New York: Vi-
       king Press.

Annotated Bibliography

Bookman, Ann, and Sandra Morgen, eds.
    1988   Women and the Politics of Empowerment. Philadelphia: Temple University Press.

An excellent collection of articles concerning women as organizers both at work and in the community. Several of the articles have been suggested as useful reading for topics covered in the modules.
The book as a whole provides a useful overview of research being conducted among women in the
United States and includes a variety of authors whose work has been important in the field. The book
demonstrates the interrelationships between women's experiences at home and at work and the importance of understanding political action across different spheres.

Chodorow, Nancy
    1978   The Reproduction of Mothering: Psychoanalysis and the Sociology of Gender. Berkeley: Uni-
       versity of California Press.

An effort to understand how women in the United States are socialized to accept their subordinate
position in the family and how such socialization fits women for their roles in the wider society. Chodorow argues that all children, across different classes and societies, are reared by women and that this
poses specific problems for girls in developing a gender identity. Chodorow presents a complex argument relating women's socialization in industrial society to the mode of childrearing. She suggests that
women are not only trained but psychoanalytically prepared for their submissive relational roles in society. Clearly, as in many feminist works of this kind, the model of women is a middle class American
model and the contrasts with the emotions and behavior of women of different classes and cultures are
not explored.

Lamphere, Louise
    1987   From Working Daughters to Working Mothers: Immigrant Women in a New England Indus-
       trial Community. Ithaca: Cornell University Press.

This book analyzes the relationship between women's employment and their domestic responsibilities in Central Fall, Rhode Island, over the past 150 years. It documents the changing ways in which
women contributed to household income and how this varied both historically and according to ethnic
group. The book provides a basis for class discussions of women's work and the immigrant experience
from the perspective of women.

Milkman, Ruth
    1987   Gender at Work: The Dynamics of Job Segregation by Sex during World War II. Chicago:
       University of Illinois Press.

This book traces the experience of women workers in the auto industry and in electrical manufacturing and explores the historical roots of job segregation. Milkman analyzes the changing conditions for women workers from the depression of the 1930s through World War II and following the war. The study presents a detailed analysis of the economic forces which allowed industry to pay women less than men. In documenting the variation in the labeling of women's work by both industry and region Milkman refutes simplistic justifications concerning strength and skill which have been used to explain job segregation by gender. This book might be read in conjunction with viewing the film *Rosie the Riveter*. It provides the historical analysis to accompany the dramatic life histories of the women in the film.

Mullings, Leith, ed.
    1987   Cities of the United States: Studies in Urban Anthropology. New York: Columbia University Press.

This collection of essays provides an introduction to current research in urban anthropology. The sections on "Public Policy and the Poor" and "Urban Kinship: generations and gender" offer important discussions on the impact of public assistance on the family and the variation of gender by class.

Sacks, Karen, and Dorothy Remy, eds.
    1984   My Troubles Are Going to Have Trouble with Me: Everyday Trials and Triumphs of Women Workers. New Brunswick, N.J.: Rutgers University Press.

This collection of articles addresses women's resistance in the workplace in relation both to old and new technologies and forms of work organization. The first section of the book opens up fundamental issues of family and community which have been neglected in studies of men workers. The second section focuses on women in the rapidly expanding service sector of the U.S. economy, including word processors, librarians, and hospital workers. An important emphasis that emerges from these articles is the stratification among women by educational background and color. The third section of the book highlights issues related to immigrant workers and women working in border factories in Mexico. The book clearly places workplace experiences in the context of class, race, gender, kinship, and community links and serves as an excellent resource for discussions of work and gender in the United States.

Sidel, Ruth
    1986   Women and Children Last: The Plight of Poor Women in Affluent America. New York: Viking Books.

This book provides an excellent portrait of women's experiences and economic status in the United States today. Sidel documents the loss of income through divorce and the difficulties facing most women trying to rear children alone in the United States. She argues that while attention has been focused on the new and high paying jobs available to some women, the variety of problems confronted by most women living on the economic margins have been neglected. She contrast the lives of American women and children and the lack of family policy with the lives of women and children in Sweden where the government subsidizes households and the provision of quality day care through a comprehensive family policy.

Stack, Carol
    1974   All Our Kin: Strategies for Survival in a Black Community. New York: Harper Torchbooks.

Carol Stack's classic ethnography of life among poor black families in an industrial town documents the reciprocal relationships developed by women in their struggle to maintain households on the margins of poverty. *All our Kin* portrays both the difficulties confronted by poor women supporting households through temporary low-paying jobs and public assistance and the strategies which allow them to survive from day to day. The book is an excellent resource for an introductory course in anthropology as it demonstrates the effectiveness of ethnography in an urban environment familiar to many students although often not understood by them.

Susser, Ida
  1982   Norman Street: Poverty and Politics in an Urban Neighborhood. New York: Oxford University
  Press.

This book describes the lives of working class women from a variety of ethnic backgrounds in
Brooklyn, New York, in the 1970s. It documents the problems confronted by the poor in seeking housing and applying for public assistance as well as modes of community organizing and the development
of community groups. The creation of broad-based community organizations is analyzed in relation to
issues of class, race, and gender which have hampered such collaboration both historically and in the
contemporary context.

15

Gender and the Application of Anthropological Knowledge to Public Policy in the United States

Leith Mullings
City University of New York Graduate School

An introductory anthropology course may be enhanced by including a segment demonstrating the relevance of anthropology to real problems in the United States. Such concerns are often considered to be the realm of applied anthropology. If one aspect of applied anthropology is its interventionist—advocacy and collaborative—direction, the other is found in its contribution to understanding social issues, specifically the use of anthropological information to challenge, develop or support public policy (Chambers 1987:319). In focusing on the application of anthropological knowledge to public policy issues, this essay will be primarily concerned with the latter aspect. After a brief discussion of some of the concerns of applied anthropologists, I will present examples of two social policy issues to which anthropology has the potential to make a contribution: ethnicity and inequality, and health and illness. I will discuss the way in which recent anthropological scholarship on gender contributes to, modifies, and in some cases restructures the basic understandings of these areas.

Applied anthropologists have been concerned with such topics as health and medicine, education, development and inequality, and have used intervention strategies such as action anthropology, community development, advocacy anthropology, and cultural brokerage (Van Willigen 1986). Though most scholars agree that anthropology—in particular the holistic approach, the concept of culture and ethnographic methodology—has the potential for a unique contribution to solving social problems, there are significant controversies about the nature and scope of the field. Among these are: the ability of anthropology to contribute to policy formation (Weaver 1985); the extent to which applied anthropology favors short-term, status quo solutions (see Chambers 1987:310), the relationship of theoretical, applied, and advocacy anthropology (see Chambers 1987; Leacock 1987; Sanjek 1987); the issue of divided loyalties, i.e., to whom is the anthropologist responsible? (see Leacock 1987); and the limitations of anthropology as a policy science (see Gibbs 1982).

There have been several recent reviews and critiques of applied anthropology, and particularly the role of anthropology in public policy (Chambers 1977, 1987; Gibbs 1982; Hicks and Handler 1987; Hinshaw 1980). However, there is very little written about the consequences of gender bias in applied anthropology.[1] Yet the same gender biases that appear in "academic" anthropology and in conventional ethnography have palpable consequences when anthropology sets itself the explicit task of helping people make decisions. Thus, conceptualizations of gender have enormous implications for public policy. Notions of appropriate gender roles, for example, have powerfully influenced policies on welfare, health care, child care, women's work, equal compensation, and the family.

Examining two examples—ethnicity and inequality, and health policy—I will argue that gender constructs have direct consequences for policy decisions and rationalizations. While suggesting that policy (in its broadest sense) often reinforces gender hierarchy, I will demonstrate how some of the new feminist scholarship raises important questions and suggests different directions. However, knowledge in and of itself does not produce structural change, which often requires social action. But scholars have at times worked with others, and I will cite examples of how feminist perspectives in health have been used to bring about change through "advocacy." Though both these topics fall within the domain of applied anthropology, it is important to note that the use of anthropological research to support, develop, or discredit policy is not limited to the work of those consciously engaged in policy-relevant research, rendering the distinction between "theoretical" and "applied" anthropology somewhat questionable.

Ethnicity, Inequality, and Public Policy

Since the beginnings of American anthropology, concern with ethnicity—group identification, by self or others, on the basis of phenotype, language, religion, or national origin—has been central to the discipline.[2] Inequality has been a pervasive feature of American life and racial and ethnic differences have often been associated with unequal positions in the stratification structure.

Specifically, African-Americans, Chicanos, Puerto Ricans, and Native Americans, as compared to European-Americans, are disproportionately concentrated at the lower end of the socioeconomic scale. In our society there is a prevailing ideology of equal opportunity. The major question, then, is: why does ethnic inequality exist? Differences in perspectives on such public policies as immigration, public schooling, housing, affirmative action, employment, and a range of other issues revolve around how the relationship between ethnicity and inequality is conceptualized. Public policy decisions are often rationalized by "scholarly" work and recent social science explanations have attributed ethnic inequality to: (1) biological or genetic differences, (2) cultural differences, or (3) structured inequality that is societally produced and reproduced.

The Prevailing Views

The notion that inborn genetic differences are primarily responsible for ethnic and class inequality continues to be found in the work of such writers as Shockley (1970), Jensen (1969, 1970), Herrnstein (1973) and Rushton (1989). Much of this work concerns IQ studies, and the policy implications are evident in the pervasive practice of "tracking" in the public school system (see Kamin 1974, 1982; Lawler 1978; and Taylor 1980 for critiques of the genetic basis of IQ). However, it is the assessment of cultural differences as determinant of inequality that has been more apparent in recent public policy.

Oscar Lewis's (1966) formulation of the "culture of poverty"—a problematic subculture characteristic of certain poor people—was perhaps the anthropological thesis that received most attention from policymakers. His description of this culture and its setting includes many ambiguities and contradictory statements that allow for emphasis on different aspects of his argument. However, policymakers chose to emphasize his analysis of the cultural, rather than the structural roots of the problem. The most influential aspect of his work for policy was Lewis's negative depiction of the way of life of the poor, and his characterization of the culture as self-perpetuating: that children absorb this "culture" by the age of six or seven and are subsequently unable to take advantage of any changing circumstances that might occur. The emphasis on culture as the major determinant of stratification is also put forward in Glazer and Moynihan's (1975) "Introduction" to *Ethnicity: Theory and Experience*. Here they elaborate their theoretical position that differences in access to resources are the result of differences in culture content:

> It is *property* that begins to seem derivative, and ethnicity that seems to become a more fundamental source of social stratification. [1975:17]

Anthropologists reacted fairly swiftly in raising questions about the culture of poverty concept and its applications. Critics cited the theoretical and methodological problems with Lewis's framework, as well as the numerous studies contradicting these generalizations about poor people (see Leacock 1971). Research in various disciplines has demonstrated how discriminatory practices and recent transformations in the larger economy (the decline of the industrial manufacturing sectors and the growth of service sectors of the economy, the movement of jobs from midwest and northeast central cities to the suburbs and "sunbelt" cities, the decline in social services) have disproportionately affected the poorest segment of U.S. society and specifically people of color. Nonetheless the culture of poverty perspective remained an entrenched assumption in public policy. Charles Valentine's (1968) analysis demonstrates how the view that the *culture* of the poor is responsible for their poverty, served as a rationale for both directing programs toward changing the culture of the poor, rather than toward eliminating poverty, and for dismantling some of the programs of the "War on Poverty."

The first wave of critiques of the culture of poverty concept (with the exception of those that were specifically directed toward reexamination of the African-American family) tended to be primarily concerned with issues of race and class, without sufficient attention to gender. Yet it was women who bore much of the brunt of the negative characterizations of poor people's culture. Women are portrayed as inadequately fulfilling their gender-based roles. Oscar Lewis describes a trend toward "female- or mother-centered families" and the "high incidence of maternal deprivation" as part of a set of negative culture traits. It is in the work of Glazer and Moynihan that this implied criticism of poor women becomes explicit. This is particularly true in Moynihan's (1965) *The Negro Family: the Case for National Action* (known as the Moynihan Report), in which the roles played by African-American women are portrayed as a causative factor in poverty and social disorganization. While Lewis had taken pains to point out that the culture of poverty is not limited to any ethnic group but is rather associated with a particular type of social structure (i.e., industrial capitalism), Moynihan applies this formulation specifically to African-Americans.

The focus of Moynihan's negative characterization of women has to do with their roles within the family. Although initially Moynihan is careful to document the negative impact of high unemployment on the African-American family and community, he then goes on to treat family structure essentially as an independent variable.

> At the heart of the deterioration of the fabric of Negro society is the deterioration of the Negro family. It is the fundamental source of the weakness of the Negro community at the present time. [1965:5]

Further,

> at the center of the tangle of pathology is the weakness of the family structure, the principal source of most of the aberrant, inadequate or antisocial behavior that did not establish, but now serves to perpetuate the cycle of poverty. [1965:30]

The major weakness of the family structure is that "in essence, the Negro community has been forced into a matriarchal structure which . . . imposes a crushing burden on the Negro male" (1965:29). Matriarchy, defined by the "often reversed roles of husband and wife" (1965:76), is reinforced from generation to generation. These "reversed roles" seem to be primarily defined by the fact that a greater proportion of African-American than European-American women work outside the home. Moynihan argues that this "matriarchal" family structure is deviant to the rest of the society and results in low educational attainment, crime and delinquency. Parenthetically, it also makes military service important for African-American men since the military "is an utterly masculine world . . . a world away from women, a world run by strong men of unquestioned authority" (1965:42). As Assistant Secretary of Labor and Director of the Office of Policy Planning and Research in the Johnson Administration, Moynihan and his report had a significant impact not only on national policy, but on scholarship and ideology. Its major effect—intended or not—was to shift attention from more structural issues such as unemployment and discrimination, to the African-American family structure and the roles played by women as primarily responsible for the condition of the African-American community.[3] (See Gilkes [1983] and Jones [1985:312] for a discussion of the effects of the Moynihan Report on gender relations in African-American communities and organizations.) An examination of more recent examples of this perspective in the popular press may be found in Collins (1989) and Baca Zinn (1989).

Unlike much anthropological research in which women were "invisible," this work was unusual in the emphasis placed on women. Indeed, one might surmise that the researchers were negatively impressed by their high visibility. At issue, however, is the accuracy of the interpretation of women's roles. These women, who often work outside the home, are portrayed as "deviant," with deviancy having negative consequences for their communities. To whom were women being compared? Recent research suggests that these women were seen as deviant to a class- and ethnic-based notion of ideal gender roles that conformed neither to the experiences of European-American working-class women nor to those of women of color.

The New Scholarship

With the impetus of the civil rights movement in the 1960s and 1970s, and the feminist movement of the 1970s, research on women and ethnicity in the United States challenged the prevailing views with studies that reexamined the roles of women in families, the workplace, and the community. Not surprisingly much of it was done by women. Basic assumptions— that the role of a woman as worker was a "deviant" one and that the roles of poor and working-class women in families and in their communities were indeed pathological—were questioned. These studies laid the basis for sophisticated theoretical examinations of the social and cultural construction of gender: the way in which the experiences of women vary with race and class, and how these compare with the dominant cultural ideology of gender roles.

Early studies such as that by Gerda Lerner (1979) pointed to the class bias of the "cult of true womanhood": the set of ideas that asserted the dichotomy between home and workplace, the contrast between male and female natures, and the idealization of domesticity and motherhood (Welter 1966). Historians and anthropologists began to give working women visibility by documenting women's participation in the labor force throughout U.S. history, and noting that only a limited proportion of the population had ever possessed the resources to be "ladies." Though much of the early work was done by historians, anthropologists have increasingly begun to study the experiences of working-class women (see Lamphere 1987, chapter 1, for a recent review of the literature on studies of working women; see also Sacks and Remy 1984). New research traced the ways in which the lives of women of color, particularly their participation in the work force, are shaped by institutionalized racism (Dill 1986; Glenn 1986; Higginbotham 1983; Jones 1985; Mullings 1986a; Zambrana 1982).[4] This work reversed the causal order of Moynihan's analysis by emphasizing the social constraints within which people created viable lives, rather than blaming the victims for social conditions they did not create.

In particular, these studies demonstrated that racial and ethnic discrimination does condition the options of women. For example, because of the discrimination against both men and women, African-American married women have historically worked outside the home in greater proportions than European-American women and as laborers have constituted a pool of low wage workers. However, participation in the work force was not deviant to the experiences of many U.S. women. European-American working-class women worked outside the home in greater numbers than an idealized version of history would have us believe. Do these conditions produce "deviant" mothers, disorganized households and alienated individuals as claimed by Lewis, Moynihan, and others?

Along with the work discussed above was a set of studies reexamining women's roles in households and communities. Carol Stack's (1970) now classic (though somewhat romanticized) ethnographic study of poor African-American families pointed to the special role women played in ensuring the survival of children in situations of high unemployment. Stack found that women were nodes in extensive networks of kin and friends that exchanged goods, resources, services, and child care in an effort to ensure the survival of children. She documented a variety of residential and domestic strategies, such as child-swapping and gift-exchange. By demonstrating that the household structure and the roles played by women, far from being pathological and disorganized, constitute a rational, highly organized response to poverty, her research speaks directly to the "culture of poverty" hypothesis. A number of studies in the 1970s and 1980s on the African-American family made similar points (see Mullings 1986b for references).

The relationship between gender roles and household structure in poor families is placed in perspective by Rapp's (1987a) comparative analysis. She summarizes much of the work to date and demonstrates that households of different classes vary in their ability to tap wages and wealth; family form and gender roles will, to some extent, reflect the household's access to material resources. Rapp notes that women-centered networks, more critical in poor and working-class families, are in part a function of the gender arrangements of urban segregation, but are also part of "community control" for women (1987a:229).

Women's work in creating networks also extends to the workplace and the community. Bookman and Morgen's (1988) edited volume provides, for the first time, a series of ethnographic case studies documenting the involvement of working-class women and women of color in community, workplace, and political struggles. Cheryl Gilkes's (in that volume and 1983) discussions of African-American women's roles as mothers, caretakers, workers outside the home and community workers deserves special mention in this regard. These studies challenge the "culture of poverty" portrayal of poor households as pathological and disorganized, and the individuals as alienated and passive. It is important, however, that these households and women not be romanticized. As will be discussed later in the essay, the inadequacy of resources takes a serious toll on these households and the women in them.

One by-product of the increased understanding of how the experience of gender differs with class and race was renewed attention to the cultural and social (although often rationalized as biological) construction of gender. It became clear that, to a great extent, how different women in the United States played out gender roles was very much a matter of the positions society had thrust upon them rather than of their physiological makeup. For example, these studies uncovered the evidence that despite the popular "mammy" stereotype, the majority of enslaved African-American women worked in the fields alongside men as field hands. After emancipation, they worked outside the home, took leading roles in their communities, and had relatively egalitarian relationships within the household. Although these roles were portrayed negatively by leading social scientists, they (along with the cross-cultural data) provide evidence for suggesting that the confinement of women to a particular set of tasks and roles is based on social, rather than biological, constraints.

Despite the variety of gender experiences, it is the roles played by elite women that become the cultural model of what womanhood should be (see Rapp 1987a). Elite women, who alone can afford to indulge in a certain life-style, set the model for femininity against which women of other classes were judged. Hence, African-American women, largely by virtue of their assertiveness on behalf of their families and communities, because they are not sufficiently economically dependent on men, become "dangerous women and deviant mothers" (Gilkes 1983:294).

These studies—by documenting the way in which the boundaries of class and race influence the meaning of gender and by highlighting the external constraints within which people operate—provided support for the structural perspectives on ethnicity and inequality. By incorporating the analysis of gender and challenging the cultural construction of normative notions of male and female roles, the structuralist position is advanced and made more compelling. But just as the structuralist critiques often missed the significance of gender, the feminist perspectives have often missed the significance of race and class. In the following curricular example the need for taking all these variables into account will be evident.

Curricular Example: Women, Households, and Poverty

Objective

To stimulate thinking about how new conceptualizations of gender might transform the way we look at public policy issues in the United States, using the example of women, households, and poverty.

Discussion

The term "feminization of poverty" has been used by a variety of scholars, policymakers and activists to refer to increasing levels of poverty among women. Social scientists disagree on how to assess the high poverty rates, but much of the recent work influential in social policy and public opinion attributes it to the rise of households headed by women. In 1984, 16% of all households in the United States were headed by women (Rodgers 1986:5).

This dialogue has particular implications for people of color who experience a proportionately greater rate of households headed by women (in 1984, 13% of all European-American households, 23% of all Spanish origin households and 44% of all African-American households were headed by women [Rodgers 1986:5]). A number of recent works assert or imply (see for example Lemann 1986; Murray 1984; Moyers[5]) that much of the contemporary poverty experienced by minority communities is attributable to the growth of households headed by women. Thus it is these women who are most frequently portrayed as "deviant" to the mainstream community—the welfare mother burdening the society with her children remains a powerful image. Jones suggests,

> The manifestations of racism—black mothers and children dependent upon the state—only reinforces racism, in much the same way that slavery was shaped by and then reinforced racial prejudice. [1985:327]

Several interrelated assumptions discussed earlier in this essay also appear in much of this work. Implicit, or sometimes explicit, is the cultural explanation for poverty—that differences in beliefs, values, etc. are ultimately responsible for disproportionate poverty and the growth of what has been called "the underclass." The argument goes something like this: the growth of households headed by women—the households themselves a result of deviant values—perpetuates poverty by providing inadequate income and socializing children into a maladaptive culture. The majority of these works assume that households headed by women are inherently problematic. Some explicitly state that they are to blame for the recent growth of poverty among some peoples of color. The role of welfare has received particular attention (e.g., Murray 1984; Moyers). It is suggested that access to welfare, by decreasing the necessity for dependence on men, encourages female-headed families and thereby poverty.

Recent studies have addressed themselves to the question of the centrality of family structure in causing poverty. Several analyses have pointed to the lack of evidence that family structure causes poverty, noting in particular that the two-parent family is no guarantee against poverty for people of color (see Baca Zinn [1989] for a review of such studies); similarly, comparative analyses of AFDC benefits in different states indicate that welfare does not have a major effect on family structure (Ellwood and Summers 1986).

Other work has pointed to economic (rather than cultural) reasons for the racial differences in rates of female-headedness. Wilson, for example, argues that while the rise in female-headship among European-American may have to do with emerging values, increasing female-headship among African-American women is directly linked to unemployment among men (see above for reasons for unemployment). Despite the picture painted by the popular press, the rate of childbearing among teenage African-American women is not increasing but rather decreased 40% between 1960 and 1983 (Wilson 1987:194). There are, however, fewer employed men to marry and the rate of marriage had declined, resulting in higher statistical rates for out-of-wedlock births for African-American teenagers. In highlighting the economic reasons for high rates of households headed by women, this work turns around the causative relationship linking female-headship to poverty and provides evidence for the view that public policies need to focus on transforming the economic situation, rather than the culture of the poor.

While this work is important in pointing to the structural reasons for the disparities in rates of families headed by women, much of it uncritically accepts normative views of the roles of men and women and the premise that households headed by women are inherently problematic, without sufficient concern for class[6] variables that bear on access to resources.

The feminist scholarship goes further in questioning the assumption that women can only have decent standards of living through access to the resources of men and questions the validity of solutions making women dependent on men, rather than on welfare, for subsistence (Baca Zinn 1989; Collins 1989). These critiques give more attention to the actual lives of women and suggest that women's reproductive and marital status are affected not only by the employment of the men in their communities, but also by their own lack of employment possibilities in a sex-segregated labor force (Gordon 1989) where women of color are disproportionately found in the lowest paid sectors.

Along these lines, scholars have examined the way in which state policies reinforce gender hierarchy. By failing to provide child care that would allow mothers to hold jobs and earn independent incomes, and by maintaining two-tiered social insurance programs that discriminate against women, public policies reinforce the traditional family structure of the male breadwinner and dependent, isolated female homemaker. Welfare and workfare programs, where benefits are even lower than prevailing wage rates, do not allow full independence for women and therefore maintain traditional gender relationships in which a woman's only option for raising her standard of living is marriage (see Gerstel and Gross [1987:461–465] for a review of such studies). The welfare and workfare programs mesh with the employment system to produce a pool of low wage labor (see Susser and Kreniske [1987] for a case study).

Finally, feminist approaches might challenge the assumption that families headed by women are inherently problematic. While single-parenting is no doubt difficult and the cost in health and realization of personal potential is often high, more attention needs to be given to the various roles played by men and how relative access to material and social resources condition the household's experience. We need to know more about the variety of ways in which people organize themselves to successfully ensure the survival of children. In this regard it may be interesting to have students discuss network formation for mutual assistance among poor and working-class women who head families (e.g., Stack 1970), as compared to that among European-American middle stratum women for whom Newman suggests

> the cultural emphasis on nuclear family independence constrains middle-class divorced women to rely on their families of origin for help and makes it difficult for them to extend ties to individuals outside this narrow range. [1986:242]

Here again, feminist writers will need to attend to race and class and the way in which it shapes the experience of gender. For example, several writers have noted that the "feminization of poverty" is a problematic phrase. It obfuscates the class and race differentiation among women and substitutes gender for class as the variable by which resources get divided up. Further, it ignores the increasing poverty of African-American men and other men of color. Indeed, not all female-headed households are poor: in 1984, though over 50% of households headed by African-American and Hispanic women were poor, only 27% of households headed by European-American women were poor (Rodgers 1986:10). As Maxine Baca Zinn put it,

> The formation of female-headed households is but one example of the closely intertwined fate of racial-ethnic women and men. [1987:24]

Policy implications that derive from this sort of analysis point to the need for societal transformations that address unemployment and race and gender wage discrimination, and strengthen commitment to the provision of social services such as child care.

Suggested Discussion Questions

1. Differences and similarities in households headed by women: Why has there been a rise in households headed by women? How do the reasons for and course of routes to independent headship differ with race and class? Is feminization of poverty an accurate description? How might differences in access to social (e.g., people) and material resources bear on the viability of households headed by women? What sorts of solutions have people devised for coping with changing family forms? (Here students might discuss the emergence of nonkin networks among middle-income women, as well as flexible networks and community organization among working-class women.) How might culture bear on both gender roles and network formation?

2. Normative notions of gender roles in scholarly work and social policy: How do specific social policies (e.g., welfare/workfare, child care, family law) reflect and reinforce traditional gender roles? How might these policies be altered if new perspectives on gender, race and class were applied? Are there alternative conceptions of primary associations that might alter our perspective on households headed by women?

Readings

Baca Zinn, Maxine
    1989   Family, Race, and Poverty in the Eighties: Cultural and Structural Models. Signs 14(4):856–
    874.
Barnes, Annie
    1987   Single Parents in Black America: A Study in Culture and Legitimacy. Bristol, Ind.: Wyndham
    Hall Press.
Collins, Patricia Hill
    1989   A Comparison of Two Works on Black Family Life. Signs 14(4):875–884.
Gerstel, Naomi, and Harriet Engel Gross
    1987   Introduction to Part IV: State Policy and Employers' Policy. *In* Families and Work. Naomi
    Gerstel and Harriet Engel Gross, eds. Pp. 457–68. Philadelphia: Temple University Press.
Gilkes, Cheryl Townsend
    1983   From Slavery to Social Welfare: Racism and the Control of Black Women. *In* Class, Race,
    and Sex: The Dynamics of Control. Amy Swerdlow and Hanna Lessinger, eds. Pp. 288–300. Bos-
    ton: G. K. Hall & Co.
Jones, Jacqueline
    1985   Labor of Love, Labor of Sorrow: Black Women, Work, and the Family from Slavery to the
    Present. New York: Basic Books.
Rapp, Rayna
    1987   Urban Kinship in Contemporary America: Families, Classes, and Ideology. *In* Cities of the
    United States: Studies in Urban Anthropology. Leith Mullings, ed. Pp. 219–242. New York: Co-
    lumbia University Press.
Stack, Carol B.
    1970   All Our Kin: Strategies for Survival in a Black Community. New York: Harper & Row.
Susser, Ida
    1986   Political Activity among Working Class Women in a U.S. City. American Ethnologist
    13(1):108–117.
Wilson, William Julius
    1987   The Truly Disadvantaged: The Inner City, the Underclass, and Public Policy. Chicago: Uni-
    versity of Chicago Press.

Health Policy

In the first part of this essay, I discussed alternative perspectives on the roles of biology, culture, and social structure in the production of inequality. This debate takes on very concrete and important ramifications when we examine the topic of health and illness. As new infectious diseases ravage our cities, health indicators decline in some sectors of our population, health costs continue to spiral and health services are less satisfactory for the majority of the population, social scientists are increasingly drawn into analyzing of the crisis in our health care system. Medical anthropology, a growing subfield, has been concerned with the interrelationship of biological, social, and cultural factors in health and illness. "Critical" medical anthropology, a relatively new field, is particularly attentive to applying the critical tools of anthropology to biomedicine as well as to the medical systems of other societies, demonstrating that biomedicine is also a cultural system and not exempt from this sort of analysis. The new scholarship on health and gender has contributed to this body of work by expanding our knowledge of: (1) the social construction of illness and health, (2) the cultural construction of medical knowledge, (3) the way in which the medical system contributes to the maintenance of hierarchy.

The Social Construction of Illness and Health

In light of the discussion in the first part of the essay, it should not be surprising that among women, health status clearly differs by race. For example, in 1980 African-American women had an average life expectancy of 72.3 years as compared to 78.1 years for European-American women, and significantly higher rates of the diseases that are the major causes of death: cardiovascular disease and cancer (Keith and Smith 1988). However the reasons for these differentials are much debated in medicine where, despite the body of literature in public health on the social causation of disease, there is a marked tendency to see differences in rates of illness and disease as a result of either genetic/biological differences on one hand, or individual life-style choices on the other. The policy result of both of these perspectives can be seen in the increased emphasis on individual, rather than social, responsibility for health and illness.

While clearly there are biological and genetic aspects of differential disease rates (see Polednak 1987), and it is often difficult to draw links between social conditions and specific disease states, the new research on gender has added to our knowledge of the way in which social conditions generate disease and influence its distribution. Some of the early studies sought to demonstrate that differences in male-female mortality could be largely attributed to behavioral rather than physiological factors (Waldrun 1986) and that as women's experiences change, so does their health status. Other studies have revealed the way in which apparent racial discrepancies (often attributed to biological differences) are mediated by class and racial discrimination (Basset and Krieger 1986; Mullings 1989; Polednak 1987). *Too Little, Too Late*, edited by Perales and Young (1988) (a special issue of *Women and Health*) brings together work on a range of issues affecting poor women. The effects of various societal forces on women's health are the subject of several chapters in Lewin and Oleson (1985).

For women of color in particular, recent work has examined the way in which the triple day—work outside the home, household responsibilities, and community work—may contribute to higher rates of disease (Mullings 1984); and how ethnicity and socioeconomic status may condition options for reproduction, contraception, and sterilization abuse (Boone 1988;

Clarke 1984; Fisher 1986; Lazarus 1988; Lopez 1987; Zambrana 1982). This research establishes that the multiplicity of roles filled under adverse circumstances takes a serious toll on the health of women of color.

Society as a whole not only bears a portion of the financial costs of preventable illnesses, but more important, loses the potential contribution of productive human beings. Weiss and Mann (1978) propose a striking way to look at the biological toll exacted by racism. The six-year differential in life expectancy between African-American and European-American women may not sound like much unless it comes off your own life expectancy. But in 1980 there were approximately 14 million African-American women in the United States, each of whom, on average, will live six years less than if she were European-American. These women, "and American society, will lose [84 million] years of human life and productivity to discrimination based on an inaccurate view of human variability" (Weiss and Mann 1978:502; U.S. Bureau of the Census, 1987:17).

With respect to health policy, this research suggests that while an understanding of cultural preferences and the role of biological/genetic differences is important, if we are to make inroads into health differentials, health strategists must also look at structural differences. This is a formidable issue to confront in the United States, which along with South Africa, is the only Western industrialized society without a national health insurance. As long as the commitment is to a fee-for-service medical system and to genetic and lifestyle explanations for racial differences in health and illness, it will be difficult to give priority to equalizing access to healthful resources—employment opportunities, adequate wages, decent housing, nutrition, education, recreational opportunities and medical care—that may make the real difference in health.

The Cultural Construction of Illness

The new scholarship on gender has raised questions about the cultural construction of medical knowledge. For many health professionals as well as consumers, biomedical definitions, concepts, explanations and models are not historically and culturally constructed, but are rather understood to be "natural" facts, applicable cross-culturally and historically. This is often rationalized with reference to "hard" sciences such as biology, physics, and physiology. Cross-cultural studies by anthropologists, however, have demonstrated that concepts of illness and health are socially and culturally constructed and distributed. Recent gender-based studies have assisted in extending this critique to biomedicine. These works suggest that knowledge is always socially constructed, that scientific knowledge is not entirely objective nor free from value judgments and cultural constructions, and that in many instances, medical knowledge is construed around cultural views of the proper place of women. Diagnosis and treatment, then, often serve to reproduce the hierarchical system they reflect.

Emily Martin (1987), for example, raises important questions about biomedicine's conceptualizations of female physiology (see also Scully and Bart 1973). Martin notes that as medical discourse began to be characterized by metaphors stressing production, menstruation was conceptualized as "failed production"—the images are those of sloughing, hemorrhaging, waste. Analyzing standard medical textbook descriptions of menstruation, she finds that

in rapid succession the reader is confronted with "degenerate," "decline," "withdrawn," "spasms," "lack," "weakened," "leak," "deteriorate," "discharge," and, after all that, "repair." [1987:47]

Similarly, menopause is seen as "a kind of failure of the authority structure in the body" (1987:45) (see also McCrea 1986). Medical terminology, allegedly value-free, contributes to negative views of these processes that find expression in women's perceptions about how medicine views their bodies as well as in their own images of their bodies. This discourse has implications for treatment, evidenced, for example, by the rate of Caesarean sections and the management of menopause. Similarly, one may question the "scientific" basis upon which signs and symptoms are organized into diseases. Laws (1983), for example, argues that medical knowledge about premenstrual tension is not really constructed out of scientifically proven facts, but is "at its roots a political construct" (1983:20).

Reproductive systems and strategies have been the focus of much of the work on gender bias in the production and dissemination of seemingly neutral medical technologies. For example, both Lorber (1987) and Crowe (1985) argue (from different perspectives) that infertility, although seen as a biological failing, is a social, rather than physiological problem in that it violates a culturally constructed notion of family and gender roles. Implicit in the use of in-vitro fertilization (IVF) are cultural values concerning the nature of femininity, masculinity, sexuality, and motherhood. Thus IVF is not a value-free technology; rather, it reinforces certain perspectives on gender roles and the family: a biological definition of motherhood, the idea that the nuclear family is a natural structure and the ideology that motherhood is a "natural" state for women (Crowe 1985). In addition, since access to high-cost technology varies with race and class, one may raise questions about the extent to which differential availability of such technology allows some couples, but not others, to have their own children.

Other work on reproduction and reproductive rights (e.g., Arditti et al. 1984) pick up these themes. Abortion "technology . . . renders the fetus visible, and the woman by implication transparent" (Rothman 1987:164). Rapp (1987b) concludes that the technology of amniocentesis gives science such authority in defining motherhood that "other voices" cannot be heard. "Other voices" are differentiated by class and race, as well as by gender. Petchesky (1983) takes on issues of class and reproduction in the history of access to abortion. Fisher (1986) discusses the way in which the incidence and consequences of hysterectomies vary across race and class. This body of work has dramatic implications for public policy relating to contraception, abortion, surrogate motherhood, fetal diagnosis, and other uses of medical technology.

These works suggest that what is seen as "neutral" scientific knowledge is, to a great extent, socially and culturally determined. This is not to assert that objective facts do not exist, but that as we perceive, organize, and apply them, we are constrained by a discourse shaped by the power interests of a hierarchical society. These interests shape medical knowledge which both reflects and reproduces notions about what women ought to be. Medical systems may do this in a particularly potent way—rendering that which is social, natural, and then utilizing natural explanations to reproduce hierarchical social relations. These studies provide the foundation for questioning whether the influence of hierarchical relations upon the metaphorical structure of medical models may impede the pursuit of health, whereas other ways of thinking may get us further.

Hierarchy and the Health Care Encounter

Although feminist critiques began with specific concerns such as negative imagery of women in medical discourse, devaluation of women's physical ills, the treatment of issues of reproduction, use of drug therapy on women, and such (see Lewin and Oleson 1985), studies of women's health status and their experiences as recipients of health care have facilitated examination of the way in which the structure and organization of the health care system, conditioned by hierarchical gender relationship in the larger society, structures the health care experience. Sue Fisher (1986), for example, analyzes discourse in doctor/patient communication to demonstrate how medical authority (generally male)[7] constructs and determines discussions about diagnoses, prognoses, and possible treatments.

Feminist scholars have raised questions about the management of childbirth and pregnancy. In particular, they have argued that the medicalization of childbirth, in which the woman is placed in a passive role and the doctor in an active role, does not serve the interests of women (Danziger 1986; Michaelson 1988; Singer 1987). As Fisher notes,

> in little more than a century, birth was redefined from a natural process in which women helped each other give birth to a dangerous, high-risk activity in which birthing women needed the medical ministrations and the interventionist practices of the male physician who would "deliver" their babies. [1986:137]

However, Michaelson (1988) suggests that the feminist critique of birth was largely pertinent to the interests of the middle class. These modes of analysis can be extended to the many other phenomena that have become "medicalized."

By elucidating the power, gender, and class relations implicit in the health care encounter, this body of work underscores the way in which health policy, like other public policies, reinforces hierarchical arrangements. It suggests that while providing access to health care is important, improving health conditions in the United States may also necessitate a restructuring of the entire health care system.

Knowledge and Action

Can the anthropological knowledge discussed in this essay be utilized to affect public policy? Perhaps one of the most striking examples of the use of the findings discussed above is the women's health movement. Using the strategies of political action organizations and self-help groups, the women's health movement sought to empower women through knowledge and to challenge the assumptions and practices of biomedicine (see Zimmerman 1987). The participants were primarily middle-stratum women (although see Morgen 1988a) and not surprisingly, the movement appears to have been more successful at challenging the cultural construction of medicine, than at addressing the social construction of disease. However, the effects of the use of such knowledge are still evident in self-help groups, the dissemination of publications (*Our Bodies, Ourselves,* being a widely read example), well woman clinics, midwifery, and other changes in the context of birthing.

As we mentioned at the beginning of the essay, anthropologists have played a variety of roles in attempting to affect public policy. Because the recent feminist scholarship emphasizes social, rather than biological or genetic, constraints to equal opportunity and consequently points to the need for fundamental structural changes rather than the short-term solutions more popular with policymakers, these findings are initially more likely to have an effect through grass-roots and community movements. Case studies of anthropologists in grass-roots organizations may be useful in giving students some flavor of the range of issues. Sanjek's (1987) account of his participation in the struggle to save a Gray Panther clinic is not specifically concerned with gender issues but his analysis of the academic, applied, and advocacy aspects of his work is very informative. Morgen's (1988b) description of her experience as a participant observer in the Citizen Action for Health, a cross-class, multiracial women's organization brings in issues of race, class, and gender. The coalition was successful in reopening a prenatal clinic and in establishing a neighborhood health center. Both accounts present challenging examples of the anthropologist as advocate, and demonstrate that when anthropologists can link their skills to an organized social movement or one on the verge of organizing, their work may attain a special significance and contribute to social change.

Curricular Example: Childbirth in the United States

Objective

To facilitate the students' thinking about the issues discussed in the essay, using childbirth as an example.

Issues to Be Discussed

1. The cultural construction of childbirth: how childbirth became an illness; views of women's bodies and childbirth; cross-cultural varieties of the childbirth experience; how does technology shape the birth experience.

2. The social construction of childbirth: how do class and race shape risk in childbirth; how do class and race bear on access to information; why do 25 percent of women in the United States receive no prenatal care or belated prenatal care (Jaynes and Williams 1989:402); to what extent does the feminist critique of childbirth obscure class and race issues?

3. The health encounter: how does the traditional management of pregnancy and childbirth reinforce gender hierarchy in the clinical setting?

4. The struggle for alternative birth contexts: midwifery, natural childbirth, control over childbirth.

5. The role of policy: the ramifications of the following issues might be discussed: the increase in households headed by women as discussed in the first part of the essay, unequal access to parental care, appropriate use of technology, increasing demand for control over childbirth.

Readings

Davis-Floyd, Robbie E.
   1988   Birth as an American Rite of Passage. *In* Childbirth in America: Anthropological Perspectives. Karen L. Michaelson and contributors. Pp. 153–172. South Hadley, Mass.: Bergin & Garvey.
Jordan, Brigitte
   1978   Birth in Four Cultures: A Cross-Cultural Investigation of Childbirth in Yucatan, Holland, Sweden, and the United States. Vermont: Eden Press Women's Publications.
Lazarus, Ellen S.
   1988   Poor Women, Poor Outcomes: Social Class and Reproductive Health. *In* Childbirth in America: Anthropological Perspectives. Karen L. Michaelson and contributors. Pp. 39–54. South Hadley, Mass.: Bergin & Garvey.

Leavitt, Judith Walzer, and Whitney Walton
    1984   "Down to Death's Door": Women's Perceptions of Childbirth in America. *In* Women and
        Health in America: Historical Readings. Judith Walzer Leavitt, ed. Pp. 155–165. Madison: University of Wisconsin Press.
Martin, Emily
    1987   Chapters 4: "Medical Metaphors of Women's Bodies: Birth"; 8: "Birth, Resistance, Race, and Class"; and 9: "The Creation of New Birth Imagery." *In* The Woman in the Body: A Cultural Analysis of Reproduction. Boston: Beacon Press.

Student Exercise

Assign the students to interview someone of their mother's and if possible, their grandmother's, generation in order to elicit their experiences with childbirth. The readings (particularly those by Lazarus 1988; Leavitt and Walton 1984 and Martin 1987) should give them ideas about what questions to ask. Information about hospital versus home births; participation by mothers, fathers, kin, friends and neighbors; the doctor's role; the mother's feelings; how mothers learned about and prepared for the birth of their first child; perceptions and description of childbirth events, etc., may be utilized to enliven discussion of the issues cited above.

Notes

Acknowledgments. I would like to thank Lynn Bolles, Lawrence Hammer, Delmos Jones, Margo Matwychuk, Sandra Morgen, Rayna Rapp and project reviewers for their comments. I would also like to acknowledge the fine research assistance of Lawrence Hammer and Margo Matwychuk.

1. It is possible, however, to find literature on specific topics of concern to applied anthropologists. In education, for example, see Pitman and Eisenhart (1988), Goetz and Grant (1988), Holland and Eisenhart (1988).

2. Boas's concern with these issues was evident in his work on European immigrants. He attempted to demonstrate that culture, not biology, accounts for differences in behavior (see Partridge and Eddy 1987). While most anthropologists would assert that anthropology, with its cultural, rather than genetic explanation of ethnic differences, has much to contribute to the public debate, there is disagreement about anthropology's effectiveness. For example, Hicks and Handler (1987) assert that anthropology has been influential in public policy and Hinshaw states that "decision makers at all levels have internalized many of the lessons anthropology has been teaching . . . with respect to race, ethnicity and multiculturalism" (1980:516). Weaver (1985), however, concludes that anthropologists have generally been ineffective in influencing public policy and that racist, exclusionary ideas such as those of Jencks had more influence on immigration policy than those of Boas and Wissler.

3. See Wilson (1987) for a sympathetic treatment of the Moynihan Report.

4. Work that attempted to conceptualize the relationships among gender, race and class was particularly important. In this regard, Angela Davis' (1981) ground breaking work, *Women, Race & Class*, followed by studies by the working group on women, race and class of the Center for Research on Women (see Resources), was critical.

5. Bill Moyers, "Crisis in Black America: The Vanishing Black Family," a made-for-television documentary.

6. The fact that there is not much information on class variables, and relatively little ethnographic work on middle-stratum African Americans and poor European-Americans, tends to structure the discussion in ethnic categories and obfuscate class by ethnicity.

7. See Leavitt (1984), Part III, for a series of articles on women in the health professions.

References Cited

Arditti, Rita, et al., eds.
  1984 Test-Tube Women: What Future for Motherhood? London: Pandora.
Baca Zinn, Maxine
  1987 Minority Families in Crisis: the Public Discussion. Working Paper: Center for Research on Women. Memphis State University. Memphis, TN. Research Paper #6.
  1989 Family, Race, and Poverty in the Eighties. Signs 14(4):856–874.
Barnes, Annie
  1987 Single Parents in Black America: A Study in Culture and Legitimacy. Bristol, Ind.: Wyndham Hall Press.
Basset, M., and N. Krieger
  1986 Social Class and Black-White Differences in Breast Cancer Survival. American Journal of Public Health 76(12):1400–1403.
Bookman, Ann, and Sandra Morgen, eds.
  1988 Women and the Politics of Empowerment. Philadelphia: Temple University Press.
Boone, Margaret S.
  1988 Social Support for Pregnancy and Childbearing among Disadvantaged Blacks in an American Inner City. In Childbirth in America: Anthropological Perspectives. Karen L. Michaelson and contributors. Pp. 66–78. South Hadley, Mass.: Bergin & Garvey.
Chambers, Erve
  1977 Public Policy and Anthropology. Reviews in Anthropology 4(6):543–54.
  1987 Applied Anthropology in the Post-Vietnam Era: Anticipations and Ironies. Annual Review of Anthropology 16:309–337.
Clarke, Adele
  1984 Subtle Forms of Sterilization Abuse: A Reproductive Rights Analysis. In Test-Tube Women: What Future for Motherhood? Rita Arditti et al., eds. Pp. 188–212. London: Pandora.
Collins, Patricia Hill
  1989 A Comparison of Two Works on Black Family Life. Signs 14(4):875–884.
Crowe, C.
  1985 'Women Want It': In Vitro Fertilization and Women's Motivations for Participation. Women's Studies International Forum 8(6):547–52.
Danziger, Sandra Klein
  1986 The Uses of Expertise in Doctor-Patient Encounters During Pregnancy. In The Sociology of Health and Illness: Critical Perspectives. 2nd edition. Peter Conrad and Rochelle Kern, eds. Pp. 310–321. New York: St. Martin's Press.
Davis, Angela Y.
  1981 Women, Race and Class. New York: Random House.
Davis-Floyd, Robbie E.
  1988 Birth as an American Rite of Passage. In Childbirth in America: Anthropological Perspectives. Karen L. Michaelson and contributors. Pp. 153–172. South Hadley, Mass.: Bergin & Garvey.
Dill, Bonnie Thornton
  1986 Our Mother's Grief: Racial-Ethnic Women and the Maintenance of Families. Working Paper: Center for Research on Women, Memphis State University, Memphis, TN. Research Paper # 4.
Ellwood, David, and Lawrence Summers
  1986 Poverty in America: Is Welfare the Answer or the Problem. In Fighting Poverty. S. Danzinger and Daniel Weinberg, eds. Pp. 92–98. Cambridge: Harvard University Press.
Fisher, Sue
  1986 In the Patient's Best Interest: Women and the Politics of Medical Decisions. New Brunswick, N.J.: Rutgers University Press.

Gerstel, Naomi, and Harriet Engel Gross
  1987   Introduction to Part IV: State Policy and Employers' Policy. *In* Families and Work. Naomi Gerstel and Harriet Engel Gross, eds. Pp. 457–468. Philadelphia: Temple University Press.
Gibbs, James L., Jr.
  1982   Anthropology as a Policy Science: Some Limitations. *In* Crisis in Anthropology, View from Springhill, 1980. E. Adamson Hoebel, R. Currier, and S. Kaiser, eds. Pp. 363–378. New York: Garland Publishing.
Gilkes, Cheryl Townsend
  1983   From Slavery to Social Welfare: Racism and the Control of Black Women. *In* Class, Race, and Sex: The Dynamics of Control. Amy Swerdlow and Hanna Lessinger, eds. Pp. 288–300. Boston: G. K. Hall & Co.
  1988   Building in Many Places: Multiple Commitments and Ideologies in Black Women's Community Work. *In* Women and the Politics of Empowerment. Ann Bookman and Sandra Morgen, eds. Pp. 53–76. Philadelphia: Temple University Press.
Glazer, Nathan, and Daniel P. Moynihan
  1975   Introduction. *In* Ethnicity: Theory and Experience. Nathan Glazer and Daniel P. Moynihan, eds. Pp. 1–26. Cambridge: Harvard University Press.
Glenn, Evelyn N.
  1986   Issei, Nisei, Warbride: Three Generations of Japanese American Women in Domestic Service. Philadelphia: Temple University Press.
Goetz, J. P., and L. Grant
  1988   Conceptual Approaches to Studying Gender in Education. Anthropology and Education Quarterly 19(2):182–196.
Gordon, Linda
  1989   Feminism and the "Underclass." Against the Current 18(Jan/Feb):42–43.
Herrnstein, R.
  1973   IQ in the Meritocracy. Boston: Atlantic-Little Brown.
Hicks, George L., and Mark J. Handler
  1987   Ethnicity, Public Policy, and Anthropologists. *In* Applied Anthropology in America. 2nd edition. Elizabeth M. Eddy and William L. Partridge, eds. Pp. 398–432. New York: Columbia University Press.
Higginbotham, Elizabeth
  1983   Laid Bare by the System: Work and Survival for Black and Hispanic Women. *In* Class, Race, and Sex: The Dynamics of Control. Amy Swerdlow and Hanna Lessinger, eds. Pp. 200–215. Boston: G. K. Hall & Co.
Hinshaw, Robert E.
  1980   Anthropology, Administration, and Public Policy. Annual Review of Anthropology 9:497–522.
Holland, Dorothy C., and Margaret A. Eisenhart
  1988   Women's Ways of Going to School: Cultural Reproduction of Women's Identities as Workers. *In* Class, Race, and Gender in American Education. Lois Weis, ed. Pp. 266–301. Albany: SUNY Press.
Jaynes, Gerald David, and Robin M. Williams, Jr., eds.
  1989   Black Americans' Health. *In* A Common Destiny: Blacks and American Society. Committee on the Status of Black Americans, Commission on Behavioral and Social Sciences and Education, National Research Council. Gerald David Jaynes and Robin M. Williams, Jr., eds. Pp. 391–450. Washington, D.C.: National Academy Press.
Jensen, A. R.
  1969   How Much Can We Boost IQ and Scholastic Achievement? Harvard Educational Review 39:1–123.
  1970   Can We and Should We Study Race Differences? *In* Disadvantaged Child: Compensatory Education, a National Debate. Vol. 3. J. Hellmuth, ed. Pp. 124–157. New York: Brunner-Mazel.

Jones, Jacqueline
  1985   Labor of Love, Labor of Sorrow: Black Women, Work, and the Family from Slavery to Present. New York: Basic Books.
Jordan, Brigitte
  1978   Birth in Four Cultures: A Cross-Cultural Investigation of Childbirth in Yucatan, Holland, Sweden, and the United States. Vermont: Eden Press Women's Publications.
Kamin, Leon J.
  1974   The Science and Politics of IQ. Potomac, Md.: Erlbaum.
  1982   IQ and Heredity: Historical and Critical Remarks. Journal of Academic Skills 3(1):30–50.
Keith, Verna M., and David P. Smith
  1988   The Current Differential in Black and White Life Expectancy. Demography 25(4):625–632.
Lamphere, Louise
  1987   From Working Daughters to Working Mothers. Ithaca: Cornell University Press.
Lawler, James M.
  1978   IQ, Heritability and Racism. New York: International Publishers.
Laws, Sophie
  1983   The Sexual Politics of Pre-Menstrual Tension. Women's Studies International Forum 6(1):19–31.
Lazarus, Ellen S.
  1988   Poor Women, Poor Outcomes: Social Class and Reproductive Health. *In* Childbirth in America: Anthropological Perspectives. Karen L. Michaelson & contributors. Pp. 39–54. South Hadley, Mass.: Bergin & Garvey.
Leacock, Eleanor Burke
  1971   Introduction. *In* The Culture of Poverty: A Critique. Eleanor Burke Leacock, ed. Pp. 9–37. New York: Simon & Schuster.
  1987   Theory and Ethics in Applied Urban Anthropology. *In* Cities of the United States: Studies in Urban Anthropology. Leith Mullings, ed. Pp. 317–336. New York: Columbia University Press.
Leavitt, Judith Walzer, ed.
  1984   Women and Health in America: Historical Readings. Madison: University of Wisconsin Press.
Leavitt, Judith Walzer, and Whitney Walton
  1984   Down to Death's Door: Women's Perceptions of Childbirth in America. *In* Women and Health in America: Historical Readings. Judith Walzer Leavitt, ed. Pp. 155–165. Madison: University of Wisconsin Press.
Lemann, Nicolas
  1986   The Origins of the Underclass, Parts 1 & 2. The Atlantic Monthly (June):31–35; (July):54–68.
Lerner, Gerda
  1979   The Lady and the Mill Girl. *In* A Heritage of Her Own. N. Cott and E. Pleck, eds. Pp. 182–196. New York: Simon & Schuster.
Lewin, Ellen, and Virginia Oleson, eds.
  1985   Women, Health, and Healing: Toward a New Perspective. New York: Tavistock Publications.
Lewis, Oscar
  1966   The Culture of Poverty. Scientific American 215(4):3–9.
Lopez, Iris
  1987   Sterilization Among Puerto Rican Women in New York City: Public Policy and Social Constraints. *In* Cities of the United States: Studies in Urban Anthropology. Leith Mullings, ed. Pp. 269–291. New York: Columbia University Press.
Lorber, Judith
  1987   *In Vitro* Fertilization and Gender Politics. Women and Health 13:117–133.
Martin, Emily
  1987   The Woman in the Body: A Cultural Analysis of Reproduction. Boston: Beacon Press.
McCrea, Frances
  1986   The Politics of Menopause: The "Discovery" of a Deficiency Disease. *In* The Sociology of Health and Illness: Critical Perspectives. 2nd edition. Peter Conrad and Rochelle Kern, eds. Pp. 296–307. New York: St. Martin's Press.

Michaelson, Karen L., and contributors
    1988   Childbirth in America: Anthropological Perspectives. South Hadley, Mass.: Bergin &
       Garvey.
Morgen, Sandra
    1988a   The Dream of Diversity, the Dilemma of Difference: Race and Class Contradictions in a
       Feminist Health Clinic. *In* Anthropology for The Nineties. Johnnetta Cole, ed. Pp. 370–380. New
       York: Free Press.
    1988b   It's the Whole Power of the City Against Us!'': The Development of Political Consciousness
       in a Women's Health Care Coalition. *In* Women and the Politics of Empowerment. Ann Bookman
       and Sandra Morgen, eds. Pp. 97–115. Philadelphia: Temple University Press.
Moynihan, Daniel P.
    1965   The Negro Family: The Case for National Action. (Reprinted *In* The Moynihan Report and
       the Politics of Controversy. Lee Rainwater and William L. Yancey. Pp. 39–124. Cambridge: MIT
       Press.)
Mullings, Leith
    1984   Minority Women, Work, and Health. *In* Double Exposure: Women and Health Hazards on
       the Job and at Home. W. Chavin, ed. Pp. 121–138. New York: Monthly Review Press.
    1986a   Uneven Development: Class, Race and Gender in the United States Before 1900. *In* Wom-
       en's Work: Development and the Division of Labor. E. Leacock and H. Safa, eds. Pp. 41–57. New
       York: Bergen Publishers.
    1986b   Anthropological Perspectives on the Afro-American Family. The American Journal of Social
       Psychiatry 6(1):11–16.
    1989   Inequality and African-American Health Status: Policies and Prospects. *In* Race: 20th Century
       Dilemmas—21st Century Prognoses. Winston Van Horne, ed. Milwaukee: University of Wiscon-
       sin Institute on Race Relations (forthcoming).
Murray, Charles
    1984   Losing Ground. New York: Basic Books.
Newman, Katherine S.
    1986   Symbolic Dialectics and Generations of Women: Variation in the Meaning of Post-Divorce
       Downward Mobility. American Ethnologist 13(2):230–253.
Partridge, William L., and Elizabeth M. Eddy
    1987   The Development of Applied Anthropology in America. *In* Applied Anthropology in Amer-
       ica. 2nd edition. *In* Elizabeth M. Eddy and William L. Partridge, eds. Pp. 3–55. New York: Co-
       lumbia University Press.
Perales, Cesar A., and Lauren S. Young, eds.
    1988   Too Little, Too Late: Dealing With the Health Needs of Women in Poverty. New York: Har-
       rington Park Press.
Petchesky, Rosalind Pollack
    1983   Reproduction and Class Divisions among Women. *In* Class, Race, and Sex: The Dynamics of
       Control. Amy Swerdlow and Hanna Lessinger, eds. Pp. 221–242. Boston: G. K. Hall & Co.
Pitman, Mary Anne, and Margaret Eisenhart
    1988   Experiences of Gender: Studies of Women and Gender in Schools and Society. Anthropology
       and Education Quarterly 19(2):67–69.
Polednak, Anthony P.
    1987   Host Factors in Disease: Age, Sex, Racial and Ethnic Group and Body Build. Springfield, Ill.:
       Charles C. Thomas.
Rapp, Rayna
    1987a   Urban Kinship in Contemporary America: Families, Classes, and Ideology. *In* Cities of the
       United States: Studies in Urban Anthropology. Leith Mullings, ed. Pp. 219–242. New York: Co-
       lumbia University Press.
    1987b   Moral Pioneers: Women, Men, and Fetuses on a Frontier of Reproductive Technology.
       Women and Health 13:101–116.
Rodgers, Harrell R.
    1986   Poor Women, Poor Families. Armonk, N.Y.: M. E. Sharpe Inc.

Rothman, Barbara Katz
  1987   Reproduction. *In* Analyzing Gender: A Handbook of Social Science Research. Beth B. Hess
    and Myra Marx Ferree, eds. Pp. 154–170. Newberry Park, Calif.: Sage Publications.
Rushton, J. Philippe
  1989   Evolutionary Biology and Heritable Traits: With Reference to Oriental-White-Black Differ-
    ences. Paper prepared for the Symposium on Evolutionary Theory, Economics, and Political Sci-
    ence: An Emerging Theoretical Convergence at the Annual Meeting of the American Association
    for The Advancement of Science. San Francisco, California, January 19, 1989.
Sacks, Karen Brodkin, and Dorothy Remy, eds.
  1984   My Troubles Are Going To Have Trouble With Me: Everyday Trials and Triumphs of Women
    Workers. New Brunswick, N.J.: Rutgers University Press.
Sanjek, Roger
  1987   Anthropological Work at a Grey Panther Health Clinic: Academic, Applied, and Advocacy
    Goals. *In* Cities of the United States: Studies in Urban Anthropology. Leith Mullings, ed. Pp. 148–
    175. New York: Columbia University Press.
Scully, Diana, and Pauline Bart
  1973   A Funny Thing Happened on the Way to the Orifice: Women in Gynecology Textbooks.
    American Journal of Sociology 78(4):1045–1050.
Shockley, W.
  1970   New Methodology to Reduce the Environment-Heredity Uncertainty about Disgenics. Paper
    read before the National Academy of Sciences, Washington, D.C.
Singer, Merril
  1987   Cure, Care and Control: an Ectopic Encounter with Biomedical Obstetrics. *In* Encounters with
    Biomedicine: Case Studies in Medical Anthropology. Hans A. Baer, ed. Pp. 249–265. New York:
    Gordan and Breach Science Publishers.
Stack, Carol B.
  1970   All Our Kin: Strategies for Survival in a Black Community. New York: Harper & Row.
Susser, Ida
  1986   Political Activity among Working Class Women in a U.S. City. American Ethnologist
    13(1):108–117.
Susser, Ida, and John Kreniske
  1987   The Welfare Trap: A Public Policy for Deprivation. *In* Cities of the United States: Studies in
    Urban Anthropology. Leith Mullings, ed. Pp. 51–68. New York: Columbia University Press.
Taylor, H. F.
  1980   The IQ Game, A Methodological Inquiry into the Heredity-Environment Controversy. New
    Brunswick, N.J.: Rutgers University Press.
U.S. Bureau of the Census
  1987   Statistical Abstract of the United States: 1988. 108th edition. Washington, DC: U.S. Bureau
    of the Census.
Valentine, Charles A.
  1968   Culture and Poverty: Critique and Counter-Proposals. Chicago: University of Chicago Press.
Van Willigen, John
  1986   Applied Anthropology: An Introduction. South Hadley, Mass.: Bergin & Garvey.
Waldrun, Ingrid
  1986   Why Women Live Longer Than Men? *In* The Sociology of Health and Illness: Critical Per-
    spectives. 2nd edition. Peter Conrad and Rochelle Kern, eds. Pp. 34–44. New York: St. Martin's
    Press.
Weaver, Thomas
  1985   Anthropology as a Policy Science: Part I, A Critique. Human Organization 44(2) (sum-
    mer):97–105.
Weiss, Mark L., and Alan E. Mann
  1978   Human Biology and Behavior: An Anthropological Perspective. 2nd edition. Boston: Little,
    Brown and Company.

Welter, B.
    1966   The Cult of True Womanhood: 1820–1860. American Quarterly (Summer): 151–171.
Wilson, William Julius
    1987   The Truly Disadvantaged: The Inner City, the Underclass, and Public Policy. Chicago: University of Chicago Press.
Zambrana, Ruth E.
    1982   Work, Family, and Health: Latina Women in Transition. Bronx, New York: Hispanic Research Center-Fordham University Monograph No. 7.
Zimmerman, Mary K.
    1987   The Women's Health Movement: A Critique of Medical Enterprise and the Position of Women. *In* Analyzing Gender: A Handbook of Social Science Research. Beth B. Hess and Myra Marx Ferree, eds. Pp. 442–472. Newbury Park, Calif.: Sage Publications.

Annotated Bibliography of Teaching Resources

The Center for Research on Women at Memphis State University conducts, supports, and disseminates research on women with a particular emphasis on race and class. In addition to their ongoing research and workshops, the Center maintains a computerized information retrieval service for bibliographic materials from the social sciences and a reference bank of scholars of southern women and women of color. The Center's publications include their *Newsletter,* research papers, bibliographies, and a working papers series. These sources are especially relevant for research on African-American, Asian American, Latina, Native American and Southern women and for issues of race, class and gender, employment, education, and inequality. For more information contact:

Center For Research on Women
Clement Hall
Memphis State University
Memphis, TN 38152

Baca Zinn, Maxine, and Bonnie Thornton Dill
    1990   Women of Color in American Society. Philadelphia: Temple University Press (forthcoming).

This collection of readings on women of color brings together studies on African-American, Latina, Native American and Asian American women within a comparative framework. The first section includes chapters on theoretical approaches and demographic analyses, the second section focuses on social organization and the third addresses strategies for survival, resistance and coping. Because several of the authors have worked together or participated in research institutes sponsored by the Center for Research on Women at Memphis State University, the volume is unified by its emphasis on the interdependent systems of race, class and gender. The reader is specifically designed for undergraduates.

Gilkes, Cheryl Townsend
    1983   From Slavery to Social Welfare: Racism and the Control of Black Women. *In* Class, Race, and Sex: The Dynamics of Control. Amy Swerdlow and Hanna Lessinger, eds. Pp. 288–300. Boston: G. K. Hall & Co.

In this article, Gilkes examines the roles of African-American women as they have responded to various mechanisms of social control. She presents a critical response to the Moynihan Report, arguing that Moynihan's images of African-American women are part of a history of negative stereotypes.

Jones, Jacqueline
    1985   Labor of Love, Labor of Sorrow: Black Women, Work, and the Family from Slavery to the Present. New York: Basic Books.

This major historical study is a useful reference on African-American women from slavery through the contemporary period. The final chapter and the epilogue present historical facts that contextualize several of the issues discussed in this essay: work, welfare and the rise of households headed by women.

Lewin, Ellen, and Virginia Oleson, eds.
  1985   Women, Health, and Healing: Toward a New Perspective. New York: Tavistock Publications.

The chapters in this edited volume analyze various aspects of women's experiences as recipients and providers of health care in the United States and the United Kingdom. The overall theme of the volume, that women's health "be considered in relation to other aspects of the societies under discussion" (p. 6), is taken up in the introduction which provides a useful overview of such issues as quality of health care, the impact of technology, and the distribution of services.

Martin, Emily
  1987   The Woman in the Body: A Cultural Analysis of Reproduction. Boston: Beacon Press.

Martin presents an insightful analysis of gender, medicine and society. She examines the way in which cultural representations of female physiology become incorporated into medical models, which influence women's own perceptions of their bodies. After tracing the way in which medical science has constructed menstruation, childbirth and menopause, she utilizes interviews to talk about how race and class mediate acceptance of the medical model.

Michaelson, Karen L., and contributors
  1988   Childbirth in America: Anthropological Perspectives. South Hadley, MA: Bergin & Garvey.

This edited volume provides a series of chapters on different aspects of the birth experience in the United States, from pregnancy through early postpartum. The introduction gives an overview of issues such as variation in the birth experience, appropriate technology, differential access, support systems, alternative birth contexts and the role of policy, and will be useful to the instructor in preparing the curricular example.

16

Women, Technology, and Development Ideologies: Frameworks and Findings

Kay B. Warren
Princeton University

Susan C. Bourque
Smith College

As anthropologists many of us want to address real world situations, such as international patterns of underdevelopment and poverty. At the same time we find it necessary to critique ethnocentrism in unilinear narratives of change that advocate and link "development," "Westernization," and "progress." The goal of this essay is to put a new generation of development critiques and ideologies in tension with anthropological studies of culture and change. This module is designed to encourage faculty (1) to integrate gender as a category of analysis in the study of social and technological change, (2) to examine the ways in which formulations of change as "development" and "technology transfer" both color our understanding of the Third World and reveal Western cultural preoccupations, and (3) to gain critical familiarity with a new generation of anthropological studies of gender, culture, and political economy, particularly as they have examined the multinational employment of Third World populations.

The explosive growth of research on gender during the United Nations Decade for Women (1975–85) resulted in new empirical work and a range of conflicting perspectives formulated by researchers studying "the integration of women into development." Anthropologists and feminist scholars sought to internationalize the study of work, family, and policy. In this essay, we evaluate the conceptual contributions that this recent research has made to formulating and answering questions about the impact of technology on women and women's responses to changing technologies. This task, though abstract at times, is important because the theoretical models that inform current research influence the direction and scope of future studies and strategies for change. As one would expect from an anthropological approach, the issue of "technology" quickly dissolves into wider discussions of the changing cultural and political situations that determine the significance of particular technologies.[1] That the international development community and other social scientists are able to identify technological concerns as primarily technical and to "factor out" or "bracket" cultural context, political economy, and history is something we need to treat in our writing and teaching.

Researchers and critics identify ironies in the need to "integrate women into development." In reality, women have always been "integrated into development" in the sense of being caught in the currents of change, forging their own understandings of change, and responding as people with multiple identities, affiliations, and concerns. A second irony involves the use of the word "development" to capture the directionality of change in the Third World. This metaphor for change commonly evokes a range of problematic associations, from evolutionary (i.e., the transformation of "primitive" to "developed") psychobiological (i.e., the individual's transformation from "infancy" to "adulthood"), and Western-focused definitions of "progress" (i.e., the movement from "traditional" to "modern") to the uncritical tendency to blame the victims of political and economic marginalization for their poverty.

For some social scientists, "development" simply refers to the actual patterns of change that nations have experienced with industrialization, mechanization, and the expansion of capitalist markets in the 19th and 20th centuries. For others, the concept involves state intervention and planning to achieve a higher GDP ("Gross Domestic Product") or other macro-level changes measurable with aggregate statistics that reflect changes in standards of living. For many scholars, the issue is both standards of living and grassroot participation in agendas for change. In this case, development is not fully measured by conventional statistical indicators, but rather by structural changes to promote equity, to widen women's and other "minorities' " economic and political participation, to recognize women as agents rather than targets of change, and to empower local groups to engage in development focusing on their own perceived needs. A concern with equity versus growth issues lies at the center of a new generation of NGO ("non-governmental organization") development activists who are promoting decentralized development projects. As our analysis of alternative perspectives on women and technological change shows, however, "decentralization" means very different things in different models of change.

In this overview, we first examine four major approaches to the study of gender and technology: the integrationist, appropriate technology, feminization of technology, and global economy perspectives. Along the way we deal briefly with studies of education and employment to consider the recent policy recommendation that higher levels of education will resolve the problem of women's limited access to technology. The overview concludes with a discussion of current anthropological literature on women in multinational "high-technology" production with special reference to Asia and Latin America. Then we turn to a discussion of alternative interpretations of women's experience in multinationals in Hong Kong and Mexico.[2] Suggestions for teaching these materials follow the essay. We have also included a selected bibliography of recent literature on development, alternative approaches to studying gender and technology; anthropological studies of gender and change, multinational employment and local culture, and rural development.

Doubts about the impact of technology transfer on the Third World began in the 1960s with the reassessment of international development programs and their impact on women. Feminist critics[3] of such programs started with the observation that women were absent from the calculations of most development planners. As a result women's economic contributions were ignored or underestimated, and the negative effects of imposed change on women's lives were not considered (Boserup 1970; Chaney and Schmink 1976; Rogers 1980).

Critics argued that contemporary patterns were reflections of a long history in which Western technology, particularly agricultural technology for the production of commercial and export crops, was differentially available to men and women in rural communities. European colonial administrators, applying their own notions of appropriate gender roles, made men the preferred recipients of training by Western technicians, even in areas where women were the primary agriculturalists. As a result of the differential access of each sex to new technology—be it plows, commercial seed varieties, fertilizer, mechanized equipment, or transportation—women's powers in community affairs were eroded. Moreover, local cultural values reflecting male dominance in community politics, rather than female involvement in productive activities, were often transferred to the new tools and crops (Boserup 1970:53–54; Etienne and Leacock 1980). Of course this process did not occur in a vacuum: changing modes of production and the introduction of commercial plantations, which bought up land resources, often meant that men were caught up in cyclic migration in search of income-generating employment while women specialized in production of food crops for family consumption. As internationally oriented commercial agriculture displaced small-scale agriculturalists—creating new forms of class stratification and rural poverty in an increasingly monetized economy—it also created gendered cleavages in access to resources.

To the extent that *access* was defined as a major issue, the logical solution—from the point of view of women and development critics—was to equalize it. Poor women needed the ability to use tools and machines, as well as literacy and education.[4] The message was explicitly pro-technology: women had lost ground because of restricted access. The solution to inequities was to open the restricted channels of education and training.[5]

Early analyses of development of modernization often assumed that the process was progressive and unproblematic. Like wider access, national development might be difficult to achieve in the 20th century given the legacies of colonialism, but it was clearly the goal. Development, however, was to come under closer scrutiny. In the late 60s and early 70s, critics of development theory pointed out that industrialization and modernization policies were not producing the expected social and economic improvement in Third World countries. They argued that conditions in the Third World were deteriorating, due to the dependence of these economies on the capital, credits, technology, training, and markets of the developed nations. This troubled dependency led many scholars to the conclusion that the wide-ranging adoption of Western models and technologies might not be the solution to the problems of developing nations.

Women and development, as a field of inquiry, and technology transfer to developing societies, as a strategy for change, have been criticized for reflecting Western ethnocentrism. Many Third World scholars argue that the concept of "technological development" is an invention of the industrialized states, intended to serve their own economic interests as producers of capital-intensive technology. Similarity, they argue that Western feminism as a political movement and a scholarly tradition has paid too little attention to imperialism, colonialism, racism, and differences among women. Moreover, they contend that Western priorities are very different from those appropriate to the Third World (D'Onofrio-Flores 1982; Srinivasan 1982; Tadesse 1982). Specifically they find that Western development strategies have been insensitive to cross-cultural differences in the significance of the family and kinship groups, the value of children, the devastating inequities born of class differences, and the economic realities of impoverished dependent economies.

The 1980s have witnessed the growing recognition of women's economic contributions to urban and rural households in developing countries, concerns about the feminization of poverty and the high rates of female-headed households, and questions about the costs, in terms of productivity, of discrimination against women (Charlton 1984:63).

Alternative Perspectives on Technology

Distinctive lines of argument have been developed to conceptualize the impact of international development on women. Some approaches see technology as a potential liberator for women, who often without any mechanization are forced to spend hours every day in labor-intensive food processing on top of other heavy family and agrarian duties. Other approaches see technology as an integral part of national and international political economies with complex, differential consequences for women and men given culturally specific sexual divisions of labor. Our recent review of the literature suggests that these diverse approaches have coalesced into several distinctive viewpoints (Bourque and Warren 1987). Each approach elaborates a social critique and strategies to enhance women's position in the face of technological change. A spectrum of distinctive political positions is reflected in these perspectives, as our overview will show. Here we critically examine the following four approaches: (1) integrationist, (2) appropriate technology, (3) feminization of technology, and (4) global economy.

The Integrationist Strategy

The integrationist framework is a liberal, reformist analysis largely focused on the professional and technical classes. In arguing for the integration of women into formal decision-making positions in government, business, and the professions, it is the flip side of the grassroots-appropriate technology model. Its adherents are concerned about the limited number of women trained as scientists and engineers, and the absence of women from positions of scientific leadership. They share a belief in the possible benefits of technology and a desire to see women participate in its development. This perspective argues that the "integration" of women will result in the transformation of basic institutions because comprehensive female participation would challenge existing sexual divisions of labor and authority, as well as differential male-female earnings. While this view does not assume that wider female participation would result in a political feminization of technology and industry, it does hold that women would introduce distinctive values and concerns to the work world (Jahan 1985).

If one's faith does not reside in a socialist government to end the inequities of capitalism, or in a burst of technological invention following the replacement of men by women and men who advocate a feminization of technology, what are the possible avenues for change? Women's expanded participation in nontraditional jobs and professions resulting from higher levels of scientific education is one answer, and clearing away the obstacles to that education and subsequent employment an essential part of the solution (Anderson 1985; Hall 1979). The integrationist perspective seeks to account for women's low enrollment in fields directly related to technology, to identify obstacles to women's educational and employment achievements, and to devise programs to reverse gender asymmetries (Briscoe and Pfafflin 1979).

Researchers from this position have focused attention on the ideologies that surround the acquisition of technical competence and the structural arrangements that reinforce stereotypes marking scientific fields and expertise as male in the West and in the Third World. Not surprisingly, they see the key to change in the political culture of education and the workplace (Namboze 1985; A. Sen 1984). In order to change gender stereotypes and widen opportunities, they argue, we must understand the processes that reproduce existing patterns. This implies that we must (1) understand sexual hierarchy as a product of culturally created social ideologies and the material conditions of women's and men's lives and (2) appreciate that sexual divisions of learning and work are not immutable behavioral specializations to be justified as functional or as vestiges of early human evolution. Rather, the school and the workplace are cultural and political environments where rules and norms are perpetuated and legitimated by contemporary ideologies of exclusion, segregation, and avoidance. Fundamental to this perspective is an understanding of how institutions shape meaning and value, as well as how individuals can both internalize and challenge social norms (Bourque and Warren

1981a, 1981b; Keller 1983). With respect to technology, these analyses extend to the fields in which women have been poorly represented, exploring ways to increase women's enrollment in science and engineering, or developing methods to deal with math anxiety and stereotypes of women that place them in the category of nonscientist (Briscoe and Pfafflin 1979).

At its best this viewpoint does not make the mistake of assuming that individuals are autonomous decision makers who decide to participate or not in technological development. Nor does it reduce education to the status of a "variable" that mechanically accounts for higher rates of technology adoption. Rather, these analysts see education as a process of structural and ideological tracking. As a result, they have had to readdress the question of wider *access* as a solution to gender inequality and to take on institutional change as necessary for structures that have constrained choice and equity.

The challenge for the integrationist perspective is that the arenas that need to be transformed have been remarkably resistant to change. Substantial reform in education or the workplace requires the intervention of political forces that must be convinced of reason and reward for pursuing substantial reform (cf. Buvinić 1983). Moreover, transformation must take place at a variety of levels: in the highest reaches of the national political system and in the political relations within the household. Since many of the changes sought can be affected by executive or bureaucratic action, it is possible to imagine a political plan of action to influence ministers of education and labor, as opposed to the broad electorate. Yet for the types of change envisioned it is often individuals, mothers, fathers, teachers, coworkers, and employers who will be the primary instruments for affecting meaningful change. Effective policies must grapple with both levels.

Amartya Sen's (1984) insightful analysis of the intrahousehold power dimensions of gender relations makes an important contribution to this perspective. Sen's work emphasizes the perceptual elements in women's contributions to the household. He notes the generalized reluctance to face the powerful conflicts of interest that exist within households and, for the Indian case, identifies a pattern of "adapted perception" that involves "systematic failures to see intrafamily inequalities and perceiving extraordinary asymmetries as normal and legitimate." Sen notes that

> problems of conflict within the family tend to get hidden by adapted perceptions both of "mutuality" of interests (going well beyond the actual elements of congruence that do, of course, importantly exist) and of "legitimacy" of inequalities of treatment. As a result no policy analysis in this area can be complete without taking up the question of political education and understanding. . . . This is an area in which social illusions nestle closely to reality, and terrible inequities are cloaked firmly in perceived legitimacy. [1984]

In addition to family perceptual and political issues, there are difficulties at the national level for the reforms proposed by the integrationist perspective. On the one hand, this is a trickle-down strategy that bets on the educationally privileged in an environment where national debt burdens have severely limited social programs for the poor. On the other hand, while most leaders must publicly declare themselves in favor of greater educational opportunity, privately they may fear that expanded education will create political problems, especially when they are unable to meet the demand for jobs from those already educated (Jahan 1985). In this context it is not surprising that educational efforts for women in many parts of the Third World are increasingly focused on nonformal education by coalitions of poor and educated women who have opted for decentralized development strategies for themselves.

Appropriate Technology

The advocates of appropriate technology (AT) hope to attack Third World poverty and underdevelopment directly by increasing local production without reinforcing patterns of dependence on industrial nations. This viewpoint has roots in those sectors of the international, but basically Western, development community that philosophically favor decentralized, small-scale approaches to development. This is a direct offshoot of the "small is beautiful" philosophy of the 1960s and 1970s involving a critique of centralization and the capital-intensive economic strategies that had dominated development planners' solutions to poverty. In practice this approach advocates scientific rationality and technical efficiency as ways to increase productivity. The strategy is to move away from capital-intensive solutions toward less expensive intermediate technologies emphasizing local resources.

Most AT development projects see cultural variability as an impediment to the adoption of more efficient technology. The technological focus of this approach has meant that local communities in the Third World are not generally consulted when decisions are made as to which local problems need to be addressed. Rather, a combination of international technical experts and state development agents work to assess which technologies to develop locally. Communities are generally consulted in the dissemination stage of the development process. As is evident from the failures of this approach, its well-meaning paternalism, reflecting a common development ideology, has undermined many of its projects.

Appropriate technology is envisioned as increasing women's productivity and giving them more time for other obligations as such community development efforts. For example, in rural societies where women spend hours every day gathering fuel for their kitchen fires, development planners have worked on new designs for low-tech mud brick stoves that would significantly cut fuel consumption. In the very common cases where rodents, insects, or rot destroy more than a third of family harvests during the early months of storage, design projects concentrate on low-cost storage practices that would increase available food. Hand-operated grinding machines for corn, wheat and millet as well as rice hullers and palm-oil presses, are promoted to free women from hours of daily drudgery without displacing workers. Solar energy, wind power, and biogas are thought of as forms of energy that would cut dependence on expensive commercial fuels (Carr 1981, 1984; Tinker 1981).

While in conception, appropriate technology seems eminently reasonable, in practice it has brought new dilemmas. Foremost is the fear of increased unemployment with new technologies. For women the cost of innovation is often high, especially when they find themselves caught in a double bind. Limited resources and cash generally restrict women's use of technologies that might increase their productivity and give them access to credit, education, and land (Ahmed 1985). Women's economically marginal position makes it very difficult to experiment with their family's welfare. For new technologies to break through women's realistic skepticism, they must substantially increase women's productivity in order to pay for the new technology and compensate women for the time lost from other work to learn and experiment with new techniques (Tinker 1981:58).

Leading exponents of appropriate technology have come to criticize top-down decision making in the development of new technologies, noting that although they may appear to be obviously appropriate in the eyes of engineers and development workers, the people who expect to use the new techniques may not find them appropriate at all (Carr 1981:193). Certainly, African women who experimented with solar cookers found serious drawbacks in an allegedly fuel-saving technology when they had to cook during the heat of the day, move the stove continually to collect the sun's rays, and were unable to fit their family-sized pots on the delicate stoves (Carr 1981).

Even if full consultation with the "end users" takes place and designs are consistent with local needs and use patterns, the concept of "appropriate" technology to lighten women's work may have fundamental pitfalls. A sexual division of technology may be created in which women gain appropriate technology for domestic work while men become the focus of wider technology training that generates new employment opportunities (Leet 1981). The issue is of particular significance in societies in which women are expected to be the financers of the traditional domestic economy with their own earnings as well as in cases where social change has multiplied the number of women-headed households.

Critical advocates of appropriate technology call for women to be involved in high-tech policy planning in order to influence the use of technology, the agenda of research priorities, the choice of government subsidies, and the discussion of needs (Leet 1981). They conclude it is not the form of technology that determines which gender uses it, but rather who controls its development, dissemination, and products. Yet the practice of AT as a development strategy continues to be top-down.

The Feminization of Technology

The feminization of technology perspective is a social critique and strategy for social change with adherents in the United States, Europe, and India. This approach is often echoed in ecological, peace, and grassroots political movements. As technological innovation is now organized, according to this school of thought, distinctive "masculinist" values determine its development and application. The result is the continual reinforcement of values emphasizing hierarchy, competition, immediate measurable results, material accumulation, depersonalization, and economic and political expansionism. It is not that bearers of masculinist views are ignorant of other values; rather, they have been forced by the economic order to suppress their "needs for subjectivity, feelings, intimacy, and humanity" and "project them onto the private life and women" (Bergom-Larsson 1982:35).

The feminization of technology position holds that technology must be redirected to serve new values, including human growth (rather than economic profit), conservation, decentralization, self-reliance, self-sufficiency, and caring. This view postulates a distinctive women's culture and sees it as a critical tool for transforming the social order toward a more humanistic, egalitarian one, concerned with relationships and welfare rather than individual success and profit. The primary source of this utopian vision is women's involvement in the family, where (this perspective idealistically holds) hierarchy is deemphasized, nonviolent persuasion is stressed, and investment is directed toward the nurturance of future generations. Women learn a wider lesson from their familial vantage point: hierarchy, whatever its form, inevitably subordinates the weaker (Bergom-Larsson 1982; Boulding 1981).[6]

Unfortunately, according to these authors, women's values are currently imprisoned by the separation of spheres of home and work. Effective change requires an expansion of women's sphere and a new political procedure for evaluating technology, one that involves women in policy-making roles and includes questions about the impact of new technologies on women and women's culture. As female values successfully inform the public world, hierarchical distinctions between "productive paid" work and "nonproductive unpaid" work will be challenged; women and men will share a personal commitment to responding to the needs of the community; and unnecessary divisions of labor will be rejected (Bergom-Larsson 1982; Scott 1982).

This perspective argues that women should not necessarily pursue integration into Western-directed development efforts. If they do so they are likely to lose the decentralized, relatively egalitarian social order of traditional society that Western women ill-advisedly gave up long ago. For those with the option of experimenting outside Western patriarchies, the best strategy would be to strengthen women's networks and expand women's sphere as a source of new economic and political organizations (Boulding 1981). Western women must cope with a more pervasive patriarchy, the sharp division of public and private, and an economic system devoted to masculinist values.

It is most useful to regard the feminization of technology as a utopian political model, rather than an accurate analysis of international development problems or realities. Its roots and values are clearly Western and Freudian, and its elaboration of an ahistorical and universal set of characteristics for women's nature is naive and inaccurate. This perspective dangerously romanticizes women's values, the family, and the nature of Third World societies. One has only to look at the rich and various constructions of gender in contemporary societies to challenge these images of male and female (see the bibliography, especially the section on anthropological works on gender). Furthermore, by distancing men from the "natural" concerns of women, this perspective limits, by definition, those with whom women might ally themselves, those whose vested interests are to question current arrangements, articulate options, and promote change to more humanistic and egalitarian social orders.

The Global Economy

The global economy perspective questions "technology" in the narrow sense as the focus of "development," arguing that, in an interdependent world system, the primary issues are economic accumulation through exploitation and dominant power relations. This critique uses neo-Marxist language to define the importance of the historical forces that shape national economies and developing countries' capacities to compete in international markets. Of central concern is the way that capitalist economies have shaped an international division of labor in which developing countries are sources of cheap labor and raw materials for technologically sophisticated countries where capital is accumulated. From this perspective, one cannot consider technology without studying the issues of production and consumption in the contexts of global economics, transforming class relations in different regions and countries, and state policies. Feminist anthropologists have contributed a gendered dimension to these analyses by studying the impacts of economic change on class formation, sexual divisions of labor, and the reproduction of the labor force in the household (Stolcke 1981).

This perspective has been very influential in international women and development circles that have been critical of the West. For many, it provides a crucial linkage between critiques of capitalism, imperialism, and gender stratification (cf. Etienne and Leacock 1980; Nash and Fernández-Kelly 1983; Nash and Safa 1985; Leacock and Safa 1986; Reiter 1975; Young et al. 1981). As Benería and Sen conclude:

> The problem for women is not only the lack of participation in this process [of development] with men; it is a system [of international capital accumulation] that generates and intensifies inequalities, making use of existing gender hierarchies to place women in subordinate positions at each different level of interaction between class and gender. This is not to deny the possibility that capitalist development might break down certain social rigidities oppressive to women. But these liberating tendencies are accompanied by new forms of subordination. [1986:150]

Stolcke, representing another current of neo-Marxist thought, stresses the function of women's forced subordination in the household in perpetuating wider inequalities:

> [T]he perpetuation of class relations and domination—mediated directly by the institutions of marriage, the family and inheritance . . . determines both women's primary assignment to domestic labour and the undervaluation of this function. In class society, in other words,

the sexual division of labour—women's domestication—is ultimately the product of man's control over women's reproductive capacity in the interests of perpetuating unequal access to the means of production. [1981:34]

Both socialists who seek redistributive alternatives to free market economies and nationalists who reject Western influence in their politics and economics find these perspectives useful. While liberal researchers do not share the utopian socialist vision, it is clear that materialist analyses have influenced their thinking about the importance of an international perspective that sees various forms of inequality as interactive and central to explanations for current patterns of development.

The insights from the global economy perspective also allow us to focus on a neglected element in many feminist analyses of technology: the interplay of national governments and international markets in shaping national planning, policy development, and the allocation of resources (Afshar 1987). Of particular concern is the state's creation of labor force policy in areas such as employment, migration, education, housing, agriculture, and industrial development. How does the state formulate priorities for its own development? For the agrarian sector, how does it balance the need to produce food crops for domestic consumption with the need to encourage the production of commodities for export? What alternatives does it see for increasing domestic production, for dealing with shifts in subsistence agriculture and wage labor, and for reducing dependency on the international market for basic food supplies?

From our point of view, the global economy perspective gives the issue of decentralized, small-scale work a much more complex shape than does the feminization of technology analysis. The latter analysts place a positive value on decentralization and tend to see it as an absolute contrast to hierarchical, centralized systems. The global economy perspective helps us see that decentralization is not inherently positive or negative, nor is it always an exclusive alternative to centralized modes of production. As in the case of multinational assembly plants, contemporary industrialization can foster decentralized modes, such as subcontracting to domestic outworkers, to produce at a lower cost (Benería and Roldan 1987). The issue is how these work patterns influence the household, whether women will be able to gain greater control of work processes in the smaller units, and whether companies will exploit a fragmented labor force by raising production quotas for constant wages.

The global economy perspective questions the common tendency to treat women as individuals without other competing identities, and to see women as a category with uniform interests and concerns. To overcome the conceptual simplification of other feminist frameworks, this view argues that, rather than studying individual women, we should instead examine household units by their class position in mixed subsistence, cash crop, and urban economies. Women's domestic responsibilities vary by class and involve intricate balances of monetized and nonmonetized activities, rapidly responding to changing market conditions (Ahmed 1985; Agarwal 1985; Bourque and Warren 1981a, 1981b; Bryceson 1985). However socially valued or devalued, women's privatized household roles are critical for the physical and social reproduction of the labor force. The central analytic project is to study women's reproductive and productive roles as they are mediated by their class positions in the wider economy (cf. Lamphere 1987). Thus, another important contribution of this perspective is to help restore concrete social contexts to women's work and perceptions.

It must be noted, however, that there are potential political drawbacks when policymakers focus their concerns about women on the household and the family. Men are seldom viewed as members of households unless it is to see them as "heads" or as "breadwinners." The focus on women's domestic and reproductive roles has tended to limit concerns to those roles. Of course, the family and household are central elements in both men's and women's lives, and reproduction and child care responsibilities affect women's labor force and political participation. However, the history of policy and development programs in this area has shown that if concern is directed at reproduction and domestic roles, those issues are likely to set limits to national policy directed to women (cf. Benería and Sen 1982, Buvinić 1983 and 1984, Evans 1985, Jaquette and Staudt 1985). As a result, women become the targets of population programs and welfare projects or they are integrated into the lowest levels of production as part-time workers. Little thought is given to providing women access to the full range of skills that would allow them to control and direct development activities (see Buvinić 1984 and Sen 1985). As long as women are primarily conceived of as members of households, there may be a tendency to leave unquestioned their absence from society's significant political, social, and economic institutions.

Multinationals: A Technological Case Study

In assessing the impact of international patterns of technological change on women's roles, a number of issues must be considered. First has been the impact of technology on agricultural production. When subsistence farming gave way to mechanized commercial agriculture for national and international markets, women's earlier work in agriculture was transformed in a variety of ways. As wage labor and migration have come to dominate rural economies, some women have specialized in the production of subsistence crops, while others have been pushed into the growing urban labor force in search of cash-generating employment (see the Bibliography, especially the section on gender and rural development). Because many women in developing countries still live in rural settlements and are engaged in agricultural work, food processing, and local commerce, this will remain an essential focus for research. In this essay, however, we have chosen to examine an urban issue: women's employment in multinational factories. Multinational employment reveals the paradoxical effects of new options in the labor force, increased education, family expectations, and young women's agency in patriarchal families. The past decade has produced a number of outstanding studies of multinational employment that are ethnographically rich while making important comparative contributions and carrying on central debates.

In the last fifteen years there has been a proliferation of industrial production in the Third World as multinational companies have searched for cheap labor to assemble high-technology products, manufacture clothing, and grow and process food. Recent relocations of manufacturing to Third World countries has been spurred by Japanese successes in capturing Western markets for consumer goods and the transformation of national firms into multinationals in Hong Kong, South Korea, and Singapore. Faced with new competition, European and U.S. companies have looked to the Third World to cut their labor costs and retain international competitiveness. In the case of the United States, this process was encouraged by new tariff regulations in the 1960s and 1970s, which allowed goods that were sent to other countries for further processing to be reimported with duty to be paid only on the value added as a result of labor (Lim 1983:71–72; Nash 1983:10).

These developments build on a long history of transnational involvement in the developing world—with a new twist, for women are now being recruited in large numbers for bench-assembly production work. "Heavy" multinational industries such as mining, petrochemicals, iron and steel, and shipbuilding continue to employ many more men than women,[7] while "light" industries like clothing manufacture, food processing, pharmaceuticals, and electronics assembly tend to have mixed labor forces where women may predominate on the assembly line. In 1980, over four million people in developing countries worked in multinational enterprises: 63% in Latin America, 31% in Asia, and 6% in Africa. Of this total it is estimated that over one million women were directly employed and an additional half million worked in national firms doing subcontracting work for multinationals (Lim 1985:7–9, 28).

For their part, national governments have often competed to attract multinational investment to deal with high unemployment and lack of capital. Multinational companies involved in microelectronic assembly, clothing manufacture, and food processing have built production plants dispersed at great distances from their corporate headquarters in the United States, Europe, or Japan (cf. Arizpe and Aranda 1981; Chapkis and Enloe 1983). New products are developed in the industrial countries and sent along with the appropriate production machinery to factories in the developing world. Local labor, which is labeled semiskilled or unskilled, is recruited for production, and the plants' output is sold in external markets, such as the United States and Europe. Manual assembly is preferred in rapidly changing industries because it successfully competes at this point with the higher cost of continually retooling automated systems to keep pace with technological, stylistic, and market-driven changes.

Two contrasting views of the impact of multinationals on women are found in the literature. One view argues that multinationals offer women important new employment opportunities in the face of rural-urban migration, urban underemployment, and cultural systems that reinforce male domination. The other view argues that multinationals lock women into new patterns of inequality, destabilize existing family forms, and socialize young women into Westernized competitive consumerism at the cost of other cultural values.

Authors such as Lim (1981, 1983, 1985) and Salaff (1981) argue that the new industrial employment is providing young women with important options and financial resources that may coexist with traditional family forms and values. While multinationals pay low wages by industrial countries' standards, Lim points out that multinational wages are generally higher and working conditions better and safer than national companies, which tend to be smaller in size and, thus, subject to greater economic pressures. The contrast is starker for women who face the exploitative and marginally paying alternatives of work as farm laborers, domestic servants, and market vendors, all typical alternatives to assembly work. The reasons for the disparity between multinationals and national firms is not due to better intentions on one side than the other, but rather to the multinationals' larger size, greater productivity, and profitability. Furthermore, multinationals tend to conform to national standards in their sexual divisions of labor (Lim 1985:24–25, 60–61).

Lim argues that without multinationals women would have fewer employment opportunities, would be forced to work for more exploitative national enterprises, and have less say in the face of traditional patriarchy:

> [a]lthough the multinational does take advantage of national and sexual wage differentials and sometimes reinforces them, it is not responsible for creating them and cannot by its own actions eliminate them. National wage differentials are the result of differences in the development of capitalist relations of production between nations, whereas sex wage differentials originate in indigenous patriarchy. [1983:85]

Many of the problems women face result from cultural expectations that they are temporary workers who will later turn their attention and time to marriage and children. As a result, national economies pay women less than men, and more young unmarried women are available for work. Young unmarried women tend to have other advantages: they can work various shifts, are more highly educated, are mobile, and at least in theory will not use pregnancy benefits. For Lim, cultural expectations about women's marriage and job commitments as well as family investment patterns that favor sons over daughters for education explain most of the earning and promotion differentials between women and men. Additionally, women's chance for promotion from the floor is unusual because of the structure of the work place. (But Lim observes that this would be true for plants in the West as well as in the Third World.) She concludes that these factors are more important than employers' gender biases in explaining female/male earning differentials in any particular country (Lim 1985:59).

Lim questions the finding that multinationals are footloose and use the threat of relocation to avoid unionization. She finds that in countries like Indonesia, the Philippines, and Thailand, where multinationals have been in place for long periods of time, their rates of unionization are higher than those of domestic industries. In these cases women may benefit by being brought together in large groups for the first time and having the opportunity to organize politically. For their part, multinationals may not fight unionization if it gives them a structure through which to negotiate efficiently with workers. Factories are more interested in political stability than they are fearful of unions; their departures are more commonly caused by business reverses, takeovers, and reorganizations. Lim argues that multinational factories have a life cycle; thus, countries with longer histories of multinational operations are more likely to have assembly plants with unions, higher wages, greater job security and worker longevity, and higher investment in capital-intensive production. They are also likely to have exported unskilled production work to countries like Bangladesh or Sri Lanka, which have still lower wages. The tendency is for multinationals to upgrade their work environments over time, especially if national governments urge these developments and the labor market is tight. The spinoffs from mature multinational operations may support the growth of national industries and an entrepreneurial middle class (Lim 1983:75–76, 83; 1985:64–68).

Salaff's in-depth study of Hong Kong reinforces many of Lim's findings, while adding an important cultural dimension to the analysis of women's industrial work (1981). Since 1949 Hong Kong has been a center of textile and assembly work promoted by local Chinese capitalists who tapped a growing international market. Their political and economic situation is unique; Hong Kong is a British colony facing an uncertain future when it becomes part of China after the British mandate expires in 1997. State policy is explicitly controlled by a profit-driven multinational commercial sector. Lacking sufficient land for large-scale agriculture while experiencing waves of migration from the mainland, the colony has both the economic policies and the labor force for multinational industrial production. The state offers very few social services beyond subsidized housing and education; there are few welfare provisions, no unemployment insurance or social security. Individuals must depend on their families for subsistence and welfare. Basic household expenses are so high in Hong Kong that multiple wage earners are necessary in every family.

Young women have played an important role in the success of multinationals in Hong Kong, and by the early 1970s they had become more than one-half the factory labor force. Typically young women from poorer families began working at the age of 12–14, though the entry age was increased to 16 in the early 1980s. Until marriage, they enjoy a three-sphered life: commitment to their natal families, industrial work, and a peer culture of friends. Their earnings are most often used to pay for a higher standard of living and for the education of sons in the family, something that Salaff argues the young women do not resent because these contributions represent a valued contribution to collective family welfare.

This situation is compatible with the Chinese value placed on the family as a joint endeavor for social survival and continuity. Chinese culture stresses a religious commitment to a male-centered conception of family ancestors. Sons are particularly valued; daughters less so since marriage will inevitably take them to their husband's family. In the past, family inheritance was equally divided among the sons; now working families invest in the future by educating their sons for higher-paying skilled jobs. In this social worldview, members of the family subordinate personal goals to their family's needs. Daughters do this by remitting three-quarters of their wages to their parents "to repay the cost of their upbringing." In return, daughters gain the right to more personal freedom: reduced demands for household work, leisure time spent free from parental control with girlfriends from work, an allowance for their own purchases, the right to choose their own husbands, and higher levels of education than in past generations. As Salaff points out, the frame of reference for these women workers is their mothers and grandmothers, rather than their brothers. As a result, while they would like more education for themselves, they do not resent the family's greater investment in sons. Women see themselves as gaining social freedom while maintaining strong family ties.

A second line of analysis is much more critical of multinationals and the opportunities they have offered women for new forms of work. This view, articulated by researchers like June Nash and Pat Fernández-Kelly (1983), emphasizes the failure of industrial work in the Third World to provide women with new options or long-term employment possibilities. Multinationals have not introduced changes that make a real difference because the recruitment of women into high-tech assembly work has not challenged the idea of a sexually segregated work force or the tacit understanding that women can be paid lower wages than men. Their analyses describe a situation in which multinationals are taking advantage and reinforcing gender, ethnic, and class inequities in industrialized and developing societies. In this respect their analysis overlaps with that of Lim and Salaff. As Nash concludes:

> [S]ectors of the labor force based on gender, ethnicity, age, and education within both industrial core and peripheral nations are differentially rewarded, and these differences, along with wage differences between nations, determine the long-run movement of capital. [Nash and Fernández-Kelly 1983:3]

Where the two schools of thought differ is that Nash and Fernández-Kelly argue that the labor practices of multinationals are challenging rather than complementing cultural practices in ways that leave women particularly disadvantaged and with less social support than they had in traditional society.

Studies of high-tech assembly plants in Mexico, Hong Kong, Taiwan, Indonesia, Malaysia, Thailand, the Philippines, Brazil, and the Caribbean illustrate the widely accepted policies of recruiting young single women, maintaining paternalistic modes of plant organization, encouraging turnover after several years of employment, and providing virtually no opportunities for advancement or job security if the market sags (Fernández-Kelly 1983, 1983b; Fuentes and Ehrenreich 1983; Lim 1981; Nash and Fernández-Kelly 1983). Employers reinforce the idea that assembly work draws on presumed womanly skills (such as manual dexterity, attentiveness, the capacity to do repetitive work, docility) and, thus, is an extension of women's conventional roles. Srinivasan notes the high cost to women of this sex role stereotyping:

> [T]he reasons for employing [women] in modern high technology companies are the same reasons for which they are *excluded* from training, technical responsibilities, and high-paying jobs. [1982:139; emphasis ours]

By defining high-tech assembly as young women's work, plants are able to maintain low wages, favorably competing with U.S. labor despite the cost of transporting goods internationally for assembly.

Within the plants, these authors argue that employers further reinforce, manipulate, and distort cultural values by bringing their own culture to bear on workers to foster control. For instance, in Japanese-managed firms there is a tendency to stress family commitments and self-discipline, while in U.S.-managed firms Western aspirations are encouraged through factory beauty contests, cooking classes, and makeup instruction, which emphasize the importance of cash incomes for competitive, consumer success and modern marriage (Elson and Pearson 1981; Grossman 1978/79; Ong 1987).

Pat Fernández-Kelly's ethnography of Mexican border industries in Ciudad Juárez (1983a, 1983b, 1983c) argues for this critical analysis. Like Hong Kong, Mexico has witnessed a growth in women's employment in multinational assembly plants. In contrast, however, Mexico's severe unemployment problems, growing population, stagnation of its agrarian base, dependence on an uncertain international petroleum market, and different cultural system mean that new work has very different implications for women, men, and their families.

Industrialization along the Mexican border has been shaped by the overshadowing presence of the U.S. economy. Assembly plants (called *maquiladoras*) are the result of the Border Industrialization Program (BIP), which was jointly developed by Mexico and the U.S. in 1965.[8] The Program was designed in part to generate local employment to counterbalance the effects of the U.S. termination of the Bracero Program, which left over 200,000 migratory agricultural workers, many of whom settled along the border, out of work. The BIP employed classical strategies learned from the Asian experience to foster multinational investment: Mexico had a rapidly growing labor force, unemployment and underemployment of about 20% in key border cities, high birth rates and internal migration to the region, and a populace willing to work for one-sixth of U.S. wages. Firms were allowed to import machinery, equipment, and raw materials free of duty into Mexico, providing all production was exported. Multinational subsidiaries were permitted to be totally foreign-owned in contrast to the limitation of 49% foreign ownership for domestic firms. For its part, the U.S. tariff policy taxed only the value added for reimported goods, including clothing and electronics. A final selling point was that U.S. managers would be able to commute to these plants from their homes across the border.

The growth in assembly plants has been impressive: in 1965 there were 12 assembly plants employing 3,087 workers; by 1979 there were 531 plants employing 156,000 persons; by 1987 there were 1,259 plants employing 322,743 persons. Between 75% and 90% of the workers in these plants are women. These factories have been the third largest foreign exchange contributor to Mexico, just behind tourism and petroleum. One-third of the multinationals' expenditures went for workers' salaries; the rest entered the Mexican economy through rents, taxes, material, and miscellaneous costs (Fernández-Kelly 1983:21, 34–35). With the devaluation of the peso and the decline in the world price of petroleum, Mexico's economy has experienced serious reverses, with increasing unemployment and great pressure on workers to seek employment in the United States (see Ruiz and Tiano 1987). While the Mexican government sees multinational assembly plants as a fundamental development strategy, it is clear that these factories will not seriously challenge their national unemployment and underemployment statistics.

Because the factories recruit many more women than men, Fernández-Kelly concludes that they have helped foster contradictory pressures on women and men in a situation where 80% of the border unemployment and underemployment is male. The companies prefer women because of women's putative greater docility, manual dexterity, and the fact that they are viewed as temporary workers who will accept the lowest possible wages. This is important, because these labor-intensive industries are intensely competitive, quick to lay off workers if demand for their products weakens, and subject to collapse during U.S. recessions. One half of the assembly plants in Ciudad Juárez closed during the 1974–75 recession in the United States. Fernández-Kelly argues, from a masculine point of view, that these factories have not reduced unemployment rates, but rather have introduced formerly "unemployable" women into the labor force. What is clear from her evidence is that women see assembly work as a step up from work as maids across the border, and they especially value the access to state medical care that they receive as a job benefit. Other women, who have worked as local secretaries, receptionists, and clerks, move to multinational jobs because the pay is higher than office positions. On the other hand, high male unemployment forces men across the border, dividing families, resulting in abandonments, and creating pressures for wives to join husbands. The fact that much of this migration has been historically illegal in the United States clearly subjects the participants to great anxieties.

Most female assembly line workers are between 17 and 25. Electronics plants recruit younger single, childless women with an average of eight years of education. Companies test women for pregnancy when they are recruited, because they do not want to pay for the eighty-two day leave women are legally entitled to with the birth of a new child. Electronics workers most often live with one or both of their parents; their income is pooled with fathers, who are often marginally employed at very low-paying positions in fields like construction. Generally they give about half their wages to the family, where the money is used for domestic expenses or higher education for a younger brother. Mothers in these households are less often members of the paid labor force, concentrating instead on domestic duties. On the other hand, older women, women with children, and less educated women, who must enter the work force, find work in apparel factories where wages are lower and working conditions less desirable. One third of the women working in clothing assembly are single mothers who have been forced into the labor market to support their families after the death or desertion of their husbands.

Women's job tenure averages three years, as they experience pressures to leave positions from companies trying to avoid payments required under the Mexican labor law for vacations, yearly bonuses, and indemnity in the event of layoffs. Factories also note a drop in women's productivity over time as they become bored of highly monotonous work. For their part, women leave positions to marry, to take care of their children, to rest and change jobs, to regain their health, and to avoid tensions with factory personnel. Women do not see themselves as permanent workers, and describe pressures from men to leave paid work to take on full-time domestic duties. Later economic need may force them back into the labor force and into less desirable positions or illegal migration.

As a result of multinational employment, older women see a shift in the value of educating daughters, noting that in their generation fathers dismissed female education as a waste of time for women who would devote their lives to their children and domestic work. Now mothers seek to persuade fathers to educate daughters to meet the mininum educational requirements for electronic assembly employment. Yet they worry that fathers will take advantage of daughters, reducing their own financial contribution to the family.

Fernández-Kelly feels very strongly that the multinational industrialization has not solved existing problems, particularly male unemployment after the end of the Bracero Program, nor has it created new options for women. Rather, the border industries have reinforced the magnetic attraction of the Mexican-U.S. border, resulting in continuing migration from other regions of the country and growing unemployment. Women are caught in complex countercurrents: they are actively recruited for work, yet thought of as supplementary and temporary by companies and themselves; they are major wage earners in families fighting for subsistence, yet pressured to retire from the labor force by husbands who seek submissive wives; they are often abandoned by men discouraged by poverty and unemployment on the Mexican side of the border. Young women have been recruited as a vulnerable and docile labor force, stereotyped as supplementary and temporary workers at plants and as submissive wives and mothers at home by patriarchal traditions. While neither stereotype is accurate, they are used by institutions and individuals to constrain women's lives in important ways.

Comparing two societies as different as Hong Kong and Mexico is a very tricky matter; their histories, cultures, state politics, international contexts, and development problems could not be more different. Yet, both societies have been touched in important ways by the new wave of multinational expansion, which has recruited young women as a first generation of female industrial workers in their families. Lim would account for the differences between the countries' multinational experiences in part by noting that multinationals have a more mature profile in Hong Kong, where women workers find the experience a more positive one economically and personally, families have adapted old cultural patterns to new modes of economic participation, and wages are higher and working conditions better. Fernández-Kelly would respond with an argument that the issues are structural, and that the basic asymmetry of the U.S. and Mexican economies has been intensified through the Border Industrialization Program. As a result, cultural patterns have been distorted, populations relocated, development priorities skewed, and families put under unbearable pressures that have intensified male-female tensions. Both would agree that the chronically high rates of unemployment in Mexico and the full employment in Hong Kong create different options for individuals, families, and multinationals expanding production in these countries.

In Hong Kong the strong cultural consensus about family economic strategies focuses the extra earnings of daughters to finance the education and upward mobility of sons. This appears to be a successful reconciliation of traditional Chinese values and the new industrial sexual divisions of labor. It allows poor families to amass funds and bet on one or two individuals, who with better schooling and high test scores might gain entrance into the university and professional work. From an analyst's point of view, of course, these cultural values direct the choice of the individual by gender, not by scholarly potential. That these decisions have not provoked tensions between daughters and sons is attributed to the fact that the daughters' frame of reference is still their mothers. Significantly, it is not clear that this family strategy for mobility actually bears fruit for the working class, given an educational system that tracks upper middle-class children rather than working-class children toward the very few available university positions.

Along the Mexican border there are crosscurrents and multiple family strategies that reflect the mixture of cues families receive from the economy. On the one hand, traditional values call for a greater educational investment in sons. Some families report saving daughters' assembly earnings to do this, although it is unclear how this might translate into upward mobility, since most men focus on crossing the border for higher earnings as manual laborers in the United States. On the other hand, the economy is demanding that daughters receive higher educational investments than formerly in order to qualify for what is considered high-status, well-paying work. This situation appears to translate into some intergenerational tensions, but, more important into increased tension between young spouses when husbands put traditional patriarchical pressures on wives to leave work, to join them in the United States in very uncertain circumstances, or to face abandonment. What is not clear is if these tensions are greater than they might be in areas of Mexico where multinationals have not dominated local economies, but internal migration for work is common.

Frames of reference influence women's consciousness in Hong Kong and Mexico; they are also an issue for the analyst. What is clear from our comparison of Lim and Salaff with Nash and Fernández-Kelly is that these analysts are operating with distinctive economic models. Both lines of analysis acknowledge structural inequalities, seeing individual actions as shaped by wider economics and politics. Each finds areas of creative choice and challenge. They find gender dimensions in international economics and in the traditional patriarchies of developing societies. What distinguishes them is one side's view that national labor markets operate with a certain level of independence and that integration into the world order will benefit women and workers, even as it brings new problems and inequities. The other side of this debate finds that capitalism has a long history of determining local and international markets and economic opportunities. This point of view seriously questions the benefits of increased economic involvement on developing societies that have different needs and dilemmas than industrialized countries. This contrast parallels the tendency of analysts who focus their work on the domestic domain to stress traditional patriarchy as shaping women's subordination, while those who examine the public domain more commonly emphasize capitalist economics as the primary shaper of gender inequality (cf. Leacock and Safa 1986:x).

Conclusions

Recent scholarship has helped us understand that many of the institutions and forces that are thought of as autonomous and neutral—like technology—are neither. Clearly a comprehensive consideration of "technology" must include a consideration of the changing social relations involved in its production, distribution, and use. As has become clear in this overview, gender—that is, the cultural construction of "female" and "male" through the family, the workplace, the state, and international business—is a very important dimension of the study of technological change. These gendered social realities are, in turn, shaped by larger economic and historical forces, often bearing cultural values and social functions that appear to be distinct from particular technological intents. In the "development" field, for instance, we have found that "technology transfers" embody cultural and political values that often reinforce international and local inequities.

Our review of four approaches to the study of women, technology, and development demonstrates that adding gender as a category of analysis to current social science involves more than just recovering women's experience. Rather, gender differences call for the explanation of male/female inequalities, much as the study of cultural constructions of racial differences calls for the explanation of racial inequalities. Consequently it should not be surprising that alternative approaches to the study of gender, technology, and development involve social critiques and oppositional discourses. The approaches are all the more important to understand because they inform the actions of groups involved in development projects and policy-making, both in the West and in the Third World.

One goal of this essay has been to put a new generation of development ideologies and critiques in tension with anthropological studies of culture and change. As anthropologists we study development ideologies as cultural constructions with political implications. This, of course, is not the full story of cultural transformation. In addition we seek to document and understand local cultural diversities and patterns of change, which are so often overlooked or ignored by development ideologies. Here our goal is to understand social change in a more subtle, comprehensive sense, one that does not use economic indicators or Western experiences as the yardstick with which to measure national transformations and one that self-reflexively questions the language of analysis.

Notes

Acknowledgments. Our thanks to Sandra Morgen, Ralph Faulkingham, and the anonymous reviewers for their critical readings of the drafts of this module.

1. For anthropologists this means a concern with the related processes of the concentration of land resources and growing landlessness in rural areas, state intervention in rural affairs, population growth, rural-urban migration, the importance of marginal service sector employment for underemployed urban populations, and national policies that define development priorities in economic planning, agrarian reform, education, labor, housing, social services, and political participation. Women play significant roles in these processes and are disproportionately affected by many of them, as is clear by differential rates of female/male subsistence crop cultivation, access to cash incomes, involvement in agrarian reforms, migration to urban centers, literacy, marginal service sector employment, and responsibility for the economic support of urban families. For historically and culturally sensitive treatments of these issues, see Benería (1982), Bourque and Warren (1981), Deere and León (1987); Nash and Fernández-Kelly (1983), Nash and Safa (1986), Ong (1987), Stoler (1985).

2. In an essay of this scope we are very aware of the limits of our cultural comparisons. No doubt there is a Latin American twist to our discussions because of the research backgrounds of both authors. We refer readers to the regional essays in this book for discussions of colonial history, rural patterns of change, and a fuller cultural presentation.

3. Our notion of feminist research includes scholarship by women and men who have taken gender as a central category of analysis and who are interested in understanding the diversities of experience both within and between genders. Internationally this research tends to examine not just the cultural construction of ''female'' and ''male,'' but rather the interplay of gender, class, ethnic, religious, and national stratifications and identities.

4. Of course this is only one stream of the history of development strategies. Another important focus of international concern has been population control, which has defined women's fertility as a major cause of Third World poverty. Here women have often been conceptualized as ''targets'' of new technologies.

5. Boserup's pioneering work has sparked insightful critiques by Benería and Sen (1986).

6. Much of this discussion is reminiscent of psychoanalytic claims that women engage in a gender-distinctive form of maternal thinking (cf. Chodorow 1978 and Gilligan 1982).

7. Accounts like Barrios de Chungara's make it clear, however, what a vital, though unpaid role women play in reproducing and sustaining this labor force (1978).

8. Fernández-Kelly notes that this development was part of a longer historical trend of Mexican industrialization through free-trade privileges begun in the 1930s in response to the Depression and the end of prohibition, which hurt Mexican liquor production along the border (1983:25).

References Cited

Afshar, Haleh, ed.
  1987 Women, State, and Ideology: Studies from Africa and Asia. Albany: State University of New York Press.
Agarwal, Bina
  1985 Women and Technological Change in Agriculture: The Asian and African Experience. *In* Technology and Rural Women: Conceptual and Empirical. Aftikhar Ahmed, ed. Pp. 67–114. London: George Allen and Unwin.
Ahmed, Iftikhar, ed.
  1985 Technology and Rural Women: Conceptual and Empirical Issues. London: George Allen and Unwin.
Anderson, Mary B.
  1985 Technology Transfer: Implications for Women. *In* Gender Roles in Development Projects. Catherine Overholt et al., eds. Pp. 57–78. West Hartford: Kumarian Press.

Arizpe, Lourdes, and Josefina Aranda
    1981   The "Comparative Advantages" of Women's Disadvantages: Women Workers in the Strawberry Export Agribusiness in Mexico. Signs 7:453–473.
Benería, Lourdes, and Martha Roldan
    1987   The Crossroads of Class and Gender: Industrial Homework, Subcontracting, and Household Dynamics in Mexico City. Chicago: University of Chicago Press.
Benería, Lourdes, and Gita Sen
    1982   Class and Gender Inequalities and Women's Role in Economic Development—Theoretical and Practical Implications. Feminist Studies 8:157–176.
    1986   Accumulation, Reproduction, and Women's Role in Economic Development: Boserup Revisited. *In* Women's Work: Development and the Division of Labor by Gender. Eleanor Leacock and Helen I. Safa, eds. Pp. 141–157. South Hadley, Mass.: Bergin and Garvey.
Bergom-Larsson, Maria
    1982   Women and Technology in the Industrialized Countries. *In* Scientific-Technological Change and the Role of Women in Development. Pamela M. D'Onofrio-Flores and Sheila M. Pfafflin, eds. Pp. 29–75. Boulder: Westview Press.
Boserup, Ester
    1970   Woman's Role in Economic Development. New York: St. Martin's Press.
Boulding, Elise
    191   Integration into What? Reflections on Development Planning for Women. *In* Women and Technological Change in Developing Countries. AAAS Selected Symposium 53. Roslyn Dauber and Melinda L. Cain, eds. Pp. 9–30. Boulder: Westview Press.
Bourque, Susan C., and Kay B. Warren
    1981a   Women of the Andes: Patriarchy and Social Change in Rural Peru. Ann Arbor: University of Michigan Press.
    1981b   Rural Women and Development Planning in Peru. *In* Women and World Change: Equity Issues in Development. Naomi Black and Ann Cottrell, eds. Pp. 183–197. Beverly Hills: Sage.
    1987   Gender, Technology and Development. Daedalus 116:173–197.
Briscoe, Anne, and Sheilla Pfafflin, eds.
    1979   Expanding the Role of Women in the Sciences. Annals of the New York Academy of Sciences, Volume 323.
Bryceson, Deborah A.
    1985   Women and Technology in Developing Countries: Technological Change and Women's Capabilities and Bargaining Positions. Santo Domingo: UN/INSTAN.
Buvinić, Mayra
    1983   Women's Issues in Third World Poverty: A Policy Analysis. *In* Women and Poverty in the Third World. Mayra Buvinić et al., eds. Pp. 14–31. Baltimore: Johns Hopkins University Press.
    1984   Projects for Women in the Third World: Explaining Their Misbehavior. Washington, D.C.: International Center for Research on Women.
Carr, Marilyn
    1981   Technologies Appropriate for Women: Theory, Practice and Policy. *In* Women and Technological Change in Developing Countries. AAAS Selected Symposium 53. Roslyn Dauber and Melinda L. Cain, eds. Pp. 193–203. Boulder: Westview Press.
    1984   Blacksmith, Baker, Roffing-Sheetmaker. London: Intermediate Technology Publications.
Chapkis, Wendy, and Cynthia Enloe
    1983   Of Common Cloth: Women in the Global Textile Industry. Washington, D.C.: Transnational Institute.
Chaney, Elsa M., and Marianne Schmink
    1976   Women and Modernization: Access to Tools. *In* Sex and Class in Latin America. June C. Nash and Helen Safa, eds. Pp. 160–182. New York: Praeger.
Charlton, Sue Ellen
    1984   Women in Third World Development. Boulder: Westview Press.

D'Onofrio-Flores, Pamela M.
  1982   Technology, Economic Development and the Division of Labor by Sex. *In* Scientific-Technological Change and the Role of Women in Development. Pamela M. D'Onofrio-Flores and Sheila M. Pfafflin, eds. Pp. 13–28. Boulder: Westview Press.
Elson, Diane, and Ruth Pierson
  1981   The Subordination of Women and the Internationalisation of Factory Production. *In* Of Marriage and the Market: Women's Subordination in International Perspective. Kate Young et al., eds. Pp. 144–166. London: CSE Books.
Etienne, Mona, and Eleanor Leacock, eds.
  1980   Women and Colonialization. New York: Praeger.
Evans, Judith
  1985   Improving Program Actions to Meet the Intersecting Needs of Women and Children in Developing Countries: A Policy and Program Review. With Robert G. Myers. The Consultative Group on Early Childhood Care and Development. High/Scope Educational Research Foundation.
Fernández-Kelly, María Patricia
  1983a   Gender and Industry on Mexico's New Frontier. *In* The Technological Woman: Interfacing with Tomorrow. Jan Zimmerman, ed. Pp. 18–29. New York: Praeger.
  1983b   For We Are Sold, I and My People: Women and Industry in Mexico's Frontier. Albany: State University of New York Press.
  1983c   Mexican Border Industrialization, Female Labor Force Participation, and Migration. *In* Women, Men, and the International Division of Labor. June Nash and María Patricia Fernández-Kelly, eds. Pp. 205–223. Albany: State University of New York Press.
Fuentes, Annette, and Barbara Ehrenreich
  1983   Women in the Global Factory. Boston: South End Press.
Grossman, Rachael
  1978/79   Women's Place in the Integrated Circuit. *In* Changing Role of Southeast Asian Women. Joint issue of Southeast Asia Chronicle, Number 66, and Pacific Research 9(5–6):2–16.
Jacquette, Jane, and Kathleen Staudt
  1985   Women "At Risk" Reproducers: Biology, Science, and Population in U.S. Foreign Policy. *In* Women, Biology and Public Policy. Virginia Sapiro, ed. Pp. 253–268. Beverly Hills: Sage.
Jahan, Rounaq
  1985   Participation of Women Scientists and Engineers in Endogenous Research and Development. *In* Science, Technology and Women: A World Perspective. Shirley Malcom et al., eds. Washington, D.C.: AAAS and Centre for Science and Technology for Development, United Nations.
Keller, Evelyn
  1983   A Feeling for the Organism: The Life and Work of Barbara McClintock. New York: W.H. Freeman.
Lamphere, Louise
  1987   From Working Daughters to Working Mothers: Immigrant Women in a New England Industrial Community. Ithaca: Cornell University Press.
Leacock, Eleanor, and Helen I. Safa, eds.
  1986   Women's Work: Development and the Division of Labor by Gender. South Hadley, Mass.: Bergin and Garvey.
Leet, Mildred Robbins
  1981   Roles of Women: UNCSTD Background Discussion Paper. *In* Women and Technological Change in Developing Countries. AAAS Selected Symposium 53. Roslyn Dauber and Melinda L. Cain, eds. Pp. 220–236. Boulder: Westview Press.
Lim, Linda Y. C.
  1981   Women's Work in Multinational Electronics Factories. *In* Women and Technological Change in Developing Countries. Roslyn Dauber and Melinda L. Cain, eds. Pp. 181–192. AAAS Selected Symposium 53. Boulder, CO: Westview Press.
  1983   Capitalism, Imperialism, and Patriarchy: The Dilemma of Third-World Women Workers in Multinational Factories. *In* Women, Men, and the International Division of Labor. June Nash and María Patricia Fernández-Kelly, eds. Pp. 70–91. Albany: State University of New York Press.

    1985   Women Workers in Multinational Enterprises in Developing Countries. Geneva: ILO.
Namboze, Josephine
    1985   Participation of Women in Education and Communications in the Fields of Science and Tech-
        nology. *In* Science, Technology and Women: A World Perspective. Shirley Malcolm et al., eds.
        Washington DC: AAAS and Centre for Science and Technology for Development, United Nations.
Nash, June, and María Patricia Fernández-Kelly, eds.
    1983   Women, Men, and the International Division of Labor. Albany: State University of New York
        Press.
Ong, Aihwa
    1987   Spirits of Resistance and Capitalist Discipline: Factory Women in Malaysia. Albany: State
        University of New York Press.
Reiter, Rayna, ed.
    1975   Toward an Anthropology of Women. New York: Monthly Review Press.
Rogers, Barbara
    1980   The Domestication of Women: Discrimination in Developing Societies. New York: St. Mar-
        tin's Press.
Ruiz, Vicki, and Susan Tiano, eds.
    1987   Women on the U.S.-Mexico Border: Responses to Change. Boston: Allen and Unwin.
Salaff, Janet
    1981   Working Daughters of Hong Kong: Filial Piety or Power in the Family? New York: Cambridge
        University Press.
Scott, Hilda
    1984   Working Your Way to the Bottom: The Feminization of Poverty. Boston: Pandora Press.
Sen, Amartya
    1984   Women, Technology and Sexual Divisions. Santo Domingo: UN/INSTRAW.
Sen, Gita, with Caren Grown
    1985   Development, Crisis, and Alternative Visions: Third World Women's Perspectives. DAWN
        (Development Alternatives for Women for a New Era). Norway: A.s Verbum.
Srinivasan, Mangalam
    1982   The Impact of Science and Technology and the Role of Women in Science in Mexico. *In*
        Scientific-Technological Change and the Role of Women in Development. Pamela M. D'Onofrio-
        Flores and Sheila M. Pfafflin, eds. Pp. 113–148. Boulder: Westview Press.
Stolcke, Verena
    1981   Women's Labours: The Naturalisation of Social Inequality and Women's Subordination. *In*
        Of Marriage and the Market: Women's Subordination in International Perspective. Kate Young et
        al., eds. Pp. 30–48. London: CSE Books.
Tadesse, Zenebeworke
    1982   Women and Technology in Peripheral Countries: An Overview. *In* Scientific-Technological
        Change and the Role of Women in Development. Pamela M. D'Onofrio-Flores and Sheila M. Pfaf-
        flin, eds. Pp. 77–111. Boulder: Westview Press.
Tinker, Irene
    1981   New Technologies for Food-Related Activities: An Equity Strategy. *In* Women and Techno-
        logical Change in Developing Countries. AAAS Selected Symposium 53. Roslyn Dauber and Mel-
        inda L. Cain, eds. Pp. 51–88. Boulder: Westview Press.
Young, Kate, Carol Wolkowitz, and Roslyn McCullagh, eds.
    1981   Of Marriage and the Market: Women's Subordination in International Perspective. London:
        CSE Books.

Teaching Modules: So How Can I Fit This All into a Week?

There are a variety of ways to deal with gender, culture, and development ideologies in the classroom, depending on the nature of level of the course. The following suggestions are for undergraduate courses with discussion sections or for seminars. We assume that time is a major constraint and that a great deal of background work will be taken care of in lectures. The following ideas for a one-week segment on gender and social change build on the Hong Kong/Mexico comparison presented in the overview. [There are many other possible comparisons which could be developed from sources cited in the multinational section of the bibliography. For example, Malaysia could be included with the excellent book by Ong (1987) supplemented with Daud (1985) *or* the United States with articles on the Silicon Valley from Nash and Fernández-Kelly (1983). Alternatively, development projects could be examined using the international case studies from Overholt (1985), Carr (1984), and Wasserstrom (1985).]

A week-long session could begin with the striking film "The Global Assembly Line," which shows the viewpoints of women working on assembly lines in Asia, Latin America, and the United States.

Reading Assignments

Bourque and Warren. "Gender, Technology and Development" *Daedalus* 116 (1987):173–197. [Overview of the four schools of thought on women and development].

Salaff. *Working Daughters of Hong Kong*, pp. 1–122. [Background on multinationals in Hong Kong and case studies of individual women and their families. Very readable].

Fernández-Kelly. *For We Are Sold, I and My People*. [This is a rich and highly analytical neo-Marxist ethnography with the "anti" side of the debate. Her article in Nash and Fernández-Kelly's *Women, Men and the International Division of Labor* is another option.]

Lim. *Women Workers in Multinational Enterprises in Developing Countries*. [A fast 98 pp. overview of multinationals in Asia with the "pro" side of the debate].

Alternatives for Small Group Discussions

One Plan:

(1a) Divide the class into small groups, assigning either Mexico or Hong Kong to each group for discussion. Ask each group to *identify all the dilemmas facing young women who are working in MNCs* in their case study. Call for volunteer scribes for each group, so people will pull together at the end of the group discussions and effectively summarize their findings.

(1b) Bring the class back together to compare findings. Raise the wider question when everyone is back by asking: How do *culture* and *economy* shape moral dilemmas for young women in Hong Kong and Mexico? You might add a debate between the Lim and Fernández-Kelly views of the impact of multinationals on women's lives.

This discussion should help students see that there is no universal female experience or universal impact of MNCs on young women. Dilemmas are shaped by contrasting economies, family forms and gender expectations, cultural values, and the agency of young women who embrace, resist, and reformulate the life scripts of their parents and their societies.

Another Plan:

(2a) Alternatively, one might give the groups, after assigning them either Mexico or Hong Kong, the following questions: How do *mothers and fathers* perceive their *sons and daughters?* How do sons and daughters perceive their families? How do these perceptions inform family dynamics? How are perceptions changing? How do families create and resolve conflicts?

(2b) Then bring the groups together to compare the two case studies. As a wider question, ask: What is the *relation of families to the economy?* Do families have a life of their own? Or is their experience and existence a function of the wider political economy?

This discussion has the same goals as the first plan with the addition that students should see that there is no universal "mother," "father," "daughter," or "son." [Take that, Freud!] Also that we can understand families both as structural arrangements and as meanings that are created and negotiated in action.

One More Plan:

(3a) Divide the class into four groups, one for each of the approaches to gender and technology. Ask each group to advocate its approach and to consider ways in which *education* could be transformed to meet the needs of young workers in MNCs in Hong Kong and Mexico. The educational issue might generate the following questions for the specific groups:

Integrationist: What would education for higher positions mean for these women, assuming some positions in supervision and management would be open to them? What are likely reactions to the possibility of women's mobility in the plants?

AT: What would "appropriate education" be in these circumstances?

Feminization: Does the family embody a distinctive array of values from those of the workplace? Would contrasts serve as the basis for a critique and utopian vision?

Global: How would women's construction of their own work change with an education informed by this view? [n.b.: Both Fernández-Kelly and Salaff show that women workers have little knowledge of the global system in which they are embedded, tending to blame speedups and layoffs on the personalities of their supervisors rather than on multinational demands for new production quotas, competition from countries where labor is cheaper, or recessions in the countries where their products are sold. This should raise important issues about women's organizing in grassroots political organizations, unions, and religious groups. This is an area where additional research needs to be done (cf. Ruiz and Tiano 1987 for articles on worker attitudes toward gender and resistance on the assembly line).]

(3b) Then bring the groups together to discuss what education would look like as each perspective is mediated by the cultural system in question.

The goal here is to help students see these stances as ones with strikingly different implications for change. It will also show them how the terms of these approaches must change when they are put in very different cultural contexts. Finally there should be an interesting educational message here, perhaps even some questions about the educational system in which our own students are operating.

Selected Bibliography

Critiques and Frameworks for Studying Gender and Development

Anderson, Mary B.
   1985   Technology Transfer: Implications for Women. *In* Gender Roles in Development Projects. Catherine Overholt et al., eds. Pp. 57–78. West Hartford: Kumarian Press. [Very accessible, general critique of technology transfer projects when they do not examine gender roles in rural societies.]
Benería, Lourdes, and Gita Sen
   1982   Class and Gender Inequalities and Women's Role in Economic Development—Theoretical and Practical Implications. Feminist Studies 8(1):157–176. [A powerful class-based critique of development.]
   1986   Accumulation, Reproduction, and Women's Role in Economic Development: Boserup Revisited. *In* Women's Work: Development and the Division of Labor by Gender. Eleanor Leacock and Helen I. Safa, eds. Pp. 141–157. South Hadley, Mass.: Bergin and Garvey. [A Marxist critique of Boserup's neoclassical formulation of gender and modernization.]
Bergom-Larsson, Maria
   1982   Women and Technology in the Industrialized Countries. *In* Scientific-Technological Change and the Role of Women in Development. Pamela M. D'Onofrio-Flores and Sheila M. Pfafflin, eds. Pp. 29–75. Boulder: Westview Press. [Feminization of technology approach.]
Boserup, Ester
   1970   Woman's Role in Economic Development. New York: St. Martin's Press. [The classic critique of the introduction of plow agriculture and its disproportionate impact on women in Africa.]
Boulding, Elise
   1981   Integration into What? Reflections on Development Planning for Women. *In* Women and Technological Change in Developing Countries. Roslyn Dauber and Melinda L. Cain, eds. Pp. 9–30. AAAS Selected Symposium 53. Boulder: Westview Press. [Short statement of the feminization of technology approach.]
Bourque, Susan C., and Kay B. Warren
   1987   Gender, Technology and Development. Daedalus 116:173–197. [Overview of the four approaches discussed here.]
Briscoe, Anne, and Sheila Pfafflin, eds.
   1979   Expanding the Role of Women in the Sciences. Annals of the New York Academy of Sciences, Volume 323. [See for critical integrationist arguments.]
Buvinić, Mayra
   1983   Women's Issues in Third World Poverty: A Policy Analysis. *In* Women and Poverty in the Third World. Pp. 14–31. Mayra Buvinić et al., eds. Baltimore: Johns Hopkins University Press.
   1984   Projects for Women in the Third World: Explaining Their Misbehavior. Washington, D.C.: International Center for Research on Women. [Examination of the environment and characteristics of income-generating projects and why they turn into welfare projects.]
Carr, Marilyn
   1981   Technologies Appropriate for Women: Theory, Practice and Policy. *In* Women and Technological Change in Developing Countries. AAAS Selected Symposium 53. Roslyn Dauber and Melinda L. Cain, eds. Pp. 193–203. [The Appropriate Technology framework by one of its main proponents.]
   1984   Blacksmith, Baker, Roofing-Sheetmaker. London: Intermediate Technology Publications. [Concrete case studies of appropriate technology projects. Good example of the innocence of this approach in practice to local culture.]
Chaney, Elsa M., and Marianne Schmink
   1976   Women and Modernization: Access to Tools. *In* Sex and Class in Latin America. June C. Nash and Helen Safa, eds. Pp. 160–182. New York: Praeger. [Classic critique of women's limited access to technology with development.]

Charlton, Sue Ellen
    1984   Women in Third World Development. Boulder: Westview Press. [Effective and concrete
    overview of development issues, policies, and project strategies.]
Chodorow, Nancy
    1978   The Reproduction of Mothering: Psychoanalysis of the Sociology of Gender. Berkeley; Uni-
    versity of California Press. [Example of the psychoanalytic argument that stands behind the fem-
    inization of technology approach.]
D'Onofrio-Flores, Pamela
    1982   Technology, Economic Development, and the Division of Labor by Sex. *In* Scientific-Tech-
    nological Change and the Role of Women in Development. Pamela M. D'Onofrio-Flores and
    Sheila M. Pfafflin, eds. Pp. 13–28. Boulder: Westview Press. [Critique of Western science, tech-
    nology, and models of dependent development as class-bound.]
Evans, Judith
    1985   Improving Program Actions to Meet the Intersecting Needs of Women and Children in De-
    veloping Countries: A Policy and Program Review. With Robert G. Myers. The Consultative
    Group on Early Childhood Care and Development. High/Scope Educational Research Foundation.
    [Problems with a focus on women and reproductive issues in development policy.]
Gilligan, Carol
    1982   In a Different Voice: Psychological Theory and Women's Development. Cambridge: Harvard
    University Press. [Example of the psychoanalytic argument that stands behind the feminization of
    technology approach.]
Jaquette, Jane, and Kathleen Staudt
    1985   Women "At Risk" Reproducers: Biology, Science, and Population in U.S. Foreign Policy.
    In Women, Biology, and Public Policy. Virginia Sapiro, ed. Beverly Hills: Sage. [Problems with
    a focus on women and reproductive issues in development policy.]
Jahan, Rounaq
    1985   Participation of Women Scientists and Engineers in Endogenous Research and Development.
    In Science, Technology and Women: A World Perspective. Shirley Malcom et al., eds. Washing-
    ton, D.C.: AAAS and Centre for Science and Technology for Development, United Nations. [Out-
    line of barriers women face to scientific training in third world countries.]
Lamphere, Louise
    1987   From Working Daughters to Working Mothers: Immigrant Women in a New England Indus-
    trial Community. Ithaca: Cornell University Press. [U.S. case study of changing political economy,
    industrial work, gender, and ethnicity.]
Leet, Mildred Robbins
    1981   Roles of Women: UNCSTD Background Discussion Paper. *In* Women and Technological
    Change in Developing Countries. AAAS Selected Symposium 53. Roslyn Dauber and Melinda L.
    Cain, eds. Pp. 229–236. Boulder: Westview Press. [International efforts to get gender on the
    agenda for the UN Conference on Science and Technology for Development. Statement of priori-
    ties and strategies for international/national change.]
Rogers, Barbara
    1980   The Domestication of Women: Discrimination in Developing Societies. New York: St. Mar-
    tin's Press. [Critique of how planners and policymakers relate to women].
Scott, Hilda
    1984   Working Your Way to the Bottom: The Feminization of Poverty. Boston: Pandora Press. [A
    wide-ranging example of the feminization of technology framework.]
Sen, Amartya
    1984   Women, Technology and Sexual Divisions. Santo Domingo: UN/INSTRAW. [Critique of
    assumptions about household decision making.]
Sen, Gita, with Caren Grown
    1985   Development, Crisis, and Alternative Visions: Third World Women's Perspectives. DAWN
    (Development Alternatives for Women for a New Era). Norway: A.s Verbum. [Wide-ranging in-
    ternational feminist critique of development models.]

Srinivasan, Mangalam
    1982   The Impact of Science and Technology and the Role of Women in Science in Mexico. *In* Scientific-Technological Change and the Role of Women in Development. Pp. 113–148. Boulder: Westview Press. [Overview of women, science, technology and employment in Mexico.]
Stolcke, Verena
    1981   Women's Labours: The Naturalisation of Social Inequality and Women's Subordination. *In* Of Marriage and the Market: Women's Subordination in International Perspective. Kate Young et al., eds. Pp. 30–48. London: CSE Books. [Excellent statement of the global economy, class analysis framework.]
Tadesse, Zenebeworke
    1982   Women and Technology in Peripheral Countries: An Overview. *In* Scientific-Technological Change and the Role of Women in Development. Pamela M. D'Onofrio-Flores and Sheila M. Pfafflin, eds. Pp. 77–111. Boulder: Westview Press. [Critique of Western models of development by a sociologist from Ethiopia and founding member of the Association of African Women for Research and Development.]
Tinker, Irene
    1981   New Technologies for Food-Related Activities: An Equity Strategy. *In* Women and Technological Change in Developing Countries. Roslyn Dauber and Melinda L. Cain, eds. Pp. 51–88. AAAS Selected Symposium 53. Boulder: Westview Press. [Appropriate technology issues.]
Warren, Kay B., and Susan C. Bourque
    1985   Gender, Power, and Communication: Women's Responses to Political Muting in the Andes. *In* Women Living Change. Susan C. Bourque and Donna Robinson Divine, eds. Pp. 355–386. Philadelphia: Temple University Press. [Cultural construction and political construction of women's development priorities.]

Cross-cultural Case Studies: Anthologies

Afshar, Haleh, ed.
    1987   Women, State, and Ideology: Studies from Africa and Asia. Albany: State University of New York Press.
Ardener, Shirley, ed.
    1975   Perceiving Women. London: Malaby Press.
Black, Naomi, and Ann Baker Cottrell, eds.
    1981   Women and World Change: Equity Issues in Development. Beverly Hills: Sage.
Bourque, Susan C., and Donna Divine, eds.
    1985   Women Living Change. Philadelphia: Temple University Press.
Caplan, Patricia, and Janet Bujra, eds.
    1979   Women United, Women Divided: Contemporary Studies of Ten Cultures. Bloomington: Indian University Press.
Dube, Leela, et al.
    1986   Visibility and Power: Essays on Women in Society and Development. New York: Oxford University Press.
Etienne, Mona, and Eleanor Leacock, eds.
    1980   Women and Colonialization. New York: Praeger.
Leacock, Eleanor, and Helen I. Safa, eds.
    1986   Women's Work: Development and the Division of Labor by Gender. South Hadley, Mass.: Bergin and Garvey.
MacCormack, Carol, and Marilyn Strathern, eds.
    1980   Nature, Culture and Gender. Cambridge: Cambridge University Press.
Nash, June, and Helen Safa, eds.
    1986   Women and Change in Latin America. South Hadley, Mass.: Bergin and Garvey.
Ortner, Sherry B., and Harriet Whitehead, eds.
    1981   Sexual Meanings: The Cultural Construction of Gender and Sexuality. Cambridge: Cambridge University Press.

Overholt, Catherine et al., eds.
   1985   Gender Roles in Development Projects: A Case Book. West Hartford, Conn.: Kumarian Press.
      [Good case studies of development projects.]
Reiter, Rayna, ed.
   1975   Toward an Anthropology of Women. New York: Monthy Review Press.
Rosaldo, Michelle Zimbalist, and Louise Lamphere, eds.
   1974   Woman, Culture and Society. Stanford: Stanford University Press.
Wasserstrom, Robert
   1985   Grassroots Development in Latin America. New York: Praeger. [Good case studies of devel-
      opment projects.]
Young, Kate, Carol Wolkowitz, and Roslyn McCullagh, eds.
   1981   Of Marriage and the Market: Women's Subordination in International Perspective. London:
      CSE Books.

Gender and Multinationals

Benería, Lourdes, and Martha Roldan
   1987   The Crossroads of Class and Gender: Industrial Homework, Subcontracting, and Household
      Dynamics in Mexico City. Chicago: University of Chicago Press. [In-depth case study of multi-
      national subcontracting in Mexico.]
Chapkis, Wendy, and Cynthia Enloe
   1983   Of Common Cloth: Women in the Global Textile Industry. Washington, D.C.: Transnational
      Institute. [Overview of multinationals in textile production.]
Daud, Fatimah
   1985   "Minah Karan": The Truth about Malaysian Factory Girls. Kuala Lumpur, Malaysia: Berita
      Publishing. [Case study of women workers in Japanese managed multinationals in Malaysia; es-
      pecially good on race and gender issues.]
Elson, Diane, and Ruth Pierson
   1981   The Subordination of Women and the Internationalisation of Factory Production. *In* Of Mar-
      riage and the Market: Women's Subordination in International Perspective. Kate Young et al., eds.
      Pp. 144–166. London: CSE Books.
Fernández-Kelly, María Patricia
   1983a   Gender and Industry on Mexico's New Frontier. *In* The Technological Woman: Interfacing
      with Tomorrow. Jan Zimmerman, ed. Pp. 18–29. New York: Praeger. [Women working on the
      Mexican-U.S. border in multinational electronics firms.]
   1983b   For We Are Sold, I and My People: Women and Industry in Mexico's Frontier. Albany: State
      University of New York Press. [Excellent, global-economy approach to multinationals on the Mex-
      ican border. Don't miss the later chapters on workers' lives.]
   1983c   Mexican Border Industrialization, Female Labor Force Participation, and Migration. *In*
      Women, Men, and the International Division of Labor. June Nash and María Patricia Fernández-
      Kelly, eds. Pp. 205–223. Albany: State University of New York Press. [Women working on the
      Mexican-U.S. border in multinational electronics firms.]
Fuentes, Annette, and Barbara Ehrenreich
   1983   Women in the Global Factory. Boston: South End Press. [Overview of women working in
      multinationals.]
Grossman, Rachael
   1978/79   Women's Place in the Integrated Circuit. *In* Changing Role of S.E. Asian Women. Joint
      issue of Southeast Asia Chronicle, No. 66, and Pacific Research 9(5–6):2–16. [Excellent pamphlet
      on Asian women's work experiences.]
Lim, Linda Y. C.
   1983   Capitalism, Imperialism, and Patriarchy: The Dilemma of Third-World Women Workers in
      Multinational Factories. *In* Women, Men, and the International Division of Labor. June Nash and
      María Patricia Fernández-Kelly, eds. Pp. 70–91. Albany: State University of New York Press. [A
      well-argued case for benefits in multinational employment for women.]

1985   Women Workers in Multinational Enterprises in Developing Countries. Geneva: ILO [Careful overview of multinational proliferation and a well-argued case for benefits in multinational employment for women.]
Ong, Aihwa
  1987   Spirits of Resistance and Capitalist Discipline: Factory Women in Malaysia. Albany: State University of New York Press. [Sophisticated ethnographic treatment of the transformation of an agrarian community and women's employment in Japanese-managed multinationals.]
Nash, June, and María Patricia Fernández-Kelly, eds.
  1983   Women, Men, and the International Division of Labor. Albany: State University of New York Press. [The best international collection of analytical case studies on gender and multinational employment in Asia, Latin America and the United States.]
Ruiz, Vicki, and Susan Tiano, eds.
  1987   Women on the U.S.-Mexico Border: Responses to Change. Boston: Allen and Unwin. [Range of women's economic and political involvements in the border region.]
Salaff, Janet
  1981   Working Daughters of Hong Kong: Filial Piety or Power in the Family? New York: Cambridge University Press. [Ethnographic treatment of Hong Kong women working in multinationals and the service industry. Good on individual strategies, family issues, and the cultural compatability of work with Chinese values.]

Gender and Rural Development Issues

Ahmed, Iftikhar, ed.
  1985   Technology and Rural Women: Conceptual and Empirical Issues. London: George Allen and Unwin.
Arizpe, Lourdes, and Josefina Aranda
  1981   The "Comparative Advantages" of Women's Disadvantages: Women Workers in the Strawberry Export Agribusiness in Mexico. Signs 7:453–473.
Barrios de Chungara, Domitila
  1978   Let Me Speak: Testimony of Domitila, a Woman of the Bolivian Mines. With Moema Viezzer. New York: Monthly Review Press.
Benería, Lourdes, ed.
  1982   Women and Development: The Sexual Division of Labor in Rural Societies. New York: Praeger.
Boserup, Ester
  1970   Woman's Role in Economic Development. New York: St. Martin's Press.
Bourque, Susan C., and Kay B. Warren
  1981a   Women of the Andes: Patriarchy and Social Change in Rural Peru. Ann Arbor: University of Michigan Press.
  1981b   Rural Women and Development Planning in Peru. *In* Women and World Change: Equity Issues in Development. Naomi Black and Ann Cottrell, eds. Pp. 183–197. Beverly Hills: Sage.
Creevey, Lucy E., ed.
  1986   Women Farmers in Africa: Rural Development in Mali and the Sahel. Syracuse: Syracuse University Press.
Deere, Carmen Diana, and Magdalena León de Leal
  1982   Women in Andean Agriculture. Geneva: ILO.
Deere, Carmen Diana, and Magdalena León, eds.
  1987   Rural Women and State Policy: Feminist Perspectives on Latin American Agricultural Development. Boulder: Westview Press.
Dixon, Ruth
  1978   Rural Women at Work: Strategies for Development in South Asia. Baltimore: Johns Hopkins University Press.

Kader, Soha Abdel, et al.
  1986   Women and Rural Development in Africa. Dakar, Senegal: Association of African Women
         for Research and Development/Association des Femmes africaines pour la Recherche et le Devel-
         oppement (AAWORD/AFARD).
Moock, Joyce, ed.
  1986   Understanding Africa's Rural Households and Farming Systems. Boulder: Westview Press.
Stoler, Ann
  1985   Capitalism and Confrontation in Sumatra's Plantation Belt, 1870–1979. New Haven: Yale
         University Press.

17

Anthropological Perspectives on Gender and Language

Ruth A. Borker   Daniel N. Maltz
1948–1989

It is a striking irony that while the study of gender and the study of language have moved more and more into the mainstream of anthropology in recent years, the study of gender and language has not. The major reason for this situation is that anthropological perspectives have been largely ignored within the interdisciplinary study of gender and language, and the topics included within the field have been narrowly defined. Our intention in this article is to examine a wide range of anthropological material relevant to the study of gender and language and thus challenge the two major paradigms that have come to dominate this field: an oversimplified political paradigm of male power and dominance, and a behaviorist paradigm that treats both gender and speech behavior as variables and seeks to find correlations between them.

The political paradigm is based on the rather simplistic concept that if men are dominant in society they must control language. Research focuses on searching for ways in which this dominance is reflected in both the structure and use of language: the grammatical gender system, the meanings of words relating to gender, the sexualization of terms for women, and devaluations of women's speech and writing styles. Anthropology has developed more complex models for talking about hierarchy, pluralism, and hegemony than this paradigm allows. For example, the concept of female mutedness, as elaborated by such scholars as Lederman (1980) and Warren and Bourque (1985) leads to far richer models of the relation between gender, power, and speech.

The behaviorist paradigm focuses on correlating a personal attribute (gender) with specific forms of speech behavior. Gender, in this view, is an attribute of the individual rather than being culturally constructed or dependent on context. The linguistic focus is on sentences or smaller units rather than larger units of discourse. Because research of this type is rarely embedded in any larger social theory, both the specific speech patterns observed and their correlation with gender are all too often trivial from a social science point of view. As Peng (1982) argues, such studies not only fail to take into account the multiple aspects of an actor's social identity, they are also based on a model of language that is not dynamic and that focuses excessively on "structure," paying inadequate attention to function.

411

Some of the difficulties with these two paradigms can be seen in their responses to Robin Lakoff's classic formulation of the problem of understanding "women's language" in American English (1975). The political agenda focuses on specific suggestions about how English trivializes female activity and on the powerlessness of women's language. The behaviorist agenda focuses on testing a specific set of propositions about the differences between male and female registers by counting occurrences of specific features in selections of recorded speech. Both appear to miss the most valuable part of what Lakoff has to offer: she directs us to examine a "language" (a complexly patterned phenomenon, not just individual features) and the ways it might relate to social and cultural difference within society. Women, she argues, learn to speak in a particular way because they are women; they are socialized to speak "like" women. Their speech skills have power limitations, however, not because they are women, but because of the actual characteristics of the speech, the way it is heard, and the ways in which it structures the relationship between interlocutors.

An anthropological approach does not assume that all differences are direct reflections of differential power and need not begin by asking whether gender has a significant influence on language use in a particular society since, as Sherzer notes, "gender, like other major social distinctions in society, such as age, power, and intimacy, is so basic to communication that there will *always* be some reflection of it in the sociolinguistic system of particular societies" (1987:117, emphasis ours). The problem is to locate these gender differences and determine their significance in particular cultures. Beginning with this perspective, we proceed to ask what kinds of relationships have been found between language and gender in anthropological research. First, we discuss the meaning of basic terms as conceptualized anthropologically: gender, speech and language. Next we ask how gender differences within society may influence the use of language. Finally, we ask how differences in language use may involve gender.

Linguistic and Cultural Gender

From feminist theory has come a challenge, well known within anthropology, to our basic notion of gender, treating it not as a biological characteristic, but as a socially and culturally constructed system of categories. Within the study of language, however, understanding the concept of "gender" is even more complex, since the word "gender" refers to a formal aspect of a language as well as to the social and cultural world within which that language is used. Unravelling this complex relationship between linguistic gender and social or cultural gender is of major significance in the study of gender and language, but too technical and complex to be treated in more than very general terms here.

The main contribution that an anthropological perspective has made to this discussion is to argue against the position taken by many linguists, that there is a clear distinction between language and culture, that formal attributes of a linguistic system have nothing to do with the valuation or categorization of people, that the linguistic gender system has nothing to do with the "gender system" in a more general sense.

In general, a gender system is a classification system used for categorizing words, people, or objects. Although many linguists use the term "gender" broadly for a wide range of systems of grammatically relevant noun-classes, we find it more profitable to follow those who use the term in a more restricted sense to refer to categorization systems tied at least in part to actual or perceived biological or reproductive roles. Within any given culture, it is possible to separate several different gender systems used to categorize several different types of entities: words, ideas, things, and activities. Taken separately, one can distinguish between grammatical gender systems, cultural conceptualizations of masculinity and femininity, cultural concepts of reproduction, and sex role systems. A variety of studies (Fiske 1978; Jabbra 1980; Munroe and Munroe 1969; Silverstein 1985), however, have shown the nonindependence of grammatical gender from other gender systems, at least when dealing with actual linguistic usage.

Perhaps the most striking example of the complex interrelation between grammatical and cultural aspects of gender is the contrast between the cases of Native America and Melanesia. In many parts of native North America, analysts have observed a phenomena often characterized as distinct "men's" and "women's" languages (Bodine 1975b), in which the use of specific morphological or phonological forms to mark the gender of the speaker and/or hearer is required. In Melanesia, in contrast, there is not only no such required grammatical indexing of gender but also no notion of distinctive ways of "talking like a man" and "talking like a woman," although there are many differences in the ways men and women actually speak that result from differences in the roles they occupy (Schieffelin 1987). This contrast is usually thought of as a contrast between linguistic systems, between formal attributes of languages. But when language is thought of as an aspect of culture rather than a separate system, a cultural rather than linguistic explanation of this apparently linguistic difference can be found. Among Native Americans, gender was not conceptualized as an attribute of the inner self as much as of overt behavior, including appearance, social roles, and other personal actions. To be male or female in such a system is to behave as a male or female and ways of speaking indicate gender as much as other forms of behavior. In Melanesia, in contrast, one's gender is not constructed from one's actions, even sexual actions, but from nonvisible internal bodily substances like blood, milk, and semen.

Speech and Language

The dominant tradition for the study of language, that used by most linguists, makes a strong distinction between language and speech, *langue* and *parole*, language structure (including syntax, semantics, and phonology) and language pragmatics, the way language is used. As applied to the study of gender and language, it is a distinction between the ways in which sex and gender are encoded in language and the ways in which speech behavior is affected by gender. Increasingly anthropological concern with cognitive variation, discourse strategies, language styles and cultural poetics has pointed to the problematic nature of these distinctions.

The case of the generic masculine in English points to some of its limitations. In the 1970s a charge was made that English was sexist because of its use of "he" and "man" as both masculine pronouns and as generics. Those working within a strictly linguistic paradigm found this accusation absurd, based in a misanalysis of the relationship between language and social reality that mistakes language *use* for language as a referential system (Gregersen 1979; Silverstein 1985).

Discussions by Bodine (1975a) and Bendix (1979) present a challenge to the whole concept of a sharp distinction between language structure and language use. One question they raise is the relation between prescriptive and descriptive grammar. Generally, linguistic theory is concerned with descriptive grammar (the structure of a language), but, as Bodine points out, the use of "he" rather than "they" for sex-indefinite third person singular is part of the prescriptive grammar of English. Prescriptive grammar rules are not included in most linguistic theories since they necessitate taking into account a social power analysis abjured by those taking a strictly structural approach to language. It is clear speakers do not use a simple rule as suggested by the prescriptive formulation. Actual use suggests that speakers attempt to signal singular indefinite in a variety of ways, such as the use of "they," "you," or generic "she" (for roles usually associated with women).

A more general problem raised by Bendix is the difficulty of separating language structure from language use or radically separating reference from connotation, of arguing that the generic masculine causes problems simply because some speakers misunderstand the system. Determining whether "he" includes "she" in referring to an indefinite person requires looking at the way it is heard, at its use in context. The meaning attributed to a particular form depends on the alternatives available and what each is seen as signaling (Bendix 1979). To use an extreme example, while the use of the word "history" may not indicate much about a speaker, the use of the word "herstory" does. For whatever reason, the generic masculine now sounds problematic to many speakers who did not find it so in the past. Those who study language cannot say these individuals don't understand their language, for the usages they develop in their discomfort *are* the "language" as it will be identified in the future. As both Bodine (1975a) and Silverstein (1985) discuss in comparing the generic masculine situation to that of the second person pronouns of English, social ideology and the ideology of language shape and change language use and thus language structure as well.

Looking at language as a tool, as anthropology does, points to a number of specific issues regarding the generic masculine. It directs us to the significance of ambiguities in usage and the need to identify the situations and speakers/hearers for whom generic forms pose problems. It is clear that the generic masculine is often misunderstood and that there is a disjunction between what speakers encode and hearers decode. Further, the generic masculine poses greater difficulties for some speakers and hearers than for others, specifically for women and for those who wish to be clear about women's inclusion (Bendix 1979). Finally, it is clear that certain generic forms, such as the term "primitive man," allow speakers and writers to ignore women without having to be aware of it.

Gender Differences and Their Relation to Speech

One major approach to the relation between speech and gender begins with gender differences and asks how they might be related to language use. For this purpose, we find it useful to distinguish three major aspects of gender: gender as identity, gender as social roles, and gender as experience.

Gender as Identity

Identity involves both one's conception of self and the way one projects this self-concept to others through speech and action. In every society, gender is a distinction that individuals learn to recognize and to some extent to use for thinking about themselves. One major use of speech is to convey one's identity, including gender identity, to others. To project a gender identity, one must (1) learn gender categories, (2) learn the ways of acting, including ways of speaking, that are associated with these categories, and (3) learn to act and speak appropriately so as to convey signals of gender at appropriate times and places. Since gender is constructed differently in different cultures, gender indicators such as speech are used to indicate different aspects of identity in different places. Beatty (1979), for example, points out that in the United States, men use gender-marked speech to signal both "masculinity" and "virility" simultaneously, while in Japan these two are distinguished.

Some analysts (Philips 1980) have argued that language is rarely used to project gender identity. Others (Lybrand 1982) have claimed that although people may claim a cultural distinction in speech based on gender, it is not necessarily found in actual behavior. Admittedly, they are making a sharper distinction between linguistic and paralinguistic aspects of language than we find useful, but we find two other major weaknesses with this line of argument as well.

First, the claim that language is used to convey gender identity does not imply that it will be used equally in all interaction. What people learn are cultural associations between patterns of speech and gender. These gender-marking, or gender-projecting, aspects of speech are more likely to be used in some contexts than in others, particularly (1) when acting (Shibamoto 1985, 1987), (2) when imitating a voice within a narrative [consider how easy it is to identify the gender of most cartoon characters, or imagine telling the story of the three bears without signaling the gender identities of mama and papa bear], (3) when first learning gender categories during early childhood (Berentzen 1984; Meditch 1975), (4) when asserting one's sexuality during adolescence, (5) when flirting, especially with strangers, and (6) when the gender identity one is projecting contradicts the gender indicated by other signals (as in some homosexual speech and action).

Second, presentation of self, or assertion of self-identity, expresses gender identity not simply by making a statement "I am male" or "I am female," but in more complex ways as well. One's reputation includes many elements, such as honor, sexual experience, emotional responsiveness, and verbal skill, which may have complex relationships to gender. Thus, for example, a speech act that conveys the message "I am sexually experienced" may have different meanings when used by a male or a female. In the Mediterranean, the concept of honor is involved in both male and female self-presentations, but possesses different meanings and is asserted in different ways by men and women (Abu-Lughod 1985, 1986). Harding (1978) demonstrates how the public verbal conflict of Spanish women, including shouting and shunning, is used to manipulate the reputations of self and others in a gender-associated way, making public what was private and altering the reputations of the participants. Among Afro-Americans (Abrahams 1975), reputation and respectability, the two evaluative codes in terms of which individual identities are assessed, are associated with different genders and expressed through different ways of speaking. Even among young children in a Norwegian pre-school (Berentzen 1984), the use of language to assert identity is gender-differentiated, boys asserting their "tough"ness and girls asserting their ties to playmates.

Gender as Role

Even when gender is not being expressed directly, language may be tied to gender through the enactment of social roles. That is, different social roles require different ways of speaking, and social roles are gender-identified even when ways of speaking are not explicitly gender-identified (Schieffelin 1987). In thinking about gender roles, particularly as they relate to language use, we find it useful to distinguish three ways in which a social role can be genderized: sexualized roles, gender-defined roles (particularly kinship roles), and gender-allocated roles such as occupations.

Sexualized Roles. Some social interactions involve gender because they are directly concerned with sexuality, that is, the individuals involved are expressing real or playful sexual interest in one another. Interactions of this sort include flirting, courtship, sexual joking, sexual harassment, seduction, lovemaking, and even obscene phone calls. Most if not all of these interactions involve the use of language, and the gender of participants is related to the way that language is used. The more private or intimate of these forms of interaction are rarely open to outside researchers; the more public ones such as flirting and courtship have been more often analyzed. Two important dimensions distinguish interactions with a sexual focus: seriousness (distinguishing courtship from playful flirting) and assent of the two participants (distinguishing flirting from harassment).

Interaction between lovers or potential marriage partners often calls for specific styles of speech, even in public. Among the Egyptian Bedouin (Abu-Lughod 1985, 1986), poetry is the speech form used for expressing emotion, sentimentality, and romantic feelings as opposed to everyday speech, which is used to express the values of honor and responsibility. Because Bedouin marriage is arranged, the poetic forms associated with romance are quite distinct from courtship, but among the Koya of South India (Brukman 1975), it is the courtship of potential marriage partners that is characterized by a marked speech form, in this case joking. Similarly, among the Sasak of Lombok, Indonesia, Ecklund (1977) distinguishes two patterns of courtship speech: (1) standard courting, which is private, one-to-one, stiff, asexual, and circumspect, and (2) *pantun,* or rhyming verses exchanged publicly between groups of males and females, which are more overtly sexual, more direct, looser in tone and style but mediated by a rhyming poetic form.

Sexual joking and other forms of flirting also often characterize the verbal interaction between men and women who work together or socialize together. For Spain, Fernandez (1977:460–463) examines the poetics of flirtatious encounters in Asturia, and Brandes (1974) describes patterns of sexual joking in work parties in Andalusia. In both cases the use of joking defines an otherwise ambiguous relationship as sexualized without necessarily being sexual. Similar uses of flirting and sexualized joking are reported from studies of interaction in English pubs. In rural Herefordshire, Whitehead (1976) observes flirtatious giggling by unmarried women, joking and challenging of single men by elderly women and married men, and the use of aggressive sexual joking aimed at women to maintain male domination in the world of the pub. Hunt and Saterlee (1987) describe a middle-class pub in East Anglia in which groups of married couples engage in cross-gender sexual bantering of an egalitarian nature. Inequality in sexual joking is restricted to bantering between the men and the publican's wife or bar maid, a relationship that combines class and status with gender.

This inequality in relations between sexual joking partners, particularly female employees and male customers, has been described in North American contexts as well. Mann (1974) and Williams (1975) describe situations in which waitresses in bars or restaurants make use of flirtatious speech as a means of interacting with male patrons. The unequal social positions of service providers and customers or employees and employers create contexts in which flirting exaggerates social inequality and flirtatious interaction may border on harassment.

A third type of sexualized verbal interaction occurs in public encounters between strangers, particularly in areas such as the Middle East, Southern Europe, Latin America, and Afro-America, where there is a strong cultural concept of a public, male-dominated world of "the street." Here we find catcalls, whistles, verbal insults, and compliments directed at passing females by males or, more often, groups of males. Suárez-Orozco and Dundes (1984) analyze the *piropo,* a Mediterranean and Latin American form of masculine verbal art addressed to women on the street, in terms of its dual character as compliment and insult. *Piropos* are generally sexual in nature and may use poetic forms to compliment a woman on her physical attractiveness or be openly offensive sexual propositions or harangues displaying aggression rather than admiration. Gardner (1980) provides a less charitable account of male-to-female street remarks in the cities of North America as displays of male power and domination in public places.

Genderized Roles.   Certain roles, particularly kinship ones, are inherently genderized. "Mother" is probably the best example. The fact that in American English the sentence "don't talk to me like that, you're not my mother" makes sense as a response to certain kinds of speech indicates that the role of mother is in part defined by its speech qualities.

Much of the research on child socialization and language acquisition has examined the verbal interaction between mothers and children, but the focus of this research has been on the language learning of children, with mothers viewed as agents of socialization rather than as actors in their own right. By turning this focus around, however, it is possible to approach "mother talk" not simply as part of the socialization process, but as a form of genderized speech attached to the role of mother. Clearly the content of this role is neither universal nor biologically determined, but varies both across cultures and with the age of the child. The elements out of which a mother's speech role is constructed, however, tend to include authority, intimacy, instruction, caretaking, and mediation with the outside world. How these elements are combined is a major element of the cultural construction of motherhood in any particular society.

Included within the general category of "mother talk" are talk to infants who do not yet use language [baby talk], talk to young children who are in the process of learning language [caretaker speech], and talk by mothers to their older children, including even adults [motherese].

"Baby talk" in the strict sense, that is, talk addressed to infants, is a speech register with special linguistic characteristics, including modified intonation, speed, pitch, sentence length and even vocabulary used for addressing infants who are not yet able to use language. Its purpose is to attract the attention of the infant and to create or express an interactive social relationship. Research (Blount and Padgug 1976; Caudill 1972; Fischer 1970; Gleason 1987) reveals numerous variations in the linguistic characteristics of baby talk across culture and gender, and Ochs observes that in Samoa no baby talk is used at all.

Since caretaking and socialization of children are not the exclusive domain of adult women in most areas of the world, "caretaker speech" is not always synonymous with the speech role of mothers. But a comparison between the talk of mothers and other caretakers can provide some profitable insights. For Samoa, Elinor Ochs (1987) argues that the sharing of caretaking roles across age and gender is so complete that "mother" is difficult to distinguish as a social role and there are no speech forms that may be distinguished as "mother talk." Among the Kipsigi of Kenya, on the other hand, when Harkness (1977) compared the speech of mothers with that of children who care for younger children, she found that mothers were more likely to use questions and other speech eliciting forms, while children caretakers were more likely to make declarative commentary statements.

Another important element of caretaker speech is the speech of socialization, particularly explicit instruction to young children on how to speak correctly. In many cultures (Schieffelin 1979, 1987; Smith-Heffner 1988), teaching others how to speak is an important aspect of the speech behavior of mothers, and imitating this behavior is even an important distinguishing feature between the speech play of boys and girls.

The speaking roles of mothers include not only baby talk to infants and the language instruction of young children, but also the speech forms associated with protecting and disciplining their children of all ages. In Western society, the recognition of "mother talk" or "motherese" as a specific way of speaking is made most clearly in children's play, particularly playing house or playing with dolls (Berentzen 1984). Much of this play consists of speaking to dolls or other children who have been assigned the role of child, of taking on the speech role of a mother.

In their analysis of interaction in an American hospital, Tannen and Wallat (1983) examine the speech role of a mother as an intermediary in doctor-child interaction, verbally working to extract information from the doctor on behalf of her child. This role of speaking both in competition with and on behalf of her child is one common characteristic of mother's speech, at least in relation to outsiders. Tannen & Wallat (1983:211) also describe a speech register they label "motherese," marked by high pitch, elongated vowel sounds, sing-song intonation, and teasing, used by a doctor when addressing young patients to convey a relationship characterized by both authority and affection.

Larson's (1982) study of linguistic code switching by Norwegian mothers to signal a switch between intimate and authoritative aspects of her role suggests that the manipulation of intimacy in relation to authority, which so clearly characterizes the speech of mothers in many cultures, may also be a more general linguistic skill of women. Underwood (1983), for example, in analyzing the interaction between a Brahmin woman and her low-caste servant, focuses on the manipulation of intimacy and the controlling role of the mistress in shifting between intimacy and hierarchical distance.

Gender-Allocated Roles.   Many roles that are not defined in terms of either sexuality or gender are nevertheless allocated to individuals on the basis of gender. These are the roles usually included in discussions of "the sexual division of labor." When different roles require different speech skills and these roles are allocated on the basis of gender, a gender difference in language use will result. How roles are allocated in relation to gender, what kinds of language differences are connected with role differences, and the extent to which these differences will be culturally associated with gender are important analytic questions.

In nonstratified, relatively homogeneous societies, speech differences between two gender-defined categories may be relatively clear-cut (Keenan 1974a, 1974b). In stratified or other nonhomogeneous societies, gender may be an element in the allocation of roles such as occupations, thus creating complex relationships between gender and patterns of speech (Ochs 1987). Why, for example, do Americans hear speaking like a teamster (or a presidential candidate for that matter) as masculine? In part it is because the kinds of speech associated with the role, such as CB radio talk, have become identified as masculine, in part because forms of speech associated with masculinity, such as cursing, have become associated with the role. Research on language use associated with primarily female occupations include studies of cocktail waitresses (Mann 1974; Spradley and Mann 1975), waitresses (Williams 1975), prostitutes (James 1972a, 1972b; Layton 1978), and secretaries (Wynn 1980). Closely related to these issues are questions of language, gender, and power. Are women's ways of speaking heard as powerless because they are heard as "feminine," as Robin Lakoff has proposed, or do women speak in certain ways because they are powerless (O'Barr and Atkins 1980)?

Religious speech roles, like economic ones, may also be assigned on the basis of gender. One obvious example is confession in the Catholic church, a particular variant of a conversation that is of central importance within Catholicism. Since the priesthood is closed to women, so is one of the two speech roles, that of confessor. Among the Kuna of Panama (Sherzer 1987), for example, different ritual roles involve different verbal genres—speechmaking, chanting, and reciting spells—with different phonological, morphological, syntactic, and semantic features. Although there is no ideological association of these linguistic forms with gender, the fact that ritual roles are gender-ascribed means that associated speech forms are as well. In other cases, such as the Buddhist Tamang of Central Nepal, even the linguistic skills of reading and writing are defined as being male (March 1983).

Southeast Asia provides a particularly striking example of the allocation of ritual speech forms by gender, since gender is not particularly important for the organization of nonlinguistic aspects of life. Among the Weyéwa of Eastern Indonesia (Kuipers 1986), for example, men speak to ancestors, perform divination, placate spirits, and deliver celebratory speeches. The form of their speech is narrative, indirect, poetic, and formulaic. Women, in contrast, are the specialists in laments and ritual weeping, nonnarrative forms with the power to evoke emotional responses. Among the Ilongot of Northern Luzon (Rosaldo and Atkinson 1975) both men and women recite magical spells to control the behavior of spirits, but men's spells concern hunting and women's concern gardening. This difference in topic implies other differences as well. Both types of spells use plant metaphors, but they evoke different plants; and men's hunting spells are based on similes of action and violence while women's gardening spells suggest ''domesticity, passivity, and mass.''

Gender as Experience

Gender is not simply an identity or a role, but a set of experiences. An individual approaches every verbal interaction with an accumulation of personal experience that comes from enculturation not merely to adulthood in the abstract but to a particularly engendered adulthood. Among the different experiences that come from having grown up as either a boy or a girl are a number of experiences with language. They may be spoken to differently by adults or encouraged to speak differently. They may be assigned different chores involving different speech routines, as among the Kaluli (Schieffelin 1987). They may spend time in gender-segregated play groups with potentially different patterns of interaction and speech use, as in Samoa (Ochs 1987), Western Europe (Berentzen 1984), and North America (Goodwin 1980). They may be exposed to gender differentiated literature, folklore, or forms of play.

Play is one of the main mechanisms through which children learn linguistic routines, and childhood games are often gender-differentiated. Among the Eskimo of Northwest Alaska, girls but not boys learn to tell storyknife tales (Ager 1974, 1979; Oswalt 1964), using knives to draw pictures in the mud or snow as they recount traditional narratives, modified Euro-American children's tales, or accounts of personal experience. They learn the speaking role of a grandmother, and when they become adult women and no longer use their storyknives, they still accompany their narratives with hand movements learned in these girlhood games. Limón (1980) describes the game of *la vieja Inés,* in which Mexican-American girls learn and practice a mother's role in manipulating language to ''take responsibility for children by naming them and speaking for them against the world beyond the kin group.'' Goodwin's (1985) analysis of jump rope in Philadelphia reveals that girls, like boys, are capable of engaging in disputes without having to terminate their games, but that they learn different mechanisms of mediation, ''mitigated'' or modulated ways of saying things rather than ''aggravated'' or unmodulated forms of dispute. They learn to propose rather than demand, to use imperatives for asserting group rather than individual interests, and to encourage short-lived rather than protracted disputes.

Gender-differentiated experiences affect adult language use most strikingly in those areas, such as the Mediterranean (Harding 1975; Silverman 1975) and Melanesia, where men's and women's social worlds are clearly distinct. Silverman (1975) describes a village in central Italy in which both men and women experience their social worlds largely through idle talk, but with each gender experiencing in a different way. Men gather in groups of at least five or six in piazzas, bars, and other places to enjoy arguments and displays of rhetorical skill on a wide variety of topics from politics to food, from sports to ways of life. Women gather in twos and threes, arm in arm with a close relative, or they sit sewing with neighbors generating a running commentary on the female life cycle of the social behavior of others.

Harding (1975) interprets similar patterns of speech difference in Oroel, Spain, in terms of men's and women's different experiences of work. She argues that because men and women spend their time in different locales, doing different things, and operating in a differently structured social world, their experience of speech and their experience of the world through speech is significantly different. In both Iran (Wright 1978) and New Guinea (Lederman 1980), men and women have different experiences of political meetings and different experiences with political oratory. Wright (1978:106–111) compares the political meetings of men and women in southern Iran, finding men's meetings to be characterized by public debate, expressions of rank, and displays of rhetorical ability, while women's meetings involve less etiquette, less focus, less direct confrontation, and alliances that are less clear. Thus men experience the political world through public debate as advocates of specific interest groups and women experience it through convoluted and circumspect speech aimed at arriving at an understanding of the tensions and alliances in a world to which they possess a multiplicity of cross-cutting ties.

But different experiences can affect the speech of adult men and women, even when gender segregation is not so great. Where men and women are involved in different activities and have different interests, as in the middle-class English pub described by Hunt and Satterlee (1987:584), they will talk about different things, use different genres of speech, and sex segregate for purposes of conversation. This classic pattern of separate conversations may originate from differences in interests, but its sociolinguistic implications may be more profound, since any differences between the speech styles and conversational skills of the two groups are sure to increase rather than decrease with continued segregation. Finally, different experiences in childhood may affect the speech styles of adults (Maltz and Borker 1982), even when men and women are not segregated during adulthood.

Speech Differences and Their Relation to Gender

A second approach to the relation between gender and language begins with speech differences and asks how they might be related to gender. We will consider five such differences here: (1) different contexts in which speech takes place, (2) different speech resources, (3) different topics and genres of speech, (4) different ways of using language to interact, and (5) different rules for speaking.

Conversational Contexts

Different contexts require and produce different ways of speaking. It is unlikely that anyone would be surprised to find that talk between two lovers in a bedroom is different from talk between a food vendor and customer in the market, or a mother and her daughter in the kitchen. To the extent that gender affects the contexts in which one operates, it certainly affects the ways in which one speaks. Telling the same tale in different contexts involves more than a social difference; it is a different linguistic act as well.

Conversational contexts may be gender restricted through either *exclusion,* where the context itself is restricted to only one gender, or *disenfranchisement,* where the context is open but the right to speak is gender-restricted. The first is exemplified by speech within exclusive men's clubs, or women's quilting bees, by speech in work groups where work is sexually segregated (Harding 1975), or in sex-segregated play or school groups. The second is exemplified by male storytelling sessions in the general stores of Newfoundland (Faris 1966), church services among the Plymouth Brethren [studied by Borker], who believe that "women should remain silent" when men are present in church, and political council meetings in parts of Melanesia (Lederman 1980) in which political oratory is culturally defined as inappropriate for women speakers.

Linguistic Resources

In many speech communities there exists more than one major way of speaking: different languages, dialects, or speech styles. Both control over these different speech resources and patterns for using them may vary according to gender. Where different ways of speaking are equally valued, different languages, dialects, or accents may distinguish between communities in a single local area. In such a situation, the distribution of linguistic resources by gender is closely tied to marriage and residence patterns. Where residence is virilocal, for example, the men of a local community will all speak the same way while women will not share speech resources with either men or other in-marrying women.

More often, particularly in present-day nation-states, linguistic codes within a community are in a hierarchical relationship with one another. One language or dialect is a local form, the other the shared linguistic form of a larger area such as a nation. Control over and use of these different languages or dialects can be related to gender in several different ways: access, usefulness, cultural associations, and social boundary marking. First, individuals with greater contact beyond the local community are more likely to learn the second language. Since men are often the ones who must work on plantations, mines, factories, etc., or attend schools while women remain in their homes, men often have greater facility in a second language. Second, nonlocalized languages and dialects are more often learned and used by those who find them socially useful, usually men who are more likely to work outside the home. But control over a second linguistic code can be of use to women as well as men. For example, it is useful to Italian immigrant women in Toronto (Rayfield 1976) who desire access to a wider range of shopping opportunities and to the ability to deal with important bureaucracies, particularly the school system, or among Hungarian-speakers in Austria (Gal 1978), where women have a greater interest than men in marrying out of the local area, and are therefore more likely to use the nonlocal language [in this case German] than men. When the difference is one of dialect rather than language, the needs of men and women to speak the more standard, less localized form are likely to vary by class. Third, knowledge of a non-local second language or more informal speech style may have cultural associations of "worldliness." For women this may become a sign of questionable sexual reputation or immodesty leading them to avoid the language, for men a sign of status (Abrahams 1975).

Finally, shifts between local and nonlocal speech forms may be used to convey messages of social identity. In two communities in Central America (Farber 1978; Hill 1987), men have been documented as shifting between Spanish, indicating prestige, power, and sophistication, and local Indian languages, indicating community solidarity. In both cases women are constrained from using this linguistic shift to the same extent as men. Overuse of the local language is seen as backwardness and a handicap to their children. Overuse of Spanish, on the other hand, is equally criticized for distancing their children from the local community. Among women in rural Norway, in contrast, Karen Larson (1982) observes a pattern of code switching between a local and national dialect within the course of a single conversation or utterance. Local dialect is used in most mother-child conversation, but standard is used to invoke seriousness and authority.

Topics and Genres

In many societies, particularly small-scale societies, a major distinction between men's and women's speech is a difference in genres (Sherzer 1987). Folklorists (Jordan and deCaro 1986:509–514) have noted that certain genres, particularly lullabies, laments, and urban legends, as opposed to other more publicly performed genres, tend to be associated with women. All too often a difference in genres and topics is dismissed as an aspect of folklore with little linguistic significance. Different genres, however, may differ on a wide variety of linguistic features from morphology to syntax as well as discourse rules and patterns of interaction.

Topic is one basis on which a genre of speech may become gender-associated. Like pop fiction in highly literate cultures, different genres of speech may be seen as reflecting the interests and knowledge of one gender or the other. Female biology including childbirth is a topic frequently used to associate speech genres such as pregnancy proverbs, Mormon visionary narratives (Brady 1987), "procreation stories" (Ginsburg 1987), and Egyptian illness narratives (Early 1985) with women. Even specific vocabulary items, particularly those concerned with sexuality and reproduction, may be gender-associated. Menstrual terms and euphemisms (Ernster 1975; Hays 1987; Joffe 1948), for example, show variation by gender as well as culture or subculture. Vocabulary changes may also express changing relations between men and women, as in the case of the introduction of the word "menopause" into English by male doctors in the Victorian era to replace the more gender-neutral term "climacteric." This was part of the process of medicalization of an experience that women had previously considered natural and handled through consultations with female popular healers or conversations with other women (Wilbush 1981).

Cultural conceptions of gender difference may also serve as a basis for differentiating genres by gender. Such dichotomies as emotionality/rationality, nurturance/aggression, and domestic/public, which are frequently linked to gender difference, may serve to categorize genres as being either male or female. Among the Weyéwa of western Sumba (Kuipers 1986), for example, divination is male speech because men are authoritative, and laments are female because women evoke emotions.

Additional insights into the association of certain genres with women is provided by the concept of "mutedness," developed by Edwin and Shirley Ardener and further elaborated by Warren and Bourque (1985), who assert that often the official ideology of a culture is constructed and expressed by men. The alternative women's social discourse is more obscure and often embedded in more remote genres of speech, such as courtship songs (Kodish 1983), jealousy songs (Johnston 1978), and marriage laments (Blake 1978, 1979). A particularly good example of an alternative social vision expressed in women's genres is the case of the wedding songs of North India (Narayan 1986), in which the bride's childhood girlfriends express twin sentiments of sorrow at the dispersal of their friendship cohort and longing for their own weddings. In song, these girls assert a sentiment that would be unspeakable in any other context: urging their fathers to hurry up and arrange their weddings.

The personal narrative is a privileged form in Western eyes, tied to *our* concepts of self. It is the form through which the individual gives expression to his or her personal voice. But it does not exist everywhere, and in some places it appears to be more a male than a female form. This fact is another expression of the outsiders' experiences of women in some cultures as "muted." For the telling of personal narratives to make sense, there must be some balance between two conditions: the story one has to tell is both shared enough to be intelligible and interesting to one's audience and yet different enough to be worth telling.

The way in which this balance works and may be related to gender is illuminated with the three ethnographic examples that follow. Both Keesing (1985) and Young (1983) report the difficulty of collecting autobiographies from women in Melanesia, and they relate this fact to notions of cultural mutedness. Young points out that although personal narratives are not an indigenous form for either men or women, men take to them much more readily than do women. He notes that the narrative he collected from a woman still appears to present her life from a man's-eye-view rather than her own. Narrative does not appear to allow a Melanesian woman to speak with her own voice. In Kelibia, Tunisia (Webber 1985) women traditionally told fantasy stories *(khurafahs),* while personal narratives or true stories *(hikayahs)* were restricted to men. The reason was that women had little experience beyond the confines of their own homes and therefore little to tell stories about. As women have increased their contact with the outside world, they have begun telling personal experience narratives, stories of encounters with outsiders such as merchants and medical personnel. Strikingly, some of these stories resemble fictional narratives more than do the personal narratives of men. Finally, there is the case of the "kernel stories," which Kalcik (1975) reports from American women's rap groups, stories alluded to but not told when groups of women gather to provide "support" for one another as they exchange experiences. These are stories related to express commonality rather than differences in experience. Again it is striking that the topics for doing so come so often from the medical-sexual-reproductive domain, including rape and gynecological examinations.

Speech As Interaction

Speech is, among other things, interaction. Much of the work focusing on men's and women's speech styles addresses this interactional dimension of language use, showing the ways in which speech forms define options for interlocutors and structure their relationships to one another. Brown (1980), for example, looks at polite language forms as strategic responses women make to their circumstances. Arguing that the social and physical vulnerability of women in Tenejapa forces them to take a more distant and circumspect stance in interactions, she shows that men and women differ systematically in their politeness strategies. Among the Malagasy, on the other hand, women are the ones who use a more direct style, while men are indirect (Keenan 1974a, 1974b). While men's "windy speech" serves to express and create egalitarian relationships, women's speech, while barring them from public politics, provides them with the social power to bring interpersonal conflict into the open, elicit direct responses, and interact appropriately with Europeans. Among children in both the United States (Goodwin 1980) and Norway (Berentzen 1984), the difference between the more hierarchical leader-oriented play groups of boys and the more egalitarian dyads of girls is reflected in different linguistic forms.

Rules for Speaking

Differences in experience including socialization lead to different rules for speaking and interpreting speech. This is what cultural or subcultural differences in language use are all about. These cultural differences are of many kinds, including appropriate speed of speech, quantity of speech, rules for topic change, for interruption, for emphasizing major points, for shifting speakers, and for audience participation. To the extent that males and females are consciously or unconsciously socialized differently or that voluntary gender-segregation occurs in childhood, there may exist different gender cultures for speaking.

Rules for different kinds of speech are learned in different contexts, however, so the relation of gender to differences in rules for speaking is complex. As we have argued elsewhere (Maltz and Borker 1982), in contemporary North America it is rules for friendly conversation in particular that are learned in the sex-segregated contexts of childhood, so it is especially in informal friendly conversations where we would expect men and women to be most likely to use different rules. Holland (1987) extends this argument by asking more generally when culture is shared across gender. In her study of a southern university, she discovers that, contrary to expectations, male and female students are more likely to agree on the meanings of terms concerned with romance than those concerned with academics. Apparently the meaning of sexual topics is more likely to be negotiated in cross-gender interaction, while more academic topics are negotiated among single-sex groups of friends.

Differences in men's and women's assumptions about language and for interaction may mean that even when they seem to be engaging in the same types of communicative acts, men and women are in fact doing very different things. Using data from a midwestern college, Bruner and Kelso (1980) argue that this is the case in writing graffiti—women are producing interactive, interpersonal advisory communications, while men are asserting themselves in egocentric, competitive, derogatory inscriptions. Davies (1986) provides a more extended analysis of the collective advice form of graffiti that seem to be unique to women. She analyzes her West Coast data as a conversation, working out the order of contribution and demonstrating the ways in which each successive inscription responds to those that precede it. This allows her to address the use of "humor" and the need to extend notions of irony to understand women's usages.

Kalcik (1975) provides a fuller analysis of the rules that govern conversation and storytelling in women's rap groups. She reports the existence of strategies of serializing, filling in, tying together, and humor, giving the interaction an overall coherence. Although there seem to be frequent interruptions and interjections, they contribute to the coproduction of talk through establishing a framework of mutual orientation that constrains the expression of certain competitive forms. The contrast between the collective narratives produced by women and single "performer" narratives produced by men is also central to Limón's (1983) discussion of Mexican-American recountings of legends and antilegends. He contrasts a joint narration of the vanishing hitchhiker legend by a group of women with a joke based on the same narrative told later by a man in terms of differences in aesthetic, social structure, and assumptions about ethnic identity and its expression.

Conclusion

The purpose of this module has been to expand the scope of the study of gender and language and to bring it closer to the central concerns of anthropology. Language, after all, is a part of culture, and speech is a form of social action. The study of gender and language presents a significant theoretical challenge to all of the social and behavioral sciences because speech and language need to be studied from a micro perspective, focusing on specifics of individual utterances, while gender and power can only be adequately studied from a more macro perspective, focusing attention on context and on the cultural construction of meaning.

Good language-oriented research can provide a model for other anthropological studies of gender, focusing attention on cultural repertoires, choices, strategies, constraints, and the power of the cultural code itself. But the study of gender and language still has much to learn from the rest of anthropology as well. The concept of gender needs to be treated as more problematic, as an aspect of the situation rather than of the individual. There needs to be more attention given to the complexity of the relation between culture and power, which can lead to more adequate understandings of the many ways in which control over linguistic and rhetorical forms can convey power. Some forms, such as orders or commands, are inherently powerful; some are culturally attributed with power. Some forms gain their power from association with powerful individuals and groups, some gain power from association with powerful social roles, and sometimes power comes not from the form itself but from greater competence in its use. Understanding language, culture, and power as these are interconnected necessitates analysis of gender, as well as race, ethnicity, and class.

References Cited

Abrahams, Roger David
  1975   Negotiating Respect: Patterns of Presentation among Black Women. Journal of American Folklore 88(347):58–80.
Abu-Lughod, Lila
  1985   Honor and the Sentiments of Loss in a Bedouin Society. American Ethnologist 12(2):245–261.
  1986   Veiled Sentiments: Honor and Poetry in a Bedouin Society. Berkeley: University of California Press.
Ager, Lynn Price
  1974   Storyknifing: An Alaskan Eskimo Girls' Game. Journal of the Folklore Institute 11(3):187–198.
  1979   Acculturation in Alaskan Eskimo Storyknife Tales. *In* Forms of Play of Native North Americans. Edward Norbeck & Claire R. Farrer, eds. Pp. 77–88. St. Paul, Minn.: West Publishing.
Beatty, John
  1979   Sex, Role, and Sex Role. New York Academy of Science. Annals 327:43–49.
Bendix, Edward W.
  1979   Linguistic Models as Political Symbols: Gender and the Generic "He" in English. New York Academy of Science. Annals 327:23–39.
Berentzen, Sigurd
  1984   Children Constructing Their Social World: An Analysis of Gender Contrast in Children's Interaction in a Nursery School. Bergen, Norway: University of Bergen Occasional Papers in Social Anthropology, 36.
Blake, C[harles] Fredric
  1978   Death and Abuse in Marriage Laments: The Curse of Chinese Brides. Asian Folklore Studies 37(1):13–33.
  1979   The Feelings of Chinese Daughters toward their Mothers as Revealed in Marriage Laments. Folklore 90(1):91–97.
Blount, Benny Garell
  1977   Ethnography and Caretaker-Child Interaction. *In* Talking to Children: Language Input and Acquisition. Catherine E. Snow and Charles A. Ferguson, eds. Pp. 297–308. Cambridge: Cambridge University Press.
Blount, Benny Garell, and Elise J. Padgug
  1976   Mother and Father Speech: Distribution of Parental Speech Features in English and Spanish. Papers and Reports on Child Language Development 12:47–59.
Bodine, Ann Mary
  1975a   Androcentrism in Prescriptive Grammar: Singular "They," Sex-indefinite "He," and "He or She." Language in Society 4:129–146.
  1975b   Sex Differentiation in Language. *In* Language and Sex: Difference and Dominance. Barrie Thorne and Nancy Henley, eds. Pp. 130–151. Rowley, Mass.: Newbury House.
Borker, Ruth Ann
  1980   Anthropology: Social and Cultural Perspectives. *In* Women and Language in Literature and Society. Sally McConnell-Ginet, Ruth A. Borker, and Nelly Furman, eds. Pp. 26–44. New York: Praeger.

Brady, Margaret K.
  1987   Transformations of Power: Mormon Women's Visionary Narratives. Journal of American
      Folklore 100(398):461–468.
Brandes, Stanley Howard
  1974   Space and Speech at the Olive Harvest. Metaphors of Masculinity. Pp. 137–157. Philadel-
      phia: University of Pennsylvania Press.
Brown, Penelope
  1976   Women and Politeness: A New Perspective on Language and Society. Reviews in Anthro-
      pology 3(3):240–249.
  1980   How and Why are Women More Polite: Some Evidence from a Mayan Community. *In*
      Women and Language in Literature and Society. Sally McConnell-Ginet, Ruth A. Borker, and
      Nelly Furman, eds. Pp. 111–136. New York: Praeger.
Brukman, Jan C.
  1975   "Tongue Play": Constitutive and Interpretive Properties of Sexual Joking Encounters among
      the Koya of South India. *In* Sociocultural Dimensions of Language Use. Mary Sanches and Ben
      G. Blount, eds. Pp. 235–268. New York: Academic Press.
Bruner, Edward M., and Jane Paige Kelso
  1980   Gender Differences in Graffiti: A Semiotic Perspective. Women's Studies InternationaL Quar-
      terly 3(2/3):239–252.
Caudill, William Abel
  1972   Tiny Dramas: Vocal Communication between Mother and Infant in Japanese and American
      Families *In* Transcultural Research in Mental Health: Mental Health Research in Asia and the Pa-
      cific. William P. Lebra, ed. Pp. 25–48. Honolulu: University of Hawaii.
Dauer, Sheila A.
  1984   Haya Greetings: The Negotiation of Relative Status. Ph.D. dissertation, University of Penn-
      sylvania.
Davies, Catherine E.
  1986   The Anonymous Collective Conversations of Women's Graffiti: Analysis of Supportive Ad-
      vice-giving. *In* Proceedings of the First Berkeley Women and Language Conference, 1985. Sue
      Bremner, Noelle Caskey, and Birch Moonwomon, eds. Pp. 108–134. Berkeley: Berkeley Women
      and Language Group.
Early, Evelyn Aleene
  1982   The Logic of Well Being: Therapeutic Narratives of Cairo, Egypt. Social Science and Medi-
      cine 16(4):1491–1498.
  1985   Catharsis and Creation in Informal Narratives of Baladi Women in Cairo. Anthropological
      Quarterly 58(4):172–181.
Ecklund, Judith L.
  1977   Sasak Culture Change, Ritual Change, and the Use of Ritualized Language. Indonesia 24:1–
      25.
Ernster, Virginia Lee
  1975   American Menstrual Expressions. Sex Roles 1(1):3–13.
Farber, Anne
  1978   Social and Sexual Constraints on Bilingualism in a Highland Mayan Town. PhD thesis, Co-
      lumbia University.
Faris, James Chester
  1966   The Dynamics of Verbal Exchange: A Newfoundland Example. Anthropologica 8(2):235–
      248.
  1972   Cat Harbor: A Newfoundland Fishing Settlement. St. John's: Institute of Social and Economic
      Research, Memorial University of Newfoundland.
Farrer, Claire Anne Rafferty
  1975   Introduction: Women and Folklore: Images and Genres. Journal of American Folklore
      88(347):vii–xvi.

Farris, Catherine S.
  1988   Gender and Grammar in Chinese: With Implications for Language Universals. Modern China 14(3):277–308.
Fernandez, James William
  1977   Poetry in Motion: Being Moved by Amusement, by Mockery, and by Mortality in the Asturian Countryside. New Literary History 8(3):459–483.
Fischer, John Lyle
  1970   Linguistic Socialization: Japan and the United States. *In* Families in East and West. Rueben Hill and Rene König, eds. Pp. 107–119. The Hague: Mouton.
Fiske, Shirley Jeanette
  1978   Rules of Address: Navajo Women in Los Angeles. Journal of Anthropological Research 34(1):72–91.
Gal, Susan
  1978   Peasant Men Can't Get Wives: Language Change and Sex Roles in a Bilingual Community. Language in Society 7(1):1–16.
Gardner, Carol Brooks
  1980   Passing By: Street Remarks, Address Rights, and the Urban Female. Sociological Inquiry 50(3/4):328–356.
Ginsburg, Faye
  1987   Procreation Stories: Reproduction, Nurturance, and Procreation in Life Narratives of Abortion Activists. American Ethnologist 14(4):623–636.
Gleason, Jean Berko
  1987   Sex Differences in Parent-Child Interaction. *In* Language, Gender and Sex in Comparative Perspective. Susan Philips, Susan Steele, and Christine Tanz, eds. Pp. 189–199. Cambridge: Cambridge University Press.
Goldstein, Judith Lynne
  1986   Iranian Jewish Women's Magical Narratives. *In* Discourse and the Social Life of Meaning. Phyllis Pease Chock and June R. Wyman, eds. Pp. 147–168. Washington, D.C.: Smithsonian Institution.
Goodwin, Marjorie Harness
  1980a   Directive-response Speech Sequences in Girls' and Boys' Task Activities. *In* Women and Language in Literature and Society. Sally McConnell-Ginet, Ruth A. Borker, and Nelly Furman, eds. Pp. 157–173. New York: Praeger.
  1980b   He-said-she-said: Formal Cultural Procedures for the Construction of a Gossip Dispute Activity. American Ethnologist 7(4):674–695.
  1985   The Serious Side of Jump Rope: Conversational Practices and Social Organization in the Frame of Play. Journal of American Folklore 98(389):315–330.
  1988   Cooperation and Competition across Girls' Play Activities. *In* Gender and Discourse: The Power of Talk. Alexandra D. Todd and Sue Fisher, eds. Norwood, N.J.: Ablex.
Goodwin, Marjorie Harness, and Charles Goodwin
  1987   Children's Arguing. *In* Language, Gender, and Sex in Comparative Perspective. Susan Philips, Susan Steele, and Christine Tanz, eds. Pp. 200–248. Cambridge: Cambridge University Press.
Gregersen, Edgar Alstrup
  1979   Sexual Linguistics. New York Academy of Science. Annals 327:3–19.
Harding, Susan Friend
  1975   Women and Words in a Spanish Village. *In* Toward an Anthropology of Women. Rayna Reiter, ed. Pp. 283–308. New York: Monthly Review Press.
  1978   Street Shouting and Shunning: Conflict between Women in a Spanish Village. Frontiers 3:14–18.
Harkness, Sara
  1975   Cultural Variation in Mothers' Language. Word 27:495–498.
  1977   Aspects of Social Environment and First Language Acquisition in Rural Africa. *In* Talking to Children: Language Input and Acquisition. Catherine E. Snow and Charles A. Ferguson, eds. Pp. 309–316. Cambridge: Cambridge University Press.

Hays, Terence Eugene
    1987   Menstrual Expressions and Menstrual Attitudes. Sex Roles 16(11/12):605–614.
Herzfeld, Michael F.
    1985a   Gender Pragmatics: Agency, Speech and Bride-theft in a Cretan Mountain Village. Anthropology [Stony Brook] 9(1/2):25–44.
    1985b   The Poetics of Manhood: Context and Identity in a Cretan Mountain Village. Princeton, N.J.: Princeton University Press.
Hill, Jane H.
    1987   Women's Speech in Modern Mexicano. Language, Gender, and Sex in Comparative Perspective. Susan Philips, Susan Steele, and Christine Tanz, eds. Pp. 121–160. Cambridge: Cambridge University Press.
Holland, Dorothy
    1987   Culture Sharing across Gender Lines. American Behavioral Scientist 31(2):234–249.
Hunt, Geoffrey, and Saundra Satterlee
    1987   Darts, Drink and the Pub: The Culture of Female Drinking. Sociological Review 35(3):575–601.
Ide, Sachiko
    1982   Japanese Sociolinguistics: Politeness and Women's Language. Lingua 57:357–385.
Jabbra, Nancy Walstrom
    1980   Sex Roles and Language in Lebanon. Ethnology 19(4):459–474.
James, Jennifer J.
    1972a   Two Domains of Streetwalker Argot. Anthropological Linguistics 14(5):172–181.
    1972b   Sweet Cream Ladies: An Introduction to Prostitute Taxonomy. Western Canadian Journal of Anthropology 3(2):102–118.
Joffe, Natalie Frankel
    1948   Vernacular of Menstruation. Word 4(3):181–186.
Johnston, Thomas Frederick
    1978   Conflict Resolution in Tsonga Co-wifely Jealousy Songs. Africana Marburgensia 11(2):15–26.
Jordan, Rosan, and Susan J. Kalcik, eds.
    1985   Women's Folklore, Women's Culture. Philadelphia: University of Pennsylvania Press.
Jordan, Rosan, and F. A. de Caro
    1986   Review Essay: Women and the Study of Folklore. Signs 11(3):500–518.
Kalcik, Susan J.
    1975   ". . . like Ann's gynecologist or the time I was almost raped": Personal Narratives in Women's Rap Groups. Journal of American Folklore 88(347):3–11.
Keenan, Elinor Ochs
    1974a   In's and Out's of Women's Speech. Cambridge Anthropology 1(3):61–70.
    1974b   Norm Makers, Norm Breakers: Use of Speech by Men and Women in a Malagasy Community. In Explorations in the Ethnography of Speaking. Richard Bauman and Joel Sherzer, eds. Pp. 125–143. Cambridge: Cambridge University Press.
Keesing, Roger Martin
    1985   Kwaio Women Speak: The Micropolitics of Autobiography in a Solomon Island Society. American Anthropologist 87(1):27–39.
Kligman, Gail Ann
    1984   The Rites of Women: Oral Poetry, Ideology and Socialization of Peasant Women in Contemporary Romania. Journal of American Folklore 97(384):167–188.
Kodish, Debora Gail
    1983   Fair Young Ladies and Bonny Irish Boys: Pattern in Vernacular Poetics. Journal of American Folklore 96(380):131–150.
    1987   Absent Gender, Silent Encounter. Journal of American Folklore 100(398):573–578.
Krige, Eileen Jensen
    1968   Girls' Puberty Songs and Their Relation to Fertility, Health, Morality, and Religion among the Zulu. Africa 38(2):173–198.

Kuipers, Joel Corneal
1986   Talking about Troubles: Gender Differences in Weyéwa Speech Use. American Ethnologist 13(3):448–462.
Lakoff, Robin
1975   Language and Woman's Place. New York: Harper & Row.
Larson, Karen Ann
1982   Role Playing and the Real Thing: Socialization and Standard Speech in Norway. Journal of Anthropological Research 38(4):401–410.
Layton, Monique Jacqueline Berthe
1978   Street Women and Their Verbal Transactions: Some Aspects of the Oral Culture of Female Prostitute Drug Addicts. PhD thesis, University of British Columbia.
Lederman, Rena
1980   Who Speaks Here? Formality and the Politics of Gender in Mendi. Journal of the Polynesian Society 89(4):479–498.
Lewis, E. Douglas
1982   The Metaphorical Expression of Gender and Dual Classification in Tana Ai Ritual Language. Canberra Anthropology 5(1):47–59.
Limón, José Eduardo
1980   "La vieja Ines," a Mexican Folk Game: A Research Note. *In* Twice a Minority: Mexican American Women. Margarita Melville, ed. Pp. 88–94. St. Louis: C. V. Mosby.
1983   Legendry, Metafolklore, and Performance: A Mexican-American Example. Western Folklore 42(3):191–208.
Lybrand, Donna Gale
1982   Gender-specific Speech Features: A Sociolinguistic Inquiry into the Language of Males and Females in an Andalusian Agrotown. PhD thesis, Southern Methodist University.
Maltz, Daniel Nathan, and Ruth Ann Borker
1982   A Cultural Approach to Male/Female Miscommunication. *In* Language and Social Identity. John Gumperz, ed. Pp. 196–210. Cambridge: Cambridge University Press.
Mann, Brenda J.
1974   Bar Talk. *In* Conformity and Conflict: Readings in Cultural Anthropology. 2d edition. James P. Spradley and David W. McCurdy, eds. Pp. 101–111. Boston: Little, Brown.
March, Kathryn S.
1983   Weaving, Writing and Gender. Man 18(4):729–744.
Meditch, Andrea
1975   The Development of Sex-Specific Speech Patterns in Young Children. Anthropological Linguistics 17(9):421–433.
Munroe, Robert Leon, and Ruth H. Munroe
1969   A Cross-cultural Study of Sex, Gender, and Social Structure. Ethnology 8(2):206–211.
Narayan, Kirin
1986   Birds on a Branch: Girlfriends and Wedding Songs in Kangra. Ethos 14(1):47–75.
O'Barr, William McAlston, and Bowman Kimble Atkins
1980   "Women's language" or "powerless language"? Women and Language in Literature and Society. Sally McConnell-Ginet, Ruth A. Borker, and Nelly Furman, eds. Pp. 93–110. New York: Praeger.
Ochs, Elinor
1987   The Impact of Stratification and Socialization on Men's and Women's Speech in Western Samoa. *In* Language, Gender, and Sex in Comparative Perspective. Susan Philips, Susan Steele, and Christine Tanz, eds. Pp. 50–70. Cambridge: Cambridge University Press.
Oswalt, Wendell Hillman
1964   Traditional Storyknife Tales of Yuk Girls. Proceedings of the American Philosophical Society 108(4):310–336.
Peng, Frederick Che-Ching
1982   Sex Differentiation in Language Variation: A Sociolinguistic Contribution to the Language Sciences. Language Sciences 4(2):131–154.

Philips, Susan
    1980   Sex Differences and Language. Annual Review in Anthropology 9:523–544.
Philips, Susan, and Anne Reynolds
    1987   The Interaction of Variable Syntax and Discourse Structure in Women's and Men's Speech. Language, Gender, and Sex in Comparative Perspective. Susan Philips, Susan Steele, and Christine Tanz, eds. Pp. 71–94. Cambridge University Press.
Rayfield, Joan Rachel
    1976   Maria in Markham Street: Italian Immigrants and Language-learning in Toronto. Ethnic Groups 1(2):133–150.
Reynolds, Katsue Akiba
    1985   Female Speakers of Japanese. Feminist Issues 5(2):13–45.
    1986   Female Speakers of Japanese in Transition. *In* Proceedings of the First Berkeley Women and Language Conference, 1985. Sue Bremner, Noelle Caskey, and Birch Moonwomon, eds. Pp. 183–196. Berkeley: Berkeley Women and Language Group.
Riddington, [William] Robbins, Jr.
    1983   Stories of the Vision Quest among Dunne-za Women. Atlantis 9:68–78.
Rosaldo, Michelle Zimbalist, and Jane Monnig Atkinson
    1975   Man the Hunter and Woman: Metaphors for the Sexes in Ilongot Magical Spells. *In* The Interpretation of Symbolism. Roy Willis, ed. Pp. 43–75. London: Malaby Press.
Schieffelin, Bambi Bernhard
    1979   Getting It Together: An Ethnographic Approach to the Development of Communicative Competence. *In* Developmental Pragmatics. Elinor Ochs and Bambi Schieffelin, eds. Pp. 73–108. New York: Academic Press.
    1987   Do Different Worlds Mean Different Words? An Example from Papua New Guinea. *In* Language, Gender, and Sex in Comparative Perspective. Susan Philips, Susan Steele, and Christine Tanz, eds. Pp. 249–260. Cambridge: Cambridge University Press.
Sherzer, Joel
    1987   A Diversity of Voices: Men's and Women's Speech in Ethnographic Perspective. *In* Language, Gender, and Sex in Comparative Perspective. Susan Philips, Susan Steele, and Christine Tanz, eds. Pp. 95–120. Cambridge: Cambridge University Press.
Shibamoto, Janet Sutherland
    1981   Sex-related Variation in the Production of Predicate Types in Japanese. Language Sciences 3(2):257–282.
    1985   Japanese Women's Language. Orlando: Academic Press.
    1987   The Womanly Woman: Manipulation of Stereotypical and Nonstereotypical Features of Japanese Female Speech. *In* Language, Gender, and Sex in Comparative Perspective. Susan Philips, Susan Steele, and Christine Tanz, eds. Pp. 26–49. Cambridge: Cambridge University Press.
Siegel, James Theodore
    1978   Curing Rites, Dreams, and Domestic Politics in a Sumatran Society. Glyph 3:18–31.
Silverman, Sydel Finfer
    1975   Talking. Three Bells for Civilization: The Life of an Italian Hill Town. Pp. 36–38. New York: Columbia University Press.
Silverstein, Michael
    1985   Language and the Culture of Gender: At the Intersection of Structure, Usage, and Ideology. Semiotic Mediation: Sociocultural and Psychological Perspectives. Elizabeth Mertz and Richard J. Parmentier, eds. Pp. 219–259. Orlando: Academic Press.
Smith Heffner, Nancy J.
    1988   Women and Politeness: The Javanese Example. Language in Society 17(4):535–554.
Spradley, James Phillip, and Brenda J. Mann
    1975   The Cocktail Waitress: Women's Work in a Man's World. New York: John Wiley and Sons.
Stoeltje, Beverly June Smith
    1973   Bow-legged Bastard: "A manner of speaking" Speech Behavior of a Black Woman. Folklore Annual [Austin, Texas] 4/5:152–178.

Suárez-Orozco, Marcelo M. & Alan Dundes
  1984   The Piropo and the Dual Image of Women in the Spanish-speaking World. Journal of Latin
     American Lore 10(1):111–133.
Tannen, Deborah
  1983   "I take out the rock—Dok!": How Greek Women Tell About Being Molested (and Create
     Involvement). Anthropological Linguistics 25(3):359–374.
Tannen, Deborah, and Cynthia Wallat
  1983   Doctor/Mother/Child Communication: Linguistic Analysis of a Pediatric Interaction. *In* The
     Social Organization of Doctor-Patient Communication. Sue Fisher and Alexandra Dundas Todd,
     eds. Pp. 203–219. Washington, D.C.: Center for Applied Linguistics.
Ullrich, Helen E.
  1975   Etiquette Among Women in Karnataka: Forms of Address in the Village and Family. *In*
     Women in Contemporary India: Traditional Images and Changing Roles. Alfred deSouza, ed. Pp.
     54–72. Delhi: Manohar Book Service.
Underwood, Kelsey Clark
  1983   The Bounds of Intimacy: Interactions among Women in Madras, India. Kroeber Anthropo-
     logical Society. Papers 61/62:69–77.
Warren, Kay Barbara, and Susan C. Bourque
  1985   Gender, Power, and Communication: Women's Responses to Political Muting in the Andes.
     In Women Living Change. Susan C. Bourque and Donna R. Divine, eds. Pp. 255–286. Philadel-
     phia: Temple University Press.
Webber, Sabra
  1985   Women's Folk Narratives and Social Change. *In* Women and the Family in the Middle East.
     Elizabeth Fernea, ed. Pp. 310–316. Austin: University of Texas Press.
Weil, Shalva J.
  1983   Women and Language in Israel. Journal of the Sociology of Language 41:77–91.
Whitehead, Ann
  1976   Sexual Antagonism in Herefordshire. *In* Dependence and Exploitation in Work and Marriage.
     Diana Leonard Barker and Sheila Allen, eds. Pp. 169–203. New York: Longman.
Wilbush, Joel
  1981   What's in a Name? Some Linguistic Aspects of the Climacteric. Maturitas 3:1–9.
Williams, Brett
  1975   Serving up Selves and Preserving the Self: Waitresses at Work. Journal of the Steward An-
     thropological Society 6(2):90–116.
Wright, Susan A.
  1978   Prattle and Politics: The Position of Women in Doshman-Ziari. Journal of the Anthropological
     Society of Oxford 9(2):98–112.
Wynn, Eleanor Herasimchuk
  1980   The Secretary as an Information Resource. Working Papers in Sociolinguistics, 78.
Young, Michael W.
  1983   "Our name is women": We Are Bought with Limesticks and Limepots: An Analysis of the
     Autobiographical Narrative of a Kalauna Woman. Man 18(3):478–501.

Curricular Examples

Gossip and Gender in Western Society

In Western society, gossip is a speech genre frequently associated with women. Why it might be associated with women and what this says about language and social structure provides a valuable topic for class discussion and analysis. For structuring such a discussion, we find it useful to distinguish five aspects of speech acts that might cause them to be classified as gossip and be associated with women: content, participants, social structure, location, and linguistic/rhetorical form.

First, gossip is defined by content as talk about people not present but known by the participants in the conversation. Students may be asked what differences in the content of women's as opposed to men's speech make it more likely to be classified as gossip. If women talk more about people and less about things than men, if women tell fewer personal narratives, fewer jokes, and fewer tall tales, then the talk of women is more likely to be called gossip.

Second, the identity of the participants themselves is a possible basis for labeling a speech act as gossip. The same speech act is more likely to be labeled gossip if the participants are female rather than male. A prototype of gossip is the talk at a coffee klatch or bridge party of housewives and mothers. The more the participants in a conversation resemble this prototype, the more likely the conversation is to be seen as gossip.

Third, the location of a speech act may contribute to its being labeled as gossip. The prototype of gossip is conversation that takes place in private, particularly in homes and yards (perhaps over the back fence) rather than at work or other "public" locales. To the extent that the home is the domain of women rather than men, gossip may be identified with women.

Fourth, gossip may be associated with a certain social organization of talk. Speaking in large groups with a primary speaker and an audience is less likely to be considered gossip than speaking one-to-one in smaller groups. To the extent that this social form is more characteristic of men than of women, gossip is a characteristic of women's speech.

In the Newfoundland community of Cat Harbour, James Faris (1966, 1972) found that residents distinguish two major types of verbal exchange, "news" and "gossip," and "only women gossip; men don't gossip, they tell cuffers" (Faris 1972:144). One of the major bases for making this distinction, Faris observes, is the social organization of talk. Gossip, he notes, takes place in private, in kitchens and across back fences between two women at a time. News is discussed in the general store, a more public locale, where groups of men gather together to share information. Women's talk, called gossip, is dyadic exchange, while men's talk is performance before a group. When men have information to relate, they wait until they have gathered a large enough audience. Women prefer to exchange their information on a one-to-one basis.

Finally, a speech act is more likely to be considered gossip if it has certain linguistic and rhetorical features. The same statement made in slightly different ways will be more or less likely to be heard as gossip depending on the specific way in which it is said. It is a valuable exercise to take a simple declarative sentence and reword it in various ways to discover what structural features make it sound more like gossip. Several such features come to mind. First, a statement in the third person such as "Maria is getting married" sounds more like gossip than a statement in the first or second person, such as "I am getting married" or "So you're going to Maria's wedding." Second, including the source of one's information or a history of its transmission within a statement makes it sound more like gossip. Consider, for example, "I heard that Maria's getting married" or even "Sue told me that Judy heard that Maria's getting married." Finally, a question-and-answer structure makes a statement sound more like gossip. Consider again such statements as "Did I tell you that Maria's getting married?" or even "Do you know what I heard? [No, what?] Maria's getting married." To the extent that the speech of women is less often in the first person, more attentive to the context in which speech takes place, and more likely to use questions and other interactive devices, it is more likely to be heard as gossip.

Women, Authority, and Language: The Case of Japanese Teachers

One of the major theoretical points made in Robin Lakoff's classic study of women's language, and one that is all too often overlooked, is that women who occupy positions usually filled by men find themselves in a double bind. If they speak in a manner appropriate to the role, they are heard as unfeminine. If they speak in a manner that is heard as feminine, it is often inappropriate to the role, particularly for displaying power. Japanese women are in such a linguistic double bind. Cultural expectations about the way to sound "like a woman" make it virtually impossible for woman to exercise authority.

Japan is a highly status/rank conscious society, and speech is a primary means through which status is negotiated and maintained. A range of linguistic forms, including lexicon, honorifics, pronouns, verb inflections, and final particles are available in speech for expressing deference, politeness, solidarity, and formality, and serve to define different levels of speech. Final particles, in particular, are used to express speakers' attitudes toward their listeners (Reynolds 1985) and their stance toward their utterances (Shibamoto 1987). They may be used to make some sentences more assertive than others or to increase the degree to which an utterance demands a response.

Japanese is also a language that has long been characterized as having distinct male and female ways of speaking. Features characterizing "women's speech" include special self-reference and address terms, special final particles and exclamations, distinctive pitch and intonational contours, frequent use of honorific style, avoidance of *kango* (Sino-Japanese lexical items), and avoidance of vulgar language (Shibamoto 1985). These elements are seen as giving women's speech its tone of greater politeness and formality (Ide 1982; Reynolds 1985; Shibamoto 1985). The cultural connection made between female speech and womanhood, male speech and manhood, "has been so strong in Japanese culture that use of male speech by a woman tends to be taken as an intention to claim manhood rather than as an intention to fulfill her social role as well as men" (Reynolds 1985:41).

The extent of the problem is illustrated by the case of a female department head in a museum (Gregersen 1970) who found it a "linguistically intolerable situation" to try to sound feminine without undercutting her own authority. She solved her problem by speaking English to her male subordinates. This inventive solution is obviously not an option open to all Japanese women, nor is it appropriate to many situations. One group of speakers for whom it is clearly inappropriate are junior high school teachers, as analyzed by Katsue Akiba Reynolds (1986).

Teaching requires that a woman exert control, as classes typically have 40 or more students. Further, to be effective a teacher must be both attentive and friendly to her students even as the students display a defensive and resistant attitude (Reynolds 1986). What is important for the problem of women teachers is that women have limited access to the particles that are most assertive, that is, particles that impose the speaker's viewpoint or demand a listener's opinion (Reynolds 1985). The pressure on women to display modesty and geniality constrains not only the final particles they can use in declarative and confirmative sentences but also the forms of question they may ask. It forces them to either use a more formal style that creates distance or to undercut the force of their utterance with copula deletion or softening syntax and intonation (Reynolds 1985). Women speakers run into problems as well in the use of imperatives—forceful command forms that not only require that the speaker be superior or at least equal to the hearer but also have an informal/intimate relationship with him or her. Assertive brusqueness and informality together for men can signal solidarity and authority, but women can only use the more assertive forms when combined with ellipsis or in combination with a very formal style. This constrains women from expressing solidarity through informality except with other women in relatively private settings.

Women who deviate from the expected speech styles run the risk of seeming not only unfeminine but also impolite or inappropriately intimate in mixed gender settings. Male teachers can employ a shift between formal speech and an informal male style that asserts both authority and intimacy as a means to engage students and effectively elicit student response through the use of assertive final particles and copula variants. Women teachers do not have these same options. Women's informal style is inappropriate to public and mixed-sex settings and does not maintain authority. Formal style maintains authority but also creates distance. Unlike men, women cannot shift between formal and informal, distant and intimate forms. To be effective teachers, women have no option but to use "defeminized" patterns to strengthen the bond to their students without losing authority. While this works in the classroom, it creates problems with principals and parents as well as creating discomfort for the teacher herself, who feels the contradictory demands of gender identity and professional role. Reynolds cites both a female principal who warned a young woman teacher about her language and a mother concerned that her daughter's speech was becoming "too rough" because of her "teacher's influence."

Teaching Resources

The most useful resources for teaching about language and gender are audiotapes made by the students themselves. Given the ubiquity of cassette tape recorders, it is relatively easy to have undergraduate students record, transcribe, and even analyze conversations that can be further discussed and analyzed in class. Guidelines for such recordings and their analysis as either written assignments or as topics for class discussion include the following:

1. Choose a context in which gender or sexuality is likely to be an important element. This tends to mean either intimate or casual conversation rather than the more official or formal types of conversation that take place in classrooms or other institutional contexts.

2. Analyze in depth the social context of the conversation in terms of opportunities and resources provided and constraints implied. What relationship exists between the participants, and what limitations are being placed on possible actions of participants?

3. Analyze the role of gender and sexuality in both the general social context and the specific interaction. Is a sexual relationship, either serious or playful, being expressed? Are any of the roles of participants genderized (e.g., mother to son)?

4. Examine the specific speech of participants as a series of purposeful social actions. Ask what individuals are doing, what acts are they performing, each time they speak. To what extent are each of these actions expressing gender or sexual identity? To what extent do gender-specific experiences or assumptions come into play in the interaction?

5. Examine patterns of discourse, the linkages between utterances, in terms of the kind of relationship between participants being expressed or created and the models of appropriate interaction being used by participants.

6. Examine syntactic forms (e.g., questions, directives, various pronominal forms) in relation to their functions in social interaction. Are any differences in usage based on the

gender of the speaker, and, if so, how might these differences be related to gender-specific experiences and assumptions?

7. Examine the ways in which things are said, the intonational and prosodic features of the speech. What do these features indicate about the speakers' intents and self-presentations? Are there gender differences in the way these forms are used or interpreted?

Annotated Bibliography

Abrahams, Roger David
  1975   Negotiating Respect: Patterns of Presentation among Black Women. Journal of American Folklore 88(347):58–80.

  Speech patterns of black women are discussed in terms of cultural concepts of "respectability," "talking sweet," "talking smart," and the opposition between house and street.

Berentzen, Sigurd
  1984   Children Constructing Their Social World: An Analysis of Gender Contrast in Children's Interaction in a Nursery School. Bergen, Norway: University of Bergen Occasional Papers in Social Anthropology, 36.

  Among 4- to 7-year-old children in a Norwegian nursery school, gender differences in the organization of play involve significant differences in the use of language.

Borker, Ruth Ann
  1980   Anthropology: Social and Cultural Perspectives. *In* Women and Language in Literature and Society. Sally McConnell-Ginet, Ruth A. Borker, and Nelly Furman, eds. Pp. 26–44. New York: Praeger.

  From an anthropological perspective, gender differences in speech are interpreted both as strategies for dealing with the constraints of social position and as enactments of cultural models of gender and speech. Relevant literature is reviewed, and the case of gossip in Europe is examined in detail.

Faris, James Chester
  1966   The Dynamics of Verbal Exchange: A Newfoundland Example. Anthropologica 8(2):235–248.

  When news reaches a small village in Newfoundland, men transmit it in public as a storytelling event performed before an audience in the shop, and women transmit it privately as "gossip" passed between individuals.

Gal, Susan
  1978   Peasant Men Can't Get Wives: Language Change and Sex Roles in a Bilingual Community. Language in Society 7(1):1–16.

  In a Hungarian-speaking area of Austria, young women, not men, are the furthest advanced in the move toward greater use of German. This fact is explained in terms of women's increasing desire to marry industrial workers rather than remain in the peasant community.

Goodwin, Marjorie Harness
  1980   He-said-she-said: Formal Cultural Procedures for the Construction of a Gossip Dispute Activity. American Ethnologist 7(4):674–695.

  Examination of gender differences in patterns of speech and play among black children in Philadelphia reveals a female form of "gossip dispute" known as "he-said-she-said," which focuses on accusations and denials about who said what to whom about whom.

Harding, Susan Friend
  1975   Women and Words in a Spanish Village. *In* Toward an Anthropology of Women. Rayna Rei-
     ter, ed. Pp. 283–308. New York: Monthly Review Press.

  In northeastern Spain, gender differences in patterns of work are expressed as well in patterns of
speech. Women develop verbal skills of gossip, intuition, and manipulation of others, skills that grant
power, but not power equivalent to that of men.

Keenan, Elinor Ochs
  1974   Norm-makers, Norm-breakers: Use of Speech by Men and Women in a Malagasy Commu-
     nity. *In* Explorations in the Ethnography of Speaking. Richard Bauman and Joel Sherzer, eds. Pp.
     125–143. Cambridge: Cambridge University Press.

  In central Madagascar, men, but not women, avoid direct expression of sentiments and admire the
use of subtlety in language. Men's indirect speech is used to maintain social relationships and women's
direct speech to express conflict, each associated with a different type of power.

Larson, Karen Ann
  1982   Role Playing and the Real Thing: Socialization and Standard Speech in Norway. Journal of
     Anthropological Research 38(4):401–410.

  Norwegian women make use of a pattern of metaphoric code switching between local dialect and
standard Norwegian to increase the force of their utterances as a strategy for disciplining unruly children.
This skill is learned in the role play of girls.

Lederman, Rena
  1980   Who Speaks Here? Formality and the Politics of Gender in Mendi. Journal of the Polynesian
     Society 89(4):479–498.

  Among the Mendi of the New Guinea highlands, formal political oratory, from which women are
excluded, expresses hierarchical gender relations and social group membership, in contrast with informal talk between individuals, which reflects gender equality and social network relations.

Limón, José Eduardo
  1983   Legendary, Metafolklore, and Performance: A Mexican-American Example. Western Folk-
     lore 42(3):191–208.

  Among Mexican Americans relating the vanishing hitchhiker legend, women opt for a collective
narration predominantly in English, a performance aesthetic criticized by males who view the women's
performance as flawed.

Maltz, Daniel Nathan, and Ruth Ann Borker
  1982   A Cultural Approach to Male/Female Miscommunication. *In* Language and Social Identity.
     John Gumperz, ed. Pp. 196–216. Cambridge: Cambridge University Press.

  Gender differences in patterns of friendly conversation resulting from different patterns of play
among boys and girls in North America are used to explain possible miscommunication between adult
men and women.

Mann, Brenda J.
  1974   Bar Talk. *In* Conformity and Conflict: Readings in Cultural Anthropology. 2nd edition. James
     P. Spradley and David W. McCurdy, eds. Pp. 101–111. Boston: Little, Brown.

  At a college bar in the Midwest, differences in the speech behavior of bartenders and waitresses
reflect differences in gender, in power, and in relationship to customers.

Narayan, Kisrin
  1986   Birds on a Branch: Girlfriends and Wedding Songs in Kangra. Ethos 14(1):47–75.

Analysis of wedding songs in Northwest India reveals that unmarried girls express publicly in song ideas they avoid speaking directly, including desire for their fathers to be quick in arranging their marriages and sadness over the splitting of girlhood friendship groups.

Schieffelin, Bambi Bernhard
   1987   Do Different Worlds Mean Different Words? An Example from Papua New Guinea. *In* Language, Gender, and Sex in Comparative Perspective. Susan Philips, Susan Steele, and Christine Tanz, eds. Pp. 249–260. Cambridge: Cambridge University Press.

Among the Kaluli of New Guinea, there is no cultural notion of differences between men's and women's speech, but because women are the primary caretakers and linguistic socializers of young children, their linguistic repertoire includes devices for eliciting repetition and imitation that are not part of the repertoire of men.

Smith-Heffner, Nancy J.
   1988   Women and Politeness: The Javanese Example. Language in Society 17(4):535–554.

In Java, women are less experienced than men at the use of politeness forms associated with public power, but as linguistic socializers of children, their speech involves both the authoritative forms appropriate to the superior status of parents and the deferential forms used when acting as examples and speaking from the perspective of the child.

Warren, Kay Barbara, and Susan C. Bourque
   1985   Gender, Power, and Communication: Women's Responses to Political Muting in the Andes. *In* Women Living Change. Susan C. Bourque and Donna R. Divine, eds. Pp. 255–286. Philadelphia: Temple University Press.

Examination of the ''mutedness of women'' in two Peruvian communities reveals a range of variation, including exclusion from public discourse, alternative discourse forms such as songs, the constraint of having to translate ideas into the dominant discourse, and even withdrawal into silence.

18

Sex, Sexuality, Gender, and Gender Variance

Sue-Ellen Jacobs
University of Washington

Christine Roberts
University of Washington

There is a general tendency to describe sex and gender in terms of polarized categories of two opposing and non-overlapping groups: sexual orientation is seen as homosexuality *versus* heterosexuality; gender identity as feminine *versus* masculinity. [Birke 1986:75]

Although sexuality, like all human cultural activity, is grounded in the body, the body's structure, physiology, and functioning do not directly or simply determine the configuration or meaning of sexuality; were this so, we would expect to find great uniformity across the world's cultures. Yet the sexual diversity we see is startling: activities condemned in one society are encouraged in another, and ideas about what is attractive or erotic or sexually satisfying or even sexually possible vary a great deal. [Vance 1985:7–8]

This module provides an overview of core concepts and ethnographic examples of sex, sexuality, gender, and gender variance to facilitate expanded coverage of these topics in introductory anthropology. We present elementary materials for teaching about a range of sexualities and gender expression rather than a full coverage of the recent studies and theoretical debates on these issues, since to do the latter requires far more space than is available. Briefly, we introduce two curriculum modules (to which we have appended questions for use in class discussion or research). Then we give a brief overview of key issues in the literature, which include operationalizing definitions of sex, sexuality, gender, and gender variance. We conclude with an annotated bibliography, a glossary of terms, and a list of films.

In writing this module, we have taken the positions that sex, sexuality, and gender have biosocial dimensions. While we do not accept the cliché that "biology is destiny," neither do we accept that these qualities are culturally or socially constructed in the absence of perceived biological realities. As Vance (1985:8) has argued, within every culture "the body and its actions are understood according to prevailing codes of meaning." Moreover, it is important to remember "that there is diversity in the patterning of sexuality from one culture to the next" (Broude 1981:634) and that within each culture there are various measures used for the management of sexuality and gender expression. In addition, "Because there is pleasure and danger in sexuality, there are problems and possibilities in every aspect of sexuality. Sexual behavior may become both liberating and enslaving. Sexual choices, although deeply personal, may also be of far-reaching political consequences'' (Espin 1986:283).[1] In taking our position we come up against academic and popular ideas about biology, anatomy, and physiology, and highly debated theories that see sexuality as either fully culturally constructed or biologically determined. We are also entering into a largely tabooed domain of both academic and popular discourse.

In 1975, Kay Martin and Barbara Voorhies published the first anthropology textbook specifically dealing with human females cross-culturally. *Females of the Species* considers the biological bases of being female, then makes clear distinctions between sex and gender, discusses gender variation and, in the second half of the book, presents a thorough comparative study of women's roles. In their landmark work they discuss sexuality only as it pertains to reproduction; this is a criticism stated to point out that the data on women's sexuality cross-culturally had not accumulated sufficiently for an in-depth discussion.

In her consideration of the paucity of information on sexuality, Frayser suggests American scientists have avoided discussion of sex and sexuality in their writings because of the taboos in American society surrounding these topics.

> At the very least, Americans are ambivalent in their attitudes about sex. This . . . has hampered the scientific study of sexuality. Researchers are scientists, but they are also members of American culture and are subject to many of the beliefs of the general public. Personal discomfort with discussions of sexuality in a public context extends into the professional arena. Many scientists hesitate to place their professional reputations on the line by studying sexuality as a legitimate area of research in its own right. [Frayser 1985:12–13]

Gender and gender variance are even less likely to be discussed in ethnographic reporting. When ethnographies do contain discussions of sex and sexuality, they are usually embedded in a section which deals with institutional or structural aspects of culture (e.g., marriage and the family) and sections on ''women'' and ''abnormalities.'' While most anthropologists have not been concerned with systematic reporting of data on sexuality and gender this is beginning to change, due to public attention to issues such as pornography, teenage pregnancy, sexual abuse of children, and AIDS. As these issues are increasingly addressed by the American public, studies of sexuality are becoming more legitimate.

Nevertheless, the study of sexuality is a relatively new research emphasis, and even terminology is confusing and problematic. During the 1970s sex and gender were sometimes conflated; the words *sex* and *gender* were used to mean the same thing. At other times, these terms were used in a manner opposite to the current accepted definitions. By 1981, with the publication of Ortner and Whitehead's *Sexual Meanings* and subsequently the journal *Gender and Society,* fairly successful attempts have been made to operationalize the terms (see Glossary).

Gender is the sociocultural designation of biobehavioral and psychosocial qualities of the sexes; for example, woman (female), man (male), other(s) (e.g., berdaches[2]). Notions of gender are culturally specific and depend on the ways in which cultures define and differentiate human (and other) potentials and possibilities. While many people in Western society may think first of heterosexual women and men when the word ''gender'' is mentioned, there are more gender possibilities than just those two. Around the world, gender is not always perceived ''as a pair of discrete binary opposites but is often seen as a continuum'' (Edgerton 1964:1288). Linguistic markers for gender reveal culturally specific epistemological categories. For example, the Mohave reportedly recognize four genders. An individual may be either a woman or a *hwami* (female berdache), or a man or an *alyha* (male berdache). If one uses the criteria of linguistic markers alone, it suggests that people in most English-speaking countries also recognize four genders: woman, lesbian (or gay female), man and gay male.[3]

Borgoras (1908) reported that the Chuckchee counted seven genders: three were female and four were male.

Sex refers to the observable biophysiological, morphological characteristics of an individual. Anthropologists have customarily proclaimed that there are only two sexes: female and male (e.g., Schlegel 1985). This proclamation is linked to a declaration that there are only two genders: woman and man. The paired sets, female-woman, male-man leave no room for culturally defined variance in sex or gender, thus creating empirical and theoretical problems. Current research makes it clear that we should open the categories of sex and gender to reflect the epistemological diversity reported cross-culturally. Research suggests that there are at least three phenotypic *sexes* acknowledged in human cultures: females, males, and androgynes or phenotypically hermaphroditic or intersexed persons (although the latter may not be found in some societies). This generalization refers to cultural conceptions regarding the possibilities of sex variation, as well as the macro phenotypic characteristics observable to the naked eye. We are not referring to medical classifications of sex-types that are based on microscopic studies of genetic variation, particularly on combinations of the X and Y chromosomes, which lead to terms such as "superfemales" (XXX) and "Y-males"'s (XYY) (Martin and Voorhies 1975; Money 1980; Money and Ehrhardt 1972). Here we are concerned only with the ways in which ordinary people respond to and culturally construct sex. This includes their responses to readily observable phenotypic and macro biological characteristics (e.g., menstruation) of others by naming and expressing cultural values for them, as well as social categories reflecting sexual and gender identities.

Davis and Whitten have stated that

> Some anthropologists have suggested that extreme cross-gender behavior should be understood in terms of a "third sex" (Martin and Voorhies 1975; Wikan 1977). The individual may be locally understood, and may understand him or herself, as incorporating aspects of both maleness and femaleness into a distinct kind of person. The person is not parody, not fetishistic, and not a woman trapped in a man's body, but rather a unique sexual and social being (Fry 1985; Nanda 1984, 1985; Parker 1984). If this is the case, even the term "homosexual" may be inappropriate for the individual or for his or her sexual partners. [Davis and Whitten 1987:81]

This interpretation of recent cross-cultural studies of sex, sexuality, gender, and gender variance is contested. In the example of the Chuckchee mentioned above, there are seven recognized genders. It is too limiting to confine our understanding of cross-gender behavior to consideration of a "third sex." Furthermore, studies of transsexuals reveal that some individuals indeed report feeling that they are "a woman trapped in a man's body" and vice versa. There are cultures in Latin America where different gender designations are applied to men who engage in same-sex sexual activities according to the role individuals assume in the sexual encounter: a man who inserts his penis into another man's body may be classified as heterosexual if he also engages in sex with women. A man who receives the penis is the one viewed as a homosexual (Lancaster 1988; see also Williams 1986 for further information on this cultural belief and practice throughout Latin America). The matter is far more complex emically when we closely examine recent studies. Our etic categories should reflect this complexity.

Sex also refers to sexual intercourse, often glossed as "making love" or "making out," whether recreational or for reproduction. The definition of *sexuality* is more problematic (cf. Ross and Rapp 1983). It refers to sexual behaviors, feelings, thoughts, practices, and people's sexually based bonding behaviors (e.g., bisexuality, heterosexuality, homosexuality, etc.) which may be a response to, or may inform, sexual identity. *Sexual identity* refers to an individual's self-attribution of sexuality. It involves sexual preferences, desires, and practices and gender identity. *Gender identity* refers to individuals' self-definition or attribution based on their acceptance, manipulation, rejection, or redefinition of their culture's gender role expectations. It includes consideration of sexuality, sexual identity, and sociocultural roles. It may or may not have anything to do with sexual preference.

> Sexuality can overlap with gender and sex, but remains a separate domain of desire and erotic pleasure (Vance 1985:9). Sex, gender and sexuality may be related but are not the same thing. The degree of their relationship, or the lack thereof, is sociohistorically negotiated and negotiable . . . [gender] is by no means an immutable assignment. [Robertson 1988:2]

Reproduction and sexuality are codependent variables in the human life cycle. But sex and sexuality are much more complex than linking them with reproduction. If a cultural belief holds that reproduction is the only objective for sexual relations, an individual is expected to engage in sexual behavior only with those persons who are considered, by sociocultural norms, to be proper other parents of the potential offspring. Cultural norms may dictate who one should have sex with and define the punishment for those who break the rules of cohabitation, but they do not fully control sexuality for all individuals. To this end, "adultery" is included as a standard category in anthropological research outlines. It is expected that a fieldworker will be able to locate, with appropriate questioning, individuals who engage in sexual relations outside the prescribed marital norms. "Prostitution" (also called "sex work" and "sex trade" by American and European activists for prostitution rights) is also a standard category in cultural trait lists, but may be more difficult to find in field situations because of the variance cross-culturally of what is considered to be "sex for sale, barter, or exchange." The terms *homosexuality, heterosexuality,* and *bisexuality* all refer to sex behavior but also carry with them other meanings (see *sexuality* above and the Glossary).

Over the past two decades, feminist studies of sex, sexuality, gender, and gender variance have given explicit attention to and challenged androcentric research on these four intertwined aspects of being human (Goodale 1971; Hanna 1988; Martin and Voorhies 1975; Ortner and Whitehead 1981; Ross and Rapp 1983). Topics range from purported female sexual promiscuity to frigidity, prostitution to total abstinence, incest victimization to pedophilia, protected property to rape victim, eroticism to pornography, and more. There have also been empirical studies of child abuse and child prostitution, historical analyses of morality and sexual behaviors, field studies of primate sexuality and theoretical treatises on the evolution of human sexuality. These writings can be readily found in journals and monographs.

In this module, we could not possibly cover the full range of research reported. What we will do is examine two ways to introduce undergraduates to issues related to sexuality, particularly as sexuality is related to gender. The first curriculum example uses the work of Jane C. Goodale and Marjorie Shostak. Goodale conducted fieldwork in several Kaulong communities in Papua New Guinea. Shostak gathered information on the !Kung.

The second curriculum examines heterosexuality and homosexuality to show how biological, physiological, and cultural factors are all interwoven in our consideration of sexuality and gender. We suggest that these examples be introduced with a brief coverage of the debate on biological bases for and sociocultural constructions of sexuality and gender. Due to space limitations we have left out discussion of transsexuality and intersexuality.

Kaulong and !Kung Sexuality

Teaching about sexuality and gender is both exciting and difficult because there are such strong emotions associated with both topics. Studying sexuality and gender in cultures other than our own gives us a chance to step outside personal and societal experiences; we gain perspective and a starting point from which to gain further understanding of our own society. Two ethnographic works particularly useful with undergraduates are "Gender, Sexuality and Marriage: A Kaulong Model of Nature and Culture" (Goodale 1980) and *Nisa: The Life and Words of a !Kung Woman* (Shostak 1983). Jane C. Goodale and Marjorie Shostaks have investigated sexuality and gender within a larger cultural context, including methods of subsistence and shelter, kinship and reproduction, and overall community organization. Goodale's study of the Kaulong demonstrates that a person's marital status is at the same level of significance for the Kaulong that one's sex is for most people in the Western world. Shostak's story of Nisa includes Nisa's sexual experiences from childhood sex play through marriage and love affairs.

Marriage and Nature in Kaulong Society

Jane C. Goodale[4] specifically examined gender and sexuality in her fieldwork in several Kaulong communities of Papua New Guinea. The Kaulong live in small horticultural communities, where both women and men raise food and parent the children. However, their tasks and behavior are influenced largely by whether they are female or male. Goodale found that both women and men in these communities have the same primary life goals. She describes these goals as "(1) immortality through reproduction of identity, and (2) self-development through production and social activity" (1980:139). The first goal can only be achieved through parenting. Since sexuality is an essential part of becoming a parent and, in Kaulong culture, sexual intercourse is only socially sanctioned for married people, one must marry in order to achieve the first life goal. The second life goal is attained by maintaining the clearing (or *bi-*[5]), participating in rituals, and raising food and trading or selling the excess. Either married or single women and men can achieve this goal. However, different conflicts arise for each sex in their attempts to achieve what Goodale has identified as their main life goals.

Among the Kaulong, an individual's self-development reflects that person's relations with others on a social level.

> The self is that part of the body in which all experience and knowledge is internalized and, as experience and knowledge accumulate, the self grows in volume independent of the natural growth of the container, the body. . . . The variable size, health and effectiveness of individuals is directly related to the health and quantity of self. [Goodale 1980:127][6]

The work that one does to achieve full self-worth is done in the *bi-* in full view of others: trading, keeping the forest cut back and participating in rituals. Both married and single women and men join in these activities (1980:139–140). However, only single people live and raise food in the *bi-*. Because the sexual intercourse engaged in by couples is considered animal-like by the Kaulong, and animals are seen as part of the forest and nature, the gardens of married couples are located away from the *bi-* and deep in the forest, which, in the view of the Kaulong, is closer to nature (1980:123–125).

The only purpose of marriage/sexual intercourse[6] for the Kaulong is to achieve their first life goal: immortality through reproduction. Prior to European contact, suicide was the accepted course for a childless couple or a couple whose child/children died before them, when the couple was too old to have more children. Once childbearing could no longer be said to be the goal, marriage/sexual intercourse was considered "without meaning and caused them shame" (1980:134). In other words, marriage is simply undesirable and is done with the hope of achieving immortality through the production of children.

Without children, a Kaulong woman or man's "identity is considered to have been lost" (1980:127). Although it is desirable, the reproduction of one's identity does not require a matching of sexes; boys can replace women and girls replace men (1980:127). Children are labeled at birth as either male or female (1980:129). Goodale did not report either sex or gender variation among the Kaulong.

Achieving the goal of reproduction of identity entails risks for both females and males, and both have reason to fear marriage/sexual intercourse. Men fear marriage/sexual intercourse because of what Goodale states is men's fear of women's lateral and vertical polluting abilities (i.e., the potential of women to make men ill and even cause death). Lateral pollution is temporary and can occur during menstruation and following childbirth. This type of pollution spreads laterally to surrounding areas to "a distance of approximately 10 to 15 metres" (1980:131). To prevent lateral pollution, a menstruating or postpartum woman moves to a distant area, away "from the *bi-*, . . . clear of all gardens and dwelling places located there and all drinking water supplies and sources" (1980:129). Women also avoid touching anything belonging to men and other items with which a man may come in contact.

Vertical pollution is permanent and occurs when mature women pass over or rest upon an object. Therefore, men never pass under bridges or fallen logs because a woman might have walked over these objects in the past. This fear of pollution among men is so pervasive that the government's plan for raised houses to reduce health problems was not adopted. To the Kaulong men, raised houses held more danger than those built on the ground, because the area underneath a house would be permanently polluted if a woman walked across the floor of the house above (1980:129).

Women also have deep fears regarding sexuality and reproduction. Goodale notes that

It is not entirely right to say that reproduction of identity is more dangerous to men. Female informants frequently discussed with me the difficult and sometimes fatal instance of childbirth and consider that a woman's womb should be fully developed (by the mid-twenties) before she can safely bear a child. Sexual activity is differentially dangerous to men and women. [1980:140, n. 18]

Although Goodale did not explore the women's fears in any more detail than with this footnote, it appears that those fears are present and do influence women's behavior. Even though women are the aggressors in courtship among the Kaulong, and thus have the prerogative to marry when and whom they want, they usually do not marry until they are in their twenties (1980:135). While other factors surely influence this decision (such as, perhaps, the advanced age of the men when they are willing to marry),[7] it seems logical that fear of childbirth and the risks associated with it would delay women's achievement of their goal to bear children in order to replace their identity.

In summary, the two goals of self-development and reproduction of identity are common to both sexes, but paths to the achievement of those goals are different for each sex. While there is nearly equal task performance of females and males in manual labor, women are prevented from attaining the highest degree of self-development possible because of the rule of isolation during menstruation and childbirth. They are prevented from working as many hours as men by the enforced menstrual and postnatal seclusion. Men do not appear to face such obstacles in working toward their goal of self-development.

However, both women and men face conflicts in achieving the goal of reproduction of their identity via childbearing. Men fear "marital contamination" from women's pollution because of the risk of illness or death associated with it, and women fear the pain and possible death associated with childbirth, especially if they become pregnant too early in life. Women, the aggressors in courtship, usually marry in their twenties and men wait until their later years.

Kaulong married couples live separately from single people because of the couple's association with sexuality, and thus with the forest and nature.

Nisa's Sex Life

Nisa is a pseudonym for a 51-year-old !Kung[8] woman who stood out as an excellent
storyteller when Marjorie Shostak conducted her fieldwork in the early 1970s. The !Kung
have traditionally been a gathering and hunting society that live on the edge of the Kalahari
desert in southern Africa. Shostak reports that adults work two or three days a week away
from home on subsistence activities and spend the rest of their time preparing food they've
collected, making or repairing tools or other belongings, and socializing. They have very few
personal belongings, no more than they can carry. Several families may live beside one another in grass huts during the rainy season, then travel and form larger villages during the
winter. Women have high status in the mostly nonhierarchical !Kung society; they gather
approximately 60% of the food supply. Children have no responsibilities until they are 15
years old and receive little formal training, learning everything from sex to survival through
observation and practice. (Shostak 1983:8–13, 106–108).

The !Kung believe that "just as people cannot survive without eating, hunger for sex
can cause people to die" (1983:265). This demonstrates how important being sexual is in their
view of life. Shostak states:

> Talk about sex seems to be of almost equal importance [to eating]. When women are in the
> village or out gathering, or when men and women are together, they spend hours recounting
> details of sexual exploits. Joking about all aspects of sexual experience is commonplace—
> except between people who maintain "respect" relationships and are forbidden to make sex-
> ual references in each other's presence. [1983:265]

Nisa was no exception to this. She stated that "If a woman doesn't have sex, . . . her
thoughts get ruined and she is always angry" (1983:31).

!Kung children first become aware of sexual intercourse by observing their parents. One
room huts make privacy impossible, and children, who sleep beside their parents, see and
hear their parents' lovemaking. Nisa's response to seeing and hearing her parents having sex
was " 'So, that's another thing people do with their genitals' " (1983:111). She also stated
that at first she thought her father was killing her mother when they made love.

While parents go gathering or hunting, children stay home with a few of the adults.
Girls and boys together often set up separate "villages" close to their own village and play
at adult activities: "hunting, gathering, singing and trancing, playing house, and playing at
parenthood and marriage" (1983:106–108). Adults do not usually interfere with the sex play
of children as long as it's kept out of sight; they often deny its existence, although they remember their own childhood sex play more vividly than other types of play. If children are
caught playing at sex, "they are scolded and told to 'play nicely,' but that is all" (1983:110).
"Because the !Kung impose no responsibilities on their children, place no value on virginity,
and do not require that the female body be covered or hidden, girls are as free and unfettered
as boys" (1983:108).

By the time she was a young teenager, Nisa was offended by her parents' having sex
when she thought they knew she was still awake. She moved out of their hut and built her
own hut where she lived alone (1983:113). Then her parents began trying to talk Nisa into
getting married. This is common among the !Kung, where early marriages are arranged by
parents. These marriages are not expected to be permanent or even of long duration. Nisa was

reluctant to get married, refusing time and again her parents' efforts (1983:127–145). The first two times she did consent to marry, she repeatedly ran away into the bush or returned to her parents' hut (1983:153–158).

When a teenage girl marries, she is not expected to have sexual intercourse until menarche, or the onset of menstruation, which is around the age of 16, on average. Until then she will have the support of her friends and family in refusing to have sex with her husband (1983:150). Nisa had sexual intercourse the first time with her husband Tashay. They did not make love until they had been living together "for a long time" and they "started to like each other with [their] hearts" (1983:158).

Nisa believed that orgasms are very important to women. She stated that

> All women know sexual pleasure. Some women, those who really like sex, if they haven't finished [orgasmed] and the man has, will wait until the man has rested, then get up and make love to him. Because she wants to finish, too. She'll have sex with the man until she is also satisfied. Otherwise she could get sick. Because if a woman doesn't finish her work, sickness can enter her back. [1983:287]

Approximately five percent of !Kung marriages consist of two women and one man. Love affairs are more common among the !Kung than the practice of having or being cowives, however, and a great deal of discretion is used, as jealousy has been known to lead to violence and even death. One's spouse is always put first in terms of time and energy, or suspicions and accusations will occur. Shostak stated, "Partly because of the lack of privacy in !Kung life, actual extramarital sexual encounters seem to be infrequent" (1983:268). However, Nisa claimed to have had many love affairs during her life. She told Shostak why she had affairs:

> [W]hen you are a woman, you don't just sit still and do nothing—you have lovers. You don't just sit with the man of your hut, with just one man. One man can give you very little. One man gives you only one kind of food to eat. But when you have lovers, one brings you something and another brings you something else. [1983:271]

Conclusion

In North America, it seems the training of teenagers in how to deal with relationships and the problems and joys they entail is an idea just beginning to catch on. Although sex education has long been a part of most public schools' curriculum, there is far more to a relationship than sex. By using the Kaulong and !Kung from Goodale's and Shostak's work in introductory anthropology courses, we can find some elements about sex and sexuality which are similar to experiences found in U.S. society.

For instance, the lack of restrictions on !Kung children as they learn about sex through observation and experimentation give us reason to wonder how our society developed the rules it has regarding children and sexuality. In the !Kung tradition of teenage or trial marriages, adolescents can learn firsthand what a relationship is like. These marriages are interesting concepts in a society where there is little formal education. Like the Kaulong, some people in the United States consider that sexual activities are appropriate only between monogamously married partners and that sex should be primarily for procreation. Others are more inclined to agree with Nisa's characterization of sexuality among the !Kung: that engaging in sex is an important part of being human; both heterosexual and homosexual experimentation with sex play during adolescence is permissible; and sexual liaisons with individuals to whom one is not married are also permissible.

In the process of comparing our society to others in any fashion, we can learn about ourselves as well as the range of possible human behaviors. We can make judgments about our behavior and rules and decide whether we like them the way they are or if some other way would be better. But until we know of other ways and view them with open minds, we are left either with never examining our society or having to imagine other ways to be, which can be very difficult.

Questions for Class Discussion or Assignment

Note: In guiding discussions that compare U.S. society with Kaulong or !Kung societies, try to encourage discussion or provide material that reveals diversity in the United States, especially by race, class, or ethnicity.

1. Opportunities to achieve life goals differ for women and men in Kaulong society. What are some differences in opportunities for women and men to achieve life goals in U.S. society?

2. The value of childbearing in Kaulong society seems to center on the replacement of identity for adults, giving them immortality. In what way is childbearing valued in the United States?

3. Many gender-based divisions exist among people in Western societies. In the Kaulong world, divisions are based primarily on marital status. Give examples of gender-based divisions in the United States and Kaulong societies and explain how these divisions affect people's lives.

4. What are some of the issues connected with sexuality for !Kung teenage girls? Are they similar to those for teenage girls in the United States? Explain.

5. Would the !Kung method of using observation and experimentation to acculturate their youngsters be appropriate for U.S. children? Why or why not? How might population density influence this issue?

6. Contrast the attitudes and behavior of Kaulong women with those of !Kung women in regard to marriage.

Teaching and Research about Lesbianism

Gender is the cultural construction of perceived biophysiological facts. This means that within any given culture, genders are recognized, named, and given meaning and attributes (including role expectations) in accordance with that culture's rules or customs for categorizing life. People interpret what they see and hear according to the limits of perception their culture (and language) make available to them. Different cultures may have different criteria for gender determination. When a baby is born, people generally rely on the appearance of the infant's external genitalia to determine whether that child will be treated as female or male, at least in the child's early years. As a child grows, more criteria come into play, such as "the phenotypic expression of sex—facial hair, voice, breast development, and general body configuration" (Edgerton 1964:1288). In some societies, the child's spiritual development and interests are also used as criteria for gender attribution (this has been shown to be especially true for the gender forms categorized as "berdache" among many American Indian tribes and similar forms found in Polynesia and Asia). Gender categories are marked with names in every culture. They are often, but not always, associated with specified roles within the community.

It is important to note that the labels we use for people do not always imply both gender and sexuality at once. Gender identity includes many different areas of a person's life; it typically includes sexuality, sexual identity and sociocultural roles. Sexual identity, on the other hand, refers to an individual's self-definition based solely on their sexual preference and practices.

Due to space limitations we will not discuss transsexualism or intersexuality (hermaphrodism). Instead, we concentrate on heterosexuality, followed by a more lengthy look at homosexuality and the wide range of relations within these two categories. We look specifically at lesbianism and how women fare in the United States and Canada.

Heterosexuals

The word *heterosexual* is a combination of the Greek word *hetero,* meaning other or different, and the Latin word *sexualis,* meaning having to do with sexual gratification or reproduction or the urge for these (Random House Dictionary of English Usage 1987). In recent literature the term is also used to refer to a person's sexual identity, that is, their own perceptions of their sexuality (who they are sexually attracted to and with whom they prefer to have sex). In everyday language in the United States, "heterosexual" refers to people whose sexual preference and behavior, and thus their sexual identity, is directed toward individuals of the "opposite" sex (meaning that women who are heterosexual seek sexual relations with men).

Depending on cultural definitions, people can think of themselves and be classified as heterosexuals yet also engage in sexual liaisons with people of their own sex. For example, Lancaster reports that in Nicaragua some men who have sex with other men are viewed as heterosexual as long as they are the ones who insert the penis into the other man's body. The man who receives the penis is the one viewed as a homosexual (Lancaster 1988; see also Williams 1986 for further information on this cultural belief and practice throughout Latin America). It is important to realize there may be variance within the notion, or behaviors, of heterosexuals cross-culturally, just as with all other categories of sexuality and gender.

In addition, it is interesting to note that individuals may be exclusively heterosexual and strongly homosocial. This means that individuals may limit their sexual activities to relationships with the opposite sex but spend the majority of their social time with individuals of the same sex. The combination of heterosexuality and high homosociality is found in most societies that stress sex segregation for work and other purposes. In East Africa, Maasai warriors (Moran) travel in groups between villages in their respective territories and have consorts and lovers among the women of the villages. Maasai women spend most of their waking time together: working and sharing affection as they raise children, tending to their husbands' cattle and maintaining their homes (Llewellyn-Davis 1978). Similarly, women who live in many Muslim societies focus their affective relations on their children, cowives, female relatives and friends, while simultaneously being classified as heterosexuals because of the public and private focus of their sexuality (Fernea 1978). People who are classified as heterosexuals may restrict their sexual relations to one other person, engage in serial sexual liaisons, be sexually abstinent, or combine several sexual strategies over the course of their lives.

Most of the literature on cultural norms concerning expressions of sexuality is concerned with regulating female heterosexual conduct and beliefs associated with the regulations. In some societies, women are considered such strong sexual attractions to men that they are to be seen in public only if they are nearly completely covered (e.g., purdah as described by Fernea 1976 and Mernissi 1987). In other societies, women are thought to have such strong "sexual desires" or "instincts" that measures are used to restrict their sex behaviors (e.g., clitoridectomy, glossed as "female circumcision," and infibulation performed in some African tribes, such as the Maasai). Elsewhere, it may be thought that women are "frigid" and incapable of sexual arousal, or have no interest in sex, but will "succumb" to sex with their husbands in order to have children (e.g., Ireland).

It can be argued that the primary reason for defining appropriate sexual behavior and punishing violations of sex codes is the control of reproduction.[9] Punishment for misconduct is intended to provide external or societal control over individuals who violate prescribed sociocultural norms. Premarital sex is severely punished in some societies where premarital pregnancy is considered illegal (e.g., Tanala) or, at least, a "shame" (e.g., Lapps), while it may be encouraged in societies where these values are not held (e.g., Aleut, Balinese, and Comanche). Extramarital sex, adultery, or fornication may be severely punished where postmarital fidelity and paternity certainty have high cultural value (e.g., Lapps and Klamath), whereas elsewhere it may be considered acceptable behavior (although less often for women than it is for men) and thus not punishable. Homosexual relations (from casual sex to pair bonding of adolescents or adults) are severely punished[10] in societies that define such relations as culturally antithetical (e.g., on religious, political, or procreative grounds), while in other societies homosexual relations are considered to be within the range of normative sex behavior (e.g., North American Indian tribes where berdache is found).

Lesbianism

People in Western society tend to view lesbianism only or primarily in sexual terms instead of as a sociocultural identity. Lesbians thus become unidimensional (Zitter 1987:187), enabling objectification. When a person or persons are labeled and objectified, the larger society tends to feel less responsible for meeting their needs. They become invisible to the rest of society. Most researchers, including anthropologists, have contributed to the problem of invisibility by not addressing issues of gender variance in their fieldwork, either on-site or in their reports. The following discussion relies on cross-disciplinary writings by lesbians. Our information is divided into sections on adolescent, middle-aged, and older lesbians, all women "whose primary erotic, psychological, emotional and social interest is in [members of their] own sex, even though that interest may not be overtly expressed" (Martin and Lyon 1983:ix).

Adolescent Lesbians.   The word *lesbian* derives from the Greek word *Lesbos,* and its use alludes to the poet Sappho of Lesbos, whose verse deals largely with her emotional relationships with other women. Colloquially, "lesbian" pertains to female homosexuality (Random House Dictionary of English Usage 1987). Homosexuality, gay, and lesbian are concepts that have different connotations in different cultures (Herdt 1989:18–20).

> Rather than one narrow definition of homosexuality, there are many different kinds, all within the context of same-sex loving; differences in sex, class, education, age, politics, [physical ability], culture, ethnicity, and race all influence the "style" (for lack of a better term) of homosexuality. The majority of data on homosexuals that has been gathered and published to date has been on gay males. [Herdt 1989:22–24, 32]

Here our focus will be on the lives of lesbians in America and Canada.

Margaret Schneider studied the development of gay identity among adolescent self-identified lesbians in Toronto, Canada, in 1984 and 1985.[11] Following are the responses of four of her informants when asked what being lesbian meant to them.

> You have to drop a lot of options. Like economic security. Women don't usually have a lot of money (Wendy, age 18). It's a real love and trust of women, and respect. It's something inside me that I can't explain (Brenda, age 17). It's not that important. Like, it's the most important unimportant issue. It's not a way of life. It's just a part of my life. You have to sneak around. It's difficult that way (Ann, age 17). It means a certain amount of independence and dependence on women . . . a sense of democracy, and strength and power in women (Carrie, age 16). [Schneider 1989:128–129]

In her research, Schneider focused on the coming-out process and how young women socialized after they became self-identified as lesbians. Schneider utilized De Monteflores and Schultz's 1978 definition of coming-out,[12] which is "the developmental process through which gay people recognize their sexual preferences and choose to integrate this knowledge into their personal and social lives" (1989:59). Adolescence is a time of conflict, as people go through the search for self-definition and identity. Adolescent lesbians have an even greater struggle than nonlesbians.

Heterosexual dating may be a way to try to conform to expectations of heterosexual friends or parents. It may also be a way young women try to see if they're "really lesbian." Schneider quotes a personal communication from J. Hunter to the effect that the pregnancy rate among teenage lesbians is increasing (Schneider 1989:117), sometimes an obvious potential, and heart-breaking, side-effect of a young woman trying to prove she is not gay.

Teenage lesbians of color or ethnicity who come out in their racial or ethnic community may experience more alienation than their white peers, as they may feel rejected by their community (the majority of whose members may feel lesbians reject the values of and bring shame to their culture) (Zitter 1987:186). This was found to be especially relevant in Toronto, where there are enclaves of different cultures in the city, and retaining cultural values of the homeland is a priority for many (Tremble et al. 1989:255). Tremble et al. found there may be more of a problem with ethnic community acceptance than with family acceptance (1989:260). But Betty Berzon, a clinical psychologist, states that

> For gay people, this is particularly important—the demystification of gayness through personalized disclosure: The simple words, "I am gay." The affirming act that says, "I will no longer be silent. I will no longer be invisible. I am understandable. I am natural. I have the right to live my truth rather than a lie to preserve someone else's fantasy of how the world should be." [Berzon 1979b:10]

For young lesbians living in rural areas of Canada and America, seclusion from other lesbians can be difficult. They may not have role models or reassurance from others about their feelings and concerns. Lesbians in urban areas do not always fare much better. Theresa, a 19-year-old lesbian living in Toronto, reported that being around other lesbians would have helped her develop a stronger self-identity:

> "Connecting with people my own age who were lesbians would have made my life a lot easier, or being told that it was okay. I didn't know where to go to find them. I didn't know if I wanted to find them on my own, alone. I needed someone to say, 'It's okay. It's okay to feel confused or to be a lesbian.' And all around me were girls my own age who were dating guys, who seemed to be enjoying that, and my parents who are heterosexual. I was sur-

rounded by all that. So I felt like there was a part of me that wasn't being acknowledged. That it didn't exist, and it made me feel alone and depressed.'' [Schneider 1989:123].[13]

A 20-year-old lesbian living in the midwestern United States looked back on her life in a more positive light. She had grown up in a town with an active women's community. Her mother was lesbian and, although they had fought often because she wanted more attention as a teen, she nonetheless felt she had gained inner strength from her mother and the lesbian community (Krieger 1983:119–120). One issue that appears to concern some teenage lesbians is growing older. As Naomi stated,

> I worry about being alone ten years down the road. I see a lot of young lesbians out there. What happens when you get old? What happens to old lesbians? I don't know. I mean, do they live together and move out to the suburbs or something? [Schneider 1989:121]

Middle-aged Lesbians. We will now try to look ten years and more down the road. Labels are not always appropriate to the people being labeled, and such is the case with referring to women from age 20 to age 60 as being ''middle-aged.'' Here, we have chosen those ages because the published research focuses on the age sets of ''adolescents'' and ''older lesbians''; there is no age referent for individuals between those categories. We will limit our discussion to the experiences of lesbians as parents, as employees in the workplace, and as partners in relationships with one another.

Parenting. Most ''studies on female homosexuality [are based on samples of] exclusively white, predominantly well-educated, and upwardly mobile [women]'' (Hill 1987:215). This is also true of most studies on lesbian parenting. As of 1978, it was estimated that approximately one-fifth of lesbians become mothers or are mothers when they first identify themselves as lesbians (Hill 1987:215). There have been several recent studies of lesbian parents, including co-parenting (Baptiste 1987; Crawford 1987; Hill 1987; Lewin 1981; Matteson 1987; McCandlish 1987; Ricketts and Achtenberg 1987). Lesbians have chosen artificial insemination (whether through a doctor's office or a community network), sexual intercourse with a male friend, or adoption as ways to become mothers. The types of choices available to lesbians who wish to raise children require some serious effort, implying that this is not a decision made lightly (McCandlish 1987:23).

Lesbian families are not just like any other family, for they have the added stress of living in a homophobic society that not only, by and large, disapproves of gay sexual identity but of gays raising children (Crawford 1987:195). Lesbians of color or white lesbians with children of color face the additional burden of racism. Audre Lorde, a well-known black lesbian poet and mother of two children, wrote, ''Black children of lesbian couples have an advantage because they learn, very early, that oppression comes in many different forms, none of which have anything to do with their own worth'' (1984:75).

Wage Work. Most research on gays in the workplace has been on gay men, and thus does not consider or explore ''the greater importance women as a group, and lesbians specifically, attach to emotional support and relationships'' (Schneider 1984:214). Those relationships can be absent or diminished for lesbians due to homophobia on the part of coworkers, which can lead to harassment and isolation from interpersonal networks and a need to prove one's worth in the workplace through overachievement.

For most lesbians, wage work is an essential part of their lives because they must support themselves (Schneider 1984:211). However, lesbians have to work under the same conditions all women do: on average, women make 65% of the wages men make. (Comparable increases in education do not result in comparable wage increases.) Women usually have less education than men, which means they are often left with jobs in the ''pink collar ghetto''[14] with low prestige, few benefits, and few unions (meaning their only recourse is through the courts when lesbians experience discrimination on the basis of sexual identity). In addition, there is the expectation, particularly infuriating to lesbians and feminists, that women on the job will "appear (through dress and demeanor) sexually attractive to men, who tend to hold the economic position and power to enforce heterosexual standards and desires" (Schneider 1987:212). The specter of sexual harassment on the job can be of particular seriousness for lesbians who may not be able to determine if it was due to being a woman or a lesbian (Schneider 1987:224).

In light of such potential difficulties, it should be no surprise when a lesbian chooses to keep her sexual identity to herself. Several women in midwestern America were of the opinion that dealing with bigotry just takes too much energy. For example, a woman named Gàyle felt that trying to make the decision of whether to come out at work or not was similar to worrying about whether you should tell the Nazis you were a Jew (Krieger 1983:149–151).

Other lesbians feel such a sense of split personality by trying to show two faces (passing as straight at work, gay otherwise) that they reject the hiding. One woman reported that lesbianism and feminism together made up an enormous part of her life. She felt she was a different person if she denied that part of her life. A university professor with tenure came out on campus because she wanted to educate people and, in the process, gained a sense of release and decreased paranoia about being gay (Krieger 1983:148, 152–53).

Stories of coming out do not always have happy endings. The following tragedy was reported by Del Martin and Phyllis Lyon in their book *Lesbian/Woman:*

> Unfortunately many Lesbians who have tried to step out of the closet . . . have found the price is martyrdom. . . . Such a martyr was Jean, of Wichita, Kansas. She made the mistake of revealing herself as a Lesbian to this small uptight American community that had bought lock, stock and barrel the "sin-crime-sickness" syndrome. Jean's family disowned her. Her girl friend left her, and the homophile community likewise shunned her. Neither she nor they could afford to associate with a "known" Lesbian. Jean couldn't find employment either, needless to say. She had no one to turn to for support, economically or emotionally. . . . The Reverend Troy Perry happened to be traveling in the area. He heard about Jean and made a special trip to Wichita to see if he could help. But the day before Troy arrived Jean committed suicide. [1983:270–271]

Committing to a lesbian relationship for the first time is a statement that one truly is lesbian and is going to live a lesbian lifestyle (Toder 1979:45). Most lesbians grow up in a family with nongay parents and thus have no role models on which to base their relationship. This can be freeing in that the couple is able to develop its own unique relationship, yet it also means that heterosexual patterns may be incorporated into their lives without their even realizing it (Berzon 1979a:30). The traditional heterosexual model of a relationship consists of one superior and one inferior partner, with the inferior partner (generally the woman) at the mercy of the superior partner for having her physical and emotional needs met (Sang 1984:54).

Deciding whether to be monogamous or not is a choice lesbian couples make that has inherent conflicts. Often monogamy is seen, especially by radical lesbian feminists, as a remnant of heterosexual relations and is therefore of highly questionable worth. Some couples even hesitate to be affectionate with their partner at women's gatherings out of concern that someone will think they're behaving too much like nongays (Krieger 1983:60–62). However, many lesbian couples choose to be, or become, monogamous, and there are often hurt feelings and guilt because of being jealous while one is trying not to be (Toder 1979:48). Margaret Nichols, a clinical psychologist and sex therapist, writes, "Every gay relationship is flawed.

Every human relationship is flawed'' (Berzon 1979:36). However, it is important to realize that not every lesbian couple has major problems with their relationship. As Nancy Toder notes,

> In a lesbian couple, both women can freely develop strength and competence. In addition, having been socialized as women, we have been trained to be interpersonally sensitive, nurturant, gentle and compassionate. In a heterosexual relationship, these qualities are used primarily to serve the man and to oppress the woman, who often must bear full responsibility for the emotional quality of the relationship. These same attributes, however, can create a miraculously high-quality relationship when shared by two women who are matched in their capacities to share and to love. [Toder 1979:55]

Older Lesbians.   The oppression lived under for so many years is evident in many older lesbians' lives today; for example, their reluctance to make use of community services or their tendency to stay closeted (i.e., to project an image and to live their lives as though they were not gay) for safety. Because they tend to stay closeted, there is little opportunity to receive support during times of emotional distress, such as following a partner's death or the end of a relationship for other reasons (Martin and Lyon 1979:136). Some of the reasons today's older lesbians tend to stay closeted are because of the conservative sexual attitudes prevalent throughout much of their lifetimes. One's sexual identity was seen as no one else's business. Also, many women have a fear of bringing hurt to their families. Not only do they have to face parents, siblings, and their extended family, but also their children if they have any (Dunker 1987:75–76).

   However, stereotypes of gay elderly being lonely and isolated, asexual or having only casual sex are not supported by research. Though depression and loneliness often mean an uphill battle for older people in general, this stereotype of older lesbians does not apply.

> Wolf (1978), in reporting preliminary trends in her research on close friendship patterns of older lesbians, contends that because older lesbians have less chance than heterosexuals for close family ties due to social stigma and because they are also less likely to have children, they have developed close friendships which offer support. [Raphael and Robinson 1984:68]

These close friendships have been vital in maintaining morale and self-esteem in old age (Raphael and Robinson 1984:68).

   Older lesbians complain of experiencing ageism from younger people, but, overall, they feel better prepared to cope with growing older than most individuals because they have been independent for so long and have had to take care of themselves in so many ways. Many, having been cut off from family support, knew they would have to prepare for old age (Martin and Lyon 1979:137–138). Those feelings were expressed by Elsa Gidlow in her article, "A View from the Seventy-Seventh Year:"

> For one thing, a Lesbian, unless she has wealth to some degree, knows that for all her life she is going to have to earn her own living. (I realize this is becoming true more and more for non-Lesbians today.) Women with this realization know they have no alternative but to prepare themselves accordingly. [1976:35]

We can see that the skills learned through supporting oneself for many years and the friends made during those years become invaluable in old age.

Conclusion

   More research is sorely needed on lesbians. The amount and focus of the research done thus far appears to follow Western society's priorities: they focus mainly on white, able-bodied, younger middle-aged lesbians of middle- to upper-socioeconomic status. Nevertheless, lesbians of color, those with physical or other disabilities, or those who are poor or very young or elderly are especially invisible to society, and they have double, triple, or more layers of discrimination with which to deal. Much more research is needed before the needs of lesbians can be responsibly dealt with by society.

In this brief discussion of lesbians by age groups we examined stereotypes by addressing those problems assumed to be associated with particular age groups. For example, lesbians come out at all ages, not just as adolescents. Sometimes a partner dies in her early twenties, leaving her lover to face such problems as child custody or lack of support from family and friends during her grieving. And lesbian couples or individuals can have problems with finances or sexuality at any age. Although it would have been redundant to address these issues for each age range, each age range can bring forth a different social perspective.

The range of variation in human sexual experience is not fully documented—or understood. We have only scratched the surface of sexual and gender diversity in our discussion of female heterosexuals and homosexuals. With increased funding in the form of public and private grants for research on sex and gender, more studies are being undertaken at this time. Perhaps the most important reason for undertaking these studies is to demonstrate the contemporary cross-cultural range of variation in human sexuality, in the process demystifying sex and sexuality.[15]

Questions for Class Discussion or Assignment

1. How might an anthropologist doing fieldwork go about collecting information from people about gender and sexual identities? In a culture new to her/him, how would she/he figure out when it would be appropriate to start asking questions about such sensitive topics?

2. Based on the information you have just read, how are people who self-identify as homosexuals similar to heterosexuals? Based on other information you have, what are some other similarities and differences?

3. What are the significant things that United States' adolescents experience as they grow to and achieve adulthood, such as premarital sex play, circumcision and reproduction? Include consideration of adolescent lesbians.

4. What are some of the issues lesbians face during their life course? What could be done to solve or at least lessen the impact of those problems?

5. In what ways do lesbians live similar and different lives compared to heterosexual women?

Glossary

We must be cautious in our application of the following terms and their definitions because they may be no more than Western heuristic devices for creating order in various universes—an order that reduces variance in human thought and practice for purposes of research expediency or compatibility of reported findings. One danger is that while we now have definitions that mark neat categories into which we can fit a range of cross-cultural behaviors, the categories may be too general (generic) for some cultures and too exclusive (specific) for others (i.e., they may not accurately reflect linguistic and other markers and concepts used by those whom anthropologists study). Defined by Western social scientists, the terms reflect Western systems of thought, which have the propensity to create dyadically opposed categories (e.g., nature:culture; sex:gender). Other cultures and systems of thought perceive different realities, and some view life and its components as interrelated or on a continuum.

However, for now, the literature reflects relative agreement on the following terms and their definitions:

gender—cultural construction of perceived biophysiological facts; i.e., sociocultural designation of biobehavioral and psychosocial qualities of the sexes; e.g., woman, man, berdache (such as Navajo *nadle,* Lakota *koskalaka,* Mohave *hwame,* Cocopa *warrhameh,* and Yuman *kew'rhame*), ''gay'' (gay male and lesbian or gay female) and others.

gender identity—individual's self-definition based on their acceptance (or rejection) of their culture's role expectations; includes consideration of sexuality, sexual identity and sociocultural roles; may or may not have anything to do with sexual preference. ''Gender identity refers to an individual's own feelings of whether she or he is a woman or a man, or a girl or a boy [or other]. In essence gender identity is self-attribution of gender'' (Kessler and McKenna 1978:4).

gender roles—refers to roles culturally assigned or defined according to gender criteria.

gender dysphoria—clinical expression used to cover a variety of gender identity issues (also referred to as ''gender disorders'') associated with transsexualism and sex reassignment (Steiner 1985).

gender variance—refers to cultural expressions of multiple genders (i.e., more than two) and the opportunity for individuals to change their gender roles and identities over the course of their lifetimes. Psychological literature sometimes uses this expression to refer to individuals who are ''at variance'' from the gender identity expected, given their biological sex.

heterosexual—one who has sexual relations with individuals of a sex (and usually gender) different from one's own.

heterosocial—one who socializes with individuals of different sexes and genders than one's own.

homophobia—unreasoning fear or hatred of homosexuals and homosexuality.

homosexual—one who has sexual relations with individuals of the same sex, and usually (though not necessarily) the same gender.

homosocial—one who socializes with individuals of the same gender.

sensual—pertaining to physical senses or physical responsiveness to stimulae.

sex—the observable biophysiological characteristics of females, males and hermaphrodites, androgynes or intersexed persons; i.e., a person's sex type; perceived biophysiological facts; usually only three types of sexes. ''Sex'' is also an English term used for copulation or other sexual activity that may or may not result in reproduction of members of society.

sexual desire—physical and emotional sensual and sexual response or longing; desire to have sexual relations.

sexual identity—individual's self-definitions based on their sexual preferences and practices (e.g., a woman may reveal her sexual identity with a statement such as ''I am a homosexual;'' see *gender identity* for ''lesbian'').

sexuality—sexual behaviors, feelings, thoughts, practices; also refers to people's sexually based bonding behavior, e.g., bisexuality, heterosexuality, homosexuality (see also *heterosocial* and *homosocial* below).

sexual preference—individual's preferred sexual partners, sexual relationships.

sex roles—duties and obligations of individuals in society based on their sex type (e.g., females may be the only individuals expected to bear and nurse children; males may be the only individuals expected to impregnate females).

transgender—an individual who lives as a person of a gender different from the one society defines for that person's sex (e.g., male "transvestites" who wear women's clothing, hair styles and other body accoutrements, use "feminine" speech and body language, and identify with the gender category *woman*). Also sometimes referred to as "cross-gendered people" (Blackwood 1984).

transsexual—an individual who has a surgically reassigned sex, either female-to-male or male-to-female (in the literature often noted as SRS f-m or SRS m-f) (Steiner 1985).

Notes

1. Unfortunately, there is not sufficient space to go into more detail about the relationship of sexuality to authority and power.

2. Berdache is the term used for a variety of cross-gender expressions in American Indian cultures. See Albers's module for a thorough discussion of berdache; also see Roscoe (1988:177–181) for the most extensive listing of female and male berdache to date and Roscoe (1987) for a comprehensive bibliography of berdache and alternative gender roles among North American Indians; Williams (1986) provides an interesting historical analysis of berdache in select North American Indian cultures.

3. There is considerable disagreement as to whether these terms represent gender categories. Some argue that the terms "lesbian" and "gay male" are (Western) culturally specific categories; others argue that they refer only to sexual preference and have nothing to do with gender categorization; still others argue that "lesbian" and "gay" refer to self-selected or chosen "lifestyles" and consequently do not reflect gender categories. It is curious that Western anthropologists seem willing to accept multiple genders in "other" cultures, but not their own.

4. Part of her research was conducted with Ann Chowning (p. 119, footnote).

5. *bi-* is the term Goodale chose, based on the Austronesian language of the Kaulong, to describe land cleared from the forest. There are usually 10 to 15 single, adolescent and adult consanguinal or blood relatives living in the *bi-* at any one time.

6. Marriage and sexual intercourse are considered synonymous by the Kaulong (Goodale 1980:119, 133).

7. Because of their fear of women's pollution "[m]en prefer to emphasize self-development over identity replacement [having children] in their early and middle life" (p. 140).

8. The !Kung language includes sounds not easily translated into written English; the exclamation point in the word !Kung indicates a glottal stop, which results in a popping sound.

9. Restrictions on and punishment for violation of rules regarding premarital sex, extramarital sex, and incest are coded within the Human Relations Area File, and limited cross-cultural studies of punishment for these behaviors have been done using the Standard Ethnographic Sample (e.g., Frayser 1985, Broude 1981).

10. We found no sources that use HRAF or SES to cross-culturally examine punishment for homosexuality.

11. In Toronto, there are more than 100 gay and lesbian organizations, but only one youth group. The research participants, not intended to be a representative sample, were "25 self-identified lesbians ages

15 to 20''; 2 black, 23 Caucasian. Most were middle-class from suburban areas. All of them worked for wages, either full- or part-time. All were at least comfortable with their sexual orientation. Participants were paid $10.00 each. The interviews lasted one to three hours, and were relatively unstructured. Schneider described the data in her report as preliminary and qualitative (n.d.:4–7), which means that further analysis of the data might reveal different results.

12. Ruth Baetz stated in *Women-Identified Women* (ed. by Datry and Potter) that there are many definitions of coming out: ''a woman's first sexual experience with another woman, a woman's self-realization of sexual feelings for another woman, a woman's acceptance of the label lesbian, a woman's declaration to anyone or everyone that she is a lesbian, or any combination of these possibilities. However coming out is defined, it requires a woman to take a stand against a cultural taboo'' (1984:45).

13. In Seattle, this problem has been addressed by the Mayor's Task Force on Gay and Lesbian Youth. Noting the high incidence of adolescent (i.e., minor) lesbians and gays ''crashing'' and ''sneaking into'' adult lesbian and gay bars, their 1988 Report recommended establishing special youth centers where teen gays and lesbians can legally socialize (Ravelle 1988).

14. The ''pink collar ghetto'' refers to those jobs traditionally held by women with at least a high school education and often an undergraduate college degree: secretarial or the lower levels of teaching and health care positions, for example. For facts and statistics on women and work, see *Perspectives on Working Women: A Databook,* Bulletin 2080, by the U.S. Bureau of Labor Statistics. Washington, D.C.: U.S. Government Printing Office, 1980.

15. There is another practical value for these studies: empirical research on sexual behaviors is desperately needed for use in educational intervention in the spread of the AIDS virus.

References Cited

Baetz, Ruth
    1984   The Coming-out Process: Violence against Lesbians. *In* Women-Identified Women. Trudy
        Darty and Sandee Potter, eds. Pp. 45–50. Palo Alto, Calif.: Mayfield Publishing Co.
Baptiste, David A., Jr.
    1987   The Gay and Lesbian Stepparent Family. *In* Gay and Lesbian Parents. Frederick W. Bozett.
        Pp. 112–137. New York: Praeger.
Berger, Raymond M.
    1982   Gay and Gray: The Older Homosexual Man. Urbana: University of Illinois Press.
Berzon, Betty
    1979a   Achieving Success as a Gay Couple. *In* Positively Gay. Betty Berzon, ed. Pp. 30–40. Mill-
        brae, Calif.: Celestial Arts.
    1979b   Developing a Positive Gay Identity. *In* Positively Gay. Betty Berzon, ed. Pp. 1–14. Mill-
        brae, Calif.: Celestial Arts.
Birke, Lynda
    1986   Women, Feminism and Biology: The Feminist Challenge. New York: Methuen.
Blackwood, Evelyn
    1984   Sexuality and Gender in Certain Native American Tribes. Signs 10:127–142.
    1985   Breaking the Mirror: The Construction of Lesbianism and the Anthropological Discourse on
        Homosexuality. Journal of Homosexuality 11:1–18.
Blumstein, Philip, and Pepper Schwartz
    1983   American Couples: Money, Work, Sex. New York: William Morrow.
Bolin, Anne
    1988   In Search of Eve: Transsexual Rites of Passage. South Hadley, Mass.: Bergin and Garvey.
Borgoras, Waldemar
    1908   The Chuckchee. *In* The Jesup North Pacific Expedition. Franz Boas, ed. New York: Memoir
        of the American Museum of Natural History, Vol. II, pt. 2, pp. 449–451.

Budd, Sharon E.
    1985   Proud Lesbian Motherhood. *In* The Lesbian Path. Margaret Cruikshank, ed. Pp. 131–137. San Francisco: Grey Fox Press.
Crawford, Sally
    1987   Lesbian Families: Psychosocial Stress and the Family-Building Process. *In* Lesbian Psychologies: Explorations and Challenges. Edited by Boston Lesbian Psychologies Collective. Pp. 195–214. Urbana: University of Illinois Press.
Cromwell, Jason
    1987   Transsexualism and Concepts of Gender. Unpublished Ms. Seattle: Ingersoll Gender Center.
Cruikshank, Margaret, ed.
    1982   Lesbian Studies: Present and Future. Old Westbury: Feminist Press.
Davis, D. L., and R. G. Whitten
    1987   The Cross-Cultural Study of Human Sexuality. Annual Reviews of Anthropology 16:69–98.
De Monteflores, C., and S. J. Schultz
    1978   Coming Out: Similarities and Differences for Lesbians and Gay Men. Journal of Social Issues 34:59–72.
Dunker, Buffy
    1987   Aging Lesbians: Observations and Speculations. *In* Lesbian Psychologies: Explorations ana Challenges. Edited by Boston Lesbian Psychologies Collective. Pp. 72–82. Urbana: University of Illinois Press.
Edgerton, Robert
    1964   Pokot Intersexuality: An East African Example of the Resolution of Sexual Incongruity. American Anthropologist 66:1288–1299.
Espin, Olivia M.
    1986   Cultural and Historical Influences on Sexuality in Hispanic/Latin Women. *In* All American Women: Lines that Divide, Ties That Bind. Johnnetta B. Cole, ed. Pp. 272–284. New York: Free Press. [originally published in Vance 1985.]
Fernea, Elizabeth
    1976   A Street in Marrakech. Garden City, N.Y.: Anchor Books.
    1978   Some Women of Marrakech. [Film in the Odyssey Series.]
Frayser, Susanne G.
    1985   Varieties of Sexual Experience: An Anthropological Perspective on Human Sexuality. New Haven: Human Relations Area Files Press.
Fry, P.
    1985   Male Homosexuality and Spirit Possession in Brazil. Journal of Homosexuality 11(3/4):137–154.
Gender and Society
    1987   Official publication of Sociologists for Women in Society. Newbury Park, Calif.: Sage Publications.
Gidlow, Elsa
    1976   A View from the Seventy-seventh Year. Women: A Journal of Liberation 4:32–35.
Goodale, Jane C.
    1971   Tiwi Wives. Seattle: University of Washington Pres.
    1980   Gender, Sexuality and Marriage: A Kaulong Model of Nature and Culture. *In* Nature, Culture and Gender. Carol MacCormack and Marilyn Strathern, eds. Pp. 119–142. Cambridge: Cambridge University Press.
Hanna, Judith Lynne
    1988   Dance, Sex and Gender: Signs of Identity, Dominance, Defiance and Desire. Chicago: University of Chicago Press.
Herdt, Gilbert
    1989   Introduction: Gay and Lesbian Youth, Emergent Identities, and Cultural Scenes at Home and Abroad. Pp. 1–42. Unpublished MS. University of Chicago.

Hill, Marjorie
   1987   Child-Rearing Attitudes of Black Lesbian Mothers. *In* Lesbian Psychologies: Explorations and Challenges. Edited by the Boston Lesbian Psychologies Collective. Pp. 215–226. Urbana: University of Illinois Press.
Jacobs, Sue-Ellen
   1983   CA Commentary (on Callender and Kochems' article on the North American Berdache). Current Anthropology 24:459–460.
Kessler, Suzanne J., and Wendy McKenna
   1978   Gender: An Ethnomethodological Approach. Chicago: University of Chicago Press.
Knutson, Donald D.
   1979   Job Security for Gays: Legal Aspects. *In* Positively Gay. Betty Berzon, ed. Pp. 171–187. Millbrae, Calif.: Celestial Arts.
Krieger, Susan
   1983   The Mirror Dance: Identity in a Woman's Community. Philadelphia: Temple University Press.
Lancaster, Roger
   1988   Subject Honor and Object Shame: The Construction of Male Homosexuality and Stigma in Nicaragua. Ethnology: An International Journal of Cultural and Social Anthropology 28:111–126.
Lewin, Ellen
   1981   Lesbianism and Motherhood: Implications for Child Custody. Human Organization 40(1):6–14.
Llewellyn-Davis, Melissa
   1978   Maasai Women. [Film in the Odyssey Series.]
Lorde, Audre
   1984   Man Child: A Black Lesbian Feminist's Response. *In* Sister Outsider. Pp. 72–80. Trumansburg, N.Y.: Crossing Press.
Martin, Del, and Phyllis Lyon
   1979   The Older Lesbian. *In* Positively Gay. Betty Berzon, ed. Pp. 134–145. Millbrae, Calif.: Celestial Arts.
   1983   Lesbian/Woman. New York: Bantam.
Martin, Kay, and Barbara Voorhies
   1975   Female of the Species. New York: Columbia University Press.
Matteson, David R.
   1987   The Heterosexually Married Gay and Lesbian Parent. *In* Gay and Lesbian Parents. Frederick W. Bozett, ed. Pp. 138–161. New York: Praeger.
McCandlish, Barbara M.
   1987   Against All Odds: Lesbian Mother Family Dynamics. *In* Gay and Lesbian Parents. Frederick W. Bozett, ed. Pp. 23–36. New York: Praeger.
Money, John
   1980   Love and Love Sickness: The Science of Sex, Gender Difference, and Pair Bonding. Baltimore: Johns Hopkins Press.
Money, John and Anke A. Ehrhardt
   1972   Man and Woman, Boy and Girl: Differentiation and Dimorphism of Gender Identity from Conception to Maturity. Baltimore: Johns Hopkins Press.
Murdock, George Peter
   1965   Social Structure. New York: Free Press.
Nanda, S.
   1984   The Hijras of India. Medicine and Law 3:59–75.
   1985   The Hijras of India. Journal of Homosexuality 11(3/4):35–54.
Nichols, Margaret
   1987   Lesbian Sexuality: Issues and Developing Theory. *In* Lesbian Psychologies: Explorations and Challenges. Edited by the Boston Lesbian Psychologies Collective. Pp. 97–125. Urbana: University of Illinois Press.

Ortner, Sherry B., and Harriet Whitehead, eds.
 1981   Sexual Meanings: The Cultural Construction of Gender and Sexuality. New York: Cambridge University Press.
Parker, R.
 1984   A Report from Rio. Anthropological Research Group Homosexuality Newsletter 5(1/2):12–21.
Raphael, Sharon, and Mina Robinson
 1984   The Older Lesbian: Love Relationships and Friendship Patterns. *In* Women-Identified Women. Trudy Darty and Sandee Potter, eds. Pp. 67–82. Palo Alto, Calif.: Mayfield Publishing Co.
Ravelle, Randy
 1988   Report on Gay and Lesbian Youth in Seattle. Seattle: Seattle Commission on Children and Youth.
Ricketts, Wendell, and Roberta Achtenberg
 1987   The Adoptive and Foster Gay and Lesbian Parent. *In* Gay and Lesbian Parents. Frederick W. Bozett, ed. Pp. 89–111. New York: Praeger.
Robertson, Jennifer
 1988   Butch and Femme On and Off the Takarazuka State: Gender, Social Organization and Lesbian Style in Japan. Paper presented at the 40th Annual Meeting of the Association for Asian Studies.
Roscoe, Will, ed.
 1987   Bibliography of Berdache and Alternative Gender Roles among North American Indians. Journal of Homosexuality 14(3/4).
 1988   Living the Spirit: A Gay American Anthology. New York: St. Martin's Press.
Ross, Ellen, and Rayna Rapp
 1983   Sex and Society: A Research Note from Social History and Anthropology. *In* Powers of Desire: The Politics of Sexuality. Ann Snitow, Christine Stansell, and Sharon Thompson, eds. Pp. 51–73. New York: Monthly Review Press.
Sang, Barbara
 1984   Lesbian Relationships: A Struggle Toward Partner Equality. *In* Women-Identified Women. Trudy Darty and Sandee Potter, eds. Pp. 51–66. Palo Alto, Calif.: Mayfield Publishing Co.
Schlegel, Alice
 1985   Cross-Cultural Studies of Gender. Paper presented at the Annual Meeting of the American Anthropological Association.
Schneider, Beth
 1984   Peril and Promise: Lesbians' Workplace Participation. *In* Women-Identified Women. Trudy Darty and Sandee Potter, eds. Pp. 211–230. Palo Alto, Calif.: Mayfield Publishing Co.
Schneider, Margaret
 1989   Sappho Was a Right-On Adolescent: Growing Up Lesbian. *In* Gay and Lesbian Youth. Gilbert Herdt, ed. Pp. 111–130. New York: Harrington Park Press.
Shostak, Marjorie
 1983   Nisa: The Life and Words of a !Kung Woman. New York: Vintage Books.
Smith-Rosenberg, Carroll
 1975   The Female World of Love and Ritual: Relations between Women in 19th-century America. Signs 1(1):1–30.
Steckel, Ailsa
 1987   Psychosocial Development of Children of Lesbian Mothers. *In* Gay and Lesbian Parents. Frederick W. Bozett, ed. Pp. 75–85. New York: Praeger.
Steiner, Betty W.
 1985   Gender Dysphoria: Development, Research, Management. New York: Plenum Press.
Steiner, Betty W., Ray Blanchard, and Kenneth Zucker
 1985   Introduction. *In* Gender Dysphoria: Development, Research, Management. Pp. 1–10. New York: Plenum.

Toder, Nancy
   1979   Lesbian Couples: Special Issues. *In* Positively Gay. Betty Berzon, ed. Pp. 41–55. Millbrae,
      Calif.: Celestial Arts.
Tremble, Bob, Margaret Schneider, and Carol Appathurai
   n.d.   Growing Up Gay or Lesbian in a Multicultural Context. Unpublished Ms. Central Toronto
      Youth Services.
U.S. Bureau of Labor Statistics
   1986   Perspectives on Working Women: A Databook. Bulletin 2080. Washington, D.C.: U.S. Gov-
      ernment Printing Office.
Vance, Carol S.
   1985   Pleasure and Danger: Toward a Politics of Sexuality. *In* Pleasure and Danger: Exploring Fe-
      male Sexuality. Carole S. Vance, ed. Pp. 1–27. Boston: Routledge and Kegan Paul.
Wikan, Unni
   1977   Man Becomes Woman. Man 13(4):667–671.
Williams, Walter
   1986   The Spirit and the Flesh: Sexual Diversity in American Indian Culture. New York: Beacon
      Press.
Zitter, Shery
   1987   Coming Out to Mom: Theoretical Aspects of the Mother-Daughter Process. *In* Lesbian Psy-
      chologies: Explorations and Challenges. Edited by the Boston Lesbian Psychologies Collective.
      Pp. 177–194. Urbana: University of Illinois Press.

Annotated Bibliography and Audiovisual Resources

Sources for Faculty (F) and Students (S)

(F/S)   Broude, Gwen J.
   1981   The Cultural Management of Sexuality. *In* Handbook of Cross-Cultural Human Development.
      Pp. 633–673. New York: Garland Press.

   Provides a critical analysis of the cross-cultural method, a discussion of reasons for the paucity of
data on sexuality, hypothesis building and testing, antecedents and correlates of sex norms and practices,
premarital sex norms for females, extramarital sex norms, homosexuality, sex anxiety, the patterning
of sex norms and practices, and suggestions for future research, with tables demonstrating correlates,
significance, source and interpretation for each major hypothesis.

(S)   Burbank, Victoria Katherine
   1988   Aboriginal Adolescence: Maidenhood in an Australian Community. New Brunswick: Rutgers
      University Press. 153 p.

   One of three sources listed that explicitly investigate female sexuality (see also Mernissi 1987 and
Shostak 1981). Based on interviews, participant observation, and in-depth case studies, analyzes Australian Aboriginal adolescents' new courting habits, marriage histories and conflicts, premarital pregnancies, and their statements about love, men, sex, and marriage.

(F)   Davis, D. L., and R. G. Whitten
   1987   The Cross-Cultural Study of Human Sexuality. Annual Review of Anthropology 16:69–98.
      The most comprehensive survey of the literature on human sexuality to date; has 403 citations, all
      of which are described in context of the article subheadings: cross-cultural methods of sex research,
      ethics and sex research, heterosexual behavior (background and general resources, cross-cultural
      studies of normative sexual behavior, sexual variation, sexual anxiety and pollution, and culture
      change and heterosexual behavior), and homosexual behavior (anthropology and homosexual be-
      havior, and areal overviews of the United States, Native North America, Latin America, Java and
      Indonesia, the Philippines, Australia and Polynesia, New Guinea, China and Japan, India, North
      Africa and Near East, and Subsaharan Africa).

(F)   Frayser, Suzanne G.
   1985   Varieties of Sexual Experience: An Anthropological Perspective on Human Sexuality. New Haven: HRAF Press. 546 p.

This most thorough review of cross-cultural research on human sexuality to date includes biological, psychological, sociocultural considerations, as well as a clear discussion of methods used in those chapters that draw most heavily on the Human Relations Area Files. Discussions and critiques of research focus on evolutionary changes in primate sexuality, biological bases of the human sexual cycle, biological and sociocultural aspects of human reproductive cycles, and patterns of human sexuality.

(F/S)   Hanna, Judith Lynne
   1988   Dance, Sex and Gender: Signs of Identity, Dominance, Defiance, and Desire. Chicago: University of Chicago Press. 311 p.

Hanna places her cross-cultural study of gender and sex variation in dance performance squarely within the context of feminist anthropological theory. She grounds her analysis of dance performance in appropriate cultural context indicating when, how and where dance depicts cultural values, especially gender roles and status, sex and eroticism; alternative expressions of sexuality and gender; and futuristic social organization and gender roles. Very well written and thought provoking, it also contains excellent comparative ethnographic examples and a thorough bibliography. India and the United States receive the most ethnographic attention.

(S)   Krieger, Susan
   1983   The Mirror Dance: Identity in a Women's Community. Philadelphia: Temple University Press.

Controversial study of a lesbian community in the midwestern United States. Based on participant observation and in-depth interviews.

(S)   Mernissi, Fatima
   1987   Beyond the Veil: Male-Female Dynamics in Modern Muslim Society. Revised Edition. Bloomington: Indiana University Press. 200 p.

One of three sources listed that explicitly consider female sexuality (see also Burbank 1988 and Shostak 1981). Discusses the Muslim concept and regulation of female sexuality, women's autonomy and independence, marriage conflict, economic factors that affect women's sexual expressions, with a concluding chapter on women's liberation in Muslim countries.

(F)   Ortner, Sherry B., and Harriet Whitehead, eds.
   1981   Sexual Meanings: The Cultural Construction of Gender and Sexuality. Cambridge: Cambridge University Press. 435 p.

Consists of ten important theoretical articles, including an introduction by Ortner and Whitehead, Cucchiari's essay on the origins of gender hierarchy, Whitehead's controversial essay on homosexuality in native North America, Poole's discussion of female ritual leaders and gender ideology among Bimin-Kuskusmin, Strathern's analysis of Hagen gender imagery, Shore's study of Samoa, Nadelson's analysis of six Mundurucu myths, and treatises by Collier and Rosaldo ("Politics and Gender in Simple Societies"), Llewelyn-Davies ("Women, Warriors and Patriarchs") and Ortner ("Gender and Sexuality in Hierarchical Societies: The Case of Polynesia and Some Comparative Implications").

(S)   Shostak, Marjorie
   1981   Nisa: The Life and Words of a !Kung Woman. New York: Random House. 402 p.

One of three sources listed that explicitly consider female sexuality, including the development of gender identity (see also Burbank 1988 and Mernissi 1987). *Nisa* is an autobiographical account of growing up and being a !Kung woman.

(F/S)   Vance, Carole S., ed.
   1984   Pleasure and Danger: Exploring Female Sexuality. Boston: Routledge and Kegan Paul. 462
   p. Contains 43 papers, images, and poetry that originated at the Scholar and the Feminist IX Conference, "Towards a Politics of Sexuality," held in New York City, 1982.

   Important theoretical papers include the introductory and epilogue essays by Vance, Rubin's analysis of contemporary conditions that have limited thinking, writing, and talking about sex, a review of
select antiabortion activists' values by Ginsburg, Webster's perspective on erotica for women, and Esther Newton and Shirley Walton's deduction of four concepts found in "talking sex" (sexual preference,
erotic identity, erotic roles, and erotic acts).

Films

Argument About a Marriage. (!Kung/heterosexual/charge of infidelity aired in public) 15 min.

Choosing Children. (United States/lesbian/multicultural, multiracial/documents three different situations in which lesbians have had children)

N!ai: A !Kung Woman. (!Kung/heterosexual/historical and contemporary footage of N!ai's
life; contains scenes where N!ai and her daughter are accused of inappropriate sexual behavior
and their response) 50 min.

Sandy and Madeleine's Family. (United States/lesbian/primary focus is court battle for child
custody, but includes footage of daily life of Sandy and Madeleine and their children) Approximately 35 min.